HUNTS' HIGHLIGHTS
of

MICHIGAN

Other Midwestern Guides titles

Hunts' Guide to West Michigan

Michigan Fresh: A food-lover's guide to growers and bakeries

*Hunts' Getaways on the Upper Mississippi
between Chicago and the Twin Cities*

HUNTS' HIGHLIGHTS
of
MICHIGAN

MARY and DON HUNT

Albion, Michigan

**Printed in the United States of America
by
Malloy Lithographing Inc.,
Ann Arbor, Michigan**

Cover Designer & Design Consultant: Chris Golus

Special thanks to Marion Meilaender
and Maria Sudnykovich

For a current catalog or information about quantity purchases,
Call (313) 475-5855, or write:

Midwestern Guides
506 Linden Avenue
Albion, MI 49224

Library of Congress Cataloging in Publication Data

Hunt, Mary. Hunt, Donald
Hunts' Highlights of Michigan.
Includes index.
1. Michigan — Description and travel — Guidebooks.
2. Outdoor recreation — Michigan — Guidebooks
917.74

Library of Congress Catalog Card Number: 91-062335

ISBN 0-9623499-5-X

To the memory of Fred B. Hunt
For all his generous help over the years

Credits for illustrations

Wayne Bronner 366

Sharon Burton 318

Dossin Great Lakes Museum Archives 277, 278, 691, 726

Santa Fabio 213

Henry Ford Museum/Greenfield Village 335, 342

Gregory Fox 328

Mark Gammage 688

Keweenaw Tourism Council 759

Pat Juntti 762

Balthasar Korab 294

Debbie Axerod Kruz 191

Jean Lau 608

Les Cheneaux Historical Society 671, 673

B. J. Litsenberger 771, 772, 773

Mackinac State Historic Parks 635, 638, 642

Lyla Messick 665

Michigan State Historic Parks 769

Michigan State Parks, Earl Wolf 525, 538, 569, 691

Michigan Travel Bureau 48, 113, 142, 199, 235, 268, 314,
385, 398, 477, 488, 549, 584, 631, 652, 714, 717, 735, 738,
753, 774

Glenn Calvin Moon 264

Muskegon County Museum 507, 508

Rick Neumann 618, 620

David Odette 123

R. E. Olds Museum 416

Keith Piaseczny 368

David Rau 309

Ted and Jean Reuther 708, 710

State Archives of Michigan 36, 50, 396, 466-7

Wayne State University Archives of Labor & Urban Affairs 351

Suzanne Wilson 559

J. Adrian Wylie 237

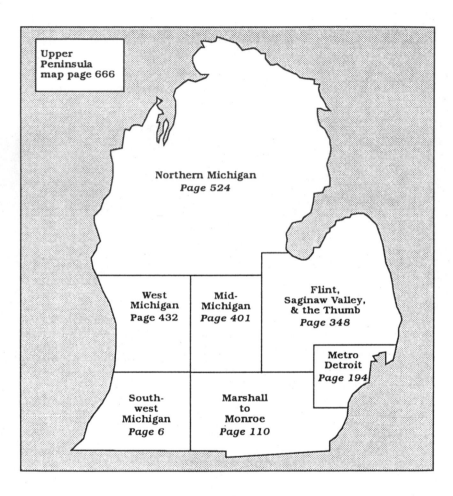

Upper
Peninsula
map page 666

Northern Michigan
Page 524

West
Michigan
Page 432

Mid-
Michigan
Page 401

Flint,
Saginaw Valley,
& the Thumb
Page 348

Metro
Detroit
Page 194

South-
west
Michigan
Page 6

Marshall
to
Monroe
Page 110

Contents

Introduction

This guidebook is the product of six years' research. We have evaluated thousands of Michigan destinations and selected only the most interesting. None of the places we include paid to be in this book, nor are there any commercial tie-ins. In every highlight we try to give enough candid information for you to decide if a destination would suit your interests and needs. Many highlights are followed with briefer notes in smaller type to tell you about other things in the vicinity you might like.

Some well-known places were left out because we don't feel they measured up to being worth a trip. Other pleasant places, where you could enjoyably spend a vacation, weren't unusual enough to be a highlight. And some small, obscure places were considered outstanding enough to be worth an entry.

We found that many of of the most interesting places were created by a person with a dream who made it work. Our bias draws us to offbeat creations like Green Top antiques mall in Allen, or Detroit's Heidelberg Project, or Legs Inn up north. This book also has a lot about old environments, whether man-made, like historic neighborhoods and parks, or natural, like virgin forests or big beech trees behind dunes.

We provide lots of logistical information on directions, hours, costs, etc. Of course, this changes. Our information was fresh as we went to press. It's still a good idea to call ahead if you need to be sure of the current situation before setting out on a trip.

Personal safety has become too big a worry for many people. The city of Detroit is too often avoided because of such fears. Bad things can and do happen everywhere, but people who live their lives in fear and don't venture beyond familiar turf miss out on a lot. Every place in this book can reasonably be visited by a single woman alone, in the daytime, taking ordinary, sensible precautions. Mary Hunt does most of the research alone.

Because this book has grown so large, we have put our recommended restaurants and lodgings in a separate book. Ask for *Hunts' Restaurants and Lodgings of Michigan* at your bookstore, or order it from us. See page 800 at the end of the book.

Michigan is a large and varied state, with many different economies, cultural regions, and even two major ecosystems in the south and north. We hope this book will help residents and visitors appreciate the rich and fascinating diversity in this sprawling state.

Helpful sources
for state-wide travel information

Local chambers of commerce are in business to provide information about the restaurants, lodgings, and other businesses that belong to the chamber. They are also good sources of community information. If directory assistance can't help you locate the chamber of commerce for an area you're interested in, call the **Michigan State Chamber of Commerce** during regular business hours. (517) 371-2100.

MITS: Customized travel information about Michigan

1 (800) 5432-YES

Hours: Weekdays 8 a.m.-11 p.m. Sundays 8 a.m.-5 p.m.

Turn-around time for mailed info: The basic information packet and brochures are mailed third-class. They take 7 to 10 business days to arrive. The customized computer info from the database is printed just for you and mailed first-class the next day.

Description: An operator answers your call, not a complicated voice mail system. You can get three kinds of information. First, you can request a basic information packet (state map, calendar of this season's events, a glossy travel planner published by *Midwest Living* magazine.

Second, you can request brochures and booklets about destinations or particular subjects that interest you: golf, canoeing, charter boats, cabins and cottages, shopping, etc.

Third, you can ask for specific customized information about, for instance, what bed and breakfasts are in Saugatuck, or which downhill ski facilities are within two hours of your home, or what's happening in Detroit next weekend. The operator then consults the MITS computer database to answer your questions. How good the database is depends on how many destinations have responded to MITS' requests for information. So far the database is far from a thorough survey of the state. (Operations began in summer, 1993. MITS is still evolving.) Commercial ventures, state parks and museums, and major lodgings and restaurants are more likely to be in the database than off-the-beaten path local parks, nature centers, and motels, for example.

Chapter 1

Southwest Michigan

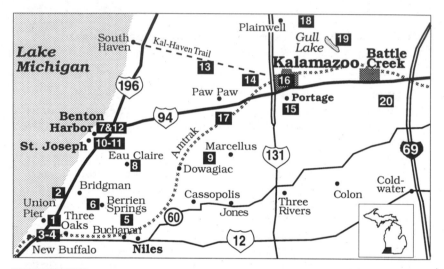

HIGHLIGHTS

For restaurants and lodgings, see *Hunts' Restaurants & Lodgings of Michigan*

INTRODUCTION
Southwest Michigan

Beaches and fruit have long drawn visitors to this pleasant region. Lake Michigan's north-south axis, coupled with winds coming from the west, has given Michigan's west coast two distinctive features: enormous stretches of sand beaches and dunes, and a productive fruit belt. Everything from peaches to wine grapes to blueberries thrives here because Lake Michigan moderates the coastal temperatures. Beautiful orchards and informal fruit stands are common sights along the hilly back roads.

The most popular beaches are at Warren Dunes State Park, St. Joseph's two beaches, and the South Haven area. The Lake Michigan shore is lined with communities developed over the decades as summer resorts for almost the whole spectrum of southside Chicago. The Irish summered at Grand Beach, Bohemians in New Buffalo, Swedes in Harbert, Jews in South Haven. Traces of bygone eras of tourism (summer hotels, motor courts, dance halls, drive-ins) arc found, now affectionately renovated, along the Red Arrow Highway, the old shoreline highway from New Buffalo to St. Joseph.

Michigan's southern tier of counties, mostly linked by the beautiful St. Joseph River and its tributaries, remains remarkably agricultural and rural. It's interesting to explore by car, bike, or canoe the area's quaint towns and villages. Settlements of Amish farmers arc centered around Nottawa and Centreville in St. Joseph County.

The old industrial and college city of Kalamazoo has evolved into the area's center of art, music, and new ideas. By contrast the cereal town of Battle Creek has languished in recent decades as automation has greatly reduced the supply of jobs at Kellogg's, Post, and Ralston Purina, and other economic mainstays have disappeared.

Harbor Country

A beguiling mix of roadside nostalgia
and international art, good food and country antiques.

In the mid-1980s the sleepy resort area around New Buffalo and Lakeside was discovered by overstressed Chicago media people seeking convenient weekend getaways.Their word-of-mouth has transformed what was once a series of low-key resort communities frequented by southside Chicago's Lithuanians, Bohemians, Jews, meat-packers, and professors. Today "Harbor Country" is home of the largest marina-condo complex on Lake Michigan. *New York Times* lifestyle articles gush over the area's exciting new shops and second homes by famous Chicago architects like Harry Weese and Stanley Tigerman.

All the exposure, plus all the new condos and renovated cottages to be decorated, have provided fertile soil for the galleries and shops strung out along and off the Red Arrow Highway from New Buffalo to Harbert, eight miles north. The four-lane road, predating interstate highways, now enjoys a growing reputation as a great place to drive, browse, eat, and see art. That is, it's great except on summer weekends. Traffic then can be fierce.

Some of the galleries go beyond the light-hearted, decorative approach typical in resort areas. There's some provocative art here as well. Harbor Country shops focusing on interior decor are unusually fresh and witty. Don't be surprised to find folk art like bottle cap figures and popsicle stick lamps. After all, these gallery owners are not self-conscious small-town folks who insist on proper English period looks, but sophisticated urban refugees, high-powered if somewhat burned out, who are attempting to slow down and enjoy life.

The Red Arrow Highway itself, named after the World War I army division in which many local men served, is a nostalgic stretch of auto-age Americana. Here roadhouses and tourist courts of the 1920s and 1930s miraculously live on. Often they've been refurbished as monuments to the childhoods of war babies and aging baby boomers who vacationed here as kids, before intestate highways and cheap air fares made more exotic vacations widely possible. The Red Arrow Highway is several

Downtown New Buffalo — part of the heated-up summer scene since a new flock of well-connected Chicagoans discovered Harbor Country in the mid-1980s. The shops and galleries along and off the Red Arrow Highway between New Buffalo and Lakeside are some of Michigan's most interesting.

blocks east of the lakeshore road that goes through the heart of resort communities, beginning with Michiana and Grand Beach on the Indiana line.

A shop and gallery tour of Harbor Country along the Red Arrow Highway seems to work best going from north (Sawyer or Bridgman) to south (New Buffalo). In that direction, it builds to a climax with the concentrated activity of New Buffalo and its busy beach and harbor. Also, more shops are on the right, avoiding left turns if traffic is heavy.

Our tour focuses on established highlights. Of course, each season brings new shops; retailing is in constant flux. It would be easy to spend a day or more browsing along these 10 miles. The Red Arrow Highway bypasses the old cottage areas that blossomed with the coming of electricity in 1918. An interesting cross-section of summer homes, from a few remaining tumble-down old resorts to gracious, sedate lakefront estates, can be seen along shady **Lakeshore Road**. Find it by turning north onto Lakeside Road in Lakeside, near the quaint Elizabethan-style shelter in the little triangular park. In two blocks, turn left onto Lakeshore and follow it into Union Pier. A gate to discourage sightseers eventually blocks the way to New Buffalo's public beach, so turn south onto the Red Arrow Highway. Lakeshore Road is fine for **biking** and **cross-country skiing** in winter. It's especially beautiful in fall and after fresh snowfall.

For a **shopping and eating tour**, start in Sawyer. Take the I-94 Sawyer Road exit and go west to the Red Arrow Highway. That improbably elegant and urbane two-story building in the heart of tiny Sawyer, incidentally, was built in the 1920s by a Chicago teamster official to house a tea room, a soda grill, and his own luxurious second-story apartment. At the triangle made where the Red Arrow Highway angles across Three Oaks Road, turn right, then left onto the highway.

Here are most of the highlights on the short but rich stretch to New Buffalo. Don't hesitate to stop in elsewhere — browsing adds to the fun.

◆ **The Book Rack.** A general line of 24,000 used paperbacks sells for half the cover price. Much more than romances — strong on sci-fi, historical novels, mysteries, children's books. *12830 Red Arrow Highway, just north of Sawyer Road in Sawyer. (616) 426-4120. May thru October: Tues-Sat 10:30-5:30, Sun 1-5. November thru April: Thurs-Sat 10:30-5:30, Sun 1-5.*

◆ **Tara Hill Antiques Mall.** 17 dealers in 17-room, 3.400-square-foot mall operated by longtime owners of Serendipity Antiques down the road and the Harbert Auction House. Specialties include folk art, tramp art, Southwestern, Mission oak, and Victorian. All booths have at least some furniture. Homey atmosphere with functioning fireplace in winter, hot coffee. *Next to the Book Rack in Sawyer. (616) 426-8673. May thru September: daily 11-5:30. October thru April: Sat & Sun 11-5:30.*

◆ **Serendipity Antiques.** Three floors of interesting, not necessarily select stuff in an old grocery store. *West side of Red Arrow Highway at Holloway Dr./Sawyer Rd., across from bank in Sawyer. Same hours as Tara Hill.*

◆ **Harbert Swedish Bakery.** Full-line bakery spotlights traditional Swedish breads and cakes. It has been here since the days when Harbert was largely Swedish and Carl Sandburg had his goat farm nearby. Tables outside and in; coffee, milk, and pop are available. *Red Arrow Hwy. at Prairie Rd. (616) 469-1777. Open 7:30-6, Fri-Sun in spring and fall, Wed-Sun in July & August, closed Thanksgiving to Easter.*

◆ **Lakeside Antiques.** Two interconnected barns and a turquoise 1950s diner out front are filled with quality pieces, including some uncommon specialties: 1950s; folk art (both antique and by living artists); bamboo, wicker, and painted furniture, plus primitive and country. Dependably interesting browsing, thanks to offbeat pieces, eye-catching displays. Different dealers run Vintage Cargo, a shop and mall next door. *(616)*

469-4467. 14866 Red Arrow Highway, just north of East Road in the center of Lakeside. Summer hours: daily except Wednesday 11-6. Winter hours: Fri & Mon noon-4, Sat & Sun 11-6. Call for transition season in spring, fall.

◆ **East Road Gallery.** Peaceful shop in a former cottage features generic Mission and related styles, never low-end but not signed Stickley, either. Room settings are fully accessorized with the likes of copper lamps, etchings, old Craftsman-style books, and some compatible paintings by living artists. Turning a 1912 Craftsman-style resort in Lakeside into The Pebble House bed and breakfast introduced gallery owners Jean and Ed Lawrence to the Arts & Crafts furniture that the old place seemed to want. Now they hold seminars on the Arts & Crafts movement and write guides to antiquing. *14906 Red Arrow Highway, between East Road and Lakeside Road in Lakeside. (616) 469 5995. Open year-round Sat & Sun 12-5, otherwise by chance or appt.*

◆ **The Silver Crane Gallery.** The picturesque half-timber building was built as the store and post office of Lakeside, the area's old-money resort, long favored by southside meat packers and University of Chicago professors. The quaint, Shakespearean look took hold in Lakeside when a Chicago replica of Shakespeare's birthplace was dismantled and moved here to become a golf clubhouse. The Silver Crane claims to have one of the Midwest's largest collections of sterling silver — mostly jewelry, but with some striking vessels like the simple pitcher from Taxco's famed Los Castillo workshop, with a sinuous lizard handle inlaid with malachite. Prices range from $20-$40 for many pins and earrings imported direct from Mexico to $800 for turquoise and sterling necklaces by Navajos. *14950 Lakeside Road, just west of the Red Arrow Highway in the heart of Lakeside. (616) 469-4000. May thru October: open daily 11-6. November thru April: open 1-4 weekdays, 11-6 weekends.*

◆ **Lakeside Gallery.** Here in the sales gallery of the nearby Lakeside Center for the Arts, art comes alive as an exciting process of exploration and experiment. Both the center and gallery were started by John Wilson, the ceramist and print dealer who organized Chicago's influential Art Expo at Navy Pier. The center, in an old Lakeside summer hotel, is a working artists' retreat that furthers artistic and cultural exchange among artists from around the world, mainly the U.S., Poland, Latvia, Lithuania, Australia, and China.

Artists donate half the work they create there to support the center; it's sold in this gallery. Works are produced under conditions of unusual freedom. They are selected after submitting proposals for projects. Sales from their works help support the center. Current works are likely to include lots of ceramics, sculpture, jewelry, and some paintings. *15486 Red Arrow Highway at Warren Woods Road in Lakeside. (616) 469-3022. Open Fri-Sun noon-6. Closed January & February except by appointment.*

◆ **Lakeside Center for the Arts.** Visitors are welcome to tour the studios at this international artists' retreat. Artists stay in the simple old inn and use the studios (painting, printmaking, ceramics, and sculpture) in the rear of the eight-acre property. It's sort of a sharecropping arrangement, in which artists give half the work made here to the center. It is sold in the Lakeside Gallery (see above). Rooms not used by artists are rented to the general public at $60/night and up, including kitchen privileges. *15251 Lakeshore Road in Lakeside. From the Red Arrow Highway, take Warren Woods Road west to Lakeshore, turn right. Center is in a few blocks. (616) 469-1377.*

◆ **Rabbit Run Antiques & Interiors.** When Chicago people like decorator Ken Gosh do country, it has a fresh, witty, comfortable look. Gosh, an early émigré to Harbor Country, sets a bright, sophisticated but informal tone that you see a lot around here. There are bright, rich colors of Amish-style quilts; American antiques; and upholstered furniture. *15460 Red Arrow Highway at the south end of Lakeside. (616) 496-0468. Year-round, daily 10-6.*

◆ **Panozzo's Cafe.** Brunch spot with odd hours, extremely pleasant garden ambiance. *15300 Red Arrow Highway on Lakeside.*

◆ **Filoni Vestimenti** Owner Shari Filoni used to rep for Chicago clothes designers; here she has assembled her favorites, along with interesting jewelry and accessories, including some nifty old watches. *In "Wilkinson Village" complex next to Panozzo's, 15300 Red Arrow Highway. (616) 469-4944. Open daily 10-6 year-round.*

◆ **Downtown Union Pier,** along Union Pier/Elm Valley Road at the Red Arrow Highway, has most requirements of a small town center, including a post office and pharmacy. **Ramberg's Bakery** is a favorite with bicyclists. **The Charcoal House** has excellent, slow-cooked BBQ ribs when it's open; call (616) 469-3737 to confirm. The **Harbert Auction House** has weekly antique auctions usually the third Monday of the month. Buyers may view items on Sunday and leave sealed bids. Call (616) 426-8673 for

Over 2,000 condos now cluster around the New Buffalo harbor. South Cove, Michigan's first condo-dock project (above), was designed by Harry Weese, one of several famous Chicago architects contributing to Harbor Country's late 1980s luxury boom. Stanley Tigerman, who has a home in the area, designed an entire subdivision near Sawyer.

particulars.

◆ **Antique Mall and Village.** An appealingly fanciful "village" in the woods, with 65 interesting dealers, largely from the Chicago area. Better quality than most Michigan malls. Don't miss the ongoing recreation of Michelangelo's Sistine Chapel ceiling in a metal building to the rear, or the log cabin and the rustic and Indian artifacts in it, *9300 Union Pier Rd., almost a mile east of the Red Arrow Highway and downtown Union Pier. (616) 469-2555. March thru December: open Mon-Sat 10-6, Sun noon-6. January & February: closed Tues & Wed.*

◆ **St. Julian Winery Tasting Room.** *Union Pier Road at I-94 exit.* A good chance to sample the interesting, constantly improving array of mid-priced wines and sparkling juices made from Michigan grapes at Michigan's largest winery. No charge for tasting. (616) 469-3150. *From mid-June thru Labor Day open 10-7 Mon-Sat, noon-7. Otherwise closes at 6 p.m.*

◆ **Local Color.** Works in many media by 80 artists and craftspeople from the area are attractively displayed in this consignment gallery. Some are whimsical, some serious, and all are contemporary in style. There's a good deal of painted furniture and hand-decorated wearable art. Usually open daily 12-5; call to confirm in off-season before making a special trip. *16187 Red Arrow Highway south of the light at Union Pier; east/side of highway.*

◆ **Kite's Kitchen.** Promising new takeout bakery/restaurant started by successful caterers Ted Wilson and Judy Kite. Known for breads, excellent dinners. They hope to grow or hand-pick all the produce they use, from basil in the pesto to raspberries for preserves. Entrees from $4-8, dinners (with appetizer and sides) $8-12 per person. Soups, desserts, salads – everything prepared on the premises. "This is a dream I've had for years," says Kite, who quit her Chicago job in planning conventions and meetings. *The shops at Union Pier, 16170 Red Arrow Highway, 1 block south of flasher light at Union Pier Road. Open Thurs-Mon 10-6 except Fri to 8. From November thru April, probably closed Mondays.*

◆ **Miller's Country House.** Woodland view from deck, cozy, casual bar, more elegant dining room. Good food, attractive setting. *Red Arrow Highway between Union Pier & New Buffalo.*

◆ **In downtown New Buffalo.** Whittaker Street, once a fairly humble place, now has some tony shops for home accessories and women's clothing in the old retail district, between the Red Arrow Highway and the lake. The **Whittaker House** at 26 North Whittaker stands out on account of its relaxed, contemporary classic clothing in beautiful fabrics of excellent quality, and also carries fashion and home accessories. *It's open daily, year-round. (616) 469-0220.*

   Hearthwoods owner/craftsman Andy Brown has long been fascinated with rustic furniture made of tree trunks, branches, and twigs. A few years ago he quit his advertising job to start this workshop and store. Here he has gathered together all sorts of contemporary rusticana — burl bowls, birchbark birdhouses, hand-made Amish rockers, and Adirondack chairs made from 100-year-old cypress wine vats. In his chunky four-poster bed ($1,600), the top canopy is formed by a lattice of thin branches that sprout directly from thick tree trunks. *116 1/2 North Whittaker, downtown. (616) 469-5551. Mem.-Labor Day: Mon-Sat 10-6, Sun 12-5. Labor Day-Mem. Day: Mon-Sat 10-5, Sun 12-5, closed Tuesdays.*

   Across the street at the corner, **Buffalo Drugs** (also called V&S Variety) functions as a community hub, with out-of-town papers, beach gear, videos, etc. A few doors down on North Whittaker, **Sweetwater Boating Supply** (616-469-5660) is an attractive, well-organized new store with enough interesting gadgets, books, and T shirts to appeal even to non-boaters. Down the hill at 125 North Whittaker, **Anchors** (616-469-6800) offers a virtually complete array of the popular Nautica menswear line — a nautical counterpart to Ralph Lauren's Polo, but a better value. No wonder — the owner's husband is Nautica's Chicago rep. Hats, ties, belts, fragrances — it's all here. Women buy the well-made jackets and sweaters for themselves. *Open year-round, daily in season. Closed Tuesdays in off-season.*

On U.S. 12 a block west of Whittaker, **Country Mates** is a rambling, hugely successful shop where the country look, complete with long skirts and teddy bears, reigns supreme. 7,000 square feet of country accessories, English, American, and Neo-Victorian, include classics like simple painted furniture, wrought-iron lamps, handwoven rugs, salt-glazed pottery in many colors, and such. Works by contemporary folk artists and craftspeople from over 40 states are shown here. The year-round Christmas shop is on two levels. Some people come just for the dried flowers and herbs, color-keyed for customers' decor. In spring an unusual variety of **ornamental and culinary herbs** is sold on the patio, along with garden statuary. *(616) 469-2890. Open 7 days year-round, daily 10-6, Sunday 12-6. In July & August, Saturdays open 'til 9.*

Half a block down North Barton at number 28 is the new, much bigger home of **Lyssa,** which its owner describes as "a bit of a curiosity shop — always something different." Unusual jewelry, accessories, and gifts from Europe, Africa, and the U.S. are played off against generally classic clothing, mostly for women. There are gifts for men and children, too. *(616) 469-1162. May thru December: open daily 11-5, to 8 on summer Saturdays. Otherwise open Thurs-Mon 11-5.*

On South Whittaker, between the old downtown and I-94, shops increasingly occupy what once were houses. The 1836 cottage at 44 South Whittaker began as the stable of New Buffalo's founder, Captain Whittaker. Today it houses **Brennen's Bookstore** at 44 South Whittaker. Its stock in trade is a wide range of vacation reading for all tastes, plus a terrific selection of greeting cards, gifts, and Dover paper construction projects. Most interesting is the local authors' section, with books by the many Chicago-area writers who have vacation homes and year-round residences here. Autograph parties on Saturday are regular summer events. *(616) 469-5730. May thru September: open daily 11-6. Otherwise: open 11-5, closed Tuesdays.*

In the two-story brick building by the train tracks, **La Grand Trunk** offers fashion-forward, contemporary women's clothes — everything from socks to black-tie formal wear. The look seems quintessentially big-city; actually, the store is a branch of a popular shop in nearby Valparaiso, Indiana, which is increasingly favored by Chicago commuters. *447 S. Whittaker. (616) 469-2122. Summer hours: 11-7, except Sunday to 6. Winter: 11-5 daily.*

AN EXCELLENT SMALL RAILROAD MUSEUM . . . . . occupies the meticulously reconstructed New Buffalo depot and commemorates the central role the railroad played in the town's history. Volunteers at the New Buffalo Railroad Museum are continually at work expanding the big working **model train display** of New Buffalo in its 1920s railroad heyday. Then the Pere Marquette Railroad up Lake Michigan's eastern shore had its shops here and employed most of the town. There's lots of information about the Pere Marquette — dubbed "Poor Marquette" by historian Bruce Catton and other Michigan boys who had to endure its bumpy ride — and its successor, the Chesapeake & Ohio. There's a photograph of the original Chessie, the pet cat of the C & O chairman and inspiration for the railroad's feline mascot. Visitors can also see a remaining part of the railroad roundhouse next door at **The Round House**, an ambitious shopping complex now occupied only by an antiques mall. *Museum is at 530 South Whittaker. (616) 469-3166. Open April thru Halloween, weekend noon to 5. Also open Fridays in summer.*

HARBOR COUNTRY'S MAIN PUBLIC BEACH . . . . . south of the spectacular, huge Warren Dunes State Park (page 18) is the **New Buffalo Beach,** within walking distance of downtown New Buffalo right at the busy outlet of the Galien River near the harbor. The swimming area here is more protected from the boating traffic than it at first seems, and the public beach is longer, with more dune grass and shrubs than first impressions suggest. There are **restrooms**, a **refreshment stand**, a small **play area** for children, and a dune **stairway** and longish **overlook and boardwalk** atop the dunes.

FOR INTERESTING HISTORIES OF LOCAL PLACES . . . . . and lots of ideas for more things to do, call the Harbor Country Chamber of Commerce and ask for the free, 60-page *Harbor Country Guide* and a lodging directory. (616) 469-5409.

FRESH-PICKED FRUIT . . . . . In Sawyer, blueberries are in season from mid-July into September at **The Blueberry Patch**, 1/2 mile west of the Red Arrow Highway on Sawyer Road. Shaded picnic area. U-pick or picked berries and preserves also for sale. *Open 10-6. Always call first; (616) 426-4521 or evenings (616) 545-8125.* . . . . Picked fruits from cherries (July) and peaches, melons, and plums (August) to fall grapes, pears, and apples are for sale at the **Phillippi Fruit and Cider Mill** (616) 422-1700. It's on Cleveland Avenue 1/4 mile south of Glendora and 5 miles east of Sawyer. Cleveland runs north-south between Sawyer Road and U.S. 12 at Galien. Many fresh vegetables, from asparagus through tomatoes to pumpkins. . . . . See also: **Lemon Creek Winery and Fruit Farm**, page 39, 5 miles east of Bridgman.

Warren Dunes State Park

Crowded beaches and remote trails,
hang-gliding and dune climbing at this splendid park

This remarkable hilly park can handle huge crowds on its beach — up to 20,000 on hot holiday weekends — and still provide a remote, rugged getaway experience on hiking trails in the dunes. Towards the shore the dunes are bare as a desert. In a textbook example of plant succession as you move inland, they are anchored first with beach grasses, then with quick-growing aspen and willows, and finally with big oaks and hickories. The northern two-thirds of the park is undeveloped except for hiking trails. The southern third contains Michigan's busiest state park facilities, planned to handle crowds of day-trippers from Chicago and South Bend. It makes for a stimulating contrast: people-watching and contemplative nature study.

The **beach** and parking area, though not exactly intimate, are far less overwhelming than most popular beaches within striking distance of urban areas. That's due to the outstanding site planning and design of three bathhouse and concession areas. The food is pretty good. By the closest parking area is **Tower Hill**, 240 feet above the lake. Kids love to climb this big, bare dune and run down and climb again — exhilarating fun, and a high point of many outings. **Hang-gliders** soar from this hill on weekends, too — more often in the spring and fall, when wind is most likely to come out of the north-northwest. Angelo Mantis gives **hang-gliding lessons** here; $70 gets you a full-day introduction, including four or five short flights. Call (312) 929-1547, and have alternate weekend dates available. Hang-gliders must be certified and have permits from park headquarters. Though hang-gliding isn't nearly as popular as it once was, a good day when the winds are right will still bring out four to six gliders.

Inland the huge dunes here are mostly covered with oak, beech, maple, and hickory woods. It's not hard to get away from the beach's crowds. Walk up the beach from the developed area — the public beach is 2 1/2 miles long — or take your car to the deeply shady **picnic area,** along a pretty creek in the relatively

Although Warren Dunes State Park attracts as many as 20,000 visitors on summer weekends, you can get away from crowds just by walking a half mile up the beach away from the developed area.

secluded back dunes. It has play equipment, grills, restrooms, and a shelter. Come early on holiday weekends — it does fill up.

For the supremely fit and energetic, a foot trail climbs to the top of the **Great Warren Dune**, then descends to an uncrowded beach. Another shorter, 1 1/2-mile section climbs **Mount Randall**. From there on a clear day you can see across Lake Michigan to the Sears Tower and Hancock Building in Chicago. There are **6 miles of hiking** and **cross-country skiing trails** (novice to intermediate difficulty). The trailhead with maps is in the interpretive area, which has pit toilets, water, and a shelter. (Go right on the first drive past the entrance, past the park office.) Trails aren't groomed, but a snowmobile does pack the novice trails. Skiers and tobogganers are welcome to use any areas at their own risk, but only the novice cross-country ski area meets all safety criteria.

The 194 **modern campsites** have more privacy than many at state parks. Some back up to a wooded dune, and many are quite shady. Three-fourths are reservable; phone reservations are recommended from mid-May through September. For people who don't have camping gear, three compact, cozy minicabins with wood stove and two double bunks rent for $30 a night.

Dune conditions fascinate scientists because they cover all possible extremes of moisture, from desert conditions to temporary ponds to constant wetness, in a geographically compact area with the same general climate. Dunes are home to plants uncommon in Michigan. Tasty wintergreen berries and cranberries grow in the interdunal wetlands of Warren Dunes and nearby Grand Mere state parks.

Preservation of this extensive area of high dunes is due to the foresight of E. K. Warren of Three Oaks, the serious-minded son of a Congregational minister who made a fortune by inventing a flexible corset stay made of turkey feathers. In the late 19th century, sand dunes were considered worthless, valued only for mining sand used in foundry molds and building materials. Warren realized the dunes' ecological value and bought 250 acres of these lakeshore dunes to preserve them for posterity. He gave them to the state as the nucleus of this park.

*On the Red Arrow Hwy. 3 miles south of Bridgman. From I-94, take Exit 16, follow the signs and go south. (616) 426-4013. Open daily, year-round, at 8 a.m. Gates close at 10 p.m. from April 1 thru Labor Day; otherwise, gates close at dusk. No alcoholic beverages March thru Sept. Restroom facilities closed Oct. 15-April 15. $4/car/day ($5 for non-Michigan residents) or $18/year state parks sticker for residents and non-residents alike. **Camping:** 194 modern sites ($14/night) open all year. Half are available on a first-come, first-served basis. Phone reservations recommended from mid-May thru September.*

A SPECTACULAR INDUSTRIAL TOUR NEAR BRIDGMAN . . . . on the shore of Lake Michigan is the **Cook Energy Information Center**. It is one of the largest nuclear plants in the U.S., providing power to over 520,000 customers in Indiana and Michigan. Next to its plant, the Indiana & Michigan Electric Company has built a lavish tourist center. Visitors can also wander among multi-level terraces towards the lake, with expensive lighting, wrought-iron tables and chairs, and abundant, well-maintained shrubs and flowers. Upstairs is a large assortment of fancy **video games** where visitors can learn about energy and how electricity is made. Every few minutes visitors are taken by a professional guide on a **multi-stage presentation**, through three impressive auditoriums. In the first, the tour guide takes the stage to interact with a full-sized computer-driven robot. Next, the visitors file into a large circular amphitheater, where an elaborate model of the nuclear plant is explained. Finally, in a third and even larger auditorium, visitors see a wide-screen film about the Cook plant. One scene shows the churning area half a mile out in Lake Michigan where the plant gets its water to cool the steam which turns the giant turbines. A quarter of a mile out, the water is returned 3° F warmer.

Visitors are welcome to **picnic** on a landscaped patio overlooking Lake Michigan, or eat inside on cold or wet days. There's an indoor snack bar and vending machines. *On the Red Arrow Highway 3 miles north of Bridgman and I-94 exit 16. A traffic light is at the entrance. (800) 548-2555. June through Sept: Wed-Sat 10-5, Sun 11-5. Other times: Mon-Fri 10-5, plus special monthly weekend events. Closed mid-Dec to mid-Jan. Handicap accessible. Group tours available. Special* **weekend collectors exhibits** *on quilts, decoys, regional art, and antiques are held once or twice a month. Free.*

A WILD DUNELAND BIRD-WATCHERS LOVE . . . . . is at **Grand Mere State Park**. Here bogs, a chain of three small lakes, and other wetlands among the dunes prevented cottage development and left the area remarkably wild, though within earshot of I-94. The Michigan Nature Conservancy gave the land to the state for a limited-development natural area. It's wonderful for spring wildflowers and migrating birds (warblers and other songbirds in spring, hawks in spring and fall). Herons, cormorants, gulls, ducks, and even shy loons are regular residents. Now an entrance road leads to a parking lot, **picnic area**, 2,200-foot, handicapped-accessible **trail**, and 2 miles of **hiking and cross-country ski trails** circling interdunal ponds, and cranberry and wintergreen bogs. A trail from the parking lot by South Lake leads to Lake Michigan and back in a mile loop. For **cross-country skiing**, the trail marked "novice" is a two-mile, flat loop, not groomed but packed with a snowmobile. More adventurous skiers and tobogganers are welcome to ski and sled through the dunes on unmarked trails, at their own risk. No camping or swimming. *Take I-94 exit 22 (Stevensville) and follow the signs onto Thornton Rd. (under the freeway to the west). (616) 426-4013. $18 state park sticker or $4/day.*

Warren Woods Natural Area

A primeval virgin woodland
an hour and a half from Chicago's Loop

These 311 acres comprise one of Michigan's few remaining virgin beech-maple climax forests. The woods you see from the car off Elm Valley Road don't look different from a hundred other places. Off the road here, a drive leads to parking, a **picnic table**, and **restrooms.** But if you take the foot trail across the Galien River to the loop along the river, you'll come to some enormous, majestic beech trees, along with maples and hemlocks — the kind of woods the pioneers encountered. The damp soil here makes for a jungly, humid environment that's sunnier and quite unlike the stand of virgin oaks and hickories on the drier upland of Russ Forest, another piece of southwest Michigan virgin forest not too far from here (page 56). Warren Woods' location on the main Lake Michigan shoreline flyway, and the abundance of dead wood for woodpeckers and for nesting, make it an outstanding place for bird-watching.

"This natural area has long been considered one of the best birding spots in the state, especially for warblers — including Hooded, Cerulean, and Kentucky Warblers — and songbirds such as Acadian Flycatchers and Louisiana Waterthrushes," says Tom Powers in his helpful *Natural Michigan* guide to natural areas. "Other birds spotted here include many that are usually only found farther south." The May **wildflower display** in this rich, damp woods is also outstanding.

The hard-packed trail loop (1 1/2 miles long) is flat except for rolling

Warren Woods is a prime birding site. It attracts many warblers and some birds like the Acadian flycatcher (above) that are uncommon in Michigan and usually seen only much farther south.

terrain along the river. For **cross-country skiing**, it's rated
novice. The section leading to the river and several overlooks is
so gently graded that **wheelchairs** can use it. An **interpretive
sign** tells about the beech-maple climax forest visible across the
river. A **self-guided nature trail** starting at the parking lot is
planned for 1994. Another section of foot trail begins at the Elm
Valley Road entrance and pullover, near the Galien River.

That this Natural National Landmark was preserved at all is
due to the remarkable foresight of E. K. Warren, the Three Oaks
storekeeper who made a fortune by inventing a better, cheaper
corset stay made of turkey feathers. Over a hundred years ago,
when most businessmen were figuring out how to exploit natural
resources, he decided to buy this virgin timberland in order to
preserve it.

*Entrances on Elm Valley Rd. and Warren Woods Rd. (both roads
go east from the Red Arrow Highway) about a mile west of Three
Oaks Rd. (which is the north-south extension of Three Oaks' main
street between U.S. 12 and the Red Arrow Hwy.). (616) 426-4013.
Always open. Handicapped-accessible in part; see above. State
park sticker required ($4/day, $18/year.)*

ANOTHER FAVORITE WOODLAND WALK . . . . . close to Harbor Country
resort communities is the **Robinson Preserve** along the Galien River. When
you leave the road and walk down into the valley, it's hard to believe you're
just a mile from the Red Arrow Highway and Lakeside's shops and galleries.
*Take East Rd. east from the center of Lakeside. Preserve is on the north side of
the road just past Basswood Rd.*

Drier's Butcher Shop

Tasty ham and bologna, sold with old-fashioned showmanship in a century-old shop in Three Oaks

They used to hold Chicago-bound trains at the Three Oaks depot so passengers could walk across to Drier's to buy some of its famous ring bologna and ham. Trains don't stop at little Three Oaks any more, but people still go out of their way to shop at Drier's. This exceptional butcher shop continues to make sausage and cure hams and bacon the old, careful, German way. The ancient frame building is an operating antique, listed on the prestigious National Register of Historic Places. Old tools and a fancy Victorian meat rack have been here over a hundred years. The four-paned windows pre-date the introduction of plate glass in the 1880s.

Despite the many old-fashioned touches — the sawdust on the floor, the corny signs like "This baloney cuts the mustard" — Drier's is actually one astute man's business response to changing times. The late Ed Drier cleverly crafted his business to preserve quality of life — his own, and his employees' and customers.' Drier's today offers a limited number of choice items: hot dogs, Polish sausage, ring bologna at about $4 a pound ("all beef, less fat, no belching," a sign points out), and liver sausage. The cheese has been made elsewhere. Bologna, hams, and bacon are smoked on the premises. Choice meat justifies the premium prices.

Back in the 1930s, in pre-med classes at the University of Michigan, a professor told Ed Drier he'd be better off making baloney than pursuing a medical degree. After getting out of the service in 1945, he did go back to work with his dad. "We always enjoyed our work," he said. Drier also enjoyed living two minutes from his shop, playing tennis with old Kalamazoo College chums, and taking a vacation from January 1 to shortly before Easter.

Antiques and art make Drier's today a lot more interesting than the plain place it used to be. Now you'll find three massive marble butcher's tables from France, picked up on Drier's midwinter travels around the world. There's a deer head, family

memorabilia, signs like *"Nicht auf den Boden spucken"* ("no
spitting on the floor" in German, a reminder that this place is
quintessentially German in its earthy, unassuming style), and
caricatures — frequently of Ed Drier, like the portrait of him as
a grumpy-looking knight, done in magazine-cover style by a
Time cover artist who was a customer.

All this stuff launched conversations with customers.
"That's part of the deal — the dog and pony show," said Drier,
who relished the personal side of the business and the nice letters that come with orders for holiday hams.

Ed Drier relied on his family, especially his daughter, Carolyn, and about a dozen young men from the area to help. Even
after they've gone out into the work world to become teachers,
dentists, engineers, and the like, some come back to the shop
to help out on their vacations. They continue to operate the

The late Ed Drier (left) with occasional helper Gary Lange, one of many
Drier friends who started working at this celebrated sausagemaker's in
high school. Above Drier is a photo circa 1900 of the butcher shop,
which looks the same today. After Drier's death at 74 in February, 1994,
his daughter, Carolyn Drier, and grandson David Wooley will continue to
run the business and make sausage the way he had ever since he went
to work here for his dad in 1945.

business the way he did. "This hooey about what's the matter with young people is mostly what's the matter with the old people," commented Drier. "It's not how many mistakes are made, it's how they are corrected."

14 S. Elm (the main business street) in downtown Three Oaks, about a block north of the intersection with U.S. 12. (616) 756-3101. Closed Jan. 1 until 2 weeks before Easter. Mon-Sat 9-5:30. The comical branch store on U.S. 12 east of town is open Sat & Sun 9:30-5, but closed in winter.

BICYCLE RENTALS AND MAPS, PLUS LOADS OF VISITOR INFORMA-TION . . . . . are now available at Three Oaks' 1899 depot, the new home of the remarkable **Three Oaks Bicycle Museum and Information Center.** It has loads of well organized free information on visiting southwest Michigan and on bicycling throughout the state. Unusual bicycles are on display. **Bike rental**s ($5 for the first hour, $10 a day) and a kids' bike cart are available. Videos feature bike safety and Three Oaks' Apple Cider Century Ride, the nation's largest 100-mile bike ride.

The **Apple Cider Century** regularly attracts 7,000 riders to three Oaks in September. The Apple Cider Century funds the museum and its enthusiastic creator, Brian Volstorf, who started the ride some two decades ago. Now mayor of Three Oaks, he's a one-man grassroots economic development whirlwind. Marked bike routes radiating out from Three Oaks range from 5 to 60 miles and go to many attractions in this book, as far north as Grand Mere State Park. Now Volstorf's nonprofit bike club has purchased the handsome brick depot, built for President McKinley's visit to present Three Oaks citizens with the first cannon captured by Admiral George Dewey in the jingoistically popular Spanish-American War. (Ask to hear the story.) Volstorf is collecting antique railroad memorabilia and more bicycle history displays for the museum's expanded quarters. *From U.S. 12, go north on Oak one street east of Elm (the main street), go two blocks. From Elm turn east just south of the tracks and two blocks north of U.S. 12. (616) 756-3361. Open daily 9-5 year-round. Call to confirm in winter. Free.* . . . . At the museum, get your **Backroads Bikeways** map of 12 marked bike routes radiating out from Three Oaks into the beautiful byways of Berrien County.

ALSO WORTH CHECKING OUT IN THREE OAKS . . . . . on the north edge of downtown are the sprawling old brick factory buildings of the **Warren Featherbone Company**, where useless turkey feathers were split and woven into improved, snap-proof corset stays. Three Oaks boomed with the widely marketed Featherbone corset stay, endorsed by no less than actress Sarah Bernhardt. Founder E. K. Warren's restored headquarters and bank, the main office of **People's State Bank,** is worth a peek inside. *3 N. Elm. Open weekdays.*

Three Oaks (pop, 1,786) has two summer ice cream shops, a corner cafe with undistinguished food, a good thrift shop near Drier's, a bar, and a big variety store with creaky wood floors. Two promising new ventures are in the works. For 1994: **Frohlich's,** an eat-in bakery/grocery/coffee-house, will open at 26 N. Elm. Home-baked croissants and bread will be served with soup at tables inside or in an out-door brick courtyard with vine-covered lattices. Planned for 1995: renovation of the old **movie theater** across from Drier's. A well heeled local businessman plans summer stage performances and "old-time movies" like Westerns, plus cold-weather movies for area kids. Food will be served. To find out more, just call Mayor Brian Volstorf at the Bicycle Museum (616-765-3361).

BICYCLING THROUGH HARBOR COUNTRY . . . . 12 marked roadside routes radiate out of Three Oaks, ranging from 5 to 60 miles. Several go to different points along Lake Michigan. Pick up a **free map/brochure** and lots of other helpful information at the **Three Oaks Bicycle Museum and Information Center** (page 20)

Fernwood

One woman's enchanted gardens

T hough Fernwood has grown into an impressive center for nature and arts education, its best part is a series of very personal gardens begun by Kay Boydston, a schoolteacher from Chicago. This serene, sensuous small universe is an inspiring example of what years of thinking about plants and working with them can create. Kay Boydston, a serious, self-taught horticulturist, discovered this ravine and brookside area with her husband, Walter, in the 1930s. From upland fields the land descends 125 feet down to the St. Joseph River, creating an exceptional range of microclimates — perfect for a gardener's and botanist's experiments with diversity. Soils vary from sand to clay, both wet and dry.

Over a 30-year period, Boydston began a **perennial garden**, a **lilac garden**, a **boxwood garden,** a **fern trail** leading to a rustic bridge by a corkscrew falls, and an enchanting **rock garden**. There in April and May bloom primroses, heathers, and many little flowers from the mountains, meadows, and bogs of the world, tucked in pockets of tufa stone. Dwarf conifers add to the effect of a delicate but tough miniature world.

These gardens have been augmented and further developed in the years since Fernwood became a public educational institution. Fully mature and filled in, they are

Kay Boydston's Fernwood gardens are relaxed, natural collections of ferns, primroses, Alpine flowers, heathers and other plants, deftly planted in and near the woods going down to the St. Joseph River. It's a serene, sensuous place many visitors long remember.

a sensory delight, filled with the sounds of splashing water and birdsong and the smells of flowers, pines, and leaf mold in the air. They form a series of picturesque small spaces like outdoor rooms, arranged around the Boydstons' simple, shingled cottage homes. (They had one small house oriented for summer, one for winter.) Arbors, bridges, benches, stone walls, and pools accent the gardens and encourage visitors to stop and contemplate a small area.

The planned and planted gardens are mixed with existing woodland trees and small plants for an enchantingly natural effect. Self-seeded wildflowers further blur the distinction between landscaping and nature.

Many famous American gardens are patterned on aristocratic European prototypes, requiring statuary, formidable garden architecture, and paid gardeners to maintain the grounds. Fernwood is more relaxed and natural; its purpose is to inspire home gardeners and show what can be grown in these climes by people of modest means. Any of the stone walls and benches could be built by an interested amateur, with local help for special projects. Maintenance isn't fussy. Bulbs poke up through fall's leaves, and fallen branches remain in place in wilder areas.

Kay Boydston's method was to choose a plant type — ferns (her favorite) or Alpine flowers, for instance — study it intensely, landscape with it, and, years later, move on to another subject. Many of her gardens are impressive collections of a type of plant, and they do have instructive labels, but her part of Fernwood wears its learning lightly.

In 1964, the Boydstons turned their home into a nature center and garden open to the public. Since then Fernwood has expanded to become a much bigger facility. Fernwood now offers a host of inexpensive and unusually wide-ranging gardening, nature and crafts **classes and workshops** for adults and children. Ask for a catalog. Full-day, week-long summer nature classes for children and Japanese crafts classes for adults could be highlights of a summer vacation in the area.

Most of the newer gardens are only now maturing to the point where they could ever approach the special magic of the gardens Kay Boydston started. The **North Vista Garden**, planted in 1964 by the late Clarence Gottschalk, longtime director of Chicago's Morton Arboretum, is the oldest and so far most satisfying. It showcases a fine viburnum collection and provides special winter twig and park interest.

Other specialized gardens south of the Visitor Center were planted much more recently, in a former cornfield acquired in 1976. They are only now filling in to create a sense of enclosure. They include:

◆ a Japanese garden
◆ a rose garden
◆ an all-American display garden, where annuals which win that collaborative seed company competition can be seen.
◆ a pioneer dooryard garden.

The **Visitors' Center** has a big fern conservatory (especially nice in winter), space for changing exhibits, horticulture classroom space, and a **gift shop**, quite romantic and feminine in mood, with garden books and a wide selection of notecards, gifts, and china with botanical and bird motifs. A very reasonably priced **tea room** looks out onto the interesting **herb and sensory garden**. The tea room is open from April through October from noon to 3, Wednesday through Friday at least; call for more details.

In April and May Boydston's rock garden is abloom with the little flowers of mountains and bogs. Primroses, iris, gentians, and wild tulips and daffodils are planted among the dwarf conifers and ferns. The gardens have been planned for year-round interest.

Fernwood is worth frequent visits. The gardens are always changing, of course, and the three miles of remarkably diverse nature trails make such an interesting contrast to the small-scale, cultivated gardens. Trail guides to five trails are available at the Visitors' Center.

Trail highlights include:

◆ The **Guide-Yourself Nature Trail** that circles a pond and goes down to the river (about 3/4 mile).

◆ A splendid **tallgrass prairie** — one of the very best prairie reconstructions around. A trail guide explains it; an overlook platform lets you survey it. The prairie blooms from May through August. (Observation deck is 100 feet from parking along a loop off the main road.)

◆ A 60-acre **arboretum** begun nearly 30 years ago. It includes a collection of 60 trees recommended for suburban lots and comparative collections of many other species, including pines, maples, oaks, crab apples, firs, spruce, magnolias, hawthorns, dogwood, arborvitae, and various flowering shrubs.

◆ The **Trail of Water** that goes past a trout pool and down to a trout pond and the river.

◆ **Fern Trail** from the rock garden along a brook to the trout pools. (No guide for this one.)

*13988 Range Line Rd. between Berrien Springs and Buchanan. From Niles or Berrien Springs, take U.S. 31/33 to Walton Rd. turn west and follow the signs. From U.S. 12 and I-94, take Red Bud Trail (in Buchanan) north to River Road, which becomes Walton. Turn left (north) at first intersection onto Range Line. Follow the signs. (616) 695-6491 or 683-8653. **Hours:** Tues-Sun year-round, 10-6 during Eastern Daylight Time, 9-5 during Eastern Standard Time. May be open Friday evenings. $3 adults, $2 seniors and ages 13-18, $1 ages 6-12. Group rates available. Pick up a free* **trail map** *with handy scale to plan your visit.*

STRIKING HISTORIC ARCHITECTURE IN NEARBY NILES . . . . .
This old city of 12,500 owes its rich if sometimes shabby architectural character to its glory days in the mid 19th century. Here the Michigan Central Railroad crossed the beautiful wide St. Joseph River and linked with the rail lines from Indiana. Paper-making continues to flourish; Simplicity Patterns are still made here and shipped all over the world.

Today, after 30 years of seeing local business siphoned off by the deceptive lure of Indiana's low property taxes, things are looking up for Niles and neighbor Buchanan, thanks to the Michigan legislature's big property tax cuts. With South Bend, Indiana and Notre Dame University just 10 miles away, "we're already starting to see the immigration of better-educated people who appreciate the good values on our fine old homes," says the local chamber of commerce director.

SURPRISES IN A SMALL MUSEUM . . . . . The interesting **Fort St. Joseph Museum** has many remarkable artifacts. Excavated from the **late 17th-century French Fort St. Joseph** just south of Niles are glass and seed beads, silver crosses, merchants' seals, and pots. The outpost served to protect the Jesuit mission here, to advance French diplomatic interests with neighboring Indians, and to supply them with trade goods in exchange for furs.

Through a historical fluke, the museum also has an outstanding collection of **Plains Indian artwork.** In the late 19th century, Niles military officers and wives, stationed in forts on the Great Plains, became friendly with Sioux leaders, who gave them many beautiful and fascinating things, including a stunning Victorian-Indian beaded dress, and large autobiographical pictographs done by the illustrious Sitting Bull and by Rain-in-the-Face. (His is in large format on cloth.) Also here: material on famous folks from Niles, including **Ring Lardner**, the **Dodge brothers**, and **Montgomery Ward**. In the works are improved interpretive displays and more material about Niles industries. *508 E. Main (U.S. 31/33) at Fifth (M-51), behind the ornate City Hall. (616) 683-4702. Tues-Sat 10-4, Sun 1-4. Donations appreciated.*

Niles' City Hall next door occupies the super-ornate **Chapin Mansion**, a Queen Anne castle of a house, lavish with many patterns of brickwork, in which each room has an elaborate fireplace made of a different imported wood. Henry Chapin was a prosperous Niles grocer in 1865 when he invested in Upper Peninsula mineral land. Years later he raked in profits when a rich iron ore deposit was discovered near Iron Mountain and became the Chapin Mine. Visitors are welcome to look around the during business hours. Ask for the interesting book about it. *Main at Fifth. Open weekdays.*

A PLEASANT WALK THROUGH OLD NILES . . . . . could begin by stopping for candy at the venerable **Veni Sweet Shop** on the southeast corner of Main at Third. (Look up to see the elegant old stained-glass sign on the front and side: black script on lavender and flowers.) The Marazita family has made candy here for 75 years, as the store changed from fruit market to soda fountain (the marble counter remains) to candy store. Favorites are peanut clusters, raisin clusters, and licorice buttons, plus peanut butter smidgens at Easter, chocolate sponge candy at Christmas. *Open 10-5:30, closed Sunday.*

Natives and visitors still mourn the loss of an even more beautiful sweet shop, the **Paris Candy Soda Lunch** — now Alice's Restaurant — at 220 South Main. Its mahogany booths with leaded glass inserts were a local landmark. Poor health forced the Patterson family to sell the business, and no local people came forth to buy the business with its furnishings (sold as a complete package). Someone from Hot Springs, Arkansas, bought them. The St. Joseph River is especially impressive at Niles — almost in a leafy gorge — though you'd never know it from Main Street, where a tacky shopping strip obscures the view. Walk two blocks south on Third, however, and you'll reach pretty **Island Park**, which follows the river almost a mile.

Of Niles's four antiques malls, one — and a good one, at that, with 70 dealers – is right downtown in the old Montgomery Ward's at 218 Second just north of Main. **Four Flags Antique Mall** (616-683-6681) is open in summer (and possibly in fall) from 10-6 Monday through Saturdays, 12-6 Sundays. Winter weekdays it closes at 5. Get directions for the three other malls, **Michiana, Picker's Paradise**, and **Unique Antiques**, all on U.S. 33 South on the way to South Bend.

If you walk up the East Main Street hill to the City Hall and Fort St. Joseph Museum, you'll pass the old **Carnegie Library** (now the **Four Flags Chamber of Commerce**, with visitor information; 616-683-3720) and the elegant **Four Flags Hotel** from the 1920s. Now a residential hotel, it's worth a peek inside for its beautiful warm tiles and carved wood details. The hotel also houses **The Colony** restaurant and **Four Flags Fantastic Flavors** ice cream parlor and espresso cafe. The adjacent **Ready Theater**, though remodeled into a triplex with budget prices, still has the roomy seating and much of the splendid mood of picture palaces from the Golden Age of Hollywood. Call (616) 683-7060 for what's playing.

Much of historic downtown Niles still suffers from the success of the homegrown Kawneer Corporation, long America's premiere manufacturers of storefront components. Kawneer pioneered maintenance-free metal panels that "modernized" many old brick commercial buildings. After covering up much of downtown, Kawneer left town and relocated in the South.

Also of interest, but farther from downtown:

◆ The magnificent brown sandstone **train station** with its great clock tower and massive Romanesque arches. The last important stop on the old Michigan Central Railroad going into Chicago, it was built as the line's show-piece to impress crowds going to the Chicago World's Fair in 1893. More recently, it has appeared in movies, including *Only the Lonely* and *Midnight Run. Fifth Street six blocks north of Main (Business U.S. 12).*

◆ The **boyhood home of Ring Lardner**, humorist and master of American vernacular, is an especially picturesque and well-preserved Gothic Revival house on a bluff overlooking the St. Joseph River. *519 Bond St., off Third four blocks south of Main/U.S. 12.*

A BLUFFTOP PARK WITH TRAILS, FINE RIVER VIEWS, AND FRISBEE GOLF. . . . . just south of Niles, **Madeline Bertrand Park** offers **nature programs** from its **visitor center** with **bird-feeding area**. Get a map there to 4 miles of **trails**, plus more in an adjacent park across the Indiana line. Trails are groomed for **cross-country skiing**, with a warming shelter. Call (616) 683-8280 for program info and ski reports. *From the U.S. 12/U.S. 33 intersection at Niles, go south on U.S. 33 about 2 miles, turn right (west) onto Ontario, follow signs to park entrance. Non-resident vehicle fee: $3/day.*

TOURS OF SIMPLICITY PATTERNS . . . . . can be arranged for groups of 10 or more (during non-summer months only) by calling (616) 683-4100. Ask for Steve Hart. Simplicity Patterns is headquartered in New York, but all the patterns, catalogs, and promotional material for their world-wide markets are printed here in Niles's 500-employee plant. Visitors see tissue paper being made in Simplicity's paper mill, then printed and folded on big web presses. The four-color in-store catalog is printed and bound here, too.

A BICYCLE PATH from South Bend and Niles to Berrien Springs and St. Joseph is in the works, to be constructed on abandoned railroad and interurban rights-of-way. A key southern link will be ready in 1995. Call Bike Specialists at (616) 683-3100 for a status report.

A WORKING 1853 GRISTMILL . . . . . complete with wooden waterwheel, can be seen right in downtown Buchanan. **Pears Mill** (pronounced "Peers") has been rescued and restored; the interior, with its massive post-and-beam construction, is handsome. Alas, the old mill stream flows not in a sylvan glade but under an ugly parking lot. Visitors can buy stone-ground flour and cornmeal, and see exhibits about local history. *Open Memorial Day thru September, weekends and holidays 1-5. (NOTE: on Sundays, the mill does not actually run.) Free; donations appreciated. (616) 695-5925. From U.S. 12, take Redbud Trail north into Buchanan; go left (west) onto Front St. (Niles-Buchanan Rd.). In 3 blocks turn south onto Oak and park at mill. From the west, Elm Valley Rd. becomes Front St.*

LIVE ENTERTAINMENT ON SUMMER WEEKENDS. . . . . can be seen and heard at the **Tin Shop Theater** in downtown Buchanan. Plays, music, children's events, and readings are performed from late May through August. Most tickets $5. Call (616) 695-6464 for program, reservations, and directions. Sponsored by the Buchanan Area Fine Arts Council.

MICHIGAN'S ONLY CAVE . . . . . can be visited for $3. At **Bear Cave**, north of Buchanan, springs formed unusual formations of tufa (a spongy limestone). Visitors get a competent 20-minute audiotaped tour of the cave's interesting, if unspectacular, chambers, tunnels, and formations. The setting by the St. Joseph River is delightful, but camping is for members only. *At the Bear Cave Campground, off Red Bud Trail 3 miles north of Buchanan. Open at most times, summers only. (616) 695-3050. $3, kids under 12 free.*

A RARE REMNANT OF A FLOWERING WET PRAIRIE . . . . . may be seen near Dayton, between Three Oaks and Buchanan. The Michigan Nature Conservancy owns 47 acres of what was once 15,000 acres of prairie in Michigan and Indiana. Curran Road and the turnoff alongside it provide a dry viewing platform from which to see prairie grasses and rare plants like rosin weed, spotted phlox, and Jacob's ladder. *From U.S. 12 at Dayton, take Dayton Rd. south a little over a mile, turn left (east) onto Curran. In about 2 miles, look for a pullover. Or, from the east, take Red Bud Trail south from U.S. 12 at Buchanan, and turn right (west) onto Curran Rd. in about 2 miles,*

Michigan Wine and Berrien County Wineries

Where you can see it all — from fruit on the vine to wine in the glass, in delightful rural settings

If you want to understand what goes into making wine, focus on small, owner-operated wineries. There you can see vines in the vineyards and ask questions of the people responsible for the entire process, from growing and picking grapes to fermentation and bottling. Winemakers, almost to a one, are direct, down-to-earth people — they're farmers and chemists, really — and often they're opinionated, crusty characters as well. At St. Julian's big Paw Paw winery, in contrast, grapes are trucked in from contract growers, and tours are given by the marketing staff. It's an interesting, informative tour but not as intimate.

The following group of three close-together wineries in south-central Berrien County provides an excellent introduction to winegrowing in Michigan, and lets visitors taste some of Michigan's most noteworthy wines. The setting is beautiful: hilly, pastoral, and remote in mood, but convenient to big population centers. **Tabor Hill**, the pioneer in the Michigan's wine industry changeover to drier, more sophisticated wines, has become the state's second-biggest winery. It's a fancy, highly capitalized place that produces mid-priced wines. Rick Moersch, who was Tabor Hill's winemaker for many years, has started his own winery, **Heart of the Vineyard**, nearby. **Lemon Creek**, a simple, 150-year-old family fruit farm, has started producing many award-winning medium-priced wines.

The Michigan wine story is a compelling agricultural drama being played out in our own time. There are many factors that affect the taste and character of wine — quality of rootstock; care of vines, temperature and humidity during the growing season; fall frost; sugar content during harvest; manner in which grapes are picked and possibly culled; winemaking style, whether skin is left in contact with the juice, whether wine is aged in an oak barrel; and winter weather. But two crucial factors affecting wine

Pub. by W. V. Hall   SHIPPING GRAPES, PAW PAW, MICH.

Paw Paw Fruit Growers' Union.
Teams Loading Grapes.

EVERY LOAD
WEIGHED HERE

For over a hundred years, Paw Paw has been a major shipping point for fruit, especially grapes. Today it is home of the innovative St. Julian Wine Company, Michigan's largest winery. In this photo, taken around 1905, wagons wait for grapes to be weighed and loaded onto trains. The tower of Paw Paw's splendid new courthouse is in the background.

quality are so site-specific as to be impossible to predict without years of experience: the exact composition of the soil on which grape vines are grown and the exact climate of the soil's location. Soil characteristics vary within small areas. And microclimate is affected by elevation, topography, and orientation to the sun, so it can vary considerably within the same neighborhood. To unlock a vineyard's winemaking potential takes years of matching different grape varieties with local soils and microclimates that suit them best.

The great vineyards of Europe have histories of hundreds of years of growing different grape varieties. Michigan, in comparison, is just moving beyond the experimental stage, along with many other regions of the U.S.

The officially recognized wine-growing regions of Michigan are the Lake Michigan Shore in southwest Michigan and, near Traverse City, the Leelanau Peninsula and the Old Mission Peninsula. Southwest Michigan has sandy soils, rolling terrain, and the same amount of heat units as the wine-producing regions of northern Europe. Michigan winters are colder than those in Europe, but more snow cover usually protects the graft union on each vine, where the bearing vine is grafted to hardier native rootstock. Occasional steamy summer weather encourages fungus, but that can be controlled with species-specific fungicide.

Historically, Michigan has used hardy native grapes like Concord and Catawba to make sweet wines that gave Michigan wines a bad reputation for many years. The first grapes suited to the contemporary taste for drier wines to prove successful here were French hybrid varieties promoted by Michigan State University. Tabor Hill showed the way in the 1970s (see page 41). St. Julian, Michigan's largest and oldest winery and the state's most important buyer of wine grapes, soon convinced its contract growers that French hybrids could be successful on a commercial scale. The hybrids Vignoles and Vidal Blanc (both white grapes and Chancellor and Chambourcin (reds) have turned out to be very well suited to Michigan. Young winemakers have since then emerged, part of the back-to-the-land movement of the 1970s. Noteworthy successes were achieved by blending hybrid varieties to create proprietary blends like St. Julian's popular Simply Red, L. Mawby's excellent blends, and Good Harbor's Fishtown White.

Then Ed O'Keefe at Chateau Grand Traverse north of Traverse City proved that a small winery could succeed growing only vinifera grapes — those prestigious "noble grapes" from the Old World that are more susceptible to freezes and disease. Riesling, a white German grape that's more cold-tolerant than most French grapes, is the vinifera variety that does best in Michigan.

Now more growers are putting more acreage in vinifera varieties, while usually still confining them to a relatively small fraction of their overall production. That way, a really cold winter like 1994 won't be as likely to wipe out all their crop, though it will reduce production of hardier hybrid varieties, too.

Sadly, financial difficulties have led Jim Eschner of Madron Lake Hills, a highly regarded premium winery in Berrien County, to get out of wine production altogether, and his former partners have gone out of business.

The recent surprise in Michigan winegrowing has been the success of Michigan red wines. Baco Noir, the first red hybrid variety widely grown here, lacked the body many people expect in a red wine. That gave rise to the notion that only white wines could really stand out in Michigan. But the hybrids Chambourcin and Chancellor and the vinifera Cabernet Sauvignon have produced full-bodied, award-winning red wines for Michigan wineries. As Chambourcin, a dry red wine grape whose taste ranks on a par with Cabernet Sauvignon, becomes better known, Michigan wines will come into their own nationally. Lemon Creek's Chambourcin won a National Gold Medal from the American Wine Society.

"For the last five to eight years, the wine industry has moved away from California," says wine-lover Christopher Cook, whose wine column appears in the *Detroit Free Press* food section each Wednesday. "We're seeing the regionalization of wines with their own regional character. It takes five to eight or ten years to get to the point where you know what you can do. California has never been able to make great Pinot Noir, which is a cold-climate grape variety. Then the French discovered Oregon Pinot Noirs were much better. Texas Chardonnay is better than 80% of the California Chardonnays, while California is ideal for Cabernet Sauvignon and Seyval Blanc.

"Michigan is really on the edge of being a very well accepted and acknowledged wine-producing state," Cook continued. "It's my belief that in five to ten years Michigan will produce some really exceptional wines: champagnes very much like the champagnes of France, made with underripe Pinot Noir or Chardonnay grapes. Typically, Michigan grapes ripen to a point, and then it's a real push at the end of the season to get enough sun to ripen fully. They have to 'strip the canopy' of leaves. Then it dawns on winemakers, they should be making champagnes! I think Rick Moersch [of Heart of the Vineyard] is a genius; he's showing the way with champagnes."

Exploiting the tourism possibilities of picturesque vineyards is a trend developed in California's wine country that will be popping up more and more in Michigan. Tabor Hill's restaurant has spectacular vineyard views but indifferent service. Paw Paw attracts busloads with the St. Julian tour, the idyllic terrace restaurant of the now-defunct Warner's Winery next door, and the Little River Cafe with its good list of Michigan wines. (See page 44.) On a much smaller scale, Rick and Sherrie Moersch of Heart of the Vineyard have a one-room bed and breakfast in their home and arrange carriage and sleigh rides. Seven Lakes Vineyard in northwest Oakland County near Holly has chosen to appeal to a broader group of prospective buyers with a series of wine-themed parties like their Hawaiian luau in August. "Any time you eat, you should have wine nearby," says winemaker-proprietor Chris Guest. His Vignoles have been deemed "exquisite" and "so similar to a high-acid French Chardonnay it's almost scary" by Chris Cook.

Recently a winemaker with lots of experience in Germany has teamed up with a well-heeled partner to build a virtual castle of a bed and breakfast inn in their Old Mission vineyard, Chateau Chantal (page 578). Alluding to the romance of wine, many wineries' labels are becoming ever more artistic.

Lest consumers get too caught up in the romance of small boutique wineries, Cook adds, "One of the best consistent wineries in Michigan is St. Julian in Paw Paw." Wine sophisticates may turn up their noses at St. Julian's tasting rooms along interstates and at tourist destinations. Furthermore, it's quite true that St. Julian aims to produce wines for all tastes and pocketbooks. But Cook praises their award-winning Chancellor and Chambourcin, bargains at $8.50 a bottle. "They'll be excellent wines 20 years from now, too. St. Julian's Rieslings are perfectly good, and their alcoholic cider, sold by the keg last year, was just spectacular."

This is an exciting time to taste Michigan wines. "Certain wines shine each year," says Cathy Lemon of Lemon Creek. "We've all got our bread-and-butter wines and our sweet wines, but each year most wineries have one wine that's really good for that year. That's why you don't go to just one winery and drink just one wine. Finding those special wines is the mystique and the fun of wine."

Though wine drinkers are often a supercilious, snobbish lot, tasting rooms are pleasantly democratic places run by people who know that ultimately, enjoying wine is all a matter of individual taste, varying from person to person. Tasting rooms let customers develop their taste inexpensively. If you decide to explore Michigan wine and wineries, it's a good idea to record your likes and dislikes in a permanent notebook. At **The Grand Grape** tasting room at the Grand Traverse Resort near Traverse City, you can compare wine from all Michigan wineries.

Here are three wineries in southwest Michigan to visit:

◆ **Lemon Creek Fruit Farms, Vineyards & Winery.** Lemon Creek offers a rare opportunity to taste a good variety of medium-priced Michigan wines (including many award-winners); to

buy and pick fresh fruit; and to see most phases of wine production, from grape growing to fermentation and bottling. (Pressing
is done at St. Julian's.) Just outside the tasting room, you can see
vines, neatly labeled by variety, and the tall grape harvester that
straddles the rows of vines and harvests the grapes. Visitors can
picnic at tables outside the tasting room. Cathy Lemon is happy
to give visitors an informal tour of the winemaking facilities.

Home winemakers can purchase grapes already picked, or
pick them themselves. Varieties include Concord and several
French hybrids (Chamborcin, Baco Noir, Vignoles, and Vidal, the
Lemons' main stock). Among vinifera varieties are Riesling and
four varieties that will be producing in 1995 and 1996: Cabernet
Sauvignon, Merlot, Chardonnay, and Pinot Noir. Fruits (sold
packaged or **U-pick**) include raspberries, four kinds of sweet
cherries, tart cherries, nectarines, pears, plums, three kinds of
peaches, and eight apple varieties.

The three Lemon brothers grew up here. They were among
the first in the area to grow grapes for drier wines. In 1981, after
years of falling fruit prices, many other southwest Michigan fruit
farmers also replaced their orchards with French hybrid grapes.
Prices fell dramatically as a result. The Lemons, like an increasing number of fruit and vegetable producers, realized they'd be
more secure financially if they marketed their own produce. They
decided to add value to it by producing wine.

Lemon Creek continued supplying Tabor Hill, St. Julian, and
Good Harbor with wine grapes but also opened its own winery in

**Tim Lemon (left), his brother Jeff, and Jeff's wife, Cathy, in their vine-
yard seven miles west of Berrien Springs. For getting a good all-around
view of growing fruit and making wine, the informal tour at their Lemon
Creek Winery is one of the best.**

1984. For newcomers to the tricky business of winemaking, the Lemons have been extraordinarily successful, with well over 100 awards for their wines thus far. Wine prices start at $5 a bottle for Ruby Rosé (a frequent silver medal-winner). The three Vidal wines (dry, demi-sec, and semi-sweet) have won the most awards; they're $5.95. And don't pass up a chance to try the outstanding Chambourcin. Sparkling juices are $3.50. *533 Lemon Creek Rd. just east of Baroda, 5 miles east of Bridgman and 7 miles west of Berrien Springs. From I-94 exit 16 at Bridgman, go north on Red Arrow Hwy. 2 miles to Lemon Creek Rd., then east 5 miles. (616) 471-1321. Open May through Dec: Mon-Sat 9-6, Sun 12-6. Also by appt. A free June festival each Father's Day weekend includes hayrides, games for kids, arts and crafts booths, and live music.*

◆ **Tabor Hill Winery & Restaurant.** A spectacular view of vineyards, orchards, and the distant Lake Michigan dunes highlights a visit to this winery and restaurant, which serves up a glamorous, California-style country ambiance for city folks.

As a winery tour, this has some pluses and minuses. The college student summer guides may not yet know much about winemaking. The restaurant may be so busy and bustling that you may have to be aggressive in asking for samples of wine at the combined tasting area and bar. July and August are especially busy. On the other hand, if you catch him at an opportune time, winemaker Michael Merchant is happy to answer questions. He can take time for group tours made by appointment.

In any case, the scenery is outstanding, and you can walk through the vineyards. The crusher-destemmer is right outside, and at harvest time in late summer, you may be able to watch lugs of grapes being dumped into the hopper. From there, they are spun in a centrifuge to emerge as juice, or they are pumped into dejuicing tanks. Some fermenting tanks are outdoors, too, chilled for free by cold winter air. Inside are memorable oak wine barrels, beautifully hand-carved with scenes from each year of Tabor Hill's early crops. The shiny German and Italian bottling equipment has a capacity of 600 to 800 cases a day — quite a contrast to the tiny hand bottle-capper at Lemon Creek.

It's all a far cry from the creative chaos of Tabor Hill's early days under wine visionary and super-salesman Len Olson. Brash and bold, Olson was convinced that Michigan could produce premium wines. When he started Tabor Hill in 1972, he was the first in Michigan to gamble and plant Chardonnay and Riesling.

Tabor Hill's winemaker, Michael Merchant, next to one of the beautiful, hand-carved wine barrels from the winery's early years. The view of vineyards and the surrounding countryside from Tabor Hill's restaurant is outstanding.

Olson's Tabor Hill "was like a commune," recalls Michigan State wine professor Stan Howell. "A lot of people came there to live and work. It was an interesting time. His wines were so much better than any others being produced in Michigan." But Tabor Hill went bankrupt under Olson, causing some area growers to lose many thousands of dollars.

Whirlpool heir David Upton rescued the financially shaky operation in the late 1970s. Today Tabor Hill is promotion-minded and rather slick in atmosphere. Its mainstays have been middle-priced wines using French hybrid grapes. Wine experts recommend its Classic Demi-Sec ($6.29), a semi-dry, easy-drinking, summer picnic kind of wine, as an excellent value. Tabor Hill's Late Harvest Riesling and Hartford Cream Sherry were 1993 Michigan State Fair gold medal winners.

A French champagne maker taught former winemaker Rick Moersch how to make outstanding champagnes the French way, fermented in the bottle. His Grand Mark Brut champagne ($19 a bottle) was named the best of show champagne at the Los Angeles County Fair, beating out many well-known California champagnes. Winemaker Michael Merchant, Moersch's longtime assistant, is following competently in his footsteps. Merchant especially recommends the vintage Chardonnays of the past four or five years ($13 a bottle), subtler than California Chardonnays; the Rieslings; and Tabor Hill's successful proprietary Blush blends of Vidal and other hybrid grapes ($6.95/bottle). "They're continually fine-tuned and improved — in our opinion — with each year's grapes," he says. "Of course, what *we* like may not be everyone's taste. That's the game in marketing — to anticipate trends in demand and taste." *185 Mt. Tabor Rd. just west of Tabor Hill, between Berrien Springs and Baroda. From I-94 at Bridgman, take Exit 16, north on Red Arrow Highway to Lake/Shawnee Road. Go east 4 miles to Hills Road, turn south (right), follow signs. From U.S. 31 bypass at Berrien Springs, take Snow Road exit west about 8 miles, follow signs. (616) 422-1161.* **Wine tastings:** *May thru September or early October Mon &. Tues 8-5, Wed-Fri 8 a.m. 9 p.m., Sat 11:30-9, Sun noon-9. Other times by appointment.* **Tours:** *May thru September or early October, noon to 4:30. It's always best to call ahead.* **Restaurant hours:** *May thru November Wed-Fri 11:30-9, Sat 5-9, Sun 11:30-9. No food service from 3 to 5 p.m. January thru April Fri 5-9, Sat 11:30-9 (no food 3-5), Sun noon to 3.*

◆ **Heart of the Vineyard.** This new winery isn't really so new. Owner/winemaker Rick Moersch was Tabor Hill's winemaker for 13 years. He first planted his eight acres of vines in 1981 on this property, adjacent to Tabor Hill. One hallmark is esoteric plantings of unusual German grape varieties like the fruity, robust Scheurebe, the spicy Gewürztraminer, and the delicate Mueller-Thurgau. Another distinguishing characteristic is Moersch's drier, French-influenced, Alsatian style of making wine with these German grapes. Now that he is a boutique winemaker, he enjoys spending less time on the road dealing with distributors and more time educating customers. He used to teach science at Berrien Springs High School, and he enjoys talking about the agriculture and chemistry of wine. In America today, wineries are, by default, the main locus of wine education, he feels.

Moersch's champagnes are celebrated (see page 38), and the **champagne cave** is a highlight of his tour. So are prearranged **carriage rides** and **sleigh rides**, on four miles of country roads in this especially scenic area. One room of Rick and Sherrie Moersch's 1881 farmhouse serves as a **bed and breakfast**. ($95/night, full breakfast, private bath, two-night summer minimum). In winter, anyone is welcome to **cross-country ski** in the vineyards and along the creek and into the woods. *10981 Hills Road, just west of Tabor Hill, between Berrien Springs and Baroda. From I-94 at Bridgman, take Exit 16, north on Red Arrow Highway to Lake/Shawnee Road. Go east 4 miles to Hills Road, turn south (right). Winery is in half a mile. From U.S. 31 bypass at*

*Berrien Springs, take Snow Road exit west about 8 miles, follow
signs. (616) 422-1617.* **Tastings:** *from Memorial Day through fall
colors, daily from noon to 6. Other times, weekends noon to 6 and
by appointment.* **Tours** *on weekends or by appointment. Three
annual benefit* **events** *include barrel tasting, disgorging champagne.* **Newsletter** *mailed to customers.*

**OTHER RECOMMENDED ATTRACTIONS IN NEARBY BERRIEN
SPRINGS.** . . . . . From the wave of plain Greek Revival courthouses
built shortly after Michigan statehood in 1837, only two survive. The dignified courtroom in the **1839 Courthouse Museum** in sleepy Berrien
Springs has been carefully restored. An outstanding museum of Berrien
County history is in the lower level. There's a restored sheriff's office,
changing exhibits, a large log house, and a book and gift shop that's very
good on regional history. *On U.S. 31 at Union, 3 blocks north of
Shawnee/Ferry. (616) 471-1202. Tues-Fri 9-4, Sat & Sun 1-5. Closed holidays. No charge* . . . . . . **Wild Birds Unlimited** features a wonderful
variety of bird feeding supplies and other bird-related stuff, from books
and binoculars to jewelry and sweatshirts. Owner Richard Schinkel
leads birdwatching trips here and around the world. *109 N. Main just
north of Ferry in downtown Berrien Springs. Mon-Fri 9-5, Sat 9-1.* . . . . .
For picnics, nature hikes, and cross-country skiing through varied
ecosystems, pretty **Love Creek County Park & Nature Center** is way
above average. Two staff naturalists lead weekend programs. *From U.S.
31/33 just east of Berrien Springs, turn east onto Pokagon Rd. and follow
signs to park on Huckleberry Rd. (616) 471-2617. Trails open daily dawn
to dusk. Center open Wed-Sun 10-5. $3/car.*

A VISIT TO PAW PAW AND ST. JULIAN WINERY. . . . . is also worthwhile. St. Julian is the big player in Michigan wine (see pages 37 and
39), and the family-owned winery does a very good job of wine education
and wine tourism. The winery is on a busy commercial strip, not in an
idyllic vineyard. The **tour** begins with an informative audiovisual show
on St. Julian and winemaking, then takes visitors to see the bottling line
and fermenting room. Wine ferments in containers from a huge, 27,000-
gallon tank down to small 50-gallon barrels. At harvest time from late
August through September, it's especially busy, as trucks deliver grapes.
A visit to the **tasting bar** completes the tour. *On M-40 a few blocks north
of I-94 exit 60 at Paw Paw. (616) 657-5568. Free tours and tastings year-
round. Tasting room open Mon-Sat 9-5, Sun noon-5 ('til 5:30 from July thru
September). Tours given every half hour from 9:30 to 4. No noon tour.* . . . . .

Warner's next door isn't a winery any more; the bankrupt winery remains in the juice business. But the **Warner Champagne Cellar Bistro** is a delightful place for lunch — especially on the shady, sunken brick courtyard between the rippling Paw Paw River and the renovated 1898 waterworks. *706 S. Kalamazoo/M-40, just north of St. Julian. (616-657-3165)* . . . . . The rest of Paw Paw is worth a look. It's an agricultural and resort village of 3,200 — a rarity for a county seat to be so small. Numerous Greek Revival buildings date from the years after 1835, when the **Territorial Road**, Michigan's main east-west artery, reached Paw Paw. If it's a weekday, look inside the elaborate **1902 Classic Revival courthouse** just east of M-40 at Territorial, for a peek at the goddess of plenty and pulchritude. The **U. S. Post Office** on North Kalamazoo (M-40) has an especially engaging WPA mural by Carlos Lopez. . . . . . **Maple Isle** is a beautiful island park with swimming beach and changing house. It's on Maple Lake off M-40 on the north side of Paw Paw. Look for the small parking area to the east, just north of the convenience store.

LEARNING MORE ABOUT MICHIGAN WINES . . . . . Pick up the free *Michigan Wine Country* newspaper distributed free at tasting rooms and wine stores. It's full of interesting, informative articles on new devel opments in Michigan wines by winemakers, wine dealers, and wine lovers. The ads spotlight all Michigan wineries and leading wine stores, too. . . . . . In Ann Arbor, the **Village Corner** on South University at Forest stocks over a hundred carefully selected Michigan wines and always features some Michigan wines in its promotions. Its super-informative catalog, published six times a year, typically has one Michigan wine feature, too. Ask for a free subscription at the store, or call (313) 995-1818. . . . . . **Chain supermarkets** may have the best prices on popular Michigan wines. Meijer, D&W Food Centers in West Michigan, and Osco/Jewel in West Michigan, Indiana, and Illinois stock Michigan wines. . . . . The **Michigan Wine & Harvest Festival**, held in Kalamazoo and Paw Paw for five days ending with the weekend after Labor Day, has wine tastings from most Michigan wineries — for a fee, to benefit local charities. The winemakers themselves, however, aren't allowed by law to be on hand and dispense samples except at the opening-night event on Wednesday. There's lots of food, music, and entertainment, an art fair, and a children's day. Call (616) 381-4003 for a brochure.

AN INCREASINGLY ENJOYABLE SCENIC ROUTE FROM KALAMAZOO TO BENTON HARBOR . . . . . is the old **Territorial Road**, also known as the Red Arrow Highway. From the west side of the high moraine west of Kalamazoo, it passes through vineyards, orchards, farm stands, and produce farms. Many old buildings in the country and in Paw Paw, Hartford, and Lawrence are quite interesting. Lately the road has attracted more small businesses like antique dealers and the Paw Paw Food Co-op a few miles west of Paw Paw. Near Benton Harbor the Red Arrow Highway passes by the **Benton Harbor Fruit Market** (page 51) and **Sarett Nature Center** (page 68).

Michigan's fabulous Fruit Belt

A 270-mile shoreline region of specialty fruits, from wine grapes of increasing note to huge crops of tasty apples, tart cherries, and blueberries.

One of Michigan's true glories is the variety and flavor of its fruits and vegetables, available at countless farm stands and many U-pick operations. A finishing touch to every summertime outing in West Michigan should be a visit to a fruit farm, to load up on fresh fruit to take home. Farm visits and picking expeditions slow down the all-too-frenetic pace of contemporary life and connect you up to the slower, older world of agriculture.

The Fruit Belt extends inland up to over 30 miles in the south. Up north it's a much narrower zone. Lake Michigan moderates the temperature of the air around it, cooling it in hot weather and making it warmer in cold weather. The lake effect tends to depress temperatures 3° to 4° F., slowing early blossoms until danger of warming followed by frosts are past. The lake also means cooler, longer summers, which let fruit ripen more slowly for more intense flavor. One Georgia native was shocked to discover that Michigan peaches tasted better than Georgia's famous peaches. The lake also elevates temperatures 3° or 4° F. in fall, extending the growing season. Wine grape varieties that need a lot of heat to ripen aren't at their best in Michigan, but varieties that prefer colder climates, like the German Riesling and the Pinot Noir and Chardonnay of Burgundy, make excellent wines.

Most winters Lake Michigan has open water, which means that winds continue to pick up moisture and deposit it as a belt of snow that protects fruit trees' roots and graft unions while keeping winter temperatures some 10° to 20° F. warmer than those in neighboring Wisconsin. Wisconsin's more extreme continental climate makes for colder and hotter winter and summer temperatures, and far more sun.

The same prevailing west winds crossing Lake Michigan are what created West Michigan's sandy, well-drained soil that's also

Those who drive along country roads in the Fruit Belt during blossomtime see beautiful scenes. Blossomtime is usually in very early May in southwest Michigan, later the farther north you go. The Southwest Michigan Tourist Council outside Benton Harbor even publishes a map of pretty blossomtime drives. Call (616) 925-6301 to get a copy.

beneficial to fruit. As the last glacier was melting some 3,000 years ago, a good deal of the sand and sediment deposited by rivers and runoff along the shore was blown back onto the land. That east-blown sand created a wide belt of sandy soil extending as far inland as Grand Rapids, and a dramatic shoreline strip of dunes, the longest freshwater dunes in the world.

Southwest Michigan's Fruit Belt first developed in the 1850s, when early farmers around Benton Harbor and St. Joseph noticed that their peach trees survived severe winters that killed off peach trees in other parts of Michigan. Demand for fruit in the booming nearby metropolis of Chicago was so great and shipping from Benton Harbor so convenient that by the 1860s, productive peach orchards fetched $1,000 an acre.

Benton Harbor's big fruit market goes back to the 1870s, when farmers' wagons lined up for a mile to load onto the fruit boats at the canal west of Main Street downtown. Steamers transported the fruit to wholesale commission houses in Chicago and Milwaukee. People began buying fruit in quantity direct from the farmers waiting in line, creating first an informal and later a formal market. That market is still operating today (see page 51).

Fruit canneries and factories making baskets and crates sprang up around and beyond Benton Harbor, and fruit-growing spread throughout much of Van Buren and Berrien counties. South Haven was long famous for its peach crop. At the turn of the century, 144,000 Michigan acres were planted in peach orchards, more than all other Michigan fruit crops combined.

A devastating freeze in 1919 killed most of the peach trees, and another freeze in the 1920s led farmers to switch to apples. Then in the 1930s Stanley Johnston developed early, cold-resistant Haven peaches at Michigan State University's South Haven experiment station. Haven peaches revolutionized peach-growing. They have an eye-pleasing reddish color. As a freestone peach, it was much easier to eat and slice than earlier varieties, whose flesh clung to the stone. Havens can be picked much earlier, and they produce over an extended period, so eating fresh peaches has become much more popular.

But even the Haven peach failed to halt the decline of peach growing in Michigan. When Chicago peach processors folded in the 1950s, Michigan peach acreage plummeted to just about 8,000. Today the figure is up a little, to 8,290.

By comparison, blueberry plantations have boomed in recent years. Stanley Johnston also started Michigan's blueberry industry when he domesticated a wild, high-bush variety quite different from low-growing Maine blueberries. Unlike most fruits, blueberries like "junk land": low, relatively chilly, swampish areas with dark, acidic, sandy soil. The area around South Haven and Grand Junction happens to have a lot of this land. It has emerged as the world's leading blueberry producer. (To see a vast array of blueberry products, visit The Blueberry Store on Phoenix Street in downtown South Haven.)

Michigan's 16,400 acres of blueberries can yield three tons of berries an acre. At a typical wholesale rate of around a dollar a pint (including packaging), blueberries are Michigan's best-paying legal crop. Those blueberry farmers within 10 or 12 miles of Lake Michigan are especially blessed because they get full benefit of the lake effect. Traditionally, migrant pickers have harvested the blueberry crop, but now $100,000 mechanical berry pickers increasingly do the job.

Michigan has 12,000 acres in grapes, centered around Paw Paw and the big juice plant in Lawton, owned and operated by the nationwide Welch's cooperative. By far the largest portion of Michigan's grapes are Concord grapes used for juice.

Especially noteworthy fruit farm destinations in southwest Michigan's fruit belt include:

Growing fruit was and is a family affair. This Michigan family posed with its apple crop in 1891. Many U-pick farm operations in Berrien County have been in the same family for five and more generations, sometimes ever since the land was settled.

◆ Wick's Apple House, just a short distance from Tree-Mendus Fruit (see page 55)
◆ Sunrise Farms near Benton Harbor. From I094, take exit 30, east on Napier 2.6 miles. Watch for signs. (616) 944-1457.
◆ Lemon Creek Winery and Fruit Farm near Berrien Springs (page 39,
◆ Crane's Orchards and Pie Pantry on M-89 between Fennville and Saugatuck.
◆ Tree-Mendus Fruit (page 53).

   Up-north fruit standouts include:

◆ Amon's cherry orchard tour near Traverse City (page 582)
◆ the beautiful Bill's Farm Market in Petoskey (page 606)
◆ Larry Mawby's winery on the Leelanau Peninsula (page 562)
◆ wineries and vineyards on the Old Mission Peninsula (p. 577-8)

   The Fruit Belt makes for a backroads adventurer's delight. Rows of vineyards and grids of orchards create an orderly, highly cultivated landscape, sprinkled with villages dating from the late 19th-century fruit boom. The area looks much more like Europe than most of the American Middle West, especially where vineyards and orchards cover high, rolling hills and glacial moraines. The **scenery** can be breathtaking in hilly parts of Berrien

County, in Oceana County south of Ludington and along the
Hart-Montague Bicycle Trail (page 526), and throughout cherry
country up north.

**MEXICAN-AMERICAN MIGRANTS WHO FOLLOW THE HARVEST TO
MICHIGAN. . . . .** have become permanent residents throughout the
Fruit Belt where permanent, year-round jobs are available. Thanks to
the big **Heinz pickle cannery** in Holland, the world's largest, over 25%
of Holland's residents are Mexican-American. Little Mexican groceries
are fairly frequent sights, though authentic Mexican restaurants are not
common. Most recently arrived Mexican-Americans prefer to save money
and cook at home. Still, it's always worth asking locally to see if there's
anything new and noteworthy. One established favorite is **Su Casa** on
M-89 by the Shell Station in Fennville. Tucked behind a grocery where
piñatas and fried pork rind hang from the ceiling, it's a hangout for local
fruit cannery workers at breakfast and lunch, and a popular dinner destination for Anglos.

**VISITORS ARE WELCOME AT THE WORLD'S LARGEST CASH-TO-
GROWER FRUIT MARKET . . . . . .** as long as they keep small children
at home and stay out of the way of the trucks and hi los moving around.
The **Benton Harbor Fruit Market** is open from May 1 (melons come
from south Florida) through October. This big (24 acres), busy wholesale
produce market is the largest cash-to-grower market in the world.
Especially large numbers of blueberries, strawberries, cantaloupe, sweet
and Indian corn, cucumbers, peaches, peppers, tomatoes, and summer
squash pass through here. The market isn't set up for outsiders, but
you can watch, and you can buy if you get a $5 permit from the **market
office**. (Check out the office for free calendars and pamphlets on buying
and using fresh fruits and vegetables.)

The most interesting place to watch the action is under the big **market shed** in the center rear. Here growers of produce that hasn't been
sold on prearranged contracts negotiate and sell direct from their trucks
to day buyers from farm stands, independent grocers, and small chains.
Trucks come about 8 a.m. and line up, six abreast, before being admit-
ted to the trading shed at 9 a.m. A U.S. Department of Agriculture
reporter takes prices from bidding there. These very prices establish
wholesale price guidelines for the entire state.

Behind that shed are direct-sales stalls where bigger growers rent
space to sell their produce. Only 7% of market transactions are of the
direct, cash-to-grower variety. The rest are deliveries on pre-sold produce. Commission houses representing firms like Meijer, and the

Spartan co-operative have little trailer-like cubes on long loading docks. Growers deliver produce to these commission brokers mostly in the afternoon.

Most produce grown elsewhere is picked green. Michigan commercial practice is to pick at the "breaker," when the tomato — for instance — is flesh-colored. Truly ripe produce would be overripe by the time it gets to the supermarket. *The market is about 2 1/2 miles east of downtown Benton Harbor at 1891 Territorial, east of Crystal and just west of Euclid. From I-94 and Kalamazoo, take exit 33, go north on Crystal, east on Territorial. From I-94 and Chicago, take exit 30, go west on Napier to Crystal, north to Territorial, then east. (616) 925-0681. Market opens May 1 with Florida melons, stays open thru October. Daily and Sunday 8-3, except Saturday 8-noon.*

WOOD FRUIT BASKETS AND CRATES . . . . . in a profusion of styles can be purchased singly at **Midwest Fruit Package** (616-927-3371), inside the Benton Harbor Fruit Market next to the market office. For gift store owners, this place is a treasure trove, thanks to low prices and the pleasantly country look. Baskets and crates are infinitely useful — for raking leaves, holding mail, storing books and toys — and attractive too.

Tree-Mendus Fruit

No other fruit farm provides visitors with so much to do, from hiking and hayrides to sampling over 200 varieties of antique apples.

Tree-Mendus Fruit artfully provides a pleasant day in the country for a generation of Americans who no longer have relatives down on the farm. In addition to 360 acres of U-pick orchards, there's a big **picnic area** and 120-acre **nature park** with **hiking trails** through wooded wildlife areas with ponds. Visitors can fill **water jugs** at a deep well. On busy weekends ushers are on hand to direct visitors to all parts of the farm. The picking, picnicking, and bus tours are all very well organized, and the place has a nice, rural atmosphere. The **International Cherry Pit Spitting Championship** is held here each year on the first Saturday in July.

Herb Teichman's tours focus on fruit and teach visitors a lot about it. He doesn't run a carnival, as some well-known cider mills and orchards do. He loves to talk to customers when time permits. His outstanding, narrated **orchard tours** cover the evolution of fruit varieties, let tour-goers sample antique apples and get a first-hand look at cultivation techniques from grafting and pruning to harvesting, depending on the season. **One-hour tours** are given by appointment, and also on short notice when possible. They cost $3 to $5 a person, depending on options, with a $40 minimum. Narrated "orchard safari" tours are offered on certain weekends. **Hayrides** and cookouts are scheduled on some evenings when the moon is full.

Teichman's **"old-time apple museum"** has grown from a few dozen antique apple trees to a remarkable collection of over 200 varieties from around the world. Here you can taste the Spitzbergen (Thomas Jefferson's favorite), the Westfield Seek-No-Further, the Fameuse (snow apple), Black Gilliflower (sheepnose), and the tasty, tart, crisp Calville Blanc d'Hiver, which goes back to 1627.

Modern marketing demands apples that look uniform and attractive, ship well, and can be picked at once. Such requirements have eliminated many old favorites. About 50 antique

At Tree-Mendus Fruit you can buy many varieties of antique apples. Old varieties have more interesting flavors than today's apples developed for mass harvesting and eye appeal.

varieties are for sale here. Much of the stock came from former GM attorney Robert Nitschke, an avid fan who collected and propagated many kinds of old apples in his Birmingham back yard. To order scions of his trees, write for the catalog of **Southmeadow Fruit Gardens**, 15310 Red Arrow Highway, Lakeside, MI 49116.

Apples you pick yourself cost 38¢ a pound, while antique and unusual varieties are about a dollar. Also for sale are jams, apple butter, frozen peaches and cherries, homemade cherry topping, and the farm's distinctive varieties of cider and cherry cider. Belgian waffles filled with the farm's Cherry Brite topping are cooked while you wait. On crisp fall days, pickers and hikers can warm themselves by the big fireplace.

Cherries ripen in July, followed by apricots, peaches, plums, nectarines, apples, pears, and pumpkins. All are grown on the farm and sold U-pick or picked. Recently the Teichmans have gotten into experimental vegetables, traditional and exotic. Gift boxes of fresh fruit are shipped from July through December.

The farm is 1 1/2 miles east of M-140 on East Eureka Road, 2 miles northeast of Eau Claire. Call first for Ripe-N-Ready report: (616) 782-7101. Open late June through 3rd week in Oct. Up to Labor Day: open daily except Tues 10-6. After Labor Day: Fri-Mon 10-6. **Group tours** *by appointment any day, starting in blossomtime (early May). Free admission to orchard/park, except on the day of the* **International Cherry Pit Spitting Contest** *(the first Saturday of July) and on Sat. & Sun. after Labor Day, when it's $4/adult, $2/child, including tour. Fee is credited toward fruit purchase.*

MORE FRUIT AND LUNCH, TOO, NEAR TREE-MENDUS FRUIT . . . . .
Scenic Indian Lake Road leads north off M-62, passing the lake and
Sprague's Old Orchard (a beautiful old farmstead and farm market) on
the way to **Wicks Apple House**, another worthwhile destination. It has a
good informal restaurant for breakfast and lunch. It's a glorified farm
market, cider mill, gift shop, bustling and friendly. Glass walls give
views of the bakery and, on October weekends, of the cider-making
process. The Wicks family raises its own asparagus, tart cherries,
Stanley plums, apples, and Concord grapes. Local produce is featured.
*52281 Indian Lake Rd. (616) 782-6822. Open Memorial Day through
October, Tues-Sun 8-6.*

MORE INFO ON FARM STANDS, U-PICKS, AND CIDER MILLS . . . . . .
For a state-wide guide that includes annotated maps to over 200 farm
stands and U-picks and 130 cider mills, see our **Michigan Fresh** in the
list of recommended Michigan travel books at the end of this book.. . . . .
For **free guides to orchards and farm stands** in Berrien, Van Buren,
and Cass counties, the heart of southwest Michigan's Fruit Belt, call or
write **Southwest Michigan Tourist Council**, 2300 Pipestone, Benton
Harbor, MI 49022. (616) 925-6301. The "Pick Michigan" booklet lists virtually all farm stands and U-picks, with some coupons. Two big, fold-out
maps show scenic routes past orchards and farms at blossom time (late
April-early May) and in fall, with those farm stands, cider mills, and
wineries that are open. Ask for "Drive among the Blossoms" and "Travel
along Jewel-Colored Roads." Inquire here also about **golf** and **events**
information.

Russ Forest

Primeval oaks and giant tulip trees,
so old they were already huge in pioneer times

An awesome stand of huge virgin oaks, hundreds of years old, surrounds the stately old Newton farmhouse at the edge of Russ Forest. It's in an undeveloped part of undeveloped Cass County. If you come to Russ Forest from the west, from Dowagiac and M-51, it appears by surprise, unannounced by signs. All this contributes to the powerful, out-of-time feeling inspired by these great, primeval trees, a rare remnant of a virgin Eastern hardwood forest.

James Newton, builder of the **Newton House** farmhouse, was an English-born orphan who came to the U.S. as an indentured servant to a Quaker family. Many Quakers came to this part of Michigan. The escaped slaves they helped to settle here formed Cass County's old rural black communities around Calvin Center, Volinia, and Vandalia. The house's older section dates from 1844; Newton's son erected the east wing in 1867. The unrestored house, finished with beautiful local hardwoods, displays historical memorabilia about Cass County and the Grange movement. The Cass County Historical Society runs this museum. To go up the unsettlingly narrow staircase to the house's cupola in the treetops is an adventure in itself. *Open Sundays from 1 to 4:30, April through October.*

Cassopolis businessman Fred Russ purchased the 580-acre Newton Woods Farm during the Depression and donated it to Michigan State University for use as a forestry research station. Such forests of sun-loving oaks and hickories cannot replenish themselves, since only shade-tolerant seedlings can survive here. This majestic stand must have established itself after a fire some 300 or 400 years ago, says the M.S.U. forester who manages Russ Forest. Gradually the old oaks and hickories are being replaced by young beeches and maples.

Russ Forest's mixed hardwoods also include a stand of immense black walnuts, as big as any you'll ever see, and the biggest tulip poplar in Michigan, 180 feet high and 15' 6" in circumference. Its sister tree, perhaps 300 years old, was the

A forest fire 300 or 400 years ago was followed by the stand of oaks that tower over visitors to Russ Forest today.

tallest recorded tree in Michigan until a wind storm toppled it in 1984. The fallen giant and its sister can be seen from the trail on the east side of the parking lot off Marcellus Highway. A spectacular **fall color display** is created by the varied trees: oak, hickory, hard maples, flame-orange sassafras, and the clear yellow of tulip trees.

Donor Fred Russ especially valued the property's huge tulip poplars, the giants of the Eastern forest, and wished to encourage research on them. In the 1930s standard forestry practice promoted planting cutover land with pines for timber and conservation. Russ was ahead of his time. He was convinced that tulip poplar plantations were a worthwhile idea. Unlike other softwoods of the poplar family, tulip poplar has a cell structure that keeps it from splintering or splitting when sawn or carved. It works and nails easily, like pine. It's naturally disease-resistant. Today the tulip trees Russ planted have reached usable size.

Eighty acres of old-growth timber along the road has been set aside as a natural area. The only cutting done here was when some walnut trees were removed for gunstocks in World War I and some white oaks for PT boats in World War II. Tree-rustling of the valuable black walnuts presents no threat here; the area is thick with relatives of the pioneer Newton family who long owned this land. They regard the forest as their own and are quick to report any suspicious strangers with chain saws.

Not all of M.S.U's Russ Research Forest was virgin forest. Most of the tree plantations are on old prairie land that was farmed. Eighty acres were owned and managed by a timber company until their recent purchase by M.S.U. (Hardwood logging is big business in Cass County.)

Cass County's adjacent **Russ Forest Park** provides parking, **picnic tables, play equipment, a small shelter, restrooms,** and access to **two miles of flat, scenic trails** that go through the research forest. They make two loops going over wooden footbridges and through virgin hardwoods and managed stands. **Cross-country skiing** on the flat, easy, ungroomed trails is encouraged. The area along Dowagiac Creek (a Class A **trout stream**) is quite open, with some low marshes.

*Park entrance and parking area is on Marcellus Hwy. just east of Newton House, 8 miles west of Marcellus and 5 miles east of Dowagiac. For **information and group tours** about forest ecology and management, contact the Michigan State University forestry research station, 20673 Marcellus Hwy., Decatur, MI 49045. (616) 731-4597. For **park information** or shelter reservations, contact: Cass County Parks Dept., 340 O'Keefe, Cassopolis, MI 49031. (616) 445-8611.*

OFF THE BEATEN TRACK NEAR RUSS FOREST . . . . . The main street of **Marcellus**, 8 miles east of Russ Forest, has lovely old homes, a quaint bank worth a visit, and the **Cozy Cupboard**, a homey restaurant where customers have assembled a collection of souvenir plates from around the world. . . . . . At **Peacewood**, a beautiful produce farm and stand that uses principles of sustainable agriculture, you can find two dozen kinds of peppers, many kinds of green and yellow beans, tomatoes and cut flowers you can pick, and other summer and fall vegetables. Farmers Judy and John Yaeger left the University of Chicago some 25 years ago for country living and physical work. They provide recipes on how to use and preserve their produce. *93356 36th St., just inside Van Buren County. (616) 423-8527. From Marcellus Highway 4 miles from Russ Forest and from Marcellus, turn north onto Lawrence Road at Thompson Corners Grocery, go 3 1/2 miles north. Farm is on west side of road.*

DOWAGIAC'S HISTORIC HOMES AND RESTORED DOWNTOWN . . . . . are remarkable. The small city (population 6,400) prospered with the phenomenal success of Round Oak stoves, once America's best-selling wood heater. Then it declined. Now Dowagiac is undergoing a downtown revival. False modern fronts from the Kawneer company of nearby Niles have been removed, historic storefronts restored, and truck traffic rerouted off Front Street. Gift and decor shops and a discount fashion store make for a modest amount of browsing. Don't miss the 1926 vintage **Caruso's Candy Kitchen**

at 130 South Front (open Mon-Sat 9:30-5:30) and **Olympia Books and Prints** at 208 South Front, a delightful used book shop where you can pick up an interesting illustrated **walking tour** to historic Dowagiac. (Open Mon-Fri 10:30-4:30, Sat 10-3).

The most impressive old houses are west of Front along High, Indiana, and Green. Most unusual of all is **The Maples** at 511 Green, which intersects West Division a block cast of West Main (M-51/M-62). Made of boulders, with a great entrance arch, it resembles some of H. H. Richardson's Romanesque masterpieces. This was only one of the homes of Round Oak's treasurer, a grandson of founder Philo D. Beckwith. He wintered in Florida and spent some of the summer at a rustic retreat for Round Oak managers. Perhaps their lavish lifestyles left Round Oak's manager/heirs unprepared for the competition brought to their ornate parlor stoves by the advent of central heating , for Round Oak failed to make the transition to more modern times.

HANDS-ON SCIENCE AND CASS COUNTY HISTORY . . . . . can be enjoyed at the newly expanded **Southwestern Michigan College Museum** outside Dowagiac. Thirty exhibits like the whisper dish and changing colored shadows convey principles of physics and light. The history gallery spotlights local industries: Round Oak Stoves, **Kitty Litter**, and James Heddon fishing lures. It also covers Cass County's important role on the Underground Railroad and its famous old **rural black community**, going back to early Quakers who helped escaped slaves. (Detroit mayor Dennis Archer grew up in nearby Cassopolis, incidentally.) *From M-51 in Dowagiac, take M-62 east toward Cassopolis. In about a mile, go right (south) onto Cherry Grove. When you come to the college entrance, park in the lot on your left. Museum is at the end of the lot. Go in the cylindrical lobby. (616) 782-5113. Tues-Sat 10-5. Free.*

CANOEING ON THE DOWAGIAC RIVER . . . . . has been called by the book *Canoeing Michigan Rivers* "one of the most interesting trips in southern Michigan." It's a short (4 hours or less), easy trip though varied, surprisingly remote terrain. Get an excellent **free pamphlet** on the canoe trip and the river's geology and history at the Dowagiac Chamber of Commerce (616-782-8212) or Olympia Books. **Doe-Wah-Jack's Canoe Livery** (616-782-9464) is 3 1/2 miles north of Dowagiac on M-51.

ANOTHER MAJESTIC REMNANT OF VIRGIN HARDWOOD FOREST . . . . . is along the Dowagiac River. The Michigan Nature Association's **Dowagiac Woods** is known for its fabulous displays of spring wildflowers and fall color. It is likely Michigan's largest moist, virgin-soil woodland. Trees uncommon to Michigan, including the chinakapin oak, blue beech, and Ohio buckeye, can be seen here. *From M-62 about 4 miles west of Dowagiac, turn south onto Sink Road. In 1 mile turn east onto Frost. In about a mile is a parking area on the north side of the road.* Wear waterproof footgear. The short trail off Frost west of the parking area is the driest, with a good view of spring wildflowers.

Downtown St. Joseph

*This quaint old place has a lively downtown,
band concerts, and an old-fashioned park
with a great view of Lake Michigan.*

Other Michigan downtowns have more spectacular
architecture or shops, but St. Joe is overall one of the
most attractive. It has healthy small-town retailing,
pleasant historic buildings, and a striking setting on a bluff overlooking Lake Michigan. Benches, sculptures, even a hot dog vendor and balloon-seller make State Street a nice place to linger.

St. Joseph enjoys unusual prosperity for a town of 9,000
because of many old-time resorters, the Whirlpool world headquarters and related facilities scattered south and north of town,
and a recent influx of second-home buyers from Chicago who are
pricing some locals out of the market.

Lake Bluff Park overlooks Lake Michigan and extends for
seven blocks along Lake Boulevard around to the St. Joseph
River on the north. It makes a wonderful walk, with flower gardens, a century's worth of sculptures, and overlook benches. Get
walking tours of St. Joseph's public sculpture and downtown
historic buildings, along with other information, from St. Joseph
Today. *(616) 982-6739. 520 Pleasant. Open weekdays 8:30-5, or
ask them to mail you information.* (Incidentally, the comfortable,
elegant Boulevard Hotel enjoys this same view.) The funny, clever
Curious Kids Museum at 415 Lake Boulevard (page 66) is a real
highlight for children.

Takeout food for a **picnic in the park** is conveniently available at **Clancy's Deli**, half a block down Pleasant, or **Mama
Martorano's**. A stairway by Ship Street descends to the old Pere
Marquette train station (now Zitta's Restaurant. From there it's
just a few blocks' walk from **Silver Beach County Park** on Lake
Michigan. The park has a wide, sandy beach, some picnic tables,
new bathhouses and a concession stand. There's little natural
landscaping and no dunes. A dramatic series of recent improvements with bright blue roofs has spiffed up the entire area, from
the blufftop stairway and restrooms to the beach itself. Silver
Beach has access to the 1,000-foot **south pier**. It's a fine place to

❶❷ Two down-towns. Unsettling & dramatic contrast between trim white city and poor black one. **Benton Harbor's** downtown (❶) almost became a ghost town, while adjacent St. Joe (❷) thrives. Don't miss **St. Joe's** Krasl Art center, band concerts in Lake Bluff Park; Benton Harbor's Wolf's Marine.

❸ Curious Kids Museum. Outstanding small hands-on museum, more kid-centered and playful than most. Zany cartoon decor.

❹ Mama Martorano's. Real Italian home cooking, redolent of garlic and wine, shines at this simple spot. Excellent food for little money.

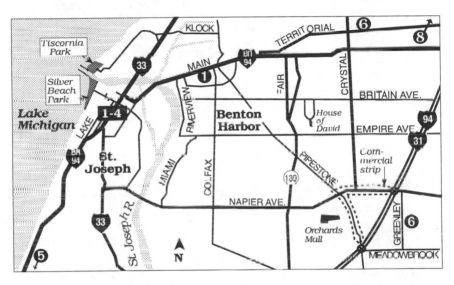

❺ Snowflake Motel. Frank Lloyd Wright conceived this once-luxurious motel which now caters to truckers, construction workers & repeat summer vacationers. Friendly staff, budget rates.

❻ The Herb Barn. A fragrant natural world a minute from I-94. Good prices on plants; lots of ideas for uses. Pretty display garden and dried arrangements.

❼ Benton Harbor Fruit Market. Watch the action at world's biggest cash-to-grower fruit & vegetable market. Good retail produce stand. Free posters, recipes.

❽ Sarett Nature Center. Bird-watcher's paradise, thanks to river wetlands, 5 miles of trails, boardwalks, and elevated viewing seats. Good gift shop, excellent talks & outings.

Highlights of
St. Joseph/
Benton Harbor

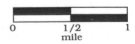

0   1/2   1
mile

fish and get a good view of the lake and shoreline.

"Silver Beach" to many Chicagoans still means the famous Silver Beach amusement park that developed into one of Chicagoland's premiere summer entertainment spots in the first half of this century. The dance pavilion and later the Shadowland Ballroom were glamorous places with big-name dance bands, visited by movie stars and celebrities. Moonlight strolls

What makes down-
town St.Joseph
special: a brick
street, attractive
landscaping and architecture, a lake
view, and many specialty shops.

along the boardwalk, giant slides, penny arcades, picnic pavil-ions, and the beach itself were the attractions. Closed in 1971, the amusement park was torn down three years later.

Back on the bluff, the **Krasl Art Center** is just across from the Lake Bluff Park's south end, at 707 Lake between Park and Pearl. It's an outstanding example of how much a small art cen-ter can do with volunteers and well-chosen changing exhibits like abstract sculptors Michael Slaski and Austin Collins from Indiana, antique maps from local collectors, and a major show in fall, 1994 of John Steuart Curry, an important American region-alist and contemporary of Grant Wood. The juried all-state com-petition in March and April is an annual highlight. The **gallery shop** is strong on jewelry, scarves, ceramics, and other gifts hand-crafted by Michigan artists in addition to having a good general line of books, cards, and gifts about art and the area, and for children. *(616) 983-0271. Mon-Thurs & Sat 10-4, Fri 10-1, Sun 1-4. Free admission.*

The heart of downtown retailing is on State Street between Ship and Elm, with its center at State and Pleasant. Typical store hours are Monday through Saturday from 10 to 5:30, Friday to 9. A small but increasing number of stores are open Sunday afternoons. **State Street stores** are mostly either small town standbys (including an old department store and a big dime store with a wonderfully creaky wood floor) or women's wear, gift, and accessory stores catering to fairly conservative, well-to-do women who expect good service and get it here. Highlights, arranged from south to north, include:

♦ **Le Verre Boutique**, *317 State*. Glasses and glass for windows, doors, and cabinetry are hand-engraved, etched, stenciled, and sandblasted here. Many unusual examples are on hand and for sale; much more can be done as custom orders. *(616) 983-4070.*

♦ **G. C. Murphy**, *307 State*. One of the last of a vanishing classic, the old-fashioned variety store. Worth a visit.

♦ **Majerek's Hall of Cards & Books**, *219 State*. Newsstand/bookstore/card shop that's much better than the average vacation reading spot.

♦ **Gallery on the Alley**, *611 Broad just half a block east of State*, offers a colorful, upbeat melange of jewelry, contemporary handcrafts, and watercolor landscapes in a tiny space. *(616) 983-6261.* Across the alley is a video and games arcade and Creative Teaching, a teachers' supply store.

♦ **The Silver Balloon**, *213 State*, is a large, attractive children's clothing store.

♦ **The Toy Company**, *505 Pleasant at State*, offers well-chosen "amusements for all ages": colorful basics like Brio trains, dolls and stuffed animals, blocks, puzzles and "Brain Boosters," picture books, plus rubber stamps and nifty crafts supplies.

♦ **Once Upon a Time**, *now at 515 Pleasant between State and Lake*, is a children's bookstore. *(616) 983-5055.*

Going north, adjoining the park on Ship at Lake Bluff is the elegant **Whitcomb Tower**, now a retirement home. It's on the very site of **La Salle's 1679 fort**, a western outpost in the great French fur-trading empire. Visitors are welcome to peek in and see the mural of Marquette and Joliet's 1669 canoe journey down the St. Joseph River. Still farther north, the **bandshell**, below Port Street between State and Lake, is much used in summer. St. Joseph has the only tax-supported municipal band in Michigan. Evening audiences can enjoy musical sunsets over the lake. **Free band concerts** are held here from July through Labor Day, Sundays and holidays at 3:30 and 7:30 (with free horse-drawn wagon rides in between), Wednesdays at noon, and on August Fridays at 7.

The St. Joseph River curves around St. Joe to the east, making a peninsula of the town. With so much riverfront and the Lake Michigan shore, St. Joe boasts more boat slips than any other town on Lake

Michigan's eastern shore. At the **Margaret Upton Arboretum**, which descends from the band shell to the river, **500 new boat tie-ups**, free to boaters, have been installed with rubberized siding and cleats.

THE BEST AREA BEACH . . . . . is **Tiscornia Park**, more scenic and secluded than Silver Beach, with low dunes and some natural vegetation. The big old resort hotels are long gone, but there's some historic flavor left, including a Shingle Style lifesaving station near the pier. The thousand-foot **North Pier** is popular for perch fishing. The pier is unusual in having **two lighthouses** that comprise one of the last remaining pier range light systems on the Great Lakes. The outer light marks the harbor to incoming boats, and the inner pier light is an additional navigational aid. The connecting catwalk survives.

Tiscornia Park is in two parts: a quarter-mile of Lake Michigan **beachfront** with restrooms, and an area on the St. Joseph River west of Ridgeway by the municipal marina, with **picnic tables** and **new rest rooms**. *In St. Joseph but north of the river. Take M-63 as if you were heading north to South Haven. See map. $3/car.*

A TEN-MINUTE WALK FROM DOWNTOWN TO THE NORTH PIER AND TISCORNIA PARK . . . . . . can be taken by walking over the St. Joseph River bridge that carries M-63 to South Haven. A bird's-eye view of the busy boat traffic at the river mouth is a bonus. Once across the bridge, cut through the parking area behind the Whirlpool offices to the **West Basin Marina**, which connects to the pier and park. Save some energy for the uphill hike back.

A THOUGHT-PROVOKING SIDE TRIP TO BENTON HARBOR . . . . . Across the Blossomland Bridge in downtown Benton Harbor, there are only a few functioning stores, mainly lunch counters. Benton Harbor (population 12,818) is still one of the most depressed cities in the U.S. How Benton Harbor went from being a prosperous city in 1960 to a 20th-century ghost town 20 years later is a story of America's post-World War II move to the suburbs at its most extreme. Mutual distrust between the white business establishment (read "Whirlpool") and leaders elected by increasingly poor black residents eventually made a shambles of the city and its government. It didn't help that Whirlpool moved all its manufacturing out of the area, mostly to Arkansas. Today, after decades of mistrust and dissension, moderate old-timers and some new urban pioneers are gaining political clout and starting moving the city in a pragmatic direction of rebuilding the local economy. Traffic signals now work, fewer streets are cratered, and vacant office buildings, which had reverted to city ownership for nonpayment of taxes, are being renovated. The long-vacant **State Theater** has been reopened to host teen lock-ins and show second-run movies selected for Benton Harbor teens, without too much sex or violence. Some critics charged the former pro-business mayor's push for fiscal stability was exploiting the city by failing to create new jobs for black city residents. He was voted out, and red ink is again flowing in Benton Harbor.

A REAL FIND FOR BOATERS AND BARGAIN-HUNTERS . . . . . Savvy boaters detour through Benton Harbor to shop at **Wolf's Marine**, a cavernous marine accessory store that claims to be the Midwest's largest and offers to match or beat any advertised price. Wolf's makes a point to stock several kinds of most accessories, plus hard-to-find parts and supplies, divers' supplies, and many kinds of smaller boats. Diving lessons are available. Even non-boaters will find lots of useful, fun stuff, like slickers, warm-up suits, seashells and netting, fishing poles, inner tubes, and inflatable boats. *250 W. Main between downtown Benton Harbor and the St. Joseph River. (616) 926-1068. Mon-Fri 9-6; Sat 9-5.*

Curious Kids' Museum

Instead of only playing up to education-minded parents, it taps into kids' own fantasies and curiosities — like 'What happens when you flush the toilet?'

This small but superior hands-on museum in St. Joseph is more tuned into kids and less out to impress their parents than many bigger children's museums. More exhibits are in good working order, and the captions are easier to understand. Bright, fanciful lobby murals are by cartoonist Nancy Drew, who draws and paints like a kid herself. They set a tone of playful messing-around that's carried on inside by bubble-blowing, face-painting, kaleidoscopes, a dinosaur gallery, a simulated apple orchard, and musical instruments to play.

The mechanical section illuminates everyday mysteries with a see-through toilet system and a transparent washing machine (compliments of local giant Whirlpool). In the handicap area, kids can learn what it's like to go up a ramp in a wheelchair or wear leg braces. There are also time-tested hands-on favorites like the giant bubble, the toaster-powered hot-air balloon, beehive, and tests of heart rate, blood pressure, and so forth.

415 Lake Blvd. between Broad and Elm in downtown St. Joseph. Park next door. (616) 983-2543. Wed-Fri 10-5, Sat & Sun noon-5. Also open Tuesdays, June through August. Closed for major holidays and two weeks after Labor Day. Adults $3, kids 2-18 $2. Kids 13 and under must be accompanied by an adult.

A GOOD CHILDREN'S PLAYGROUND . . . . . along Lake Michigan is **Lions' Park,** a few blocks south of Silver Beach in St. Joseph. There's no swimming here, however. To get there, find the Krasl Art Center at Lake Boulevard and Park up on the bluff. Take Park Street down to the lake and turn left on Lions' Park Lane.

THE ST. JOSEPH/BENTON HARBOR AREA'S MOST COMPELLING CURIOSITY . . . . . and its most popular attraction from around 1910 through the 1950s won't be found on any current visitor map. The grounds, rockery, and miniature railroad of the **House of David** amusement park and zoo, are now overgrown. The ball diamond where the famous long-haired teams dazzled tourists is long gone. And the fanciful, picturesque band stands and pavilions are rotting and gradually being taken down by the aging members of this once-vital religious commune, whose members were sworn to celibacy.

Followers of this 18th-century Pentecostal cult arrived in Benton Harbor in 1903. Under the leadership of the charismatic and astute Benjamin Purnell, they developed many successful area businesses, including this park. It's a fascinating, complex story, summarized in our *Hunts' Guide to West Michigan* (page 00), explored in detail in Claire Adkin's *Brother Benjamin*. Still to be seen are the large and ornate communal residences on Britain Avenue. *From downtown Benton Harbor, take Main a mile east to Fair, turn right (south), and in about 3/4 mile, turn left (east) onto Britain. No trespassing onto private property, but you may use public roads. The houses are on your left.* Take the drive between Shiloh and Jerusalem houses to reach the **House of David Arts**, a picture frame shop staffed by a delightful Scottish woman who came to the House of David with her parents in the 1940s. Postcards and other House of David publications are for sale, along with honey still produced by the commune. *Open Mon-Fri 8 to noon and 1 to 5, Saturday 8-noon. (616) 925-1891.*

MORE HOUSE OF DAVID HISTORY. . . . . can be seen and read at the **House of David Room** at the **Benton Harbor Public Library.** It's one of the most unusual and thorough special-interest archives of its kind, the life work of librarian Florence Rachuig. She provides interested visitors with a brief printed history and brings out, upon request, documents chosen from the contents list. The photographs are especially compelling. Rachuig has a clear-headed, sophisticated, yet sympathetic view of these talented, gullible, misunderstood people and the group psychology that attracted them. She also gives illustrated lectures — until September, 1995, when she retires and moves to Texas to honor a promise to her husband, a transplanted Texan. *The library is at 213 E. Wall in downtown Benton Harbor, a block south of Main and a block east of Pipestone. Hours: Mon-Wed 9-8, Thurs & Fri 9-6, Sat 9-5. Call first to be sure of seeing the House of David Room. (616) 926-6139.*

Sarett Nature Center

*An extraordinary place to watch birds
that even novices will enjoy*

What makes this Michigan Audubon Society sanctuary a paradise for novice birdwatchers are its many benches and elevated towers, strategically located in different habitats. They are comfortable places where it's easy to sit and stay still and quiet enough to observe birds at close range without disturbing them. Excellent **trail booklets**, available at all hours at the trailhead by the parking lot, are keyed to views you can often enjoy while sitting. You could even buy a nature book at the top-notch gift shop and read it comfortably sitting by an alder thicket, pond, or tamarack bog, observing the sights and sounds of life around you. A tree house lets you observe from a tree canopy; a bench overlooks a dogwood thicket.

These 350 acres along the Paw Paw River northeast of Benton Harbor include many kinds of prime natural habitats. Here upland meadows and forests overlook lowland marshes and swamp forests going down to the riverbank. In spring and fall the river floods, attracting many migratory waterfowl. A sedge meadow produces a **fine fall wildflower** display. Dead trees, created by rising water levels in swamps, have created plenty of tree holes for wood ducks, owls, woodpeckers, and the uncommon prothonotary warbler. Shorebirds like the Virginia rail remain north in winter if there is open water, provided here by the bayous of the Paw Paw River.

Some five miles of **trails** include quite a bit of boardwalk for good viewing of wetland habitats. The trails are planned as a series of short loops, so you could

Shorebirds like the Virginia rail remain north in winter if there is open water, like the bayous of the Paw Paw River at Sarett.

Towers and treehouses like this let birdwatchers look down on the bird life attracted by the wetlands of the Paw Paw River's floodplain. Hear you may see the unusual Pro-thonotary Warbler, which nests only in hollow trees close to the water.

plan hikes from 1/2 to 2 1/2 hours. **Cross-country skiers** are welcome in winter. Most trails are not handicapped-accessible because of occasional stairways, but they are otherwise easy. One handicapped-accessible trail is directly off the parking lot. Highway noise is occasionally distracting.

Remember, birds are most active in the morning and evening, when the sun is low in the sky. Plan your visit accordingly.

Sarett's **gift shop** is among the very best for nature publications, notecards, bird feeders, seed, and the like. The adjoining meeting/observation room has some well-done displays of mounted birds, seeds, and antlers. A naturalist is usually on hand to answer questions. The center sponsors a busy schedule of **talks**, **nature walks**, demonstrations, outings, and adults' and children's summer **classes**. Sarett naturalists lead several adult **eco-trips**; write Sarett Nature Center, 2300 Benton Center, Benton Harbor, MI 49022 for details.

*2300 Benton Center Rd. in Benton Township. Northeast of Benton Harbor/St. Joseph on the Paw Paw River, 1 mile north of the Red Arrow Hwy. From I-94, take I-196 north (toward South Haven), but get off in 1 mile at the Red Arrow Hwy. exit, go west to Benton Center Rd., then north. From St. Joseph and downtown Benton Harbor, take Main or Territorial 2 miles east to Crystal, north (left) on Crystal to Red Arrow Hwy. (616) 927-4832. **Interpretive center hours:** Tues-Fri 9-5, Sat 10-5, Sun 1-5. Trails and parking lot open dawn to dusk.*

A SPLENDID INTRODUCTION TO BIRDWATCHING IN MICHIGAN . . . . . is a free **pamphlet** from the Michigan Audubon Society detailing 15 prime sites. Look for it at Michigan Visitor Information Centers on major interstates going into Michigan, or send a self-addressed, stamped envelope with 45¢ postage to: Michigan Audubon Society, 6011 W. St. Joseph #403, Lansing, MI 48917.

ANTIQUES AND HERBS JUST OFF I-94 . . . . . It's a one-minute detour to **Bay Antiques**, a large shop south of Coloma, just east of Benton Harbor. It has lots of furniture, both rough and finished. Architectural artifacts, leaded glass, bisque dolls, and oriental rugs are other specialties. *From I-94, take exit 39 (Coloma), go south, turn onto Mountain Rd. in 1/8 mile, follow signs. (616) 468-3221. Open from April through September every day 12-5, Fri & Sat to 7. Otherwise Wed-Sun 12-5.* . . . . . Just a minute off the freeway you can enter the slow-paced, sensuous world of aromatic plants at **The Herb Barn**. The attractive display garden provides lots of ideas for landscaping with the 100 varieties of herbal plants sold here. Inside the sales room, a big selection of books, plus dried arrangements and wreaths, show how to use them. *Southeast of Benton Harbor. Take I-94 exit 30, head east on Napier Rd., then turn immediately south onto Greeley Ave. Stop behind the farmhouse at 1955 Greenley. (616) 927-2044. Mon-Fri 10-5, Sat 10-4, and May-Dec Sun 12-4.*

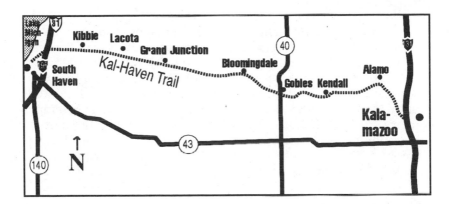

Kal-Haven Trail

*A 34-mile bike path from South Haven to Kalamazoo
passes blueberry plantations, wetlands, farms,
villages and forests.*

There's a surprising amount of variety on this enjoyable
34-mile bike path. It's on a hard, cinder-surfaced abandoned railroad bed that goes from the outskirts of
Kalamazoo through the heart of blueberry country to South
Haven. You look down steep, wooded ravines at glacial lakes on
the east, and pass flat cow pastures and blueberry fields to the
west before going along miles of wetlands with herons and
ducks.

These flat rails-to-trails bikeways are ideal for safe family
bicycling. You can see way ahead; road crossings are infrequent.
Three towns (Gobles, Bloomingdale, and Grand Junction) have
restaurants which make good rest stops. The crushed cinder
surface is compact and well-drained. Much of the way is at least
lightly shaded. Restrooms are at eight locations along the trail.

Even out-of-shape cyclists can do one way in a day, with
rests. It makes sense to start from Kalamazoo and spend the
night in South Haven, after a swim at the Lake Michigan beach.
If you don't have a bike, you could rent one at Healy True Value
Hardware in Gobles (616-628-2584) for an 11-mile shorter trip to
South Haven. Bikes may also be rented at Northside Memories
just north of the Dyckman Street bridge in South Haven (616-
637-8319). **Cross-country skiers** and **snowmobilers** are wel-

come in winter. (Long sight lines mean the snowmobilers won't suddenly come upon skiers.) A 12-mile **equestrian trail** between Kibbie and Bloomingdale should be ready by summer, 1994.

Starting from the eastern trailhead, the first part of the trail goes through a hilly, deeply shady oak forest. The terrain flattens out by **Mentha**, named for the mint plant. Once a large swamp of tamaracks and black ash, this became the experimental mint plantation of A. M. Todd, Kalamazoo's Peppermint King. The company office and social hall faces the trail; other remnants of the company town are south along 23rd Street (formerly Todd Avenue). Mentha operated here from 1900 to 1954, when wilt ruined commercial mint-growing in Michigan.

Just east of Gobles, 10 1/2 miles from the east trailhead, **Grandpa's Beehive Farm** makes a convenient snack stop. Here you can get sandwiches, drinks, baked goods, and water, and for $2 tour a funky farm animal zoo and nature preserve.

Bloomingdale (population 500) is the largest town on the route, and home of the **Bloomingdale Cafe** (616-521-6550), open Tuesday through Saturday from 11 to 8. It's across from a central park and the former **train depot**, now held open by vol-

Lake Michigan at South Haven is a refreshing destination after the 34-mile bike trip from Kalamazoo. Not only beaches but two long piers are a short trip through town from the trail's end. Tight summer parking makes bicycle transportation a real advantage.

unteers as a bike trail rest stop and little museum on summer weekends. Restrooms are in a nearby caboose.

Three miles east of Grand Junction, **Lake Eleven** has a public access fishing site. **Grand Junction** itself, surrounded by blueberry fields, is the home of Michigan Blueberry Growers, a large cooperative that markets its 800 members' blueberries within and beyond the U.S. (See page 49 for the Michigan blueberry story.) Here the Country Fare restaurant (616-434-6425) is open seven days a week for breakfast, lunch, and dinner.

On the last few miles of trail through backwater bayous of the Black River, it's well worth planning to linger to take in the wildlife from the convenient elevated platform of the rail bed.

The variety of natural and agricultural ecosystems make this trail a delight from early spring through fall and into winter. Early May brings **wildflowers** and flowering dogwood (between Kendall and Gobles) to the woods, and **fruit blossoms** to orchards. The trail's well-drained surface is relatively dry when much of Michigan is muddy with spring. **Blueberries** ripen in July and August, and the leaves turn a gorgeous reddish-purple in fall. In winter the red twigs of the blueberry bushes are striking against the snow. **Fall color** along the trail in general is excellent, thanks to the great variety of woods and wetland foliage

Kulamazoo trailhead: in Oshtemo township 1/4 mile west of U.S. 131 on 10th St. between West Main and H Avenue. Take West Main from 131, turn north onto 10th. **South Haven trailhead:** *now behind the county building on Wells Street, just west of the Blue Star Highway and about 3/4 mile north of Phoenix. From I 196, the Phoenix exit west, follow signs. Easy biking from trailhead to downtown, beaches. Call (616) 637-2788 for an illustrated map/ brochure. Trail fee: $2/day individual, $5/family; annual pass $10/$25. Register at trailheads or access points.*

Michigan Fisheries Interpretive Center

At the Wolf Lake Hatchery see millions of fish,
from tiny fingerlings to huge sturgeons,
and learn a lot about Great Lakes fishing.

Each year millions of fish are grown at this state hatchery west of Kalamazoo. It and the five other state hatcheries stock Michigan's public lakes and streams. This is one of the nation's most modern computerized and automated hatcheries. Visitors may observe, in season, its many activities, from spawning, incubating, and hatching eggs to rearing and loading millions of fish that will be released. Spawning occurs in October for lake trout and salmon, and in late March and April for walleye, northern pike, and muskellunge. Hatching, beginning in mid-April for walleye, is especially fun to watch.

In some years over 100 million walleye alone are hatched here, many of which are transported to holding ponds around the state. There they grow to a slightly larger size that is much more able to survive in the wild. Over one million chinook salmon a year are raised for six months until they are over three inches long, then released in rivers and streams in early spring. The salmon swim out into lakes Michigan, Huron, and Superior, where they are joined by salmon from adjoining states' hatcheries. Three and a half years later, those that

The bony-plated lake sturgeon can grow 200 pounds and more, and live to be well over a hundred years old.

survive will return to their original stream to spawn.

Huge **tanks** also hold the enormous populations of northern pike, sturgeon, and brown trout usually raised here. (The fish-hatching program includes both cold-water and warm-water fish, but varies from year to year.) Trout and salmon in indoor tanks are fed automatically every ten minutes. That's fun to watch, but large groups spook the fish, which are unaccustomed to people because the feeding is automatic. Back when an employee fed the fish, they were far less timid, and actually charged after the food.

Other highlights are the 15 **outdoor ponds**, especially the **show pond** with its three enormous sturgeon swimming slowly along the bottom. They are about five feet long and 30 to 50 years old. All the fish here are unusually interesting: big steelheads (also called rainbow trout), from eight to 15 pounds, some very elderly Montana grayling, and other less readily visible sport fish. Visitors can get free bags of pellets to feed the fish. A walkway out into the pond lets visitors look down at the backs of the five-foot sturgeons — even in winter. Flowing well water keeps the pond ice-free in all but the coldest weather.

In the central visitors' area are **plaques** of Michigan's record fish, including a 26-pound rainbow trout, a 46-pound chinook salmon, a 193-pound lake sturgeon, and a 47 1/2-pound catfish. Don't miss the excellent 11-minute **multi-screen slide show** in the 92-seat auditorium which tells about the mission and workings of the Department of Natural Resources Fisheries Division.

Large **historical photos** and captions tell how, in the late 19th century, Michigan commercial fishermen were taking 30 tons of whitefish a year, which led to an eventual collapse of the fishery. Four play-it-yourself **slide shows** tell the story of commercial fishing in Michigan (the parallels with lumbering are clear, about how natural resources were carelessly exploited), recount the horrid sea lamprey invasion, and describe the restoration of the Great Lakes fishery. The federal government's biggest thrust today is restoring the native lake trout, raised in the Marquette hatchery.

In 1921 the Welland Canal bypassing Niagara Falls was finished. It allowed the dreaded sea lamprey to enter the Great Lakes. By 1940 the eel-shaped parasite had spread throughout the lakes. Lampreys decimated valuable food fishes like lake trout and whitefish until a chemical was developed that greatly

Visitors of all ages are transfixed by the huge sturgeon swimming around in the show pond.

suppressed lamprey numbers, allowing for the survival of desirable food and sport fishes. The tiny fish called alewives were similarly introduced through the St. Lawrence Seaway. Depletion of large food fish by the lamprey led to the alewife explosion. Huge die-offs, peaking in the memorable year of 1967, threatened to ruin Michigan beaches until coho and chinook salmon were introduced to control the alewife population.

Ten miles west of Kalamazoo on M-43 at Fish Hatchery Road. From I-94, take U.S. 131 north to exit 38B (M-43), go west 6 miles to Fish Hatchery Rd., left (south) to second drive. (616) 668-2876. Open year-round Wed-Sat 10-5. Also open from Mem. Day to Labor Day Sundays noon to 5. Admission free.

Celery Flats
Interpretive Center

*A nifty museum remembers the glory and hard work
for one of Kalamazoo's most famous products.*

Kalamazoo's bygone fame as America's Celery City is celebrated in the suburb of Portage's inspired little museum
in a creekside park. Kalamazoo-area growers were the
first to popularize celery as an important commercial vegetable.
By the 1880s over 300 local growers were shipping huge quantities all over the United States. A quarter of this region's entire
populace earned its living from celery.

The Kalamazoo area's huge celery industry got its start in the
1860s, when one Cornelius DeBruyn developed and marketed a
sweet but stringy yellow variety of celery. Within a decade other
area celery growers were jointly marketing Kalamazoo celery as
an appetizer — "fresh as the dew from Kalamazoo." Soon celery
was touted as a relaxant in patent medicines, tonics, and sodas.
At the train station and on street corners, many boys sold
bunches of Kalamazoo's celebrated celery.

At this entertaining museum, the celery story is told not only
by gardening tools, tonic bottles, and the like, but by a demonstration greenhouse, celery beds, family photos, and retired celery farmers as weekend guides.

The museum vividly shows the very hard work of the "celery
Dutch." Like almost all of West Michigan's Dutch emigrants, they
were poor people from the rural Netherlands. Earlier settlers of
Yankee stock had passed over the wetlands so plentiful in southern and western Michigan. For little money, poor Dutchmen,
accustomed to farming wet soils, could buy swamplands and
mucklands, then gradually clear them by laboriously grubbing
out tamaracks and shrubs, then draining them by hand.

Profitable cultivation of celery depended on having large
families (typical among Dutch immigrants) to do the tedious
work: first harrowing the muck fine, then starting and coddling
the fussy seedlings, transplanting them, cultivating by hand, and
picking off insects, also by hand. (Chemicals injured the plants.)

An old postcard celebrates Kalamazoo, the Celery City, and the many celery fields in and around it. Here in the 1860s celery was first raised as a popular edible vegetable.

Celery had to be irrigated in dry weather, then blanched by covering with boards in summer and with dirt in fall. Growers had to watch for just the right time to harvest. Finally came another round of intense family activity: harvesting before dawn (thought to bring fresher celery), cleaning, trimming, and neatly tying and packing each head by elaborately wrapping it in paper, and neatly packaging the heads in crates. Kept in root cellars, celery lasted all winter — one of the few green vegetables reliably available in the 19th century.

World War II, smaller families, and scarce farm labor all hastened the demise of Michigan celery. Celery-growing shifted to California, with its reliable weather and cheaper labor. Today's Pascal celery replaced sweeter yellow varieties. Many of Kalamazoo's celery farms south of town were sold for suburban development and became the sprawling suburb of Portage. But many greenhouses and small family farmsteads continue as the basis for Kalamazoo's huge bedding plant industry today.

The celery museum is the centerpiece of a pretty (if unspectacular) linear park along Portage Creek. A two-mile, handicapped-accessible asphalt **path** along the stream forms a loop.

There's an attractive **playground, picnic tables** and **shelter,**
and, across the road, a one-room **country schoolhouse** (same
hours as celery museum) and a grain elevator used for functions.
For $6 you can take a 45-minute **canoe ride** from a dropoff point
back to the center, through woods and marshland that are good
for seeing ducks and geese. **Special events** with live music
include a crafts fair, a mid-July bluegrass festival, and harvest
day in early September, when celery is picked and farmers
demonstrate equipment.

*7335 Garden Lane in Portage. Easily reached from I-94 exit 76A.
(Take S. Westnedge 2 miles south, turn east — left — onto Garden
Lane.) From U.S. 131, take exit 31, east on Centre, north on
Westnedge, east on Garden Lane. (616) 329-4404. May thru
September, Fri-Sun & holidays noon-6. Also by appointment.
$2/adults, $1/children 5-15. Handicapped-accessible.*

FROM CELERY TO FLOWERS . . . . . Gale Arent, the longtime Kalamazoo
County extension agent, paved the way for the successful transition from celery-growing to raising bedding plants. He explains that the local celery industry "began to decline in the mid-1950s with the advent of direct seeding in
the southern and western United States. . . . Dutch farmers all had small
greenhouses used to germinate celery seeds to grow field transplants. As the
celery industry declined, the suburbanization of America was creating a
demand for flower and vegetable transplants for home garden use . . . The
former celery growers combined their horticultural experience with the
knowledge of bedding plant culture provided by Michigan State University
scientists and Extension staff to create a profitable and expanding bedding
plant industry. Today over five million flats of bedding plants are grown in
the Kalamazoo area." . . . . . Bedding plant growers show off their stuff at the
Flowerfest in late July. It includes floral displays and horticultural tours in
many parts of greater Kalamazoo. Call (616) 381-4003 for details . . . . . For
more info on **retail bedding plant greenhouses**, see page 96.

OLD WORLD WAR II FIGHTERS LOOKING LIKE NEW. . . . . can be seen at
the **Kalamazoo Aviation History Museum** (Air Zoo). The museum emphasizes military aviation, evenly balanced among the Army Air Corps (forerun-
ner of the U.S. Air Force), the Navy, and the Marines. Founders Pete and Sue
Parish both flew during World War Ii, she as a WASP. The 46,000-square-foot
museum and the recently acquired 35,000-square-foot annex feature a rotating selection of most of the museum's 50 aircraft. The classic Corsair fighter
is joined by a Wildcat, Hellcat, Tigercat, Bearcat, Warhawk, Aircobra, and

Skyraider, among other fighters. A new 12-passenger **flight simulator** gives the thrill of a flight in the museum's Corsair. Visitors can go on board the newly acquired C-47 Skytrooper and see how paratroopers arrived at the war front. For **"Flight of the Day,"** different planes are flown each day at 2 p.m., May through September, weather permitting. A 64-seat **video theater** continuously shows vintage WWII footage, drawing upon recruitment films, shorts about specific aircraft, and newsreels about important air campaigns and battles. Murals, photos, memorabilia, models, and a gift shop add to the Air Zoo's interest. *On the grounds of the Kalamazoo/Battle Creek International Airport just south of I-94 in southeast Kalamazoo/Portage. From I-94, take exit 78, go south on Portage Road to Milham, turn east (left). (616) 382-6555. Open year-round. June thru August: Mon-Sat 9-6, Sun noon to 6, Wed to 8 p.m. September thru May: Mon-Sat 9-5, Sun noon to 5. $5 adults, $3 children 6-15.*

Downtown Kalamazoo

*A delightful city park, America's first downtown mall,
a rich array of Victorian architecture, an established
microbrewery, and cheap, creative vintage shops*

Although central Kalamazoo features no major visitor destinations, it provides a surprisingly rich urban experience for anyone who enjoys the traditional (and now all
too often vanishing) pleasures of city life: walking, browsing in
stores, people-watching on streets and in a beautiful park, seeing whole streets full of elaborate, well-preserved Victorian houses and churches, and even touring a microbrewery. Resale stores
here really stand out in originality and variety, and compared to
metro Detroit or Chicago, prices seem incredibly cheap. The central district here has four new coffeehouses, lots of live music
and dancing, and a wide variety of restaurants, including the
charming and inventive Cosmo's Cusina.

Kalamazoo is just big enough to support a full range of cultural amenities, including John Rollins bookstore, unusually
large for a city of this size. It's on the long suburban commercial
strip of Westnedge south of I-94. Kalamazoo's population is
80,000 in the city proper and more than twice that in the metro
area, including 41,000 in the sprawling southern suburb of
Portage alone.

Kalamazoo's unusually balanced economy is such a cross-
section of America that the *Wall Street Journal* featured the rumi-
nations of a focus group of local residents as a regular front-page
feature during the 1992 presidential election. Principal industries are several papermaking plants, Upjohn Pharmaceuticals
(whose headquarters and research labs are here), and a big GM
plant that's about to close.

Western Michigan University, Kalamazoo College, and
Kalamazoo Valley Community College form a large educational
establishment. People who went to college here often stick
around. They form the basis for large art, folk dance, tennis, and
blues communities. There's an uncloseted gay community, a
substantial black community centered on the north side, and
more than a few Mexican Americans and Asians. Liberals and

❶ Bronson Park. Its flowers alone are worth a special visit. Historic sculptures and imposing surroundings make this one of the Midwest's finest urban parks.

❷ Kalamazoo Mall. The country's 1st pedestrian mall hasn't thrived over the years, but see neat shops, ornate old theater, and lively midday scene in warm weather.

❸ Public Museum. Small, delightful Egyptian section highlights this local museum. Major emphasis is local history. Nice gift shop. Moving in '95.

Shops. Okuns Shoe Store has huge variety of shoes. Vintage shops have great values and selection. Warehouses of antiques, arch. elements.

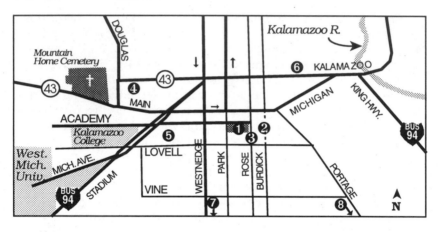

❹❺ Historic districts. On Stuart (5) and South (6) , see blocks of showy mansions built by wealthy Victorians. Most are well preserved; 4 are now bed & breakfast inns.

❻ Kalamazoo Brewery. Pick up tasty, potent stout in this small, funky brewery, and get an informal tour at the same time.

❼ Celery Flat Interpretive Center. Kalamazoo pioneered commercial celery growing. Fascinating museum shows the enormous work Dutch families did to grow this fussy vegetable.

❽ Air Zoo. Colorful group of World War II fighters, especially carrier planes like the legendary Corsair. Daily flights, films, and displays.

Highlights of
Kalamazoo

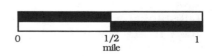

0   1/2   1
                     mile

conservatives both have strong constituencies, which means interesting politics and lots of battles over abortion. The large Dutch population includes many religious fundamentalists, yet Kalamazoo was also the home congressional district of liberal gubernatorial candidate Howard Wolpe. (When he taught political science at Western, Reagan wunderkind David Stockman was one of his students.)

Lately central Kalamazoo is developing a lively alternative scene and a certain panache. It's not uncommon to meet newcomers who are pleased to have discovered it. Low rents, a supply of artistic entrepreneurs, and a strong alternative market have joined to create resale heaven — the best array of shops in Michigan, considering goods, originality, and value. Other small, independent businesses with creative ideas have taken hold, especially in the past few years, and more often on the edges of the central area than in the middle. "People are taking chances and starting their own little businesses," says Lori Cousino, a social worker who also runs La-De-Da's vintage store (see page 88). "In college there was the idea that you had to go somewhere else to do anything interesting. We who never left were considered the losers. Now people come back from Chicago and New York, where they weren't happy, and there's a sense that we're doing pretty well."

Cousino loves it that high school students here are confident enough to be individualistic with old clothes. Compared to his old home in Detroit's Indian Village, Dale Cebelinksi, another vintage store owner with an artistic flair, thinks central Kalamazoo is heaven: a simple, friendly, heterogenous, visually rich place with great old buildings, compact enough that you can walk everywhere, where social problems are on a manageable scale.

To check out the burgeoning local **alternative music scene**, stop by the office of the State Theater at 404 South Burdick (see page 86) and pick up free papers about area music. Yamaha Award-winner Verve Pipes has Kalamazoo roots. Top local groups include the reggae band Jah Kings and Rolling Head, who have played with Cracker. The State's **Kalapalooza** show each February showcases local bands. The prestigious **Irving S. Gilmore International Keyboard Festival**, held here every other year (next in April, 1996), is a steadfastly noncompetitive, secretly juried keyboard artist award and celebration of all genres of keyboard music, funded by the estate of a self-effacing Upjohn heir and amateur pianist who loved the arts.

Because 19th-century Kalamazoo grew steadily, without big booms and busts, elaborate homes were built in a succession of historic styles in the same neighborhoods. The Vine, South Street, and Stuart neighborhoods have survived in remarkably good shape, without much demolition. These houses are in the Stuart Neighborhood a mile west of downtown north of West Main.

Kalamazoo is one of the few cities in Michigan dense enough to be a good destination for train trips. (See page 97.) Points of interest in central Kalamazoo have been arranged here as a walking tour starting from the train station and proceeding south to Vine at Forest. The route is 1.25 miles one way, plus detours out South Street and East Kalamazoo. Take the Westnedge bus back if you're tired. It's a lot to see and do in one day, depending on how many places you stop at. The best part for pedestrians is along the mall, the park, and South Street. If you're in a car, you might prefer to park on Academy, north of Bronson Park.

Kalamazoo Mall/Burdick Street

◆ **Train station/Metro transit.** *459 N. Burdick at Kalamazoo.* Get bus schedule information here. Nifty old Richardsonian Romanesque building.

◆ **Sarkozy Bakery** *(616-342-1952; closed Sat. at 3 p.m., Sun., Mon.). 335 N. Burdick at the north end of the Kalamazoo Mall.* The consummate bakery — friendly owner Judy S., diverse clientele and staff, and all sorts of great stuff, often of Eastern European inspiration. Stop for coffee or juice. Buy focaccia for lunch in the park. Join the Saturday-morning roundtable from 9 to 10:30.

◆ **Flipside Records** *(616-343-5865). 309 N. Burdick.* Recommended by new music fans as the best all-around record

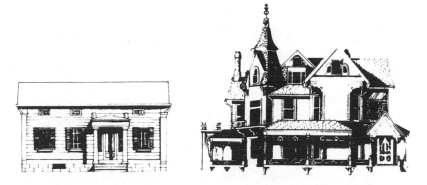

store in a town that's becoming known for alternative music. New and used, strong on jazz. Carries new vinyl.

◆ **Arcadia Commons.** *Between Kalamazoo and Michigan, along and off the Kalamazoo Mall.* Still in the works. Massive, stylish urban redevelopment of existing buildings and uncovering of Arcadia Creek with a walkway below street level. Soon to house the Kalamazoo Public Museum (projected move: fall 1995), Kalamazoo Valley Community College, parking structure, and more. East of the mall are an amphitheater and pond. An ugly duckling furniture store has been turned into a Midwestern version of the Paris Opera now that its Second Empire façade has been restored.

◆ **Kalamazoo Mall.** *Along South Burdick between Water and Lovell.* The nation's first pedestrian mall (1959) remains the nucleus of Michigan's best-balanced downtown. Playground just south of Michigan. Tables at Lovell. Takeouts encouraged. Enough specialty shopping to be interesting, especially to the south. Two department stores between Michigan and South: **Jacobson's** (616-349-6661; tea room is open for lunch, including Sun.) and **Gilmore's** (616-345-3541).

Standouts (from north to south): the **Kalamazoo Convention and Visitors Bureau** across from the Radisson hotel complex; inside the **Radisson** on the Mall at Michigan Avenue, a gift shop, coffeehouse, poster gallery, basket shop, and fashion boutique; **Caffe Casa**, coffeehouse-gallery (open 'til midnight, except Sun. 9-9); new and used mysteries, sci-fi and romance at **Deadly Passions** (tucked in the rear of number 157; 616-383-4402); **Petals & Postings** (616-342-8551), huge selection of cards and T shirts, funny and sweet; **Terrapins** (616-383-4330), jewelry, imports, alternative gear, drums; **Athena Book Shop** (616-342-4508), good browsing for new books, now twice as large, open to 9 p.m. weekdays, to 6 Sat., 1-5 Sun.; an exceptionally large **Mole Hole** (616-344-9000) geared to many tastes, from traditional to contemporary to ethnic, with lots of jewelry.

The pedestrian mall ends at Lovell. But don't stop there. The 400 block of South Burdick is especially interesting. The **State Theatre** at Burdick and Lovell is one of only 12 surviving "atmospheric theaters" designed by the famous theater architect John Eberson. Inside is a Spanish courtyard of long ago, complete with statues, fountain, and three-dimensional facades of picturesque buildings along the walls. Stars still twinkle in the ceiling-sky when the lights dim, and the cloud machine still works. The theater books live music — rock, jazz, blues, country, and gospel music, plus comedy. Occasionally the vintage Barton theater organ gets a workout at events sponsored by the southwest Michigan theater organ group that maintains the organ. Call (616) 345-6500 for program information.

South of Cedar are antiques and resale shops, a coin and stamp shop, the **People's Food Co-op** (616-342-5686), and **Lizards and Mice** (616-382-1444), with offbeat art, T-shirts, and jewelry by local alternative artists.

West of the mall on South Street, **Something's Brewing** (616-349-1295) sells coffees and teas and has a small tea room, open in the daytime. West of the mall on Lovell, **Woodrose Fine Imports** (616- 344-8220) features colorful painted wood masks, Peruvian jewelry, Guatemalan clothing, and ikat-dyed clothing from Indonesia.

BRONSON PARK AND VICINITY

◆ **Bronson Park.** *On the west side of downtown, bounded by Rose, Park, South, and Academy. Extra parking is along Academy.* Even though a deadly 1980 tornado ripped out dozens of its giant oak trees, Bronson Park is a most beautiful and interesting urban park. It's surrounded by imposing civic and church buildings. A century's worth of monuments and fountains immediately convey that this has long been an important focal point for the citizens of Kalamazoo.

Once a cow pasture, the rectangular parcel became a park in 1876, part of a great era of American park-building commemorating the nation's centennial. In the southwest corner is the area's only remaining **Indian mound**, a centuries-old Hopewell-period burial site. In the northeast corner an imposing eight-foot

bronze sculpture of an American foot soldier from 1923 com-
memorates U.S. military campaigns. **Memorial plaques** sprinkled throughout the park honor people as diverse as Adlai
Stevenson and prominent Kalamazoo feminist Lucinda Hinsdale
Stone. The 1913 U.S.S. Maine Memorial Tablet was cast from
parts of that famous Navy ship which exploded in Havana harbor. Toward the east end is a dramatic sculpture-fountain.
Erected in 1939, it commemorates the sad removal of local
Indians to the west in 1840. Another fountain features sculptor
Kirk Newman's lifelike playing children. Both **fountains and
pools** are favorite play spots for nearby children on hot summer
days.

What makes this park especially nice in summer is the
abundance of well-maintained flowers, beginning with spring
bulbs and climaxing in a spectacular floral sculpture which
changes every year. They are provided by the region's huge bedding plant industry, successors of the once-booming celery growers. Special **free festivals and events** fill the park many weekends in spring and summer; call the Convention and Visitors
Bureau at (616) 381-4003 for a calendar.

On the park's southern border, the city's distinctive 1931 Art
Deco **city hall** has lots of wonderful Egyptian-flavored embellishments outside and in. Along the tops of the four limestone exterior walls are bas-reliefs of events from the city's history. To city
hall's west, the **First Presbyterian Church** is a majestic Gothic-

At the Sarkozy Bakery, Judy Sarkozy (right) has created a participatory
workplace. Tables encourage customers to sit down and talk to each
other.

inspired structure built in 1930. To city hall's east is the imposing **Park Club**, a Queen Anne castle made of Lake Superior sandstone in 1890. Once the home of a prominent local industrialist, it is now a private club.

◆ **Michigan News Agency.** *308 W. Michigan, a block north of Bronson Park and two blocks east of the Kalamazoo Mall. (616) 343-5958. Open 365 days, 6 a.m. to 9 p.m.* A fabulous newsstand with a beat-up wood floors and a been-there-forever atmosphere (since 1947, in fact), brought into the 1990s by the founder's daughter and her husband. They are utterly devoted to serving *all* their customers, from street people to Kalamazoo's considerable number of literati, such as novelist Jamie Gordon and acclaimed short story writer Stuart Dybek, who both teach at Western. Don't miss the bulletin board! 2,500 magazine titles, with new ones constantly added. Maps, tobacco, comics, lots of out-of-town papers. Noteworthy: job search materials, job banks for many cities, national ad search.

◆ **Kalamazoo Public Museum.** *On the second floor of the city library at Rose and South.* There's a splendid Egyptian section, complete with mummy, lots of attractively displayed ancient artifacts, and good descriptions. Displays are small but choice until the museum moves into the much larger new museum in the Arcadia Commons, in fall of 1995. Learn about area Pottawatomi, southwest Michigan's oak openings and prairies, early roads and land sales, and famous bygone local products like Checker Cabs and Gibson Guitars. Interactive hands-on games for kids, and a very nice **gift shop** with educational toys. *Tues-Sat 9-5, Sun 1-5. (616) 345-7092. Planetarium shows Wed 7 & 8, Sat & Sun 1:30, 2:30, 3:30. Free.*

◆ **Two stores for used and vintage clothing and more.** The 1920s apartment block at Rose and Lovell is home to two terrific second-story resale shops: **Designer's Exchange** consignment shop (616-385-2551) and **La De Da's** (616-342-6759; open Wed-Sat 11-5), where former Western Michigan art student Lori Cousino has filled an apartment with visionary castoffs (clothing for men and women, and mostly decorative household goods), some of which she makes into her own fascinating art. She dispenses coffee, advice, and good deals to a largely alternative crowd from high schoolers to professional musicians and old hippies. Some customers get so excited they start singing. Shop Wednesday for the best deals.

The State Theater, used mostly for live music events, is a rare surviving example of John Eberson's atmospheric theaters, with an interior that recreates an exotic Mediterranean town, stars that twinkle in a deepening blue sky, and a cloud machine that still works.

◆ **Pandora's Books for Open Minds,** *around the corner in an old Greek Revival house at 226 W. Lovell. (616) 388-5656.* Rambling store with wide range of books, cards, etc., some mainstream but all of interest to feminists and lesbians in some way.

◆ **St. Luke's Episcopal Church.** *247 W. Lovell.* Exceptionally picturesque brick Gothic Revival church complex.

◆ **Ladies' Library Association Building**. *333 S. Park at Lovell.* An outstandingly bold, richly embellished brick High Victorian Gothic building from 1878-79, reminiscent of the strong, gutsy work of Philadephia architect Frank Furness. Still a private club. The group sought to stimulate learning and culture in the era before public libraries, when the educational opportunities for women were limited. Stained-glass windows depict scenes from Milton, Shakespeare, Burns, and Hawthorne. Don't miss the long-tongued copper gargoyle drain spout.

◆ **Kalamazoo Institute of Arts.** *Park at South. (616) 349-7775. Open Tues-Sat 10-5.* More about making art, teaching, and thinking creatively than about the passive connoisseurship that dominates most bigger, wealthier museums. There's no permanent collection, but the changing shows are usually stimulating. The **museum shop** emphasizes handcrafts; it's in the rear, off the parking lot entrance.

◆ **South Street Gallery.** *471 W. South, in the lower level of the Marlborough Condominiums. (616) 344-0526.* Mainly decorative works by regional artists.

◆ **South Street Historic District.** *South Street from Westnedge to Stadium.* This remarkably intact historic streetscape, 3/8 of a mile from both downtown and Kalamazoo College to the west, remained a prestigious neighborhood where impressive houses were built between 1847 through World War I. Architectural styles range from Greek and Gothic Revival through Georgian and Tudor. Kalamazoo was a wealthy town with many industries, no booms or busts, and old families who stayed in homes for generations. All this made for stable neighborhoods whose fine homes were unusually well maintained, not chopped into low-income apartments by the 1940s.

The **Red Cross** (616-382-6382) occupies the two **Upjohn houses** where widowed neighbors Carrie Gilmore and William Upjohn married each other circa 1900, founding a multifaceted business dynasty that remains extremely influential today. Visitors are welcome weekdays; phone ahead for tours. See *Walking through Time* for historical information.

VINE NEIGHBORHOOD

This central-city success story is a square mile of southside Kalamazoo, bounded by Lovell, Oakland, Howard/Crosstown Parkway, and Burdick. Some unusual historic homes and the following small businesses along South Westnedge are what would interest visitors about this unusually diverse neighborhood, where renters, owner-occupants, students, professionals, and group homes live together in a racially mixed, harmonious, well-organized area. Other college towns could learn a lot about cooperative, self-help community development in low-income and student rental areas from the **Vine Neighborhood Association** (616-349-8463) and its development arm, **Vine Ventures**, both headquartered at 913 South Westnedge and open weekdays. This dense, turn-of-the century area is on the upswing, with continuing renovation of houses that can be had for $20,000 to $40,000.

◆ **Cosmo's Cucina.** *804 W. Vine at Locust, a block west of Westnedge. (616) 344-5666. Open 11-10 weekdays, for weekend breakfasts 8:30- 3 p.m., also Sat. evenings.* Delightful, tucked-away second-floor restaurant with great atmosphere and food; a fine spot for a mid-walk pause.

◆ **Gotta Have It!** *817 S. Westnedge. (616) 342-8145. Open daily noon-6.* The owners have a way of combining unlikely things and making kitsch look good and even intelligent. Deco, Moderne, 1950s-1960s, pop, and more fills up a house.

◆ **Carousel Ice Cream and Sandwich Shop.** *819 S. Westnedge. (616) 342-8493.* Corner store with an original soda fountain.

◆ **Fourth Coast Cafe.** 418 S. Westnedge. Coffeehouse with cof fees from around the world, pastries, etc., plus chess and other games to play. Upstairs in a treetop space is the Taj Mahal Indian restaurant. (See *Hunts' Restaurants and Lodgings of Michigan.*)

◆ **Bicentennial Bookshop.** *820 S. Westnedge. (616) 345-5987. Closed Sundays.* Well organized and well stocked with used and rare books and selected old magazines.

◆ **Octagon House,** *925 S. Westnedge.* Most unusual for an octagon because it's so well preserved and because it's one story. Hard to see when the leaves are out.

◆ **Pioneer Park.** *Westnedge at Park Place.* The site of an old cemetery has been renovated with funds and work crews from the neighborhood. Benches and big trees make for a pleasant place to sit and snack, and view many of the area's nicest houses. You may notice small courts of houses built behind main streets here. Dutch immigrants often built extra backyard housing for newly arrived relatives.

◆ **Attic Trash & Treasures.** *1301 S. Westnedge at Forest. (616) 344-2189.* Used furniture, jewelry, sheet music, and lots of great middle-class 20th-century nostalgia items. Behind it, **Johnson Piano**, third-generation piano restorers, displays two elaborate small grand pianos and a showcase of miniatures.

◆ **Thieves' Market.** *1305 S. Westnedge just south of Forest. (616) 388-6166. Open daily 12-6, Sun 2-5.* A wild mix of used and new stuff, from sequined dresses to bow ties to accordions, eyeball jewelry, sentimental framed pictures, and corny souvenirs, artfully crammed into quite a small space. For people who miss the Ann Arbor of the 1960s and 1970s, it's a must. The owner stocks tarot cards and books, does readings by appointment. The bul-

Funky Kalamazoo: Lori Cousino in La De Da's, upstairs at Rose and
Lovell. It's one of Kalamazoo's many imaginative and inexpensive vintage stores. An old industrial and college city, Kalamazoo today is
spawning many offbeat shops.

letin board reflects her longstanding love of the blues.

Getting back to downtown: You can walk the 1 1/4 miles back on Park, parallel to Westnedge but a block to the east, or you could take the bus, which stops on the half-hour at Park and Forest.

EAST END WAREHOUSE DISTRICT

East of Burdick, extending south from Kalamazoo. Not as interesting when explored by foot as the Kalamazoo Mall, Bronson Park, and Vine Street areas. A .75 mile round trip from the Amtrak station. Many stores stay open to 6, 7, or 9, so you could stop here before catching an evening train.

◆ **The Emporium.** *313 E. Kalamazoo. 381-0998. Note odd hours: 2-6 p.m. Sat & Sun; 7-9 p.m. Mon-Fri.* Three long buildings packed with antique furniture attract antiquers from far and wide. Don't take the gruff owner personally; he treats everyone that way.

◆ **Kalamazoo Brewing Company** *315 E. Kalamazoo. (616) 382-2338. Open 9 a.m. 10 p.m. Mon-Fri, noon-10 Sat, noon-5 Sun. Tours Saturdays at 1, 2, 3, and 4.* This microbrewery turns out about 6,000 barrels of highly regarded beer, ale, stout, and porter a year. Lately it's become known for its vintage-style ales that are capable of being aged. Third Coast Old Ale and Bell's Eccentric Ale are two. Aged ales "smooth out and develop nice flavors," says owner Larry Bell.

Housed in an old plumbing supply building, the place has an unpretentious, friendly, funky ambiance. There's lots of beer memorabilia on the walls and bottled brew for sale. Locals rave about the new **brew pub**, one of the few smoke-free places to enjoy beer. It's more like an eclectic cafe with chess, ping pong, and a wonderful atmosphere. Seven of the firm's 20 beverages are on draft at any time, and everything's available by the bottle.

◆ **Water Street Coffee Joint.** *315 East Water at Kalamazoo, across from the brewery. (616) 373-2840. Open every morning. Stays open evenings to 10 at least, except Sun & Mon.* The interior and mood of this owner-designed coffeehouse is so artistic in every detail, you'd think the owner was an art student. But no, he studied finance at Western. He worked across the street at Heritage and had his eye on this spot for years. Pastries, muffins, and light lunches are available. Don't miss the inlaid slate and marble sunburst in the concrete floor.

◆ **Heritage Architectural Salvage and Supply Company.** *402 E. Kalamazoo at Water. (616) 385-1004. Tues, Wed, Thurs & Sat 10-4.* Long warehouses are loaded with original and reproduction doors, hardware, simple building parts, architectural parts, and garden architecture. The owners are dedicated preservationists who sometimes intervene to keep buildings from being demolished. They may start an antiques mall in their loft.

◆ **The Robinson Collection.** *505 E. Kalamazoo at Walbridge. (616) 342-8228. Mon-Sat 10-7.* Cheerful, friendly shop with an Afrocentric focus and widespread appeal: books, tapes (including storytelling, gospel, some African music), collectibles, posters, cards, and dolls.

◆ **Okun Brothers Shoe Store.** *South St. at Edwards on the east edge of downtown. (616) 342-1536. Mon-Fri 8:30-9, Sat 8:30-7.* One of the largest, most colorful shoe stores in the Midwest offers discount prices to boot. You can find everything from ballet slippers to firemen's boots, lizard cowboy boots to high-heeled sandals. This 70-year-old store is from a bygone era of retailing — bustling and never fancy. The exterior walls are plastered with painted signs of brand names. The 30 salespeople are willing to bargain even on discounted prices.

Bronson Park is in downtown Kalamazoo, bounded by Rose, Park, South, and Academy streets. Best way to get downtown: avoid South Westnedge. From west (Chicago), from I-94, go north on U.S. 131, follow Bus. Route I-94 (Michigan Ave.), turn south onto Rose. From east (Detroit), from I-94, take exit 81, which is Bus. Route I-94 (Kalamazoo St.). Turn south onto Rose. Park on the street along Academy or South.

YET ANOTHER MAGNIFICENT LATE 19th-CENTURY NEIGHBORHOOD . . . . . is on the west side of central Kalamazoo, just north of the Kalamazoo College campus. The **Stuart Avenue Historic District** is along Stuart and Woodward between West Michigan/Main and North. When a horse-drawn streetcar came out this way in 1884, professional men and business owners built huge suburban homes to display the wealth they gained in the years after the Civil War. . . . . Today, the Casteel family's five carefully restored bed and breakfast inns have done much to promote this neighborhood. Many elaborate Eastlake, Queen Anne, and Italianate houses, even student rental properties, boast classy historic paint schemes. Visitors are welcome to walk through the beautiful **gardens** on Stuart at Main, south of the Bartlett-

Upjohn House, a bed and breakfast at 229 Stuart, provided they check with the innkeeper first.

ONE MORE EXCEPTIONAL RESALE STORE. . . . . A fire forced the **Souk Sampler** (616-342-9124) to move from the Vine Neighborhood to a strip mall at 4614 West Main. The owner is "terribly creative" and the environment she has invented for her men's and women's vintage clothing store is extraordinary, says an admiring colleague on the local resale scene. The jewelry department alone, with its Bakelite, rhinestones, and beads, is amazing, and old shoes are displayed to look like art.

AN ARTS LINE WITH TWO WEEKS' OF UPCOMING EVENTS AND SHOWS. . . . . 75 member groups contribute to the **Arts Council of Greater Kalamazoo** arts line. Dial (616) 000-1000, punch in 2787 (that's ARTS), and hold on past the 15-second ad. . . . . . The arts line includes all events at the **Kalamazoo Civic Theater**, in a gem of a theater on the south side of Bronson Park. The multifaceted theater has several programs of musicals and dramas: mainstage, area theater, youth theater, black theater, and summer theater.

MORE RESOURCES FOR CURIOUS VISITORS . . . . . . You can pick up *Kalamazoo Downtown,* an interesting free tabloid with upcoming events, at area shops. . . . . . History and preservation buffs will want to buy *Walking through Time: A Pictorial Guide to Historic Kalamazoo.* It's $5 at the Athena Book Shop, 300 South Kalamazoo Mall. . . . . The **Kalamazoo Convention and Visitors Bureau** at 128 North Kalamazoo Mall offers visitor information, including a calendar of events and walking tours of historic areas. Stop by the office weekdays, or call (616) 381-4003.

ANNUAL EVENTS OF SPECIAL NOTE. . . . . include July's **Flowerfest** in Bronson Park, a celebration of the local bedding plant industry that includes horticultural tours as well as performances and food; the **Black Arts Festival** in August; spinners' and weavers' **Fiberfest** in August; the **Wine and Harvest Festival** in early September; and the new **Allegro Arts Festival**, an interactive, multidisciplinary blend of visual arts, song, and dance (616-342-5059), held on the downtown mall in mid-September . . . . . For a two-month **events calendar** or an annual one, call the **Convention and Visitors Bureau**, (616) 381-2710.

GOOD DEALS FROM THE BEDDING PLANT INDUSTRY . . . . . Family-owned greenhouses are behind nearly every house along certain streets adjacent to the productive mucklands where Kalamazoo's "celery Dutch" grew celery until World War II. (See page 77). In spring you can get **good deals on bedding plants** by buying direct. Some growers sell only wholesale, but others sell wholesale and retail. Their signs will often say whether they sell to the public, what they specialize in, and whether they sell on Sundays. (Many don't.) Look in the Yellow Pages under "Bedding Plants" for a long listing.

To see this interesting variant of family farming, drive out North Westnedge or head for Comstock, just east of Kalamazoo. To get to Comstock, take the I-94 Sprinkle Road exit, go north. After you've passed Bus. I-94/Amvet Parkway, turn right (east) onto Market Street or Comstock Avenue. Two greenhouses have a big retail trade: **Wenke's Greenhouses** on Market at Sprinkle, with annuals, vegetables, and herbs (616-388-2266) and **Bell Flowers** at 5437 Comstock (616-343-6857). Bell's specializes in perennials and sells them in large gallon sizes, in 3" pots ($1.69 each or $19 for a flat of 14), and in small 69¢ trays, grown like annuals for $9.50 a flat, less for additional flats. The selection is enormous — dozens of varieties of clematis, for instance. In winter, house plants and forced bulbs are for sale.

Amtrak between Detroit and Chicago

A slice of historic Michigan that grew up along the Michigan Central: vineyards and factories, quaint towns and depots, and the Kalamazoo River's woods and wetlands.

Most major cities of southern Michigan are lucky enough to be on the Detroit-Chicago Amtrak route over the historic Michigan Central line. It's one of the busiest passenger rail lines in the Midwest — and quite possibly the most beautiful. Michigan's historic rail stations are architecturally distinctive and unusually well preserved. They're highlights of this train trip. So is the 1 1/4-hour portion between Jackson and Kalamazoo, when the tracks parallel the Kalamazoo River valley and let you look down at the woods and wildlife by the river. This stretch is especially scenic in **fall color season**, in **early spring** leaf-out time, and in winter when **snow** is on the ground. Late summer's foliage obscures too much; it's the dullest time for this train trip.

You may be tempted by brochures and articles about short tourist railroads, which have been proliferating lately. But when you can take a real train ride on Amtrak that takes you somewhere worthwhile and has genuinely interesting scenery along the way, why bother with a pokey, overpriced little tourist train that lumbers through farm fields at 10 miles an hour?

On the Amtrak route between Ypsilanti and Kalamazoo, nineteenth-century townscapes and interesting, brief industrial landscapes flash by. They alternate with just the right amount of open farmland and densely wooded river scenes to be diverting. From just west of Jackson to Kalamazoo, the tracks parallel the beautiful Kalamazoo River valley. The wooded river views are especially glorious — in winter, when the bare tree shapes are outlined against the snow; in early May, the pointillist phase of leaf-out time; and in fall color season. With leaves off the trees, quite a bit of wildlife — birds and deer, mostly — can be seen from the train.

The trick in planning a day's outing by rail is finding a destination with enough interesting things to see and do within walking distance of the train station. A trip to the intense metropolis of downtown Chicago is best of all — and the morning train from Michigan cities does allow for six hours in the Windy City without spending the night. That's plenty of time for a walk through the Loop, a visit to the Art Institute, and a stroll down Michigan Avenue's Magnificent Mile.

In Michigan, here are your choices:

♦ **Ann Arbor** is the ideal destination for a train trip, a compact and bustling university town with some of the state's most interesting central-city shopping areas. See pages 145 to 180.

♦ **Kalamazoo** is another excellent destination, with wonderful streets of 19th century architecture, terrific vintage clothing shops, a beautiful urban park, and two museums. Train schedules from southeast Michigan or Chicago permit a full day's outing or a weekend that's enjoyable in a low-key way. See pages 82-96.

♦ **Albion** (population 10,000) is a small town with one train stop a day in each direction. Rail travelers can actually walk from downtown to some delightful riverside parks and natural areas and an orchard within their allotted four hours. See page 120.

♦ **Niles.** Main attractions within walking distance of the station are historic buildings, an antiques mall, a pretty riverside park, and a fine museum with exceptional artifacts from Potawatomi and Plains Indians and the French fur trading outpost that was here. A cab can take you to Fernwood Botanical Gardens. See pages 31-34.

♦ **Dearborn.** A cab ride for $6 or so takes you to Greenfield Village and the Henry Ford Museum, which are adding stimulating new exhibits each year. The train station is between Dearborn's two downtowns and a fair hike from either. Call the Dearborn Cab Company, (313) 562-6060. You could try getting around on a bus. Call SMART (313-962-5515) for details about your situation. See pages 333-344.

♦ **Detroit.** The new Amtrak station is on Woodward at Baltimore, two blocks south of Grand in the New Center area. The New Center is home of the fabulous Fisher Building (page 243), the G.M. Building, the Fisher Theater, and several restaurants. It's just 3/4 of a mile by foot or by cab down Woodward to the

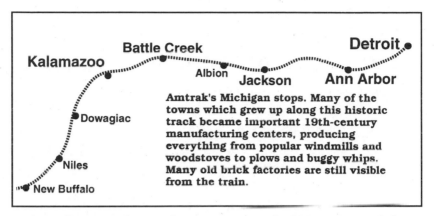

Kalamazoo
Battle Creek
Detroit
Albion
Jackson
Ann Arbor
Dowagiac
Niles
New Buffalo

Amtrak's Michigan stops. Many of the towns which grew up along this historic track became important 19th-century manufacturing centers, producing everything from popular windmills and woodstoves to plows and buggy whips. Many old brick factories are still visible from the train.

Detroit Institute of Arts, the Detroit Historical Museum, and the Wayne State University campus. It's not a charming walk past the empty spaces that make up too much of Detroit, but in daytime it's not likely to be dangerous, either. (See pages 242-252.) Rail connections now join Detroit with Royal Oak and Birmingham.

◆ In the auto-dependent 1990s, bus systems in sprawling **Jackson** and **Battle Creek** unfortunately aren't up to providing dependable, convenient transportation to major area attractions.

The ideal vantage point for looking out train windows is from the table seats in the food service cars that are on most trains. They enable you to see out left and right without seat backs blocking the view. An extra plus: the train crew hangs out there, and they know a lot about what's on the route.

For Amtrak schedule and fares, call 1-800 USA-RAIL. Four trains a day in each direction go between Chicago and Detroit. There are no reservations, and unfortunately there is no separate baggage car, so it's not possible to take your bike on the train. Fridays and Sundays can be busy, and passengers boarding on down the line sometimes have to stand during peak vacation and holiday times.

RECOMMENDED TOURIST TRAINS . . . . . include the charming **Southern Michigan Railroad** between Clinton and Tecumseh (call 517-456-7677; see page 136); the **Huckleberry Railroad** at **Crossroads Village** near Flint, with its gritty, narrow-gauge old steam engine (517-763-7100; see page 360); and the quarter-size **Junction Valley Railroad** in Bridgeport north of Frankenmuth (517-777-3480), where you can spend the day in delightfully landscaped, park-like grounds.

Gilmore Classic Car Museum

On a splendid farm near Hickory Corners,
a choice collection shows how some
of the most impressive car models have evolved.

This superb collection of old cars is located north of Kalamazoo in immaculately restored old barns moved from area farms. The late Donald Gilmore, an heir and chairman of the giant Upjohn pharmaceutical empire, clearly lavished money and attention on this remarkable collection of over 125 cars. What's special here is the opportunity to see how various makes evolved over the years. Twenty pristine Packards, the largest such collection in the world, show how that legendary car changed from 1905 through the last model in 1956. There are 15 Rolls Royces, from the 1910 Silver Ghost to the 1938 Pack Ward. Mark I and II Lincolns from 1940 and 1956 show how old that sleek line is.

Most historically important is the fascinating evolution of Henry Ford's autos from his initial 1903 Ford Tonneau to the 1906 Model N and the record-breaking Model T (19 million sold from 1907-1928) to the 1928-31 Model A. You can see the humble 1903 Cadillac grow in nine models into the flashy, finny model of the 1960s. In addition, there are fancy old fire engines, a series of Stanley Steamers, a full-scale replica of the Kitty

Two Checker Cabs, made in nearby Kalamazoo, are from the choice collection of the Gilmore Classic Car Museum. At the left is a 1922 cab from Checker's first year of production. The other is a 1936 model.

Hawk, and even a narrow-gauge steam locomotive.

Much emphasis is given to Kalamazoo cars. On display and still working are the first new car sold in the city, an 1899 Locomobile, and a variety of the popular and high-quality Roamers, last made in Kalamazoo in 1930. Last but not least are three of Kalamazoo's legendary Checker cabs: one from 1922, one from 1935, and the last Checker that rolled off the line in 1982.

On M-43 at Hickory Rd. west of Hickory Corners and just north of Gull Lake, 17 miles northeast of Kalamazoo. (616) 671-5089. Open mid-May thru mid-Oct: daily 9-5. $6 admission, children under 12 and under free.

HERBS AND PERENNIALS IN A PRETTY OLD FARMSTEAD SETTING . . . . are under three miles from the Gilmore Car Museum at **Bracloch Farms** on the west side of Gull Lake. Plants are grown in greenhouses behind the big weathered dairy barn. Its cool ground floor houses a large shop, filled with unfussy dried arrangements, floral gift items, and books on gardening. Many gardens and herb plots give visitors ideas for landscaping with herbs and perennials. *From M-43 a mile north of Richland (that's south from the Gilmore Museum), turn east onto County Road C at the Stagecoach Stop Inn. When C ends, turn left. Farm is first drive on right. (616) 629-9888. Open from mid-April to Christmas. Tues-Sat 10-5, Sun 1-5.*

Kellogg Bird Sanctuary

Where idyllic landscaping has created a paradise
of plentiful food for dramatic big birds

Walking into the Kellogg Bird Sanctuary near dusk is like walking into a dream. It's a lush, romantic landscape. Peacocks amble freely on the lawn, languorously trailing tails of brilliant blue and green. Here a normally elusive eastern wild turkey is so well socialized that it makes an excellent photo subject if you happen to meet it on its early-morning or late-afternoon foraging strolls. Inside the entrance gift shop, you pay two dollars to enter, plus 50¢ for a generous bucket of corn. Down a winding path through a wooded glade you come to lovely **Wintergreen Lake**. Birdsong fills the air. Squirrels are drawn by plentiful food from many nut trees, domestic and exotic. Arching bridges connect lagoons along the shore. Rare trumpeter swans sail up majestically to you, hoping for corn. When they emerge from the water, it's a surprise to see them plop along on huge, comical black feet. It's a terrific thrill to be able to feed the birds and see them up close in such a gorgeous setting.

The Canada Goose, now common and prolific, was endangered when the sanctuary was created to help it in 1928. Loss of habitat to agriculture and urbanization made wildlife decline alarmingly in the early 1900s.

These were barren, overgrazed hills in 1928. At that time cereal magnate W. K. Kellogg started the sanctuary as a refuge for Canada geese, threatened by loss of habitat to agriculture and urbanization. This and other conservation efforts proved so successful that Canada geese are now pests in many places. Today the sanctuary offers the public a most dramatic opportunity to see birds up close

Seeing and feeding six kinds of swan, including the rare trumpeter swan, is fun for all ages. Though several exotic species like the European black swan (above) are at the Kellogg Bird Sanctuary, its chief purpose is to improve habitats for threatened native species, and show visitors how to do the same.

and learn about them. It's a part of Michigan State University's Kellogg Biological Station. The excellent **book shop** has posters, clothing, gifts, and toys, plus an outstanding selection of publications geared to nature-lovers and teachers. Here you can find out how to transform your back yard into a paradise for birds, following the same landscaping principles and planting materials used in the refuge.

Permanent residents among the free-flying waterfowl by the lagoon include six of the world's nine varieties of swans and 30 pairs of Canada geese. In spring through fall they are augmented by 20 varieties of migrating ducks, such as bufflehead, ruddy ducks, hooded mergansers, and northern shovelers. Canadas alone number 5,000 during fall migration.

Interpretive signs along the 1 1/2-mile asphalt loop tell about the waterfowl in some detail. In a secluded area, away from the lively hubbub of waterfowl at the lake, visitors have an unusual chance to see 14 **birds of prey** up close, including a threatened red-shouldered hawk, the endangered short-eared owl, and a bald eagle. Modern zoo practice ordinarily prohibits caging such big native birds. These are injured. Some are being rehabilitated; others are so badly hurt they couldn't survive in the wild.

The sanctuary's residents and their activities change with the seasons, so repeat visits are worthwhile. Spring means the return of winter migrants to nest here or pass through. Swans and geese nest in late March, ducks start in early April. Nesting structures have been built in public areas to be easily observed by visitors. The young are hatched in May and June. Summer residents include many ducks, geese, and swans, along with over two dozen species of backyard songbirds. (To see bobolinks and such, you'd have to go out into the fields of the Biological Station.)

Beginning in October, ducks and geese stop here on their way south. Early November usually brings the greatest numbers and most varieties. Winter isn't dull, either. Swans, some geese, and diving and dabbling ducks stay near the lake, which doesn't freeze. In warm, snowless winters, geese may linger by the thousands, thrown off-kilter by confusing weather signals.

12685 East C Ave. east of Gull Lake between Kalamazoo and Battle Creek. From M-89, turn north on 40th St. In a little over a mile, go west onto East C Ave. (616) 671-2510. May-Oct: daily 9-sunset. Nov.-April: 9-5. Early-morning bird-watching by special arrangement. $2/adult. 50¢/children 4-12. Wheelchairs available at the office; barrier-free trail.

SKIERS, HIKERS, AND PICNICKERS . . . . . enjoy the quiet, scenic **W. K. Kellogg Forest**, a Michigan State University forestry experiment station on the hills and valley formed by pretty Augusta Creek. It's about three miles southeast of the Kellogg Bird Sanctuary. Cereal king and philanthropist W. K. Kellogg started it as a demonstration project in reforesting cutover, overgrazed hills — marginal farmland typical of Michigan's many areas of glacial lakes and hills.

Today the forest's 740 acres are planted in a huge variety of trees, quite possibly the largest genetic archive of temperate plant tree species in the world. From the entrance a dirt road leads back behind the "Maple Manor" sugar shack (used for **mid-March syrup-making demonstrations**) to a series of rustic **picnic areas** beneath big pines along the creek. Artificial ponds and rapids have turned the creek into a designated **trout stream**. A steep 1/4-mile trail leads to a **scenic overlook**. A **2 1/2-mile road loop** continues north from the picnic grounds and circles around, past plantations of Scotch pines for Christmas trees in which the seedlings come from stock grown in different cold climates from around the world. **Skiers, hikers**, and **bow-hunters** are all welcome to use the forest's 25 miles of ungroomed firebreaks separating experimental stands of trees. Stop for a **map and brochure** at the forest entrance off 42nd Street, 3/4 of a mile south of M-89 and two miles north of the quaint canal village of Augusta. Admission is free. Restrooms behind the office are always open. Call (616) 731-4597 for special, **forest-related events**. *Open year round from 8 a.m. until sunset, except Thanksgiving, Christmas, New Year's, and Easter.*

VISIT A STATE-OF-THE-ART DAIRY. . . . . two miles north of the Kellogg Bird Sanctuary. A free, self-guided tour of Michigan State University's **Kellogg Dairy** starts in the milking parlor and ends with a chance to pet the calves in outdoor nursery hutches. Call (616) 671-2507 for current **milking times;** they're at dawn, around noon, and at dusk. If you miss seeing milking, you can watch an interesting nine-minute video on dairy farming practices. A **free booklet** explains the basics of milk production and nutrition.

This high-tech dairy has an automatic flush system that cleans out the barn in minutes. By hand that's a three-hour job. Dairy farms can be big polluters because of fertilizer runoff and manure. In this integrated waste management system, liquid manure and flushing water are stored in clay-lined ponds, then recycled as fertilizer and irrigation water for fields. Treated manure solids are used for bedding. A high-tech dairy like this could pay off for a herd of 150 or more, the size of a family farm with some hired help. It costs more in equipment but saves on time and fertilizer. *From M-89 east of Gull Lake and Richland, turn north on 40th St. The dairy is 2-1/2 miles north, past B Ave. (616) 671-2507. Free.*

STROLL THROUGH THE BEAUTIFUL GROUNDS OF W. K. KELLOGG'S LAKESIDE ESTATE. . . . . at the **Kellogg Biological Station** Manor House. It's on 3700 East Gull Lake Drive at B Avenue. (East Gull Lake Drive joins M-89 at the lake's southern tip.) In 1926 Battle Creek's cereal king built a simple, tasteful Tudor home, Eagle Heights, at the highest point overlooking Gull Lake. It became the core of a 3,500-acre, year-round Michigan State University center for biological research (birds, ecology, forestry, agriculture), conferences, and extension programs.

The **Manor House** itself is closed to the general public, but visitors are welcome to take the health-conscious Kellogg's favorite exercise **walk down to Gull Lake**. A picturesque stone and brick stairway zigzags down the steep, wooded hill to a pagoda and boat dock that juts out into the lake. This walk is especially lovely at sunset. For a dramatic, planned vista, look back up at the house from the pergola. Just before the pergola, there's a perennial garden with a rose arbor and sundial bearing the workaholic Kellogg's favorite saying, "The early bird catches the worm." Kellogg loved to take this walk with his friend and frequent guest, science writer Paul de Kruif. Kellogg ordinarily insisted on a smoke-free environment, but he let de Kruif smoke his omnipresent pipe on these walks.

FOR A SWIM IN GULL LAKE. . . . . there's the small, oak-shaded **Ross Township Park** on East Gull Lake Drive just north of the Kellogg estate. Parking is limited. The beach is stony, with a deep dropoff. The **Prairieville Township park** on M-43 at the north end of the lake is larger but less scenic, with an improved beach, bigger parking lot, and bathrooms. Both have modest fees per car, and both are often crowded on summer weekends.

SEE HOW RIDING THERAPY HELPS DISABLED KIDS . . . . . Riding therapy is a great confidence-builder for kids with all kinds of handicaps and learning disabilities. Powerful yet gentle horses can get through even to children with severe emotional problems. The nation's pioneer in riding therapy is just southeast of the Kellogg Bird Sanctuary. The **Cheff Center for the Handicapped** welcomes visitors to observe its classes, see its stables, and picnic in the playground overlooking the pastures. By learning to ride, a disabled child "is doing something that the rest of his friends can't," says a staffer. Results can be thrilling. *The Center is on 43rd St., just north of M-89, about 8 miles west of Battle Creek and 2 miles east of Gull Lake's south tip. (616) 731-4471. The barn, at the top of the hill, is open year-round. Mon-Thurs 8-5. Fri 8-noon. Drop-ins welcome, or call to arrange a tour or find out times for year-round classes.*

Binder Park Zoo

*Naturalistic settings make this
an unusually enjoyable zoo to visit.*

This splendid, lushly planted small zoo is rapidly evolving
into a popular regional destination. You won't find caged
lions or tigers. The animals selected to live here have
places where they can feel at home. The gibbons live in a lush,
spacious area where they can swing through trees. The hand
some zebras have a long enough field to develop a full gallop. The
cheetahs' two-acre area resembles their native savannas. The
Siberian lynx live in a pine forest; visitors enter a Russian-style
log cabin and look at the lynx up close through big windows.

Elevated boardwalks add to the feeling that most of the zoo is
the animals' turf. A 2/3-mile **habitat trail** takes you through
fields, marshes, and forests, adding to the feeling that this is not
an artificial environment.

Many animals here have been chosen because of their world-
wide status as threatened or endangered species. Zoos cooperate
to keep and breed threatened species through plans that match
animals' requirements with zoo facilities and climates. Binder
Park's Chinese red pandas, cheetahs, ruffed lemurs, and gibbons
are here as part of a cooperative international species survival
plan. Other endangered animals at Binder Park are Mexican
wolves, trumpeter swans, ring-tailed lemurs, Formosan sika
deer, and bald eagles.

Less exotic animals can be petted (and fed, in the case of
goats and sheep) at the adjoining **Miller Children's Zoo.** Here
are llamas and camels, a draft horse, African cattle, dwarf zibu
and Vietnamese pot-bellied pigs, rabbits and guinea pigs. A 15-
minute **train ride** ($1 per person) takes visitors into the woods
and back.

There's a pleasant **snack bar** with indoor and outdoor seating areas; a large **gift shop** full of stuffed animals, animal
posters and cards, and books and games; and a newly expanded
picnic area by the enlarged parking lot that is the first finished
phase of zoo expansion. Inquire about **special programs** including early-morning nature walks, natural night life and zoo

Spacious, naturalistic settings make the Binder Park Zoo a splendid place to view an assortment of animals from cheetahs and vultures to the increasingly rare rhinoceros shown here. At the children's zoo, all animals can be petted.

snoozes, and big after-season Zoo Boo and ZooLights extravaganzas without animals.

Use the map to make sure you don't miss exhibits in outlying areas. Bear in mind that animals are most active in the morning or late afternoon, and when the weather is cooler. In summer the zoo stays open until 8 p.m. on Wednesdays and Thursdays.

In 1976, when zoo director Greg Geise, an animal behaviorist by training, arrived, the 50 acres of the current zoo exhibits were mostly trees and grass. A tremendous amount of planting since then created the exhibits' natural look. It's easier for newer zoos with bigger sites to follow today's naturalistic philosophy of zoo design than it is for older zoos in more constrained urban settings. Binder Park Zoo is especially fortunate because it has 400 acres and lots of mature trees to work with.

Geise carried the zoo's first animal with him, a European ferret, when he accepted the challenge to start this zoo. He began with a tiny budget and is proud to be independent of tax support and the political interference that often goes with it in municipal zoos. Geise has bootstrapped the operation and believes the zoo has ultimately profited from having to market itself and support itself like a private business that depends on visitors for revenues. Attendance has grown to almost 300,000 a year. Almost half come from beyond the immediate Calhoun and Kalamazoo County area.

Now the zoo's "Double the Zoo" plan to raise nearly $13 million has gotten off to a good start with grants of almost $6 million from the Kellogg and Upjohn foundations and the Kellogg Company. It calls for a 50-acre Wilds of Africa including a rhinoceros conservation center, primate and bird exhibits, a large conservation education center, and a 12-acre savanna with giraffe, zebra, ostrich, antelope, and more.

Zoo is 5 miles south of downtown Battle Creek at 7400 Division Dr. at Beadle Lake Rd. From I-94, take Beadle Lake Rd. Exit 100, go south 3 miles on Beadle Lake Rd. (616) 979 1351. Open mid April to mid October. Weekdays 9-5, Sat 9-6, Sun 11-6. From June thru August open to 8 p.m. Wed & Thurs. Adults $4.50, children 3-12 $2.50, seniors 65 and over $3.50. Family or grandparent memberships $40/year.

Chapter 2
Marshall
to Monroe

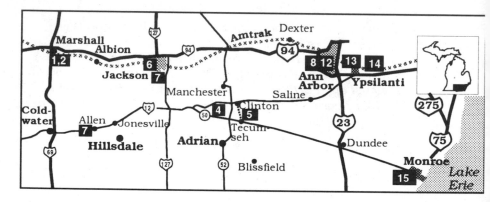

HIGHLIGHTS:

For restaurants and lodgings, see *Hunts' Restaurants & Lodgings of Michigan*

INTRODUCTION

Marshall to Monroe

In the 1820s and 1830s, many of Michigan's first settlers moved into this corridor, which stretches almost a hundred miles west from Monroe, on Lake Erie. Energetic, ambitious Yankees from upstate New York sought better opportunities in the emerging West. They traveled to Michigan on the recently opened Erie Canal and on Lake Erie steamships.

These York State Yankees followed long-established Indian trails that became Michigan's first roads. They founded towns along those corridors that often developed into prosperous centers of industry. Ypsilanti, Ann Arbor, Jackson, and Marshall developed along the early Territorial Road that turned into I-94. Growth was soon reinforced by the state's most important railroad, the Michigan Central, the route used by Amtrak between Detroit and Chicago today.

In the much more rural southern tier of counties, the old roads to Chicago were today's M-50 from Monroe through the pretty old town of Tecumseh, and today's U.S. 12 from Ypsilanti to Coldwater and on to Chicago, then hardly more than a village.

The visible evidence of New York influence is the clean-lined Greek Revival farmhouses and mansions they built. These can be spotted in many old towns and villages, where there has been less later development pressure to tear them down. Stunning Greek Revival architecture draws many visitors to the town of Marshall, which got off to a fast start but "went to sleep" in 1870 after its industrial district burned — a calamity that preserved its beautiful old homes.

More important are the colleges and universities these well-educated, ambitious people founded: Adrian, Albion, the normal school in Ypsilanti that became Eastern Michigan University. Most important of all is the University of Michigan. It owes its international research prominence to the influence of its early Yankee leaders, who brought German-style academic research to the innovation-friendly Western frontier. Soon the frontier institution became a national leader in education.

Marshall

Michigan's finest historic homes
in a picture-book small town

Peaceful and settled, this town of almost 7,000 retains the pleasant aura of its heyday in the 1850s and 1860s. Its streets are lined with big trees and attractive houses, including Michigan's most outstanding collection of Greek Revival and Gothic Revival homes from the 1840s and 1850s. Its September homes tour (page 119) is famous. So is the original Win Schuler's restaurant), which capitalized on an Old English theme and a remarkable host to become a favorite destination restaurant, especially after freeways were built in the 1950s.

Marshall boomed and grew rich in the mid-19th century, then went to sleep economically until antique-loving mayor Harold Brooks led a pioneering historic preservation crusade, beginning in the 1920s. Thanks to his success in preserving and publicizing Marshall's fabulous stock of historic architecture, Marshall gained fame as an unusually attractive version of the ideal American small town. The homes tour, started in 1964, is an all-out community effort that continues to promote awareness of restoration, preservation, and interior decorating.

There's a widespread obsession with the details of local history, usually without much of an appreciation for concepts and context. Historical plaques pop up everywhere. They are paid for by the enthusiastic historical society that earns plenty of money from the homes tour.

In the 1990s, Marshall has become more of a tourist town in all seasons. Its central location makes the National House Inn and McCarthy's' Bear Creek Inn good rural getaways from Chicago and metro Detroit. Marshall has grown into an antiques center, with nine shops, two malls, and a monthly market. Downtown has evolved a sweetly romantic Victorian theme that's so pervasive that browsing in stores is like seeing a spread of *Victoria* magazine come to life. (In fact, *Victoria* featured Marshall in 1991. So did the *New York Times* travel section, commenting that "Marshall's small-town pride is a genteel descendant of the boosterism that Sinclair Lewis savaged in *Main Street* and

This 1840s Greek Revival mansion, one of Marshall's most imposing, belonged to Mayor Harold Brooks, the man who got Marshall excited about historic preservation in the 1920s. Marshall was settled in the 1830s by industrious New York Yankees. An 1872 fire destroyed its industrial district, so financial leaders couldn't fork up the cash to keep the railroad shops in town. The resulting economic slumber preserved Marshall's beautiful houses.

Babbitt.") Winter, spring, and summer home and garden tours attract visitors, as do numerous festivals and the professional Cornwall Dinner Theatre at Turkeyville, a restaurant and gift complex at a onetime turkey farm a few miles north of town.

Marshall's quaint image belies both the aggressive real estate speculation launched by the town's founders and its present-day status as a home to large corporations. Marshall is the regional headquarters of State Farm Insurance, which employs 900, and it's the research and development center for Eaton, manufacturers of auto and truck components. It's also a light industrial center. More people work here than live here.

Today Marshall has also become a suburb of choice for commuters to Battle Creek, 15 minutes to the west. And it is the chosen residence of numerous retirees and some 400 traveling salespeople. All are drawn by Marshall's idyllic small-town image.

Marshall's lovely big homes were built by the town's go-getting early settlers who headed west to Michigan in the 1830s. They were unusually well-educated young people from wealthy New York State families, frustrated by the lack of opportunity in

the established and confining East. They went west not to
become farmers and till the soil, but to buy up large parcels of
land, promote their area, and profit from it.

They liked Marshall's strategic central location, halfway
across the state on the Territorial Road, the major artery of
Michigan settlement. At Marshall, a creek joined the Kalamazoo
River, providing water power for future mills. That site happened
to be at the center of Calhoun County, and therefore an ideal
spot for the county seat. (Marshall's splendid old Victorian courthouse was replaced by a boring low box of a building in the
1960s, shortly before the reputation of florid Victorian architecture was redeemed.)

Marshall's founders were determined to build here the same
kind of fine homes, good schools, and churches they had been
accustomed to back east. They had the money and sophistication to build them. Marshall's state representative back then,
John Pierce, devised Michigan's farsighted plan for a state
education system. His funding plan laid the basis for the early
preeminence of the University of Michigan among public universities. Pierce also fought but failed to win the state capitol for
Marshall, but failed.

Financial incentives offered by Marshall men did succeed in
wooing the Michigan Central Railroad's important machine
shops and hotel restaurant in 1844. These machine shops led to
three booming decades that ended after a 1872 fire destroyed the
entire factory district. Weakened financially, town leaders could-
n't come up with the new subsidy demanded by the railroad for
improvements. (Subsidies to railroads were a common practice in
those days.) In 1874 the railroad shops moved to Jackson, which
boomed, while Marshall went to sleep for 50 years.

Thus Marshall was spared the opportunities and stress of an
expanding industrial local economy. The town became a kind of
haven for a genteel, unhurried lifestyle. It was a pleasant retreat
for old money and some self-employed people, including William
Wallace Cook (author of pulp fiction like the Deadeye Dick and
Frank Merriwell series) and a number of purveyors of patent
medicine. Patent medicine enjoyed a boom here from the 1880s
to 1906, when the Pure Food and Drug act put a sudden end to
it. One lasting legacy of that colorful era is the Brooks Rupture
Appliance Company, makers of custom abdominal trusses. It still
occupies its historic quarters on Michigan Avenue next to the
Carver Park at Marshall Street.

Unthreatened by development pressure, Marshall's blocks of fine old homes remained little affected by competition from new subdivisions (there weren't any until after World War II), or by growing numbers of industrial workers seeking inexpensive housing in rooming houses divided from fine old homes.

Here's the basis for a satisfying, do-it-yourself tour of historic Marshall:

◆ **A walking tour map,** authoritative and free, is available from the Chamber of Commerce, 109 E. Michigan (open weekdays). Call (800) 877-5163 for it and a helpful visitor packet. Or get it at Cronin's or the Marshall House antiques centers or the National House Inn (see below). The map covers a hundred noteworthy homes — dates, styles, and interesting historical tidbits. At the Chamber, *19th-century Homes of Marshall, Michigan* ($7.95) is an outstanding value for its interesting history and pictures of nearly every noteworthy historic house.

◆ **The American Museum of Magic.** See page 121. Unmatched in Michigan for originality and substance. Well worth the trouble of calling to set up an appointment — even if you have no particular interest in magic.

◆ **The Honolulu House,** a fabulously eccentric 1860 house with a pagoda-shaped observation deck, is on Michigan Avenue at Fountain Circle on the west edge of Marshall's attractive downtown. Its builder, state Supreme Court Judge Abner Pratt, fell in love with the Hawaiian Islands when he was U.S. consul there from 1857 to 1859. His wife's poor health forced him to return to Marshall. He built this authentic tropical home with Victorian trim to house their Polynesian treasures and replicate their relaxed lifestyle. His wife soon died, and so did he, reportedly of pneumonia contracted on a cold drive from Lansing on which he wore tropical clothing, as was his wont.

This most peculiar house is lavishly decorated, with beautiful fireplaces. The meticulously restored 1885-1888 murals are a knockout — a late-Victorian reinterpretation of Pratt's original tropical murals. Their lush Renaissance blend of leaf and vine patterns and classical motifs is in rich, subtle greens, reds, purples, and pinks — 120 shades in all.

The interesting furnishings assembled here by the Marshall Historical Society do not reflect the house as it was ever really lived in. The collection's highlight is an elaborate dining-room suite, sent to the 1876 Philadelphia Centennial Exposition to

A sojourn in Hawaii inspired the Honolulu House, now a museum.

show off each kind of Michigan hardwood and help publicize the state's burgeoning furniture industry.

The basement rooms are arranged more like a typical house museum, with areas for quilts and needlework, toys, and a kitchen. Don't miss the Marshall Folding Bathtub cleverly disguised as a cabinet. It's a relic of Marshall's patent medicine boom. *Open year-round. Open daily from mid-May to October 31 from noon to 5. Otherwise open weekends only, 1-4. $3 admission. Park behind the house. You may learn more by reading the thorough 25¢ brochure than by asking the amiable volunteer guides.*

◆ **The Prospect Street hill,** two blocks north of Marshall's main street, offered the choicest building sites for Marshall's early élite. An easy hour's walk gives a good look at 29 fine Marshall homes and gardens. Take the time to look, and you'll be rewarded. (Look behind the houses, too. This area has some fabulous carriage houses.)

Two blocks north of the Honolulu House on Kalamazoo are two romantic Greek Revival temple-houses facing Prospect. The easterly one belonged to Mayor Harold Brooks for over 50 years, the west one to his brother, Louis, an authority on early chairs in the Middle West. North on Kalamazoo within the next half mile are 15 other noteworthy houses, including some picturesque Gothic Revival ones. Don't miss the square bracketed Italian Villa with the imposing setting at **603 North Kalamazoo.** William Wallace Cook, author of the Deadeye Dick, Buffalo Bill, and Frank Merriwell series, wrote up to a novel a week here between 1903 and 1933.

East on Prospect at Grand, the Gothic Revival houses at **224 Prospect** and **311 North Grand** are straight out of influential romantic architect Andrew Jackson Downing's books. Finish your tour by continuing east on Prospect to Division, then going a block toward downtown and turning back on Mansion west toward the Honolulu House.

◆ **Downtown Marshall** along several blocks of Michigan Avenue has an appealing mix of terrific Italianate architecture (look up to spot upper-floor details), upscale gift and antique shops, and wonderful small-town institutions like a good hardware store and dime store.

The chamber of commerce has a list of all area antique dealers. The biggest stores are open Sunday afternoons, but come on Saturday for biggest selection. Marshall also has several women's wear stores that offer fairly traditional fashions and good personal service. Shopping standouts (arranged from east to west) include:

Marshall House Antique Centre. *100 Exchange at E. Michigan, behind the little park. (616) 781-2112.* Quality dealers in a historic house. Good mix of furniture (largely 19th century).

Corner Collections. *103 E. Michigan. (616) 781-3050.* Big, multifaceted gift store was based on tabletop and kitchen things in its first 12 years in Eaton Rapids. Worth checking out for ideas like making lamps of Mason jars or other containers you can fill, using a fabric shade you choose yourself.

J. H. Cronin Antique Center. *101 W. Michigan. (616) 789 0077.* Large antique mall with lots of oak, printed ephemera and prints. Run by Ted and Donna Tear, who put on the monthly Marshall antiques show. He deals in signs and advertising; she has a terrific collection of White Castle mugs, promotional whistles.

Kids' Place. *106 N. Jefferson. (616) 781-3853.* A small but interesting children's bookstore that reflects the owner's offbeat sense of humor. Also stocks books on Marshall (including most John Bellairs titles) and related subjects.

Serendipity. *108 W. Michigan. (616) 781-8144.* Informally sophisticated country/Victorian mix of gifts, accessories, coffees and gourmet items, all served up with a decorator's ingenuity that approaches Martha Stewart's.

Williamson's Gift and Gourmet Shoppe. *115 W. Michigan. (616) 781-5641.* Opulent Victoriana with the light, airy touch of the 1990s, lavish with laces and flowers, and fine chocolates, too. The place to go for accessories to warm up a grand Italianate mansion.

Darling V & S Variety. *143 W. Michigan. (616) 781-0122.* Independently owned dime-store variant, oriented to crafts.

Louie's Bakery. *144 W. Michigan. (616) 781-3542.* Incredibly inexpensive and old-fashioned bakery, especially known for sweet rolls. Louie's still makes hot cross buns for Lent.

The Mole Hole of Marshall. *150 W. Michigan. (616) 781-5923.* In addition to a general line of gifts, it has antique wood fixtures, a big selection of music boxes, and a seven-rank Barton theater organ. You can ask to have it played and see the pipes operating through a window.

National House Inn. *102 S. Parkview at West Michigan on the circle, across Michigan Ave. from the Honolulu House. (616) 781-7374.* One ground-floor room of this historic 1835 inn is an antique shop. The rear herb and perennial garden is worth a look. It's the oldest operating inn in Michigan.

◆ **Postal Museum.** *Inside the Marshall Post Office, 202 E, Michigan. (616) 781-2859.* Tours can be arranged by appointment or on the spur of the moment if time permits. Inspired by his antique dealer grandmother and by Marshall's history mania, Postmaster Mike Schragg has established an impressive museum in several unused basement rooms. His tour begins with a talk about the patronage system used to appoint postmasters into the Eisenhower era, then proceeds to survey artifacts like general-store post office cases, books of postwar savings bonds sold to schoolchildren, the first RFD bag ever used in Michigan, and heavy glass mailboxes, so you could see if the mail had come. It's well worth while if you have a preexisting interest in the postal service, in bureaucratic systems, or in postage stamps and cancellations.

The post office itself is noteworthy because it's built of Marshall sandstone, in a pure Greek Revival style revived in the 1930s under the influence of Mayor Harold Brooks. The area from here to east of Jackson is the only part of Michigan not on a Great Lakes shoreline where bedrock is at the surface and able to be quarried.

◆ **Ketchum Park**, a most pleasant riverside park and playground on Marshall's humbler south side, is at the millrace of Rice Creek, just behind the dam — a popular fishing spot. This was the site of the mill and factory district, whose fiery destruction led to the economic decline of 19th-century Marshall. To get there, take Marshall Street south from the little park at downtown's east end. **Picnic tables and grills** are at Ketchum Park, or you could take out a sandwich from Mancino's on Michigan Avenue.

◆ **Capitol Hill**, the land Marshall set aside for the state capitol, is on Marshall Street south of the Kalamazoo River. Today it's

the Calhoun County Fairgrounds. The trim little 1839
"Governor's Mansion" at 612 S. Marshall at Washington is now
a Daughters of the American Revolution clubhouse. *Open
Sundays in July and August from 2 to 4.* Also open then is the
Capitol Hill School, a well-planned 1860 Gothic Revival schoolhouse, a block east of Marshall St. on Washington at Maple.
Today it contains a nifty period schoolroom and a toy collection
with a folk art masterpiece, **Hinkle's Automatic Theater** — a
traveling marionette show with mechanical band.

MARSHALL'S BIG EVENT OF THE YEAR . . . . . is the **Marshall Historic
Homes Tour,** held the weekend after Labor Day. A great many of the townspeople pitch in to work on food, musical entertainment, arts and crafts displays, and tours of half a dozen homes. For particulars on this year's tour,
call the Chamber of Commerce, 1(800) 877-5163. . . . . Another smaller, less
crowded homes tour is the **Christmas Walk,** limited to 650 tickets. Call the
chamber for details; sign up by early October. . . . . Also inquire at the chamber about the July **garden tour.**

MORE ANTIQUES FROM MAY THROUGH OCTOBER. . . . . The Calhoun
County Fairgrounds, south of downtown off Marshall Avenue, is the scene of
the **Marshall Antiques Market.** The two-day show is deliberately timed for
the same weekend as Margaret Brusher's prestigious Ann Arbor Antiques
Market, a Sunday-only show held the third Sunday of the month. That way
customers and dealers who come to southern Michigan for the Brusher show
can take in another show on Saturday. And the Marshall market appeals to
dealers who don't show in the Brusher show because she won't allow
exhibitors to do other shows in the area. Dealers (about 100 thus far) are
screened for quality, and all merchandise is guaranteed to live up to its
billing. Saturdays 8-4, Sundays 10-4. $3 admission Saturday or Sunday, $20
for first pickings on Friday 1-8. Call (616) 789-0990 for info.

EVENING ENTERTAINMENT IN MARSHALL . . . . . Small towns aren't big
on nightlife. The Chamber of Commerce (616-781-5163) can fill you in on
community events, civic theater productions, etc. . . . . Marshall is unusual
in still having an operating movie theater, the **Bogar Theatre,** at 223 E.
Michigan. (6160 781-3511. . . . . . **Schuler's Restaurant** offers participatory
dinner theater in January, February, and into March, has occasional special
dinners, and books performers in the Pub on some weekends. Call (616) 781-
0600. Then there's the professional **dinner theater** at **Cornwell's Turkey
House** outside of town. Don't expect too much from the dinner; the potatoes

taste like they're from a box. But the theater competently performs light fare, often musical revues. Call (616) 781-4293. . . . . . In Battle Creek, 15 minutes to the west, the intimate, state-of-the-art **Discovery Theatre** downtown next to McCamly Place frequently books a variety of outstanding regional performers in all musical genres. (616) 966-2560. The **Kellogg Arena** books occasional big-name performers; call (616) 965-3308.

AN INDUSTRIAL SMALL-TOWN COUNTERPART TO MARSHALL . . . . is right next door in **Albion** (population 10,000), 11 miles to the east. Its Methodist founders didn't quite have Marshall's money or style, but they did have energy and brains. Their talent went into developing industry and making **Albion College** (birthplace of both "The Old Rugged Cross" and "The Sweetheart of Sigma Chi") into one of Michigan's best private colleges. The Gale Manufacturing Company, maker of a famous steel plow, grew into a giant iron foundry, now part of Harvard Industries but still called the Malleable. Other foundries followed. Albion industries attracted workers from Germany, the Ukraine, Poland, Italy, Hungary, south Texas, Kentucky, and Florida, creating a most ethnically and racially diverse population for a small town. Today all but one of the foundries are closed, but the foundry workers and their descendants remain.

Albion's prosperity in the late nineteenth century and its location at the **forks of the Kalamazoo River** have resulted in a most **attractive townscape** — well worth a visit. Take Business 94 to Superior, downtown's main street, and you'll see some unusually elaborate Second Empire commercial buildings. You can canoe *under* one downtown building. Also worth a look: the beautifully restored **train station/Chamber of Commerce** on West Michigan and the neighborhood along Irwin Avenue. (It intersects with Superior at the south end of town.) But downtown retailing is weak; shopping centers hurt it badly. An interesting **walking tour and map** can be obtained from the Gardner House Museum (see page 126) or the Chamber (517-629-5533).

Continue south on Superior and turn left onto River, or turn and you'll reach pretty **Victory Park**, where the river's north and south forks join at a dramatic dam and picturesque series of millraces and waterways. Fishing in the south fork is pretty good. Landscaped by Genevieve Gillette some 50 years ago, Victory Park is quite possibly the prettiest all-around city park in any Michigan town.

Farther south of Superior, across the river, **Riverside Cemetery** has an exceptionally interesting mix of monument styles, from florid Victorian to Russian crosses in the southeast corner. Get an interesting guide outside the cemetery office.

American Museum of Magic

In downtown Marshall, a passionate fan's tribute
to professional magicians,
and to the sense of wonder they can create

The very best attractions are often little publicized, the products of dedicated amateurs in love with their subjects. A premiere example is the American Museum of Magic, which keeps no regular hours and distributes no brochures. Its fame extends mainly within the fraternity of magicians. Many magicians make annual pilgrimages here when they gather for the Magic Festival in nearby Colon (see page 125). Magician David Copperfield has called the museum "one of my favorite places on earth. No matter how much time I set aside to enjoy it, it is never enough." If you want to understand the soul of magic, he advises, visit this museum.

You may arrange for a 1 1/2-hour museum tour at your convenience with proprietor and guide Robert Lund. A devotee of magic since the age of seven, he's not a magician himself. He is a most gracious and enlightening guide, no matter how superficially his visitors are interested in magic, provided they follow his rules. First, DO NOT BE LATE. (He won't wait.) Second, once he explains that all the magic props and artifacts you see are originals, NEVER ask again if they're the real thing. "I may throw a tantrum," he says sternly.

Even if you're altogether uninterested in magic, you may well be won over by the dazzling visuals. A 1868 commercial building with a splendid cast iron front has been handsomely refurbished by Bob Lund and his wife and collaborator, Elaine. It is full of posters, beautifully decorated antique magic props, collections of magic sets, and porcelain figures of magicians.

Equally impressive are Lund's intelligence, wit, and commitment to his life's mission: the preservation of the artifacts and archives of many of the past century's magicians. Lund retired to Marshall ("paradise," he calls it) and opened the museum in 1979 to house and display his collections. He refers to his illustrious career as a writer for *Popular Mechanics* and automotive magazines as autobiographical detail of no interest.

The museum tour consists of stories illustrated by Lund's vast collection of old promotional posters from touring magicians. Obscure dead magicians come to life again. For example, "Here's one of my favorites, John C. Green, a crusty old coot and tough as the territory he played. Green worked the same small towns in Canada for 50 years. That indicated that he was a good magician, because you can only cheat the same people once. He left me his route books, with the towns he played and money he took in." A case contains Green's ledger, which shows the fate of most of the few full-time professional magicians: they gained little from a life of hard work and hard traveling.

To give a sense of the size and complexity of many props, there's a bulky 5' x 4' x 4' carrying case, one of scores that famed magician Harry Blackstone traveled with. They filled a 90-foot, double-size baggage car. Each piece, save one, was painted orange for quick identification at train stations. Lund points to the lone exception, a black tool chest with "Peter Bouton" stenciled on it. He opens it to show a neat array of the varied tools of the trade. Bouton was Blackstone's real name, and Pete, his brother, was his key offstage man, a gifted carpenter, chemist, painter, even a seamstress. Lund reckons the Blackstones, senior and junior, as the best all-round magicians he's seen. He knew Harry, Sr. well. Harry Blackstone, Jr. is an occasional visitor to the museum. Many of the Blackstones' papers are in Lund's extensive archives of magic.

Some highlights of the museum tour, which spans four centuries and six continents, include:

♦ Mandrake the Magician comics.

♦ an 18th-century book by Jean Eugene Robert-Houdin, the Frenchman who took magic out of the supernatural closet and promoted himself frankly as a performer.

♦ posters of magician Marjorie Waddell. "See a man sawed in half," they proclaim. Lund says she was one of several "very good lady magicians who didn't go anyplace because many men don't like to be challenged by women."

Retired automotive writer Bob Lund leans on Houdini's milk can, the escape stunt which made Houdini famous. Lund's magic museum in downtown Marshall is so filled with significant material about magic that famous magicians make regular pilgrimages to take in the glories of their profession.

◆ a century's worth of sets of magic tricks for children.

◆ the original prop for the giant milk can stunt that rescued the young Harry Houdini's career. A St. Louis theater owner had threatened to book another act if he didn't draw more customers — soon. Houdini constructed it in a weekend. The audience filled the "milk can" with water, the lid was locked, but Houdini survived — thanks to a specially designed dome top with air holes, so he could tip back his head to breathe.

Houdini, Lund says, "is one of my least favorites — a man of all-consuming ego, among other failings. It's a myth that Houdini's secrets died with him. He had no secrets. He was the greatest stunt man and daredevil of his day. But we can't confuse stunts with magic. He thrived on confrontation, as if he were saying, 'You dummies! Can you figure it out?'"

The tour ends with a touching tribute to David Bamberg, also known as Fu Manchu. He was, Lund says, "the man who taught me what magic is all about — not tricks, but wonder and make-believe." Bamberg was the sixth and last generation of a family of magicians that began with a one-legged Jewish street magician in 18th-century Holland.

The big names in magic in the early 20th century acted as if they were geniuses and exploited a hostile, superior relationship with their audiences. Bamberg achieved a more marvelous effect with imagination and kindness, warmth and mystery. His magic lives on in a dazzling troupe of mostly volunteer performers, Le Grand David and His Own Spectacular Magic Company of Beverly, Massachusetts. Troupe members pay frequent visits to Lund's museum in Marshall.

In the end, what makes this place so special — sublime, even — is not at all the rarity or extent of the museum's artifacts or the learning behind the collections. It's the spirit behind it — the sincerity and integrity. Today, it seems, "everybody is somebody's minion," says Teller, one half of the Penn and Teller magic team. He is a big fan of Bob and Elaine Lund. "So few people today have anything they love that's really theirs. Bob and Elaine have this incredible independence, work like crazy, and have this great sense of humor. They have this incredible museum — and their chief fascination is with magicians that you've never heard of."

In downtown Marshall at 107 E. Michigan between Madison and Jefferson, kitty-corner from the handsome sandstone post office. By appointment only. Call (616) 781-7674 at least a day or two

*ahead of time. $3/person. Children must be accompanied by an
adult.*

TIDBITS AND TRIVIA . . . . . about the American Museum of Magic are
served up in a delightful little book, *The American Museum of Magic: Its
True Story* by Daniel Waldron. It's for sale for $5 at the museum. One
example concerns the seance held at the museum on October 31, 1978. "In
keeping with Houdini's promise that 'if there was any way to communicate
from The Beyond, he would find it,' [it] was conducted at daylight at the very
hour of his death, featuring a plate of bagels and lox as an added lure to
Houdini, who was Jewish."

"THE MAGIC CAPITOL OF THE WORLD" . . . . . summer home of the great
magician Harry Blackstone, **Colon**, Michigan, 40 miles southwest of
Marshall, is today the home of **Abbott's Magic Manufacturing Company**,
the world's largest producer of magic paraphernalia, and the site of Abbott's
famous annual **Magic Get-Together**, four days usually around the first
weekend in August. For more on Colon and Abbott's Saturday magic shows
(1 p.m. from Memorial Day through Labor Day), call (616) 432-3235.

BICYCLING AROUND MARSHALL AND ALBION . . . . . can be fun. Bikes are
the ideal way to view Marshall's historic architecture. Back roads into
Calhoun County's smaller towns don't generate a lot of traffic, and it's easy to
get in and out of Marshall itself. Biking 11 miles to the college town of **Albion**
along the **Kalamazoo River valley** is an easy drive, and Albion offers numerous low-key destinations. The best route: Take B Drive North on the south
side of Marshall just north of the river all the way east to Austin Avenue and
into Albion. Or turn left (north) from B Drive North onto 25 1/2 mile Road
and go a mile uphill to visit the picturesque and interesting campus of **Starr
Commonwealth** (see page 126). The 15 miles from Marshall to **Homer** on
Homer Road via the hamlet of Eckford are pretty but more demanding for
out-of-shape cyclists, and the route jigs and jogs considerably. A good map is
recommended. **Bernie's** on Homer's quaint main street has terrific hamburgers and olive burgers. A fine nine-mile route from Homer to Albion takes 25
1/2 Mile Road north out of town. Turn right (east) immediately onto L Drive
South, then take the first left onto 25 Mile Road to see an exceptional **octagon house**. At J Drive South jog left (west) and then right (north) onto Condit
Road to pass **Harrison's Orchards** a mile south of Albion. It's open for
apples, cider, and popcorn from September-December.

A BEAUTIFUL RIVERSIDE REFUGE FOR BIRDS AND WILDLIFE . . . . . is part of Albion College's **Whitehouse Nature Center.** Over half a mile of Kalamazoo River frontage and an unusual variety of ecosystems make the 125-acre center special. In an hour you can visit a tallgrass prairie, marshes, ponds, a wildflower garden, upland and flood-plain woods, old fields, and an old gravel pit planted to encourage wildlife. The trails, not the interpretive building, make this place special. Best for first-time visitors are the half-mile **Marsh Trail** (a boardwalk path along the river; 20 minutes) and the one-mile **Prairie Trail** (40 minutes) along the river to the prairie and wildflower garden. Remember, the plentiful birds and rabbits are most active early and late in the day. Pick up free trail guides, engagingly written and illustrated, by the building. Inside you can see an example of **home vermicomposting** (composting by earthworms), as developed by *Worms Eat My Garbage* author and worm expert Mary Appelhof of Kalamazoo. *Take Erie St. east from downtown Albion. Turn south on Hannah at the train tracks, and look for the signs for Farley Dr. and the nature center before you get to the football stadium. (517) 629-2030. Open year-round, dawn to dusk. Interpretive building open weekdays 8 a.m.-5 p.m., Sat & Sun noon-5. Free.*

MICHIGAN'S PREMIERE INSTITUTION SERVING TROUBLED YOUTH . . . . . is between Marshall and Albion. Visitors are always welcome to tour the beautiful, college-like campus and lake at **Starr Commonwealth.** If it's a weekday, stop in at the impressive main office and conference center nearest the entrance, to learn about Starr and its positive peer culture treatment method. You may be able, even on the spur-of-the-minute, to visit Starr's art collection at the **Brueckner Museum** and **Gladsome Cottage,** the former home of founder Floyd Starr. The house gives a good look at the earnest, positive, confident world view of early 20th-century Methodism. For people who had parents and grandparents from backgrounds like Floyd Starr's, the house is a magical window on a not-too-distant past. Starr believed that beauty instructs, and he urged Starr's friends to leave paintings and sculpture to the school. Famous friends memorialized at the Brueckner Museum included Helen Keller and George Washington Carver. *To arrange outstanding student-led tours of Starr, call (517) 629-5591, extension 431. Just south of I-94 exit 119 on 26 Mile/Starr Commonwealth Road, 3 miles west of Albion.*

A TREAT FOR LOVERS OF QUALITY VICTORIANA . . . . . is the **Gardner House Museum** in Albion, with its rich 1880s period rooms of choice furniture, paintings, and objects from local families. Exhibits on Albion's interesting history are featured in upstairs and basement rooms. *509 S. Superior, just south of downtown. (517) 629-5100. Open last weekend April through last weekend October, Sat. & Sun. 1-4 and by appointment.*

Green Top Country Village and Antique Mall

In Michigan's "antique capital" of Allen,
a whimsical group of orphaned historic buildings

This remarkable spot just west of Allen on U.S. 12 thankfully makes no pretense at being a real country village. Green Top is a fanciful collection of some 30 old buildings filled with antiques for sale. They include country stores and schools, granaries and barns, a root beer stand and a work-crew trolley car. The effect looks as if pieces of Midwestern towns were sucked up in a tornado, transported to Oz, and rearranged and painted by Munchkins in combinations of soft earthtones and dulled pastels. Maturing lilacs, daylilies, and evergreens serve to root the transplanted village to Earth again. Low stone walls, inspired by the Depression-era roadside attractions along U.S. 12, organize the place into gardens. Woodchip paths wind through a grove of shady young maples to courtyard groupings of the orphaned buildings.

This is a much more diverting way to look at a lot of antiques than the usual warehouse-like malls. When looking at stuff gets to be too much, you can stroll through the grounds. They are accented with benches and various ornaments, including an elaborate Italianate outhouse. Pick up a **flyer** on the buildings' origins at the front sales desk in the main building.

The original Green Top Lodge and Cabins (the name comes from their green roofs) are the core of this inspired confection. The onetime roadhouse opened in 1925, the year the Chicago Road out front was paved. Motor touring was then fast becoming a popular middle-class pastime. Green Top, one of the favorite stops between Detroit and Chicago, hosted salesmen, truckers, and tourists. The cabins were among the first around to have their own toilets. Jim Klein, a native of nearby Adrian, bought the old place to use as an antique shop in 1982, when the village of Allen was far less lively than it is today. Soon after that, his friend Norma Kaetzel despaired of being able to fix up a dilapidated historic building on her property, a plain little Greek Revival schoolhouse from 1840. Her dilemma inspired Klein to expand Green Top by moving such endangered buildings onto the five-acre site. Since then Green Top has become "a home of last resort for orphaned buildings," says Klein.

In some ways the place *is* like a real village, with a friendly atmosphere and some real characters among the dealers. If malls full of slicked-up, overcategorized antiques and collectibles turn you off, Green Top may be a place you'll like a lot. Its 35 dealers cover a lot of territory, mostly moderately priced: Victoriana, oak, walnut, and a good deal of furniture in the rough to balance the small things and collectibles. Today Green Top has evolved from a wide-ranging mall into more of a group shop of dealers who think somewhat alike. The Green Top look is mainly eclectic Americana with good lines, everything from bamboo to mahogany, with quite a few primitives and Victorian and folk art pieces. There are fewer dealers and less clutter than a few years ago. Much more of the stock has been acquired by Jim Klein and his energetic wife, Beth. Pieces are priced to move; if you take too

Tourist cabins (here) and a roadhouse in front of them formed the original Green Top. To them have been added some two dozen orphaned buildings and various rockery like this bird bath, inspired by the Depression-era rock roadside attractions along this part of U.S. 12. This unusual antiques mall has become a celebrated local attraction.

long to make up your mind about something, it may well be gone.

Green Top is a natural for Hillsdale County. As is common in Michigan's southern tier of counties, many of its towns are hardly bigger today than they were in their prime in the 1870s. Some, like Allen, almost became ghost towns. Derelict buildings are in good supply here. The land is variously too gravelly, hilly, or wet to pay off for large-scale, mechanized agriculture, but it is well suited to Amish methods of small-scale, general, self-sufficient farming. Several Amish communities have moved into the area. Amish men are excellent house-movers. To move the new 1,100-square-foot Methodist church to Green Top, teams of Amish workmen carefully pried the walls apart (a crane then lifted them onto a truck), dug the new foundation by hand, and put the building back together.

Green Top is on U.S. 12, 12 miles east of I-69 at Coldwater and half a mile west of Allen. (517) 869-2100. Open daily including most holidays, year round 10:30-5.

🌲🌳🌲

"THE ANTIQUE CAPITAL OF MICHIGAN" . . . . . is what the village of **Allen** calls itself. Allen consists of a four-corners and a strip of 19th-century stores and houses along U.S. 12, the old Chicago Road. Founded in 1827, Allen had 500 people in 1880, but has dwindled to 200 today. Its tiny downtown has been revived by an increasing number of antique shops. Today Allen numbers six antiques malls and many freestanding antique shops (over 100 dealers in all), plus an in-town herb shop. The very first antique shops, here and elsewhere along the Chicago Road, date from the road's paving in 1925. That spawned tourists courts, gas stations, and curio shops.

Many Allen shops from the 1960s, especially the older ones like **Poor Richard's Antiques and Books** and **Michiana Antiques**, have room after room of stuff piled high, not overly categorized or showcased. For people who like to paw through stuff, there's the alluring hope of hidden treasures.

Andy's Antiques is another old shop in the onetime general store and post office. At the **Little Farm Herb Shop** (517-869-2822), Susan Betz offers over 250 kinds of herbs, everlastings, and cottage flowers in season (from Mother's Day through early summer). There's a sizable display garden behind the shop, which is in an old chicken coop. **Simple Treasures Antiques** also has classes and supplies for porcelain dolls. **Lakeview Antiques** specializes in Depression glass, china, and pottery. **Chesney's Antiques** in the Olde Chicago Pike Mall sells refinished furniture and cane chairs. **Poor Richard's** has a vast stock of framed popular pictures and books. At **Hand & Heart Antiques**, Brent Barribeau is an American Indian folk artist and woodcarver.

In the **Old Allen Township Hall Shops** (517-869-2575), John Alward and Janine Fentiman have created in the former town hall an attractive two-level space for appealingly presented booths. Their own eclectic merchandise includes masks from Nepal, rocks and minerals, trade beads, and African crafts. "For the last 20 years we have run a world-wide business out of Allen," she says. When she or Alward is in town, visitors can see their **First People American Indian and Eskimo Museum,** by chance or appointment.

When you get to Allen, look for the bold black-and-white **brochure and map** to plan your visit. *Malls and larger shops are open daily from 10 or 11 to 5 throughout the year. Some shops are open weekends only.* **Summer festivals** *have open-air antiques, flea market stalls, and barbecues put on by the volunteer firefighters. They are held on Memorial Day, Independence Day, and Labor Day. Winter weekdays are hit-or-miss at many Allen shops.*

A SPRINGTIME DELIGHT . . . . . is the **Slayton Arboretum** at nearby Hillsdale College. Even in winter, this arboretum is exceedingly picturesque — the epitome of that informal rock-garden romanticism so popular in the 1920s. In May and June it is spectacular with displays of flowering crabs and peonies. Clumps of white birch and Norway and white spruce, planted in 1929 in this former gravel pit, now loom tall above fieldstone walls and gazebos, rustic footbridges and goldfish ponds. Lagoons and nearby lakes attract many birds. Paths wind up a steep slope from the gazebo and outdoor amphitheater. An overlook terrace permits views of a landscape studded with specimen plantings and quaint little structures like the English cottage-style horticultural laboratory. *On Barber at Union, east of the college. From U.S. 12 at Jonesville, take M-99 almost into downtown Hillsdale, but turn east at Fayette. In about 1/2 mile turn north onto Union.*

A RICH BANKER'S PALATIAL HOME . . . . . designed by Elijah Myers, the architect of Michigan's state capitol, has been splendidly restored as the **Grosvenor House Museum** in Jonesville, 5 miles east of Allen on U.S. 12. Jonesville banker E.O. Grosvenor's 1870s house is full of elaborate details and the then-latest tricks in modern engineering and planning. It has that rich layering of exotic objets d'art, patterned motifs, and wood surfaces that gives high Victorian style its eclectic, opulent effect. An upstairs **museum room** presents ordinary Jonesville history well, featuring local products from Jonesville's old cigar factory and dairy to recent plastic dollhouse play sets from Kiddie Brush and Toy — "toys that mold character," says the ad, like Susy's Superette and the Friendly Folks Motel. *From U.S. 12 at the park in downtown Jonesville, take Maumee south 3 blocks to 211 Maumee. (517) 849-9596. Open the first full weekend in June through September, Sat. & Sun 2-5.*

Hidden Lake Gardens

*A lovely spot in the Irish Hills pairs
picturesque landscape gardens with woodland trails.*

This 755-acre arboretum is a very special place year-round. It was first planted by Harry Fee of Adrian, who used the striking terrain to create memorable scenes with plants. He assembled a property that took advantage of the unusually varied glacial landscape in this band of hills and lakes known as the Irish Hills. In this region huge ice chunks from the last Ice Age left a crazy-quilt landscape of round kettle-hole lakes, steep-sided valleys, and dramatic vistas interspersed with sweeping meadows and marshes.

Fee's plantings, begun in 1926, provide a mature backdrop for later collections and gardens planted by Michigan State University since 1945. He donated his gardens to M.S.U. because of its outstanding landscape and horticulture programs, and left a substantial endowment to provide for their future maintenance. The Herrick family of Tecumseh (Ray Herrick founded Tecumseh Products, a Fortune 500 firm that makes engines and compressors) donated a handsome and impressive visitor center and separate conservatory. They are used as a **center for landscape education**.

The front part of Hidden Lake Gardens has been landscaped for maximum picturesqueness, while the back oak uplands, laced with **five miles of hiking trails**, remain in their natural state. (Get a **trail guide** at the visitor center.) Six miles of beautiful **one-way drives** wind through the front part so close to branches of flowering magnolias, crabs, and cherries that even from the car you notice individual flowers. A bike drive through this part lets you stop and smell the flowers, but bikes are prohibited on Sundays. You can also park your car on one of many pullovers, and get out and walk.

It all makes for an especially nice blend of the cultivated and wild. You can go for a vigorous hike (a good mix of hardwoods makes **fall colors** gorgeous), then learn about Michigan forest communities in the visitor center, or take in the damp, fragrant atmosphere of the tropical house, or see rare dwarf conifers in a

One of Hidden Lake Gardens' many unusual horticultural attractions is the Harper Collection of Rare and Dwarf Conifers (here). A woods with fine fall color and an indoor conservatory make the gardens a worthwhile year-round destination.

special garden. The gardens are especially beautiful after a fresh snowfall; skiing is not allowed. Everywhere you can glean ideas for your own yard from the many identified plantings. Lists of nursery sources for plants are provided whenever possible.

Here are some highlights not to miss:

◆ The **front road system** artfully invites you into a special world and manipulates the views to give a fresh, intimate perspective on the trees and shrubs you see. Lilacs, flowering crabs, and cherries are wonderful in May. At the far west end is a choice collection of evergreens.

◆ There's **Hidden Lake** itself, beneath overarching willows next to the visitor center. A pair of swans, often with baby cygnets, will come up to the pullover area and eagerly eat bread visitors bring. (No moldy bread, please! It makes them sick.)

◆ **Hosta Hillside** by the lake has been planted and maintained by the Hosta Society of Michigan. Inquire about the society's big May hosta sale, with unusual plants from members' collections.

◆ Naturalized **primroses and daffodils** bloom in the last two weeks of April. The primroses are at the lake's north end; daffodils are all over.

◆ **Exhibits in the visitor center** cover topics like the development of plant aristocrats through hybridization, the life and death of a glacial lake, forest communities in southern Michigan, conifer classifications, and Michigan geology. They're dense yet satisfying to the inquiring lay mind. Take one or two topics on a visit, and you could learn a lot of botany and horticulture basics fast.

◆ The large **conservatory** is unusually enjoyable, especially in winter. Some very large, luxuriant specimens in the **tropical house** make you feel like you're in a rain forest; it's fun to see grapefruit, figs, guava, and tangerines growing on trees. There's also an **arid house** and a **temperate house**, where you can see **orchids, ferns, fuchsia,** and some remarkable **bonsai**, artistically pruned trees up to 25 years old but only a foot high. Well-written signs about plants' culture and uses in food and ornament are good reading. Among the featured indoor plants are bamboo, banana, cactus, camphor, cocoa, coffee, fig, palm, sugarcane, tapioca, and vanilla. After a thoughtful visit to the temperate house, you will see familiar house plants in a new way.

◆ **The Harper Collection of Rare and Dwarf Conifers** are behind the conservatory. Some are bluish or gold, some weep or lie flat on the ground. Many come from genetic mutations or witch's brooms: small, thick growths on the limbs of a tree that grow true to form when propagated by cuttings.

A **picnic area** with restrooms has been provided behind the Harper Conifer collection. The excellent visitor center **gift shop** has many books and pamphlets on nature and gardening, plus nature-related notecards, T-shirts and sweatshirts, rock samples, and bird feeders and houses. Classes and workshops on gardening, birds, and more are held on many Tuesday evenings, Saturdays, and in summer on Wednesday afternoons. Fees: $2-$12. Call for info. The big **spring plant sale** on a mid-May weekend features lectures on hostas and conifers and choice plants from the collections of American Hosta Society's and American Conifer Society's members.

The Gardens are on M-50 8 miles west of Tecumseh and 7 miles east of Cambridge Junction, the historic crossroads where M-50 joins U.S. 12. From Adrian or Chelsea, take M-52 to M-50, turn west. (517) 431-2060. Grounds and conservatory open 365 days/ year, April thru Oct. 8 a.m.-dusk, Nov. thru March 8 a.m.-4 p.m. Visitor center open 8-4:30 weekdays, 12-6 weekends; in winter 8-

*4 weekdays, 10-4 weekends. $1/person weekdays, $3/person
weekends, children under 2 free.*

BEEKEEPING SUPPLIES, HONEY, AND CANDLE MOLDS . . . . . along with
a **working beehive** (cut away so you can see inside) and all sorts of gifts and
books pertaining to bees, are sold a few miles west of Hidden Lake Gardens
at **Hubbard Apiaries**. $120 buys you everything needed to get started in bee-
keeping, including a bee suit. Pick up a free catalog. *On M-50 at Springville
Rd., east of U.S. 12. (517) 467-2051. Open weekdays only, 7-4:30.*

SIGHTSEEING ALONG U.S. 12, THE OLD CHICAGO TURNPIKE . . . . .
through the Irish Hills, can be fun. Along the road is a weird blend of pioneer
Michigan history and 20th-century tourism: 1920s gas stations and lookout
towers, the Prehistoric Forest, Mystery Hill, water slides, bumper boats, go-
cart raceways, and Roger Penske's Michigan International Speedway (517-
592-6666), which packs the area four weekends a summer. A few remaining
farmhouses and taverns date to the old Indian trail's first round of improvements in the 1830s. Neglect, unsightly sand and gravel pits, and care-
less development have increasingly taken their toll on this interesting route.

Here's a short list of additional recommended sights for a pleasant drive
along the 18 miles of U.S. 12 between the interesting village of Clinton on the
east and U.S. 127 on the west. All except Stagecoach Stop are free or inexpensive. List reads from east to west. For other sights on and near U.S. 12, see
Green Top and Allen (pp. 127-130). *Most sights are open daily in summer only.
Call (517) 592-8907 weekdays for more Irish Hills information.*
◆ **Eisenhower's Presidential railroad car**. Original interiors, memorabilia.
Furnished as if Ike were still on the campaign trail. Well worth the modest
entrance fee.
◆ **Stagecoach Stop**, a make-believe 19th-century village theme park just
west of Ike's railroad car, is more of an all-day attraction. It blends soap
opera, nostalgia, arcade games, wild game park, and crafts demonstrations.
Not for the kitsch-aversive. More for kids today; not nearly as widely appealing to adults since the wonderful antique coin-operated musical devices have
been removed. *7203 U.S. 12, near Onsted. (517) 467-2300.*
◆ **Irish Hills Towers**. Corny, fun lookout is best in fall. Big **adventure golf**
course next to it.
◆ **St. Joseph's Shrine.** An inspired folk art environment. The Stations of the
Cross behind the parking lot leading down the hill to the lake were made of
colored tile and cement during the Depression. The way traces Christ's walk
to the crucifixion on Cavalry. The historic marker explains, "The footpath

begins at a replica of Pontius Pilate's palace, then winds past balconied houses, through the judgment gate and ends at Christ's tomb." The rustic arch-
ways and railings were made to resemble logs by two Mexican artisans who
did other work in the area. *8743 U.S. 12 in Cambridge Township, Lenawee
County, south of Brooklyn.*

◆ **Walker Tavern Historic Complex.** Fine small state historical museum
and restored 1832 tavern tell the story of the Chicago Road, a chief route of
settlement during Michigan's pioneer boom years of the 1830s. Travelers
piled into a few sleeping rooms, shared beds, spent much time in the barroom. Daniel Webster and James Fenimore Cooper stayed here on expeditions to what was then the American west. Pleasant picnic area in large park.
*At U.S. 12 and M-50. Enter off M-50 north of U.S. 12. (517) 467-4414. Open
summers only due to lack of funds. Call for hours.*

◆ **Mary's House of Rosaries.** Lots of different kinds of rosaries, and statues
of famous and obscure saints. Good religious pictures, too. Well worth a stop
for fans of popular religious art. *On U.S. 12 about 3 or 4 miles east of U.S.
127, south side of road. In a house; open daylight hours.*

◆ **McCourtie Park.** More rustic structures done in cement on the former
estate of the cement king of nearby Cement City. Bridges and some remarkable cement birdhouses are along a pretty creek. Poor maintenance is threatening these unusual structures. **Flavor Fruit Farms** (517-688-3455) is an
orchard and farm market in a handsome old farm a short ways north on S.
Jackson Rd. *McCourtie Park is on U.S. 12 in Somerset Center, in the far
northwest corner of Hillsdale County.* **To enter:** *turn north onto South Jackson
Road.*

Southern Michigan Railroad

*A scenic trip along a river valley between two
quaint old towns: a relaxing glimpse of rural America.*

This short train ride is a low-key delight. The 45-minute
trip between the picturesque old towns of Clinton and
Tecumseh passes by woods and marshes full of wildlife,
farm fields, and some terrific vegetable gardens. A 116-foot timber trestle over the River Raisin is a special thrill. It seems like a
real event when you arrive at Tecumseh's handsomely restored
downtown — much more than when you come by car. You can
make the return trip immediately, but many passengers prefer to
spend two hours looking around Tecumseh (if they started in
Clinton) or Clinton (if they started in Tecumseh). The historic
Clintonian Inn is a fine place for a lunch or dessert.

This is an historical stretch of railroad, with real, workaday
equipment, not a scaled-down steam engine and cute open-air
cars. The 1938 Plymouth switch engine, long used by the Hayes
Albion Corporation, now pushes the train to Tecumseh and pulls
it back to Clinton. The passenger cars aren't fancy. There's an
open-air freight gondola that now seats 60 people on wooden
benches. And there's a covered commuter car that spent most of
its working life on the old Chicago South Shore line. Cabooses
are used when additional seating is needed.

On the train, look for informational handouts on the track
and railroad. In the typical style of true rail fans, the line's equipment and history is minutely described. The Southern Michigan
Railroad is in operation because of a small group of high school
students. For generations of Tecumseh boys, a favorite pastime
was to hitch rides on the slow-moving freight train that connected Clinton with Adrian. The line, originally known as the
Palmyra & Jacksonburg Railroad, goes back to 1853 and is an
offshoot of the first railroad west of the Alleghenies, between
Adrian and Toledo. 1982 brought the closing of the line's last
customer, the Budd plant that made wheel and brake assemblies
in Clinton. Conrail abandoned the track. But a group of high
school juniors, aided by a lawyer father, formed a nonprofit corporation, raised a down payment, and bought 13 1/2 miles of

track for $100,000. Now local kids still ride the rails as staff of the popular weekend train.

Plan to spend some time in the Clinton depot, originally built as part of a municipal power plant. Its **gift shop** is full of nifty railroad insignia items on mugs, patches, and T-shirts, plus trainmen's caps, postcards, and other memorabilia. There's also an informal **museum**, and you can go downstairs to see work in progress restoring hand cars, baggage trucks, and the like.

Station and museum at 320 S. Division at Clark in Clinton. (517) 456-7677. From U.S. 12 in downtown Clinton, turn at Comerica Bank and take Division three blocks south to the depot. Runs Sundays, June through September, plus weekend color tours in October (leave from Tecumseh). Summer schedule **trains leave Clinton** *at 11, 1, and 3. The Tecumseh stopover and loading point is at downtown light, M 50 and Evans.* **Trains leave Tecumseh** *at 12 and 2. Arrive 15 minutes before departure; limited seating. $6 adults, $4 children 2 12.*

WELL OVER TWO DOZEN ANTIQUE SHOPS . . . . . are in or near the Irish Hills. Among the best are the **Manchester Antique Mall** (313 428-9357) in delightful downtown Manchester, the **Hitching Post Antiques Mall** (517-423-8277) on M-50 near M-52, two miles west of Tecumseh, and the **Brick Walker Tavern** (517-467-4385) on U.S. 12 at M-50 (closed Mon & Tues). Clusters of antiques shops and/or malls are in downtown Clinton, Tecumseh, and Allen, and lately there are more antiques in Jonesville, too. Look up Pluck's in Jonesville, in a big Italianate house a block north of U.S. 12 on M-99. *Ask for a helpful shop guide and map to other area dealers.*

Jackson Cascades

This huge man-made waterfall in a baroque
pleasure park is a nostalgic sight from the 1930s.

There's nothing subtle about Jackson's best-known sight — an illuminated 500-foot artificial waterfall cascading down a hill at 3,000 gallons a minute, in three pools and 16 falls. After dark, shifting patterns of colored lights turn the Cascades into a baroque fantasy in vivid Technicolor. Recorded show tunes underscore its theatricality.

Every evening from Memorial Day to Labor Day the Cascades offer low-key summer entertainment for $3 a head. The falls, fountains, and music are turned on from 7:30 to 11 p.m. You can climb the 129 steps that flank the 30-foot-wide falls and watch the sun produce repeating rainbows in the spray. (Kids love this!) A hand stamp lets you leave and reenter, so you can picnic, fish, feed ducks, play, and enjoy the numerous facilities and scenic hills and waterways of the surrounding **Cascades Park** (see below).

The Cascades are so grand and monumental, you'd expect them to have been built only in a very large metropolitan area, not in a small but enterprising city of 55,000. That was Jackson's population at its peak in 1930, two years before the Cascades were finished. (Today the population of Jackson has declined to 37,500.) In Jackson's glory years of the 1920s, it prospered and made many local fortunes in auto parts. "Little Detroit" was Jackson's nickname.

One especially forceful and enthusiastic local magnate was Captain William Sparks. He had immigrated from England with his family, had grown up in Jackson, and had became rich as a

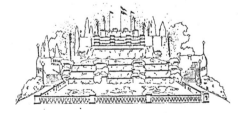

At the Cascades, baroque grandeur was brought to Jackson by Cap Sparks, radio manufacturer and local booster par excellence.

parts supplier. By 1920, the Sparks Withington Company, originally formed to make buggy parts, employed over 7,000 people.
They made Sparton radios, electric auto horns (which Sparks
pioneered), and other automotive accessories.

Sparks's lifetime goal was to put Jackson on the map. A
three-term mayor, he was once simultaneously the city manager
and Chamber of Commerce president. His Sparks-Withington
Zouaves (pronounced zoo-AHVS) were a kind of quick-stepping
precision drill team, patterned after a colorful Algerian infantry
unit. Many American towns had their own Zouaves units. "Cap"
Sparks (the title was honorary; he never served in the military)
and his Zouaves toured the world, bringing fame to their home
town. While in Barcelona, Sparks was so taken by a grand, cascading waterfall that he later determined to build a version of it
on the marshland behind his magnificent Tudor home. Soon
what began as a plan for a skating pond at the foot of the
Cascades blossomed into 465 acres of lagoons, picnic areas, and
an 18-hole golf course and clubhouse.

The **Cascades-Sparks Museum**, just inside the entryway to
the amphitheater, is a quirky, often amusing collection of old
Sparton Electronics radios, colorful Zouaves costumes, and
memorabilia, including photos of the Jackson Zouaves performing in *The Court Jester* with Danny Kaye, and scenes from the
very successful concert Harry Chapin performed here shortly
before his death.

The Cascades did succeed in putting Jackson on the national
showbiz map during the 1930s and 1940s, as attested by press
clippings from major U.S. cities about the seven-stage extravaganzas staged there. Today Sparks's mansion on West Street has
been replaced by apartments after two feuding women's clubs
torpedoed plans to reuse it. But its impressive Tudor garage and
guest house can still be seen on Kibby Road, across from the
matching Tudor **Cascades Clubhouse** at the entrance to the
Sparks Foundation Park. The renovated clubhouse opens for
weekday **lunch** and **Sunday buffet** in fall 1994. Call directory
assistance (517-555-1212) and ask for Cascades Manor House.

Air-conditioned movies and TV took their toll on Cascades
attendance. The concrete crumbled, and Sparks' magnificent gift
to the city threatened to become an obsolete white elephant. But
local construction workers restored the Cascades and built the
amphitheater and museum building. The new sound system is
excellent. A second round of renovations, half a million dollars'

worth, was finished in 1993. It includes a new water recircula-
tion system that's both filtered and chlorinated for cleanliness.

Today the Cascades are an entertainment anachronism.
Some Jacksonians consider them irredeemably tacky, unsophis-
ticated, and dumb. To others, the Cascades' direct, childlike
charm evokes a wonderful, nostalgic period. Gigantic **fireworks
shows** with live entertainment are held at the Cascades on the
Saturday of each summer holiday weekend – Memorial Day, the
Fourth of July, and Labor Day. The last weekend of August
brings the largest **Civil War Muster** in the Midwest, with major
battle re-enactments, camp life, battalion parades, a dress ball,
and music festival. It's free; call (517) 788-4320 for a brochure.

*S. Brown at Denton Rd. in the Cascades County Park, Jackson.
From I-94, take West Ave. exit 138 at Jackson Crossing mall and
follow the signs south. (517) 788-4320. Memorial Day through Labor
Day, 7:30-11 p.m. daily. $3 per person, ages 5 and under free.*

BY THE CASCADES, A BIG PARK WITH ACTIVITIES AND GREAT GOLF . .
. . . Inspired by his dream of creating a magnificent landscaped waterfall on
his estate, industrialist William Sparks went on to create **Cascades Park**,
where meadows and wetlands meet rolling hills. Adjoining the Cascades are a
fanciful **playground** with cast concrete animals and a moonwalker, and an
18-hole miniature golf course ($2, open daily in summer 11-11). Across
Denton, behind the Tudor-style Cascades clubhouse is a **duck pond**, a **par-
cours/jogging track** with 21 exercise stations on a 2.2 mile trail, and two
miles of **lagoons** for fishing and boating with a **handicapped-accessible fishing pier**. Here paddleboats can be rented for $4/half-hour.

Golf is an obsession in Jackson. The high quality of its public and municipal courses makes it available to virtually everybody. Two courses are in
Cascades Park. **Hill Brothers Golf Course** is a 9 hole, par 3 "executive
course" with shorter holes; $3.75 ($1.75 before 11 weekdays). Call (517)
782-2855 for reservations. The **Cascades Golf Course** is an 18-hole course,
and quite challenging. Its front 9 are longer and easier, the back 9 shorter
and more difficult. Call (517) 788-4323 for reservations and prices.

In winter, the park's glacial hills lends themselves to **cross-country-ski-
ing** (trails begin south of the Clubhouse), **sledding** down the Cascades hill,
and **skating** on the duck pond behind the Clubhouse (warming house open
weekends 11-7).

FAMOUS FOR ITS GIANT SUNDAES . . . . . the **Parlour** soda fountain at the
Jackson All-Star Dairy is the most popular spot in town. No super-premium

ice cream here, just the basics — chocolate syrup, nuts, whipped cream, good ice cream made at the ice cream plant right next door, and lots of it. (A single scoop here is closer to two normal scoops.) The $4.50 banana split (6 scoops, piled in a foot-high pyramid) is more than three people can comfortably eat. "Dare to Be Great" ($14.95) is a 21-scoop monster. Typical three-scoop sundaes are $2.95. Obliging counter girls will honor requests for extra sides of whipped cream and toppings (you do pay for them) and for special fountain treats — lemon malts, or hot fudge malts, for instance. (Malts are made with soft ice cream unless you specify extra rich.) Expect a wait in summer, longer on weekends or after the malls close and movies are out. The entire fountain menu, plus big $1 cones in 31 flavors, is available at the faster **takeout** line. A few picnic tables are outside. *On Higby at Daniel, just east of Brown and the Westwood Mall. From I-94 exit 138, take West Ave. to Michigan Ave., turn west; in 7 blocks turn north on Higby. (Brown Street runs from the Dairy to the Cascades.) (517) 782-7141. Open daily 10-10, to 11 in summer.*

JACKSON'S HIDDEN SECRETS . . . . . hidden to outsiders, that is, include a wonderful large outdoor sculpture by the late, great **Louise Nevelson**, so poorly sited (in front of the closed hotel on East Michigan just east of Mechanic) as to be almost invisible, and an amazing number of good, moderate-priced **public golf courses**. Call the Chamber of Commerce at (517) 783-3330 for the Jackson golf guide, or stop by the 24-hour tourist info center by the McDonald's at I-94 Exit 145 east of town. Golf is so popular in Jackson it ranks with bowling and softball as one of the three blue-collar sports. . . . . . . Jackson (its environs, actually) is the home of Republican rocker Ted Nugent. His musical tributes to hunting and his bowhunting mentor, Fred Bear, are available along with archery gear and his published musings on the subject at **Ted Nugent's Bowhunters' World** at 4133 West Michigan west of town. Call (517) 750-9060 for directions.

Michigan Space Center

*A fascinating, up-close view of America's great leap
to dominance in space exploration*

Housed in a big geodesic dome on the Jackson Community
College campus south of Jackson, the Michigan Space
Center manages to take a complex topic —America's
space ventures of the 1960s and 1970s — and illuminate it in a
way that entertains and educates rather than overwhelms the
visitor. There are background displays on the Solar System and
the evolution of rocketry. But most of the displays pertain to that
amazing era when the U.S. moved from far behind the Soviets in
rocket design to become the first and only country to land
humans on the moon.

Liberally scattered throughout the Center are historically im-

portant space equipment,
such as a prototype of the
Mariner IV spacecraft
which flew close to Mars in
1964 and a Lunar Rover
Vehicle. Most spectacular
is the actual Apollo 9 command module used to link
up in space with a test
Lunar Excursion Module
three months before the
first moon landing. You get
to look right inside the
module to see the cramped

**The Apollo 9 command mod-
ule used for a key test mission three months before the
first moon landing. The
Space Center's many exhibits
illuminate the spectacular
American advances in space
exploration made from 1960
to 1980.**

quarters. An array of spacesuits shows their rapid evolution from the stiff early Mercury suits (1958-1963) to the flexible Apollo suits of the 1970s. Especially fascinating for children is the detailed explanation of how astronauts go to the bathroom. Also interesting are displays of the food eaten in space. Get on a big digital scale and compare your weight on earth with what it would be on any of the other planets. The large but primitive-looking computer console which guided John Glenn's historic first Earth orbit in 1962 shows how much more sophisticated today's space electronics are. A moon rock was brought back by Jackson native Al Worden and other members of the Apollo 15 crew. There are **films** on space topics, a self-guided tour, a **gift shop**, and a **picnic area**.

2111 Emmons Road. Take exit 142 from I-94 to 127. Take 127 to the Monroe and M-50 exit. Turn left onto McDevitt Ave. Turn left onto Hague at the first traffic light on McDevitt. Take Hague to Emmons Road and follow the signs. Plenty of free parking at the Space Center. (517) 787-4425. May through Labor Day: Mon-Sat 10 5, Sun noon-5. Call to check on hours from after Labor Day through April. Adults $3.50, students and seniors $2.50, children under 5 (with parents) free. Groups of 15 or more may get discount rate of 50¢ off regular admission prices by calling in advance.

A FIRST-RATE NATURE CENTER . . . . . not far from the Michigan Space Center has five miles of **trails** through woods and over streams with excellent interpretive markers. It also has some indoor exhibits and a nature-oriented gift shop. To get to the **Dahlem Center** from the Space Center, go south (left) on Browns Lake Road where the entrance drive is. In about a block turn west (right) onto Kummel. In one mile, turn north (right) onto South Jackson Road. Dahlem Center entrance is in two blocks. Call (517) 782-3453 for info.

AN OUTSTANDING VICTORIAN HOUSE MUSEUM AND MORE . . . . . is a short, scenic drive from the Space Center. **Ella Sharp Museum** consists of an especially elegant 1857 farmhouse; an authentically furnished settlers' log cabin, circa 1840; a schoolhouse; several 19th-century businesses; and three galleries with regularly **changing exhibits on arts and local history**, plus the hands-on **Discovery Gallery** for children.

Tours of the house, given every half hour and customized to each small group's interests, go way beyond Victorian decorating to point out things like how quickly industrialization changed people's everyday lives in the late 19th century, and how fascinated the Victorian middle class was with nature and its spiritual power. Ella Sharp's mother was a wealthy Easterner who invested in Michigan land and actually came out to live on it. With her husband she developed Hillside Farm into a showplace of progressive agriculture. Ella herself was a successful reformer. Her causes were good government, improving town and rural life through women's clubs, and conservation. Don't miss a trip to the house's treetop cupola.

The Granary restaurant is a most attractive lunch spot (open Tues-Sat). There's a good **gift shop** in the main exhibit building. *The museum is in Ella Sharp Park on the south edge of Jackson, on Fourth just south of Horton Rd. From the Space Center take Browns Lake Rd. past the Jackson Community College Campus. It turns into Stonewall and leads to the museum. Enter the park and park behind the museum. From I-94, take M-50/Business 127, exit 138 at Jackson Crossing, go south on West and follow the signs. (517) 787-2320. Tues-Fri 10-5, Sat & Sun 12-5. $2.50/person, $1 child, $5 family*

ADVENTURE GOLF AND SWIMMING AT SHARP PARK . . . . . At the Sharp Park entrance on Fourth Street, just north of the Ella Sharp Museum, an **18-hole minigolf course** occupies a manmade hill with two cascading waterfalls and rivers emptying into a large pond with a 25-foot fountain. Trees, shrubs, and seasonal flowers turn this into a three-acre multilevel garden. There's a small snack concession. *The Sharp Park East Miniaturized Golf Course (517-788-4696) is open from April through October. Summer hours are 10 a.m. to 10 p.m.; spring and fall hours start and end with weekends (Fri-Sun) only; call for specifics. Cost: $2.50 per person (all ages), $2 in groups of 5 or more. Half price before noon.* . . . . . Next door, the **Sharp Park Swimming Pool**, an Olympic-size Z-shape pool with diving and instructional wells, is open to all. *Season: school summer vacation, usually from the 2nd week of June to the last part of August. Open swim hours: 1-3, 3:15-5:15, adults only 5:30-7; late-evening hours in hot weather. (517) 788-4050. $1/person.*

THE BIRTHPLACE OF THE REPUBLICAN PARTY . . . . . is Jackson's biggest claim to fame. A meeting of Free Soilers, abolitionists, anti-slavery Whigs and Democrats, men concerned about the growing power of the railroads, and others was organized in Jackson by local attorney Austin Blair and other dissidents. It proved so large it had to be held outdoors, **"under the oaks"** in a grove just west of town. Blair went on to become Michigan's beloved Civil War governor, a staunch backer of Lincoln, before being thwarted by Michigan big-money interests who came to dominate the party he helped found. The oak grove was later subdivided and built up, but two city lots now make up a small **park** commemorating the historic site. One of the trees was hit by lightning during Watergate – the stuff of enduring local legend. But some big oaks remain. *On Franklin at Second. Take West Ave. from I-94 exit 38 to 2 blocks south of Michigan Ave., turn east onto Franklin for 4 blocks.*

Ann Arbor shopping and nightlife

Michigan's liveliest downtown, cosmopolitan and dynamic, has a dazzling mix of unusually specialized shops, from pop culture of the 1950s to Chinese art.

Ann Arbor is not just the home of one of the country's most distinguished universities. Over the past couple of decades it has become one of the most interesting spots to visit in the Midwest. Walking down Main Street or State Street on a Friday or Saturday evening, you'll find the sidewalks crowded with a colorful mix of people, from the elegantly attired to street people, from professors to punks. Coffeehouses (16 of them so far, with more on the way) have popped up everywhere. They often have live entertainment, and they're ideal places to observe the local scene. Most shops stay open late, augmenting the busy bars and nightspots. Many restaurants spill out onto the sidewalks. The cultural and entertainment options are almost overwhelming.

Even on an ordinary winter weekend with no particularly big events, central Ann Arbor is alive with activity. Out-of-town visitors are an increasing part of the crowd, drawn to what for many is the most interesting place in Michigan. Some Ann Arbor store managers say half their checks are from out of town. Lines form outside popular restaurants, and shops on Main Street are packed with after-dinner browsers until 10 p.m. Restaurant competition has become so fierce, most of the food is at least pretty good.

Enough traditional old German businesses such as **Ehnis & Son** work clothes shop and **Schlenker Hardware** (both on West Liberty) remain downtown to give some historical continuity to the area. Remnants of Ann Arbor's once-lively counterculture live on at the **Del Rio Bar** at 120 West Washington, the **Old Town** at 120 West Liberty, and upstairs over the **Heidelberg Restaurant**, 214 North Main, where monthly "poetry slams" are held. But people who remember the laid-back Ann Arbor of their college days are surprised by its big-city intensity, its traffic (often

❶ Downtown. Interesting concentration of restaurants & shops. Lively Main Street scene on into the evening with plenty of good open-air summer cafes.

❷ Kerrytown. Lively restaurant/shop complex. Popular bistro, large farmers' market, outstanding kitchenware shop, Nearby **Treasure Mart** is must visit for bargain-hunters.

❸ Zingerman's. Extraordinary deli and fancy food shop. Delicious huge sandwiches, outstanding bread & interesting selection of cheeses, meats, and ethnic dishes.

❹ State-Liberty shopping area. Anchored by Borders Books. Great record & book shops, many other interesting stores & coffee houses. Cosmopolitan street scene.

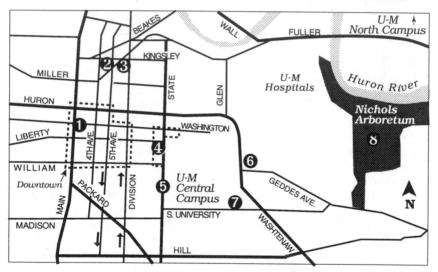

❺ Two U-M museums on State St. At the **Kelsey**, priceless ancient Egyptian, Greek, and Roman pieces. **Museum of Art** has important paintings, medieval to modern.

❻ U-M Exhibit Museum. Extraordinary natural science displays with prehistoric scenes, dramatic dinosaur skeletons, many rare specimens.

❼ Middle Earth. Entertaining shop in student-oriented commercial strip. Full of all sorts of amusing items, many outrageous. Nearby **Village Corner** has one of state's best selections of wines.

❽ Nichols Arboretum. Delightful hilly 126 acres. Paths down to Huron River. Over 2,000 kinds of plants, outstanding peonies. Beautiful Forest Hills Cemetery is next door.

Highlights of
Ann Arbor

0   1/2 mile   1

approaching gridlock, though still light by New York standards) —
and its expensive merchandise. It's not hard to find a $1,500
sport coat, a $5,000 painting, or a $20,000 ring in central Ann
Arbor.

Ann Arbor has become more than a college town. It has
become a regional research and development center. And it's also
a suburb of choice for metro Detroit's intelligentsia. Downtown
Detroit is barely 45 minutes away. People like Ford Motor president Alex Trotman and many *Detroit Free Press* editors and writers
find this the most congenial place in Southeast Michigan to live.

What sets Ann Arbor apart from other downtowns that
experienced rampant gentrification in the 1980s is that many —
maybe even most — stores haven't simply jumped onto the latest
hot trend. Stores here are usually owned and run by knowledgeable people with longstanding interests in what they sell,
whether it be backpacking gear or Chinese art. Upscale specialty
chains like Benetton and J. Crew, which threaten to overwhelm
downtown Birmingham and Grosse Pointe, have made few
inroads in Ann Arbor. Shops with crafts, decorative arts, and
home accessories are much stronger in Ann Arbor than clothes.
Ann Arbor *really* shines in books (page 169) and CDs (page 174);
some say it's the best book and record town in the U.S. Now
Borders, the homegrown bookstore that originated the superstore concept in bookstore chains, has taken over the Liberty
Street space vacated when Jacobson's moved to Briarwood, and
is adding a sizable music, video, and multi-media department to
its huge book inventory. (See page 169.)

In recent years, the **State Street area** has seen bookstores
expand and its retailing mix lose clothing stores and older customers. **South University** has become overwhelmingly oriented
to undergraduates. General retailing has nearly vanished from
Main Street, except for **Kline's Department Store** at 306 South
Main, where some very good deals are to be found. The phenomenally successful Zingerman's deli and Sweet Lorraine's restaurant generate daytime traffic that have brought new stores to the
Kerrytown area, the near north side specialty shopping complex
by the Farmers' Market. Central-area parking is so tight, interesting specialty stores geared more to local people are now found
in shopping centers along **Plymouth Road**, including Traver
Village on Plymouth Road west of Nixon and the Courtyard
Shops at North Campus Plaza.

Here are some standouts, arranged by areas. For readers'

convenience in planning a route, bookstores and CD stores have been briefly noted here. They're treated more fully in separate chapters on pages 169 and 174.

DOWNTOWN: ON AND OFF MAIN STREET

As recently as 20 years ago, downtown Ann Arbor was dominated by longtime German businesses. But over the past decade it has become a stylish place for eating, drinking coffee, and browsing. The block of South Fourth Avenue between Liberty and Washington attracts interesting start-up stores and is always worth checking out. The 200 block of Washington is becoming a gallery destination. *Parking: street spots are hard to find. There's a big surface lot at Washington at Ashley. (Remember that Fourth and Fifth avenues are just east of Main St., Fourth and Fifth streets are just west of Main.)*

◆ **Arcadian II.** *322 S. Main. (313) 994-8856. Mon-Thurs 11-6, Fri 11-9, Sat 10-9. Sun noon-5.* Second location of the successful Nickels Arcade antique store has the same sweet flair for displaying things that could look dull and ordinary. Quilts as backdrops set off flowered china, early 20th-century bedroom and dining room suites. Wonderful selection of antique jewelry, including many cameos. Most items are between 1880 and 1930 or so.

◆ **Generations: The Children's Store.** *337 S. Main. (313) 662-6615.* Great browsing for parents and for kids, who can play at Brio and other playtables. Books, jewelry and nifty little toys, puppets, and educational toys that are really fun. Colorful, relatively pricey kids' clothes take up less and less space. A beehive of activity on weekends, Friday night, and summer evenings. Inquire about special events.

◆ **Selo/Shevel Gallery.** *335 S. Main. (313) 761-6263. 10-7 Mon-Thurs, 10-10 Fri and Sat. Summer thru Christmas: noon-5 Sundays.* Functional and art glass, and perhaps Michigan's best single collection of handmade contemporary American jewelry, from $40 to $1,000 and up, in gold, silver, brass, with semi-precious and precious stones, including diamonds. Back-lit blown glass makes the mood here colorful, clear, and shimmering. Glassmakers include Josh Simpson and his paperweights encasing "little worlds" of freeform colors and shapes; clean freeform, bevel-cut glass sculpture from Blake Street Glass; and Matthew Buechner's Art Nouveau-style trumpet vases in combinations of clear and frosted glass. The gallery's folk art, wood, ceramics, textiles and metal crafts are on Main at Liberty.

◆ **Wilderness Outfitters.** *333 S. Main. (313) 761-8515. Mon-Thurs 10-6, Fri & Sat 108, Sun 12-5.* Well-equipped shop features camping, climbing, and backpacking gear. Cross-country ski equipment a specialty. Widest selection of backpacking boots around. Tends toward classic lines of outdoor apparel as compared with flashy new ones.

◆ **Ayla & Co.** *323 S. Main. (313) 665-7788. 10-6 Mon-Sat.* Fashion-forward contemporary classic clothing for the rich and the thin. A decade ago, it looked as if upscale clothing boutiques were becoming a big part of central Ann Arbor. Now only Ayla remains.

◆ **Collected Works.** *317 S. Main. Mon-Thurs 10-9, Fri & Sat 10 10, Sun 12-5. (313) 995-4222.* Lots of jewelry, cards, accessories, mostly with a look that's multicultural and hip but soft and on the romantic side. Natural-fibers clothing, mostly for women but with some sweaters, shirts, and pants for men. Rayon is considered natural, and there's lots of it, flowery and loose. Relaxed, comfortably sophisticated look plays off ethnic prints and textures against basic solid colors in unstructured clothing, often knit. Prices from inexpensive to moderate.

◆ **Selo/Shevel Gallery . . . at Liberty.** *301 S. Main at Liberty. (313) 761-4620. 10-7 Mon-Thurs, 10-10 Fri and Sat. Summer thru Christmas: noon-5 Sundays.* Stunning corner space at Liberty and Main has an earthy, rich mix of ethnic art and contemporary crafts from leading American craftspeople: exotic wood boxes; ceramics of porcelain, stoneware, and raku; chimes and Swedish door harps. Ethnic handcrafts regularly on hand include puppets from Bali and Thailand, African masks and sculpture, Turkish and Moroccan kilims, Mexican rugs and pillows, and fantastic carved and painted armadillos, iguanas and such from Oaxaca.

◆ **The Conservatory.** *111 W. Liberty. (313) 994-4443. Mon-Thurs 10-6, Fri & Sat to 8 or later.* Subdued but dazzling shop with products of good design. This delightfully serene gift shop is run by an architect. Jewelry, home accessories, and unusual baskets. The eclectic assemblage increasingly emphasizes paper in many forms: cards, unusual playing cards, blank books, stationery, and striking Japanese paper.

◆ **West Side Books.** *113 W. Liberty. (313) 995-1891.* Used and antiquarian books and prints in an old storefront with atmosphere. See page172.

◆ **Rider's Hobby.** *115 W. Liberty. (313) 668-8950. Mon-Fri 10-8, Sat 10-6.* Among Michigan's best hobby shops: trains, radio-control planes, adventure games, kits. Flagship of the small regional chain with other more spacious locations.

◆ **Ann Arbor Art Association.** *117 W. Liberty at Ashley. Mon noon-5:30, Tues-Sat 10-5:30.* The expanded gallery shop in this one-time carriage factory presents an interesting mix of member artists — largely painters, weavers, jewelers, printmakers, and lots of ceramics. Quality can be high. Some work retains a refreshingly uncommercial sincerity; much is sophisticated and with-it in both positive and negative senses. Changing exhibits are always worth checking out.

◆ **Ehnis & Son.** *116 W. Liberty. (313) 663-4337. Mon-Sat 8-6.* A genuine working man's clothes store, descended from a harnessmaker whose sideline was shoes. Quality overalls, work shirts, and boots. Authentic old-time interior worth a look.

◆ **Occasionally.** *223 S. Main. (313) 769-5151.* Lots of souvenirs from the U-M (Go Blue T shirts in many languages) and the state of Michigan.

◆ **After Words.** *219 S. Main. (313) 996-2808.* Large store with many well-chosen remaindered books at deep discounts. See page 172.

◆ **Falling Water Books and Collectibles.** *213 S. Main. (313) 747-9810.* A store that has its finger on the pulse of the times. Often miscategorized as a New Age store, it's a feel-good gift store that mixes mainstream and New Age self-help, inspirational, and women's books with jewelry, cards, fossils, and music.

◆ **16 Hands.** *216 S. Main. (313) 761-1110. Mon-Thurs 10-6, Fri & Sat 10-10, Sun 12-5.* Attractively displayed contemporary crafts and cards at a wide range of prices. Cheerfully sophisticated, often with a colorful primitivism that plays off simple dark silhouettes with glowing colors. Jewelry, furniture and wood accessories, metal work, weaving, blown glass, and other media by talented artists with regional and national followings.

◆ **The Peaceable Kingdom.** Warm, clever, personal shop has become an Ann Arbor institution with its potpourri of imaginatively displayed things, from small inexpensive toys and gadgets to imported and contemporary American folk art. Don't be so distracted by the novelties that you forget to look up on the walls and see Mexican and African masks and Ann Arbor artist Charla Khanna's compelling one-of-a-kind dolls. *210 S. Main. (313) 668-7886. Mon-Thurs 10-6, Fri & Sat 10-10.*

◆ **Grace's Select Second Hand.** *122 S. Main, just below Republic Bank. (313) 668-0747. 11-9 Mon-Sat.* Unpretentious mix of Middle American furniture, household goods, often from house sales. Offers some good pickings. Akin to the Treasure Mart, but with fewer antiques. 4,000-square-foot consignment shop for clean, selected furniture and household goods, from kitchen utensils to bedroom sets and hutches. Three 80-foot walls allow lots of space for framed paintings and prints, old and new.

◆ **Lotus Gallery.** *207 E. Washington. (313) 665-6322, Tues-Sat 11-5:30.* Antique art and furniture of southeast Asia, including Chinese jades, Japanese netsuke and simple 19th-century wood chests of drawers, antique porcelain and stoneware, and unusual things like an opium scale. Also, contemporary Chinese paintings, outstanding Southwest Indian pottery. Owner-collector Les Werbel is available after 5 and on many Saturdays.

◆ **Rage of the Age.** *220 S. Fourth. (313) 662-0777. Tues-Sat 12-6, otherwise by appointment.* The Fifties revisited, with everything from rhinestone brooches ($25-$200) and Renoir Matisse and Frank Rebajes' hand-wrought copper bracelets to mix-and-match anodized aluminum tumblers ($25 for 6 or 8). Ask about modernist furniture classics. Clothing and textiles a specialty.

◆ **Common Language.** *215 S. Fourth. (313) 663-0036. Tues-Fri 12-8, Sat 12-8, Sun 12-4.* Cards, posters, books, T-shirts about subgroups of the human rainbow: gays, lesbians, African-Americans, and more. Also non-lesbian women's issues, books on pregnancy and childbirth. See page 171. More of a sense of humor than you might expect.

◆ **Aunt Agatha's Book Shop.** 213 S. Fourth. (313) 769-1114. New and used mystery and crime. See page 172.

◆ **Whole Cloth.** *206 S. Fourth. (313) 668-8028. Mon-Sat 10-6.* Fabrics from around the world, including Austrian lodencloth, Nigerian cottons, Liberty prints, basic high-quality wools, cotton sheeting, 100% cotton knits, many expensive silks and crepes you'd expect to see at English tea parties. Unusual buttons: wood, shell, antiques.

◆ **Art Deco Design.** Most of the artfully displayed Art Deco furniture, accessories, and jewelry here was made between 1925 and 1939, but 1950s modernist classics add extra zing. Prices are reasonable (a long, useful Florence Knoll sideboard was $500), and reproductions are few and far between. Owner Constance Basil loves to talk about Art Deco. "Art Deco was, and still is, glamour, nostalgia, and frivolity. It was the last attempt made in Europe to create a perfectly coherent design," she states in a fascinating handout on the style she treasures and studies. Don't miss the beautiful wall of Bruce Barrett's vintage lighting. May move; call for new location. *207 E. Washington. (313) 663-DECO. Tues-Sat 11-6.*

◆ **The Artful Exchange.** *215 E. Washington. (313) 761-2287. Wed-Fri 11-5, Sat 10-5.* An eclectic variety of fine art — paintings, sculpture, drawings, ethnic art, and prints — sold on consignment. Prices start as low as $15 and go up into the thousands, for "investment art" by the likes of Chagall, Dali, and Calder. Most are from $300 to $900. Here can be found anything from works by Robert Motherwell and Albrecht Dürer to contemporary Tibetan paintings and Chinese peasant art. A good place to find works by former U-M art school faculty like Emil Weddige, Guy Pallazolla, and Richard Wilt. Frank Cassara, well known in the 1930s and still painting today, is a regular exhibitor. Now about half the gallery is devoted to contemporary gallery artists.

◆ **Levy's ArtCafe.** *211 E. Washington between Fourth and Fifth avenues. (313) 665-6464. Breakfast and lunch Mon-Fri 8-4. Dinner Wed-Sun 4-10. Sat and Sun brunch 1-4.* Levy's is a full service restaurant (including bar) and coffeehouse inside an art gallery. Artists from across the country, working in all kinds of media, have their art on display. Proprietors are the sons of Audrey Levy, whose indoor art fairs have long been popular.

◆ **Barrett's Antiques and Fine Arts.** *212 E. Washington. (313) 662-1140. Thurs-Sat 11-6, sometimes later.* Victorian antiques, art glass, clocks, quilts, and more, most attractively displayed. There's a good deal of Rookwood pottery, the owner's specialty. Don't miss the toys and collectibles in the basement.

◆ **The Bead Gallery.** *309 E. Liberty between Fifth and Division (lower level). (313) 663-6800. Tues-Fri 10-6, Sat 10-5.* A fabulous array of beads is enough to inspire you to make your own creations. Ceramic beads from Thailand, charms, gemstones, Ethiopian silver beads, wonderful glass beads, old and new. Plus the requisite cords and other findings, and artfully displayed examples of jewelry to inspire you. Books and instructional sheets.

◆ **Creative Tattoo.** *307 E. Liberty. (313) 662-2520.* Degree-holding artist and former art teacher Suzanne Fauser has won national awards with her beautiful tattoos and relieved a lot of embarrassment by modifying ill-advised body ornament.

KERRYTOWN AREA/NORTH FOURTH AVENUE

Not many years ago a struggling commercial district just north of downtown, the Kerrytown area has come on very strong recently, with Ann Arbor's hottest restaurant in town (Sweet Lorraine) and many of the most interesting new shops. The area includes the big Kerrytown complex (actually three joined old buildings), the adjoining Farmers' Market, and nearby shops and restaurants. *Parking often quite tight in this area. Best last resort is the parking structure on Ann Street between Main and Ashley.*

◆ **Near Kerrytown.** The entries below are just south of the Kerrytown complex.

Ann Arbor's Farmer's Market. *Open-air sheds run from Detroit and N. Fifth Ave. to N. Fourth. (313) 761-1078. Wed & Sat 7-3.* One of Michigan's most robust, colorful (and crowded) farmers' markets. Not cheap, but quality of the fresh produce and fruits is excellent. Good selection of herbs and other plants.

DeBoer Gallery. *303 Detroit. (313) 741-1257. Tues-Thurs 10-6, Fri 10-9, Sat 9-5.* Quirky, whimsical art in all media; many animals. Everything from coffee mugs and T-shirts to jewelry and tiles. Most are one-of-a-kind, handpainted.

ATYS. *303 Detroit. (313) 996-2976 Tues-Thurs 10-7, Fri 10-8, Say 10-5, Sun 12-3.* Stylish, well-designed, sleekly functional contemporary living accessories. Everything from a toothbrush to a $68.75 bottle opener. Says the owner, "Living in Europe taught me that the things you use everyday can be pieces of art."

Gothic Proportions. *303 Detroit. Tues-Sat 10-6. Sun 11-2.* Reproductions — most of them unpainted — of gargoyles, imps, classical Greek torsos, Egyptian sphinx, columns and pedestals. An amusing collection, from $8 to $250.

◆ **Kerrytown** *(between N. Fourth and Fifth. Most stores are open between 10-8 on Thurs and Fri, Mon-Wed 10-6, Sat 10-5, Sun 12-5.)* Noteworthy shops inside include:

Monahan's Seafood Market. *(313) 662-5118.* Fresh fish for serious fish-lovers. A quarter of the customers are foreigners used to more fish in their diets. The Japanese like "sanma," a mackerel pike, monkfish livers, and asari. The French like red mullet, flown fresh from Paris. Koreans like skate wings. Germans like smoked eel and a variety of herrings. You can get huge shrimp, wonderful flounder.

Partners in Wine. *(313) 761-6384.* Good buys in California, Australian, and French wines. The three proprietors taste all the wine they carry.

Kitchen Port. *(313) 665-9188. Mon-Fri 9:30-8, Sat 9-6, Sun 11-5.* An exceptionally fine kitchen store, with considerable selection in everything from utensils to tableware. Largest selection of cookbooks, placemats, napkins, pot racks in southeastern Michigan. Call for times of cooking demonstrations.

Moveable Feast. Takeout shop of the bakery of one of Michigan's finest restaurants. Great sourdough French bread, croissants, pastries.

Hollanders. *Kerrytown, 40 N. 5th Ave. (313) 741-7531. Mon-Wed 10-6, Thurs & Fri 10-8, Sat 9-5, Sun noon-5.* Hand-crafted desk accessories and gift items using decorative papers. Everything made right here, using wide variety of paper imported from around the world. Desk boxes range from $10 to $40.

◆ **Treasure Mart.** *529 Detroit, between Kingsley and Division. (313) 662-1363. Mon-Sat 9-5:30.* Ann Arbor's legendary resale shop has a sprawling array of home furnishings and knick-knacks at all price levels, sometimes at prices far lower than an antique shop would charge. The quality of its used furniture, col-

Busy to the point of bedlam on summer Saturday mornings, the Ann Arbor Farmers' Market is one of the few in Michigan where growers must jockey for space. The result is lots of choices for visitors

lectibles, lighting, china, linens, framed pictures, and the like reflects the broad range of Ann Arbor lifestyles, from the ordinary to the affluent. Large and fast-moving stock.

◆ **Zingerman's Delicatessen.** See page 176.

STATE STREET AREA

Although just north of the U-M campus, this area has far transcended a student shopping area. Its shops draw people not just from other parts of Michigan, but other states and countries. It has become the center of Ann Arbor's outstanding concentration of bookstores and CD stores (see page 169 and page 174). **Nickels Arcade,** an historic 1915 European-style arcade of small shops, runs between State Street and Maynard. *Parking: one of the toughest places to find a space in town. Safest bet is the structure entered from Washington between Main and Division.*

◆ **Chris Triola Gallery.** *5 Nickels Arcade. (313) 996-9955. Tues-Fri 11-7, Sat 10-5.* Very chic pullovers, simple and boldly patterned in themes from African and jazz to Celtic, from $350-$450. Designed by Lansing's Chris Triola. Also skirts, scarves, jackets and sweaters.

◆ **Clay Gallery.** *8 Nickels Arcade. (313) 662-7927. Mon-Fri 9:30-5:30, Sat 9:30-5.* Beautiful pottery, much of it in subdued earthtones, by a cooperative of 12 Ann Arbor potters. Everything from small gift items to large architectural pieces.

◆ **Alexa Lee Gallery.** *201 Nickels Arcade (upstairs). (313) 663-8800. Tues-Sat 10-6.* Purple wood floors set off this Soholike gallery that features important Midwestern artists in all media. Exhibits change monthly. The quality of the work makes this well worth a visit.

◆ **Matthew C. Hoffmann Studio.** *16 Nickels Arcade. (313) 665-2122.* This annex from the pricey main shop half a block away on Maynard features silver for those who don't want to faint from sticker shock. Rings, bracelets, and necklaces. Fancy belt buckles run from $200 to $750. This shop attracts many Scandinavians partial to white metal. Check out the stunning framed insects on the wall collected by Bob Natillini.

◆ **Renaissance.** *336 Maynard. (313) 769-8511. Mon-Thurs 10-6, Fri 10-7, Sat 10-6.* Fashion-forward Euro-style clothing for men. Sportcoats run from $295-$1295, shirts from $65 to $295.

◆ **Matthew C. Hoffmann.** *340 Maynard. (313) 665-7692.*

The members of the
Clay Gallery coopera-
tive, an exceptionally
pleasant shop in the
historic 1915 Nickels
Arcade. The pedestrian
space runs from North
State and the U-M cam-
pus to Maynard Street.

Wealthy folks come from far and wide to buy Matthew
Hoffmann's expensive contemporary creations. Hoffmann calls
his jewelry "portable sculpture."

◆ **Van Boven Clothing.** *326 S. State. (313) 665-7228.* Ann
Arbor's classic men's clothing store, where professors go to buy
their tweed sportscoats and Oxford shirts.

◆ **John Leidy.** *Both sides of the Michigan Theater, 601 E. Liberty.
(313) 668-6779.* Well-stocked gift shop with many of the top lines
of china and silver.

◆ **Harry's Army Surplus.** *500 E. Liberty. (313) 994-3572. Mon-Fri
9-8, Sat 9-6, Sun 11-5.* Wild selection of everything from cheap
camping gear and East German border guard overcoats to paint
splat guns and throwing stars. A neat place to browse.

◆ **Herb David Guitar Studio.** *302 E. Liberty. (313) 665-8001.
10-6 Mon-Sat, Thurs & Fri to 7.* Custom made guitars from Herb's
shop range from $200 to $3500. Best repair shop in Midwest.
Also for sale here are banjoes, hand drums, acoustic guitars.

◆ **Bivouac.** *336 S. State. (313) 761-7206.* Popular outfitters for
campers, hikers, climbers, skiers. Big and bustling. You may
stand in line for help on Saturdays.

◆ **Espresso Royale**. This hangout sells a delicious cup of cappuccino or espresso, plus muffins, bagels, croissants, and European treats like poppyseed bread. Part of a college-town chain, ER has recreated slick, high-tech Italian cafes without being offensively cute or self-conscious about it. The State Street location is phenomenally popular; be prepared to stand in line. Solo performers and small ensembles perform Sundays, Tuesdays, Thursdays, and Fridays, 8-10 p.m. No cover or dancing. *324 S. State. Mon-Fri 7 a.m.-midnight, Sat & Sun 9 a.m.-midnight.*

SOUTH UNIVERSITY COMMERCIAL DISTRICT

Three blocks of stores and restaurants along South University connect the central campus with the fraternity and sorority area along Washtenaw and Hill. Over the past ten years, the area's character has come to be almost exclusively oriented to undergraduates, with a proliferation of fast-food chains. If you are unfortunate enough to arrive by car at the top of the hour when classes are getting out, you'll just have to wait, as there is no doubt in these students' minds that pedestrians have the right of way. *Parking: On South University, the city structure on Forest just south of South University is your best bet.*

◆ **Middle Earth.** *1209 South University. (313) 769-1488. Mon-Sat 10-7, Thurs & Fri 'til 9, Sun noon-5.* One of the most entertaining shops in the entire state. Nostalgia candy and novelties compete for space with a striking display of beautiful jewelry, some quite expensive, including thousands of earrings. You'll find a wild and outrageous variety of constantly changing "cheap thrills": Elvis troll dolls, inflatable pink Cadillacs. T-shirts are also a big deal here — you'll find some of the hippest (and funniest) in the country. The first shop in town to sell bawdy greeting cards, Middle Earth still has the most ribald selection, though there are plenty of lovely, artistic cards any mother would love to get. Over 20,000 offbeat postcards.

◆ **Village Corner.** *Southeast corner of South University and Forest. (313) 995-1818. 7 days 8 a.m.-1 a.m.* The VC keeps its scruffy, vaguely counter-culture ambiance in the face of Ann Arbor's rampant gentrification. Clerks, often outlandishly clad, wait on you in amusingly surly fashion. You'd never realize a nationally known wine shop is in the back. The VC has one of Michigan's most sophisticated and wide-ranging selections of wine, from inexpensive to very fine — 4,000 kinds, along with 600 kinds of spirits. In the wine section, sales people are knowledgeable and willing to take the time to advise customers on their selections, even if it's a $5 bottle to accompany spaghetti and meatballs. Prices are reasonable, and deals on cases of wine are especially good. Masterfully clear and informative shelf descriptions of wines are written in part by Village Corner owner Dick Scheer, a well-known wine authority and judge. Ask for the free annotated catalog and newsletter. For picnics, the VC has a good selection of convenience and takeout food (fresh fruit, sandwiches, good bread and cheese) and groceries.

ANN ARBOR NIGHTSPOTS

◆ **The Ark.** *637 S. Main. (313) 761-1451.* Admission is usually $8-$10. Shows begin at 8 p.m. Attracts top folk performers from all around the country.

◆ **Bird of Paradise.** *207 S. Ashley. (313)-8310.* Pleasant jazz club with live music nightly.

◆ **Blind Pig.** *208 S. First. (313) 996-8555.* This popular local rock 'n' roll club provided one of the first audiences beyond Seattle to give Nirvana a boost. Live music includes blues, rock 'n' roll, reggae.

◆ **Espresso Royale Caffe.** *214 S. Main. (313) 622-2770.* This coffeehouse features acoustic jazz, classical, and folk performers Fridays and Saturdays (9-11) and Sunday at noon.

◆ **The Heidelberg.** *215 N. Main.* This old German restaurant now uses its top floor for live bands, who play Fridays and Saturdays (10:30-1:30) and Sundays (7-9:30). Recently it's become a stage for established Ann Arbor groups and performers: Steve Nardella, George Bedard, Steve Somers, Steve Newhouse, and others.

◆ **Michigan Theater.** *Liberty at Maynard. (313) 668-8480 for program info.* Ann Arbor's 1928 picture palace was threatened with conversion to a shopping arcade. Now it is a successful community-owned theater, much used for concerts, occasional plays, and films. The interior gilding and other decoration has been restored. On weekends, before the main event, the original Barton Theater Organ is often played. It's a chance to see movies the way they were once meant to be seen on the big screen.

◆ **The Nectarine Ballroom.** *510 E. Liberty. (313) 994-5436.* A New-York-style dance club with DJs six nights a week. Various themes on different nights: gay, Eurobeat, alternative, disco.

◆ **Rick's American Cafe.** *611 Church. (313) 996-2747.* Near the

U-M campus. Many students flock to this rock 'n' roll club, with strong bookings of out-of-town bands.

◆ **Cava Java.** *1101 S. University. 741-5282.* Right next to the U-M central campus, gifted local Ann Arbor impresario Joe Tiboni picks interesting musical groups to play downstairs at this coffee shop, from blues and boogie to rock 'n' roll and folk. Thurs-Sat 9:30 p.m. to past midnight.

A 1928 PICTURE PALACE . . . . . the **Michigan Theater** was bought by the city in the 1980s for use as a community venue rentable to any group. Splendidly restored to all its gilded grandeur, it has blossomed by filling in gaps in the city's formidable array of entertainment. The **drama series** features big-time productions from Broadway and leading regional theater companies. **Not Just For Kids** offers big-name family entertainment. The **Serious Fun** series consists of commercially tested avant-garde performers such as Laurie Anderson, Sankai Juku, and frequently Philip Glass. **Revival films** (\$4.50) fill in the off nights. Music on the big Barton theater organ frequently precedes movies. *Call (313) 668-8397, or stop by the theater entrance on Liberty at Maynard for a schedule.*

INTENSE STREET LIFE . . . . . comes to Ann Arbor each July during the **Art Fair** — actually three big fairs with a thousand artists, stretching from South University to Main Street. There's too much of everything — bargain-priced merchandise, art, food, hot weather — but people come back year after year. Two fairs include art of the highest caliber found at street fairs anywhere, while a third is more pedestrian but continually being upgraded. Some terrific area musicians perform on several stages. Wednesday through Saturday, in the last part of July. (313) 994-5260.

THE ANN ARBOR ART SCENE . . . . . is lively, but more oriented to showcasing the area's unusual number of productive artists than to an art-hungry market. There are dozens of places that exhibit visual art, but no single gallery guide. The cultural smorgasbord of **performances, lectures,** etc., is similarly rich. Your best bet for an overview of what's going on is to pick up a copy of the *Ann Arbor Observer* monthly magazine, with a calendar of events and exhibits that's easy to use and virtually complete. The current day's main events are on the Observer's calendar information line, (313) 665-6155.

GOOD MOVIES DOWNTOWN . . . . . are shown at the small, easy-to-miss **Ann Arbor Theater,** 210 S. Fifth Avenue between Liberty and Washington. (313) 761-9700. Tuesday matinees and weekday shows at 4:40 are a fine alternative to fighting rush-hour traffic.

FUN WITH SCIENCE . . . . is the mission of the popular **Ann Arbor Hands-On Museum** downtown. Over 250 science exhibits for children. Some of the most popular are the giant soap bubble capsule, the "double piddler" (two colliding streams that a strobe light illuminates), the giant zipper, the operating cut-away toilet, and the large PVC pipe organ kids can play. Educational computer games for kids. Good educational **gift shop**. It's in a landmark 1879 fire station, and a major expansion is in the works. Call (313) 995-KIDS for info on one-day workshops and free demo topics. *Huron at N. Fifth. Tues-Fri 10-5:30, Sat 10-5, Sun 1-5. Adults $4, seniors, children, and students $2.50.*

University of Michigan Museums

In a small part of campus are three of the state's finest museums and other places to visit.

Bcause the University of Michigan has been a leading American research institution for over a century, it has had the collections and research staff to develop three exceptional museums. They are:

UNIVERSITY OF MICHIGAN EXHIBIT MUSEUM. Not many other natural science museums in the country match the rarity and breadth of items on display here. Areas explored include prehistoric life and dinosaurs, anthropology and Native American cultures, Michigan wildlife, astronomy, biology and ecology. The very number of displays can be overwhelming, however. Up until now most of the explanatory signs have been more appropriate for college students than for the general public.

New leadership is gradually changing museum signs to be more attuned to the general public. A new outreach philosophy means the museum will offer more of interest to all ages, host more **events** and **workshops** (call for info), be more interactive, and have different things to see throughout the year.

There is much here to interest most visitors, and kid-friendly docents know how to overcome the rather stiff exhibit style in popular group tours.

The second floor holds many museum highlights, including the big draw – the **dinosaur section**. Also here are dozens of meticulously constructed dioramas — miniature three-dimensional scenes which vividly show life on Earth in the distant past. View a lush scene from a Pennsylvania forest 300 million years ago when giant insects abounded, dragonflies had 30-inch wingspans, and huge roaches crawled among gigantic palm trees. Another diorama shows what Nebraska looked like 10 million years ago when populated with camels, primitive elephants, short rhinoceroses, and rodents the size of woodchucks. You can see Los Angeles 15 million years ago when sabertooth tigers roamed the region.

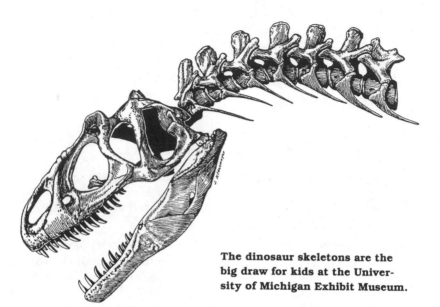

The dinosaur skeletons are the big draw for kids at the University of Michigan Exhibit Museum.

Another series of seven dioramas reveals the evolution of life, beginning back in the Cambrian age 575 million years ago when crab-like creatures were the most sophisticated beasts around. You also get an intriguing glimpse into the villages of the various Indian tribes who inhabited Michigan before Europeans arrived.

The dinosaur section, seven skeletons strong, is highlighted by the looming remains of a big allosaurus that roamed Utah 140 million years ago. The flesh-eating giant had forbiddingly long claws and sharp, menacing teeth. More subtle but also evocative are the various fossil footprints made by dinosaurs millions of years ago.

The fourth floor best shows the museum's new approach. An **interactive weather-wall** display is connected by Ethernet to global weather information and atmospheric phenomena. The transparent anatomical mannequin (a see-through woman whose organs are visible) is the centerpiece of the redone Human Anatomy Alcove, opposite the popular planetarium and astronomy exhibits. Weekend **planetarium shows** ($2.50/person) change several times a year. They consist of **family star talks** geared for all ages (Saturday at 10:30, 11:30, 1:30, 2:30; Sunday at 1:30 and 2:30) and **feature shows** geared to adults (no one under 3rd grade age is admitted). They are at 12:30 and 3:30 Saturday and 3:30 Sunday. Weekday shows are by reservation only.

The museum has a nifty **museum shop** on the ground floor, full of inexpensive mineral and fossil specimens, dinosaur items, and all sorts of small items to delight kids, along with nature publications. *1109 Geddes Ave. where it intersects with North University. Parking hints: on weekends the small lot behind the museum, entered off Geddes, sometimes has spaces. It always has* **handicap spaces.** *Otherwise, public parking is available (about $1/hour) in the Fletcher Street ramp between the dental school and Power Center. (313) 764-0478. Mon-Sat 9-5, Sun 1-5. Free.*

KELSEY MUSEUM OF ARCHAEOLOGY. This small but important museum has two special attractions. The first is the 1891 building itself, made of local fieldstone in the Richardsonian Romanesque style. Originally called Newberry Hall, it was built to house the private Student Christian Association. Great pains were taken in choosing beautiful stones for the structure. The large Tiffany window on the north side, the elaborate woodwork, blue slate roof, and imposing front turret combine to make this a memorable campus landmark.

Inside is stored one of the most important collections of ancient Greek, Egyptian, Roman, and Near Eastern artifacts. Only a fraction of the 100,000-piece collection is on permanent display. What you see is very choice indeed, and accompanied by informative explanations of these artifacts' place in ancient life. Colorful Egyptian mummy masks, exquisite Greek black-and-red-figured vase paintings, rare and amazingly intact Roman glass are all presented in a comfortable, intimate setting which encourages close study. Most surprising of all, perhaps, are the early Egyptian sculptures, dating from 2400 to 200 B.C. They reveal remarkable artistic skill. Group tours are most welcome. Traveling educational kits can be borrowed for classroom use. *Closed through August, 1994. 434 S. State, across from Angell Hall. September-April Mon-Fri 9-4, Sat & Sun 1-4. May-August: Tues-Fri 11-4, Sat & Sun 1-4. Call (313) 764-9304 for general information and special exhibits.*

UNIVERSITY OF MICHIGAN MUSEUM OF ART. This is considered among the top ten university art museums in the country. The permanent collection of over 12,000 includes works by Dürer, Delacroix, Rodin, Picasso, Rembrandt, Corot, Millet, Monet, Cezanne, Miro, and Klee. Well-known paintings on permanent display include Expressionist Max Beckman's *Begin the*

One of many treasures at the University of Michigan's Kelsey Museum of Archaeology is this second-century Roman sarcophagus showing a Bacchic revel.

Beguine, the Italian Baroque painter Guercino's *Esther before Ahasuerus*, and Carl Wimar's dramatic portrayal of the American West, *Attack on an Emigrant Train*.

Collections of Whistler prints and German Expressionist paintings are outstanding, and there is a large collection from China and Japan. From Italian Renaissance panel paintings to Han Dynasty tomb figures to African sculpture and contemporary photography, the museum collection is notable for both its range and quality.

Special exhibitions include both national and international loan shows and small exhibits drawn from the Museum's permanent collection. Interpretive **programs** range from lectures, symposia, and gallery talks by artists and curators to chamber concerts, multimedia performances, and other special events.

The **museum gift shop** has a choice assortment of cards, art publications, posters, handmade and ethnic jewelry, folk art and craft collectibles. An enthusiastic, high-caliber staff of volunteer docents conducts free private tours for school and other groups as well as public **Sunday Tours** of special exhibitions and the permanent collection on Sundays at 2 p.m. During the academic year, the Museum presents **Midweek at the Museum**, a weekly series of gallery talks, art videos, and slide lectures each

Tuesday, Wednesday, and Thursday at noon. For exhibit and program information, phone (313) 764-0395. To schedule a group tour, call (313) 747-2067. *525 S. State at South University. (313) 764-0395. September-May: Tues-Fri 10-5, Sat-Sun 12-5. June-August: Tues-Fri 11-5, Sun 12-5. Closed Mondays, New Year's Day, Independence Day, Thanksgiving Day, and Christmas Day. Free. Donations welcome.*

U-M NORTH CAMPUS. This outlying 800-acre campus across the Huron River northeast of the Central Campus was planned in the 1940s, when residential neighborhoods blocked future growth of the university in central Ann Arbor. Architect Eero Saarinen planned the new campus, which includes the College of Engineering, School of Music, and the combined School of Art and College of Architecture and Urban Planning.

Major public attractions are:

◆ **Phoenix Memorial Laboratory.** The two-megawatt experimental nuclear reactor built here in 1954 was one of the first university reactors in the postwar surge of research interest in peaceful applications of atomic energy. Thirty- to sixty-minute tours are available by appointment (48 hours' advance notice is requested) Monday through Friday. *Bonisteel Blvd. near Beal. (313) 764-6220.*

◆ **Gerald R. Ford Presidential Library.** This is one of only nine presidential libraries in the country. It's here because Ford was a 1935 graduate of the U-M. Interested citizens and scholars from around the world come here to delve into myriad issues affected by the Ford presidency. The library's 15 million pages of documents brought from Washington include all of Ford's White House papers as well as the papers of certain key advisors such as economist Arthur Burns and energy chief Frank Zarb. Some papers remain classified and are kept in locked vaults, but most are available for public scrutiny. *1000 Beal south of Bonisteel Blvd. (313) 741-2218. Mon-Fri 9-4:30.*

◆ **Bentley Historical Library.** Home of the Michigan Historical Collections, one of the three big archives of Michigan history. The others are the State Archives in Lansing, housed in the Historical Museum complex (page 00) and the Burton Collection in the Detroit Public Library. A gallery shows exhibits that change every two months. The general public is welcome to look at original documents, which include the papers of many political figures (governors Frank Murphy and Bill Milliken, Senator Phil Hart, and many more), health food progenitor Dr. John Harvey Kellogg, 1960s radical John Sinclair, and the Detroit Urban League. Civil War letters and C. H. Stoner's collection of historical railroad photos are outstanding. Inexpensive copies and enlargements of the over one million graphic images can be made, including postcards of Michigan hometowns of any era– and University of Michigan campus scenes. They're nifty gift ideas. *1150 Beal at Bonisteel. Park by building or across the street. (313) 764-3482. Mon-Fri 8:30-5, and from September thru May, Sat 9-12:30.*

◆ **Stearns Collection of Musical Instruments.** The core of this unusual collection is 1,400 instruments collected by wealthy Detroit drug manufacturer Frederick Stearns and donated to the university in 1899. They include some extremely rare Asian and African instruments along with European instruments like a Baroque cello in almost-original condition and a recorder from the time of Bach.

The collection, now over 2,200 items and growing, is encyclopedic, representing instruments of all sorts from throughout the world. New acquisitions, including the first Moog synthesizer to be sold, reflect an effort to collect 20th-century materials. Interesting **lecture-demonstrations** are held at 2 o'clock on the second Sundays of September, October, January, and February. *In the new Dow Towsley south wing of the Moore Building, the main part of the School of Music, at the end of Baits Dr. (Baits is off Broadway at the top of the hill, about 1/4 mile west of Plymouth Rd. Or, from Murfin on North Campus, take Duffield to Baits.) (313) 763-4389. Wed-Sat 10-5, Sun 1-6. Free.*

THE HEART OF THE U-M CAMPUS . . . . . is the **Diag**, the diagonal walk crossing the original 40-acre campus between the retail districts on State and North University and on South University at East University. Many major classroom buildings are clustered here, backing up to a plaza in front of the **Graduate Library**. (Its eighth-floor map room has one of the best views in town.) Countless rallies and demonstrations have been held here. On pleasant days, this is a good place to see students and their myriad organizations and causes set up here to garner support. The action spills over into the adjacent **Fishbowl**, a large-windowed connecting hall between classroom buildings to the west.

THE FIRST STUDENT UNION . . . . . was the venerable **Michigan Union** on State at the head of South University, built in 1920. On its front steps President Kennedy first announced the Peace Corps, saying, "Ask not what your country can do for you, but what you can do for your country." For many years women were only allowed entrance to the Union through a side door, and then only for special events. (Women alumnae built the much smaller Michigan League.) The second-floor **billiard room** was the last male bastion to fall, in the late 1960s. It remains one the Union's most interesting areas. With oak paneling and quality tables, the room retains the atmosphere of gentlemen's gaming rooms in decades past. Some of the country's best players still drop in to play here. In the slickly remodeled Union basement is a big **Barnes and Noble student book store** and large **food court**.

CARILLON CONCERTS BY A PLAYFUL FOUNTAIN . . . . . . The Union's female counterpart as a student center was the 1929 **Michigan League** on North University at the Ingalls Mall, a rather grand axis between the graduate library and the monumental Art Deco/neoclassical Rackham Building on Washington Street. Smaller than the Union, the League has long been popular for its well-stocked newsstand at the front desk, its large and excellent **cafeteria**, and its basement grill. The League also houses the 700-seat **Lydia Mendelssohn Theater**, Ann Arbor's most congenial space for theatrical performances. . . . . . Between the League and tall Burton Tower is the delightful **Cooley Fountain** created by Swedish sculptor Carl Milles in 1940, when he was on the Cranbrook faculty. It shows Triton, the Greek god of the sea, frolicking with his children. . . . . . Across from the League is **Burton Tower**, a campus landmark. At its top is the **Baird Carillon**. Its 53 bronze bells weigh from 12 pounds to 12 tons. **Half-hour concerts** begin weekdays at noon when school is in session. During that time you can go up to the top and see the single player pound hand and foot levers in quick succession to ring the bells. The tower offers a fine view of the campus. On the eighth floor is the **Japanese music room**, with tatami mats. Its instruments can be heard when School of Music students practice there Tuesdays between noon and 9 p.m., September through April. Likewise, the **gamelan** or Indonesian orchestra can be heard in practice on the fourth floor Thursday afternoons and evenings.

A BIT OF OXFORD AND CAMBRIDGE IN THE MIDDLE WEST . . . . . Right across State Street from the Union is the **Law Quadrangle**, home of the U-M's highly ranked law school. This picturesque court of Gothic buildings was built between 1923 and 1933 and largely modeled on Cambridge University in England. The Law Quad's quality of workmanship was rare even in the 1920s. The striking reading room of the **old Law Library** at the south side of the quadrangle has richly ornamented blue and gold plaster medallions decorating the ceiling.

1920s. The striking reading room of the **old Law Library** at the south side of the quadrangle has richly ornamented blue and gold plaster medallions decorating the ceiling.

THE BIGGEST COLLEGIATE STADIUM IN THE U.S. . . . . . . is Michigan Stadium on Stadium at Main. It seats over 101,000, but they're packed in mighty tight. The stadium is dug into the side of a valley wall; the football field lies directly over Allen's Creek. If you put your ear down on the 50-yard line when the stands are empty, you will hear the creek running below. Next door is **Crisler Arena**, which seats 1,360. It hosts concerts, NCAA wrestling and gymnastics matches, as well as U-M basketball and gymnastics.

A MUST FOR MICHIGAN SPORTS FANS. . . . . is the impressive and extensive permanent exhibit on Wolverine athletics at the new **Margaret Towsley Sports Museum** at **Schembechler Hall**, on South State near McKinley, just south of Yost Ice Arena. The short entrance hallway with a visual timeline of great events in Michigan sports history is just an introduction. (Interesting how the first female athlete appears only in the 1970s.) . . . . . The snazzy visuals go way beyond the usual trophies and action photos. They're accented with objects like an ancient football uniform (the shoes alone weighed several pounds). The teams of Michigan's legendary football coaches get several display cases each, but each minor sport has a case, too, in which far more women are seen. The evolution of various sports is interestingly told. . . . Visitors to this nostalgic trip down memory lane are likely to include former varsity players and their relatives. The museum is said to be a first for a single university. A rousing, rah-rah **video** extolling Michigan's long tradition of "student athletes, the best and brightest in the land" (!!??) can be viewed in a small theater. *Hours are 11-4 Mon-Fri, Sat 10-2, plus Friday evening hours from 5:30 to 7:30.* . . . . . Next door at Yost (entered from the north end) is the **Go Blue Shop** of M paraphernalia. A branch store is at Briarwood Mall. Michigan logo items are reportedly the most widely seen and purchased college logos in the world.

Bookstores in Ann Arbor

The bookstore mecca of the Midwest is centered at Liberty and State, near the U-M campus.

Few places in the country have as lively and high-quality a concentration of bookstores, both new and used, as does central Ann Arbor. Its anchor is the fabulously successful Borders. Increasingly the town has become a magnet attracting book-lovers from distant cities.

Connoisseurs of antiquarian books would do well to pick up a listing of area dealers at any used-book store. It will direct them to several distinguished home book shops, such as Jan Longone's internationally known **Wine and Food Library**, which deals exclusively in out-of-print and rare publications on wine, food, and gastronomy. It's by appointment only; call (313) 663-4894.

◆ **Borders Books and Music.** Ann Arbor was a virtual trade book wasteland in 1971 when the two Borders brothers, former grad students, started their store in an obscure second-story retail space on William. It has become one of the very finest U. S. bookstores; now it's the flagship of the rapidly-growing, high-quality chain that launched the superstore concept. Secrets of its success: knowledgeable, helpful clerks; a relentlessly attentive manager, Joe Gable; pleasing ambiance; and outstanding back list. Quality remainders. Big children's and young adult section, with tables. An impressive selection of maps and better posters. The new location features an espresso bar, a video and CD section, and a multi-media area. *Liberty between State and Maynard. (313) 668-7652. Mon-Sat 9-9, Sun 11-6.*

◆ **Shaman Drum Bookshop.** This serene shop specializes in serious books in the humanities, chosen by its highly knowledgeable staff. Important books in religious studies, classical studies, literature and literary studies, poetry, Native American culture (owner Karl Pohrt's specialty), and anthropology. Frequent book signings. Trade manager Keith Taylor, winner of a major poetry award, is most helpful at recommending good books for many tastes. A fine place to connect up with area book people. Now in

Fellow booksellers regard Jay Platt of the West Side Book Shop as one of the real gentlemen in the business. The Victorian building is a gem, and the selection of books and Edward Curtis photographs is choice.

a much-expand first-floor location, it is greatly enlarging its collection of literary fiction. *311 S. State. (313) 662-7407. Mon-Fri 10-5:30, Sat 'til 4:30.*

◆ **The Hundred Acre Wood.** Small shop with children's classics, carefully selected new titles, and a big Pooh section. *10 Nickels Arcade. (313) 663-2411. Mon-Fri 10-5:30, Sat 10-5.*

◆ **Kaleidoscope.** Big space full of oddball old stuff: lots of books, also cameras, toys, magazines, sheet music, posters, and more. A knack for presentation makes it look great. Book condition isn't choice (some are library discards), but ample room means you can find things smaller stores couldn't afford to keep around. Stories for kids are help at 3 p.m. on Sundays. *217 S. State. (313) 995-9887. Mon-Wed 10-6, Thurs-Sat 10-8, Sun 1-5.*

◆ **David's Books.** Legendary, somewhat scruffy upstairs store, crowded with some 50,000 used books at quite reasonable prices. An important part of the Ann Arbor book scene. Good collection of new books on chess. *622 E. Liberty at State. (313) 665-8017. Mon-Sat 9:30 to 9 or 9:30, Sun 12-9.*

◆ **Dawn Treader.** Rambling spaces with general line, specialties in sci-fi, mysteries, natural history, math, science, philosophy, art, Americana, exploration. Some rare and early printing books in Liberty store. *514 E. Liberty near State. (313) 995-1008. May-Oct: Mon-Sat 10-9, Sun 1-6. Winter: closes at 8. Second location: 1202 South University (downstairs). Mon-Sat 11-10, Sun 1-6.*

◆ **Books in General.** Big, airy, loft-like space A large, round table makes this a pleasant place to sit down and browse through a huge stock of used books in literature, science, humanities. General line, better than usual sections in science and technology, foreign languages. *332 S. State (upstairs). (313) 769-1250. Mon-Sat 9:30-9, Sun 12-8.*

◆ **U-M Barnes & Noble Bookstore.** Spiffy big college textbook store also has, among its general reading books, a special section with English and American paperback editions of the classics. *In the basement of the Michigan Union, on State at South University. (313) 995-8877. Mon-Thurs 9-6, Fri 9-5, Sat 10-4, Sun 12-4. Shorter summer hours.*

◆ **Ulrich's Book Store.** The oldest textbook store in town, Ulrich's also has a good art supplies department and a big selection of U-M insignia items and inexpensive posters. *East University at South University. (313) 662-3201. Mon-Fri 8:30-5:30, Sat 9:30-5.*

◆ **Hall of Fame Sports Books.** Both new and used sports books (some quite rare). Also includes sports magazines, games, gifts, and collectibles. *311 S. Fifth Ave. between Liberty and William. (313) 995-8811.*

◆ **Common Language.** "For women and their friends." Feminist and gay studies, erotica, also mainstream books like detective series where the detective is not a white man. Kids' books stress positives of being different, having a gay parent, etc. *214 South*

Fourth, downtown between Liberty and Washington. (313) 663-0036. Tues-Fri 12-8, Sat 11-8, Sun 12-4.

◆ **Aunt Agatha's Book Shop.** Delightful ambiance in this mystery book shop. Knowledgeable owner sells both new and used. Also includes true crime books, puzzles, and related items. *213 Fourth. (313) 769-1114.*

◆ **Falling Water Books and Collectibles.** New Age books, plus crystals, other minerals, gifts. See page 150. *213 S. Main. (313) 747-9810. Mon-Sat 10-10, Sun 12-6.*

◆ **After Words.** Attractively laid out and good for browsing, this good-sized store carries drastically discounted new books. A third are remainders, two-thirds are still in print but at least 40% off. *219 S. Main. (313) 996-2808. Mon-Sat 10-10, Sun 12-8.*

◆ **West Side Book Shop.** This delightful shop fits the traditional image of a used bookstore: antique in a comfortable way, cluttered, accented with old prints, and personal — conducive to browsing and chatting. Space constraints make for higher quality. General-line, with nautical topics, exploration, and photography as specialties. Edward Curtis Indian photographs, other old photographs in antique-filled back room. *113 W. Liberty just west of Main. (313) 995-1891. Mon-Fri 11-6, Sat 10-5.*

◆ **Wooden Spoon.** A venerable used book shop, the Wooden Spoon is in the very spot where the legendary Joe's saloon once was. Its many rooms have a distinctly dusty, well-worn aura. Long-time manager David Dye died in 1993. The new owner is bringing an almost entirely new stock of books. *200 N. Fourth Ave. at Ann. (313) 769-4775. Mon, Tues & Thurs 9:30-4, Wed & Fri 9:30-6, Sat 7:30-5, Sun 1-5.*

◆ **Crazy Wisdom.** The owners have expanded and deepened titles in metaphysical and holistic subjects, including holistic health, bodywork, Jungian and transpersonal psychology, Buddhism, and women's spirituality. Also, audiotapes, jewelry, and interesting objects. *206 N. Fourth Ave. (313) 665-2757. Mon & Tues 10-6, Wed-Fri 10-8, Sat 10-6, Sun 12-6.*

◆ **Barnes & Noble.** Another in the fast-growing B&N superstore chain. Especially big children's section. Lots of bargain remaindered books. Espresso bar. Long hours. *Washtenaw at Huron Parkway on Ann Arbor's east side. (313) 677-6475. 9-11 daily.*

◆ **Little Professor.** This is one of the largest stores in the Little Professor franchise system. Nowhere nearly as complete as

Borders, but better than a mall bookshop. *Westgate Shopping Center (Stadium between Liberty and Huron). (313) 662-4110. Mon-Sat 9-11, Sun 8-10.*

◆ **Geography Limited.** Carries wide selection of maps, including every Michigan topo map. Wide selection of atlases, tour guides, and geography-oriented games. *2390 Winewood (close to Jackson and Stadium).(313) 668-1810. Tues-Wed noon-6, Thurs & Fri Noon-8, Sat 10-6.*

◆ **Webster's.** Large bookstore in northern Ann Arbor shopping center includes good magazine selection. *2607 Plymouth, in Traver Village. (313) 662-6150. 8-11 daily.*

A HANDY MICHIGAN GUIDE TO ANTIQUARIAN BOOK DEALERS . . . . . in homes as well as shops can be had through the Curious Book Shop, 307 E. Grand River, East Lansing, MI 48823. Stop by, or send a check for 75¢ or a $1 bill plus self-addressed, stamped envelope. The well-organized booklet lists some 150 dealers and specialties (Civil War, cookbooks, radical politics, fishing, Masons, African-American and much more.

RARE BOOKS IN A STATELY SETTING . . . . . Next door to the President's House on South University across from Tappan, the **Clements Library** has one of the country's leading collections of rare books, manuscripts, and maps on America through the 19th century. The library is patterned on an Italian Renaissance villa. The style was chosen to reflect the age of great explorers and cartographers who opened up the Americas. Beyond the ornate bronze grilles on the entrance doors is the grand main reading room. Antiques are on display throughout. A grandfather clock comes from George Washington's 1782-83 headquarters at New Windsor, New York, a gift from Carl Van Doren, who used the library to write his *Secret History of the Revolution.* A collection of Amberina glassware, fashionable in the 1880s, was made by the New England firm which eventually moved to Toledo, Ohio, and became Libbey Glass. At the west end of the room is one of the most popular paintings of 18th-century England, Benjamin West's *The Death of General Wolfe.* The painting shows British General Wolfe, fatally wounded, surrounded by his staff. The year was 1759, just after Wolfe had completed a victory over the French at Quebec, sealing British control over North America. *909 S. University at Tappan. (313) 764-2347. Mon-Fri 10:30-12, 1-5.*

Ann Arbor record stores

For CDs, tapes, and even vinyl,
central Ann Arbor is the best between the coasts.

Many music-lovers from across the U.S. consider Ann Arbor the best place to shop for recordings because of the outstanding comparison-shopping permitted by the concentration of high-quality stores. In its 15 years here, Schoolkids has grown into the musical equivalent of the Ann Arbor Borders Books. Most record stores are open evenings and Sunday afternoons.

◆ **Schoolkids Records & Tapes**. Early on, Schoolkids learned that having a great back list in the right town can build a market dramatically. Its strength is its breadth and depth in everything from rock and jazz to country, folk, blues, and new age, including esoteric labels and foreign pressings. Some CDs it imports direct. Vinyl, which held on longer here, is being phased out. No returns. Good place to pick up information; the staff is knowledgeable and helpful. And now they've opened The Annex next door for alternative music and used recordings. *523 E. Liberty. (313) 994-8031. Mon-Sat 100-9:30, Sun noon-8.*

◆ **SKR Classical**. SKR's classical music store is bigger than ever, with 20,000 titles. It's a Schoolkids' subsidiary, managed by Jim Leonard. Passionately opinionated when he was a music critic, Leonard is a most approachable advisor for people who are intimidated by classical music and their ignorance of it. He strives for a user-friendly, anti-snobbish store, started a **newsletter**, and instituted Sunday **music appreciation classes** from 1 to 2 p.m. SKR Classical has the state's biggest collection of classical compact disks, and a great many tapes. It also has scores and many pirate tapes of live performances. *539 E. Liberty. (313) 995-5051. (800) 272-4506. Mon-Sat 10-9, Sun 12-6.*

◆ **Borders Books and Music**. Following the pattern established by the Borders chain's newer stores, its Ann Arbor flagship is now into CDs in a significant way. *(313) 668-7652. Mon-Sat 9-9, Sun 11-6.*

◆ **Discount Records**. Discount covers all the pop, jazz, and classical bases and keeps local prices competitive. Though part of a chain, its Ann Arbor outlet has an intelligent selection. *State and Liberty. (313) 665-3679. Mon-Thurs 9-9, Fri & Sat 9-10, Sun 12-8.*

◆ **State Discount.** A campus general store, State is known by music buffs not as a source of shampoo and snacks but as the cheapest place in town to buy just-released, mass-volume CDs. *309 S. State. (313) 994-1262. Mon-Fri 8:30-9, Sat 10-7, Sun 12-6.*

◆ **Borders Books and Music.** Now into CDs in a significant way. Liberty between State and Maynard. *(313) 668-7652. Mon-Sat 9-9, Sun 11-6.*

◆ **Wazoo Records.** This upstairs store has a well-organized stock of CD records and tapes with some vinyl (mostly rock, but with big sections of jazz, country, folk, classical). Reasonable prices ($4.50 for most vinyl records, $5-10 for used CDs, tapes $4 to $5). A stock of newly released CDs encourages trade-ins. Everything is guaranteed. The only scratchy records you'll find here are rare ones. Good prices paid for used records. *336 1/2 S. State (upstairs) (313) 761-8686. Mon-Fri 10-8, Sat 10-6, Sun 12-6.*

◆ **PJ's Used Records and CDs.** PJ's is a hip, intense used record store run by knowledgeable jazz, R&B, and blues enthusiasts. "Opinions rendered on all subjects," they advertise. Jammed with recordings, it keeps adding more as music fans abandon their vinyl collections in favor of CD. *617B (upstairs above Subway) Packard between Hill and State. (313) 663-3441. Mon-Thurs 10-9, Fri & Sat 10-10, Sun noon-8.*

◆ **Earth Wisdom Music.** A purveyor of New Age music for meditation, relaxation, guided imagery, "creative ambiance," and dance, Earth Wisdom has been around since before the genre became a Muzak for the 80s. *Inside Seva Restaurant, 314 E. Liberty. (313) 769-0969. Mon & Tues 11-7, Wed-Sat 11-8:30, Sun 11-2:30.*

◆ **Tower Records.** Big outlet of the coast-to-coast outlet. Local manager keeps unusually strong collection of obscure rock imports. *1214 South University (upstairs). (313) 741-9600. 9-midnight daily.*

Zingerman's Delicatessen

This fantastic deli also showcases
choice foods from around the world.

Depending on who you talk to, this is the best deli in the Midwest or even the world. Sandwiches (over 100 in all) are huge and delicious; the $7.75 corned beef Reuben is the best-seller. The extensive takeout counter offers tempting salads and favorites, from deli classics like coleslaw ($1.50/side), chicken soup, and noodle kugel ($2.50/slice) to inventive potato salads, the popular Thai noodle salad, and salmon-dill pasta salad ($5/side) made with Irish smoked salmon. With Bruce Aidells' sausages from San Francisco and unusual hand-made cheeses, domestic and imported, the deli counter is absolutely top-of-the-line. The selection of olive oils, vinegars, and mustards is outstanding. The owners do a great job of searching out exceptional jams, relishes, and goodies of all kinds. Free samples are plentiful. The fun, information-packed free handouts are a short course in food. Call (313) 663-0974 to subscribe to their monthly **newsletter** ($10/year).

Food writer and *Atlantic* senior editor Corby Kummer enthused in *Eating Well* magazine, "How does a store in such a town offer an unquestionably great selection of the world's cheeses, perhaps the finest teas sold in America, corned beef and pastrami so richly flavored as to make even New Yorkers jealous, a brilliantly edited collection of olive oils, vinegars, fruit preserves and pastas – in all, between 2,500 and 3,000 of the best foods and flavors anywhere? And why is the service in this remarkable store the sort of utterly professional and knowledgeable service Americans expect to find in Europe – gently blended with the concern and warmth that Europeans think of as American? In short, what has Ann Arbor done to deserve Zingerman's?"

Jim Harrison, novelist and noted cook, seems to come close to a spiritual epiphany in the former neighborhood grocery store on Detroit Street, between Kerrytown and the Treasure Mart. "In Zingerman's, I get the mighty reassurance that the world can't be totally bad if there's this much good to eat, the same flowing emotions I get at Fauchon in Paris, Harrods' food department in

From this old neighborhood grocery on the edge of the Kerrytown commercial district, Zingerman's has built a nationwide reputation.

London, Balducci's or Dean and DeLuca in New York, only at Zingerman's there is a warmth and goodwill lacking in the others" (*Esquire*).

In 1982, when they started Zingerman's, Paul Saginaw (from Detroit) and Ari Weinzweig (from Chicago) wanted to start the kind of deli that would sell the kind of food your grandmother cooked and used, whether she was Jewish or German or Italian. And they wanted to create a workplace that they would enjoy coming to every day.

Those values are in good part responsible for their success — along with a lot of smarts and passion and hard work and study. For years Zingerman's searched out better and better sources for the cheeses and olive oils and meats it sells. Now they are taking a more active role in supporting emerging producers of hand-crafted foods. Zingerman's is one of the biggest customers of Loomis Great Lakes Cheshire cheese ($8.99/lb.), made a few blocks away on Felch Street. "The Loomis family has gone to extraordinary lengths to make a world-class cheese right here in Ann Arbor," proclaims the *Zingerman's catalog of good food*, developed as a way to expand Zingerman's customer base without creating multiple stores. "Their milk is organic, from a local herd of Holsteins. The cheesemaking is done by hand, the pressing takes place on an antique Welsh press. It is aged on wooden shelves and the cheese is allowed to breathe, age, and develop a natural rind, bringing out its full, rich flavor."

Weinzweig writes much of the catalog and the store's vast amount of promotional and educational material about food. (He's the outgoing front man, while the intensely focused, no-nonsense Saginaw deals more with behind-the-scene operations and Food Gatherers, the leftover food-for-the-poor community service arm Zingerman's founded.) Weinzweig has even joined a writers' support group to improve his writing; he aspires to become a published food writer. Most of Zingerman's treatises on food categories (olive oils, cheeses, olives, salsas, etcetera) are available free as handouts at the deli. The catalog and mail-order business was conceived as a way to build on Zingerman's out-of-town customer base and expand sales without cloning the original store.

But other places can and do carry off the hand-made food thing. What makes Zingerman's stand out from its New York and continental counterparts is its Midwestern-ness. The friendly, knowledgeable staff is astoundingly polite and patient. No matter who you are and what you know or don't know, they are nice. No matter how overbearing and picky the customer, they're almost incredibly polite and helpful.

Because Zingerman's refuses to grow by starting branches or franchises, it has legions of imitators intent on ripping off its interior design and display techniques and tracking down its food sources. What these wanna-bes ought to focus on is how Zingerman's hires and trains a staff that serves customers so cheerfully and becomes so knowledgeable about food.

Zingerman's started its own bakery, **Zingerman's Bakehouse**, in 1992, because Weinzweig and Saginaw weren't happy with the rye bread they could get for sandwiches. "Unfortunately, much of what has passed for rye bread in this country over the years is merely bland wheat bread made with a dash of rye flour and a few caraway seeds for flavor," Weinzweig writes. "They have little in common with the rye bread my grandparents were eating in New York and Chicago 70 or 80 years ago. Jewish-style breads are the core of what we do at Zingerman's. . . . [They] are made with a natural sour starter, a bit of yeast, rye and wheat flours. . . . These rye breads have a shiny, crackling crust when they come out of the oven, a crust that's chewy and satisfying every time you bite into it." Plain Jewish rye is $3.50 for a two-pound loaf.

Not all breads are traditional. Some are originals, like the moist, rich chocolate cherry bread ($6.95 for a 1 1/2-pound loaf), and farm bread with scallions and toasted walnuts ($3.95 for a 1 1/2-pound loaf).

If all this sounds too good to be true, it is. The down side of Zingerman's is its customers. Often there arc too many of them. Sometimes they are extremely pretentious, self-important, inconsiderate people who are quite comfortable spending what seems like hours tasting and coming to a decision. That's fine when the store is uncrowded, but if you're in a long line behind an overbearing foodie, it's an ordeal waiting to buy your simple loaf of bread to take home to dinner. At the wrong time, Zingerman's can seem far more like hell than heaven — a peculiarly contemporary form of hell, at that.

Straight from Zingerman's deli employees, here are **tips for shopping and eating** at Zingerman's. The store is divided into the deli counter, where groceries are bought, and the sandwich counter, where customers order sandwiches to eat here or to go, and other deli items to eat on the premises. Then they arc seated at **Zingerman's Next Door**, the sit-down area in a neighboring house, or at picnic tables in the court, and called when their order is ready. The atmosphere at Zingerman's Next Door is quite relaxed; coffee drinkers are encouraged to linger in the evening over coffee and dessert.

◆ **Order ahead**. Call (313) 663-DELI and leave your name and estimated time of arrival. This works great for sandwiches, but it means you can't taste before you decide on deli items. Piles of takeout menus are at cash registers by every counter, and by the espresso machine at Zingerman's Next Door. Request the mail-order *catalog of good food* from a cashier, but be aware that its selection is more limited than what's in the store.

◆ **Have your food delivered** by Food By Phone (995-3663). The delivery charge is 15% of whatever the food order costs. Delivery to parks within Ann Arbor is available.

◆ **Early in the morning and early in the week is less crowded.** Monday and Tuesday mornings are usually the least crowded times, unless it's a holiday. Weekends are unpredictable but usually busy. When the nearby Farmers' Market is underway, there's a line by 7 a.m. on Saturdays. In winter, weekend mornings are slower.

◆ The **retail deli counter** is busiest from about 9 a.m. to 11 a.m., after work, and probably all day on weekends. Breads are 25% off after 9 p.m.

◆ The **sandwich counter** gets busy by 11 a.m. on weekdays, with a lull from 2:30 to 3:30 and even 4 p.m. Evenings it slows down after 8 p.m.

422 Detroit at Kingsley. From Huron (Bus. I-94) or Catherine, take North Fourth Ave. north to Kingsley, then turn right. Look for a parking place along Kingsley or Detroit. (313) 663-DELI (also call DELI to order ahead). Mail-order: (313) 663-3400; FAX: (313) 769-1235. **Deli** *open Mon-Sat 7 a.m.-10 p.m., Sun 9 a.m.-9 p.m.* **Zingerman's Next Door** *(313-663-JAVA) open to 11 p.m.*

Miller Motors

In Ypsilanti's historic Depot Town, a Hudson auto dealer, little changed from the 1940s.

In front of this old Hudson dealership is a vintage HUDSON sign, and in the show window is a spiffy-looking Hudson coupe. This isn't a mirage — or a museum. It's the business of Jack Miller, whose father started selling Hudsons here in 1933. Though production ceased in 1957, Miller still trades in Hudsons. His place is probably the best in the world to get Hudson parts, still in their original cartons, some half a century old. They have been bought up from old warehouses around the country.

In the service area behind the sales room are an array of Hudson cars for sale, as well as Miller's private collection. These have included a 1953 Hudson Hornet, the 1946 Hudson pickup Miller drives to work in the summer, a 1946 Hudson convertible, and a 1956 pink and grey Hudson. In an adjoining area Miller repairs old Hudsons.

Hudson aficionados often stop by to chat. Miller affably shares his wealth of knowledge about Hudsons with visitors. He

Miller Motors' Hudson dealership in 1946. It doesn't look much different today, even though Hudsons haven't been made since 1957.

❶ Huron St. historic buildings. Impressive 19th-century mansions line bluff overlooking Huron River. Evokes a more scenic, preindustrial Ypsilanti.

❷ Historical Museum. Humdrum Victorian rooms, but great display of underwear which made Ypsi mills famous. Wonderful arrowhead collection, eccentric items.

❸ Depot Town. Old, once-bustling commercial district fueled by two train depots. District now home to bars and antique shops, highlighted by the Side Track with great hamburgers and ornate big bar.

❹ Miller Motors. Long after the beloved Hudson auto ceased production, this Hudson dealership keeps trading both parts and cars and retains its 1940s look.

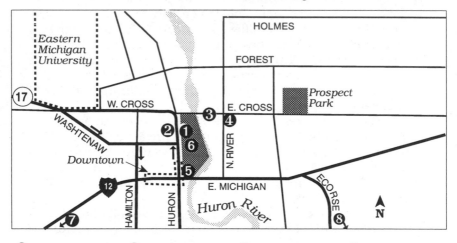

❺ Materials Unlimited. Extraordinarily big selection of vintage architectural items, both antiques and repros. Many ornate fixtures, including stained glass, columns, and hardware, make it good for browsing.

❻ Riverside & Frog Island Parks. Scenic Huron River parks host great events— June's Frog Island Blues/Jazz Festival, August's big Heritage Festival, and holiday light display (313) 482-4920.

❼ Schmidt's Antiques. One of country's best places to get English antique furniture. The monthly auction is a comic treat just to watch. 5138 W. Michigan. (313) 434-2660.

❽ Yankee Air Museum/ Willow Run Airport. Interesting collection of old military aircraft at the historic and now crumbling Willow Run Airport, where Ford built bombers during WWII.

Highlights of
Ypsilanti

0   1/2   1
            mile

explains that they were first manufactured in 1909 and named after financial backer J. L. Hudson, the Detroit department store magnate. The Hudson name was sullied in the mid-1950s when Nash took over the firm and turned out what some consider gaudy imitations of the real thing. But the Hudsons of the 1940s were extraordinary automobiles, Miller points out, fast but stable highway cars engineered and built extremely well.

Looking around the showroom is a treat. The walls are covered with old Hudson promotional posters, as well as with photos and other antique artifacts. Visitors are welcome to browse. And you can also kick the tires of what a *Car and Driver* article called the "vaguely eccentric" array of cars other than Hudsons.

100 E. Cross Street at River just east of Depot Town. From I-94, take Huron St. exit 183 north about 1¹/₄ miles, then east on Cross. (313) 482-5200. Open Saturdays 9-5 (except for lunchtime). Open during the week for group tours, but only by advance arrangement.

ANOTHER STOP ON AN AUTOMOTIVE NOSTALGIA TOUR . . . . . is, just a block east of Depot Town, the former home of **Preston Tucker**, father of the innovative **Tucker automobile**, and hero of Francis Ford Coppola's movie Tucker. He lived in the big white house at 110 North Park, just north of Michigan Avenue. From River Street in Depot Town, go east a block to Park and turn right. As owner of the Ypsilanti Machine Tool Company on Grove Street behind his house, he built a remote gun turret for the Army, in addition to racing Indy cars and customizing automobiles.

SAY IT LIKE A LOCAL . . . . . It's pronounced "IPP-si-lan-tee." Never be tempted to say "YIP-si-lan-tee." Detroit judge Augustus Woodward platted the town in 1825. Ever prone to the magnificently complex (he designed Detroit's circle-and-square street layout), Woodward shrugged off ordinary suggestions like Waterville and named the town after the Greek general who had just become a hero in the battle for Greek independence against the Turks.

INTERESTING ARCHITECTURE AND ANTIQUE SHOPS . . . . . are in the 19th-century commercial district along East Cross called **Depot Town**. It features some popular bars, several antique and resale shops, a food co-op, and other attractions. Depot Town actually became the city's main downtown for awhile after the railroad arrived in 1838 from Detroit. The passenger and freight depots are still here. The **Michigan Central passenger station** on North River Street, now one story high, is a pale shadow of the ornate three-

story building and tower built here in 1863. A fire and train collision have
reduced it to its present humble state. . . . . Across the tracks, the **freight
depot** is a long Italianate structure from 1875. It is now headquarters for the
Ypsilanti Farmers' Market, open Wednesdays and Saturdays from 8 a.m. to
3 p.m. Many of the upper stories of the 1850s and 1860s brick storefronts
along Cross are now apartments, and the area, with its own sprightly neighborhood publication, has a sense of camaraderie. The 1859 **Follett House** at
17-25 E. Cross was known as one of the finest hotels on the Michigan
Central line. The third-floor ballroom hosted Buffalo Bill, Tom Thumb, and
other 19th-century celebrities. . . . . The **Side Track** at 56 East Cross is a
very popular watering place, with excellent hamburgers and a massive back
bar. **Aubree's Saloon** at 39 East Cross is a lively, upscale gathering place
with billiards, a sidewalk cafe, and a rooftop deck where barbecued ribs,
chicken and fish are cooked outside. Call (313) 483-1870 for entertainment.
Often it's well worth checking out. Around the corner of North River Street is
the **Ypsilanti Food Co-op**. *East Cross St. between the Huron River and River
St. Many stores open Sundays 11-5; some antique shops are closed Mondays
and Tuesdays.*

OTHER YPSI STANDOUTS FOR ANTIQUERS . . . . . **Materials Unlimited** is
one of the biggest and best places in the Midwest to find attractive architectural artifacts, new and old: stained glass windows, ornate brass door hinges,
carved oak column capitals, 19th-century building ornaments, etc. Also:
some antique furniture here, eccentric items like wooden masks and cigar-
store Indians. *2 W. Michigan Ave. between Huron St. and the river. (313)
483-6980. Mon-Sat 10-5.* . . . . . **Schmidt's Antique Shop** is widely known
for its entertainingly funny monthly auctions that often have high quality furniture. For decades Schmidt's imported mostly middle-quality English
antiques by the container load, but shifting exchange rates have diminished
that trade. Still, the gallery sales room makes for interesting browsing. *5138
Michigan Ave., 4 miles west of Ypsilanti. (313) 434-2660. Mon-Sat 9-5, Sun 11-
5. Auction: first Saturday of month, 11 a.m.*

IN AN IMPRESSIVE MANSION . . . . . perched on a bank of the Huron River,
the **Ypsilanti Historical Museum** has an amusing assortment of local artifacts. You can see the long underwear that gave the city a national reputation in the 19th century. A poster touts the woolen garments as "the perfect
underwear for progressive people" with the jingle: "*Never rip and never tear/
Ypsilanti underwear.*" A back room is full of old dolls. Kids are said to be
most intrigued by the large dollhouse made from crates during the Depression. *220 N. Huron St. near Cross. (313) 482-4990. Thurs, Sat, Sun 2-4. Free.*

Yankee Air Museum/ Willow Run Airport

At a legendary, aging airport, an imposing collection of famous American fighting planes

Part of the fun of visiting this military air museum is roaming around Willow Run Airport. It's a remarkable place built in the early 1940s to test the long-range B-24 bombers built in the huge adjacent factory. Today the airport has a rather seedy, almost disreputable look to it. The carcasses of old planes are strewn around the fringes of the giant field, some partially devoured for spare parts. Big old four-engine propeller-powered cargo planes still lumber into the air from the long runways. Many rush critically needed parts to keep auto plants around the country in production.

Just west of the field is the gigantic **GM Hydra-Matic Plant**, so big that specially-made superhighways funneled workers in and out of the complex. This was initially the famous **Willow Run Bomber Plant**. Erected by Ford Motor in 1941, it was the largest building ever built. The monster covers 70 acres at the eastern edge of Washtenaw County. It sprawls over 3/4 of a mile. Architect Albert Kahn built it in an L-shape to keep it from spilling into Wayne County, which Ford considered unfriendly Democratic territory with higher taxes. The big plant proved to be a big boost to American morale after Pearl Harbor. But Ford Motor was in such a state of confusion under its aging, suspicious founder that Willow Run's production goals weren't met until the war was almost over.

When the giant facility was planned, it wasn't clear whether or not the Allies would lose Great Britain to the Nazis, so Willow Run had to make quickly thousands of bombers big enough to fly missions across the Atlantic to reach Germany. Between 1942 and 1945, some 42,000 women and men worked in the plant. Midgets were hired to fit parts in the nose section and other hard-to-reach areas. By the time the bomber plant closed in June of 1945, it had produced 8,685 B-24 Liberators.

GM purchased the plant in 1953 to make automatic transmissions. The big Hydra-Matic plant has actually been expanded over the years to 4.8 million square feet. It now employs about 9,300 workers. Next door is a Chevrolet assembly plant which makes Caprices.

On the airport's other side, off Beck Road, is the **Yankee Air Museum**, housed in a cavernous 1941 hangar. It has the interestingly scruffy atmosphere of a bootstrap creation by dedicated fans. Although the museum was only organized in 1981, the huge hangar is already crowded with aging military aircraft. Some are in the process of being renovated. On weekends you'll often see an elderly volunteer mechanic working on an engine.

Some of the 28 planes here already fly. One is a 1945 C-47, the cargo version of the classic DC-3. Another is a 1943 B-25 gunship that saw action in Europe, providing close ground support and flying 90 bombing missions. This is the same model used in the Doolittle raid of Japan. Museum members will soon have finished work on a classic B-17 "Flying Fortress," the Allies' largest heavy bomber during most of World War II. Also on display in the hangar is another classic military aircraft: the F-86 Sabre jet, a famous Korean War fighter.

On the second floor of the hangar complex are rooms with memorabilia on display: Air Force patches and medals, old newspaper clippings, paintings and photos of planes in action, engines, shells, radios, flights suits, goggles, and so on. Just outside the hangar are even more planes, highlighted by the hulking, rather ominous presence of a camouflaged B-52 bomber. The **gift shop** is well stocked with books on aviation, model airplanes, postcards, T-shirts, and other souvenirs.

Willow Run Airport, off Beck Rd. Take exit 190 from I-94. (313) 483-4030. Tues-Sat 10-4, Sun 12-4. $4.00/adult, $3.00 seniors over 60, $2.00 children over 5, children 5 and under free.

Monroe

It reached its zenith well before the Civil War. Now it's an interesting backwater where you can see a War of 1812 battlefield, well preserved old homes, and Custer memorabilia.

Just up the beautiful River Raisin from the marshes along Lake Erie, Monroe is a settled old industrial city, originally French. For centuries Indians harvested wild rice in these marshes. Lotuses blossom here every August, giving a spectacular view to visitors who head east out Dunbar Road just south of town. Hunters and bird-watchers are attracted by the huge flocks of migrating waterfowl which come to the marshes, home of some of the state's best bird-watching.

The equestrian sculpture of General George Armstrong Custer, on Monroe at Elm just north of the Raisin River, was dedicated by President Roosevelt and the general's spirited journalist widow. The famously impetuous general regarded Monroe as his home town.

Monroe is one of Michigan's most historic cities. Only Detroit was incorporated earlier. But relative to the Motor City, Monroe has stagnated over the decades. Today the historic city center seems curiously remote from the busy highways that go past it connecting Toledo to Detroit.

Monroe was founded by French-Canadians who grew disenchanted with life in Detroit under the British after France lost control in 1760. Some natives still speak in the area's distinctive French accent. The Indians taught Monroe's French the custom of eating muskrat (pronounced "mushrat" in these parts), and it is still considered a delicacy here. Trapped before the spring thaw, muskrat is often featured at late winter dinners of Monroe fraternal orders and charitable organizations.

The most colorful and exciting era in the city's history occurred between 1825 and 1837 when thousands of Easterners landed here on their way to settle Michigan, Indiana, and Illinois. The Erie Canal, opened in 1825, brought settlers to Buffalo, where they boarded sailing ships or steamers to make the sometimes dangerous and usually uncomfortable 10-day voyage to Monroe.

Highlights of the Monroe area:

◆ **Monroe County Historical Museum.** Housed in the old post office, this interesting general museum of local history has many memorabilia about **General George Armstrong Custer**, the most famous person associated with Monroe. Custer spent much of his youth in Monroe and visited it often afterwards. Before his famous demise at Little Big Horn in 1876, Custer had been a heroic Civil War officer, promoted to general at the unheard-of age of 23 because of his aggressive, courageous leadership.

Here you can see Custer's swords and beloved rifles, a map he made of a Confederate camp while he was held aloft by balloon, and his big buffalo robe worn during the Washita Campaign of 1868 when he defeated a bigger band of Sioux. People come from around the world to visit the museum and the Custer collection of the **Monroe County Library** on 3700 S. Custer Road (M-50) at Raisinville Road (313-241-5277). Much of the library's big collection of photos, films, tapes, and written matter was assembled by the late Dr. Lawrence Frost, Monroe podiatrist, mayor, and Custer authority.

The museum, outstanding for a town of Monroe's size, has much more than Custer memorabilia of interest, although the most extensive exhibits are now housed at the River Raisin Battlefield site. A display about the pride of Monroe, Kaye Lani Rae Rafko, Miss America 1988, features the revealing green sequined Hawaiian costume she made for her hula dance in the pageant's talent competition. Beauty pageants are *big* in Monroe. *126 S. Monroe St. (313) 243-7137. May-Sept: Tues-Sun 10-5. Oct-April: Wed-Sun 10-5. Free. Pick up a **walking tour brochure** for a walk through old Monroe.*

◆ **Downtown.** Plans to revitalize the downtown with a riverwalk have stalled for lack of money to complete the construction. The most interesting part of this faded commercial and civic area is **Loranger Square**, at the intersection of First and Washington, a block east of Monroe Street, the town's main drag. This New

England-type square, unique in Michigan, shows how much older Monroe is than other cities in the state. The unusual, impressively ornate 1880 **County Courthouse** is on the square's southeast corner. In front is a cannon that dates to the reign of George II of England. Across First Street is the site of the **First Presbyterian Church,** built in 1846. Next to the church on First is the **Dorsch Memorial Library**, located in the former home of Dr. Eduard Dorsch, a Bavarian physician who fled after the failed 1848 German revolution. On the square's northwest corner, a plaque commemorates the spot where a **whipping post** once stood. Whipping posts were a rarity in the Midwest.

Along Washington Street (one street over from Monroe) are some attractively restored commercial buildings north of the courthouse. The **Monroe Bank & Trust** is a fine example of early 20th-century Beaux Arts architecture. It's worth a peek inside to see the imposing interior. A map on the kiosk outside orients visitors to major Monroe sights. At **River Run Patisserie** across the street, you can buy tasty fresh pastries and coffee to go.

North of the river across the Monroe Street bridge is the impressive **Custer Monument** at Elm and Monroe. It was unveiled in 1910 by his widow, by then a well-known New York writer, with President Taft at her side. Behind it is **St. Mary's Park,** just north of downtown, a pleasant riverside picnic spot. You can pick up a coney island at downtown's most popular and quaintest eatery, **Coney Island Lunch** (4 W. Front) and saunter across the pedestrian bridge to the park. The impressive complex of Art Deco buildings across Elm Street from the park is **St. Mary's Center**, a conference and retreat facility, and the Mother House of the **IHM Sisters** (Sisters, Servants of the Immaculate Heart of Mary), the order of nuns which governs Marygrove College in Detroit.

Several noteworthy establishments are on Monroe Street. The tidy, well-organized **Thrift Shop** at 119 S. Monroe sells its merchandise (used clothes, furniture, dishes, etc.) at amazingly cheap prices. *(313) 242-1082. Open Mon-Fri 9:30 to 3:30, except for closing at 11:30 on Tuesday; Saturday 10-2.* **Spainhower's Auction House** has a wild variety of antique items for sale. *Open 9-5 Mon-Fri. Call 313-242-5411 about upcoming auctions held every three to four weeks.* Celebrating its 25th year in 1994, the **Book Nook** at 42 S. Monroe sells books and religious articles geared to Monroe's big Catholic community. Lots of material on Custer is available here. *(313) 241-2665. Open Mon-Fri 9:30-6,*

Sat 9:30-5.

Finally, if you walk west on Front Street past Monroe Street, you'll soon see the home of the **Monroe Evening News** at 201 W. First. Giant glass windows let the passing public see its big web presses in action. Around 2:30 on weekday afternoons, you can see that day's edition roaring off the presses. *Centered at the intersection of Front St. with Monroe and Washington, extending south from the River Raisin.* A **walking tour brochure** available at the museum takes you on an interesting walk through Old Monroe's historic commercial and residential districts.

◆ **River Raisin Battlefields and Massacre Site.** The War of 1812 pitted the British and Indians against the Americans. At stake was the extent of American holdings on the continent. One of the major battles in that often ineptly led war occurred on the River Raisin between Dixie Highway and Detroit Street. A sequence of dioramas at the interpretive museum shows what Frenchtown (Monroe's former name) looked like in 1813 when an American army was badly mauled here in an early-morning surprise attack by British and Canadian soldiers. Nearly 280 Americans were killed, and a brigade of 600 militiamen surrendered. Wounded Americans, left in the homes of Monroe settlers, were set upon by Indians a day later. Over 60 were murdered. This famous "River Raisin Massacre" later ignited the American troops. A series of metal markers along the river explains its major incidents.

The new battlefield interpretive museum now houses the Monroe County Historical Museum's most comprehensive exhibits. In addition to a number of dioramas, a fiber optic map program provides a fourteen-minute audio-visual summary of the War of 1812 in the region. *Open daily 10-5, May 15 thru Labor Day; Sat and Sun 10-5 from October thru April, although weekday tours can be arranged in advance. 1403 E. Elm Avenue, just west of Detroit St. (between M-50 and I-75). Call (313) 243-7136 to verify hours.*

◆ **Navarre-Anderson Trading Post.** The centerpiece of this three-building complex is the plain house built in central Monroe in 1789 by fur trader François Navarre. It's believed to be the oldest surviving house in Michigan, and it has been restored and furnished with simple French-Canadian furniture to look as it might have when the Navarres lived there between 1789 and 1802. The brick schoolhouse built on this site in 1860 has been interpreted as a **country store** from between 1910 and 1920. The third building is a replica of a 1790s **French-Canadian barn.** *N. Custer Rd. at Raisinville Rd., 4 miles west of downtown Monroe. From M-50 (S. Custer Rd.) turn north onto Raisinville Rd. and cross the river. (313) 243-7137. Open Memorial Day-Labor Day, weekends 1-5; other times, by appointment for groups. Free.*

◆ **Sterling State Park.** Sterling State Park, just north of Monroe, is western Lake Erie's only park with camping and swimming. From the beach, swimmers and sunbathers get a stark view of the giant cooling towers of the Fermi Nuclear Plant four miles north.

Half of this 1,000-acre park consists of water — lagoons that are excellent habitats for migrating and nesting shore birds. A 2.6-mile loop along the **Marsh View Nature Trail** surrounds the park's largest lagoon. (It's open for **cross-country skiing** in winter.) A mile-long walk leads to its **observation tower.** A causeway leads to the large **beach**, beach house, parking area and, behind it, the partly shaded **picnic area** and **playground** on a rise offering a panorama of Lake Erie.

Western Lake Erie is often referred to as the "walleye capital of the world." The park has a large **boat launch** area with twelve launch lanes and parking for over 500 cars/trailers. People from

A walking tour brochure from Monroe's fine historical museum takes you past many well-preserved blocks of mid 19th-century houses south of the courthouse and on the north bank of the River Raisin. They are an unheralded treasure of the settled old town of Monroe.

all over the U.S. come to camp at Sterling and leave with a freezer full of one of the best-tasting fish. The park has 288 modern **campsites** without privacy or shade, overlooking the boat basin. *Camping fee: $11/night. On State Park Rd., off Dixie Hwy. 1 mile northeast of I-75 exit 15. (313) 289-2715. 8 a.m.-10 p.m. $4/day or $18 annual state park sticker.*

◆ **Fermi 2 Power Plant & Visitors Center.** These tours of Detroit Edison's only nuclear power plant get high marks from radiation experts for straightforward information about nuclear power and about the much-publicized delays and cost overruns in 1988 in starting up Fermi 2. The visitor center tours combine a **film** on how nuclear energy is produced, a tour of the facility, a **bus tour** of the site layout, and lots of chances for questions-and-answers. Not surprisingly, the tour emphasizes safety and environmental issues. There's a scale model of Fermi 2's drywell primary containment system.

Fermi 2 is Detroit Edison's cheapest source of power, so the Christmas Day fire that triggered an emergency shutdown in 1993 really hurt. The plant was shut down for months. *On Enrico Fermi Drive off Dixie Hwy., 7 miles north of downtown Monroe. (313) 586-5228. Advance reservations of 2-3 weeks required for free group tours conducted Mon-Fri between 8 and 4. Individuals may join scheduled group tours. Some evening and Saturday tours may be arranged on request.*

◆ **Manufacturers Market Place.** Discounts of 30% to 70% at 64 stores make this outlet mall Monroe's #1 visitor destination. But the sister mall at Birch Run near Frankenmuth (p. 377) has more stores and a neighboring designer outlet mall. Tenant stores here include **Van Heusen, Izod, Jonathan Logan L'eggs/Hanes/Bali, Bass** shoes, **Famous Footwear, Toy Liquidators, American Tourister, Corning/Revere, Sportsland USA,** and **Pepperidge Farm.** Places with especially good deals are **Carter's Childrenswear, Socks Galore, The Paper Factory** (giftwrap and school supplies), and the large **WestPoint Pepperell** store (the only one in Michigan). *14500 La Plaisance at I-75 (exit 11), 2 1/2 miles southeast of downtown Monroe. Mon-Sat 10-9, Sun 11-6. Closed Easter, Thanksgiving, and Christmas. Hours are subject to change. For information call (800) 866-5900.*

Chapter 3
Metro Detroit

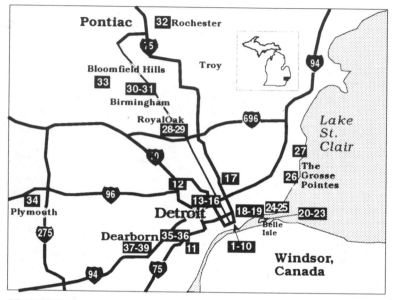

HIGHLIGHTS

For restaurants & lodgings. see *Hunts' Restaurants & Lodgings of Michigan*

INTRODUCTION

Metro Detroit

Less than one-thirtieth the size of Michigan, Metro Detroit has some 4.5 million people, half the state's population. It's a region of stark contrasts. Oakland County (Birmingham, Bloomfield Hills, Royal Oak, Southfield) is one of the wealthiest counties in the U.S. The city of Detroit, shrunk to just one million citizens, has become a national symbol of urban poverty, though its problems are shared by many other cities.

The auto industry continues to dominate this region's economy. Not only do the Big Three have their headquarters here, but hundreds of sizable Detroit-area auto parts suppliers prosper and languish as auto sales nationwide rise and fall.

Detroit was a medium-sized city of 285,000 in 1900, on the eve of the auto boom. In 1905 autos were made in 175 American cities. With surprising quickness, Detroit became the nation's auto capital because of some remarkably capable, aggressive entrepreneurs: Henry Ford, the Dodge brothers, the Fisher brothers, Henry Leland, among others. Huge lumbering profits from northern Michigan provided lots of available capital to invest in the new industry. And Detroit already had a strong base in working with metal and manufacturing engines from its 19th-century shipbuilding, stove, and rail car industries. The city's central Great Lakes location made it easy to ship iron ore, limestone, and coal to local factories.

By 1910, Detroit had exploded to become the fifth biggest U.S. city. From 1905 to 1924, immigrants flocked to Detroit, giving it a far wider variety of peoples than older Midwestern cities. Metro Detroit has more Arabs than any place else in the U.S., large numbers of African-Americans, Albanians, Belgians, Maltese, and Poles, plus many Germans, Hungarians, Irish, Italians, Jews, Mexican-Americans, and Appalachian southerners.

The enormous wealth from the auto industry has left many extraordinary sights in and around Detroit. The city has one of the world's top art museums, a fantastic island park in Belle Isle, a great zoo, and remarkable historical museums. Majestic 1920s skyscrapers still loom over the town, and flamboyant mansions of four auto barons are now open to visitors.

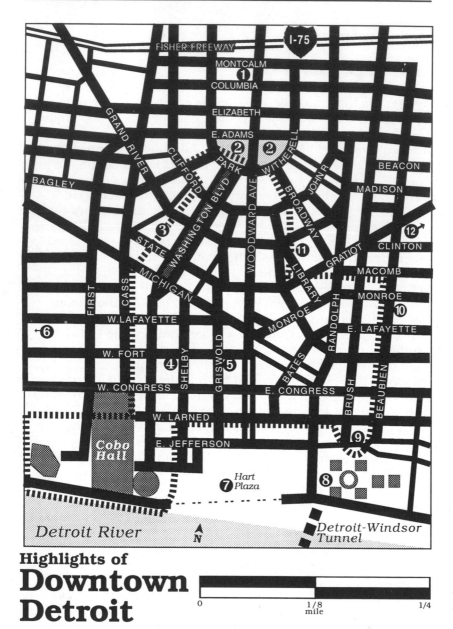

Highlights of

Downtown
Detroit

1 Fox Theater. Restored "Siamese Byzantine" extravaganza, one of the most lavish U.S. picture palaces, has become nation's top-grossing venue for big-name acts. Nearby **Gem** presents revues,plays.

2 Grand Circus Park. Once a 19th-century jewel, this old park has many important historic statues. The heart of Detroit's grand Theater District, now coming to life again.

3 People Mover. A must for visitors, this 2.9 mile elevated train gives a spectacular view of the entire downtown. Terrific public art in the 12 stations. Despite ailing finances, not likely to close.

4 Silver's. Interesting office supply/gift store has an excellent cafeteria in the basement, Britt's Cafe (faces Congress). Old bank an architectural gem designed by Stanford White.

5 Guardian Building. One of the country's great skyscrapers. Flamboyant 1929 Art Deco tower has a stunning main lobby and adjacent banking hall. Open weekdays; ask for nifty brochure.

6 John King Books. Big old glove factory now houses one of country's biggest used book stores. 1 million books plus collectibles like postcards and framed pictures.

7 Hart Plaza. Views of river, city, fountain-sculpture. Good free weekend entertainment from mid-May to Labor Day's great Montreux-Detroit Jazz Festival.

8 Renaissance Center. Huge & disorienting modern landmark includes large hotel, shops, and restaurants. Catch great view from the 72nd-floor steak house or 71st floor observation lounge.

9 DuMouchelle Gallery. Michigan's premiere auction gallery, featuring expensive possessions of the rich and sometimes famous.

10 Greektown & Trappers Alley. Downtown's liveliest, most colorful spot. Authentic old Greek bakeries and restaurants next to a beautiful 4-level festival marketplace.

11 Grand River art galleries. New focus of evolving downtown art scene. Sherry Washington Gallery shows top black artists.

12 Eastern Market. Hard-to-match mix of shops for cheese, meat, fish, poultry, spices, nuts, produce, wine plus open-air market. Bargains, selection, earthy atmosphere. Coffeehouse inside Rocky Peanut Co.

INFO SOURCES

◆ For a **downtown Detroit map** and metro Detroit **visitor packet,** or for information on attractions and events, call the What's Line, (313) 567-1170.

◆ For a **People Mover map** and attractive **Art in the Stations guide,** call (800) 541-RAIL.

◆ For a **Detroit parking guide** to lower-cost city-operated parking, call (313) 224-0300, or write Municipal Parking Department, 200 Civic Center, Detroit, MI 48226.

Hart Plaza

*At the historic site of Fort Pontchartrain,
it's a lively riverfront scene in the summer.*

Highlights of the past and present converge at this popular
riverfront gathering place. Eight acres of multi-level
paved park lead down from Jefferson Avenue to the
Detroit River and the very spot on which Cadillac built Fort
Pontchartrain in 1701. One side of the plaza looks out onto the
river, with views of the **Ambassador Bridge** and **Windsor**,
Ontario. On the other side is a view of Detroit's impressive **skyline**. The bright-painted antique **trolley cars** wait on Jefferson at
the side of **Mariners' Church** (page 202) between regular runs to
Grand Circus Park (page 215) from 10 a.m. to 6 p.m. The giant
sculptural fist at Woodward and Jefferson memorializes Joe
Louis, Detroit's famous Brown Bomber, who became the world
heavyweight boxing champion in 1938.

Hart Plaza is a splendid place to be in nice weather. On
weekdays at lunchtime it's crowded with downtown workers.
Regulars play chess at concrete tables near the **Dodge Fountain**,
by famed sculptor Isamu Noguchi. It's easy to be mesmerized by
the fountain's changing water patterns. Quite possibly you'll
catch a look at the perennially dapper Bulldog Joe. A well-known
Detroit character, he's the very embodiment of a man-about-
town of the 1920s, in a Panama hat, white gloves, ivory-headed
cane, and white spats.

From late May through September, Diamond Jack **tour boats**
leave from Hart Plaza on a
26-mile, two-hour narrated
tour. The cruise travels to
the St. Aubin Marina, under
the Belle Isle bridge, circles
Belle Isle, then moves down
the Canadian shoreline,

**The 1849 Mariners' Church,
just east of Hart Plaza, remains
the spiritual focus of a far-flung
maritime community.**

The Detroit riverfront, seen from Windsor sometime about 1980. Hart Plaza is the lit-up place between the Renaissance Center complex to the right and Cobo Hall, the low, dark complex to the left. On Hart Plaza's riverfront side was the site where the French nobleman Cadillac built a fort in 1701 to control the rich fur trade of the western Great Lakes.

passes under the Ambassador Bridge, and loops back along the U.S. side when it reaches Fort Wayne. Detroit maritime buffs from the Dossin Great Lakes museum helped put together the commentary. *Wed-Sun from late May until September at 2, 4, and 6 p.m; in September, Fri-Sun only. (313) 843-9376. $9/adults, $8/seniors, $6/kids under 16, kids under 5 free.*

Free Riverfront Festivals are held on selected weekends (Friday through Sunday) throughout the summer. Music, dance, food, and national talent characterize **ethnic and theme festivals** such as the World's Largest Free Circus (mid-June), the Latino World Festival (early July), the Motor City Praise Festival (late July), the Arab World Festival (early August), and the African World Festival (mid-August). The free **Montreux-Detroit Jazz Festival** on Labor Day weekend elicits raves from critics and fans. It's a wonderful glimpse of Detroit at its best – fabulous music and a mellow crowd. Other big, free events are the mid-May **Downtown Hoedown**, the world's largest free country music festival, and the **Detroit-Windsor International Freedom Festival** with fireworks just before the July 4 weekend.

*Hart Plaza is at the foot of Woodward between Jefferson and the Detroit River. People Mover stop: exit at Millender Center and walk across Jefferson or the RenCen skywalk. Call (313) 224-1184 weekdays 9-6 for a **Riverfront Festivals schedule**.*

Renaissance Center

A symbol of Detroit's attempt to bounce back,
this confusing complex has a stunning view.

The gigantic Renaissance Center complex, four cylindrical office towers grouped around a 73-story cylindrical hotel, looks all too much like a fortress intended to protect its occupants from neighboring vandals outside the gate. It's Detroit's tallest building and most recognizable landmark. The five-star view from the circular observation floor or the Summit Steak House is a real-life map of the Detroit River and its islands, up to Lake St. Clair and down almost to Lake Erie.

The project was spurred by the 1967 Detroit riot, which accelerated the exodus of whites from the city's center. Henry Ford II pushed it through, cajoling Ford suppliers and other major area businesses to invest the hundreds of millions to build the riverside complex. Like his grandfather and namesake, Ford had a deep if erratic idealistic streak. He felt the RenCen was essential to reverse the Motor City's decline.

The architect was John Portman, whose spectacular multi-story interior atriums in Hyatt Hotels in Atlanta and Los Angeles had revolutionized hotel design. When the RenCen opened in 1977, it was full of glamorous shops – Gucci, Cartier, Mark Cross – part of what was to lure suburbanites downtown.

But the RenCen quickly became notorious as a bewildering circular maze for casual visitors. Without memorable landmarks, the space connecting four look-alike round towers around the hotel proved disorienting. Monied suburbanites were not drawn to the forbidding, confusing place. Many luxury retailers, intended to be a big draw, pulled out, while the huge hotel suffered from a low occupancy rate. The RenCen came to symbolize to many not a renaissance but wrong-headed urban revitalization schemes cut off from the communities they were devised to serve. By 1983, the original investors had defaulted on their loans.

Today's RenCen is better but still confusing, and it still doesn't draw many suburbanites downtown. Nonetheless, the massive complex is credited with helping to launch the succeed-

ing wave of riverfront office and residential projects. The Ren-
Cen's 50-odd shops and service businesses and 23 or so eater-
ies have achieved a stable presence, due mainly to the 16,000
people who work for the companies with offices here.
Restaurants range from numerous fast-food outlets (some open
for breakfast) to the spectacular, 71st-story **Summit Steak
House & Lounge** (313-568-8600), with Tex-Mex, Japanese,
Greek, and seafood sit-down restaurants in-between. The
Renaissance Theaters (313-259-2370) have four screens.

The shops include Gebran's menswear, Gantos, Winkelman's, other women's wear stores, and a small assortment of
typical mall outlets for cookies, books, cards and gifts, plus a
complete range of office and visitor services. The Waldenbooks
here is very well run.

One remarkable RenCen attraction is the **view** from the
revolving 71st-floor **Summit Steak House** or the **observation
deck** just below it. A trip on the elevator to the lounge, without
a meal or drink, isn't cheap ($3/adults). But you can look out
from comfortable, pod-like lounges in many directions. It's especially interesting if you know Detroit streets and landmarks and
bring binoculars and a map. Of course, you can see pleasurable
boats and freighters, too. The view is especially impressive
toward sunset and at night. Lunches at the revolving restaurant
begin at just $5.95 and let you take in the view at your leisure.
Sunday brunch (10:30-2:30) is $18.95/adults, $8.95/children
ages 3-10, free/kids under 3. For a quick, **free view** from not
quite so high up, take one of the glass-sided elevators attached
to each office tower. From the 400 Tower you can see Hart
Plaza, downtown, and downriver.

E. Jefferson at Brush on the Detroit River. Open 7 a.m.-11 p.m.
***Shop hours** vary; most are generally open 10-6. Second-story
bridges across Jefferson connect with the Millender Center and
People Mover Station. **Information kiosk** in Jefferson Ave.
lobby. **Park** in Lot A or Lot B off Beaubien, east of Jefferson.
Rates encourage short-term and off-hours parking: $1 for 3 hours
weekdays 10-6, $2 week nights after 6, 12 hours for $2 weekends. To get a helpful **directory and map,** call (313) 568-5600
weekdays, write Renaissance Center Venture, 100 RenCen
#1400, Detroit 48243, or stop at the information kiosk in the Jef-
ferson Ave. lobby.*

UNDER THE RIVER TO CANADA . . . . . It's a bit eerie taking the dark, damp **Detroit-Windsor Tunnel** to Canada under the Detroit River — certainly not as scenic as the Ambassador Bridge downstream. The 5,135-foot-long tunnel was finished in 1930. The center 2000-foot section was created by sinking nine steel tubes, each 31 feet wide, in a trench 45 feet under the riverbed. At times there are considerable delays waiting to get through customs on either side. Weekday mornings are least busy. *Foot of Randolph St., just west of the Renaissance Center.*

AN ANCIENT DETROIT CHURCH ON THE RIVER . . . . . Adjacent to the RenCen and at the tunnel to Canada is **Mariners' Church,** founded in 1842 as an autonomous ("Free") Church by a bequest from Julia Anderson. By the authority of the will of Julia Anderson, the act of the State Legislature, and as noted in a recent and favorable court decision, Mariners' Church is "owned, controlled and directed by a self-perpetuating Board of Trustees," and *not* by the Episcopal diocese. The building dates from 1849. The church and its charismatic minister remain a focal point for sailors on freighters and for a sizable community of Great Lakes maritime aficionados.

Mariners' Church, "A House of Prayer for All People," uses the traditional Anglican liturgy. At the **Blessing of the Fleet** on the second Sunday of every March, dozens of ship masters and pleasure-craft owners bring the flags of their ships to be blessed. The closest Sunday to November 10 is a **memorial service** for the crew of the **Edmund Fitzgerald**, whose crew was first remembered in 1975 at Mariners' Church by the Rector's ringing the bell 29 times, as recorded in Gordon Lightfoot's "Ballad of the Edmund Fitzgerald." *170 E. Jefferson east of Woodward. (313) 259-2206. Guided tours by appointment. Open for casual visitors Mon thru Fri 10-5. Services Thurs noon, Sun 8:30 & 11.*

Greektown

*Long a Greek commercial and restaurant district,
this is Detroit's liveliest block.*

With its many Greek restaurants and the five-level
Trappers Alley shopping and restaurant complex, this
bustling, busy block of Monroe Street has long been one
of Detroit's most popular tourist attractions. It's one of the few
areas in Detroit where the 19th-century city holds its own.
Greektown, wrote *Detroit News* editor Martin Fischhoff, "is a success story right out of some urban planner's dream (though
planning had nothing to do with it). It's about the only place in
Detroit that's alive around the clock." Trappers Alley shops have
come and gone. But area developers Ted Gatzaros and Jim
Pappas have scored some successes with their beautiful and
conveniently located Atheneum Suite Hotel a block away at
Brush and Lafayette, and their popular New Orleans-style
Fishbone's Rhythm Kitchen on Monroc at Brush, in the
International Center Building. (Check out the long, tall waterfall
behind the restaurant!)

Now they're lobbying hard to establish Greek town as the
first downstate Indian gambling casino. But anti-gambling sentiment, backed by Detroit's powerful black churches, runs deep.
Even the efforts of longtime mayor Coleman Young to pass a vote
for casino gambling proved futile.

This area is the core of a Greek neighborhood going back to
1915, with its bakeries, grocery stores, and coffee houses where
a few old-timers still come to drink coffee and play cards. The
coffee houses are now tucked behind profitable video arcades. A
block south, at 349 Monroe is **The Old Shillelagh,** an Irish pub
with darts and weekend folk music (313-964-0007).

The neighborhood, like much of Detroit's east side, was originally German. The beautiful red-brick **St. Mary's Catholic
Church** complex at 646 Monroe houses the city's third-oldest
Catholic parish, dating to 1835. Almost as old is the congregation of the **Second Baptist Church** at 441 Monroe, founded by
13 former slaves in 1836. Its first pastor was an antislavery
activist, its basement the last stop on Michigan's underground

railroad.

Overpopulation caused hard times that drove over a fourth of the Greek labor force off their native rocky farmlands between 1890 and 1920. Greek men found their way to then-booming industrial towns throughout Michigan, from Detroit and Flint to Dowagiac and Calumet. They parlayed earnings from factory and construction work into small businesses opening up in a rapidly urbanizing America: shoe repair, groceries, rooming houses and downtown commercial property, and above all, confectioneries and restaurants. Greeks did it so quickly and successfully that it's hard to believe that they were mostly farmers from primitive Greek villages thrust into a totally unfamiliar environment.

Greektown families have long since moved onward and upward. They are scattered throughout the metro area. But many Greek-Americans still patronize Greektown establishments. Restaurant menus feature gyros, shish kebob, spinach pie, Greek salads, egg-lemon soup, rice pudding, baklava, and the like. Locals joke that it's really all prepared in one kitchen, though the new Cyprus Taverna at 512 Monroe is setting a new standard for Greek restaurants on the street.

For restaurants, see *Hunts' Restaurants and Lodgings of Michigan*. Greektown points of interest in addition to restaurants are:

✦ **Trappers Alley** is a pleasant place to wander around. The rich brick facades of old buildings are juxtaposed with crisp, colorful tiles and lush foliage. These buildings once were part of the huge tannery operations of Traugott Schmidt and Sons, one of the country's largest tanneries in the late 19th century. A leading attraction here is the **Blue Nile** Ethiopian restaurant. The complex is struggling to maintain a strong array of interesting shops. At this point, noteworthy Trappers Alley stores include several fashion boutiques, the **Jill Perette Gallery**, with attractive African-inspired gifts on the second level, and on the third level, **Michigan Memories**, with Up North sweatshirts and regional books, oven mitts and cutting boards shaped like Michigan's mitten, and long-lasting fragrant candles made by the proprietors.

Tucked away on the east end of the third level, **Urban Park** (313-963-5445) is a rambling, nonprofit art gallery with separate galleries clustered around two open courtyards. It is devoted to mounting changing shows of local, regional, and national artists who are often on hand to answer questions about their work. Music performances and poetry readings are also occasionally held here. It's well worth checking out for the art *and* for the lively bulletin board and handouts on the local arts, music, and coffeehouse scene. Nearby, **Comix Oasis** puts together arresting windows of pop art and collectibles. Another intriguing window display is at **Amie's D'Elegance Unique Doll Shop and Accessories** across the way, geared to serious collectors of African-American dolls. By appointment only; (313) 393-3547.

On the ground level, the **Athens Bookstore** (313-963-4490) is *the* place to find Greek-language publications, cassettes of Greek music, ornate coffee urns, and gaudy religious icons, along with lots of tacky Detroit souvenirs.

Trappers Alley is on Monroe at Beaubien, five blocks north of the Renaissance Center and 2 blocks west of I-75. Follow I 75 South to 375 South and take the Lafayette exit. If you turn right on Lafayette and go up 1 1/2 blocks, you'll come to an entrance for the parking lot located behind Trappers Alley. The Greektown People Mover station is on the third level of Trappers Alley. (313) 963-5445. Mon-Thurs 10-9, Fri & Sat 10-11, Sun noon-7,

♦ **International Center of Apparel Design.** The second-floor showrooms of clothing, jewelry, and accessories designers are just getting off to their first full season. Look for Caribbean, African, and other ethnic influences. *Detroit Free Press* business writer Anthony Neely thinks this could develop into an expanding local crafts economy. *Main entrance at 1045 Beaubien at Monroe. (313) 963-3357. Tues-Wed 11-7, Thurs-Sat 11-8, Sun 12-5.*

♦ **Astoria Pastry Shop.** The spiffy new location of this old Greek pastry shop has been expanded to appeal to strolling Greektown crowds, with ice cream, cappuccino, and quite a few tables. The spinach pie is a nice snack if you don't feel like buying an entire meal at nearby restaurants. Crusty yet soft Greek breads are made for sopping up salad oils and pan juices. All the traditional Greek and Middle Eastern filo-honey-nut pastries are here, some with a new twist, like chocolate baklava. Astoria offers a wide range of baked goods, including American favorites and Italian standards like toasted biscotti (some dipped in chocolate and walnut) and cannoli. *541 Monroe. (313) 963-9603. Sun-Thurs 8 a.m.-11:00 p.m., Fri-Sat 8 a.m.-1:30 a.m.*

♦ **Athens Grocery and Bakery.** Both Greektown groceries enjoy good reputations among Greek-Americans, and they smell wonderfully of fresh bread (in the morning) and spices. The crusty loaves, soft in the middle, sell for under a dollar apiece. The

Athens' old-fashioned front window, filled with neatly arranged groceries, nicely balances Greektown's neon glitz. *527 Monroe. (313) 961-1149. Mon-Thurs 9-9, Fri & Sat 9-11, Sun 9-7.*

◆ **Monroe Grocery and Bakery.** Open the beat-up wood screen door, and you feel you're in a time warp. Ornate, shiny tins of olive oil and imports have a turn-of-the-century look, while pistachios, Greek cheeses, olives, pastas, and filo dough are sold in bulk at the counter. *573 Monroe. (313) 964-9642. Sun-Thurs 9:30-8:30, Fri & Sat until 10 or 11.*

*Greektown is on Monroe St. between St. Antoine & Beaubien. Follow 75 South to 375 South and take the Lafayette exit. Most restaurants open 11 a.m.- 2 a.m. or later, 7 days a week. **Park** at large, 24-hour city structure just east of Greektown, entered off Monroe or Macomb. **People Mover Stations:** Greektown (Monroe and Beaubien), Bricktown (Beaubien and Fort).*

GROCERIES IN GREEKTOWN . . . . . . Hours at Greektown's two old-world grocery stores are so long ('til 9 p.m. at the earliest) that you can both dine and shop for groceries. Greek bread, cheese, and wine can be the center of simple, delicious meals. **Greek feta cheese**, made from sheep's milk, is richer and quite unlike the domestic variety. Creamy white **kasseri cheese** is like a mild cheddar. It can be cut into cubes, dredged in seasoned flour, and pan-fried 'til it's soft. Greeks serve it with lemon, crusty Greek bread, and a **red wine** like the dry red from the highly recommended Nemea (pronounced "nuh-MAY-uh") region. An excellent, very light white wine is made by Boutari. Both are about $7 a bottle. **Retsina wine**, flavored with resin, is admittedly an acquired taste even when served correctly (very, very cold). Greeks like to drink it with fish, or with olives, bread, and fresh tomatoes.

THE CRIMINAL JUSTICE SYSTEM AT WORK . . . . . Criminal mystique has been one of Detroit's hottest cultural exports lately, thanks to area detective writers Elmore Leonard and Loren Estleman, who set many of their stories here. **Detroit Recorder's Court** is where Leonard and Estleman get much of their material, and where Harrison Ford hung out to pick up atmosphere for the movie *Presumed Innocent.* A model of efficiency under difficult conditions, the court recently won a prestigious national award for its operation. "Watching criminal investigations in Recorder's Court is better than going to the movies, and it's free," says a Leonard character. *Frank Murphy Hall of Justice, 1441 St. Antoine south of Gratiot, a block northwest of Greektown.*

Detroit People Mover

*Get a spectacular bird's-eye view
of downtown Detroit on one of the country's
most lavish public transportation systems.*

This elevated rail system runs in a 2.9-mile loop around downtown. It offers extraordinary views of the central city, the Detroit River, and Windsor. Even in winter, it's a memorable ride. As a bonus, big, colorful works of art make it an adventure to enter the platforms in each of the 13 stations. Call the People Mover for a splendid brochure on **"Art in the Stations."** Especially memorable are Stephen Antonakos's neon at Greektown, Charles McGee's African-inspired Noah's Ark at the Broadway station, and rich, dynamic designs in Pewabic tile by Tom Phardel and Al Loving, Jr.

The People Mover is the most expensive public transportation project in history. The 2.9 miles cost federal and state tax-

Vibrant art, mostly in tile and richly colorful, makes the People Mover experience even more exciting — alternating views of art and slice-of-life reality as you look into the buildings and streets along the route. Art is in each station. Pewabic tile is often featured in this important and successful public art project. Here arc (left) Al Loving Jr.'s subtly colorful work in Millender Center and Kirk Newman's hurrying commuters in the Michigan Avenue station.

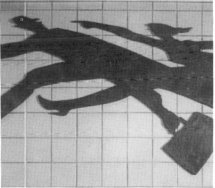

payers a whopping $200 million, vastly more than initial projec-
tions. Unfortunately, there are one-third fewer riders than projected, requiring the financially strapped city to subsidize it
heavily.

Still, the People Mover is a visitor's delight: beautifully
designed, clean, safe, and frequently patrolled. It's a smooth-
working system which gives the rider an unparalleled view of the
glories and desolations of downtown Detroit. The entire loop
takes only 15 minutes. Cars come at least every two minutes.
Maps with all the stations and what's near them are available in
each car.

You may want to make several trips to take it all in: the
beauty of the aqua Detroit River on a sunny day, the ornate
1920s skyscrapers, the VIPs' cars double-parked for lunch at
the elite Detroit Club, historic Grand Circus Park, the once
proud and now sadly abandoned hotels and office buildings on
the north part of the loop, the towering Renaissance Center,
lively Bricktown and Greektown. Special highlights: the swing
out over the Detroit River by the Joe Louis Arena and the up-
close glimpse of City-County Building employees at their desks.

*Downtown Detroit (see map for route). 1-800-541-7245; from
Detroit, 962-RAIL. Current operating hours: Mon-Thurs 7 a.m.-11
p.m., Fri 7 a.m.-midnight, Sat 9 a.m.-midnight, Sun noon-8 p.m.
Fare: 50¢, children 5 and under free. (Call to confirm; budget cuts
may necessitate changes.) Handicap-accessible by elevator, esca-
lator, and wheelchair lifts.*

FOR A HANDY PEOPLE MOVER MAP . . . . . with clear indications of nearby destinations, call (800) 541-7245 or, from Detroit, 962-RAIL. Ask for the
"Art in the Stations" brochure while you're at it.

Guardian Building

One of the country's most remarkable Art Deco skyscraper is an original visual feast.

This colorful, richly decorated Art Deco skyscraper, finished in 1929, is a flamboyant banking tribute to the go-go years of the 1920s. It also is linked to the financial excesses of that time, for its occupant and owner, Guardian National Bank, was the very first in a nationwide domino-like chain of banks to close in 1933, greatly intensifying the national Depression.

The notched Aztec facade is unusual in itself. The 32-story building is faced with specially made reddish-orange bricks, which bands of green and white tiles enliven. The bricks, less costly than the granite or limestone exteriors of most skyscrapers of the era, allowed architect Wirt Rowland to use the savings on a variety of spectacular visual effects, designed to make the building noticeable and inviting.

Most stunning are the **main lobby** and the adjacent **banking room** half a story up. Over the main entrance is a half dome covered in colorful tiles from Detroit's famous Pewabic Pottery (page 280). Concealed in the 1950s, the dome has since been restored by the Guardian's present owner-occupant, Michigan Consolidated Gas. The walls of the main lobby are blood-red Numibian marble. Rowland had to reopen an African mine to get such a vivid natural hue. The lobby's mosaic mural was designed by noted artist Ezra Winter. The ceiling of the main banking room is painted on canvas, behind which is a horsehair mat to mute sound in the vast room. Ask at the lobby informa-

Blue, green, and red tiles in geometric Indian motifs decorate not only the Guardian Building's outside entrance but its roof line and lobby. Inside a Michigan map dominates the grand banking hall.

tion desk for an interesting historical **brochure** on the building.

Ernest Kanzler, brother-in-law and close friend of Henry Ford's son, Edsel, built the Guardian Building. His Guardian Group became the major banking power in Detroit. Edsel Ford put millions of his and Ford Motor Company's money into Kanzler's banking syndicate, So successful was this group that there was even talk that Detroit would overtake Chicago as the financial center of the Midwest. Then the 1929 stock market crash put increasing strain on the overextended bank. Despite a personal plea from President Hoover, Henry Ford refused to bail the bank out at a critical juncture, even though his son lost up to $20 million with its failure.

500 Griswold at Congress. (313) 965-2430. Mon-Fri 9-5.

🌲🌲🌲

**OTHER FINE DOWNTOWN ARCHITECTURE FROM THE EARLY 20TH
CENTURY . . . . .** The 1925 **Buhl Building** feels like a church, a true temple
of commerce, with the dark, enclosed, rich effect of heavy medieval masonry
and Romanesque decorative embellishments. Italian bronzes accent the
marble lobby. *Southwest corner, Griswold at Congress. Open Mon-Fri . . . . .*
In the 47-story **Penobscot Building**, finished in 1928, architect Wirt Rowland designed one of Detroit's most endearingly appealing buildings.
Setbacks above the 30th floor form an interesting cubistic pattern topped by
an observation deck (now closed) and a big, illuminated ball, once a hallmark of the city. Inside, the warm-colored marble floors feature geometric
designs, with Indian eagles on the elevator doors and mailboxes. The interior
shops include a **C&L Books** (formerly Doubleday, now owned by its longtime
manager and a co-worker) and **John T. Woodhouse Sons** tobacconist,
whose wood-inlaid interior is a period delight. In the basement, the
Epicurean Cafe is a big place with breakfasts and lunches that are a terrific
deal. *Corner of Griswold and Fort. (313) 961-8800. Mon-Fri 8 a.m.-6 p.m. . . .*
. . The former People's State Bank is Detroit's only building designed by the
famous Beaux Arts architects McKim, Mead and White. It dates from 1900
and is now occupied by **Silver's**, a stylish office supply firm. Balustrades,
allegorical sculpture, and two Ionic columns make it appropriately bank-
like, but huge arched windows let in lots of light. Today the dignified banking floor showcases gifts and accessories, plus room arrangements of office
furniture. It feels a little like a museum of serious good design. The gifty,
impulse-oriented lower level (opening onto Congress) is jazzy, with trendier
items, cards, candles, and good sales on glassware and dishes. In the rear is
very popular cafeteria style **Britt's Cafe**. *(313) 963-4866. Enter on Congress
at Shelby. Mon-Fri 8:30-3 p.m. Silver's main entrance is on Fort.*

Fox Theatre
and the Theater District

A restored Siamese-Byzantine-Indian picture palace
anchors the revival of one of America's
great entertainment centers from the 1920s.

Detroit's extraordinary auto boom decade of the 1920s resulted in an unusual concentration of theaters. The city's explosive population growth coincided with the era of palatial movie theaters put up across America by Hollywood studio owners. Detroit's Grand Circus Park area attracted many opulent theaters, each designed to outdo the last. None was more utterly and unabashedly gaudy than the 5,000-seat Fox Theatre on Woodward, opened in 1928 and restored in 1988. Part of the nationwide 250-theater Fox chain, this picture palace, built for $6 million, was the flagship of the empire and the pinnacle of Detroit architect C. Howard Crane's successful career as one of the nation's preeminent designers of movie theaters. (The Detroit Fox was later duplicated by St. Louis's Fox Theatre.)

The eclectic Asian interior was designed by owner William Fox's wife, Eve Leo. She humorously called it "Siamese Byzantine." The six-story lobby was intended to look like an ancient temple in India. In the main auditorium you can see a two-ton stained-glass chandelier. Walls feature peacocks, serpents, Buddhas, Chinese tomb guardians, Greek masks, Egyptian lions, and other motifs from Hindu, Persian, Indian, Chinese, and southeast Asian art. This era of unbridled opulence was not to last long. Fox lost control of his theaters during the Depression, which left him $91 million in debt.

The Fox was designed for both movies and live performances. A careful $15 million restoration was completed in 1988 thanks to hometown boosters Mike and Marian Ilitch, owners of Little Caesar's Pizza, the Detroit Tigers baseball team, the Red Wings hockey team, and the Detroit Rockers soccer team. Now the Fox is packing in crowds with over 250 acts a year — a heartening boon for a troubled downtown abandoned by major retailers. Ilitch business and family interests have established North

America's third Second City comedy troupe in the building next door and launched three new restaurants in and around the Fox: **Tres Vite**, superchef Jimmy Schmidt's sophisticated yet rustic Italian restaurant in the Fox office building; **America's Pizza Cafe**, where specialty pizzas are made in a wood-fired oven, also in the Fox building; and **Risata**, a contemporary Italian restaurant in the Second City building.

For several years in a row, the Fox has been the top-grossing venue in the U.S. Wide-ranging attractions have included Barbara Streisand, David Copperfield, the New York City Ballet, *Grease*, Bonnie Raitt, *Gone with the Wind*, and President Bill Clinton speaking to the G-7 economic conference. The Ilitches have renovated the 10-story office building attached to the Fox as the world headquarters of Little Caesar's, making the firm the first major corporation to move to Detroit in over 30 years.

Now Mike Ilitch, as owner of the Detroit Tigers, is trying to build a new Tiger Stadium in "Foxtown," across Woodward from the theater. The plan has been controversial because of the state

Little Caesar pizza baron Mike Ilitch with his wife and partner, Marian, and daughter Denise in the Fox's fabulously ornate foyer. Deals between the Ilitches' organizations and the city of Detroit have been the prime force behind revitalizing downtown Detroit. Ilitch wants to build a new Tiger Stadium near the Fox.

tax money it would take to complete the big project.

Other theater restorations are underway or talked about. Most dramatically, the **Michigan Opera Theater** (313-963-7474) is transforming the water-damaged wreck of the delicately detailed Grand Circus Theater into its future home – a massive and meticulous restoration project.

All this has happened because of Detroit real estate executive/investor Chuck Forbes and his long-held dream to save the grand theater district he had loved growing up in Detroit. First Forbes bought numerous threatened theaters, including the Fox. Brought together by the city of Detroit with bigger investors, like the Ilitches, he made deals to assure the theaters' preservation and reuse. His own flagship is the intimate, stunningly restored 1927 **Gem Theater**, across Woodward from the Fox. On a bigger scale, Forbes's 1925 State Theater, half a block down Woodward from the Fox, has cabaret seating, a 64-screen video wall, and a dance floor. Designed by C. Howard Crane in an opulent Renaissance style, the theater is now used for concerts and plays, dancing, and private parties and meetings.

Here's information about attending events at current theater district venues. For freeway directions to the Theater District, see end of theater entries.

◆ **Fox Theatre.** *Woodward at Montcalm at the northwest edge of downtown. (313) 396-7600. Parking (maximum daily or evening rate $5) is off Woodward across the street or in the eight-story parking deck behind the theater off Montcalm.*

◆ **Second City Theatre.** Young actor/comedians on an empty stage create topical sketches and improvise. Second City developed talent and set the style for *Saturday Night Live;* the father of Gilda Radner, one of its most talented alums, managed a Grand Circus Park hotel a few blocks from here. *Woodward at Montcalm, next to the Fox. (313) 965-2222.*

◆ **Gem Theatre.** Splendidly detailed restoration of the intimate, 450-seat Spanish Revival theater built for the 20th Century Club. The Gem now books long-running revues like "The All-Night Strut" and has also had success with a play by movie star/playwright Jeff Daniels, launched in the Purple Rose Theater in his hometown of Chelsea. In the early 1960s, actor George C. Scott founded and directed a theater company at the Gem, then known as the Vanguard. *58 East Columbia across Woodward from the Fox. (313) 963-9800.*

◆ **State Theater.** Call (313) 961-5450 for concert and nightclub information. *On Woodward a block east of the Fox.*

◆ **Music Hall Center for the Performing Arts.** This elegant theater, built as a legitimate theater in 1928 by Dodge widow and heiress Matilda Dodge Wilson, now books a wide variety of music, dance, and dramatic performances. (313) 963-7680. Weekends it's home to the very popular **Detroit Youtheatre**, with Saturday children's programs and the Wiggle Club on Sundays (both October through May). *350 Madison at Witherell on Grand Circus Park. (313) 963-7663.*

Freeway directions to Woodward and the Theater District: From I-94 east or westbound, take the Woodward exit, go south on Woodward (toward downtown), theater is on the right after 2 miles. From I-75 southbound, take Mack Ave. exit, go right onto Mack, go about 3/4 mile to Woodward, turn south onto Woodward (toward downtown); the Fox is on the right in 1/2 mile. From I-75 northbound, take Woodward exit, follow signs to Fox Center, taking two immediate right hand turns and you'll see the theater. From I-96, go toward Detroit to I-75 north and follow directions above. From Lodge Freeway, take I-75 north and follow directions above.

A STATELY DOWNTOWN PARK . . . . . is **Grand Circus Park** on Woodward and Adams, a block southeast of the Fox. Its semi-circular shape was created by Judge Augustus Woodward's neo Parisian, circle-and-spoke plan for rebuilding Detroit after an 1805 fire. Once a jewel, the park remains an interesting blend of old and new sculpture and pleasant trees, set against a backdrop of handsome buildings from downtown Detroit's apogee between 1915 and 1925. The staffed underground **parking garage** is reasonably safe, inexpensive, and never full.

THE GRAYSTONE JAZZ MUSEUM . . . . . has moved downtown to 1521 Broadway, just down from Grand Circus Park. Founder/director James Jenkins is enthusiastically devoted to keeping Detroit's great jazz tradition alive with concerts, book signings, a film series, and the videos, memorabilia, and instruments you can see here. Named after the celebrated Graystone Ballroom. Detroit jazz greats include Betty Carter, Donald Burrd, Sonny Stitts, Milt Jackson, and Barry Harris. *Open Tues-Fri 10-5, Sat 11-4. (313) 963-3813. $2.*

Downtown Detroit shops and galleries

Tucked away in quaint, odd corners —
established galleries and creative new shops

Contrary to the popular impression, quality retailing in downtown Detroit isn't dead. Urban pioneers and holdovers are just scattered in pockets that can be hard for outsiders to find. Seeking out the city's half-hidden jewels can be a tonic to the jaded, because doing business in the city, much more than in malls, is still about personal relationships. Downtown Detroit in the 1990s is a village — a friendly, cozy village where everybody knows one another, said longtime downtown women's fashion retailer Lynn Portnoy when she reluctantly decided to move to Royal Oak. What's unsettling is that the village occupies buildings erected when downtown Detroit was the hub of a booming early 20th-century metropolis. Still, out-of-towners can enjoy discovering these diverse spots.

Another point about shopping downtown: shopping in the city of Detroit is one thing any consumer can do to make a positive difference, albeit a small one, in the great urban problems of our day. Increased revenue builds local employment, adds revenue to city coffers with taxes, and preserves historic buildings by keeping their tenants. That's the way diehard Detroiters think — the committed urbanites who always shop local whenever they possibly can. Detroit's black churches and business groups organize Shop

Elaborate bronzes, furniture, silver, and such are auctioned off monthly at DuMouchelle Art Galleries, along with occasional choice collections of more interesting things. The showroom on Jefferson across from the RenCen offers a fascinating look at the ornate trappings of success from an earlier generation.

Detroit campaigns to combat the widespread, understandable, yet destructive preference of African-Americans for brand-name, shopping-center retailing which is almost inevitably suburban.

However, a new mood has been developing since Dennis Archer became mayor in 1994. Downtown's specialty retailers are busier on weekends, not just with their regular customers but with new ones, too. They can only attribute the change to a new mood of confidence and enthusiasm for Detroit brought by the new mayor. Another promising trend: more artists with studio-lofts right downtown and near it, and a burgeoning showcase for Detroit-area art in five galleries initiated by Christine Biagas in a most attractive space on Grand River at Library behind the old Hudson's, owned by her and her husband, a professor of bicultural studies at Wayne State. Artists' energy and artists' visions of urban life have been the initial chapters of more than a few urban success stories.

This chapter focuses on scattered and unusual specialty shops and galleries. Areas are arranged from southeast near the river to northwest at the Theater District. For an overview of all downtown shopping, see the attached note.

◆ **DuMouchelle Art Galleries.** The region's premier auction spot, this is where the furniture, art, jewelry, and bibelots of the very rich are put on the block. Once Detroit's first Cadillac dealership, the building has big display windows today full of things like chandeliers (over 60 are typically on hand), porcelain, paintings, cut crystal, silver, rugs, and furniture. These are priced items for sale right from the floor.

Auctions take place once a month, usually the second or third week. The event attracts collectors from all over the world. Items may be inspected the week before the auction from 9:30 to 5:30. The three-day auction begins Friday at 6:30 p.m., Saturday at 11 a.m., and Sunday at noon. Items go for anywhere from $10 to $200,000. A Tiffany lamp recently sold for $49,000. A silk Oriental rug from the Shah of Iran's palace was picked up for $60,000. And the high bid for an Andy Warhol "slipper collage" was $10,000. *409 E. Jefferson at Brush across from the RenCen. (313) 963-6255. Mon-Sat 9:30-5:30. Free valet parking on auction dates. Pick up a **free illustrated brochure** for the upcoming auction here or at the Hart Plaza visitor information booth.*

◆ **Muccioli Studio Gallery.** An elegantly renovated Italianate townhouse serves as the studios of jeweler Nate Muccioli and his mother, Anna Muccioli, both graduates of the Center for Creative

Studies. She's a painter and sculptor; he does custom creative jewelry and uses the gold and stones in customers' old jewelry in new designs. *511 Beaubien near Greektown. (313) 962-4700. Tues-Fri 11-6, Sat 11-4.*

◆ **Broadway at Gratiot** has long been a center of men's clothing, and a half a dozen good shoestores and menswear stores remain. The range of styles is enormous, from the carefully elegant to the urban hip. **The Broadway** at 1247 Broadway is loaded with designer names, leather coats, and beautifully accessorized displays — the GQ look. It's favored by style-conscious men, including famous rock and sports stars and occasional drug dealers like the one assassinated in the store itself. Despite that incident, it's a friendly place, with terrific sales. *(313) 963-2171. Mon-Thurs 9:30-6 p.m., to 7 on Fri & Sat.* Across Gratiot at 1307 Broadway, **Henry the Hatter** is in its 97th year. "Everything that's made, we carry," claims its owner, including $8 wool berets, British silk hats, Western hats, and the flat-top black hat with a snap brim ($65) favored by jazz great Dexter Gordon, a favorite with women and men. *(313) 962-0970. Mon-Sat 9-6.* A new addition to the area: **Abraham's Coffee Exchange**, a coffeehouse that opens around 9:30 or 10 a.m. and closes around 10 p.m. Monday through Friday. *225 Gratiot. (313) 965-1213.*

◆ **On Grand River at Library,** two blocks toward Woodward from Harmonie Park, a gallery center with lots of surprises is developing behind the old Hudson's. The **Sherry Washington Gallery** represents three internationally acclaimed African-American painters, Benny Andrews, Richard Mayhew, and William T. Williams, as well as Shirley Woodson, Charles Burwell, David Driskell, and David Fludd, all with national reputations and all of African descent. Big windows and a splendidly restored Beaux Arts building make this a fine place to look at art. *(313) 961-4500. Open Tues-Fri 10-5, Sat 12-6, Sun & Mon by appointment.*

Kitty-corner from it at 35 East Grand River, **Gallery Biegas** presents an eclectic mix of established artists from around the world and emerging artists in a striking modernistic former bank building. Occasional one-person shows highlight artists from other countries. *(313) 961-0634. Tues-Fri 12-6, Sat 12-5.* Building owners Christine and Miguel Biagas have reached out to enable several other galleries to open in the adjoining storefronts. "We envision a gallery complex as a forum for local artists, for new artists, for nationally and internationally known artists," she says. Energy is something she greatly values, sometimes over polish and maturity.

Here, after 18 months in limbo, the respected **Detroit Focus Gallery** has found a home. The artist-run, nonprofit gallery shows the work of established and new artists, including some big environmental installations, in shows decided by its exhibition committee. No media are excluded. *33 E. Grand River. (313) 965-3245. Tues-Fri 12-6, Sat 12-5.*

At the **International Artists Gallery**, another Biagas' tenant, partners Julian Chiu (a Romanian painter) and Richard Griesbeck show work by American and international artists, thus far from East Africa, Hungary, Romania, and Russia. *27 E. Grand River. (313) 961-1188. Thurs-Sat 12-5.* The final gallery in the Biagas's building is **AC, T** (that stands for Artists' Cooperative, The). AC,T's anti-elitist philosophy is that it's up to the artists, not to a jury or director, to decide what and when they are ready to show. *29 E. Grand River. (313) 961-4336. Thurs-Sat 12-5.* If you're doing downtown galleries, don't forget the interesting **Urban Park** in Trappers Alley (page 202).

◆ In the **Harmonie Park** area, two blocks east of the Broadway People Mover station, a fountain and park occupy one of the odd triangles created by Judge Woodward's circle-and-spokes street layout after the 1805 Detroit fire. Street people sit in the park; creative shops are scattered nearby. The area's longtime anchor, the Detroit Artists Market has moved to Stroh River Place, freeing up its large, two-level space at 1452 Randolph for the **Dell Pryor Galleries** *(313-963-5977; Tues-Sat 11-5).* As a widow with six children, Pryor built up Cluttered Corners antiques in Greektown using her interior design background and her love of the old Greektown's artistic ambiance. Then her charming old alleyway was developed into the rehabbed Trappers Alley. The Attic Theater and later Pryor herself had to move. Harmonie Park, with its long history as a local arts center, seemed a logical new home for her store. It mixes unusual, reasonably priced antiques with contemporary crafts, all displayed in striking room settings. Also on hand: interesting estate and modern jewelry, including African-face cameos.

Now, ironically, upscale renovations have shunted out Harmonie Park's resident studios and performing spaces. Of all the artistic enterprises, only Pryor remains. The extra room and mezzanine wall space have enabled Pryor to add a fine arts

Hopeful sign: Pam Duvall in front of her charming gift shop on John R at Elizabeth, a block from the Fox. After downtown retailing's precipitous decline, scattered shops and a gallery area behind the old Hudson's may portend a modest renewal geared to the arts.

gallery to her store. Her daughter Sharon, back from New York where she was a freelance photographer for the *Village Voice* and a photo editor for *Essence* magazine, organizes shows of contemporary painters, sculptors, photographers, and other artists. *1452 Randolph, across the way on Centre at Randolph. (313) 963-5977. Tues-Sat 11-5.*

Architects Schervish Vogel Merz, who helped orchestrate the successful revival of Rivertown as an entertainment district, have moved to the old Harmonie Hall and acquired rights to much area property. They have rehabbed upper-level office and apartment space and plan to bring restaurants to the area.

Half a block south from Harmonie Park, **Spectacles** is the quintessence of cool, Spike Lee-style urban hip. It features pricey Ts, sweats, jackets, and caps with designs from his movies. Other sportswear, jewelry, accessories, leather goods, and shades are also on hand. *230 E. Grand River. (313) 963-6886.*

Mon-Sat 11-6 except Fri to 7.

◆ **Along Washington Boulevard**, designed about 1915 to be the Paris of Detroit and now a poignant shadow of its former glory, two upscale apparel stores stand out that are "fashion-oriented but not trendy." Buyer Meta Fluker-Yett says, "We buy New York-inspired clothes for fashion staying power." Her **Rio Boutique** offers contemporary women's clothes and accessories for play, career, and after 5. Image consulting and free makeup consultation are extra services offered to customers. *222 West Grand River at Washington Blvd. Times Square People Mover Station. (313) 961-6056. Mon-Sat 10-6.* **Rio Kids** offers cleanly styled, contemporary clothes for infants through size 14, boys and girls. Kids love the play area with videos. Right now Guess is "on fire," but less widely known lines set Rio Kids apart from department stores. *1258 Washington Blvd., kitty corner from the Rio Boutique. (313) 963-0180. Mon-Sat 10:30-5:30.*

◆ Facing **Grand Circus Park**, the David Whitney Building has unfortunately lost many interesting tenants in its beautiful arcaded spaces. But on the other side of the park, east on Adams from the Central Methodist Church, the church-sponsored **Swords into Plowshares** peace art gallery and adjoining thrift shop are worth checking out. The gallery space permits some passionate multimedia explorations of the themes of war and peace that can be very moving. *45 E. Adams. Tues, Thurs, & Sat 11-3. For info, call Central Methodist at (313) 965-5422.*

◆ **On John R at Elizabeth**, two blocks northeast of the Fox. **Twenty One 10 Elizabeth's** is a tucked-away treasure, charmingly cluttered with interesting jewelry, baskets, pottery, stationery, and cards — multi-cultural in origin, arranged with a gentle sort of Victorian flair. There's so much to see, you might easily miss the nifty rubber stamps and beads for necklaces and earrings. A friendly, savvy staff makes this a good stop for scoping out downtown happenings. *2110 John R at Elizabeth. (313) 964-2102. Mon-Sat 11-5.*

◆ **Little Foxes.** This tiny, luxuriously layered gift shop/flower shop behind Tres Vite restaurant in the Fox Theatre Building is worth checking out not just for the sterling jewelry, crystal, cards, and gifts, but for the miniature fountain and beautiful, ivy festooned ceiling paintings. *2211 Woodward at Montcalm. (313) 983-6202. Tues-Fri 10-6. Also open about 2 hours prior to shows on weekends.*

FOR DETROIT EVENTS INFORMATION . . . . . and a visitor packet, call the 24-hour **What's Line**, (313) 567-1170. . . . . The **Visitor Information Center** near the RenCen and Hart Plaza is in front of Ford Auditorium off Jefferson at the foot of Woodward. It's open 9-5 Mon-Fri and for special events.

A TREASURE FOR SERIOUS FILM FANS. . . . . The **Detroit Film Theater** shows high-caliber films Friday through Sunday that haven't been seen locally. The plush auditorium in the Detroit Institute of Arts boasts excellent acoustics and technical equipment, and there's even a bar for socializing and refreshments. At $5 a ticket, it's an outstanding entertainment value. Call (313) 833-2323 for program information and to get on the mailing list.

JAZZ FOR EARLY BIRDS . . . . . . Clean, well-run, not too smoky, no cover, and good, reasonably-priced down-home food like pork chop sandwiches and macaroni. The crowd is mixed, and the atmosphere is wonderfully friendly. Most music clubs are never as organized as **Bo-Mac's Lounge** at 281 Gratiot between Broadway and Randolph, around the corner from Harmonie Park. It's open from 11 a.m. to 2 a.m., and Thursday through Sunday the live music starts at 8 p.m. (313) 961-5152.

OF INTEREST NEAR DuMOUCHELLE . . . . . A beautifully renovated Italianate townhouse, the **Beaubien House**, is a good first stop for people interested in making their own tour of downtown and Rivertown historic architecture. The historic home is now headquarters of the Michigan Society of Architects, and several **free pamphlets and maps on area architecture** are available. In the elegant front parlor are worthwhile changing exhibits related to architecture or people involved in architecture in Michigan. *553 E. Jefferson just east of Beaubien. (313) 965-4100. Mon-Fri 8-5.*

OTHER SHOPPING IN AND NEAR DOWNTOWN. . . . . The **Financial District** centered at the historic office towers at Griswold, Congress, and Fort has the outstanding **Silver's** gift and office store (page 211) and a very friendly bookstore, but they're only open Monday through Friday. . . . . The **RenCen** (page 200) has dozens of chain stores geared to officeworkers and an exceptionally good Waldenbooks. . . . . . For **Trappers' Alley, Greektown**, and the beautiful new **International Design Center**, see page 205. . . . . **John King Books** (page 224) on downtown's south edge is a big draw for many people, as is **Eastern Market** and its wholesale-retail specialty shops (page 226). . . . . . **Woodward Avenue**, once Detroit's equivalent of Fifth Avenue, isn't just wig shops and discount stores. There's a big, bustling **Winkelman's** at 1448 Woodward near Grand Circus Park, and a **Sibley's**

Shoes for men just north of the park. . . . . Not far from downtown, the **New Center** has a **Crowley's** department store, a **Winkelman's**, and a **Waldenbooks** in its small mall, and the stunning **Detroit Gallery of Contemporary Crafts** and the **Poster Gallery** are in the amazing Fisher Building (page 243). No mall could hold a candle to it for atmosphere. Two leading luggage stores are in the New Center area. . . . Then there are the **museum shops** at museums from Motown to the DIA, from the Dossin Great Lakes Museum to the Museum of African-American History. . . . . Out Jefferson, near the river, are the **Detroit Artists' Market** (page 266) and **Pewabic Pottery** (page 280). Some visitors will enjoy the Mexican groceries in Mexicantown southwest of downtown, along Bagley and Vernor. **The Luna Bakery** at 5620 West Vernor at Junction is open seven days from 8 a.m. to 7 p.m. at least.

CRIME IN DETROIT . . . . . is what outsiders worry most about. But downtown Detroit, Rivertown, and the New Center are frequently patrolled. The People Mover has been virtually incident free. Recent national statistics confirm the notion held by most people who live and work in Detroit that crime in the city is no worse than in other big American cities. Panhandlers are plentiful, to be sure. . . . Normal discretion about avoiding deserted places is advisable, of course. At night, take advantage of lighted, guarded parking whenever possible. . . . . . The biggest danger in Detroit at night, insiders say, is **car theft**, not muggings. For some reason, GM products are most in demand. . . . . The attended city garage under Grand Circus Park is inexpensive, reasonably safe, never full, and close to the People Mover route. Open daytimes only.

John King Books

In an old glove factory near downtown Detroit,
one of the biggest used book stores in the country.

Housed in a one-time work glove factory just west of downtown, John King Books has become a national leader in
used and rare books. Its workaholic owner, John King,
flies all around the country in search of big lots of used and
remaindered books to fill his store's over 30,000 square feet. (A
separate warehouse has another 20,000 square feet. King also
owns the Big Book Store near Wayne State University that sells
comic books, magazines, and paperbacks and a smaller store in
Ferndale that sells books similar to those downtown.) At nearly a
million volumes, his may be the biggest book store in the
country. The stock is well organized, and browsing on four floors
is comfortable despite a sign that warns, "You have to be tough
to shop here — we don't serve coffee." On the second floor, tables
of irregular Penguins sell for $1 each.

The store also sells a fascinating variety of framed pictures,
printed ephemera, postcards, and collectibles, artfully displayed
in several first-floor rooms of this pleasant catacomb. The store
will search for hard-to-find titles for a dollar. There's always a
box of free books out front.

King's philosophy for acquiring books is to stay general,
partly because he finds it "too boring" to specialize. He and his
staff do a good job weeding out the drivel. Prices can vary widely. One serious book collector says you can find some terrific
bargains here, like the first English edition of Chekov letters he
found for $12.50.

Take the south bound Lodge Expressway (U.S. 10) to the Howard
Street exit ramp. Just off the Howard Street exit ramp service
drive on 901 W. Lafayette at Fifth Street. Park on expressway
side of building. (313) 961-0622. Mon-Sat 9:30-5:30.

Bookseller John King in his mammoth used book emporium, a four-story building that used to be a glove factory. He flies around the country buying large lots of books, so he can offer a terrific selection (over a million books) in his well-organized, pleasant book store.

Eastern Market

A colorful, earthy vestige of old Detroit, with wonderful food appealing to the city's diverse population.

Since the 1890s, this colorful, bustling market has been where Detroiters come to buy produce from local farmers and to purchase meats, fish, coffee, nuts, produce, fruit, spices, wine, and cheese from the stores around the market. Surrounding the large open-air stall area called "the sheds," where up to 800 farmers can sell their produce, are wholesale-retail specialty shops. The entire area is rich in atmosphere.

Today Eastern Market shoppers take advantage of all kinds of bargains – buying in quantity in 50-pound bags, buying seconds, buying late in the day on Saturday when vendors need to sell out, bargaining with vendors, buying from stores with prices well below standard retail prices. Eastern Market wholesale/ retail stores are also the nucleus of a thriving little gift basket cottage industry, what with the inexpensive baskets at R. Hirt and the goodies to put in them at Hirt, Rafal Spice, and Rocky Peanut Company.

The Market is a genuine vestige of old Detroit: a great medley of smells and sounds and colorful sights, and a vast variety of food appealing to the city's diverse cultures. Much of the market's color comes from the old wholesale/retail businesses clustered around the square (used for parking) in front of the main market sheds. In front of **Ciaramitaro's**, the third-generation Italian produce business on Market and Winder, you'll see dozens of crates of onions being unloaded, followed by piles of burlap bags of potatoes, as customers buy grapefruit and celery from the stand that's in front of the store, winter and summer.

Next to the **Gratiot Central Market**, southeast of the Eastern Market sheds across the recessed Fisher Freeway, the aroma of nuts pervades the air at **Germack's**, the oldest pistachio importer in the U.S. Pungent spices greet you in several Middle Eastern shops; an Islamic slaughterhouse is a few blocks away. Nearby at **Capital Poultry**, live ducks (a favorite with Detroit's many Poles) and chickens cackle away. Feathers are mixed in the dirt in the gutter outside.

Sal Ciarmitaro of Ciarmitaro Brothers Produce is one of many third- gene-ration Eastern Market wholesalers. Part of the market's charm is its conti-nuity with the past and its emphasis on food as a basic bulk commodity.

Wholesalers at the market today are likely to be descended from Belgian, German, and Polish farmers who sold at the market generations ago, or from Italian and Lebanese produce peddlers who first catered to Detroit's booming population of industrial workers beginning about 1910. In a city that's known great ups and downs, people love the Eastern Market because it's still pretty much the same.

In the past two decades artists have been moving into the market area. The five-story building on Gratiot with Fuchs Religious Goods on the ground floor is almost entirely occupied by artists, as is a good deal of second-story space near Rocky Peanut Company. More studios are in the Russell Industrial Center. Detroit's prestigious Center for Creative Studies near the Detroit Institute of Arts attracts art students and faculty, but space in that area isn't as cheap as you'd think. Hence, the interest in the Eastern Market area.

The Winder Street Gallery, on Winder Street a few blocks northeast of the market sheds in the old brewery district, is one place where the area's artistic energy is on public view. Here, next to his colorful, playful yet functional office/studio, designer and furnituremaker Alan Deal recognizes noteworthy Detroit-area artists in well attended quarterly shows. *1568 Winder St. at Orleans. (Winder joins the marketplace between Ciarmitaro's and R. Hirt's.) (313) 259-0710. Open Saturdays.*

The market changes with the time and day of the week. Something's happening almost around the clock.

◆ **Saturday mornings.** The market is a madhouse, especially from 7 to 10, when the crowds are largest. Food-lovers from far and wide converge here for weekend shopping.

◆ **Weekend and weekday nights.** The market area's energetic night life is epitomized by the literally till-all-hours activity at **Bert's Marketplace.** This jazz club has a menu featuring soul food; ribs and baked chicken are popular items. Jazz-lovers can find a range of jazz musicians performing throughout the week. *2727 Russell. (313) 567-2030. Mon-Thurs 11 a.m. until about 2 or 3 a.m. Fri-Sat 10 a.m. until 5 or 6 a.m.*

◆ **Early weekday mornings.** The wholesalers' weekday work is mostly done before sun-up. Around 1 a.m. trucks from the South and Southwest arrive to be unloaded. Throughout the early-morning hours, trucks of all sizes are coming and going, unloading and loading. Some produce is already destined for distributors like I.G.A., Spartan, and Abner Wolf, and some is sold at the market. By the time restaurants open around 6 or 7 a.m., the main part of the work day is over, and it's time for a break.

Farmers in market stalls compete with these out-of-state producers for retail buyers, and a lot of bargaining takes place. They are prepared to sell wholesale to distributors, retailers, and restaurants, and retail to the general public, but consumers can try their hand at bargaining down to wholesale prices, especially if they buy in quantity.

◆ **Weekdays in the mid-morning and afternoon.** Now the atmosphere is leisurely — a good time to get the undivided attention of the knowledgeable clerks at market shops. The farmers are gone by late morning, but wholesale/retail produce places remain well stocked.

The thickest concentration of retail stores is on Russell just north of the market. There, low new buildings house a variety of retail stores, including the venerable and highly recommended **Al's Fish and Seafood** (2929 Russell, 313-393-1722) and **B & S Produce** (3111 Russell, 313-833-6133), where you can get big

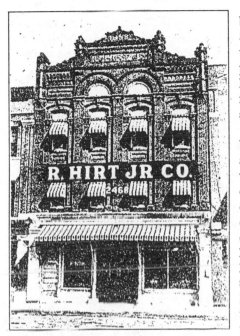

Shopping at R. Hirt in the Eastern Market is a weekly tradition for quality- and value-conscious customers. Swiss immigrants started it as wholesalers in cheese, butter, and eggs. The building was erected just after the market opened in 1893. Today R. Hirt's focus is on cheese, fancy foods, and basketware, with some bulk groceries like rice.

bags of onions and potatoes, 5 pounds of raw peanuts for under $5, fresh-roasted peanuts for little over a dollar a pound, or choose from five kinds of watermelon in season.

North of the market between Gratiot and Mack are several more blocks of wholesalers and meat packers, who cut up and package carcasses for retailers. Every odd turn reveals something else: **Rudy's New and Used Restaurant Equipment**, **Berry & Sons Islamic Slaughterhouse**, **Amrine's** Middle Eastern grocery near the Gratiot Central Market, the **Jenuwine Candy & Tobacco** wholesale/retailers on Russell (pun intended), **Fuchs Religious Goods** across Gratiot from the Gratiot Central Market (where you'll find jinx-removing incense and herbal remedies), the **Farmers' Restaurant** on Market and Division, and the **Meat Cutters Inn** at 2638 Orleans ("Fine Food, open 7 a.m.-7 p.m., Hires Root Beer").

Here are some of the Eastern Market's most notable shops, arranged from east to west:

◆ **Cost Plus Wine Warehouse.** It's a real pleasure to deal with Irishman Tim McCarthy. Knowledgeable without being condescending, he is a terrific guide to wines. He puts his own label (Tara Hills) on a very good Michigan Riesling produced by Chateau Grand Traverse. *2448 Market. (313) 259-3845. Mon-Fri 8:30-6, Sat 7-4:30.*

◆ **R. Hirt Jr. Company.** This century-old Detroit grocery has a great range of merchandise: cheese, sausage and ham products, crackers, bottled waters, beans and rice, coffees and teas, mustards and condiments, chocolates and cookies, and all sorts of imported pastas, jams, sparkling waters, olives, and fancy foods. As at many Eastern Market wholesale/retailers, prices are somewhere between wholesale and normal retail prices.

Hirt's is big-hearted and resolutely old-fashioned, even when old-fashioned means somewhat inefficient. Here's the system for shopping at Hirt's: You take a basket, load up on shelved merchandise, then go to the counterperson. He or she gets your cheese from the ancient, walk-in wood refrigerator, cuts it straight from the wheel (you can often get samples), wraps your purchases, and writes up a bill. This you pay at the separate cashier's, then return to pick up your purchases. Saturdays are crazy, what with the big, convivial crowds who seem to enjoy the opportunity to socialize in line and pick up food ideas. On weekdays, it's quiet, and the service is attentive, prompt, and knowledgeable.

Hirt's non-food treasure trove is the third-floor **wicker and basket department**, where you can find classics (laundry baskets, door mats, tomato, bushel, and berry baskets, covered picnic baskets), decorator items (including decorative tins, hampers, Adirondack chairs), and a huge variety of shapes and sizes of all kinds of baskets. *2468 Market at Windsor. (313) 567-1173. Mon-Fri 8-5, Sat 7-4.*

◆ **Ciaramitaro Brothers Produce.** Ciaramitaro's (pronounced "SHERM-uh-ta-ro's) and many other market old-timers started as commission houses that took farm produce and resold it at a percentage. Today Ciarmitaro's is mainly a wholesale food purveyor. The colorful, year-round produce stand on the sidewalk is more of a sideline run by retirees. The ancient-looking frame building was used as a tavern and inn going back to the 1840s. Slaves fleeing to Canada were housed in its basement. *2506 Market at Winder. (313) 567-9064. Mon-Sat 5:30 a.m.-2 p.m.*

◆ **Eastern Market Trade Center.** Friendly indoor bazaar of small merchants who sell everything from West African sculpture and musical instruments to antiques to baseball cards to gold jewelry to African-theme sportswear. *2530 Market, next to Farmer's Restaurant and Adelaide St. (313) 259-0042. Mon-Thurs 8-5, Fri-Sat 8-6.*

◆ **Joe's Wine and Liquor.** Known for its extensive collection of beers. *2933 Russell. (313) 393-3125. Mon-Sat 7-6, Fri until 7.*

◆ **Rafal Spice Company.** Even if you don't need any spices, be sure to stop in here just to smell the cumulative effect of 400 herbs and spices on hand. It's a visual treat, too, to see row upon row crammed with everything from asafetida powder to burdock root. Rafal also carries 85 kinds of coffee beans (at attractive prices), 60 kinds of bulk teas, and a large assortment of hot sauces, plus potpourri, oils, and books with recipes for concocting your own scents. Pick up a mail-order catalog, and you can conveniently inventory and restock your spice rack from home. *2521 Russell. (313) 259-6373. Mon-Fri 7-4, Sat 7-2.*

◆ **Rocky Peanut Company.** In addition to a very wide variety of bulk nuts, snack mixes, and dried fruit, this updated grocery stocks many oils, vinegars, condiments, packaged cookies and tinned and packaged gourmet items, coffees, teas, spices, and more. What's especially dazzling are the bins of bulk candies – over 400 kinds, perfect for assembling your own gift baskets. A slick new coffeehouse with espresso, cappuccino, and more is open during regular hours. *2489 Russell facing the marketplace. (313) 567-6871. Mon-Fri 7-4; Sat 7-5.*

◆ **Gratiot Central Market.** This colorful amalgam of butchers and other shops is in the white building with the terra cotta cow heads over the entrances. **Ronnie's Meats** (313-567-3226) offers a wide range of meats, including portions of a sheep's or cow's anatomy most Americans never consider edible. *Detroit Monthly* has called its baby back ribs the best in town. Goat is butchered to Islamic halal standards. **Joe Wigley Meats** (313-567-2857) is famous for its lamb and kosher-style corned beef. *1429 Gratiot. It faces Gratiot on one side and the Fisher Freeway Service Drive on the other. Mon-Fri 8-5, Fri until 6, Sat 7-7.* **Park** *on the service drive or Gratiot, or take the pedestrian walkway over the Fisher Freeway from market square parking.*

◆ **Capital Poultry.** Here you can actually pick out a live chicken to be dressed and picked up later. Free-range chickens grown by northern Indiana Amish are sold for very reasonable prices. Other poultry is also available, including guineas, pigeons, and wild game in season. *1466 E. Fisher Freeway next to the Gratiot Central Market. (313) 567-8200. Tues-Sat 7:30-5.*

◆ **Germack Pistachio Company.** America's oldest pistachio processor (since 1924) offers natural and red pistachios and many kinds of nuts, seeds, and dried fruits. Roasting is done on the premises. *1416 E. Fisher Freeway, near the Gratiot Market. (313) 393-0219. Mon-Fri 8:30-4:30, Sat until 2.*

The Eastern Market is just north of Gratiot 1 mile east of downtown. From Gratiot, take Russell north over the Chrysler Freeway. Signs clearly direct visitors from Gratiot to the market. Eastern Market Central Administration: (313) 833-1560. **Market hours:** *Mon-Fri 5 a.m.-noon (but most farmers are gone by mid-morning), Sat 5 a.m.-6 p.m.* **Retail store hours:** *typically 8 a.m. (earlier on Saturday) until 4 p.m. or 2 p.m. Sat.*

EASTERN MARKET RESTAURANTS . . . . . There are a variety of popular eating places in the Market to pick up a cheap breakfast or lunch. The **Russell Street Deli** (2465 Russell, 313-567-2900; current hours Mon-Fri 11-2:30, Sat 8:30-2) stands out above the rest with its excellent homemade soups, changing daily, and fresh-roasted turkey sandwiches. Classic deli sandwiches mostly around $4. Also in the vicinity: the venerable **Roma Cafe**, **Joe Muer's** outstanding fish restaurant on Gratiot at Vernor, and, on the inexpensive, takeout end, the highly regarded **Louisiana Creole Jambalaya** just north of Joe Muer's on the opposite side of Gratiot. See also *Hunts' Restaurants and Lodgings of Michigan.*

Tiger Stadium

*One of very last of the legendary old ball parks,
it's got atmosphere the new ones can't beat.*

The old ball park at Michigan and Trumbull may have only a few more years before it may be replaced by a new stadium downtown. The exploits of Tigers past — Ty Cobb, Charlie Gehringer, Mickey Cochran, Al Kaline, not to mention Lou Gehrig's last game and Reggie Jackson's 1971 All-Star home run onto the upper-deck roof — all these resonate in the minds of knowledgeable visitors to the venerable park. Tiger Stadium has no plush suites, several hundred seats behind iron pillars, and more cheap seats than any other major league ball park. That jeopardizes it in the new economics of baseball.

The Tigers were already playing at this site (then called Bennett Park, capacity 8,500) when a 23,000-seat stadium was built in 1912. It is the core of today's Tiger Stadium. In 1924 double decks were constructed from first to third base. They extend all the way out over the lower deck, providing some of baseball's best upper-level seats, right on top of the action. In 1936 more double decks in the right field pavilion and bleachers were added, and still more seats in 1938, bringing the capacity to 53,000.

Today Tiger Stadium is the only major league ballpark with upper deck and lower deck outfield seats. That makes it "the best fan ballpark in the country," says Los Angeles baseball consultant John Pastier, who has written about stadiums since 1973. The new stadiums, he says, are geared to affluent fans.

On the other hand, the old ballpark has its problems. Up to 7,000 seats are obstructed. Lines for restrooms and concession stands are sometimes long.

And then there's the Corktown neighborhood — a typical Detroit landscape consisting of a few old buildings and too much vacant space. That puts off the suburbanites who are baseball's biggest fans. In truth, those old bars on Michigan Avenue are lively remnants of an Irish community that still comes to the neighborhood to get together in places like George Reedy's Saloon and the Irish-American Club. As the Irish have moved out, they have been replaced by Maltese — a little-known ethnic group initially drawn by the auto plants. (Metro Detroit has more Maltese than anywhere else aside from the Mediterranean island nation itself.) Corktown is a remarkably stable neighborhood. Offspring of suburbanized Corktown Irish often move back. But the bleak view on and off Michigan Avenue is so off-putting, it's hard to convince suburban visitors that the area is pretty safe.

New Tigers owner Mike Illitch is known as a marketing prodigy who built Little Caesar's Pizza into the foundation for a flourishing sports and entertainment empire. **Tiger Plaza**, an arcade of souvenir stands and fast food outlets, wraps around the stadium's front corner. Ilitch brought back live organ music (its removal was one of many PR blunders by the organization of former Tiger owner and rival pizza baron Tom Monaghan). And he has introduced a host of promotions and giveaways unequaled in major league ball. Monday night, kids can run the bases after the game. Friday nights there are **fireworks** after the game. **Seniors** 62 and over pay $7, not $11, for weekday day games. There's an **alcohol-free family seating section** and **group discounts** for 20 or more. Call for info on more promotions and giveaways.

Michigan Ave. at Trumbull, one mile west of downtown Detroit. Call (313) 962-4000 for schedule and ticket reservations.

A TASTE OF MEXICO NEAR TIGER STADIUM . . . . . Just half a mile southwest of the stadium on Bagley is **Mexican Town**, with several popular Mexican restaurants and an interesting Mexican import shop. Businesses here and on Vernor between Grand River and Livernois serve southwest Detroit's sizable Hispanic population of over 30,000. A wide selection of Mexican groceries and beers is at **La Colmena** grocery to the east, on 2443 Bagley at 17th. It stays open until 8.

Historic Fort Wayne

Built to defend Detroit from the British,
this fort now dramatizes Detroit's military history.

This old star-shaped U.S. Army fort has been connected with a good deal of important U.S. military history. Today it is a museum operated by the Detroit Historical Museum. Due to budget cutbacks, it's open for special public events only (see below). Fort Wayne is so unusual for the Midwest, a visit is well worth the effort. Though it was built in the 1840s and 1850s, its design was based on principles of warfare developed in the 17th century. The fort is closer to a medieval fortress than a 20th-century military base. It's a reminder of how rapidly warfare has changed in the past century, compared with the previous six centuries.

Like a castle, Fort Wayne depends on an encircling moat, thick walls, and heavy, studded doors. Its star shape allowed cannon to fire grapeshot out of embrasures to repel attackers who approach the 22-foot-high outer walls. Fort Wayne also harks back to the time when the U.S. was still in conflict with Great Britain. It was built on a narrow bend in the Detroit River three miles south of downtown Detroit in order to stop enemy vessels from heading up the river.

On the occasions when the fort is open to the public, visitors can explore the tunnels and casemates (chambers for guns) within the outer walls and walk through the handsome three-story barracks near the fort's parade ground. The fort's first two

Built more like a medieval fortress than a modern military camp, Fort Wayne shows how much military strategies have changed since it was built in 1840. A moat and thick walls and doors were then significant ways to repulse potential British invaders.

floors house exhibits telling the story of Detroit's military history, from the coming of the French in 1701 through the Indian Wars of the 1890s.

Smaller museums are housed in the separate buildings of officers' row, outside the old star fort. The **commanding officer's house** has been restored to an authentically furnished 1880 Victorian residence. The **guardhouse** is furnished as it was during the Spanish-American War in 1898.

6325 W. Jefferson at Livernois. (313) 297-9360. Budget constraints have eliminated regular hours, but the fort and museums are open during special events; call for information.

BLACK FLIERS AND WOODLAND INDIANS AT FORT WAYNE . . . . . The **National Museum of the Tuskegee Airmen** tells the story of American black servicemen's struggle to achieve equality during World War II. The Airmen were an all-black Air Force unit, formed in 1942 at the instigation of civil rights leaders, and stationed at Tuskegee, Alabama. In the North African and Italian campaigns, the Airmen proved their skill as pilots, bombardiers, navigators, and ground crew. *Tours available by appointment only. Call (313) 965-8858.* . . . . . The **Great Lakes Indian Museum** has an exceptional collection of Woodland Indian artifacts, including beautiful quillwork, beaded moccasins and ceremonial clothing, and early trade goods. *Open for touring only when Fort Wayne is open for special events.*

OUTSTANDING SPECIAL EVENTS AT HISTORIC FORT WAYNE . . . . . Sadly, budget cuts mean that **tours** of the fort are now special events. In 1994, two Saturday walking tours (in late May and late August) offer not only a chance to get inside the commanding officer's house and the barracks, but interpreters from the Fort Wayne Living History Society and a box lunch in the mess hall. 1994 events also include a winter **lecture series** and a **Commanding Officers' Dinner** in mid-May. Events most likely to be held annually are several weekend **flea markets** and a huge family picnic, **Detroit's Birthday Party**, complete with birthday cake and lemonade, period bands, and children's activities. Call (313) 297-9360 for information on all events and future scheduling.

Shrine of the
Black Madonna Bookstore

*A terrific selection of books on Africa
and African-Americans, plus African fabrics and artifacts*

The attractive cultural centers/bookstores of the Shrine of
the Black Madonna present the largest selection of books
on Africans and African-Americans anywhere in the U.S.
The Detroit store, though not as big as the Shrine's Houston
facility, is most impressive: spiffy, well-organized, and serene in
mood. The staff is knowledgeable and friendly to customers of all
races. Long before multicultural chic and African fashions
showed up in malls and department stores, people who cared
about African cultures came here.

The Shrine is a black church founded in Detroit over 40
years ago by the Reverend Albert Cleage to promote African-
American self-sufficiency and to stress black Americans' con-

**Long before African design became chic, the Shrine of the Black
Madonna bookstore and gallery carried traditional African artifacts like
the sculpture store manager Ayele Bennett shows here.**

nectedness with African culture. It describes itself as a Pan-African orthodox Christian church; today it's part of the United Church of Christ with churches in Detroit, Atlanta, and Houston.

The large bookstore and import shop is also a **gallery** (on the second floor) with space for occasional lectures and readings by visiting authors and others. Here you can find an unparalleled range of books on Africans and African-Americans, from mainstream bestsellers like Taylor Branch's biography of Martin Luther King, to obscure publications by small political and literary presses here and abroad. This is the place to find the complete works in print of Langston Hughes, Zora Neale Hurston, and James Baldwin, as well as a passel of biographies of Motown stars and numerous scholarly and popular histories by black and white historians. Egyptology is another specialty. The children's book section is large and especially inviting.

Scott Nearing's 1930s classic on subsistence farming reminds visitors that self-sufficient agriculture is what the Shrine's Beulahland project is all about. Beulahland is an 5,000-acre farm planned for the South, where young African-American boys can grow up off the streets and help feed the poor in American cities.

Other sections of the store feature jewelry, imported fabrics, and handcrafted objects from Africa. Prices are lower than what you'd expect to pay at gift shops. Fabrics, mostly $7 to $12 a yard, include woven kente cloth strips, once worn only by Ghanaian royalty; vivid aso-oke from Nigeria, accented with metallic threads; heavy cotton mudcloth in bold patterns and muted, neutral colors; long pieces of khorogo cloth, with designs of animals, birds, and village life; and batiks from Nigeria and Ghana. For inspiration on how to use these beautiful fabrics, there's a book on 101 ways to wrap kanga cloth.

The shop offers quite a range of African artifacts: little thumb pianos, wonderful wood elephants for $6, copies of Ashanti kings' stools, and carved stone chess sets for $96 to $110. Considering the craftsmanship, prices are low. Kissi stone plates, incised with etched designs of plants and fish, are $35. Hand-painted papyri in beautiful golds and bronzes are copies of ancient pictures of Egyptian deities.

13535 Livernois just west of Davison in Detroit. From I-96, get off at the Davison ramp and go east. Turn left at Livernois and immediately look for the parking lot and sign. This is a rough part of town but OK in daytime. (313) 491-0777. Mon-Sat 11-6.

Motown Museum

*In a simple neighborhood home, hit after hit
was churned out with assembly-line regularity.*

Pop music legends — scores of them — were created during the Sixties in these two adjacent homes. The genius behind Motown's amazing hit factory was Berry Gordy Jr. a former boxer and autoworker. His father, a Georgia farm worker who came to Detroit in 1922, was a part of the Great Migration from the agricultural South to the industrial North.

Under Gordy, Motown Records launched stars whose music is part of American life today: Michael Jackson, Stevie Wonder, Diana Ross and the Supremes, Marvin Gaye, Martha Reeves and the Vandellas, Smokey Robinson and the Miracles, the Four Tops, the Temptations, Lionel Richie, Gladys Knight and the Pips, the Isley Brothers, Junior Walker, and more. Motown's Black Forum label made the only authorized recording of Martin Luther King's "I Have a Dream" speech. "Lift Every Voice and Sing," considered the black national anthem, was first recorded by Motown and Kim Weston, who is today a tireless organizer and supporter of local talent in Detroit.

Records produced in the small, crudely fashioned rear studio were among the first 45s by black artists to break out of the R&B charts into mainstream popularity. Within a few years of its founding in 1959, Motown became America's biggest black-owned company. In 1972 Gordy left Detroit for Los Angeles to pursue movie and television projects. Music industry analysts date the decline of Motown Records to its departure from Detroit and its inability to develop new talent in Los Angeles to replace its increasingly independent stars and songwriters from the Motor City. In 1988 Motown sold its recording arm to MCA-linked investors for $61 million.

The Motown Museum takes you back to an earlier, much simpler era. By the early 1960s, so many local kids flocked to the Motown studio here that traffic on West Grand was jammed for blocks. Some wanted to glimpse the stars who recorded here. Others hoped to audition informally on the front porch, an approach that had succeeded for more than one Motown star.

Gordy grew up in the neighborhood behind the Detroit Institute of Arts. Each member of his hard-working family contributed $10 a month to build an enterprise fund from which any family member could draw. (Family cooperation like this was what enabled many African-Americans to pursue higher education and build businesses.) After his jazz-oriented record shop went bankrupt, Gordy began focusing on writing and producing rhythm and blues songs for local groups. At a critical juncture, Gordy borrowed $800 from the family fund to start his own record production company. "Shop Around," written by Smokey Robinson, was the first big hit he produced.

A talented manager and an autocratic disciplinarian, Gordy perfected the assembly-line style of hit production. He hired teams of writers who, as one critic describes it, put out "a wholly mechanical style and sound that roared and purred like a well-tuned Porsche." The Supremes recorded 12 #1 pop hits in five years, all written by the great songwriting team of Lamont Dozier and Eddie and Brian Holland. Gordy so carefully orchestrated Motown affairs that charm coaches were hired to polish the manners and dress of Motown recruits.

In the museum, rooms are crowded with Motown memorabilia. On display are publicity photos and scrapbook shots, letters, album jackets, newspaper clippings, plaques and gold records. Highlights include Studio A, where all Motown's early hits were recorded, with the modest four-track board from which most of Motown's greatest hits were engineered. Original sheet music is on the music stands, just as it would have been during a recording session.

Esther Gordy Edwards, Berry Gordy's sister and herself an

early Motown executive, founded the Motown Museum to keep the Motown spirit alive in the Motor City and share the story of Motown's roots with fans who come from all over the world. Volunteer help is welcome. Her philosophy is reflected in the excellent **introductory video**. It points out that Motown's genius was in organizing and marketing talent that was already right here in Detroit, for the most part, and that its success was the work of many, many people, not just well-known figures like Berry Gordy and the stars.

For years the museum was an admittedly homespun operation. Myopic sophisticates sniffed at display techniques (thumbtacks held up record covers and photos) but weren't able to recognize that the museum had spirit and heart that more professional museums often lack. Today the museum has a museum professional as director, to help realize Esther Edwards' dreams while maintaining its intimacy and her clear sense of purpose. The Motown Museum has joined the Henry Ford Museum in Dearborn (the indoor counterpart to Greenfield Village) in a pioneering $1.7 million partnership between a large, established museum and an emerging one.

Displays have been professionalized. The sequence of

The Supremes were only one of many extraordinarily popular groups developed by Hitsville USA from their modest studio-offices on West Grand Boulevard.

exhibits traces the Motown story, beginning with the Gordy family and the trials of Berry Gordy's early years in the music business, followed by rooms focused on talent recruitment and artist development. The musicians' gallery shows the people (and often the very instruments) that created Motown's distinctive instrumental sound. Finally the stars take the stage.

In 1995 Hitsville USA, as the house on Grand Avenue was known, will be restored to its appearance in the 1960s. Visitors can see Berry Gordy's living quarters and the business office. A Motown exhibit with visuals and sound, created by museum design guru Ralph Applebaum, will open simultaneously at the Henry Ford Museum and the Motown Museum. Each museum will tell a different part of the story. After 18 months, both parts will be housed in an expanded Motown Museum that incorporates Motown's original home here. Possibly it will be attached at another site.

2648 W. Grand Blvd., a few blocks west of the GM Building, New Center, and Henry Ford Hospitals. From the Lodge/U.S. 10, take W. Grand Blvd. exit, head west. From I-96, take West Grand exit, go east. From I-94, take the Lodge/U.S. 10 north, get off at the next exit (Grand) and go west. (313) 875-2266. Mon-Sat 10-5, Sun 2-5. Fan club membership ($30 individual, $45 family of 4) includes free annual admission, Grapevine newsletter, notices of museum events. Admission: adults $3, 12 and under $2.

Fisher Building

An office building with 1920s-style Persian grandeur,
thanks to the brothers who started Fisher Body

The Fisher Building ranks with the Guardian Building
downtown as the most fantastic of Detroit's remarkable
collection of 1920s office buildings. The seven Fisher
brothers had become enormously rich by developing the enclosed
auto body and then selling Fisher Body to GM. They planned the
New Center complex across from the General Motors headquarters as a second major commercial center in the city. It was supposed to rival the increasingly congested downtown area.

Here the brothers set out to create the world's most beautiful
office building. The architect was Albert Kahn, famed for his factories. Plans called for erecting another identical 26-story building, with a 60-story tower between them. But before these other
buildings were begun, the Depression stopped them cold.

When the Fisher Building opened in 1928, it sported one of
the most fabulous interiors of any office building in the world.
It's full of what Detroit architectural historian Hawkins Ferry
called "pagan splendors" — mosaics and inlaid marbles patterned in geometric and stylized naturalistic motifs. "Upon the
walls gleam 40 different varieties of marble that would dazzle
even the most jaded Roman emperor," re-
marked Ferry. In the magnificent three-
story arcade of shops, the ceiling and
walls are covered with cherubs and
muses, orange trees and hemlocks,
eagles, vines, and folk art motifs.
Rich greens and oranges, lavishly
gilded with gold leaf, make for a
warm and welcoming effect that
makes an ordinary office worker
or shopper feel like royalty. The
original interior decorations of
the adjoining Fisher Theater,
which uses the arcade as its
lobby, were based on Central

**The depression curtailed the
Fisher brothers' grand plan to build
a copy of the existing Fisher
Building and connect them with a
much taller 60-floor tower.**

American art. In visual splendor they rivaled those of the fabulous Fox. They were removed in 1961, at the end of the theater's moving picture days, when it was transformed into Detroit's preeminent legitimate theater. Its acoustics, stage, and orchestra pit make it superb for even the biggest and most elaborate musicals. Hits including *Hello, Dolly* and *Fiddler on the Roof* originated here before moving to Broadway.

As in most fancy office towers of the 1920s, elevator doors and mailboxes are treated as works of art. Unusual amenities here included free babysitting in a richly decorated nursery, white-dressed parking attendants, and, in the theater lobby, banana trees, a pond of goldfish and turtles, and wandering macaws fed by moviegoers.

In an era and a city where a good many historic jewels have faded or disappeared, it's a pleasure to visit the Fisher Building, impeccably maintained by the Canadian real estate firm, Trizec Properties. It was named Historic Office Building of 1993.

A bank's sumptuous Aztec plaster decoration and ornate vault are now part of the affordably priced **Pegasus in the Fisher** restaurant facing Grand Boulevard. Shops catering to office workers (including stores for women's and children's fashions) line the main arcade and elevator wing. Two standouts toward the Lothrop entrance of the main arcade are open Mondays through Saturdays 10-6 and on theater nights. The **Detroit Gallery of Contemporary Crafts** offers a select and beguiling array of American contemporary crafts by top craftspeople, priced from $25 to $500 and up. Displays mix media to good effect: jewelry, ceramics, rugs, toys, a little furniture, clothing, quilts, and dolls. Don't miss the sunburst of tiles from Detroit's famous Pewabic Pottery (page 280) on the floor in the rear. The **Poster Gallery** includes an outstanding selection of quality posters with African-American themes, along with a general poster line. Also on hand: interesting musical chimes for wall or table. Next door, **Cultural Accents** carries dolls, jewelry, and gifts from many peoples and cultures. Another new store, **Facets Jewelry Design Studio**, features unusual designs and stones from award-winning jeweler Todd Terwilliger.

W. Grand Blvd. at Second Ave. Rear entrance on Lothrop. Open Mon-Fri 8 a.m.-9 p.m., Sat 9-6. Freeway directions: take the Lodge (U.S. 10) to Pallister exit, turn left onto Lothrop. 3 hours free parking in New Center One lot, Lothrop between Second and Woodward with validation from any New Center store.

🌲🌳🌲

THE REST OF THE NEW CENTER IS ALSO WORTH A LOOK. . . . . The
lobby of the massive, sprawling **General Motors world headquarters** (1922);
Albert Kahn, architect) across the street is loaded with a sense of both
Renaissance grandeur and high-stakes corporate drama. Will the brisk-
paced, blue-suited executives seen in the lobby regain market share for the
automotive giant? Displayed on the lobby's east hall (toward Woodward) are
current-model GM cars, plus **historical displays. . . . . . Free summer concerts** with top local musicians are held at the New Center park on Grand at
Second across from the GM Building. *Current time: Fridays 11:30 a.m. to 1
p.m. (313) 874-4444 for details* . . . **New Center One** is an attractive small
shopping center anchored by Crowley's Department Store, with Winkelman's,
Gantos, and Waldenbooks. It's across from the Fisher Building on Grand
Boulevard at Second. For dedicated Detroiters committed to keeping their
dollars in the city, it's a godsend. (Hudson's, having debilitated the city by
leading the way in suburban retail and housing development, closed its flagship Detroit store in 1982, then prevented competing retailers from leasing
the space.) . . . . . North of the Fisher Building, **New Center Commons**, a mix
of new and renovated housing, is a successful GM project to rehabilitate the
neighborhood around it.

NEW CENTER ENTERTAINMENT IS FIRST-CLASS. . . . . For program and
ticket information about the **Fisher Theater**, where most major Broadway
road shows perform, call (313) 872-1000. The **Attic Theater**, Detroit's resident professional theater company — artistically respected, fiscally plagued
— is across Third from the Fisher Building, near Grand. Call (313) 875-8284.
Club Penta, in the Fisher Building lower level, presents first-rate jazz music
of the sleek, sophisticated variety, in an atmosphere of quiet elegance. Wed-
Sat at 9. (313) 972-3760.

**FOR AN INTIMATE, DOMESTIC VERSION OF THE FISHER BUILDING'S
WAY WITH ART DECO . . . . .** be sure to visit the home of Lawrence Fisher
(page 283), one of the Fisher brothers and the president of Cadillac Motors.

Detroit Institute of Arts

One of the nation's most extraordinary collections of great art, with special strengths in American art, German Expressionism, and Italian Renaissance art

Detroit is blessed with one of the nation's half dozen leading art museums. The collection is encyclopedic. Virtually every period of Western art is creditably represented, from the Mesopotamian through modern eras. In non-western art, the Asian and African collections are especially strong. Works by every major American artist are here.

The museum's greatest strengths are in American, Italian Renaissance, Dutch-Flemish, and German Expressionist art. While there are dozens of masterpieces throughout, the following (arranged in chronological order) are considered the museum's most important:

Gudea of Lagash (Mesopotamian), ca. 2141-2122 B.C. Superb stone sculpture of the ruler of a city-state.

Early Autumn (Qian Xuan), 13th or 14th century. Delicate handscroll in ink and color of insects in autumn.

Nail Figure (from the Western Kongo), ca. 1875-1900. 46-inch wooden icon served an African community's mystical needs.

Saint Jerome in His Study (Jan van Eyck), ca. 1390-1441. Small, richly symbolic oil painting by the great Flemish painter.

The Wedding Dance (Pieter Bruegel the Elder), ca. 1566. Colorful, realistic view of a peasant wedding.

The Visitation (Rembrandt), 1640. Dramatic presentation of the Biblical scene in which Mary and Elizabeth encounter God.

Cotopaxi (Frederic Church), 1862. Grand, mystical oil painting of an active volcano in the Andes.

Self Portrait (Vincent van Gogh), 1887. One of the great artist's sunnier self-portraits.

Seated Bather (Pierre-Auguste Renoir), 1903-6. Sensuous, languid nude painted when the artist was in his sixties.

Detroit Industry (Diego Rivera), 1932-33. Rivera's masterpiece. An enormous series of frescoes focusing on Detroit's auto industry.

Reclining Figure (Henry Moore), 1939. Large female sculpture in elmwood.

Many other important works are worth mentioning — major pieces by Whistler, Picasso, Modigliani, Miro, Kokoschka, Gauguin, Seurat, Degas, Cezanne, and Matisse, among others. A popular favorite is Romare Bearden's **Quilting Time** (1986), a large, colorful work showing African-Americans and their quilts outside a tiny house in a field. To find specific works, ask a staff person to note their locations on a map as you enter.

The museum's huge size and disorienting labyrinth of halls and corridors present the visitor with the problem of excess. You need to be careful not to become numbed by the thousands of pieces on display. One helpful antidote is a free one-hour **guided tour** *(given Wed-Sat 12:15, Sun at 1 & 2:30)*. It gives a quick view of the highlights.

The Motor City, a product of the 20th century, was a relative latecomer to matters of collecting art and establishing a public museum to showcase it. The late 19th-century wealth that launched most great American museums wasn't widespread enough here. Detroit was merely a medium sized city until the auto boom took off around 1910.

When Detroit did finally open its museum, in 1927, it had the talent and resources to build a great museum quickly. Its first director, William Valentiner, a friend of many German Expressionists, bought their work as it was being produced, before the art market escalated its cost. In Detroit, Valentiner proved a gifted teacher of wealthy, well-connected Detroiters like Robert Hudson Tannahill and Eleanor Clay Ford, cousins belonging to the J. L. Hudson department store family. They contributed enormously to the museum, not only through their donations, but through their advice, taste, and connections.

Edsel Ford, Henry's son and Eleanor's husband, had the enthusiasm to take up Valentiner's suggestion and commission Diego Rivera, the great Mexican socialist muralist, to create his masterpiece, *Detroit Industry*, in the DIA's main courtyard. And Edsel Ford had the courage to stand up to virulent criticism of this powerful but controversial celebration and critique of Detroit's economic base. Its social criticism and modernist look went way beyond the bounds of the genteel good taste wealthy Detroiters expected from art.

The down side of Detroit's late entry into the art museum game is the DIA's skimpy endowment. The DIA is far more

In the lower right corner of the south wall of "Detroit Industry" are portraits of art patron Edsel Ford, Henry's son (left), and his friend and aesthetic mentor William Valentiner, founding director of the Detroit Institute of Arts. Edsel Ford and his wife, Eleanor Clay Ford, were enormously helpful and generous to the fledgling art museum. Their unpublicized financial assistance enabled the museum to stay open during the Depression.

dependent on subsidies than museums that have had more money given over a longer period of time. A recent funding crisis cut back hours and had museum galleries open in shifts for awhile. Now, thanks to volunteers, all galleries are open, and a scaled-back program of **special exhibits** (usually $3 extra fee) is in place. Call also for upcoming lectures and events.

Unfortunately, the museum can often feel like a stage set or lofty Temple of Art for an elite crowd of carefully dressed Oakland County suburbanites, rather than a people's institution where all kinds of area kids come on Saturdays for classes and treasure hunts, and where ordinary families show up for casual Sunday outings. Comparisons with the much smaller Toledo Museum of Art,which has long been oriented to broad-based art education, put the DIA to shame. Even casual visitors immediately pick up on the difference in atmosphere.

The DIA staff knows it has a problem being user-friendly. The huge museum with its multiple additions is made even more confusing and hard to grasp because the ground-level side entrance on Farnsworth has become the major entrance. Visitors have to thread their way through hallways, stairways, and eleva-

Diego Rivera's masterpiece, "Detroit Industry," was made possible through the
patronage of Edsel Ford with the encouragement of DIA director William
Valentiner. Radical in its critique of capitalism, the mural depicted
manufacturing processes with faultless accuracy. Edsel Ford defended it
against the predictable outcry of criticism, unlike the Rockefellers, who
capitulated to similar criticism and destroyed the Rivera mural they had
commissioned for Rockefeller Center.

tors to the main first-floor galleries.

The museum has created a **visitor center** off the Farnsworth
lobby. It's easy to miss. Here in a short video, museum director
Sam Sachs, hand in blazer pocket, invites visitors to "have fun.
You're going to have a great experience." He urges them to think
and explore art, points out that reproductions are no substitute
for seeing the original, and dispenses sensible advice. The museum can't be seen in a day. Choose a part to look at more closely.
When concentration wanes or arches collapse, take a break and,
he suggests, patronize the museum's two restaurants. The striking **Kresge Court Cafe** (Wed-Fri 11-3, Sat-Sun 11:30-4) is a
vast, open dining area inspired in part by the courtyard of the
Bargello Palace in Florence. Here you can eat cafeteria-style, sip

coffee, or drink beer and wine. The new **American Grille** restaurant offers table service and a Sunday brunch (Wed-Fri 11:30-2, Sun 11-3); for reservations, call (313) 833-1857.

The **Museum Shop** by the Farnsworth entrance (open 9:30-5:30) carries a sophisticated selection of art books, cards, reproductions, jewelry, and gift items, but is weak on inexpensive things that appeal to kids. Marketing stuff is getting to be a major revenue source for strapped museums; the DIA shop has outlets at Twelve Oaks mall and the Somerset Collection.

5200 Woodward between Kirby and Farnsworth, 1/4 mile southeast of I-94. From I-94 east or west, take the Woodward/John R exits, go south on John R approximately 4 blocks. From I-75 south, take the Warren Ave. exit, proceed on Warren to Woodward, and go north on Woodward. From U.S. 10 north or south, take the Forest Ave. exit, go east on Forest, then north on Woodward 1/2 mile. (313) 833-7900. Wed-Fri 11-4; Sat-Sun 11-5. Pay what you wish, but you must pay something. Suggested admission: adults $4, students and children $1. Occasional charge (typically $3) for special exhibitions. **Parking** *in a secure, lighted parking garage on Farnsworth: $2 maximum. Surface Science Center lot at John R and Farnsworth, $1.25.* **Guided tours:** *Wed-Sat 12:15; Sun 1 & 2:30 (call to confirm).*

TWO OTHER NEARBY MUSEUMS OF NOTE . . . . . The handsome **Museum of African-American History** documents the history and culture of African-Americans from pre-slavery life in African villages through the Underground Railroad to the Civil Rights Movement. The museum's most dramatic display is a full-scale mock-up of part of a slave ship below deck, complete with sound effects. *301 Frederick Douglass between John R and Brush. From Woodward, take Kirby to John R, turn right, then left. (313) 833-9800. Wed-Sat 9:30-5; Sun 1-5. Suggested donation: $2/adults, $1/children. . . . . .* **The Detroit Science Center** has items now familiar in hands-on museums: computer games, a giant soap bubble device, anatomical displays, geological formations, fossils. The big draw is the **Omni-Max Theater**, a huge tilted screen which conveys a sense of motion in specially filmed movies. Science-related films are shown every hour on the half hour from 10:30 until 3:30. *5020 John R. From Woodward, take Kirby to John R. (313) 577-8400. Mon-Fri 10-2, Sat 11-5, Sun noon-5. Adults $6.50; ages 4-12 $4.50; under 4 free.*

PRESERVATION WAYNE'S DETROIT HERITAGE TOURS . . . . . give the general public an insider's view of some of Detroit's grand architecture and exciting renovation projects, in tours given by the principal historic preservation organization in the city. . . . . For information on upcoming tours and events, or to volunteer for tour guide training, call the Preservation Wayne 24-hour **tour and events line** at (313) 222-0321. Regular Saturday walking tours, generally at 10 a.m., include an **African-American heritage tour,** "Magnificence on Woodward" (with a look inside the sumptuous French chateau of a house designed for railroad car magnate Frank Hecker), a **Theater District tour** of restored theaters and restorations in process, and "Mansions of Ferry Avenue," in which visitors can go inside famed art collector **Charles Freer's 1893 Shingle Style house,** one of the finest works of noted Philadelphia architect Wilson Eyre. One room was built to house Whistler's Peacock Room before Freer started Washington's Freer Gallery and moved it there. Preservation Wayne has convinced Wayne State University to invest $2 million in restoring or renovating the historically and architecturally significant building. Most tours are $8, $5 to members.

Occasional Preservation Wayne bus tours cover **Detroit stained glass,** Cranbrook's origins in **Detroit's Arts and Crafts movement,** and the auto industry and unions in Detroit.

FOR OTHER ART GALLERIES NEARBY . . . . . look in the index of this book for the Sherry Washington Gallery, Dell Pryor Gallery, Detroit Focus and Gallery Biegas downtown; the Detroit Gallery of Contemporary Crafts in the Fisher Building; Detroit Artists' Market and Pewabic Pottery on East Jefferson; the Birmingham gallery area (page 304); Book Beat in Oak Park; and Habatat in Pontiac.

FOR CURRENT GALLERY SHOWS . . . . . see listings in the Friday *Detroit Free Press* and *Detroit News.*

THE MAIN GALLERY OF THE CENTER FOR CREATIVE STUDIES . . . . . is a stone's throw from the DIA in the Park Shelton Apartments on East Kirby at Woodward. The campus of the prestigious professional school's College of Art and Design is two blocks east on Kirby, behind the DIA. The **Center Galleries** show stimulating exhibits of national, local, and student work in all media. Call (313) 874-1955 for info on the current show. Hours are Tues-Sat 10-5; admission is free. Ring the buzzer at the main entrance, 15 E. Kirby, to get in on Saturday!

Detroit Historical Museum

From fort to Motor City, Detroit's past
is illuminated with bold, insightful exhibits.

Detroit has had an especially rich, eventful history. Founded in 1701, it has changed sovereignty five times. Its strategic location at a narrow point on the Detroit River made the fort town a keenly fought-over prize, ruled by France and then England before joining the U.S. in 1796. This museum, one of the best in the state, captures much of that history quite well.

The new **Furs to Factories** exhibit of Detroit history to 1901 traces Detroit's development from a fur-trading outpost to a major industrial giant. Wall murals and lifelike scenes with mannequins recreate the French wilderness settlement of the 1700s. On the second floor, **"Doorway to Freedom"** traces the Underground Railroad routes leading to Detroit, just across the river from escaped slaves' ultimate destination in Canada, and highlights area churches, homes and other buildings where they found refuge. Opening in June, 1994, **"World War II Remembered"** features posters, newspapers, and unusual toys bringing the war effort to everyday life across America.

The museum's changing shows and semi-permanent exhibits are some of the most vivid and memorable parts of the museum. Through November of 1994, **"Feeling Groovy: America, 1969"** displays artifacts of that year, many related to the Viet Nam War.

A longtime highlight is **The Streets of Detroit** exhibit in the basement. It's a three-quarters-scale, realistic nighttime recreation of Detroit commercial streetfronts in the 1840s, 1870s, and at the turn of the century. Along cobblestone and then brick streets you walk by banks, a printing shop, a drug store, a bicycle shop, and a grocery store, among others. The darkened ambiance makes the settings seem lifelike. The street is a rich step back into the past, no doubt magical for many children. Particularly wonderful is the old Kresge & Wilson Big 5 and 10¢ Store, which once occupied the spot where the National Bank of Detroit now stands across from Kennedy Square. "Nothing over 10¢ in this store" was its motto. S.S. Kresge went on to establish dime stores across the nation, building the giant company which evolved into today's K Mart Corporation, now headquartered in nearby Troy.

Behind the Streets of Detroit is the **National Toy Gallery**, with changing exhibits from one of the world's largest collections of toys, including the notable Glancy Trains. Upstairs, the **Tavi Stone Fashion Library** (limited hours) is a rare resource for fashion historians, with magazines, videos, books and slides about all areas of fashion. It's next to the **Booth-Wilkinson Costume Gallery,** where "Quilts around the House," featuring historic quilts, is on exhibit through March, 1995.

In the Round Hall near the entry is a 15-foot-high carved mahogany **clock** from the turn of the century. At noon a procession of figures from around the world marches in native costume around a globe while a music box plays. The attractive first-floor **gift shop** features a wide assortment of antique reproductions, posters of Detroit scenes, books, toys, and souvenirs.

5401 Woodward at Kirby (across from Detroit Institute of Arts). Park free behind museum off Kirby. (313) 833-1805. Wed-Fri 9:30-4, Sat & Sun 10-5. Freewill donation: adults $4, others $1.

DETROIT HISTORICAL TOURS, LECTURES, DINNERS, AND EVENTS . . . . . are previewed in the annual 48-page program guide, available at no cost through the **Detroit Historical Society.** Call (313) 833-1805 or write the Society at 5401 Woodward Avenue, Detroit, MI 48202. Tours (mostly by bus) include black historic sites, the auto industry and its unions, dinner tours in lavish mansions, Latino Detroit, Eastern Market, the Theater District, and neighborhood strolls from Corktown to Northville and Wyandotte.

DETROIT HISTORICAL SOCIETY MEMBERSHIP . . . . . helps support its museums, brings free admission to the Detroit Historical Museum and Dossin Great Lakes Museum, a free subscription to *Michigan History* magazine and the society's quarterly, a 15% discount at the Old Detroit Museum Shop, the annual program guide, and invitations to special events like seeing the July 4 fireworks from historic Fort Wayne. Send checks ($60/family, $30/individual, $15/student) to Detroit Historical Society, 5401 Woodward, Detroit, MI 48202.

FOR A SURPRISINGLY PLEASANT WALK THROUGH THE WAYNE STATE UNIVERSITY CAMPUS . . . . . walk down Kirby (it's the side street between the historical museum and the library) to Cass. Across Cass, the street has been turned into a beautifully landscaped **pedestrian mall,** studded with sculpture. Its main corridor is along what used to be Second Avenue, parallel to Cass. Points of visitor interest: changing exhibits at **Walter Reuther Library of Urban Affairs** and in the gallery at the **Art Building** (both at Kirby); **Student Center** with food court, campus events info on the mall at what was Kirby.

Hangouts on Cass include **Alvin's Finer Delicatessen,** 5756 Cass near Palmer (known for blues, rock); **Cosmic Cafe** vegetarian restaurant (87 W. Palmer).

VISITOR HIGHLIGHTS AT AN OUTSTANDING PUBLIC LIBRARY . . . . .
The **Detroit Public Library,** across Woodward from the art museum and across Kirby from the historical museum, is in a grand Beaux Arts building (1921), designed by Cass Gilbert to resemble the Boston Public Library. The grand staircase is full of murals in the Italian Renaissance style; Detroiters may enjoy **Gari Melchers' romantic historical scenes** of early Detroit in the second-floor Adam Strohm Hall. Here are interesting **changing exhibits.** . . . . . Library hours: Tues-Sat 9:30-5:30, except Wed 1-9. . . . . . The **Burton Historical Collection** (Detroit history) and **National Auto History Collection** (limited hours) are tops of their kind.

Hamtramck

*This Polish autoworkers' enclave
has a bustling, nostalgic, 1940s-era commercial district
with good shopping and eating.*

This city of just two square miles, totally surrounded by
Detroit, has been a Polish stronghold since the First
World War. Drive along its bustling main street of Joseph
Campau and you'll see Polish bakeries, Polish meat shops, Polish
bookstores, Polish clubs. At the corner of Belmont and Joseph
Campau is a tribute to the Polish Pope, a large statue of Pope
John Paul. For a **free guide to Polish Hamtramck** – its bak-
eries, delis, restaurants, and shops – stop at the Polish Art
Center, 9539 Joseph Campau (page 258).

For years now, Detroiters have been discovering the gritty
charm of a trip to Hamtramck: eating heartily in its good, cheap
restaurants; browsing in the small, budget-oriented shops, bakeries, and meat markets; and, more recently, dancing to some of
the area's most innovative rock at Lili's 21.

For years numerous artists have had studios in second-story
storefront space, invisible to public view. Now two cool coffeehouses on side streets, the Shadow Box Cafe and Planet Ant,
cater to working artists in the daytime and to alternative music-
lovers and an alternative crowd at night.

Joseph Campau's long retail blocks still have the vintage
appeal of a living, thriving blue-collar relic from the 1930s or
1940s, before chains came to depersonalize retailing and before
malls had sucked the vitality out of most American downtowns.
Hamtramck's downtown today presents an amazing contrast
with the boarded-up bleakness of similar 1920s shopping strips
in nearby Detroit. Many value-conscious Detroit-area shoppers
with casually urbane good taste do a large part of their shopping
for clothes and household goods in Hamtramck's cozy shops.

Hamtramck's Polish population is declining, from a high of
60% to under 40% today. Taking up the slack are Albanians
from Yugoslavia. They are now over 20% of the population.

The dense workers' neighborhoods here were built for autoworkers' families in one amazing gush between 1914 and 1920,

Hamtramck's bustling commercial district along Joseph Campau is a reminder of what urban America looked like in the 1940s, before suburbanization and the big change in retailing.

when the village's population skyrocketed from 3,589 to 45,615, the largest increase in that decade anywhere in the U.S. The sudden growth occurred because in 1910 the Dodge Brothers built Dodge Main, a huge auto factory on the south edge of what was then an old German farming village.

Today, even with the declining Polish presence in Hamtramck, its commercial district has a distinctly Polish feel to it. But city services are suffering as the population, which peaked in 1930 at 56,000, has dropped to just 18,400 today. A major blow to the community was the closing of Dodge Main in 1979. The GM Poletown plant, built on some of the same land, sits two-thirds over the Detroit border. Its approximately 5,200 jobs haven't come close to replacing the 11,000 Dodge workers.

Hamtramck highlights, arranged from north to south, include:

◆ **Shadow Box Cafe.** College students and locals mingle at this intimate, 40-seat cafe, where jazz and folk artists and alternative bands play on weekends. There's no cover charge. *2917 Trowbridge, 1 block south of Caniff and just east of Joseph Campau. (313) 873-2233. Open Fri-Sat 11 a.m.-4 a.m.; Tues, Wed,*

Thurs and Sun, 11 a.m.-midnight; Mon 4 p.m.-midnight.

◆ **Planet Ant.** This busy spot seats 50 or 60 inside and, in summer, opens a back patio with a garden and tables sculpted by Detroit artist Brian Lehto. The menu of desserts, muffins, and bagels is expanding to include other light food such as pasta salads. Every night except Sunday has an event scheduled: Monday–open mike poetry; Tuesday–"Drum Circle" (an open jam session for percussionists); Wednesday–live bands; Thursday–open mike night (so popular that people have to be turned away); Friday and Saturday–live music, often folk performers. *2357 Caniff between Joseph Campau and I-75. Sun-Thurs 11 a.m.-1 a.m., Fri-Sat until 3 a.m.*

◆ **Monument to Pope John Paul II.** It's not surprising that this distinctively Polish city would want to do something special to commemorate the installation of the first Polish pope. Much of the funding has come from the proceeds of an annual festival held for four days around Labor Day, when over 700,000 visitors flock to the city. The austere little park is enlivened by the colorful and well-executed mural of costumed folk dancers in a historic Polish street scene. The fence is formed by the original entrance gates to the late, lamented Dodge Main plant, Hamtramck's reason for being. *Corner Belmont and Joseph Campau.*

◆ **John Paul II Bookstore.** Religious articles are sold here, but the store has erratic hours, and it's closed more often than it's open. *10304 Joseph Campau. (313) 873-3588.*

◆ **New Palace Bakery.** Hamtramck is known for its Polish bakeries, and the New Palace is a favorite among the locals. One Polish specialty is angel wings, a very light dough fried with a powdering of sugar. Another favorite is paczki, or jelly-filled doughnuts. On the day before Lent, lines form by 7 a.m. to buy them. Lemon tortes, cinnamon-raisin breakfast rolls, and pumpernickel and rye breads are other standbys, and cookies come in many, many shapes. *9833 Joseph Campau between Yemans and Evaline. (313) 875-1334. Mon-Sat 5 a.m.-7 p.m., Fri 'til 8.*

◆ **Ciemniak Meat Market.** Lots of people around Hamtramck think this is the best meat market in town. Ciemniak's own smokehouse is in back, where they make such things as hunter's sausage and smoked kielbasa. Kiszka is made with buckwheat, beef blood, liver, and pork. *9629 Joseph Campau between Norwalk and Edwin. (313) 871-0773. Mon-Sat 9-6.*

◆ **Polish Art Center.** This delightful shop has such an attractive array of Polish arts and crafts that people visit it from all over the U.S. Here you can find Polish folk art rugs ($35 to $300), beautiful wooden plates inlaid with metal ($8 to $50), Polish leaded glass ($11.50 to $500), costume dolls ($7.50 and up), and brightly painted Russian nesting dolls starting at just $12 a set. Sparkling and intricate tinfoil nativities, called *szopka,* are $75.

Colorful Easter eggs, including Ukrainian goose and ostrich eggs, are on hand, as are egg-decorating supplies (dyes, wax, tools, unfinished eggs). There are inexpensive paper cuttings (and books on creating this cheery Polish folk art), amber jewelry, replicas of antique Polish swords, and Polish greeting cards.

New to the store are Polish music CDs (mostly $16), videos ($25-$79), and thousands of Polish-language books – everything from novels and encyclopedias to Polish language courses to children's books to self-help books on health and using Macintosh computers. Striking contemporary Polish posters of movies are back – for $12. FAX inquiries are welcome (313-874-1302), and a mail order catalog is in the works. *9539 Joseph Campau at Norwalk. (313) 874-2242. Mon 9:30-7, Tues-Thurs 9:30-5, Fri-Sat 9:30-5.*

◆ **Henry the Hatter.** Like its downtown parent store, this shop offers a wide range of hats, from wool berets to Western-style. *9307 Joseph Campau. (313) 875-5587. Mon-Sat 9-5:30.*

◆ **St. Florian Church.** This magnificent Gothic church, completed in 1926, is on the scale of a great European cathedral. Serving one of the region's largest parishes, it holds 1,800. The church was designed by Ralph Adams Cram, America's high priest of the 20th-century Gothic Revival. The interior is awesome, with an enormously high ceiling. All the windows are true stained glass windows – not the painted colored glass of most American churches, but windows where the designs and figures are made of individual small pieces of glass of different colors. Seen in daytime with only natural light filtering through the windows, the effect is the same as in medieval churches. *2626 Poland. Faces Florian St. one block west of Joseph Campau. (313) 871-2778. Church is open to visitors 8:30 a.m.-6 p.m.; enter from back door on Poland St.*

◆ **Cadillac Detroit-Hamtramck Assembly Center.** The highly roboticized new Poletown plant makes Cadillac Sevilles, Buick Rivieras, and Oldsmobile Toronados. An extended, wrenching controversy and much pain were created when the city of Detroit condemned and tore down a whole neighborhood and the Immaculate Conception church so GM could build its big new Poletown plant, incorporating the site of the old Dodge Main plant. A vital retail district along Chene Street south of I-94 was turned into a ghost town in the process. Plant tours have unfortunately been suspended. Try calling (313) 972-6000 to see if they have resumed. *Just north of I-94 between Mt. Elliot and I-75.*

GETTING TO HAMTRAMCK . . . . . isn't all that easy. It's isolated by freeways, a rail line, and the big G.M. Plant. From Woodward in Detroit, turn east onto Holbrook, a mile north of I-94. From northern Detroit, take McNichols (6 Mile) 1 1/2 miles east of Woodward to Joseph Campau. From the east side, take Mt. Elliot north and veer to the left onto Conant, on Hamtramck's eastern perimeter. **From freeways**, take I-75 (the Chrysler Freeway) to Caniff, about 1 1/2 miles north of I-94. If you're northbound, from Detroit's downtown/New Center, turn right onto Caniff, then right onto Joseph Campau in three blocks to reach the main drag. If you're southbound from the suburbs, turn left onto Caniff. If it's late at night, pay attention to these directions, or you'll end up lost in a creepy part of Detroit.

NEIGHBORHOOD TAVERNS . . . . . off the main drag are enduringly popular Hamtramck institutions best observed after work. Many have inexpensive food and/or entertainment. They include:
♦ **Artie's Locker Room**, 3141 Caniff at Charest, (313) 893-8088.
♦ **G's Place**, 2764 Florian. (313) 871-9641.
♦ **Paycheck's Lounge**, 2932 Caniff. (313) 874-0909.
♦ **The Attic Bar**, 11667 Joseph Campau. (313) 365-4194. Popular hangout for blues musicians who drop by to play and listen. Live blues featured seven nights a week. Call after 5 p.m. for listings. *Open daily 5 p.m.-2 a.m.*

LATE-NIGHT HAMTRAMCK ROCKS . . . . . The streets are empty, all the Polish widows are asleep, and the serious drinkers in the after-work crowd are lingering in the front rooms of their favorite taverns when they're joined by the late wave of hip young people from every social class, from Birmingham and Royal Oak and Detroit. They've come to hear new music – not oldies and covers of current hits. The opening band plays around 10 p.m., followed by the headliner at midnight, so sometimes people first stop by **Planet Ant** or the **Shadow Box Cafe** (page 255-256), where an acoustic act might be playing. The "biggest" club that books the best-known acts is **Lili's 21** at 2930 Jacob, 3 blocks south of Holbrook (313-875-6555), followed by **Paychecks** at 2932 Caniff (313-874-0909).

Heidelberg Street Project

*Color and castoffs turned a decaying neighborhood
into a curiously moving fantasy environment.*

Tour busses stop regularly to see the constantly evolving
art environment on Heidelberg Street, in the oldest and
most decrepit part of Detroit, the near east side. Here are
street after street of modest worker homes from the 1880s. Most
are older and run-down. A few look well-maintained. Many more
are boarded up. There are so many vacant lots that pheasants
are known to thrive in these parts.

Artist Tyree Guyton grew up on Heidelberg Street, and here
he started creating remarkable inner-city environmental art. His
first work was "Fun House," an abandoned house next to his
grandfather's neat, grey and green home. He splashed the weathered frame house with color and covered it with old toys, doll-
houses, pictures, signs, plastic bottles and the like.

Guyton's Heidelberg Project has grown beyond individual
buildings until the pavement of Heidelberg Street sports a tangle
of colored lines. Bright shoes march up tree trunks. A crowd of
stately pedestal drinking fountains gathers in the vacant lot
across the street. Smiling faces painted on Naugahyde-type
chairs enhance the party atmosphere of a vacant lot. Black and
white splotches decorate the dead tree behind them. New discards arrive regularly, dropped off by Guyton's many fans, and
the project is always evolving with new ideas and new material.

For Guyton, the project became both a way to stabilize the
neighborhood, now turned into a tourist attraction, and to work
out his own personal demons. As a child he lived in poverty on
this street. His mother was overwhelmed by family responsibili-
ties. He was abused by a family acquaintance and teased for his
interest in art. Only his grandfather encouraged his art.

As an adult, Guyton studied briefly at Detroit's Center for
Creative Studies and has pursued art as a career. "Fun House"
got him started using color, imagination, and cast-off toys to
transform a depressing environment into a wild and appealing
fantasy of the childhood he never enjoyed. Sometimes it's a
social critique. The effect is loose and not conventionally cute. It

evokes strong reactions — pro and con.

Photos couldn't convey the magical, powerful feeling of this place. Coming here can be a very special experience. Guyton's late grandfather, Sam Mackey, lived next to the Fun House for 40 years. He saw the neighborhood become spotted with abandoned homes that invite arson, drugs, and other crimes. A philosopher and preacher, he was often out on the park bench installed for the steady stream of visitors, happy to share his experience and thoughts. His grandson's art inspired him to take up a brush and create shapes and figures in a child-like fashion; a gallery in Paris exhibited these works.

In spring of 1992, the city of Detroit, responding to unidentified neighbors' complaints, gave Tyree Guyton 15 minutes to salvage bits of his assemblages before demolishing Fun House and several other city-owned buildings he had decorated. In June Sam Mackey died; hundreds of people who loved the Heidelberg Project attended his funeral. His house has now been decorated with multicolored designs. Tyree Guyton's work has been exhibited at the Detroit Institute of Arts and elsewhere; his career as an artist seems on its way.

Detroit's Archer administration is on record as being "not against" the Heidelberg Project. Guyton is trying to buy up vacant lots to assure a permanent exhibit space.

Heidelberg Street has to be seen in real life, and not just from a car, to have a chance to work its often-powerful effect. Some people never do feel it, but skeptics may well be won over. Guyton's outdoor arrange-

Some find Tyree Guyton's fanciful assemblages on Heidelberg Street weird and disconcerting. Others find his work a powerful artistic vision made all the more affecting because of its real-life setting in a deteriorated neighborhood.

ments of pedestal sinks, shoes marching up spotted trees, assemblages of doors, and such remain and continue to grow. Since the art environment is always changing, it's worth checking out whenever you're in the area. Lately classical music comes from speakers concealed in the art environment.

On Heidelberg between Mt. Elliott and Ellery. From downtown, take Gratiot to Mt.Elliott, turn right. Three blocks past Mack, turn right onto Heidelberg Street. Or, go east on Jefferson, turn left onto Mt. Elliott, and turn left onto Heidelberg in about a mile.

IN THE VICINITY AND WORTH A LOOK. . . . . The well-known **Capuchin monastery and soup kitchen** is a few blocks southeast on Mt. Elliott. . . . . For almost two centuries Detroit notables have been buried at picturesque **Elmwood Cemetery**, entered off Elmwood just north of Lafayette. At the cemetery office, pick up information on graves of noteworthy burials. Notice, too, the gentle rise and fall of the land. Much of Detroit looked like this in the 1840s, before it was leveled for high-density real estate developments. . . . . . If you take Mt. Elliott all the way southeast to the river, you'll be at **Mt. Elliott Park**, one of the new riverfront parks. It's a good place to fish and watch river traffic and activities at the **Coast Guard station** for ice-breaking, rescue, buoy-tending, and policing operations. Pick up a snack or deli food at the upscale Harbortown Market on Jefferson at Mt. Elliott.

ANOTHER MEMORABLE HOME-BASED ART ENVIRONMENT . . . . . is in Redford Township, between Detroit and Livonia. Here in a courtyard between Silvio Barile's **Redford Italian Bakery and Pizzeria** and his house, he has used Kwikcrete to create an elaborate sculptural homage to things he cares about: America, freedom, family, mama's love, Roman and Italian heroes and selected American presidents (Washington, Lincoln, Roosevelt, and Kennedy). You have to walk through it to take it all in. Another part of the magic on this modest city lot: productive fruit trees and vines, including things like figs that ordinarily don't grow in Michigan. How is love of family consistent with bare-breasted pinups? Ask the artist! The bakery is also an Italian grocery. You can sit at tables and eat Etruscan pizza, his specialty, with pop. *26417 Plymouth Road. From I-96, take the Beech-Daly Exit 178, go south on Beech-Daly to Plymouth, then right (west). Bakery is across from Long John Silver. (313) 937-2288.*

East Jefferson Avenue and the riverfront

History, good music, Detroit's oldest historic architecture, and striking scenery in a series of riverfront parks

In 1980 the three-mile stretch of riverfront between the RenCen and Belle Isle bridge was industrial. The river was blocked off from public use by old warehouses and factories, and by remnants of docks and ship yards. Today the departure of most industry has paved the way for the Rivertown entertainment/office/apartment district of the most expensive land in Detroit. Scattered nightspots and restaurants range from the Woodbridge Tavern, an old speakeasy with a nifty terrace, and the earthily casual and eclectic Soup Kitchen Saloon blues and jazz club, to famed chef Jimmy Schmidt's Rattlesnake Club restaurant. Ample parking and safe streets are plusses. For more on the Detroit River and shipping, see pages 276-279.

The city's three new riverfront parks at the feet of St. Aubin, Chene, and Mt. Elliott streets have proven aesthetic and popular successes. Chene Park outdoor jazz and pop music concerts at sunset are a don't-miss attraction worth a visit to Detroit.

Harbortown and Stroh River Place, two large mixed-use luxury housing developments, have proven popular with upper-income empty-nesters and young professionals. But enough old buildings and businesses like Medusa Cement remain to give the place a kind of gritty, real-world visual atmosphere.

Here are Rivertown highlights, arranged from west (the RenCen end) to east, toward Belle Isle. Easiest access is from Jefferson; all the mentioned streets that end at the river (Chene, St. Aubin, etc.) intersect with Jefferson.

◆ **Jefferson Avenue historic buildings.** Pre-Civil War Detroit, with its gentle Federal-style townhouses and Gothic revival churches, has largely been erased by the industrialization spurred by the War between the States. But scattered pieces of antebellum Detroit can still be seen on Jefferson, especially on the two blocks east of the Chrysler Freeway (I-75/I-375). The parade of old houses is occasionally interrupted by turn-of-the-

Detroit's riverfront, with Chene Park in the foreground and downtown Detroit in the background. Just behind the park are the giant Medusa cement silos, which Medusa's big bulk carriers supply regularly with limestone from Charlevoix and elsewhere.

century apartment buildings and clubhouses built by the wealthy before they left the city for the suburbs in the 1920s. For an interesting brochure on historic Rivertown architecture, stop by the Beaubien House (page 222).

Two fine old buildings are regularly open to the public:

◆ **Christ Episcopal Church** is a beautiful 1863 Gothic Revival church designed by Gordon Lloyd, a star of 19th-century Michigan architecture known for his Episcopal churches all over the state. Weekdays ask at the office to look inside and see the beautiful stained glass windows. A Tiffany window depicts the legend of St. Elizabeth of Hungary. A portrait window honors the family of the church's first rector, William Lyster. As a missionary in pioneer Michigan, he coined the name "Irish Hills" for the glacial hills of Jackson and Lenawee counties. *960 E. Jefferson just east of I-75. (313) 259-6688. Sunday morning services 8:15 and 10:30.*

◆ The 1840s **Moross House**, Detroit's oldest existing brick dwelling, is the headquarters of the **Detroit Garden Center**. Portions of it have been furnished with mid-19th-century antiques from old Detroit families. Its walled rear garden is a lush, vine-clad oasis planted with favorites from the mid-19th century: peonies, lilacs, spring bulbs, and wisteria. There is an excellent **horticultural library**. The center sponsors one-day classes and workshops, trips, and special events like a Christmas open house the first weekend in December and an orchid show the weekend closest to Valentine's Day. *1460 Jefferson west of Riopelle. (313) 259-6363. Open Tues thru Thurs 9:30-3:30 and by appointment.*

◆ **St. Aubin Park.** This park features two fishing shelters, a grassy picnic area, and two river overlooks, plus a 67-slip transient pleasure boat marina (the only one in Detroit) handy to downtown. A series of creative **outdoor history exhibits** interpret the Detroit riverfront. A coalition of government agencies and civic groups funded them. History plus riverfront scenery make the park a fine place for a leisurely stroll. Call (313) 224-1184 for info on tours of riverfront history.

Many exhibits are on the river's edge buffer between the river and the marina. A path to it starts at St. Aubin and Atwater. Along the riverwalk, on the north end of the river's edge buffer, are inscriptions with a dozen moments in the riverfront's history. Some of the largest marine steam engines ever made were built across the street at the Detroit Drydock Company. In fact, the city's auto boom of the early 20th century built directly on skills and technologies of shipbuilding. A seven-foot model of a drydock shows an 1892 freighter being worked on.

By the marina office and restrooms is a Play Area with **Land of Boats**, the first play sculpture designed by the internationally known sculptor **Vito Acconci**. On a curved wall on the north end of the park, three markers give a historical overview of **African-Americans in Detroit**. *On Atwater between Orleans and St. Aubin about a mile north of the RenCen. Open for fishing during daylight hours. For marina reservations and docking fees, call (313) 259-4677 or 1-800-338-6424. For a fee, a costumed guide from the Rec. Dept. offers group tours (313-224-1184).*

◆ **Chene Park.** Chene Park combines low-key fishing and riverfront access with an expanded, 6,500-seat riverfront amphitheater that is a major regional **concert venue** for top performers in blues, jazz, classical, and adult contemporary music. Concertgoers can get up during concerts and walk along the river and small pond. At sunset and after dark, the effect of lights reflected in the water is fabulous. And during a concert, the combination

of spectacular scenery, good music, and mellow crowds along the
river is hard to equal.

Every 10 days or so, the **Medusa Challenger**, a freighter as
long as two football fields, unloads cement from Charlevoix to the
Medusa silos next to the park. Call (313) 496-0555 to find out
when it is coming. *On Atwater at the foot of Chene and Dubois,
between St. Aubin Park and Stroh River Place. For specific information on* **concerts***, call (313) 224-1184 between 8:30 and 5:30,
or the pre-recorded Rec. Dept. Fun Phone at (313) 252-2200 + code
3501 (toll-free in Detroit).*

◆ **Stroh River Place.** The giant Parke-Davis pharmaceutical
company began here in 1873. Today architect Albert Kahn's
handsome brick buildings from the early 1920s have been stylishly renovated and developed by the Stroh Brewery. River Place
has offices (including Stroh corporate headquarters), apartments
and townhouses, the elegant River Place Hotel, and Jimmy
Schmidt's celebrated **Rattlesnake Club**, with innovative
American regional food. *At the foot of Joseph Campau, corner of
Atwater. Valet parking, or park on a nearby street and walk.*

Changing exhibits are held in the large, two-story exhibit
space of the **Detroit Artists Market**. Shows feature new and
established artists in the area. Some are juried, others are selected by a single curator. The Detroit Artists Market was established by collectors and art-lovers to provide a place where new
art could be seen and sold. Board members typically include
leaders of the Detroit Institute of Arts and other notables, not
artists. The **gallery shop** carries two-dimensional art, sculpture,
jewelry, and other crafts. *1452 Randolph at Centre. (313) 962-
0337. Tues-Sat 11-5. Park on Harmonie Park next door ($2 all
day) or on the street.*

◆ **Mt. Elliott Park.** The Lighthouse Depot of the 1870s became
a Coast Guard center of operations for the region from Lake Erie
to Lake Superior. Coast Guard operations for maintaining lighthouses and river channel markers are headquartered at the foot
of Mt. Elliott, readily observable from the park, which is under
construction. Coming: an interpretive center on Detroit riverfront
history in a building formerly owned by the Coast Guard. *On
Atwater at the feet of Mt. Elliott, Iron, and Meldrum.*

Belle Isle

A top Michigan attraction, this 3-mile-long island features great views, a splendid zoo and aquarium, a nature center, conservatory, and much more.

Belle Isle is one of the most interesting and beautiful urban parks in the world. Here you can get a dramatic **view of downtown Detroit**, a panoramic **view of the Detroit River** with its international freighter traffic, and an equally sweeping **view of Canada**. Right across the river is the big Hiram Walker distillery, moved from Detroit to Windsor during Prohibition.

On the 981-acre island itself, you can find waterfront **picnic areas** throughout, two long **fishing piers**, and an elaborate **playground** for kids along with a **giant slide**. There's a delightful **zoo**, an extraordinarily beautiful freshwater **aquarium**, a fascinating **Great Lakes shipping museum**, a sizable plant **conservatory** and formal gardens, and a **nature center** with nature trails through forests filled with deer. A quaint **floral clock** still graces the entrance in summer. Even if you don't get out of your car, it's pleasant to drive around the park with its antique cast-iron street lights, fanciful old picnic pavilions, and frequent monuments. A herd of some 90 fallow deer, tame and very small, roam the island, especially around the nature center.

The crush of visitors (10 million a year) creates problems on this attractive island. At times maintenance personnel cannot keep up with the accumulation of trash. Some areas are scarred and need upgrading. On warm evenings teenagers cruising with loud portable stereos can create so much congestion that this is one of the last places you would want to be. Evenings and weekend afternoons from the first warm days of spring into midsummer are best avoided. As we go to press, it seems possible that entrance fees ($3/day/car or a $15 annual pass) will be imposed. That will improve maintenance and may cut down on teen cruising. There is a quaint **police station** on the island, at Inselruhe and Central Avenue, with enough patrols to make it safe for visitors day or night. (The island is never closed.) By big-city standards, Belle Isle is quite safe.

Scott Fountain at Belle Isle's western end offers a splendid view of downtown Detroit.

The city bought Belle Isle in 1879 for $200,000. A century earlier, it had been a common grazing ground for the French farmers whose narrow ribbon farms fronted on the river. Today the major thoroughfare is around the island's perimeter. Originally swampy throughout, most of the park has been elevated with fill. Only the eastern wooded area looks the way it did a century ago. Canals allow canoeists to traverse the length of the island, but the canoe livery is currently closed.

The one-way perimeter road goes counter-clockwise. Sights are arranged in the order in which you come to them. Of special interest on Belle Isle are:

◆ **Scott Fountain.** To make room for this huge and ornate fountain, Belle Isle's western end was extended a thousand yards. From that western tip you can see not only the fountain but its reflection in the specially constructed lagoon. Italian white marble — some 20,000 square feet of it — was used to create the monument, which the city was at first reluctant to build. The half million dollars were supplied in the bequest of James Scott when he died in 1910. But Scott was viewed as such a scoundrel that the city at first refused to honor his request to spend the donation on an imposing monument in his honor. Eventually the city held an international competition, won by the eminent Beaux-Arts architect Cass Gilbert. (The following year he also was hired to design Detroit's Public Library.) For the fountain, Gilbert came up with a complex series of bowls, basins, and fountains, complete with spewing turtles, dolphins, lionesses, Neptunes, and animal horns. Sculptor Herbert Adams created the required bronze statue of Scott. It graces the fountain's west side. Some say the spot was chosen so that prevailing winds keep him wet much of the time. For the first time in decades, all four pumps work, and the central spray reaches a height of over 75 feet.

◆ **Dossin Great Lakes Museum.** Not to be missed. One of the country's leading maritime museums. Outstanding river views, in all weather, from the pilot house of the William Clay Ford. See separate entry, page 274. *Open Wed-Sun 10-4. $1.*

◆ **Aquarium.** Another must-see, both for dramatic tanks of fish and its striking architecture. See separate entry, page 272. *Open daily including holidays 10-5. $1.*

◆ **Whitcomb Conservatory.** Capped by an imposing 85-foot glass dome, this 1904 building was made of parts from an exhibit at the St. Louis World's Fair. The giant palms in the central space are spectacular. Adjoining rooms feature cacti, ferns, tropical plants, a large collection of orchids, and seasonal floral displays. The bulletin board is a good place to catch up on horticulture events in the area.

In front are **formal gardens** and a delightful fountain capped by a **bronze gazelle**, created by Marshall Fredericks in 1936. At the base are four animals native to the island: a hawk, rabbit, otter, and grouse. *Inland from Dossin Museum. (313) 267-7134. Open 9-5, every day of the year. $1 admission for everyone over 2 years; also allows access to the Aquarium next door.*

◆ **Belle Isle Zoo.** Set amid splendid, shady trees, this small, 13-acre zoo is an exceptionally pleasant place to spend a summer day. The key to its charm is the 3/4-mile-long elevated

The Belle Isle Conservatory and Aquarium are wonderful places to visit any time of year. $1 gets you into both.

walkway from which most of the animals are viewed. Looking down into the animals' settings gives a more three-dimensional, interesting view. The naturalistic settings are ample enough to allow most of the 30 species to roam freely. For brief visits or people with small children, a visit to the Belle Isle Zoo may well be more satisfying than seeing the much larger and more expensive Detroit Zoo.

Among the rarer animals on display are endangered spectacled bears, the only bear native to South America, and maned wolves, also from South America. These wolves are known as "foxes on stilts" because their long legs enable them to see over tall vegetation. The "World of Spiders" is a popular exhibit that showcases about a dozen types of spiders. A new carnivore exhibit of lions and tigers opens in mid-June, 1994. *On Vista, just south of Central Avenue in center of island. (313) 398-0900. Open May thru Oct, 10-5 daily. Admission: 13 and older, $2, seniors $1, ages 2-12 50¢.*

◆ **Nature Center.** Belle Isle's nature center is on the eastern side of the island where the forest and marsh remain in their natural state. Two self-guided **nature trails**, one 3/4 of a mile long, the other 1/4 mile, give good views of the native wildlife in the 200-acre natural area. For **wheelchair users** there's a short paved trail as well. Here you can also see the now tame and abundant European fallow deer, brought to the island in the1930s. In April the trails are likely to be underwater.

Though the indoor part of the nature center isn't large, it's well worth a visit any time of year. Intelligent, clear displays explain the area's interesting natural history and dramatically spotlight selected aspects of animal anatomy and behavior. Lively bulletin boards make this a good place to learn about area natural history programs.

Most of the snakes, birds, turtles, and mammals inside are temporarily held injured animals or illegal confiscated pets such as ferrets and foxes. *North end of island on Oakway. (313) 267-7157. Wed-Sun 10-4. Donations welcome.*

◆ **The Livingstone Memorial Lighthouse**, made of Georgian marble, is topped by a bronze lantern cap. It's almost 70 feet tall; its light can be seen 15 miles away in the middle of Lake St. Clair. *The light is on the east tip of Belle Isle. As you follow the island perimeter road to the right around the island, past the Coast Guard station and park where the road veers left. Walk the asphalt path to the island's tip.*

In Belle Isle's wooded eastern third, small fallow deer wander about freely, to the delight of children. French farmers in the 18th century used the island for grazing cattle.

To get to Belle Isle from the intersection of I-375 and Jefferson in downtown Detroit, go 2 1/2 miles east to East Grand Blvd. Turn right onto the MacArthur Bridge to Belle Isle. (313) 267-7116. Possible auto fee: $3/car/day or $15 annual pass.

A BROCHURE WITH MAP . . . . . "Detroit's Beautiful Belle Isle Park," describes the full range of activities and sights. It is available weekdays 8-3:30 at the park office, which is in the White House on Inselruhe, or by writing Detroit Recreation Dept., 735 Randolph #2006, Detroit, MI 48226.

KEEPING BELLE ISLE NATURAL . . . . . and keeping it a clean, attractive, public pleasure park is the aim of **Friends of Belle Isle**. They organize a spring clean-up and other volunteer activities, raise money for island renovation projects, publicize the many activities and events held on the island, and act as a watchdog advisory group to Detroit Common Council about the many development projects proposed for the island. They opposed former Mayor Young's proposal for casino gambling on Belle Isle (earning his enduring enmity) and don't like the zoo-horse equestrian center or the permanent grandstand proposed for the Grand Prix races either. Their **newsletter** is newsy and excellent. To get involved, call (313) 331-7760 Mondays or Fridays, or become a member ($15 individual, $25 family). Write Friends of Belle Isle, 8909 E. Jefferson (after September, they move back to the island, so write "Belle Isle"), Detroit, MI 48214.

Belle Isle Aquarium

A fantastic freshwater world of strange fish
and a noisy electric eel in a most beautiful setting

Not only is this the oldest public aquarium in the U.S. but one of the most visually striking. It was built in 1904, designed by Albert Kahn, the architect who shaped much of Detroit. Carved dolphins, now mostly covered by vines, grace the entrance. The interior, with muted, indirect lighting, has a delightful aura created by the serene green-tiled ceiling contrasted with the black-tiled lower level. The effect, augmented by the many strange fish in crystal-clear aquaria, is that of entering a fantastic new world.

Over 100 species of freshwater fish are here. The rarest is the tiny and endangered desert pupfish from the southwestern U.S., where rampant development is dangerously lowering the water table. Most popular is the huge, ugly electric eel, which delivers a hefty 650 volts to stun prey. Through a speaker visitors can hear the big eel's electric output when it is fed at 10:30, 12:30, and 2:30 daily (and at 4:30 Sunday). Often big crowds gather to experience the noisy performance.

Informational signs in this striking aquarium are excellent, and interior "waterscaping" in the big tanks realistically emulate

The long-nose gar fish is one of many large Great Lakes fish you can see in their huge 2,800-gallon tank. The Belle Isle Aquarium's biggest attraction of all is the noisy electric eel.

the fishes' natural environments. Neither frustratingly brief nor overly long, the signs provide interesting nuggets of information. The sign next to the piranha exhibit reads: "Outside of the movies, piranhas have never been known to kill a person. In fact, people swim and bathe in rivers where piranhas live. Piranhas use their razor-sharp teeth and strong jaws to feed on fish. An injured animal that falls into piranha-infested waters may be reduced to bones in minutes."

Because of corrosive vapors from salt water, the aquarium no longer keeps saltwater fish. But you can see most major groups of freshwater fish, including a big 4,000-gallon tank of Great Lakes fish: Largemouth Bass, Lake Sturgeon, Spotted Gar, and Long-nose Gar. Ten thousand gallons of refrigerated water is used to keep pike, walleye, perch, bass, panfish, and trout.

Inland from Dossin Museum. (313) 267-7159. 10-5 daily, including holidays. $1 admission for all over 2 years old, also allows access to the Whitcomb Conservatory next door.

FISHING ON BELLE ISLE . . . . . The island has four special fishing spots. The two long piers at either end of Inselruhe are especially interesting. Fishing bulkheads are at the island's east end, one on the south side (just west of the Coast Guard Station) and one on the north, across a channel from the Detroit Yacht Club. Sizable catches are common. Among the fish caught are silver bass, bluegill, perch, sheephead, catfish, salmon, pickerel and pike. A bait shop is four blocks west of the MacArthur Bridge: **Jefferson & Meldrum Service** (6220 E. Jefferson, 259-1176). It can fix you up with a pole, hook, line, and sinker for under $10. Don't forget a fishing license. Minnows are $2 a dozen, worms $1.50 a dozen. Worms are used in summer, while minnows are used in the winter for pike and pickerel.

Dossin Great Lakes Museum

*It spotlights Detroit's important role in Lakes shipping
with an elegant passenger lounge,
meticulous models, changing exhibits,
and a pilot house with a grand river view.*

This superb museum is an ideal place to launch a season
of boat-watching. All sorts of questions can be fielded by
its knowledgeable staff and, on weekends, by its enthusiastic volunteers. Broad-based support by maritime fans has kept
Dossin fresher and more vital than others operated by the City of
Detroit's financially strapped Museums Department. A well-
stocked **bookstore/souvenir shop** is housed in an elegant
tobacco stand from a passenger ship. Groups of 10 or more can
call ahead for a tour. (Donations appreciated.)

Outside you'll find two big cannons from Commodore Perry's
key naval victory in the Battle of Lake Erie, the turning point of
the War of 1812. Just beyond the entrance is a splendid oak and
stained glass interior from the 1912 steamer, the *City of Detroit*.
This was the Gothic Room, where male passengers came to
smoke and talk. The ornate room suggests that vanished era
when passengers cruised the Great Lakes in luxurious comfort.

In the next room leading toward the river, a giant three-
dimensional relief map of the Great Lakes shows the relative
depths of the five lakes, from shallow Lake Erie (only 210 feet at
its deepest) to Lake Superior (1,333 feet).

Among models of Great Lakes ships and large photos of boat
christenings and spectacular wrecks, a display promotes Great
Lakes shipping, which today takes a back seat to railroads and
trucks. It points out that a boat delivering 15 million tons to
Chicago from the East Coast takes just 24 million gallons of fuel,
compared with 35 million gallons by rail and 123 million gallons
by truck.

Other museum highlights include:

◆ the **modern-day working pilot house** of the William Clay Ford
(1953), flagship of the fleet that hauled iron ore, coal, dolomite,
and limestone to Rouge Steel in Dearborn. Visitors can steer the

surprisingly small wheel, check the chadburns at the front for direction and speed, and look up and down the river. Over the functioning **ship's radio**, you can hear ships radioing their expected time of arrival to the J.W. Westcott mail boat station four miles downriver. (See page 278.)

On the river's near bank are signs showing the distance and direction to frequent freighter destinations:

> < Marquette 481 miles
> < Green Bay 507 miles
> < Alpena 219 miles
> < Duluth 728 miles
> Montreal 618 miles>
> Toronto   299 miles>

♦ a **working submarine periscope** at the base of the stairs to the pilot house is the museum's most popular exhibit. Looking past crosshairs designed to guide torpedos at enemy ships, you can get a great view of what's coming up and down the river and a view of Belle Isle, too.

♦ big **picture windows look out and down the river** in De Roy Hall, to the right of the pilot house, along with **displays** of things like torpedo boats at Detroit's Fisher Boat Works (once the most complete boat works on the Lakes), and superbly detailed **ship models** of ships associated with Michigan, from LaSalle's ill-fated Griffon through the Boblo S.S. Columbia, the famous luxury passenger S.S. South American, and the Edmund Fitzgerald.

♦ **Miss Pepsi** (1963), the first hydroplane to break 100 mph, is in the pavilion opposite the entrance. (The Dossin family who paid for half the original museum owned Miss Pepsi and the local bottling company that was bought out by Pepsi-Cola.)

For information on the Detroit-based **Great Lakes Maritime Institute** of maritime fans, and for many of their publications, stop at the Dossin Museum's shop.

Open Wed-Sun 10-4. (313) 267-6440. Closed holidays. Suggested admission $1; more is welcome.

Detroit River

One of the world's major freighter highways
is beautiful on a sunny day.

This wide, deep river connects the upper Great Lakes (Huron, Superior, and Michigan) with the lower Great Lakes of Erie and Ontario. Three centuries ago, when French fur-trading interests dominated the region, the river's almost half-mile width made it difficult in wartime for shore batteries to stop ship traffic. So in 1701 the French set up a fort at the relatively narrow point now marked by downtown Detroit. They perched cannon on the high northern bank to repel enemy English ships.

For Detroit's first two hundred years, shipping from the downtown wharfs was central to its economy, connecting the city with New York to the east and Chicago to the west. The river still carries the world's largest tonnage of cargo, but Detroit is no longer a significant port. Today the old riverfront industries that once separated the river from the city are gone. The riverfront from downtown to Belle Isle has emerged in the 1970s and 1980s as the magnet for the only new office and residential development in Detroit.

On a warm, not-too-windy day, the banks of this attractive aqua river are a wonderful place to watch the big boats go by. In

The highly recommended Diamond Jack river cruise takes visitors up and down the historic Detroit River, which has been one of North America's busiest waterways for three centuries.

Riverside Park, at the foot of West Grand Boulevard in southwest Detroit, is one of the many tucked-away nooks that reveal less obvious aspects of Detroit life. Here are the J. W. Westcott marine supply company, open around the clock during shipping season, and the Detroit fireboat Curtis Randolph.

the 1960s, freighters passed an average of once every 12 minutes. Today only about 25 to 35 a day pass by Detroit. One reason is the giant thousand-foot-long Great Lakes freighters, which can do the job of six conventional freighters. It's a thrill to see these massive boats pass by. Some have up to 60,000 tons of cargo. It adds to the mystique that a freighter may be coming from any port in the world.

Binoculars add to the fun of watching the passing boats. Good boat-watching sites, arranged from Windmill Point at the Detroit/Grosse Pointe Park line southwestward, are:

♦ **Mariner Park and the Windmill Point Light.** Looks out into Lake St. Clair. *Take Jefferson east to Alter, about 1/2 mile past Golightly Vo-Tech Center. Go east 1 mile on Alter; park is just past the bridge.*

♦ **Belle Isle.** From the island's east tip you can see out into Lake Clair. Ships on the horizon are half an hour away. On the island's south side, take Strand out past the Coast Guard Station and park soon after it. A long fishing pier is at the end of Inselruhe just east of the Dossin Museum. *Take the bridge off Jefferson, two miles east of downtown Detroit.*

♦ **Chene Park.** Fishing and benches within view of the big Medusa Cement silos, where every 10 days or so the *Medusa*

Challenger, a boat as long as two football fields, unloads cement from Charlevoix on Lake Michigan. The smaller *Medusa Conquest* also docks here. It may portend the new age of more flexible Great Lakes shipping with smaller manpower requirements. It's an old tanker cut down into a barge whose stern has been notched so a tugboat fits into it. Call (313) 471-6250 weekdays to find out when deliveries are being made. *At the foot of Chene or Dubois streets east of Jefferson, 1 1 /4 miles past the RenCen.*

◆ **St. Aubin Park**. Two fishing shelters, a picnic area, and two river overlooks abut a 67-boat transient marina. Creative outdoor **exhibits** relate riverfront history. By the marina office and restrooms is celebrated sculptor Vito Acconci's *Land of Boats*, a play sculpture.

The *Diamond Jack*, docked here, gives excellent **two-hour boat tours** of the Detroit and Windsor riverfronts. Call (313) 843-7676 (recording) or 843-9376. Costs $9 for adults, $6 for kids.

Looking fragile as a toy boat, the J. W. Westcott pulls up to a passing freighter to deliver mail. It's the only place in the U.S. where mail is delivered to moving vessels. You can see it in action just below the Ambassador Bridge.

*Take St. Aubin or Orleans from Jefferson south to the river and
park.*

◆ **Hart Plaza.** The very spot Cadillac chose for Fort Pontchartrain in 1701. Fishing, benches and picnic tables along the river.
The *Baja Beach Club*, a **floating nightclub** permanently docked
below, is the lake's last remaining sidewheeler. *At the foot of
Woodward. Park free on weekends along adjoining streets west of
Jefferson (Shelby, Griswold, Brush, Beaubien) or use the RenCen
lot A off Beaubien east of Jefferson.*

◆ **Riverside Park.** This grassy park, almost beneath the impressive Ambassador Bridge, is a terrific spot for boat-watching. The
little **mail boat** of the J.W. Westcott marine supply company is
docked next door. It's quite a sight to watch the 45-foot boat sail
out and pull up to passing freighters, looking alarmingly fragile
next to the giant it is servicing. The freighter's crew drops down a
line with a bucket for mail and supplies. The Westcott Company
provides ships with everyday supplies, nautical charts, and river
pilots for foreign vessels. Visitors are welcome to browse in its little **Great Lakes bookstore.** Open 24 hours a day during shipping season (April through December). (313) 496-0555.

Just down from Westcott are the City of Detroit's fireboat,
the *Curtis Randolph*, and past that, carferries that shuttle railroad cars between Detroit and Windsor. Also downriver is the
Detroit Harbor Terminal, periodically busy shipping and receiv-
ing manufactured parts. Directly across the river are Windsor's
harbor facilities. *At the foot of West Grand a block east of Fort.*

SPLENDID RIVERFRONT LODGING . . . . . An especially good overnight
place to watch the freighters go by as well as get a dramatic view of downtown Detroit is the **Ramada Inn** of Windsor. It's on Riverside Drive West. Be
sure to ask for a room on the Detroit River side, and you'll get your own personal outdoor porch overhanging the water. Call ahead for reservations at
(800) 228-9898. Rooms are regularly about $70 American a night and up,
but ask for special promotions.

Pewabic Pottery

Since 1903, some of the world's finest pottery and tile has been made at this quaint studio.

The art pottery and architectural tile made here since the early 20th century is famous for its beautiful, subtle glazes. Pewabic's founder, Mary Chase Perry Stratton, is best known for her six iridescent glazes, which were used extensively on both vessels and tile. She had been prompted by a local industrialist, Charles Freer, who was also one of the world's foremost connoisseurs of Oriental art. He showed Stratton a piece of Babylonian pottery which had a mysteriously beautiful patina. After years of experimentation, she was able to emulate it.

Stratton was an important figure in the Arts and Crafts movement that flourished in Detroit at the turn of the century. It promoted a return to simple, pre-industrial handcraftsmanship. True to its ideals, Stratton never attempted to exploit her glaze formulations by mass-producing her art. Her work maintained its artistic integrity, involving constant experimentation and change. Some of Stratton's most striking work was in architectural tiles, which can be found in public places, from the Nebraska State Capitol to the Shrine of the Immaculate Conception in Washington, D.C. Pewabic tiles can be seen all over Detroit, including the entrance of the Guardian Building in downtown Detroit and Christ Church in Bloomfield Hills.

Stratton named the fledgling pottery "Pewabic" after a Keweenaw Peninsula copper mine near Hancock, Michigan, her hometown. Her work was so well received that she was able to build this pleasant gallery and workshop built in the style of an old English country inn. She later married its architect, William Stratton. The pottery declined after her death in 1961.

But since 1981 there has been a revival under the auspices of the non-profit Pewabic Society. Production is once again underway, in the spirit of Stratton's work. To see what contemporary artists do with tiles commissioned for their work at Pewabic, take a look at the UAW Monument in downtown Flint (page 353), Detroit's Times Square and Millender Center *People Mover* stations (see page 207). Vintage Pewabic murals are at the Cadillac Center station in downtown Detroit.

Continuing to reflect Mary Stratton's vision, Pewabic today is a multifaceted place involved in education, exhibits, museum collections and archives, and in increasing production of hand-crafted architectural tile for buildings. Designers and craftspeople make tiles for homeowners and design professionals who want distinctive custom tiles for fireplaces, countertops and backsplashes, bathrooms and spas, and for walls. Pewabic also offers **classes**, workshops, lectures, internships and residency programs for studio potters and other artists, as well as outreach

to students from pre-school through high school. **Historic exhibits** tell the story of the pottery's role in the history of Detroit, the growth of the American Arts and Crafts movement, and the development of ceramic art.

Visitors can wander freely throughout the two-story building, which looks much as it did decades ago. In its **production studios**, artists

Pewabic founder Mary Chase Perry Stratton in her studio. Her glaze for pottery and tiles became a celebrated part of Detroit's Arts and Crafts movement early in this century.

mix clay, create molds, press and glaze tile, shape vessels, and fire a variety of kilns. Its **consignment galleries** showcase ceramic works in varying styles and techniques by established and emerging artists nationwide. The **gift shop** features reasonably priced Pewabic gift tile and vessels in both reproductions and adaptations of its historic designs. Motifs include animals, themes from fairy tales and fables, and geometric shapes. There are displays of tile tables, garden ware, jewelry and commemorative tiles.

10125 E. Jefferson between Cadillac and Hurlbut, across from Waterworks Park and about 1 1/2 miles east of the Belle Isle bridge. Park in courtyard in front of the building. (313) 822-0954. Mon-Sat 10-6. Free admission; donations welcome.

AN ENDURINGLY ELEGANT NEIGHBORHOOD . . . . . is **Indian Village**, between the Belle Isle bridge and Pewabic Pottery. The large mansions on three long streets were built between 1895 and the mid-1920s on land that used to be 18th-century French ribbon farms. *Indian Village is on Burns, Seminole, and Iroquois between Jefferson and Mack.*

Fisher Mansion

*Amusingly lavish, this auto baron's mansion
recalls the excesses of the Roaring Twenties.*

This fancifully lavish mansion is one of the extraordinary sights of Detroit. It was built in the 1920s by the talented playboy head of Cadillac Motors. Its style has been described as "glitz bordering on garish." Neglected after owner Lawrence Fisher's death, the mansion has been purchased, restored, and maintained as the Bhaktivedanta Cultural Center by Alfred Brush Ford, great-grandson of Henry Ford, and Elisabeth Reuther Dickmeyer, daughter of legendary UAW chief Walter Reuther. Ford and Dickmeyer donated the mansion to the International Society for Krishna Consciousness (ISKCON) to which they belong. It is one of 300 ISKCON centers world-wide.

Today the mansion also serves a small community of Hare Krishna followers, who use the ballroom for their temple room. They are pleasant, gentle people who do not proselytize visitors in any way and don't wear orange robes, either. They do offer, upon request, an audio-visual presentation on the religiously-based Bhaktivedanta culture.) On the second floor is the excellent **Govinda's** vegetarian restaurant, also run by the Hare

The Fisher Mansion is a cozy, comfortable version of San Simeon, the California palace of Lawrence Fisher's friend, publishing magnate William Randolph Hearst.

Krishnas. The grounds and gardens with their fountains and wandering peacocks are peaceful retreats in the Spanish style of the house.

Lawrence Fisher was one of the seven Fisher Brothers who helped revolutionize the auto industry in the early 20th century by building enclosed bodies for cars. Lawrence was a big, beefy bachelor who squired the likes of Jean Harlow and threw opulent parties. No elitist, he invited local tradespeople as well as celebrities to these events. Champagne flowed continuously during parties from the mouth of a solid silver head of Neptune in the entryway.

The home of publishing magnate William Randolph Hearst, Fisher's good friend, inspired this mansion on the Detroit River. Hearst's San Simeon then set the standard for California opulence, mixing an eclectic array of florid architectural styles. Fisher's mansion follows in this tradition. The effect of all the pattern, texture, and color is dazzling and surprising, not overwhelming or pompous. The scale is intimate; the house only has three bedrooms. The entranceway has black Majorcan tiles on the floor with gold insets. Tiles in Art Deco patterns surround the silver head of Neptune. Long Roman tiles alternate with Pewabic tile. The marble columns are Corinthian Greek. The bathrooms are especially memorable. In all, 75 ounces of gold leaf and 140 ounces of silver were used on the mansion's ceilings and moldings.

Always impeccably dressed, Fisher remained a bachelor until, at 62, he married his childhood sweetheart, then 67. One of his great loves was his dogs. He frequently dined alone with his cocker spaniel, who ate out of a silver bowl. When the dog suddenly disappeared one day, the disconsolate auto baron personally went door to door in the neighborhood, offering a $10,000 reward for its return, to no avail. When another dog drowned in the adjacent swimming pool, he had the pool filled in. He buried two of his beloved pooches in signed, silver Tiffany caskets on the mansion's grounds. One of the first things a subsequent owner did was to dig up the caskets, dump the bones in the trash, and sell the silver.

Sailing was another of Lawrence Fisher's passions. Hence, the mansion is strategically situated with canal access to the Detroit River. Fisher had the Grayhaven Canal built up to the house, with large enclosed boat houses on each side. The larger held his 106-foot yacht. The smaller housed the vessel which

From this silver head of Neptune, champagne flowed continuously at the parties of Cadillac Motor chief Lawrence Fisher. The variety of dramatic tile designs in this foyer only hints at the exuberant, eclectic decor throughout this amazing mansion.

later became President Kennedy's presidential yacht.

The ballroom emulates a Spanish courtyard, complete with Venetian parapet and delicate white clouds painted on the blue ceiling. During Fisher's festive parties, a machine projected stars on this ceiling, and lighting was adjusted to simulate dusk or dawn, whichever time it might be. Some of the world's top wood-carvers were brought to work on detailing. In some cases a carver would spend over a year on a single door. Not much of a reader, Fisher ordered the hand tooled leather books in the library by color rather than title.

Amazingly, this splendid mansion was sold by a bank in the early 1960s for just $80,000. ISKCON have respected the historical integrity of the place. Their own colorful religious paintings hang on some walls, but they don't obscure the feel of the place when Fisher lived there. In fact, they are well suited to the vivid, exotic atmosphere. One startling exception is an upstairs room in which sits a full-sized, bluish seated statue of their deceased guru.

383 Lenox, off E. Jefferson in Detroit, about 3 miles east of the Belle Isle Bridge and 5 miles east of downtown. From Jefferson, turn onto Dickerson. Look for the sign to Victoria Park, Detroit's new showplace subdivision. Dickerson becomes Lenox. From I-94, take the Conner exit; go south on Conner, which ends at E. Jefferson, and turn left onto E. Jefferson. At the second traffic light, turn right onto Dickerson, where you will see a billboard for

*Victoria Park. (313) 331-6740. Tours Friday thru Sunday at
12:30, 2, 3:30, and 6; also at other times by prior arrangement.
$6 adults, $5 seniors, $4 children.*

JUST WHAT ARE THE 'HARE KRISHNAS'? . . . . . A note from a Detroit
disciple of the International Society for Krishna Consciousness (ISKON):

"The Society was founded in 1966 by His Divine Grace A. C.
Bhaktivendata Swami Shrila Prabhupada. The society currently operates
temples, preaching centers and farming communities on six continents. His
Divine Grace brought from India the ancient teachings of The Vedas.
"The two primary theological texts, The *Bhagavad Gita* and The *Shrimad
Bhagavatam*, were written 3,000 years B.C. and existed as an oral spiritual
tradition for 2,000 years before that.

"Modern-day members of ISKCON have realized that the teachings of
the Swami do not just take us back to Godhead but also show us a way to
live and conduct our lives. Many members are mainstream professional people like doctors, engineers, and lawyers."

Grosse Pointe

A haven for Detroit's old money,
the Pointes offer lovely views of Lake St. Clair
and lavish early 20th-century estates.

This famous string of five affluent suburbs is a splendid place to tour by car or bicycle, thanks to beautiful Lake St. Clair and the handsomely landscaped estates. "Grosse Pointe" is actually five separate municipalities stretching along and off the lake just east of Detroit. Driving out Jefferson from Detroit into Grosse Pointe Park, there is a dramatic change. As you cross Alter Road, you go from close-packed Detroit blocks and enter a green, kempt domain of big trees and beautiful homes. In recent decades, much of Detroit's east side has become blighted, so the contrast is even more striking.

The prominent old families of Grosse Pointe, Grosse Pointe Shores, and Grosse Pointe Farms are about as close as Metro Detroit comes to having an aristocracy. Many scions of the founding auto barons still live in the Pointes. This is definitely George and Barbara Bush territory, with the tone set by low-key people with inherited money.

Actually, there's more diversity of income and ethnicity here than the WASP stereotype suggests. Away from the lake, especially toward Detroit in the planned buffer suburb of Grosse Pointe Park, there's a good deal of modest, middle-class 1920s housing. The Grosse Pointes offer better housing deals on comparable houses than Ann Arbor. Grosse Pointers reflect the ethnic mix of Detroit's old east side: Italians, Belgians, Poles, and Lebanese, plus a few old French families — and lots of executive transfers.

Property on the lake is always expensive — often over a million dollars per home. Some of the choicest streets are Vendome, Provençal (overlooking the Country Club of Detroit), and Lake Shore Road. There still aren't many Jews or Democrats or blacks in the Pointes, though their numbers are gradually increasing. For years through the 1950s, prospective Grosse Pointe home buyers were screened by the Grosse Pointe Realtors' infamous

Grosse Pointe is famous for its lakefront mansions, though many of the biggest have been demolished for subdivisions. One elegant mansion you can visit is the Grosse Pointe War Memorial at 32 Lake Shore, once the home of a Packard Motor founder.

point system – a source of sensitivity and embarrassment today. Private detectives hired to fill out reports didn't even bother to rate blacks or Asians. They were automatically banned. Other prospective home buyers were secretly rated on such issues as:

1. Is their way of living typically American?
2. Appearances—swarthy, slightly swarthy, or not at all?
3. Accents—pronounced, medium, slight, not at all?
4. Dress—neat, sloppy, flashy, or conservative?

The screening maintained a homogeneous population of whites.

The shoreline of these affluent communities was first settled by Detroit French who left the city after England took it over in 1760. The French established distinctive ribbon farms along Lake St. Clair. Only 300 to 600 feet wide, they extended a mile or more inland, permitting each farmer crucial access to Lake St. Clair for transportation.

Wealthy Detroiters began building summer homes in the Grosse Pointe area as early as the 1840s, but few who worked in Detroit dared live year-round so far out. Wealthy businessmen often commuted by yacht to Detroit from their summer Grosse Pointe residences. A few of these fine old Victorian mansions still stand, such as the 1895 Queen Anne house at 365 Lake Shore.

Beginning around 1910, wealthy Detroiters withdrew from the city, with its booming factories they themselves built, and with the masses of immigrants who came to work there. Grosse Pointe became famous for its magnificent lakeshore estates that imitated elegant country houses in England, France, and Italy.

More typical were straight streets of large, ten-room Tudor or Georgian Revival houses. Some of the most spectacular lakefront mansions have been razed to make way for more modest half-million-dollar homes. But many remain.

A trip out Jefferson and Lake Shore Road from Detroit to Grosse Pointe Shores is a fine drive, especially when the sun is shining on the stunning turquoise blue of Lake St. Clair. The wonderful Art Deco storefronts on Jefferson remind you just how urban these close-in suburbs of the 1920s really are. They were laid out along streetcar lines, in fact. To see Windmill Point or the house built by Pewabic Pottery founder Mary Chase Perry Stratton and her architect husband, turn right from Jefferson onto Three Mile Drive, about a mile west of the entrance to Grosse Pointe Park. The Strattons" informal multi-level house at 938 Three Mile is oriented to the garden. It combines Arts and Crafts principles with balconies, bays, and beamed ceilings of Mexican architecture.

To see one of the prettiest parts of the Pointes, continue on Three Mile to Esser. Go right onto Esser, left onto Bedford or Harcourt, and right onto Windmill Pointe Drive. It terminates at a small park. The **Windmill Point Lighthouse**, where Lake St. Clair joins the Detroit River, sits at the south edge of Mariners' Park in Detroit. From Windmill Point Drive, turn left at Alter Road to get to the lighthouse.

Where Jefferson becomes Lake Shore Road, no houses obscure motorists' views of the lake. You could park on a side street and walk along here. But don't venture into the public parks. They're for card-carrying residents only — and always have been. (Suburbs of this era throughout the U.S. were developed with the explicit intention of providing a wholesome, healthy life for "our kind of people" and keeping the growing central cities and their exotic immigrant populations at bay.)

Stop in at the **Grosse Pointe War Memorial** at 32 Lake Shore Road in Grosse Pointe Farms. Originally the home of Russell Alger, Jr., a Packard Motor Company founder and son of the Governor/Senator/Secretary of War, it is now the hub of recreational and cultural activities in the Pointes. Visitors are welcome to peek inside the meeting rooms and see the stunning lake views, framed by elegant, formal interiors in 15th-century Florentine, 16th-century Venetian, and Italian Baroque styles.

A particularly striking sight is the private **Grosse Pointe Yacht Club** off Lake Shore at the foot of Vernier Road. What began as a ice boating club in 1914 had, by 1929, become an Art Deco version of Venetian splendor. The picturesque tower, almost 200 feet high, has ship bells which strike the hours during sailing season. This remarkable yacht club, finished just before the Depression, turned out to be Grosse Pointe's last gasp of gilded grandeur. The Thirties ushered in a sober Georgian neoclassicism, which set the tasteful, albeit dull, tone for nearly all Grosse Pointe construction ever since. A visit to the Cotswold-inspired **estate of Edsel and Eleanor Ford** (page 293) is a worthwhile end to this drive. Shortly before you get there, look for the new lakefront French chateau with the sweeping curved entrance stairs, and steep, slate mansard roof. Built by Art Van Elslander of Art Van furniture, it's far larger than anything else around to fit in all the extras like indoor and outdoor pools, toy room, game room, massage room, etc.

To get from Jefferson to Kercheval, Grosse Pointe's main shopping street, is tricky. You have to go west on a street going in from Lake St. Clair that is south of the Country Club of Detroit. In Grosse Pointe Farms to the north, Moran is a good cross street. So is Maryland, in Grosse Pointe Park to the south. The rest of the Pointes' retailing, restaurants, and services are on Mack Avenue, the major artery which goes from downtown Detroit to St. Clair Shores and beyond and is on or near the Pointes' northeastern border.

Shopping in the Pointes is famously dull, compared to glitzy, trendy Birmingham in the heart of Oakland County's nouveau riche affluence. The Pointes' pervasively preppy look — traditional good taste, little makeup — barely changes from one generation to another. **The Hill,** on Kercheval in Grosse Pointe Farms between Fisher and Muir, has non-chain shops and upscale services. **The Village**, Kercheval's chief shopping area, is between Cadieux and Neff in Grosse Pointe. It's now almost completely dominated by chains: Talbot's, Laura Ashley, Jacobson's, Waldenbooks, Winkelman's, etc. The wonderful old **Sanders Confectionery** at 17043 Kercheval has a popular soda fountain and lunch counter in the vintage 1935 interior. Just south of the main retail area, at 11 Kercheval, is a **Brooks Brothers** discount outlet (313-886-2300), where suits retailing for $400 to $500 sell for $300 and $38 ties are $9. Next door at 15 Kercheval, the showroom of **Kennedy and Company** (313-885-2701), decorators, displays its trademark look, traditional but not timid, with rich fabrics and saturated, deep colors. Of the accessories sold here, candles and votives are a specialty. On Kercheval at Fisher, the mostly glass **Grosse Pointe Public Library** stands in striking architectural contrast to the conservative revival styles favored in the Pointes. No wonder – it was designed by Bauhaus-trained Marcel Breuer, a master of the International Style. Dexter Ferry, Jr., an heir to the Detroit seed company family, donated it to the school system. Breuer wanted to make the main reading room homelike by furnishing it with art, including a tapestry based by a Kandinsky painting and a Calder mobile.

Grosse Pointe's most interesting browsing is on **Kercheval in the Park**, between Wayburn and Beaconsfield in Grosse Pointe Park, just across from the Detroit line. The popular Sparky Herbert's restaurant inspired its revival. Now higher rents have forced some really distinctive tenants, like James Monnig Booksellers, to relocate. Still, there are some distinctive old and new spots here.

◆ **Grosse Pointe Reliques.** Crowded consignment shop full of quality antiques and used furniture at reasonable prices. It contains **Shaw's Books**, specializing in automotive books and ephemera, open by appointment (313 0824-0816). *(313) 822-0111. 14932 Kercheval. Mon-Sat 11-5.*

◆ **Third Coast Booksellers.** Self-described as "Detroit's literary bookstore." Owner/novelist Michael Goodell decided to borrow some money and open a first-class bookstore on the east side modeled on personal European bookshops, after his chosen calling of writing fiction failed to take off. The result is a beautiful, service-oriented store that aspires to be a Borders in a tenth the size — strong on literature, women's studies, art and architecture, travel, and children's books. (Don't miss the specially commissioned stained-glass versions of "Goodnight Moon" and "Peter Pan.") It's "a Danielle Steele-free zone" — no romances; no sports, sci fi, New Age, or westerns, either. *15129 Kercheval. (313) 822-1559. Mon-Fri 9-7, Sat 9-6, Sun 10-4.*

◆ **Cup A Cino.** A coffeehouse that doesn't open until well into the evening; call for hours. *15104 Kercheval. (313) 822-3888.*

◆ **Gallerie 454.** An eclectic gallery that mounts a new show every month. The art on display ranges from early American Impressionism to contemporary. Some months feature thematic exhibits: May is flower month, June is nautical month. *15105 Kercheval. (313) 822-4454. Tues-Fri 10-6, Sat 10-5.*

◆ **Rustic Cabins Bar.** In the early 1930s, when this onetime blind pig went legit, the façade was adorned by two northwoods cabins outlined in round log slabs. Inside, this favorite hangout has barely changed. It has original booths and beat-up old tables, a moose head and mounted fish on the knotty-pine walls, and an Art Deco bar. There's pool, foosball, pinball, but no food. Old-timers stop by in the afternoon, a young crowd comes in the evening. *15209 Kercheval. Mon-Sat 11 a.m.-2 a.m.*

◆ **Mulier's Omer Market.** Fourth-generation grocer-butcher has evolved from a neighborhood store geared to nearby Belgians into a gourmet grocery, without losing any of its earthy character. They make liver paté, meat loaf, sausage, and Rose Mulier's famous potato salad. *15215 Kercheval. Mon-Sat 8-6.*

LAKE ST. CLAIR . . . . . named by La Salle in 1679, is a heart-shaped body of water 400 square miles, sandwiched between Lake Erie and Lake Huron. It separates the Detroit River from the St. Clair River above. The lake is shallow, averaging just 10 feet in depth. A 700-foot-wide shipping channel has been dredged for 18 1/2 miles, giving freighters the needed 27 feet of water to pass through.

TWO WONDERFUL BAKERIES ON MACK AVENUE . . . . . Top-of-the-line baked goods, from danish and rye breads to cookies and beautiful whipped cream pastries, can be enjoyed at tables at **Josef's French Pastry Shop**. Fresh fruit, semi-sweet chocolate, good cream and custard fillings, and not too much sugar make the pastries stand out. Prices are reasonable. Quiche, pizza, and pasta salads are available for quick lunches. *21150 Mack at Brys, a few blocks past the Farmer Jack at the northeast edge of Grosse Pointe Woods. Look for the purple awning. (313) 881-5710. Tues-Sat 8-6, Sun 8-1:30. . . . . .* An Italian bakery with all the trimmings (lemon ice, candy almonds, pizza by the slice, Italian bread, a substantial section of imported pastas, canned goods, and wines), **Bommarito Bakery Dolceria Palermo** is advertised as "the original Italian bakery, family owned and operated since 1925." There's nothing fancy or pretentious about this place. Eastside Italians agree their cannoli are outstanding. Chewy sub rolls make their subs terrific, too. A boon for busy families: Mrs. Turri's frozen ravioli, around $3 a pound. *21830 Greater Mack at Avalon, east side of street, just inside St. Clair Shores, across from Meldrum Bros. Nursery. (313) 772-6731. Open Tues-Sat 8-8. . . . . .* **Freeway directions** for both bakeries: take I-94 to Vernier exit, east on Vernier to Mack, then west onto Mack.

Edsel & Eleanor Ford Home

A beautiful Cotswold manor house and grounds,
just as they looked when the Fords lived there

Built on 87 acres at Gaukler Point, overlooking Lake St. Clair, this splendid mansion takes the prize for formal good taste among the homes of Detroit auto barons. A large, rambling house, designed by the eminent Detroit architect Albert Kahn, it mimics on a grander scale Cotswold cottages a hundred miles west of London. Much of the interior paneling and furniture come from distinguished old English manors. The roof is of imported English stones expertly laid by Cotswold roofers. Interior hallways are of limestone, which gives you the feeling of entering a centuries-old manor, though the house was actually completed in 1929.

Visitors first see a 15-minute video, then go on an informative, entertaining one-hour tour, led by a professional staff member of the estate. What makes this house especially interesting is that it remains as it was when the Fords lived here. Edsel, Henry Ford's son and the president of Ford Motor, died in 1943. His wife, Eleanor Clay Ford, left the estate virtually untouched. Some of the priceless paintings — by Renoir, Degas, Titian, Van Gogh — have been donated to the Detroit Institute of Arts and replaced by copies. Originals by Cezanne, Matisse, Diego Rivera, and others remain here. And the original furniture and carpeting are intact.

Most rooms have a stately, formal feel. A striking exception is what the Fords called the "Modern Room," executed in harmonious Art Deco style in 1938 by famed industrial designer Walter Dorwin Teague. This casual gathering place is a stylishly sophisticated yet comfortable room.

Eleanor left Edsel's personal study unchanged after his early death from stomach cancer. It was here that the capable executive was reportedly seen bent over his desk, weeping in frustration from the abuses heaped on him by his father. Edsel, an intelligent, modest, gentle man, was Henry and Clara Ford's only child. President of Ford Motor since he was 25 years old, Edsel was widely respected by Ford workers and managers. His work in developing the 1940 Lincoln Continental resulted in a classic

The grounds of Edsel and Eleanor Ford's estate were designed by Jens Jensen, one of America's most influential landscape architects, a proponent of naturalistic design and native plant materials like these American elms. The grounds make a pleasant place to linger and enjoy the splendid view of Lake St. Clair.

automobile honored by the Museum of Modern Art. His influence on the visual arts in Detroit, through his public and financial support, was tremendous. Money given by the Fords kept the Detroit Institute of the Arts open during the Depression, though their gift was never made public. Advised by his friend William Valentiner, director of the Detroit Institute of Arts, he commissioned the radical Mexican muralist Diego Rivera to paint his masterpiece Detroit Industry murals in the DIA main court.

As the years went by, Edsel was at times sadistically treated by his father, who became more curmudgeonly and autocratic as he aged. More than once Henry publicly demolished badly needed auto innovations that his son had spearheaded. Edsel and his co-workers had to watch helplessly as Henry refused to upgrade his Model T while Chevrolet surged into the lead as the nation's best-selling automobile. Ford Motor didn't begin to rebuild until

Edsel's son, Henry II, with Eleanor's backing, wrested control from company thugs after Henry died.

The estate's lakefront setting is as remarkable as the manor house. It was planted in native Michigan trees and shrubs by the famous landscape architect Jens Jensen, an influential proponent of loose, natural landscaping using only native species. Now his plantings are mature, and the effect is hauntingly serene. Here Jensen created a large meadow, a lagoon, a peninsula that formed a cove, and plants to enhance the property at all times of year.

Another treat is daughter Josephine's playhouse, a gift on her sixth birthday. It is carefully crafted in a similar Cotswold style but executed in 3/4 scale so that the ceiling is only six feet high. The furniture is similarly proportioned. Boys weren't permitted in the playhouse, the tour guide says, but Josephine sometimes spent the night there, alone except for her two bodyguards.

Plan to take a tour before 4 p.m. or even 3 so there will be plenty of time to **walk the grounds**, see the pool house and gardens, and revisit the playhouse, if children are so inclined. Wednesday through Saturday from 11:30 to 2:30 a **lunch** of very reasonably priced soups, sandwiches, salads, and desserts, catered by ONE23 restaurant in Grosse Pointe, is served in the tea room in the adjacent activity building.

For info on upcoming exhibits; **lectures** on art, gardening, and other subjects; and **children's activities**, call (313) 884-4222. Shows for 1994-1995 include imperial Russian porcelain, contest quilts from the 1933 Chicago World's Fair (the boldest designs lost), and decorative nature motifs in East Asian art.

Eleanor Ford left her beloved home to the public when she died in 1976. Tours to groups of children are free; an **activity center** with meeting rooms encourages additional public use. An interesting illustrated booklet is for sale at the **Gallery Shop** for $4.

1100 Lake Shore Rd. at the north end of Grosse Pointe Shores. (313) 884-4222. Tours Wed-Sun 1, 2, 3, 4 p.m. A noon tour is given from April thru December. Adults $4, seniors $3, children under 12 $2.

Detroit Zoo

Long a pioneer in creating natural settings,
it has a spectacular four-acre chimp compound.

The world's finest zoo **chimpanzee exhibit** is the center-piece in this 125-acre zoo. Its four acres are enough to provide a natural habitat for 18 chimps. The rolling, sylvan setting allows the chimps to establish a natural social order, so that visitors can see them acting as they would in their indigenous habitats. Numerous viewing points allow visitors to see the chimps up close. The animals are outside almost every day, but when weather is too severe, they can be viewed in two large indoor day rooms behind one-way glass.

As many people actually come to ride on the **Miniature Railroad** as to see the animals. The free train carries visitors from the Main Station 1 1/2 miles to the back of the zoo at the African Station. For visitors' comfort, adult rolling chairs, "Kids Kabs," and wagons for children offer alternatives to walking.

Another popular exhibit is the **Holden Museum of Living Reptiles**, which houses a wide variety of snakes, frogs, lizards, and crocodiles from around the world. In the **Penguinarium** live four species of penguins (blue, king, macaroni, and rockhopper) in three different habitats. The outer, triangular ring of the exhibit is water. The penguins can swim around continuously, giving visitors a wonderfully close underwater view of the birds through glass walls. The **Wilson Aviary Wing** provides a big free-flight space for birds. In this horseshoe-shaped space are a waterfall, stream, pond, and many tropical plants. The birds fly unrestricted in this scenic space, which visitors traverse on a walkway.

New in 1994 is the **Mandrill Exhibit**. This multi-level, airy, glass-fronted exhibit houses mandrills, members of the baboon family. They are distinctive for their wildly hued faces and rumps in shades of blue, red, and purple. Excellent viewing sites allow visitors to get acquainted with the Zoo's newest residents. Other recent additions are the aardvark and anteater.

This pioneering zoo opened in 1928 to huge and wildly enthusiastic crowds. Detroit's was the first American zoo to emphasize barless exhibits rather than more confining and jail-like cages typical of the day. This more modern and humane approach to zoo design is most dramatically seen in one of the zoo's first displays, the dramatic, enormous **Bear Hill**. It features both grizzly and polar bears. Instead of fences, large moats protect visitors from the huge bears. But the moat proved ineffective on opening day in 1928. A big bear leaped the moat and approached Detroit's mayor, who affably — and foolishly — reached out to shake its paw.

Open daily, year-round, 10 a.m.-5 p.m. Ten Mile at Woodward in Royal Oak just north of I-696 (take Woodward exit). Enter from Woodward or I-696 service drive. Information line: (810) 398-0900. Admission: $6 for adults and teens 13 and over $5.75; ages 2-12 $2.50; under 2 free.

Flamingos have become such a common ornamental motif, it comes as a surprise at the Detroit Zoo to see how they move and behave in real life.

Royal Oak shops and galleries

The hippest, most idiosyncratic retailing in Metro Detroit

Before 1980, Royal Oak's twin commercial boulevards, Main Street and Washington Avenue, had fallen into decline, like most aging American downtowns upstaged by shopping malls. That trend began to reverse itself in 1980 when energetic Patti Smith started her vintage clothing shop on Washington. Hip and affordable, Patti Smith Collectibles attracted customers from far and wide with both its interesting vintage clothing and its inexpensive original designs. Smith set a successful example, and her Sixties-style, community-minded spirit has been infectious.

Although Smith has recently abandoned her retail shop to focus on design and manufacturing, the trend she started continues. More and more interesting shops are popping up here. Some have moved from Birmingham, where expensive rents inhibit innovation. Others are talented newcomers to retailing. So many good restaurants have recently moved to Royal Oak or opened here that it's Metro Detroit's restaurant hot spot. (See *Hunts' Restaurants and Lodgings of Michigan* or Molly Abraham's *Restaurants of Detroit*).

Here are some of the shops that make Royal Oak's downtown one of the Midwest's most interesting:

ON AND OFF WASHINGTON

◆ **Duke Gallery.** Arts and Crafts Furniture, lighting, pottery, and art glass. Other distinctive 20th-century design movements are also represented: Art Nouveau, Art Deco, and Art Moderne. The work of Frank Lloyd Wright, Gustav Stickley, Charles Eames, and Louis Comfort Tiffany is often found here. *312 W. Fourth (Washington Square Plaza). (313) 547-5511. Mon-Tues-Sat 11-6, Wed-Thurs-Fri 11-9.*

◆ **Dave's Comics and Collectibles.** Boomer collectibles are artfully displayed. Here you'll find lunchbox collections (1985 was the year the last metal lunchbox was made), cereal-box rings, vintage trucks, plastic figures of comic book heroes, sports cards, and even Transformers. *407 S. Washington. (810) 548-1230. Mon-Wed 11-8, Thurs-Fri 11-9, Sat 11-7, Sun 11-4. In winter, Mon & Tues until 6 only.*

◆ **Gayle's Chocolates.** Gayle's is a jewel of a shop, one of the most pleasing Art Deco makeovers to be found. Its designer, the acclaimed Ron Rea, also helped renovate the interesting Washington Square Building up the block. Outstanding chocolate truffles ($1.10 each) are the main attraction. Some say Gayle's are the best available. You can also buy excellent espresso and cappuccino, hot chocolate, or steamed milk and honey. A front area with tables lets you sit back and enjoy the decor and people on the street. *417 S. Washington. (810) 398-0001. Mon-Sat 10-6, open later in summer.*

◆ **Lotus Import Co.** Ethnic jewelry, clothing, and decorative accessories from all continents, with quite a few Asian selections — all appealingly displayed in this visually rich shop. The Indones-

Deborah Roberts in front of her shop on 11 Mile just east of Main. She's a more recent example of the creative energy that has made Royal Oak into an exceptionally exciting place to browse and eat.

ian clothing, made from old sarongs of ikat fabrics, includes patchwork coats, dresses, shirts, blouses, jumpers ($50-$200). Also a good selection of Indonesian masks ($14-$200). *419 S. Washington. (810) 546-8820. Mon-Tues 10-6, Wed 10-7, Thurs-Fri 10-9, Sat 10-6.*

◆ **Vertu.** Vertu is known for its collection of furniture from the mid-1930s to the late 1950s, especially pieces by Eames, Nelson, and other Herman Miller designers. More generally, it deals in objects of modern design (largely furniture and ceramics) from 1900 to 1960. Owners Roger Ellingsworth and Robert Rozycki are quite knowledgeable about mid-20th-century design. *511 S. Washington. (810) 545-6050. Tues-Sat noon-6.*

◆ **World of Kites.** Here you'll find over 250 varieties of kites and an amazing array of accessories: kite ferries which go up and down the kite string ($13), kite parachutes ($4.50), and even kite strobe lights ($30-$50) to light up your kite in the night sky. *525 S. Washington at Sixth. (810) 398-5900. Tues-Fri 11-5, Sat 10:30-5.*

◆ **Dos Manos.** Well-chosen, affordable handcrafts from Latin America. Tin mirrors from Mexico, Mexican pottery, jewelry from Mexico and Peru, wool and cotton purses from Guatemala and Bolivia. Terra cotta planters in the shapes of frogs and turtles are $18 to $65. *210 W. Sixth. (810) 542-5856. Mon-Wed 11-6, Thurs-Fri 11-8, Sat 11-5, Sun 12-4.*

◆ **Deco Doug.** Radios, clocks, lamps, vintage watches, and some furniture, exclusively Art Deco from the 1920s into the 1950s. *106 W. Fourth. (810) 547-3330. Mon-Sat 12-6 unless at a show.*

◆ **Neon Images.** Owner Darcy Salbert searches far and wide for old neon clocks, then refurbishes them to like-new condition and sells them for $250-$775. You can also find old gum ball machines ($65-$275), slot machines ($1,100 and up), and new small neon advertising signs ($125 and up). *108 W. Fourth. (810) 543-5063. Mon-Fri 11-5, Sat 12-5.*

◆ **Stamping Grounds.** Rubber stamps here are taken as serious fun, a means for inspired creative expression, and not just a passing fad or cute gift item. There are plenty of nifty examples and idea books to get you started, and special inks for stamping on fabrics. The selection of rubber stamp designs goes way beyond the usual lines to include offbeat new releases and lots of alphabets. *228 W. Fourth. (810) 543-2190. Mon-Sat 10-5.*

◆ **Chosen Books of Michigan.** Metro Detroit's only gay bookstore. The shop is well-stocked with books, magazines, cards, novelties, gifts, videos, and various paraphernalia. *120 W. Fourth. (810) 543-5758. Noon-10 daily.*

◆ **Deborah Roberts.** This small, crowded shop is a visual delight. New York native Roberts has an uncommon eye for finding and arranging interesting things from toothbrushes to toys. *206 W. 11 Mile Rd, just east of Main. (313) 543-7372.*

ON MAIN BETWEEN THIRD AND LINCOLN

◆ **Bright Ideas.** The Midwest doesn't have many contemporary home furnishings stores featuring original new Italian, Swedish, and German furniture designs. Bright Ideas has them, plus accessories like halogen lighting. *220 S. Main at Third. (313) 541-9940. Mon, Thurs, Fri 10-9; Tues, Wed, Sat 10-6; Sun 12-5.*

◆ **Carol/James Gallery.** An exceptionally pleasing contemporary arts and crafts gallery, Carol/James carries glass, decorative and functional ceramics, wood, jewelry, and fiber by 75 craftspeople. The blown glass paperweights and perfume bottles ($55-$365) stand out. *301 S. Main. (313) 541-6216. Mon-Wed 10:30-5:30, Thurs 10:30-9, Fri 10:30-5:30, Sat 10-5:30.*

◆ **Incognito.** Clothing related to popular music (rock 'n' roll, hip-hop) takes up most of the space in this shop, but there is also an extraordinary selection of sunglasses in over 300 styles. *323 S. Main (at Fourth). (313) 548-2980. Mon-Sat 11-7, Sun 12-5. Summer: Mon-Thurs 11-8, Fri 11-9, Sat 11-8, Sun 12-5.*

◆ **Noir Leather.** Downtown Royal Oak can boast of some genuinely eccentric shops. Noir Leather is the most notorious. "It is certainly one of the few places in the Midwest where you can buy how-to videos on body piercing and tattooing, underwear that glows in the dark, and a range of political buttons fit for everyone from peacenik to storm trooper," wrote *Detroit Free Press* reporter Lewis Beale. "Where else could you see in-store signs that read, 'Absolutely no return on Bondage items for sanitation reasons?' " Most Noir customers are punks interested in fairly conventional things like its big selection of leather motorcycle caps and leather sheath skirts, but there's an ample supply of handcuffs, ominous-looking leather masks, and crops for customers with kinky sexual tastes. Owner Keith Howarth is no punk himself but an art historian and former art conservator with exceedingly polite manners. Also check out Vintage Noir around the corner at 124

Washington, anchored by six-story Washington Square, is not Royal Oak's only major retail street. Main Street, two blocks east, also has many specialty shops, from punk paraphernalia to exotic birds.

N. Fourth, which sells used counterparts to what you find new here. *415 S. Main. (313) 541-3979. Mon-Sat 11-8, Sun 1-9.*

◆ **Aquarium Shop.** Owners Dave and Mike have a reputation for good service and a quality selection of well-cared-for pets. Tropical fish and birds are the main attractions. One of the most popular birds is the quaker, a smart, small parrot ($249). Lily pads ($20-$30) and Japanese koi (colorful fish which grow up to two feet) are sold to stock backyard ponds, an increasingly popular home hobby. Check out the new reptile department, where you'll find snakes and frogs. *504 N. Main. (810) 544-FISH.*

GETTING TO THE ZOO AND ROYAL OAK. . . . . Now that I-696 links Metro Detroit's east and west sides, it's a snap. Take I-696 and get off at the Woodward/Main St. exit, go north on Main, less than a mile. The retail area is just south of 11 Mile Road. To get to Washington, go left on Fourth. Peripheral parking is clearly marked. From I-75, take the 11 Mile exit 62, go west on 11 Mile about 1 1/4 miles, then south on Main or Washington.

GOOD FRESH FOODS AND GOOD STUFF . . . . . Many discriminating cooks shop for in-season produce and fruit at the year-round, 110-stall **Royal Oak Farmers' Market**. Most stalls are indoors, and there's a big parking lot. *Open May through October on Tues, Fri, Sat 7 a.m. -1 p.m. Open year-round on Saturday.*

Sundays year-round from 10-5 the market changes into a highly regarded **flea market** that's better than the name implies. A number of the 75 dealers have permanent booths set up, from which they sell everything from dried flowers and crafts to precious metals and coins. Lots of clothes (both old and new) and antiques and collectibles are always on hand. Patti Smith got her start selling vintage clothing here. *316 East 11 Mile Rd., 1 1/2 blocks east of Main St. (313) 548-8822.*

THE RADIO PRIEST'S LEGACY . . . . . The impressive **Shrine of the Little Flower** Catholic Church at Woodward and Roseland just north of 12 Mile Rd. was built by the famous radio priest Charles Coughlin. The genial, theatrical priest sympathized with the Depression-era plight of his autoworker parishioners and became an influential New Deal backer. But by 1935 Coughlin had become a blatant anti-Semite and almost a fascist. He denounced Roosevelt as a tool of Jewish bankers. His admirers contributed to the church, completed in 1933. Stones from each state are inscribed with that state's flower. (Note. antiwar activist Tom Hayden was an altar boy here.)

ENTERTAINMENT IN ROYAL OAK . . . . . is anchored by the metro area's leading comedy club, **Mark Ridley's Comedy Castle** (810 542-9900); the **Royal Oak Music Theater** (810-546-7610), a major venue for various rock/pop genres; and the **Main Art Theatre** (810-542-0180), limited distribution art and foreign films.

Birmingham galleries

In an intensely fashion-conscious downtown,
one of the most important concentrations
of art galleries in the Midwest

During the Eighties, Birmingham became a major Midwestern center of important art galleries. They focus on
everything from museum-quality ancient artifacts to
contemporary art by internationally known artists. Catalyst for
this convenient concentration was the prestigious Donald Morris
Gallery on Townsend, which moved from Detroit in 1975. Now a
number of galleries are near it, and some are scattered along
Woodward in downtown Birmingham. So many galleries have
come to occupy a charming strip of small shops on Woodward
north of downtown that it's now known as "gallery row."

ON AND NEAR TOWNSEND STREET

◆ **Donald Morris Gallery.** Morris primarily sells the established
20th-century American and European masters: Milton Avery,
Alexander Calder, Joseph Cornell, Jean Dubuffet, and Piet
Mondrian, to name a few. The gallery also handles classic
African art and turn-of-the-century decorative arts. This is the
state's most expensive gallery, with many prices in the hundreds
of thousands of dollars. *105 Townsend. (810) 642-8812. Tues-Sat
10:30-5:30.*

◆ **G. R. N'Namdi Gallery.** Paintings, sculpture, and a good number of collages, all characteristically vibrant and colorful, by contemporary artists with national and international reputations,
including many African-American and Latin American artists,
such as Carol Ann Carter, Perez Celis, Al Loving, Jean Miotte,
and Howardina Pindel. *181 Townsend. (810) 642-2700. Tues-Sat
10:30-5:30.*

◆ **Hill Gallery.** Building on its longtime base of museum-quality
American folk art (mostly historic, some contemporary) and
interesting regional artists, Hill has become a leading Michigan
gallery. It now also shows contemporary paintings and, especially, sculptures by nationally well-known artists. Among the
artists exhibited are Mark DiSuvero, Ralph Fasanella, Carol

Hepper, Heather McGill, and Donald Sultan. *163 Townsend.* *(810) 540-9288. Tues-Sat 10:30-5:30.*

◆ **Robert Kidd Gallery.** Contemporary paintings and sculpture by Harry Bertoia, Helen Frankenthaler, Sam Gilliam, James Havard, Ida Kohlmeyer, and others. *107 Townsend. (810) 642-3909. Tues-Sat 10:30-5:30.*

GALLERY ROW ON NORTH WOODWARD

Don't overlook second-story shops on the upper end. Salvatore Scallopini across the street is a fine spot for a quick meal or snack. *N. Woodward between Harmon & Oak, a few blocks north of downtown.*

◆ **Lemberg Gallery.** Contemporary paintings, drawings, and graphics by artists who are locally and nationally prominent. A $30,000 Jasper Johns work may hang on one wall, and on another a $1,000 oil painting by Stephen Magsig. *538 N. Woodward. (810) 642-6623. Tues-Fri 11-5:30, Sat 11-5.*

◆ **Halsted Gallery.** This gallery has a national reputation for its 19th- and 20th-century photography. It also carries out-of-print and rare books on photography. *560 N. Woodward. (313) 644-8284. Tues-Sat 10-5:30.*

◆ **Xochipilli.** Pronounced "ZO-sha-pee-lee," it's named after the Aztec god of the arts. Director Mary Wright gets raves from area artists as one of the most interesting, committed, supportive, and discriminating gallery directors around. She shows paintings and sculpture by contemporary artists known nationally and internationally. *568 N. Woodward. (810) 645-1905. Tues-Sat 11-5.*

◆ **Donna Jacobs.** This fascinating gallery specializes in ancient art: Greek, Roman, Egyptian, Etruscan, Near Eastern, and Pre-Columbian objects. These include pottery, glass, bronzes, stone, textiles. Many of these museum-quality pieces sell in the $200-$500 range. *574 N. Woodward. (810) 540-1600. Thurs-Fri 11-5:30, Sat 1-5.*

◆ **Elizabeth Stone Gallery.** Original paintings and drawings by book illustrators — mostly contemporary, and some old masters of the genre — are gathered here by a longtime children's librarian at Cranbrook's elementary school. Media range from large oils to pastels to very detailed watercolors. Prices range from $100 for spot illustrations to $7,500, with most from $800 to $3,500. *536 N. Woodward. (810) 647-7040. Tues-Sat 10-6.*

◆ **Mettal Studio.** Highly original sculptural art jewelry by Center for Creative Studies alums Patrick Irla and Cary Stefani. *534 N. Woodward. (810) 258-8818. Tues-Fri 10-6, Sat 10-4.*

◆ **Arkitektura/In-Situ.** Reproductions of classic 20th-century modern design. It was started in 1984 by the grandson of Eliel Saarinen and two other alums of nearby Cranbrook, where the great Swedish designer lived and worked for many years. In addition to Saarinen designs, Arkitektura/In-Situ sells authorized reproductions of classic furniture by late, great architect/designers like Le Corbusier, Mies van der Rohe, and Charles Rennie Macintosh, and current names like Robert Venturi, Stanley Tigerman, Michael McCoy, and Joe D'Urso. Prices range from $100 to over $15,000, but few of these careful reproductions are cheap. The gallery is branching out into carrying more Italian lines. *474 N. Woodward. (810) 646-0097. Mon-Fri 9:30-5, Sat 1-5 after Labor Day until Memorial Day; closed Sat in summer.*

◆ **O.K. Harris/David Klein Gallery.** Paintings by modern and contemporary masters, with some emphasis on New York and California artists. Prices range from $1,000 to about $30,000. New exhibitions mounted every month usually focus on one or two artists. On the first Thursday of every month, the gallery stays open for a 6-8:30 p.m. opening of its new exhibition. *430 N. Woodward. (810) 433-3700. Tues-Sat 11-6.*

🌲🌳🌲

OTHER SPECIALIZED GALLERIES NEARBY . . . . . In the relatively new field of contemporary glass art, the **Habatat Gallery** has developed a national reputation. The field got its start at workshops held in a garage behind the Toledo art museum in 1962, when a Libby Glass chemist gave University of Wisconsin art professor Harvey Littleton technical information enabling artists to work in glass using only small kilns, without big factory facilities. Glass can be cast, blown, sandblasted, or slumped. Some is clear, some is brilliantly colored, some is like a painting. Prices can run from $3,000-$80,000 for works by leading glass artists like Dale Chihuly, Joel Philip Myers, Howard Ben Tre, and Klaus Moje. In September, 1994, Habatat will move to Pontiac, but the exact location wasn't known as we went to press; call the gallery for information. *32255 Northwestern Highway in the Tri-Atria center, midway between Middlebelt and Orchard Lake Roads in Farmington Hills. (810) 851-9090. Tues-Sat 10-6. . . . . .* The **Backdoor Gallery** is devoted exclusively to nontraditional cloth art dolls, showing the work of 18 artists from Michigan and throughout the U.S. Prices range from $45-$900; $300 is average. Artists Kath Lathers and Kathleen Brickler presently run the gallery in a homey setting that adjoins Lathers' living room, but it will move to a more traditional retail space in downtown Farmington in September, 1994. The gallery name and phone number will remain the same, so call for info on the new location. *37220 Eight Mile Road, Farmington. (810) 474-8306. Thurs-Fri 11-3, Sat 12-5.* . . . . . . **Book Beat** is a photographic art gallery showing vintage and original works of the 19th and 20th centuries. Here you'll find works by Alfred Stieglitz, Margaret Bourke-White, James Van Der Zee, Weegee, and Carol Wald, among others; Hollywood images of Marilyn Monroe, Josephine Baker, and other stars, as well as silent era stills; Detroit-area images by David Griffith, Jim Klein, and Jeffrey Silverthorne; Dadaist and Surrealist works such as 1920s images of Berlin and Paris. Other specialities: children's books, rare and out-of-print art, and photography books are also sold here. *26010 Greenfield in Oak Park. (810) 968-1190. Mon-Sat 10-9, Sun 11-6.* . . . . . Contemporary works in all media are on view at **Revolution**. It features ceramics and experimental shows or installations. Prices run from $500 to $15,000. Recently, the gallery has begun hosting events on **new music**; for now, the music is on CD, but plans call for live music in the near future. *23257 Woodward Avenue in Ferndale. (810) 541-3444, Tues-Sat 10-6, except Thurs until 8.* . . . . . Another cluster of galleries is in **downtown Detroit**, on and near East Grand River behind the old Hudson's. See page 216-217.

MICHIGAN'S MOST FASHION-CONSCIOUS, GLITZIEST DOWNTOWN . . . . is in **Birmingham**, centered at Woodward and Maple. Blessed with virtually the only functioning downtown in this booming suburban region of central Oakland County, the prestigious residential suburb of 20,000 has assumed a new role, unwelcome by many longtime residents, as the shopping mecca for one of the 10 wealthiest counties in the U.S. Twenty years ago downtown Birmingham wasn't all that different from Grosse Pointe: somewhat clubby and preppy, and fairly traditional and sedate in tone. Today it is alive with the latest upscale trends and creative ideas, with cafes and unusual shops, prestigious offices, even a luxury hotel and legitimate theater. Stylish people come to see and be seen. Attitude is everything for these self-conscious fashionplates, adolescent and adult, and you don't see many smiles on the street. The place is mellower, less crowded, and more pleasant in summer. **Shain Park**, two blocks west of Woodward and a block south of Maple, is a lovely place for a relaxing takeout meal from the Merchant of Vino.

Turnover is continual in this high-rent area, and upscale national chains with deep pockets are driving out independent merchants. *Store hours are generally from 10 to 5:30 or 6, Monday through Saturday, Thursday to 8.* Easiest parking is in city ramps; look for signs.

Cranbrook

*Here famed architect Eliel Saarinen created
an extraordinarily beautiful environment
for artists and students.*

This educational complex on 315 rolling acres has several claims to renown. Internationally, Cranbrook is known for its Academy of Art, a graduate school of art, design, and architecture. Locally it is known for its distinguished private elementary, middle, and upper schools, as well as for its art and science museums.

Finally, Cranbrook is also known throughout the world for the total aesthetics of its built environment — a careful integration of buildings, gardens, sculpture, and interiors. The noted architectural photographer Balthazar Korab, who lives nearby, expressed this nicely. "Cranbrook is my place of recreation. Walking there, you find yourself in a different atmosphere. It's like a large private estate that has been opened to us pedestrians, where you can inhale a time past, an era of great patrons and great ideas. . . . . . The gardens, the grounds, and the buildings have a definite, luxurious cohesiveness."

Two remarkable men, a patron and an artist, joined their energies to create this special place. The patron was Detroit newspaper magnate George Booth. The artist was Eliel Saarinen. In 1904 Booth bought a rundown Bloomfield Hills farm and commissioned Albert Kahn, on his way to becoming Detroit's leading architect, to build a large, Tudor-style mansion there. Booth, the grandson of an English coppersmith from Kent, was a leading proponent of the Arts and Crafts movement, which stressed a greater unification of life and art through handcrafted artistic production by individual craftspeople. It was a total approach to design that blurred the distinction between fine arts and crafts. Before he married into a newspaper family, Booth had owned a successful ornamental ironwork factory in Windsor. A trip Booth took to Rome in 1922 was the catalyst for the Cranbrook schools, which would gain worldwide attention. There he saw the American Academy and decided to create a school of architecture and design. He persuaded the well-known Finnish

Now restored and open to the public: Saarinen House, designed by and for Eliel and Loja Saarinen. He was Cranbrook's Finnish-American architect in residence (1925-1950) and the head of its art academy (1932-1946). She was an influential weaver. The dining room here, done in coral, red, dark and light woods, and a gold ceiling oval, shows their rich yet simple style. He designed the furniture; her tapestry is on the wall.

architect, Eliel Saarinen, along with Saarinen's wife and children, to move to Bloomfield Hills in 1925 to lay the groundwork for the Cranbrook community.

The Brookside elementary school, built up close to Cranbrook Road, shows the rustic charm of the cottage style. It has a wonderful iron gate, Scandinavian-style brickwork, and numerous sculptural accents. Saarinen's first designs were for an Academy of Art and Cranbrook School for boys in 1925. In 1928 he designed his own house (now completely restored, along with the furnishings designed by him and his wife, Loja, and open to the public) and a second along Academy Way off Lone Pine Road. Saarinen and Booth had begun to bring distinguished artists to assist in creating many buildings within the complex (most are not viewable by the public) and to teach at the Academy, which opened in 1931.

The Cranbrook Academy quickly gained a reputation as one of the world's top artistic communities. It continues today to be an important advanced art institute, with internationally known artists in residence in nine departments: architecture, ceramics, design, fiber, metalsmithing, painting, photography, printmaking, and sculpture. A high point of Cranbrook was just before World War II, when Saarinen's son, famed architect Eero Saarinen, together with Charles Eames, created a new, leaner interior design look in frankly machine-made furniture. By the 1950s, Cranbrook alumni Charles Eames and his wife, Ray, along with Florence Knoll and Harry Bertoia, had popularized the look so much that it has become the very essence of International-style "modern" design. Examples of their work can be seen at the Academy of Art Museum (see below).

Cranbrook is a wonderful place to take walks at every time of year. Covered with fresh snow, it's a magical place. In spring and summer the formal gardens at Cranbrook House are a special delight. The outstanding buildings, many with engaging decorative details, combine with the hilly setting and mature landscaping to create a memorable environment. Throughout the grounds are 60 sculptures by the prominent Swedish sculptor Carl Milles, who headed the sculpture department for 20 years, and Marshall Frederick. Fredericks was Milles' protegé. His "Spirit of Detroit" and other sculptures are familiar Detroit-area landmarks. A map of the grounds is available from the Cranbrook House.

Four Cranbrook buildings are open to the public:

◆ **Cranbrook House & Gardens.** The 1908 mansion designed by Albert Kahn is now the Cranbrook community's administrative office. It features leaded-glass windows and tapestries and art objects collected by Cranbrook founders George and Ellen Booth. The stunning, impeccably maintained **gardens** around the house are marked by dramatic vistas, fountains and cascades, sculptures and architectural fragments. *380 Lone Pine Road. (313) 645-3149. Gardens open: May thru August, Mon-Sat 10-5, Sun 11-3. September, daily 11-3. October, weekends only 11-3. Combined house and garden tour: $6. Call (313) 645-3149 by Tues. for Thurs. lunch reservations. Park at Christ Church Cranbrook.*

◆ **Saarinen House.** The 1930 home, studio, and garden of Eliel Saarinen, Cranbrook's resident architect from 1925 to 1950 and the art academy's first president, from 1932 to 1946. Now completely restored down to the important decorative accessories, the extraordinary interiors feature Eliel 's furniture and architectural detailing and tapestries, rugs, curtains, and other textiles designed by his wife, Loja. *Open May through October. One-hour tours held Thurs, Sat & Sun at 1:30, 2, 3, and 3:30. Adults $5, students with I.D. and seniors $4, no children under 7. Fee includes admission to art museum. Tours involve stairs.*

◆ **Academy of Art Museum.** On permanent view are works by the Cranbrook Academy's many prominent faculty and students, including Carl Milles, Florence Knoll, Charles and Ray Eames, Maija Grotell, Eero Saarinen, and Marshall Fredericks. Many examples of Eliel Saarinen's decorative work and architectural drawings are here. **Changing exhibits** focus on contemporary trends in the visual arts, with one-person shows of nationally and internationally known artists and group shows of Cranbrook's emerging artists and designers. The bookstore offers books on arts and crafts related to Cranbrook. *Enter on Academy Way, 500 Lone Pine Rd. (810) 645-3312. Turn right and park behind the museum. Open Wed thru Sun 1 5. Adults $2.50; $1.50 students and seniors. Call for information on frequent lecture series and special exhibits by noted artists.*

◆ **Institute of Science.** This exhibit museum is filled with displays illuminating key aspects of the physical sciences, botany, biology, anthropology, and archaeology. Here you can find one of the most extensive and well arranged **mineral collections** in the country. One room is devoted to hands-on exhibits, mostly demonstrating scientific principles. The **hall on Native**

American culture is especially noteworthy. Full-scale tipis are on display, along with many artifacts and dioramas showing what life was like in villages of various native peoples. The **observatory** is open to the public Saturday evenings after dark. Planetarium and laser shows are held on weekends. Two **gift shops** are here, one especially for children. *Enter on Academy Way, 500 Lone Pine Rd., and proceed straight back to Institute Way. Park in the lot by the entrance. (313) 645-3200. Mon-Thurs 10-5; Fri-Sat 10-10, Sun 1-5. Sept thru May: adults $5, students and seniors $4. June thru August: adults $6, students and seniors $5.*

*Cranbrook is at 1221 North Woodward Avenue in Bloomfield Hills. The new **public main entrance** is marked by a sign. A **map** of the grounds and general brochure about the Cranbrook Educational Community is available from the Public Relations office in Cranbrook House, or call (313) 645-3142.*

NEAR CRANBROOK . . . . . Christ Church Cranbrook, an imposing English Gothic-style Episcopal church, was the gift of Cranbrook founder George Gough Booth and his wife, Ellen Scripps Booth. The excellence and diversity of the craftsmanship throughout the building speak to George Booth's interest in the British-inspired Arts and Crafts Movement of his era. He sought out the finest artists and craftspersons when the church was built. Although most of the woodcarving, stained glass, and mosaics are contemporary with the construction of the church in the 1920s, many of the objects in Christ Church Cranbrook are centuries-old treasures found by the Booths on their travels. . . . . The 118-foot tower holds the Wallace Carillon, whose 50 cast bronze bells weigh between 16 and 6,720 pounds. **Sunday summer carillon recitals** by carillonneurs from across North America and Europe are offered free of charge at 4 p.m. from Independence Day weekend through Labor Day weekend. **Tours of the tower,** from which you can get a spectacular view of Bloomfield Hills and a particularly nice view of Cranbrook next door, are available by appointment. *Main sanctuary open to visitors 8:30 a.m.-5 p.m. daily. Services held at 8, 9:15, and 11:15 a.m.; 8 and 10 a.m. during the summer. 470 Church Road, at Lone Pine and Cranbrook Roads (across from the Cranbrook House entrance). (810) 644-5210.*

Meadow Brook Hall

Built by the widow of automaker John Dodge,
this 100-room mansion is a joy to visit.

Of the four large mansions of Detroit auto barons on public view, this is the warmest and most pleasing. The other
mansions, each interesting in very different ways, are
Henry Ford's Fair Lane (page 345), Edsel Ford's Grosse Pointe
estate (page 293), and Cadillac president Lawrence Fisher's flamboyant Detroit River mansion (page 283). It's a remarkable feat
to make a 100-room Tudor mansion feel comfortable and inviting. The credit goes to Matilda Dodge Wilson, the daughter of a
German immigrant from Canada who ran the Dry Dock Saloon
on Detroit's riverfront.

Second wife of the great automaker John Dodge, she was left
over $150 million after he died in 1921. At age 41 she married
Alfred Wilson, a wealthy lumber broker. In 1926 she began
building her long-planned Tudor home at Meadow Brook.
Industrious, warmhearted, and strong-willed, Matilda was closely involved in Meadow Brook's design, construction, and decor.

Happily, the interior of this magnificent home is still quite
close to what it was when Matilda Dodge Wilson lived here.
Although she ultimately spent $4 million on the home, she
resisted overpowering effects. In a very natural way, priceless
works of art occupy the same rooms as works of purely personal
interest. Most of the rooms, big and small, pleasingly combine
fine works of art (including paintings by Van Dyke, Reynolds,
and Rosa Bonheur), ornate carved wood and plaster architectural detailing, carpeting, and furniture.

Matilda Dodge Wilson donated her estate and $2 million to
help start **Oakland University** on these grounds. The well-
known **Meadow Brook Theatre** on campus offers professional
performances between October and May. Call (313) 377-3300 for
information. The outdoor **Meadow Brook Music Festival**, just
over the hill from Meadow Brook Hall, runs June through
August, and includes pop, classics, rock, and jazz. Call (313)
377-3300 for information.

Built in the late 1920s for $4 million (a tremendous amount of money in those days), Meadow Brook Hall is surprisingly homey for a 100-room mansion. The winged horse is by prolific Detroit-area sculptor Marshall Fredericks of Cranbrook. Dodge heir Matilda Dodge Wilson closely supervised its construction, proud that her English Tudor estate was built with mostly American materials.

On the Oakland University campus off Walton Rd. on Adams Rd. 3 miles northeast of downtown Pontiac. From I-75, take Exit 79 (Pontiac Rd.) east one mile to University Dr. (313) 370-3140. Self-guided tours year-round Sun 1-4. Guided tours in July & August, Mon-Sat 10:15-3:45. Public tour (1 1/4 hours) also offered at 1:30 p.m. Mon-Sat from Sept. through June. Open some holidays and daily in early Dec; call to check. Adults $6, children under 12 $3 . Group rates and special services available; call to check.

Holocaust Memorial Center

*Grim and disturbing, this outstanding museum
illuminates what led to the mass murder of Jews.*

The murder of 6 million Jews by Hitler's Nazis during
World War II is documented in a chilling, almost low-key
manner in this multifaceted, superbly designed museum.
Visitors to the $7 million center begin the self-guided tour hear-
ing the sweet, haunting voice of a mother singing a Jewish lulla-
by. You enter a darkened, ominous-looking tunnel and pass a
video of Hitler bombastically shouting to a throng of Germans his
racist message and world view. Displays put into historical context Germany's suffering after World War I and the punishing
peace imposed by the French. It becomes clear how humiliation
and economic distress led many Germans to turn upon their
Jewish fellow Germans as scapegoats.

Displays use a sophisticated combination of historical artifacts, photos, dioramas, and film footage, so that no visitor can
escape the Holocaust's horror. What comes across is the almost
incredible act of the systematic extermination of millions of men,
women, and children by an industrialized, Western society quite
similar to our own. The Nazis' blatant sadism is also evident.
These victims not only died but experienced extraordinary suffering before death.

This obviously isn't a pleasant place to visit. Children under
12 aren't advised to come. But the Holocaust museum exposes
us to sad truths about what the human race is capable of.

*6602 W. Maple in West Bloomfield Township, 2 miles west of
Orchard Lake Rd. In the Jewish Community Campus across from
Henry Ford Hospital. From I-696, take Orchard Lake Rd. exit 3
miles north to Maple, turn left. (810) 661-0840. Sun thru Thurs 10-
3:30. 1 1/2 -hour public tour held Sundays at 1 p.m. No admission
charge.*

ALSO AT THE HOLOCAUST MEMORIAL CENTER . . . . . is the Bernard L.
Maas **Garden of the Righteous**, where marble plaques commemorate the
heroism and unselfishness of only a handful of the many who helped save

lives. Among those honored are governments, diplomats, communities, and individuals. . . . . . The **Morris and Emma Schaver Library-Archive** is one of the most comprehensive collections of Holocaust materials in the U.S. Everyone is welcome to read, browse, or do research here. Copy service is available. Educators are urged to make full use of the HMC **documentary video collection.** . . . . . The **communities retrieval service** gives visitors a printout highlighting the history of every European Jewish community of 500 families or larger. It is the first such service in the U.S. Cost: $10 per retrieval.

100 KINDS OF YARMULKES . . . . . plus sterling menorahs, Israeli recorded music, books and games on Jewish subjects are a few miles away at **Esther's Judaica Giftworld**, in Crosswinds Mall on Orchard Lake at Lone Pine Road (810-932-3377).

THE EPICENTER OF JEWISH BAKERIES . . . . . is at Greenfield and Ten Mile in **Oak Park**, one of the first postwar suburbs of choice for Jews, long before the move to West Bloomfield Township. Today Oak Park has large communities of Orthodox Jews and recent Russian Jewish immigrants, along with many Chaldeans and African-Americans.

Plymouth

This sedate suburb's downtown has blossomed into a center of interesting and unusual shops.

Few towns of 10,000 come close to the vitality of Plymouth's downtown and Old Village. For years, this bedroom community was home of the Daisy Air Rifle Company, known far and wide as the air rifle capital of the world. Daisy was initially the Plymouth Windmill Company, but when sales declined, the firm decided to make and give away an all-metal air rifle to any farmer who would buy its windmill. The air rifle sold briskly while windmill sales languished. So the company stopped making windmills and changed its name to the Daisy Manufacturing Company in 1895. It moved to Arkansas in 1958. You can still see its big brick buildings off North Main close to the railroad tracks.

Today Plymouth has almost a movie-set look of wholesome small-town America. Neighborhoods of well-maintained, unpretentious homes are considered so safe some residents don't even lock their doors. Summer evenings find entire families walking downtown to visit the park, the bookstores, and coffeehouses. A community band still gives concerts weekly on Thursday evenings in the park. Now more and more visitors are coming to town, attracted by a variety of surprisingly exciting shops.

Highlights of Plymouth are:

◆ **Kellogg Park.** A shady triangular downtown park that creates a pleasant center to the city. It was donated by John Kellogg, who arrived in 1832 with a chest full of gold coins, having just sold a hotel and warehouse on the Erie Canal in Palmyra, New York. Opposite the park on Penniman is the **Farmers' Market**, where fresh produce is sold Saturdays from 8 a.m. to 1 p.m., May through October. At the **Penn Theatre**, facing the park, not-quite-first-run movies are shown, usually at 7 and 9, for $2. *(313) 453-0870.*

◆ **Penniman Showcase,** on a pleasant block of shops just west of Kellogg Park. The work of some 150 American craftsmen in porcelain, stoneware, fibers, and jewelry is attractively displayed. The richly colorful display of blown glass is a special treat. Prices

Right across from Main Street is delightful Kellogg Park. Plymouth residents walk here for free summer concerts Wednesdays at noon and for Thursday-evenings band concerts. Call (313) 453-1540 for details.

range from $10 to $500. *827 Penniman. (313) 455-5531.*

◆ **Muriel's Doll House.** The downstairs is crammed with a big selection of dolls ranging from $10 to $9,000. Upstairs you'll find elaborate dollhouse kits (some costing as much as $3,600) and an enormous selection of accessories. This place has customers from all over the world. *824 Penniman. (313) 455-8110.*

◆ **Plymouth Coffee Bean Co.** Sip cappuccino in inviting overstuffed chairs and sofas. Newspapers, books, and board games are also on hand. *884 Penniman. (313) 454-0178.*

◆ **Country Charm.** One of the town's biggest draws, this is a country decor shop executed with out-of-the-ordinary taste. From the inviting scents when you enter to the elegant presentations, this is a pleasant place to visit. One big seller is handcrafted furniture by a Michigan craftsman. Check out the nifty personalized family necklaces, from $6 to $22. *322 S. Main. (313) 454-3612.*

◆ **Memory Lane**. Of Plymouth's many antique shops, this one stands out for jewelry and china. *336 S. Main. (313) 451-1873.*

◆ **Chameleon Galleries.** This contemporary art shop features wood, porcelain, pottery, among other things. Most striking are the blown glass and strikingly beautiful handcrafted kaleidoscopes ($125-$500). In back is a **coffeehouse**, which also connects to the adjoining **Little Professor bookstore**, a major

Plymouth hangout. *370 S. Main. (313) 455-0445.*

◆ **Maggie & Me.** Maggie LaForrest designs wonderfully exuberant, oversized women's shirts, pants, and dresses. They're so distinctive you can spot a design a mile away. Not trendy, this is what some call "fun clothing," embellished with lace, baubles, beads, and buttons. From this store Maggie has started satellite stores in Royal Oak and Harbor Springs. *880 W. Ann Arbor Trail, one block south of Penniman.*

◆ **Native West.** Well selected Native American art, mostly Southwestern, includes hot pepper wreaths, drums, Navajo sand paintings, and alabaster sculptures. The shop also carries lodge pole furniture made of sturdy pine. *863 W. Ann Arbor Trail. (313) 455-8838.*

◆ **Harvest Moon.** A combination juice bar, coffee and sandwich shop, this place has an inviting counterculture flair, with homespun aphorisms tacked to the walls. Try the $2.25 "Red Roar" — "NOT too much beet but the right amount of this iron-rich, blood-cleansing, nutrient rich powerhouse." The yummy Yamalicious salad combines apples, yams, cabbage, walnuts in a tangy sauce. *545 Forest Ave. (313) 454-7593.*

◆ **Georgia's Gift Gallery.** This big emporium of collectibles grew out of a modest space to become perhaps the biggest of its kind in the state. For those who have become addicted to collecting pricey plates, dolls, Snow Village items, Disney figures, etc., etc., this is the place to go. *575 Forest Ave. (313) 453-7733.*

◆ **Michael Camp.** At this showroom for Plymouth master cabinetmaker Michael Camp, you can get discounted prices on his many Early American pieces, from a Dunlap candle stand ($295) to a Massachusetts highboy ($3,795). Camp's parents also sell early American antiques here. *331 N. Main. (313) 459-0367.*

◆ **Old Village.** An intriguing, eclectic commercial district dating from the simultaneous arrival of two railroad lines to Plymouth in 1871. It became a busy railroad area, with as many as 18 passenger trains arriving a day. What you find here now, and in houses along Starkweather and Mill, are a number of funky resale and antique shops. But two recent arrivals have considerably elevated the quality of offerings here. **M. Hubert** has a fine selection of quality art glass and art pottery along with clocks and a dazzling array of commemorative medals. *198 W. Liberty. (313) 451-1505.* Across the street is Sharon McInturff's **Pansy's,**

The boy pictured in Daisy's 1947 American Boy's Bill of Rights responded to post-World War II anti-gun sentiment by proclaiming his right to learn to shoot safely.

an alluring shop filled with select little treasures. *181 W. Liberty. (313) 451-1850.*

Les Bebe de Bea. In the front of this unusual doll shop is a year-round Victorian Christmas room, complete with an elaborately adorned tree. In the back Bea Roderick teaches doll-making classes and makes her own distinctive dolls, including pouring, firing, and painting the porcelain bodies. In the rooms in between are displayed dolls by Bea and many other artists. Worth a peek even if you're not into dolls. *774 Starkweather. (313) 451-5525.*

Petticoats. Earlier called Mountain Rags. Diana Licht has earned a considerable reputation for her designs of children's clothing. The styles are heavily influenced by turn-of-the-century classics like sailors' suits and pinafores. She makes wonderfully creative use of fabric, taking, for example, a colorful old bed-spread for the fabric of a playsuit. *643 N. Mill. (313) 455-5109.*

◆ **Plymouth Historical Museum.** A highlight here is the BB-gun room displaying the locally manufactured Daisy and Markham

BB guns and fascinating advertising for them. One 1910 Daisy Air Rifle ad proclaims, "Boy, you ought to have a gun this summer. Make up your mind to get one, and learn to shoot straight." In the basement is a wonderful model of the countryside along the Middle Rouge River showing the village industries Henry Ford built. Two bargains in the **gift shop** are a $2 paperback on the history of Daisy Air Rifle and an especially well written hardbound history of Plymouth by Sam Hudson for $8. *155 S. Main St. (313) 455-8940. Wed, Thurs, Sat 1-4, Sun 2-5. Adults $1.50, children 5-17 50¢, families $4.*

ALSO IN PLYMOUTH . . . . . are two notable restaurants which attract people from many miles around: the Sweet Afton Tearoom near Old Village and the Cafe Bon Homme on Penniman. See *Hunts' Restaurants and Lodgings of Michigan* for details.

ANOTHER CHARMING TOWN NEARBY . . . . . just four miles north of Plymouth, **Northville** has a smaller, older downtown with a number of upscale gift and antique shops in various traditional styles. One special standout: **La Belle Provence**, known for French country antique and reproduction furniture and accessories. *119 N. Center. (810) 347-4333.* . . . . For entertainment there's the **Marquis Theatre**, with professional productions (313-349-0868). For amusing mystery whodunits, check out the casual, funny **Genitti's Hole-in-the-Wall** restaurant. *108 E. Main. (810) 349-0522,*

❶ Greenfield Village. Henry Ford's extraordinary collection of important American buildings brings history to life.

❷ Henry Ford Museum. Stunning displays of recent technological eras. Sweeping "Made in America" exhibit a must-see.

❸ Fair Lane. Henry Ford's final home, built on picturesque spot of River Rouge, complete with massive water-powered electrical plant.

❹ Rouge Plant. Awesome auto complex where 100,000 once worked. Iron ore came in ships; Fords rolled out.

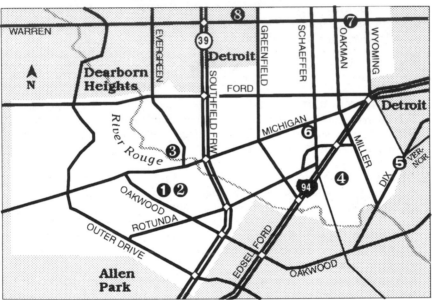

❺ Southend Arab shops. Port of entry for Arabs. Nice Arab culture museum. Good Yemeni restaurant, Lebanese bakery.

❻ Alcamo's Market. Outstanding Italian grocery with hard-to-find cheeses, sausage, imported pastas.

❼ Arab shops on W. Warren. Thousands of Arab immigrants have created good bakeries, restaurants, groceries.

❽ Judy's Cafe. Very good food in homey atmosphere. Everything from spaghetti to Cuban black bean soup.

Highlights of
Dearborn

0   1   2
miles

Ford Rouge Complex

An awesome historic symbol of American industry
at its most vibrant and oppressive

This historic colossus of American industry is, sadly, no longer open for tours, but you can drive around the complex to take in its awesome magnitude and powerful visual forms. The Rouge was where Henry Ford put it all together. It was the world's first vertically integrated factory, an idea much copied but later discredited as too centralized and massive. At one end iron ore came in by ship; at the other cars rolled out the auto assembly plant.

Dredging the shallow River Rouge for three and a half miles up from its mouth at the Detroit River enabled freighters to deliver limestone, coal, iron ore, and other raw materials to the 1,100-acre site. The huge factories Ford built here turned the raw materials into auto parts made of steel, plastic, rubber and glass. They were then assembled into Ford automobiles.

By the 1920s this had become the world's biggest manufacturing complex. 10,000 cars a day were made here. The Rouge became a potent symbol of the machine age.

Henry Ford's historic Highland Park Plant, where just a few years earlier he introduced the assembly line, was only five years old when he started planning for the much bigger Rouge plant in 1914. It was located not far from the Dearborn farm where he grew up. The 1,100 acres were marshy farmland when Ford sent his agents to buy up the component parcels all in a single day. The Rouge's first products were submarine-chasing Eagle boats made at the tail end of World War I.

By the late 1920s, 75,000 workers were making Model As at the Rouge, turning raw materials into completed vehicles in just 33 hours. Immigrants from much of Europe and the Middle East flocked here to work. Just east of the factory gates, on Salina Street, there were bars for nearly every nationality. Fifty languages were said to be spoken at the elementary school serving Dearborn's South End. As older immigrants left, they were replaced in the 1960s and 1970s by countrymen of the original Syrians, Lebanese, and Palestinians, and by fellow Arabs from

The Rouge River, still a natural-looking waterway as it passed Henry Ford's home a few miles upstream, was deepened at the Rouge complex to admit giant freighters. They brought the coal, iron ore, and other basic materials that built the 10,000 cars a day produced in the huge plant.

Yemen and Iraq. They form the largest Arab community in North America. Since Arabs eschew alcohol, the bars have vanished.

It was an extraordinarily bold move for Henry Ford to invest the hundreds of millions of dollars needed to make this giant car-manufacturing complex, including a state-of-the-art steel-making plant. Another Rouge plant turned 210,000 bushels of soybeans a year into paints, plastics, and binders. An electrical power plant added in 1920 was one of the world's largest. One plant made the tires for Ford cars, while another made the glass windshields. Yet another made the famous Ford V-8 engine, Henry Ford's last engineering triumph.

But the Rouge was also the scene of terrible labor strife. The aging Henry Ford lost interest in industrial production. And he couldn't relate to the new immigrants and their foreign cultures. "The Rouge isn't fun any more," he explained, and he turned his interests to Greenfield Village, *McGuffey's Readers*, and an idealized American past — ironically, the pre-industrial, rural past of Ford's hometown of Dearborn before his own factories transformed it.

As Henry Ford aged, the dark, suspicious side in him grew. It allowed little sympathy for the workers. They were pushed to exhaustion and spied upon. At Ford Motor Company, Henry's capable son, Edsel, was cruelly frustrated by his father, while Henry empowered the notorious Harry Bennett and his security department — virtual thugs and spies who infiltrated many potential organizing meetings. Symptoms of oppressive working conditions were many. Innocent protesters were slaughtered during the 1932 Hunger March. In the 1937 **Battle of the Overpass**, Walter Reuther and other union organizers passing out leaflets were flagrantly beaten up by Bennett's goons, even though photographers were present. The resulting photographs helped turn public opinion in the union's favor. Finally, a strike in 1941 prompted the company to recognize unionized workers.

Labor difficulties, along with the threat of German bombing attacks at the huge complex, led Ford management to decentralize operations after World War II. The Rouge's equipment grew outdated until its very existence was threatened during the auto depression of the early 1980s. Workers at the complex dwindled to about 15,000.

But a 1983 labor-management agreement prompted the company to invest $500 million to modernize its Rouge Steel operations, including Double Eagle Steel Coating. They now make galvanized (rust-resistant) steel. Rouge Steel is the new blue-colored plant you see at the east side of Miller Road near Rotunda Drive. Finally, Rouge Steel became profitable. Ford sold it in 1989.

The entire Rouge complex seems to be experiencing a renaissance. The soybean and tire plants were scrapped long ago, but the Rouge Power House still generates enough power to serve a city the size of Boston. Mustangs roll off the assembly line at the rate of one a minute. Each year freighters carry 5 million tons of coal, iron-rich taconite pellets, and limestone to the complex. The blast furnaces can produce over 2 million tons of iron and the steelmaking facilities make 3 million tons of molten steel a year. An engine plant makes some 600,000 of the 1.9 liter, four-cylinder engines for Ford Escorts each year.

A DRIVE AROUND THE ROUGE . . . . . Start at the north. Take Miller from Michigan Avenue, or take the Rotunda Drive exit from I-94 (Exit 209). As Miller Road passes high over the rail lines, a vast panorama of this awesome industrial complex opens up. Unfortunately, it's almost impossible to park near here and take in the view. A little farther on, by Gate 4, the main gate, you can pull over to look at the Dearborn Historical Society's marker — which neglects to mention the historic Battle of the Overpass that took place on a bridge near here. The attack on labor organizers played a key role in the history of the United Auto Workers. That bridge is gone, but it looked like the current overpass you see leading to the employee parking lot.

Turn west onto Dix Avenue just as it passes over the River Rouge. The drawbridge here rises to let big freighters come in from the Great Lakes. The once-meandering river is now dredged straight and so polluted with chemicals that it never freezes in the winter. In the distance you can often see freighters unloading at the huge steel foundry to the north.

Along Dix west of here is an ugly but powerful and fascinating landscape created by piles of raw materials and byproducts of industry. Firms like a refinery and Detroit Tarpaulin are mixed in with factory-gate bars and junkyards advertising for wrecked cars. At this point you may want to turn around and head back on Dix into Dearborn's Arab South End (page 327), the working-class neighborhood at the factory gates. Or you can continue onto Schaefer Drive and back to I-94 or Michigan Avenue.

A SNACK OR MEAL IN THE NEARBY MIDDLE EAST . . . . . Directly in front of the Rouge is a bit of the Middle East, not five miles from Greenfield Village. There you can buy delicious, healthy breads, meat pies, meals, and ingredients for Middle Eastern cooking. The **Red Sea** Yemeni restaurant at 10307 Dix at Salina serves huge portions of good food in pleasant surroundings.

Two Arab neighborhoods in Dearborn

The largest Arab community in the U.S. offers exceptional bakeries, a variety of good restaurants, and Arab hospitality in a familiar but exotic setting.

Today Dearborn's South End seems as exotic as anyplace in the U.S. The working-class neighborhood near the Ford Rouge factory gates is the point of entry for Dearborn's large (20,000) and growing Islamic Arab community. Signs are in Arabic as well as English, head scarves are common among women, and Yemeni men wear traditional skullcaps. The call to prayer can be heard from a nearby mosque five times a day. Storekeepers uncover small prayer rugs on their counters and pray. And yet, in other ways, the area seems quite familiar to anyone who grew up in a city neighborhood where kids played pick-up games of ball and went to the corner store for their mothers, where several families on every block had fabulous rose gardens in their small yards, and on summer nights grown-ups sat on their porches after dinner and talked.

People from around much of the world came to work in Detroit during its 1920s boom years. The first mosque in the U.S., in fact, was near Ford's Highland Park plant. Before the wars in the Middle East in the 1970s created so many Muslim refugees, most Arabic-speaking immigrants to the Detroit area were Christians, usually from Lebanon or the Chaldean part of Iraq.

One legacy of metro Detroit's big and diverse Arab population is an increasing number of very good Middle Eastern restaurants and a few really outstanding ones, including La Shish in West Dearborn, Phoenicia in Birmingham, and the unassuming Steve's Back Room in Harper Woods.

THE SOUTH END

Dearborn's South End residential neighborhood grew up quickly in the early 1920s around the factory gates of the famous Ford Rouge plant, which once employed over 90,000 workers. The Rouge's smoke stacks loom over the neighborhood's modest

Afrah Pastry on West Warren is one of dozens of Dearborn retail businesses aimed primarily at Dearborn's big and growing Arab-American community. Many non-Arabs in metro Detroit have discovered the good food, low prices, and friendly service at these Arab businesses. Hospitality is highly valued in Arab cultures.

houses. The South End was a true American melting pot of dozens of nationalities working at Ford, until well after World War II. Today newly arrived Arab immigrants have replaced the older-generation autoworkers who have died or moved to better housing elsewhere.

Now that the South End has become a port of entry for Islamic Arabs, its dozens of bars have disappeared, while Arab bakeries, groceries, hair salons, and meat markets have blossomed. These serve neighborhood residents, plus the larger Islamic community which attends the big Sunni Moslem Mosque on Vernor at Dix.

The children of Muslim autoworkers who started building the mosque in 1939 have mostly moved on "into business" — the second stage of Arabs' preferred career pattern that ends up, one or two generations after immigration, in "the professions," especially law. Now the South End is the reception area for a continuing stream of immigrants. When they can afford it, they'll likely move to the middle-class part of east Dearborn around Warren and Schaefer, where roomy brick houses were originally built for Ford foremen and craftsmen. The Lebanese and West Bank Palestinians, escaping wars at home, have come to America as families. Yemeni men usually come alone. They frequent the South End's coffeehouses, patronized by Arab men only. Yemenis in America long dreamed of saving enough money to return and live comfortably with their families in their beloved but impoverished homeland. Now, finally, they're resigned to a life across the ocean in America.

To learn more about Arab culture over the centuries, plan a visit to the excellent **Arab-American Community Center for Economic and Social Services** (better known as **ACCESS**). Outstanding displays of interesting artifacts, photos, and text feature Islamic contributions to science, coffee-drinking, beautiful embroidered garments, architecture, and calligraphy. One interesting exhibit tells how Arab culture is rooted in a common language, not ethnicity or religion, and explains how the Virgin Mary is revered in Islam as the mother of one of its great prophets. Look for exhibits on music and local Arab history (Arab peddlers' wagons were a neighborhood staple in much of Det ·· and the beginnings of many successful businesses) in the library. Its comprehensive collection of books and videos on the Arab world is open to the general public. *Take Dix east of Miller 7 blocks, turn north (left) onto Saulino Court. Open weekdays 9-5. Call (313) 842-7010 to schedule weekend group tours.*

South End stores are on Dix and Vernor just east of Miller. Take Miller south from I-94 or Michigan Avenue. *Many stores are open from 9 a.m. to 9 p.m., 7 days a week.* Two shops that stand out are:

◆ **Arabian Village Bakery.** This small, family-run, homestyle bakery occupies part of a neighborhood grocery. For about a dollar each, there are meat pies and baked kibbee (cracked wheat) stuffed with lamb. You can warm them up in the oven for healthy fast-food meals or fry them. (For takeout eating on the run, the clerk will microwave them and squirt on a hummus sauce.) *Zahtar* are delicious flat breads flavored with oregano, sumac, and sesame. *Kaak* are spice cookies attractively stamped with decorative molds. *10045 W. Vernor at Dix. (313) 843-0800.*

◆ **Arabian Gulf Market.** At Middle Eastern groceries like this, you'll find many kinds of rice — in bulk (mostly 50¢ a pound) or in huge bags, imported olives at $1.29 a pound, unusual baked goods and candies, chunks of pressed tobacco, exotic tins of olive oils and fruits, and other staples, along with brass coffee boilers for making Turkish coffee. *1001 W. Vernor near Dix.*

West Warren between Schaefer and Miller

Arab culture, with its long tradition of trading, dovetails with the American dream of success through entrepreneurial energy and hard work. Storefronts along West Warren were largely empty 15 years ago. Today they are bursting with immigrant energy. Signs are in Arabic and English, giving the ordinary 1920s shopping strip an oddly exotic air.

Arabs set great store by fresh fruit, good breads, and pastries. Prices are often astonishingly low. "Shopping is a social event," says an Arab woman, "and the price is always questioned." Bargaining is never considered rude.

Competition is fierce, and most Arab restaurants here are good, with similar menus. Many are quite popular with non-Arab customers, who enjoy the healthy food and hospitable service. The restaurant scene here is in constant flux. New ones are opening all the time, ownership changes frequently — the restaurant business lacks status among most Arabs — and some restaurants that still have good reputations among outsiders have gone way down hill.

From the car, everything blurs together on this busy street. The area is best enjoyed on foot — window-shopping, buying food, stopping for pastry or coffee. Gift shops featuring fashions, coffee sets, and games are becoming more common. Many stores stay open late, so you can shop after dinner. For restaurants, see *Hunts' Restaurants and Lodgings of Michigan.*

West Warren businesses are patronized mostly by Arab speakers — not only neighborhood residents but academics and Oakland County professionals and businesspeople who make special shopping trips here. But a surprising variety of non-Arabs also come here to shop and eat out, attracted by the tasty, healthy food and extremely reasonable prices. The meat stores offer lamb and goat, slaughtered to halal standards akin to kosher rules.

Here is a selection of noteworthy shops, arranged from north to south and east to west:

◆ **Eastborn Fruit Market.** Arabs eat prodigious quantities of fresh fruit, and Dearborn produce markets offer low prices and unusual things like fresh figs and crunchy, tart-sweet fresh dates in season. This popular store is the area's first Arab produce store that's fairly large and well lighted. It also carries imported oils, rice, and other grains. *7431 Wyoming north of Warren. 8 a.m.-8 p.m.*

◆ **Bon Juice.** Snazzy juice bar with tables offers fresh fruit juices and concoctions like Kashta (sweetened milk curds; $2) and the Energizer (a refreshing combination of bananas, strawberries, milk, and honey; $1.50). *10621 W. Warren. Open 'til 9 p.m.*

◆ **Afrah Pastry.** Small shop well thought of by locals. Afrah offers beautiful honey-filo-nut pastries, and some French pastries, at lower prices. The bird's nest with pistachios (60¢) is excellent. Tables make this a nice place to stop in an interesting area. *12741 W. Warren.*

◆ **Express Jewelry.** Middle Eastern jewelry and gold. In the fluid, war-torn Arab world, gold jewelry is as esteemed as a portable form of wealth as it is for display and status. *12817 Warren at Appoline.*

◆ **Coffee and Nut Gallery.** The smells of coffee beans and spices in this tiny grocery are wonderful. *13029 W. Warren next to the Cedarland Restaurant.*

◆ **New Yasmeen Bakery.** New Yasmeen's pita bread has become a familiar staple at many metro Detroit groceries, and its *fatiya* (spinach pies) are considered the best around. Lebanese spinach pies are much simpler and healthier than the familiar Greek spinach pies in filo dough that's flaky with butter. The dough is plumper and more substantial, and the spinach filling is deliciously lemony. One and a half or two *fatiya* make a handy, satisfying lunch. Meat pies, filled with a ground lamb mix, come in the same plump triangular pocket and also cost 75¢. The same dough is used for round, 10-inch open pies topped with cheese, meat, or thyme mixed with sesame and oil ($1.25 each).

New Yasmeen has a deli and large streetfront area with tables (the door is on the side). It's easy to stop for a quick meal and go home with an array of breads, spreads like hummus, and salads like tabooli and fatoush, so you wouldn't have to cook for days. Big refrigerator cases have deli items like stuffed grape leaves, and several kinds of olives and cheese.

The helpful, friendly staff is happy to provide samples and advise non-Arabs about what to eat with what and when. *Labne,* for instance, is a thickened form of yogurt that makes a terrific, healthy breakfast when spread, with or without jam, on date-filled bread rings, raisin bread, and other breakfast breads. But ask first what you're getting. A fair number of those beautiful-looking breads are flavored with cardamom, a taste many Americans can't deal with for breakfast. *13900 West Warren at Horger, 3 blocks west of Schaefer. (313) 582-6035. Daily 5:30 a.m.-8:30 p.m., including Sundays.*

◆ **Sultan's Bakery.** Meat and spinach pies, fried kibbee, and such, not fancy pastries, are the focus of this attractive new bakery/deli started by the owners of the Arabian Village Bakery, a longtime fixture in Dearborn's South End. Also on hand, to take out or eat in at tables: deli salads (parsley-rich fatoush and tabooli, garlicky hummus chickpea spread, babaganoush(eggplant spread), falafel sandwiches, fried kibbee, and rotisserie chicken, plus olives and other deli items. "They will become a favorite in East Dearborn," predicts a resident. "Their prices will make them popular." *6851 Schaefer. Watch for the red awning. (313) 581-6688. Open daily 7 a.m. to at least 8 p.m.*

◆ **Shatila Bakery.** Long the big name among Dearborn's Arab bakeries, Shatila is owned by a noted pastry chef from Beirut. It also serves coffee and has a few tables which are great places for people-watching, since so many people in the line at the counter know each other. All signs are in Arabic.

Generous hospitality and entertaining at home are hallmarks of Arab culture. It's important to have a tray of pastries on hand to serve with Arabic coffee, that thick, cardamom-flavored brew served in tiny cups. Honey-nut-filo pastries are traditional. Beautiful, light French pastries with whipped cream and icing flowers are a legacy from the era when the French dominated Lebanon in the 19th and early 20th centuries. (In fact, the French colonial government shoulders the blame for stirring up rivalries between previously peaceful peoples by elevating the Maronite Christians above the Muslims.) *6914 Schaefer two blocks south of Warren, opposite L'Opera Banquet Hall. (313) 582-1952. Mon-Sat 8 a.m.-11 p.m., Sun 9-9.*

◆ **Joe and Ed's Schaefer Market.** Larger than most convenience stores, Joe and Ed's has a big selection of Middle Eastern food, from produce and breads to canned goods, bulk rice, and beans.

Long hours make this convenient. *5635 Schaefer near Ford Rd. (313) 846-5725. Daily 9:30 a.m.-1 a.m.*

♦ **El-Masri Bakery.** Founded in Palestine shortly after the turn of the century, and recently moved to Dearborn. Known for *kanify,* a Palestinian delicacy something like a pizza made with sweet, soft cheese — sold by the slice or by the pie. Also on hand: an extensive variety of traditional honey-nut-filo pastries and beautifully decorated French pastries (actually lighter and less buttery) with whipped cream, at incredibly low prices like 60¢. Tables let you sit, eat, drink coffee, and watch people. El-Masri has fast become a very popular local gathering spot. *5125 Schaefer 1 block north of Michigan. (313) 584-3500. Daily 9 a.m.-11 p.m.*

OTHER GOOD ETHNIC FOOD SHOPS IN AND NEAR EAST DEARBORN . .
. . . When you walk in the door of **Alcamo's Market**, East Dearborn's celebrated Italian specialty store, you're overwhelmed by the beguiling fragrances of spicy salamis, garlic, cheeses, coffee beans, and breads. There are two aisles of imported pastas in this spiffily updated old-time grocery, along with Italian specialties like fava beans, imported Italian cookies, crackers, appetizers, and sauces. Produce is gorgeous. There's some Greek food, too. *4423 Schaefer, 2 blocks south of Michigan in downtown East Dearborn. (313) 584-3010. Mon-Thurs 9-6, Fri and Sat 9-7. Easy to miss. Look for the red awning. Park in lot on Schaefer and Osborn.* . . . . In the stable Polish neighborhood in a part of Detroit's west side wedged between East Dearborn and Dearborn Heights, two longtime retail neighbors have combined. **Kowalski Sausage** sells takeout Polish favorites like stuffed cabbage, in addition to its well-known kielbasa and such. At the **West Warren Bakery** good pumpernickel and rye breads are under a dollar a loaf. There are Polish specialties like angel wings and jelly donuts, and a very good sourdough French bread, great for toast, also baked as submarine rolls that are served next door at the highly regarded Judy's Cafe. They're chewy, with a crunchy crust that holds in the juice from tomatoes, and only a quarter apiece. Order ahead to be sure of availability. *15708 W. Warren at Montrose, 2 blocks west of Greenfield and about a mile east of the Southfield Freeway in Detroit. (313) 584-2610. Mon-Sat 5 a.m.-7 p.m.*

Henry Ford Museum

A world-famous collection of American products, along with remarkable exhibits that entertain and explore the American cultures of cars and manufacturing.

Henry Ford's squadrons of pickers spread over the Midwest and New England to come up with an astounding array of artifacts for this vast (12 acres) indoor museum next to Greenfield Village. The museum's dignified exterior is an exact copy of Philadelphia's Independence Hall. Inside is one colossal collection after another. There's the world's greatest collection of 19th-century farm and kitchen implements. The exhibit on the history of lighting, from candles through electric bulbs, is immense enough to comprise a substantial museum in itself. The same could be said for the large collection of airplanes and cars. Nowhere will you find a more complete collection of American tractors.

Over the years the museum staff has worked to give shape to this huge, at times bewildering, hoard of items. Director Harold Skramstad came to the Henry Ford Museum/Greenfield Village in 1980 with the mission of reinvigorating the institution and reviving it financially. Its new direction is to use the splendid collection to illuminate people's work lives and social lives. This approach has only become apparent since 1991, when the immensely popular **"The Automobile and American Life"** opened. This lavish series of full-scale displays nostalgically shows the car's effect on the American roadside landscape. There's a vintage McDonald's sign, complete with oversized golden arches, a Holiday Inn guest room, and a diner plucked from Marlboro, Massachusetts, lovingly refurbished to its pristine state in 1946, when an egg salad sandwich cost 15¢. At a gleaming green and white 1940 Texaco service station, you can even peer into the full-scale garage and see the tools used at the time.

The **evolution of the auto industry** is brilliantly elucidated by using a sequence of TV monitors showing short historical film clips alongside splendidly restored automobiles from each period. To see the restored cars/auto history in chronological order, find the ramp in front of the Oscar Meyer Wienermobile and follow it

How the automobile changed
the American landscape is one
of several themes of the Henry
Ford's sprawling, riveting
exhibit on "The Automobile
and American Life." This giant,
neon-trimmed McDonald's
arch from the 1950s is a crowd
favorite.

up. Videotaped **interviews about design concepts** with illustrious automobile designers like Gordon Buerig, Raymond Loewy,
and Harley Earl are fascinating even for people with little previous interest in car design. But the exhibit's tone remains cele-
bratory and barely touches on the negative aspects of America's
love affair with the automobile: urban sprawl, impersonality,
dependence on foreign oil, pollution, and increased isolation of
the poor and old.

The new **"Made in America"** permanent exhibit goes beyond
mere celebration. It deals with American manufacturing – its
technological development and social impact. It presents the
subject in such an entertaining and illuminating way that there's
something in it for everybody: film clips of Lucy from the "I Love
Lucy" show messing up the candy-making production line; a
huge operating painting robot used in auto factories; a life-size
clean room where microchips are made; and 1930s miniature
furniture (used by salesmen) of Herman Miller Inc.'s trend-setting modular system.

Video stories are told in the voices of people who came to
America from all over the world. The factories they worked in
that epitomized the American System of manufacturing first
developed here in Southeast Michigan. The **American System**
came to feature long production runs, low prices, a mass market,

and eventually plenty of styling and advertising to promote planned obsolescence. Here, finally, is the Big Picture about the American age of industry from the 18th-century crafts era to today and into an uncertain future— honestly represented, replete with tradeoffs about industrial growth and its impact on the environment or the quality of work life. Visitors can look through the 19th-century *Scrapbook of Censure* and see that criticism of materialism and consumption is far from new. A video show on efficiency expert Frederick Winslow Taylor and the assembly-line speed-up he inspired shows its terrible effects on worker morale. Henry Ford emerges with some warts in the museum he founded.

"Made in America" is meant to be grazed. There's no designated sequence. But it's easy to miss a lot, including the exhibit's centerpiece video, "America in the Making."

Here is some useful advice for a visit.

◆ **Buy an annual pass and come back several times.** Single-day admissions to either the museum or Greenfield Village are expensive ($11.50/adult, $5.75/child 5-12), and the new exhibits are so extensive and interesting, return visits are well worthwhile. The Henry Ford Museum/Greenfield Village combined annual pass ($25/adult, $12.50 child) and $80 family membership are bargains if you go four or five times a year and attend a few of the many special weekends with no additional charge.

◆ **Look for the "Made in America" layout map** as you enter the main entrance. Getting an overview of what you most want to see will keep you from missing out on personal highlights. (A printed map for visitors is in the works.)

◆ **See the first section (up to the raised platform) carefully and thoroughly.** It incorporates large and sophisticated machines, several of which operate. The display cases spell out the problems and trade-offs involved, without oversimplifying. For instance, robots can substitute for human workers in dangerous, unhealthy jobs like spray painting, but they also take away good jobs workers enjoy. Small items like book covers, pamphlets, ads, and objects are effectively used to illustrate and amplify ideas. If you skim over the display cases, you'll miss some of the exhibit's most interesting parts.

◆ **Talk to the interpreters.** The part-time staff who greet visitors in the entry area are trained to demonstrate and explain many parts of the exhibit. They can show how things work that you might well not understand by yourself. They are also free to offer candid personal perspective on the big questions raised here. It's quite a surprise to hear a retired GM engineer say, "It took three million years to develop the fuel resources we use, and we're using them up so fast, I think we need to slow down and smell the roses. We're such a pell-mell society, rushing headlong into what could be a real calamity."

◆ **Watch the frequent short videos.** They can be the exhibit's highlight, because they add a thoughtful dimension of historic depth, with lots of old film footage. The 1950s smarmy, smug advertising pap about the wonders of American consumerism is shown for what it is. Over an hour's worth of videos are shown on a dozen small video monitors and two large theaters.

◆ **Don't miss "America in the Making" shown on the raised deck.** Displays here relate manufacturing and its consequences to choices we have to make today. The **11-minute film in the glass theater** shows how decisions and choices made by companies and governments have shaped today's realities. It points out how most Americans assumed continuous growth was a national birthright, and shows how prosperity bred complacency, but ends on a brighter note: "History has shown that our ingenuity and resourcefulness can help us adapt to challenges." The four-station **interactive computer kiosk** nearby focuses on decisions made at other key times: the 1930s, just after the crash of mass production; the 1950s during the Cold War build-up; and the oil embargoes of the 1970s. Another video shows industrial themes in movies and TV, from Spencer Tracy as an efficiency expert to the plutonium plant in *Silkwood.*

◆ **After the raised deck, choose "The Craft Era" and "The Making of Mass Production"** over the exhibit on Power. These complete the historical overview of where we are and how we got there. Manufactured goods illustrate points like "Americans have always preferred or relied on foreign products" (18th and 19th century Chinese export porcelain) and "Silversmiths catered to customers who used silver to illustrate their wealth and taste" (Paul Revere pitcher). The giant interior photo of the revolutionary Ford Highland Park plant is impressive; the **"Workers' Lives"** video is not to be missed.

The **power exhibit**, replete with several huge steam engines, is visually impressive. But unfortunately it assumes some familiarity with the basics that aren't explained – like knowing that boilers made the steam and used coal to do it. An interpreter to explain what you don't understand might make this come alive.

In counterpoint to these mammoth display areas and the longtime collections of items by category (glass and dishes are in front, for instance), the museum also holds an assortment of fascinating isolated items. There's the rocking chair in which Lincoln was murdered. You can see the huge, 600-ton 1941 "Allegheny" steam locomotive, one of the last and largest of a proud era, displayed to great effect next to the cute life-size replica of the third-oldest train in the U.S. A Lunar Roving Vehicle, one made by NASA to transport astronauts on the moon, is in the concourse.

Hands-on exhibits are generally entertaining but don't add much to big-picture ideas. The elaborate **Innovation Station** participatory production line, aimed at kids, requires getting a free ticket and takes about half an hour. At the supervised **Activities Center** children can operate an assembly line, pedal a high-wheel bike, and do other hands-on things.

At the end of the walk from the entrance, the **American Cafe** and soda fountain is open 9-4:30, year around. No museum ticket is required. Here the hot dogs cost almost $2, but the beef stew lunch at under $6 is hearty and filling. Thrifty visitors are well advised to bring bag lunches to eat at the Corner Cupboard **picnic area** within the museum. The **Plaza Store** within the museum sells handcrafts (many made in Greenfield Village) and a wide range of toys for children and adults.

Temporary exhibits are quite elaborate, semi-permanent in nature. A major exhibit on the Motown Sound opens in June, 1995. (See page 239.)

See Greenfield Village above for directions, phone, and prices. To learn about upcoming events, order an info packet, or talk to a live operator, call (800) 835-5237.

A GREAT MUSEUM STORE . . . . . . You don't have to have a museum ticket to shop at Henry Ford Museum's **Museum Store** (open 9-5 daily). Its outstanding book section is especially strong on automobiles and roadside architecture, Henry Ford and Ford Motor, antiques, crafts, Detroit history, and inexpensive Dover paper toys and coloring books. Many of the dolls, crystal, china, and other gift items reproduce objects in the Museum's collections.

THE STORY OF THE HUGE, AMBITIOUS TWIN MUSEUMS HENRY FORD FOUNDED . . . . . is recapped, briefly, in a video on the main concourse of the Henry Ford Museum. Look or ask for **"Beyond the Factory."** In many ways, it's the most fascinating story of all, rich in paradox and irony. It tells how Ford, the genius of mass production, wanted to develop a popular priced automobile and tractor to help free farmers from the burdens of animal power and rural isolation. How, a few miles downstream from his boyhood home and baronial mansion on the River Rouge, he built the world's biggest factory, the Ford Rouge, the consummate example of vertical integration — iron ore came in by ship, finished cars rolled out. How a hundred thousand workers from all over the world came to work there, creating a polyglot proletariat Henry Ford neither understood nor respected. And how Ford then declared, "The Rouge isn't fun anymore," and set about developing Greenfield Village and the Henry Ford Museum to recreate the rural world of middling people, farmers and craftsmen, a world he had done much to destroy.

The museum, village, and related elementary school were at once Ford's personal retreat and a very forward-looking vision, museum staffers say. By drawing on the past and on the history of change and innovation, Ford wanted to train people to continue to be resourceful in the modern industrial era he had helped create.

TO UNDERSTAND THE EPIC DRAMA OF FORD . . . . . — and a good deal of Detroit — you have to *read* it. A good place to start is with Robert Lacey's ***Ford: The Men and the Machine*** or with ***The Fords*** by Peter Collier and David Horowitz (also available complete on audiotape at many libraries). In this book, if you look up Henry Ford and Edsel Ford in the index, you'll come upon the main visitor sights associated with them, and some worthwhile background, too.

While Ford was absorbed by his museums and experimental interests like exploiting the manufacturing possibilities of soybeans and developing seasonal "village industries" to enable people to stay on the farm, he insisted on keeping control of Ford Motor Company. He actively thwarted plans of his astute son, Edsel. The results for the company were disastrous. (See pages 293 and 323.)

OTHER THINGS TO DO IN DEARBORN . . . . . if you're staying over on a trip to Greenfield Village/Henry Ford Museum:
Visit Fair Lane, the Henry Ford Estate, and have lunch (weekdays only) in the dramatic swimming pool room. See page 346. . . . . . **Explore Arab Dearborn** for dinner and food shopping; pastry shops and groceries are open until 9 at least. West Warren between Schaefer and Wyoming is the main drag. See pages 327-333. . . . . . **Hear blues and related music** forms at **Sully's** (313-846-5377) and **Moby Dick's** (313-581-3650). . . . . . **Eat out** at these recommended restaurants: M & M Cafe (Lebanese-American; 1-581-

5775); La Shish (Lebanese; 313-584-4477); Buddy's Pizza (313-562-5900).

THE MOST HANDS-ON ACTIVITIES . . . . . in the Henry Ford Museum and Greenfield Village are for **Summer Festival**, from June 18 through August 22. . . . . . Special **holiday programs** also feature participatory activities. For more information on upcoming activities, call (800) 835-5237.

HELP IN CONSERVING YOUR HISTORIC ARTIFACTS . . . . . Conservators at the Henry Ford Museum are happy to share their expertise. **Preservation fact sheets** ($2 each, prepaid) include care and cleaning tips, plus a resource list and bibliography. They cover archival material, autos, brass, clocks, textiles and clothing, furniture and wood, glass and ceramics, structures, iron, paintings, phonographs, photos, plastic, silver, and art on paper. . . . . . Consultations about artifacts brought to the museum ($50/hour in donation to museum and village) require filling out an order/info form in advance. . . . . . Call (313) 271-1620 for conservation particulars.

MUSEUM REPRODUCTIONS . . . . . of furniture and decorative accessories in the museum collections are for sale at the **American Life Collection Gallery** (open during museum hours) on the first floor of the Henry Ford Museum, next to the American Cafe.

AN INEXPENSIVE SHUTTLE TO MAJOR AREA DESTINATIONS . . . . . including Henry Ford's estate, major hotels, the Detroit Institute of Arts, RenCen, Greektown, New Center, and (evenings) the downtown theater district is new for 1994. $3 ticket can be used all day. Call (800) CALL DTW.

WAGONS AND STROLLERS . . . . for children, and strollers for adults, are available at both Greenfield Village and the Henry Ford museum.

Greenfield Village

*A product of Henry Ford's great interest
in American history, it's a major American attraction.*

This famous outdoor museum is a direct outgrowth of
Henry Ford's desire to show how technology has changed
the lives of ordinary Americans. Its indoor counterpart is
the Henry Ford Museum next door. As Ford entered his sixties,
he developed a passionate interest in the tangible manifestations
of American history. Ford had a different collecting agenda from
most of his wealthy contemporaries, who sought out the pinna-
cles of achievement in the arts and crafts. In the Henry Ford Museum and Greenfield Village, Ford wanted mainly to document
ordinary life from the past, that of farmers and shopkeepers and
artisans, the more common people. He focused on America's industrial transformation in the late 19th and early 20th centuries.

Not only did Ford spend millions to obtain the many buildings and artifacts assembled here, but he also personally spent
months actively seeking them out. He supervised their placement
here, and would spend hours in these historic buildings — often
alone — savoring their connection with the past.

In layout and landscaping, no real village ever resembled
Greenfield Village. It is simply a collection of historic buildings.
Some were idealized and upgraded when they were "restored,"
decades ago.

Village highlights include:

◆ **Firestone Farm.** A real Ohio working farm from 1882, the
boyhood home of tiremaker and Ford friend Harvey Firestone.
Merino sheep were the farm's main cash product. Visitors can
see big Percheron draft horses at work, and short-horned
Durham cows and Poland China pigs for household food. From 9
to 5, museum employees actually "live" there, doing normal farm
work: milking, working with the animals, laundry, gardening. If
you come at noon, they're eating the noon meal the women have
prepared. Inquire about the dates for **Spring Farm Days** that
kick off the season.

◆ **Wright Cycle Shop.** Here, in the famed birthplace of aviation,
Orville and Wilbur Wright built kites, gliders, and ultimately the

Percheron draft horses do much of the work at the Firestone Farm, restored and operated as it was in the 1880s. It was the boyhood home of tiremaker Harvey Firestone, a close friend of Henry Ford.

world's first successful flying machine. By 1903, the American bicycle craze of the 1890s was on the wane. The Wrights eked out a living selling bicycles and bicycling paraphernalia from the store and repairing bikes in the room behind it. In the very back, they built their flying machines. Moved from Dayton, Ohio, in 1936, the building has been restored to look much as it did in 1903, the year of their first motorized flight.

◆ **Susquehanna Plantation.** This Maryland plantation house is shown as it would have existed in 1860. It illuminates the economic and social basis of slavery — who the slaves and masters were, their various roles, and the relationships among them.

◆ **Glass, pottery, printing, tinsmithing, and textile demonstrations**. Using 19th-century techniques, craftspeople show how these important products were made.

◆ **Ford's birthplace.** This simple Greek Revival farmhouse was built on Ford Road in Dearborn by Henry's father William in 1861. Widespread fascination with Henry Ford makes this exhibit popular.

◆ **Ford Mack Avenue Factory**. In 1903 the first production-model Fords were manufactured in the original of this building. This factory turned out up to 18 cars a day and quickly made Henry wealthy. The 4- horsepower vehicles started at $800.

◆ **Mrs. Cohen's millinery shop.** A Detroit widow ran this shop at the turn of the century to support her family. Visitors enjoy seeing hats made and trying them on.

◆ **Armington & Sims Machine Shop.** Many visitors are unexpectedly fascinated by the awesome turn-of-the-century steam engines demonstrated here.

◆ **Edison's Menlo Park Compound.** In this complex of six plain New Jersey buildings, one can relive one of the most extraordinary phenomena in American history. Thomas Edison's 1880 laboratories were the world's first commercial research and development center. Edison gathered chemists, machinists, craftsmen, glass blowers, and other specialists and gave them a wide assortment of tools and materials. The results were spectacular. In just 10 years, 420 of Edison's 1,093 patents came from here, including the electric light bulb, phonograph, and electric sewing machine.

◆ **Noah Webster House.** Here Noah Webster completed his famous dictionary. An upstairs room displays the extraordinary number of his accomplishments, from founding Amherst College to serving in his state legislature.

◆ **Eagle Tavern.** Transported from Clinton, Michigan, this 19th century tavern is complete with ladies' parlor, sitting room, and bar. Here you can buy weak versions of authentic drinks from the 1850s such as a "Jersey Lightning" ($3.75). In back, a **restaurant** serves huge, reasonably-priced meals from recipes of the era such as stewed rabbit and pork loin. Recommended: lemon trout. Entrees around $9.

◆ **J.R. Jones General Store.** Waterford, Michigan's general store has been meticulously restored to the year 1886, when the proprietor retired. Most museum stores have a range of contents that date over several decades at least. Here the shelves are stocked with 3,000 authentic artifacts and 2,500 reproductions of merchandise available in 1886, when consumerism and brand names (Heinz, Arm & Hammer, Borden's Eagle Brand condensed milk, Louisville Slugger baseball bats) were beginning to take hold. Authentic local notices are posted on the wall.

◆ **Cotswold Forge.** A gifted blacksmith/ interpreter fascinates visitors of all ages as he explains his work (two hundred years ago, most everyday tools and fasteners were made by hand by the village blacksmith) and makes heated iron bend and curve, as if by magic. Things made here are used in the village and sold at the gift shops. The nearby 17th-century stone cottage and barn were brought from southwestern England, 175 tons in all. Some of Henry Ford's ancestors came from the Cotswolds.

◆ **Daggett Farmhouse.** Kids and adults love seeing the everyday activities of this spare New England farmhouse from the 1760's: spinning (visitors help card wool), cooking on the open hearth, gardening in the beautiful big garden, where many plants are unfamiliar. Medicinal herbs grown and used include hyssop (for coughs) and angelica (used in liquors and perfumes, also believed to ward off evil spirits).

◆ **Suwanee Lagoon.** Idyllic, shady park-like area with a snack bar and terrace seating overlooking the lagoon where the paddle-wheel steamboat Suwanee docks. Boat rides are $1; rides on the **antique carousel** are 75¢.

More of Greenfield Village's buildings are open during the peak summer season, from mid-June through the latter part of August. This season, billed as **Summer Festival**, has the most hands-on activities in both the village and Henry Ford Museum. The Mr. Wizard organization has helped devise the **"Wizard of Tuskegee"** activities involving George Washington Carver's peanut products, and Wright-related **"Wizards of Flight"** activities. If you're planning a visit in the slow season (April, for instance, or November), you might call to find out what's open.

Greenfield Village's mammoth size is a strength and a weakness. The quality of interpretation is uneven. You may only want to see part of the big complex at one visit. Here's some advice from the staff about enjoying Greenfield Village. Plan on making a day of it. Pace yourself. Take a break and sit in the park-like areas scattered throughout the village. Slow down. Don't see so many buildings that they blur together. The **annual pass** and **membership** allow for repeat visits and bring the cost per visit way down. Study the map and daily activities upon arrival and decide what you want to focus on. Visitors can break up their walking tour with a narrated **train ride** on the village's splendid steam locomotive that circles the entire complex. It stops only at the entrance and the Suwanee lagoon. $2 gives you unlimited rides for the day. Or you can take a horse-driven **carriage ride** ($4 per person) or **bus ride** ($3 per person); both are narrated and last 30 to 35 minutes.

Another good way to take a break is to have a meal or a snack. Picnics are encouraged. The snack bar food, scattered throughout the village, is uneven and not cheap. Food is served at the historic Eagle Tavern and, next to it, the new **Taste of**

History cafeteria (open 10-5) right next door. Here you can sample some of the dishes also prepared at the Firestone Farm and 18th-century Daggett Farmhouse, and try Dandy Weed Salad (George Washington Carver's favorite), or Abraham Lincoln's chicken fricassee, or Elvis Presley's favorite pound cake. Entrees are around $5; soups and pastries between $2 and $2.50; tastings 50¢-75¢. Bag lunches (around $5) reflect themes from the Firestone Farm, Carver's peanuts, or a railroader's meal. The big, airy room, by the inventive metro Detroit restaurant design firm Peterhansrea, is something to see. It combines some carnival glass and Haviland china from the museum with corn-art murals and a pie clock.

The **Greenfield Village Store** gift shop has many toys and games for children, in addition to reproductions of antiques and jewelry in the collection here, handcrafts made in the village, and an outstanding book store like that in the Henry Ford Museum.

Greenfield Village is in West Dearborn, about 8 miles west of downtown Detroit. From I-94, take the Southfield Freeway north and follow signs for the Village. From Michigan Avenue, turn south onto Oakwood at the green-roofed Westborn Market. (313) 271-1620. **For 24-hour taped info,** *call (313) 271-1976.* **For personal help,** *brochures, events info, classes, etc., call (800) 835-5237, 9-5 weekdays (outside area code 313). A real person will talk to you. TDD for the Deaf: (313) 271-2455, 10-5 daily.* **Open** *daily 10-5. Buildings are closed Jan-mid-March, but the exteriors can be viewed for free with a ticket to Henry Ford Museum.* **Admission to** **either** ***Henry Ford Museum or Greenfield Village:*** *adults $11.50, seniors 62 and over $10.50, youths 5-12 $5.75, under 5 free. 2-day unlimited-admission ticket to Museum and Village $10 youths, $20 adults. The Museum/Village* **annual pass** *($25 adults, $12.50 youths) makes frequent visits affordable. Call for membership options. Members get free admission, discounts in shops, classes, members-only events. Sample family rate for 2 adults (can be parents or grandparents) and children: $80/year.*

Fair Lane, the Henry Ford Estate

*Here's the huge, quirky home
the industrial legend created once money was no object.*

By the time his estate was completed in 1914, Henry Ford's interests and activities were already expanding beyond manufacturing cars. His wife Clara and son Edsel moved into Fair Lane without him in December while he was taking his peace ship to Europe in a quixotic attempt to stop World War I. Fair Lane is a gigantic, park-like spread, 1,600 acres in all, and for many the splendid landscaping is the high point of a visit.

The home itself shows that aesthetics were not the legendary auto magnate's strong suit. It's a strange amalgam of Frank Lloyd Wright's naturalistic Prairie Style and the medieval-influenced Scottish baronial style. Ford changed architects in midstream, and it shows. The grandiose home seems a bad fit for Henry Ford's down-to-earth tastes. Not surprisingly, a favorite room was the rustic, less pretentious Field Room. Its raw-timbered ambiance is unlike the ornate interiors in the rest of the house.

Although the heirs auctioned off most of the original furniture after Henry and Clara died, Edsel Ford II is leading the Ford family and the community in a joint four million-dollar restoration effort that has recovered many of the furnishings and placed them back in their original spots. A posthumous painting of Henry's mother, Mary Litogot Ford, once again hangs in the music room. The English Room, where Thomas Edison stayed, has been restored, as has the dining room.

Ford applied his restless, creative energy not to the house but to its huge hydroelectric power plant and laboratory. It occupies a separate structure and is connected by a long underground tunnel with the mansion. Ford teamed up with friend Thomas Edison to create an extraordinary 110-kilowatt electric system — quite a feat, given the small size of the River Rouge which powers it. The 1915 plant is once again generating all the electricity for the estate. The independence provided by having his own power plant must have fulfilled a deep-seated need in

Ford; he later built another 20 hydroelectric plants on small rivers in southeastern Michigan.

The grounds are the high point of a visit to Fair Lane. The mansion overlooks a beautiful, wooded portion of the River Rouge at the point of a delightful man-made waterfall. After seeing garbage floating past his mansion, Henry Ford was personally responsible for getting the upstream towns of Plymouth and Northville to stop dumping raw sewage in the river.

The surrounding 1,600 acres were transformed by the famous landscape architect Jens Jensen into a series of naturalistic meadows and forests. With the aid of a well-designed $1 map of the grounds, you can take your own tour of this vast area. The map is available at the gift shop or reception desk inside Fair Lane. **Burroughs Grotto** was dedicated by Ford and naturalist John Burroughs in 1918. The **Ford Discovery Trail**, open from June 15 through Labor Day, is an outdoor walk that acquaints visitors with Ford and his friends, known as "the wizards of Fair Lane." A replica of Ford's **tree house**, the **root cellar**, and the **boathouse** are among the exhibits.

Nature was one of Ford's many passions. An avid bird-watcher, he installed hundreds of birdhouses — eight of them were even heated in winter! Almost 600 deer roamed the woods and fields. Clara Ford's taste was for more formal English gardens. She appropriated one of Jensen's meadows to create a fantastic rose garden that gained national attention in its day. Today you can see its ruins, for it would cost $400,000 a year to maintain.

It's worth having lunch at **The Pool**, a restaurant in the dramatically illuminated space which was initially the mansion's swimming pool. It's open weekdays from 11 to 2. Various entrees, salads, and sandwiches are under $6.50. In addition to daily specials and homemade soup, the restaurant also serves soybeans and Poland spring water, special favorites of Ford.

In west Dearborn, west off Evergreen between Michigan Ave. and Ford Rd. From I-94 or I-96, take the Southfield Freeway (M-39) to Michigan Ave. in Dearborn, go west to Evergreen, north to Fair Lane. Park at the Henry Ford Estate lot, marked by a brown sign. (313) 593-5590. Open year-round. Always open Sundays 1-4:30, with tours on the half hour. From April thru Dec: Mon-Sat tours from 10-3 on the hour, except no tour at 12. Jan-April: 1 tour daily, Mon-Fri. Call for time. $6/adults, $5/seniors and students, 5 & under free.

Chapter 4
Flint, Saginaw Valley & the Thumb

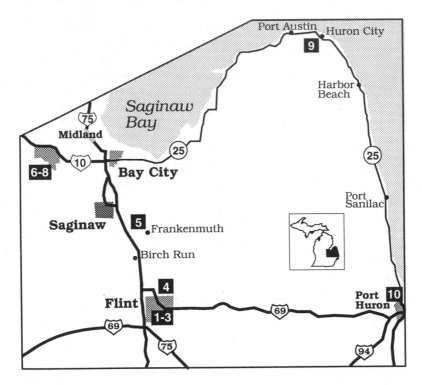

HIGHLIGHTS

1 **Sloan Museum** – 350
2 **Flint Institute of Arts** – 355
3 **G.M. Truck Plant Tour** – 358
4 **Crossroads Village** – 361
5 **Frankenmuth** – 365
6 **Dow Chemical Tour** – 378
7 **Dow Gardens** – 382
8 **Chippewa Nature Center** – 387
9 **Historic Huron City** – 390
10 **Port Huron** – 395

For lodgings and restaurants see *Hunts' Restaurants & Lodgings*

INTRODUCTION

Flint, Saginaw Valley & the Thumb

This was one of the country's most important lumbering regions in the late 19th century. Millions of logs were floated down the Saginaw river to mills in Saginaw and Bay City. Logging generated huge fortunes, which later helped fund the start of the auto industry

Among the many area factories using lumber was Flint's successful Durant-Dort Carriage Company, started by Billy Durant. That visionary entrepreneur later assembled Buick, Oldsmobile, Cadillac, and Oakland Motors (renamed Pontiac) to create General Motors.

Saginaw and Bay City are classic lumber towns, where lumber barons built elaborate houses, libraries, and churches. Lumber towns with extensive sawmills needed nearby foundries to make equipment for loggers and mills. Saginaw's foundries expanded into huge facilities incorporated into General Motors.

Bay City today is a poor but remarkably preserved place with an illustrious industrial past. Bay City made giant cranes and hoists, and kit homes from Aladdin and other makers. The many Poles who worked in those factories give the town an enviable, well-kept solidity.

Nearby Midland enjoyed little of the money reaped from logging. When Herbert Dow came to develop its bromine deposits into a chemical industry, the devastated landscape of tree stumps fostered in him and his family a love of gardening and conservation that still makes Midland distinctive place to visit.

After the Thumb was logged off, professors at East Lansing's Michigan Agricultural College (now Michigan State) drew on their climate and soils research to encourage the Polish, German, and Canadian farmers moving into the area to grow sugar beets and dry beans. Today the huge bean silos and colossal piles of sugar beets in fall stand out as landmarks on the flat skyline, along with the spires of Catholic churches and the stubby towers of Lutheran ones.

Sloan Museum

*Flint's local history, of unusual interest and importance
to American labor and manufacturing, is told
with uncommon candor, sympathy, and perspective.*

The vibrant new 10,000-square-foot permanent exhibit on
"Flint and the American Dream" adds new dimensions
of Baby Boom nostalgia and contemporary social rele-
vance to an already outstanding museum of local history and
culture. An extra bonus for car-lovers is a **choice collection of
cars,** including the oldest production-model Chevrolet in existence, a sporty red 1910 Buick "Bug" raced by Louis Chevrolet,
the famous Chevy "490" (the world's top-selling line in 1918),
and a futuristic 1959 Cadillac Cyclone, a non-production concept car that still looks avant-garde.

As long as Flint's G.M. plants were booming, the local official
popular culture consisted of a bland, self-congratulating (and
usually dumbed-out) faith in the status quo, in GM, and in a
basically sunny future. But by the late 1980s, that confidence
had been fundamentally rocked – by severe unemployment,
made worse by decades of easy living; by prospects of continued
corporate downsizing; and by global competitors and GM's inter-
nal problems, long masked by lack of competition.

Flint has been accurately billed as the town that built
General Motors, not the town that GM built. Its story, as told in
the Sloan Museum, begins like that of many Michigan towns:
first, with native Indians' hunting and agriculture, in tune with
the seasons; followed by Europeans exploiting natural resources
through commercial fur-trapping, then through lumbering,
which spawned heavy industry needed to make equipment for
sawmills and logging equipment. Each of these eras is illustrated
by a fully furnished, **life-size interior** of unusual interest. The
tipi can be entered, a great hit with children. A vast and realistic
miniature model of a logging company, from camp to mill, is
compelling for anyone interested in the subject.

In the 20th century, hometown carriage manufacturer Billy
Durant created General Motors with his stock market winnings.
Flint history becomes so dramatic and fascinating that it's
nationally significant. First, more than any other event, the 1937

Flint's dramatic, important labor history is well told at the Sloan Museum and at the Labor Museum and Learning Center. This photo shows the famous 1937 Sit-Down Strike, an event that led to unionization of all American autoworkers.

Flint Sitdown Strike was the birth of the modern labor movement. It led to the UAW becoming the only recognized negotiating representative of labor in the auto industry, ushering in a long era of high wages and good benefits for Michigan's many autoworkers. Flint had the highest concentration of autoworkers of any metropolitan area in the United States – and probably still does.

What makes this new exhibit so compelling is its honest, complex look at Flint's evolution into a company town and a consumption-oriented boom town without equal – and at the painful shock that came when jobs dwindled and the GM market share plummeted in the 1980s. This local museum stands out by not flinching at many less attractive aspects of local history. Americanization campaigns of the 1920s bordered on harassment of foreign immigrants. Easy credit sold more cars but made the Depression worse by repossessing workers' homes and cars. The postwar suburban dream of the 1950s was available to white people only. The local government and press were all too willing to support GM corporate goals without criticism. The AutoWorld indoor theme park and downtown festival marketplace, supposed to launch tourism to bolster the local economy, proved embarrassing failures.

Highlights of "Flint and the American Dream" include:
◆ pennants for Good Roads Day (1912): "No more mud!"
◆ factory life shown in huge photos and a movie
◆ compelling quotes from many kinds of observers on labor issues. "I ain't got no kick on wages," said a GM worker in 1935, "but I just don't like to be drove."
◆ a 1930s home movie tour of downtown Flint
◆ a newsreel of the 1937 Sit-Down Strike and two front pages (one from the UAW, one from the GM house organ) to take home
◆ consumer ads, signs, and products from Flint's 1950s boom, photos and memorabilia of drive-ins. Teen car culture was an especially lucrative market in Flint.
◆ a lobby display for **"Roger and Me,"** Michael Moore's documentary movie hit satirizing Flint and General Motors. (Moore ignored the museum's requests for memorabilia until his mother was contacted.)

It's too bad the exhibit didn't draw on Moore's comments or those of other gifted culture critics from the Flint area. They include 1960s activist and White Panther Party founder John Sinclair; Ben Hamper, "the Rivethead," celebrated autoworker/columnist; the late raconteur and novelist Ed Love, author of "Subways Are for Sleeping" and several funny, poignant reminiscences; comedienne Sandra Bernhard; and gadfly/philanthropist Stewart Mott. The museum did make special efforts to include photos of immigrant European and African-American families, which unfortunately aren't very interesting.

Even for people who don't care much about cars, the **car collection** is worthwhile for its business and social history. The cars convey the principles of **"Sloanism,"** as developed by Durant's successor in the 1920s, the young MIT grad who had developed a reputation for turning around troubled companies. The principles: clearly segment the market by price and prestige, and introduce the annual model change.

Finally, the Sloan Museum does include an exhibit on human health and anatomy that lays out the basics of reproductive health. Short, clear displays show birth-control methods and explain how effective each is; tell in vivid detail about sexually transmitted diseases; and show the stages of gestation in three-dimensional models, from a tiny embryo to a nine-month fetus. It could be a boon for parents who find it hard to discuss sex with their kids. The sensible blue sheets on "There's No Place Like Home . . . For Sex Education" are available to take home.

1221 East Kearsley in Flint's Cultural Center. From I-75, take I-475 north to Exit 8A (Longway Blvd.), turn right at the first light, turn right at the next street (Forest). To park in free lot down the hill from the museum, turn right onto Matthew and left into the lot. (810) 760-1169. Tues-Fri 10-5, Sat-Sun 12-5. Open Mon in July & August. $3 adults, $2 children 5-12.

THE STORY OF WORK AND WORKING PEOPLE IN MICHIGAN . . . . . is told in huge photo panels of exceptional interest, with well chosen, accessible text, at the **Labor Museum and Learning Center of Michigan.** You may opt for a **guided tour** by a UAW retiree that's simpler but also interesting. Written material is objectively presented and no more pro-labor than a state historical museum might be. Thoughtful displays begin with the egalitarian crafts era of small shops, where owners and workers labored together. By the late 19th and early 20th centuries, the crafts era was replaced by impersonal mass production; productivity and profits increased and wages decreased as a result. Early labor leaders disagreed on how to organize – trade by trade (the American Federation of Labor's approach) or the Wobblies' "One Big Union."

Displays look at work and conditions in lumber mills (lumber barons greatly influenced Republican state politics), in Upper Peninsula mines, and in the huge manufacturing plants of the stove, railroad car, and automobile industries. Strong-arm tactics, blacklists, and Flint's well-meaning welfare capitalism were all used to keep out unions. Grievances behind the historic 1937 Flint Sit-Down Strike that paved the way for the United Auto Workers Union are explored: wages, unpaid down time, speed-ups, seniority (foremen often fired older workers and favored younger ones), and piece work.

This museum is still in progress. It now ends just after World War II, which brought more women and minorities into the workforce. It has a small labor book shop and gift shop. *711 N. Saginaw in the Walter Reuther Bldg. on the Mott Community College Campus 2 blocks north of downtown. From Saginaw and downtown, turn left onto Fifth, then immediately into parking lot. From I-475, take the Longway Blvd. exit. Go west 6 blocks on Longway, look for Reuther Bldg. between Saginaw and Martin Luther King Blvd. (810) 762-0251. Tues-Fri 10-5, Sat noon-5. $2/adults, $1/children and seniors.*

A SCENIC PICNIC SPOT IN DOWNTOWN FLINT . . . . . Riverbank Park along the Flint River is an unusually elaborate urban park, the outgrowth of needed flood-control measures. Four and one half blocks long, it has flower gardens, picnic sites, a **playground**, a large amphitheater, and a fish ladder for the big salmon migrating upriver in the fall. There is even a water-powered **Archimedes screw** which lifts water to create multiple waterfalls. In the fall it's exciting to see the **fish ladder** and watch for giant salmon swimming upriver from Lake Huron to spawn. The greatest migration is usually from late September through October. . . . . . The 50th anniversary of the **UAW Flint Sitdown Strike** is commemorated in a nifty pictorial **monument**. It's across the river from the University of Michigan Flint, at the park's east end. The handsome display features big, rather primitive mural paintings on Pewabic tiles. One shows the great Flint Sitdown strike of 1936-37 at Fisher Body Plants 1 & 2. The other shows workers in an automobile plant. An amusing touch is the benches in front of the displays: tan concrete car seats.

HISTORIC MIDWEST PIPE SHOP . . . . . Paul's Pipe Shop (810-235-0581) at 647 S. Saginaw in downtown Flint stocks over a million pipes ranging from a $1.49 corncob to a $5,000 Dunhill. Pipes cram the shop; even more are stored on the second story. Owner Paul Spaniola's best selling tobacco is his "58th Anniversary" blend — $2.25 for 2 ounces. Cigars fill another climate-controlled room. Paul boils his own Cayuga pipes in a special South American nut oil and claims flatly that it is "the best pipe you ever smoked." Paul himself is a five-time winner of the world pipe-smoking title. (The person who can smoke his pipe the longest wins.) Neither pipe-smoking nor downtown Flint is what it used to be. Paul's has more the air of a party store than a gentleman's pipe shop. *Mon-Sat 9-7.*

A GOOD WEEKEND FAMILY DESTINATION . . . . . There's so much to see and do in **Flint's Cultural Center** alone, what with the museums, planetarium, events at the Whiting Auditorium, Flint makes a worthwhile destination any time of year. Call the visitors' bureau at (810) 232-8900 for upcoming events. Call Whiting Auditorium (810-760-1138) to receive info on the coming seasons of its Classical, Broadway, Showcase, and Family series. Flint offers an impressive array of reasonably priced offerings, and visitors won't have a hard time finding their way around. In summer, with **Crossroads Village** and related areas in gear, you could just about spend an enjoyable week in Flint, and camp at the county's attractive campground. The failed AutoWorld theme park was derided when it sought to build on that tourism infrastructure.

Flint Institute of Arts

Splendid 19th-century French paintings help make this a leading Midwestern art museum.

Generous donations from wealthy Flint citizens have built this into the state's second most prominent art museum, behind only the Detroit Institute of Arts. It's an unusually appealing museum, worth a look even for people who don't think they like art. It's small. Admission is free. The changing exhibits are interesting and diverse. The permanent collection is strong in accessible but radically different areas.

The **contemporary paintings and sculptures**, nearly all representative in some way and often quite realistic, are bold and stimulating. Often they incorporate pop images or optical tricks. Look at them and you see things in a new way, without having to be inducted into an arcane art theory.

Broadly appealing in a much softer, more romantic vein, is the exceptional collection of **19th-century French paintings**, mostly landscapes. It includes works by Corot, Courbet, Renoir, Toulouse-Lautrec, Bonnard, Pissarro, and Vuillard.

The **Bray Renaissance Gallery** is a Renaissance-style hall, with an ornate coffered ceiling and marble floor. It houses an impressive collection of 15th- to 17th-century European works of art, including furniture, paintings, a monumental set of ten 17th-century

American art at the Flint Institute of Arts is unusually appealing, even for people who don't think they like art. John George Brown's How D'Ye (circa 1875-1880) is an uncommon depiction of an African-American boy.

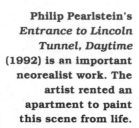

Philip Pearlstein's *Entrance to Lincoln Tunnel, Daytime* (1992) is an important neorealist work. The artist rented an apartment to paint this scene from life.

French tapestries, and an angel by Rubens. A series of six Sunday-afternoon **classical music concerts** is held in this stately marble hall.

Other highlights include Chinese sculpture and porcelains, African art, and a collection of 19th-century paperweights. The museum's collection of Oriental vases and sculptures is also noteworthy. Some exhibition highlights: The Walter Evans Collection of African-American Art (Sept. 1 through Nov. 7, 1994) and Romare Bearden as Printmaker (Feb. 7 through April 15, 1995). Call for upcoming **events**, which include frequent workshops, a Wednesday noon film series, and evening lectures.

The **museum shop** includes decorator items, handmade contemporary jewelry, scarves, art books, toys, and cards.

1120 E. Kearsley, in Flint's Cultural Center. From I-475 from the south, get off at the Court St. exit, turn right, go to 2nd light, turn left onto Crapo. At the next light, turn right onto Kearsley. Park in lot south of museum. (313) 234-1695. Tues-Sat 10-5, Sun 1-5. Tuesday-evening hours; Oct-May: 7 p.m.-9 p.m. Free admission; donations appreciated.

OTHER ART STOPS IN FLINT . . . . . Right down a hall from the Flint Institute of Arts in the sprawling DeWaters Art Center is the **Mott Community College Fine Arts Gallery**. From October through December and February through April, it mounts one-person shows by some prominent Michigan artists. . . . . It's not exactly art, but the **Flint Public Library**, just west of the art museum, hosts crafts and collectibles exhibits and a huge range of free talks, readings, workshops, and performances for all ages. Call (810) 232-7111. The library on school nights is a lively place that sheds a more hopeful light on urban education than you get in the media. . . . . . The **Buckham Gallery** in downtown Flint is one of Michigan's premiere alternative galleries and performance spaces. It is run by artists to show "contemporary, cutting-edge art . . . with no censorship or interference." Though some art is for sale, it has not been chosen for its marketability. Its big space encourages large environmental installations and dance performances. (Performance art and poetry are also featured.) Artists and poets may have international reputations or local ones. *The gallery is at 134 W. Second a block off Saginaw in downtown Flint. Phone (810) 239-6334 for upcoming shows and events. Hours: Wed & Thurs 11:30-5, Fri 2:30-8, Saturday by appointment.*

MICHIGAN'S LARGEST PLANETARIUM . . . . . is the **Longway Planetarium**, with a 60-foot domed screen for an especially realistic depiction of the skies. It's the same size as the big planetaria in Chicago and New York. Entertaining multi-media shows change every three to five months and explore the skies, ancient mythology and the constellations, science fiction, and space travel. An excellent **gift counter** has astronomy- and space-related T-shirts, stickers, books, posters, and hard-to-find educational items. Gift and **exhibit areas** are open 9-5 weekdays. Individuals are welcome to tag along with any school group coming to see shows during the week. *1310 E. Kearsley in the Cultural Center. From I-475 from the south, take Longway Blvd. exit, go 2 blocks east to Walnut and turn right. (810) 760-1181.* **Regular astronomy shows** *($3/adults, $2/kids and seniors) are scheduled Saturday and Sunday. Spectacular* **laser light shows** *with rock music can be seen on Fri. and Sat. evenings. Call for current program info.*

GM Truck & Bus
Flint Assembly Plant Tour

An old auto plant shows a new, participative management philosophy at work.

For anyone interested in seeing a real, unscripted look at a typical auto assembly plant, this tour comes highly recommended. The guide, veteran autoworker Ed Campbell, encourages visitors to stop and ask questions at any point on the 1 1/2 mile, 1 1/2 hour walking tour. (The tour is also fully wheelchair accessible; call for details.) Workers enjoy talking about what they do. The tour is so unstructured that if you don't ask questions, you won't get much out of it.

This historic plant was built to make Chevrolets in 1947. The first Corvairs were made here; so were military vehicles used in World War II and in Desert Storm. After the tour, visitors are welcome to linger in the **display area** where interesting photos and text illuminate the plant's history. Books and plant souvenirs are for sale at the nearby **gift shop**. GM Truck & Bus has been through a lot of changes since the days when Ben Hamper, "the Rivethead," worked on its rivet line. From 1977 through 1987, the celebrated gonzo autoworker/author riveted frames of GM Suburbans and Blazers, which are now made in Janesville, Wisconsin. The rivet line is gone, replaced by the plant's only robots.

Products are always being shuffled among auto plants because it takes a year to install new manufacturing lines for redesigned products. Most new product lines are installed in available empty space, so that production of popular models can keep going without interruption on the old manufacturing line.

Since mid-1993 this plant has made GMC and Chevrolet "G" vans, moved in from plants that were closed in Lordstown, Ohio, and Scarborough, Ontario. This van, a favorite for RVs and delivery trucks, hasn't been redesigned since 1971. The current version stays in production here in Flint through 1995. Then the new version will be up and running in Wentzville, Missouri, outside St. Louis. Employees don't know what the plant's new product will be, nor do they know whether the plant will close down during the retooling process. Around August, 1994, the plant will also begin producing dual-wheel pick-up trucks of the kind used to pull horse trailers.

Fifty-six acres (3.3 million square feet) are under one roof here. The plant used to employ up to 8,500 workers making several products, compared to today's work force of 3,500. Seven rail lines ended here; now only one is in use. The current just-in-time manufacturing system means far fewer large deliveries by rail, but hourly deliveries at four or five truck docks.

An auto assembly plant like this assembles several thousand parts and subassemblies. On each 10 hour shift, 340 workers build 34 vehicles per hour. Each worker has 1 minute and 47 seconds to complete his or her operations, which range from bolting on separate parts (gas tanks, body parts, etc.) to applying seals and filling each brake cylinder with brake fluid. There's a surprising amount of variety within that 1 minute and 47 seconds. Several tasks may be performed. And not all vehicles are the same. They have been ordered to different specifications. Workers check the manifest for each vehicle and the directions on their computer screens.

The tour starts with the most dramatic assembly step, gate-keeping, where the side (gate) is married to the floor panel. (The old body-drop construction, where a completed auto body is dropped onto the chassis, has been abandoned.) Then the tour goes back to the ladder line, where the frame is riveted together, and across to the finishing line, where vehicles are road-tested on rollers.

Everyone here is consistently busy, unlike workers at Flint's heavily roboticized Buick City, who have time to read on the job. Maintenance workers with walkie talkies circulate on bicycles. Occasional supply baskets of fresh parts roll down wide aisles to workstations. The whole scene is like a calm, steady, complex ballet choreographed by engineers for a cast of hundreds. That's the industrial aesthetic that mesmerized artist Diego Rivera when he was researching and creating his vast *Detroit Industry* mural at the Detroit Institute of Arts.

Tour visitors are impressed with how clean the plant is, and how mature and serious the workforce is. No wonder – the minimum seniority is 15 years. Most of the $38,000-a-year workers are fortyish: many look like casually dressed college teachers. Plant morale is high, thanks to changes introduced after plant manager Jim Cirar took over in the late 1980s. "Every employee has had an opportunity to set their operation up," says tour guide Ed Campbell. "GM now recognizes that autoworkers have brains."

Cirar also introduced the factory tour, largely as a way of letting the public, and autoworkers' families in particular, see what actually happens in the plant. "Ten years ago GM wouldn't consider using an hourly employee like me to show people around," Campbell says. "I can say anything I want."

The plant is on Van Slyke at Bristol Rd., on the southwest side of Flint near Bishop Airport. From I-75/U.S. 23, take the Bristol Rd. exit 116A, go east, in 1 mile turn north onto Van Slyke. Enter Gate 6, park in visitor parking. From I-69, turn south onto I-75, then take first exit at Bristol Rd., follow above directions. (810) 236-4978. Free one-hour tours are available at 9 a.m., <u>but only by</u> <u>advance request</u>.

Crossroads Village
and Huckleberry Railroad

Charming 19th-century settings
and the grit, noise, and smoke that went with them

This museum village is an outstanding destination for
families and history-lovers, but with certain caveats.
Crossroads Village is the only place in Michigan where
you can see a big variety of 19th-century industries in action
every day: a pre-Civil War **gristmill**, a **sawmill**, and a **cider mill**,
along with more common things like a **print shop**, **blacksmith
shop**, and **toymaker's shop**. Outside the toy shop kids can roll
hoops and play with other old-fashioned toys. Some longtime
demonstrators are experts in their fields. Generally competent
costumed workers make simple tools, cornmeal, and cider,
which visitors can purchase.

A special attraction is a 35-minute ride on the **Huckleberry
Railroad**, a narrow-gauge steam engine similar to those built for
logging camps and mines, with a train of open-air cars. The train
ride's grit and jolts do much to de-romanticize 19th-century train
travel. Watching the old steam-powered machines in action
sheds a perspective on how hard people had to work under
noisy, dangerous conditions to make basic products.

Bees swarm around the apple pulp at the cider mill. Belts

**Historic Genesee County buildings threatened by demolition were
moved to Crossroads Village and restored. The three-story brick buildings (right) were moved when Fenton replaced much of its downtown
with a shopping center. The depot in Davison (left) dates from lumbering
days. The 1854 Buzzell House (center) is one of several authentically
furnished buildings.**

The jolts and gritty smoke of a ride on the Huckleberry Railroad at Crossroads Village dispel many notions about the romance of train travel in the good old days. The name goes back to when this stretch of track went past huckleberry marshes.

whir overhead in the grist mill. The smell of coal smoke and sawdust irritate your eyes. Most historic recreations are only for looking, and never confront all your senses with these realities.

Other things at Crossroads Village, however, can be so annoying that they can threaten to spoil the whole visit. Suburban-style landscaping near the train station is bright and cheery but completely inauthentic. The staged train robbery melodrama is corny, even for some children. If things like this bother you, plan to concentrate on the buildings and activities on the periphery first, and save the downtown and train trip for later. Bring a picnic for the flavor of an old-fashioned outing, or go to the **chicken broil** ($6.50-$9.50) weekends from noon to closing. That way you'll avoid the mediocre snack shop.

Crossroads Village highlights include:

◆ **Atlas Mill.** A pre-Civil War grist mill sits on a splendidly lazy "mill pond" that's actually part of Mott Lake. The whole building shakes when the watergate is opened up to move the grindstones and make cornmeal.

◆ **Carousel.** Music from an antique organ that imitates a whole band accompanies the chariots and 36 horses of this 1912 carousel. It was manufactured by Charles Parker, "America's Amusement King." Rides are 75¢. Tucked away beyond the chapel and sawmill, it's easy to miss.

◆ **Ferris wheel.** A 1910 Parker "Superior Wheel." 75¢ a ride.

◆ **Sawmill** with demonstration.

◆ **Cider mill** with demonstration.

◆ **Restored, 19th-century buildings** authentically furnished with antiques include a lawyer's office and home, a church, a school, and a recreated doctor's office. (These are quite well done, unlike the historic buildings which conceal souvenir and snack shops.)

◆ **Durant barn** with toymaking demonstrations.

◆ **Print shop** in the Manwaring Building downtown. The Cross-roads Chronicle is a good read in the lively, folksy style of small-town journalism.

For a **daily schedule** of hourly demonstrations and special performances in the Opera House, consult the map given to you on arrival. **Weekends** have more activities. Some summer weekends feature a **special show** of some sort at no extra charge. Annual events include an antique machine show; a special for rail fans; an old-fashioned Fourth of July (no fireworks); encampments of Civil War and Revolutionary War troops; a September Harvest Jubilee; and February ice harvesting. Call for annual events brochure.

October weekends feature the **Ghost Train** or trick-or-treating at haunted village buildings. **Christmas at Crossroads** combines a train ride, visit with Santa, decorated historic homes, an extensive holiday light display, music and entertainment, crafts, and more. $2.75-$6.50 depending on age and whether you take the train or not. *Call 800-648-PARK for events info.*

If you plan to spend a half day or more, Crossroads Village is an excellent entertainment value.

Bray Rd. north of Coldwater Rd. east of I-475. From I-475, take Saginaw St. (exit 13) and follow signs. (313) 763-7100. **Summer season:** *mid-May through Labor Day. Mon-Fri 10-5:30, weekends & holidays 11-6:30.* **Fall:** *open weekends in September. Summer rates: adults $7.50, children 4-12 $5.50, seniors over 60 $6.50.*

MORE FAMILY SUMMER ATTRACTIONS NEARBY. . . . . make Crossroads Village an ideal low-cost summer destination. (All these destinations, including the village itself, are operated by Genesee County Parks and Rec.) There's nearby scenic camping on the Flint River at the **Timber Wolf Campground.** . . . . **Penny Whistle Place** is a spiffy, creative play environment with 10 activities aimed at toddlers to pre-teens — easy, fun ones like the Ball Crawl, Cloud Bounce, and Music Machine (a sort of giant calliope with keys you step on), or challenging, scary ones like climbing high on a net, or swinging from platform to platform on a gliding cable. A real hit with kids. **Bluebell Beach**, using the same parking area, provides a convenient place to swim, but without much shade. *Penny Whistle Place and Bluebell Beach are on Bray Road just south of Crossroads Village. Open Memorial Day to Labor Day, daily 10-7, $3.00/person.* . . . . . **Stepping Stone Falls** has wooded picnic spots. It's especially nice near dusk, when the man-made falls at the outlet of Mott Lake are illuminated with **changing colored lights.** The water flows over rectilinear platforms with stepping stones across the shallow parts. *From Crossroads Village and Penny Whistle Place, take Bray south to Carpenter, then east, north on Branch. From I-475, take Carpenter exit 11, go east 1 1/2 miles to Branch, north briefly on Branch to falls. Open daily from Memorial Day to Labor Day, noon-11. Free.* . . . . . *For* **info on all these destinations**, *call 1-800-648-PARK.*

Frankenmuth

An insider's guide to the real Frankenmuth —
and the best things to do there

This former German farm town of 4,400 has become Michigan's top tourist draw. An estimated three million visitors a year flock to its Bavarian-themed street of gift shops, now two miles long. Two mammoth restaurants anchor the bustling pedestrian strip. Zehnder's and the Bavarian Inn rank among the 10 biggest-volume restaurants in the U.S., serving up to 10,000 guests on a weekend. The entire commercial area is dolled up in a relentless Alpine manner: chalet-type buildings with cutout wood balconies and wavy trim on the eaves. Geraniums are everywhere in warm weather; the streets and sidewalks are Disneyland-clean.

It's easy for purists and sophisticates to dismiss Frankenmuth as an overcommercialized tourist trap. But it would be a shame to miss some delightful experiences: a leading small American brewery, outstanding shops for high-quality German toys, hobby and crafts shops (for woodcarvers, quilters, and dollhouse fans in particular), and some good German food, especially sausages. The best shops are small and personal. Customers enjoy developing relationships with the staff over the years.

The secret to enjoying Frankenmuth lies in being selective. The town works on two levels at once. The applied surface is completely and innocently phony, a marketing ploy pure and simple. For instance, Franconia, the northern part of Bavaria where Frankenmuth's founders came from, isn't culturally Bavarian at all (it wound up in the large state of Bavaria after Napoleon reorganized his German conquests), and it certainly doesn't have chalets designed to stand up under the heavy snows of the Bavarian Alps. The picturesque Baroque onion towers you see in Frankenmuth were architecture of the Counter-reformation, favored by Catholics; Frankenmuth was and is devoutly Lutheran. Real Bavarians are Catholic, notably easygoing and fun-loving, while the Germans who settled Frankenmuth in 1845 were devout Lutherans, serious and extremely hard-working, just like their descendants today.

But on a deeper level, Frankenmuth is quite genuine, and

The scene outside of Bronner's, Frankenmuth's most famous attraction. Started in a garage, it has grown to become the world's largest Christmas store, as big as four football fields.

friendly, too. It's very German. You can meet locals under 50 who speak English with a slight German accent even though their ancestors have been in Michigan well over a hundred years — because they didn't learn English until school. And it's very much a community. Everybody knows everybody else, and quite a bit about their family history, too. Cleanliness and local pride are pervasive. Even the bank president can be seen picking up stray trash on his way to work; it's bad form in Frankenmuth to ignore litter. The unassuming Zehnder brothers, who own Zehnder's and the Bavarian Inn, live right in town in the main visitor area. They are hands-on managers, and everybody seems to like them.

Frankenmuth's fame began with chicken dinners at several hotels that took advantage of their convenient location between Detroit, Flint, and Saginaw. These all-you-can-eat dinners drew traveling salesmen at first. Then, in the 1920s and 1930s, when auto touring was a novelty, families came out for a drive on weekends. During the 1950s, the Christmas decorating shop begun as a sideline of Wally Bronner's sign shop quickly grew into a famous institution advertised on billboards as far away as Pennsylvania and Florida. Gift shops by the score followed suit, building on the reputation long established by Frankenmuth breweries and sausagemakers. Today, with Michigan's largest discount shopping mall at Birch Run, seven miles away on I-75, the Frankenmuth phenomenon seems to be gaining momentum, even benefitting motels in Flint and Saginaw. Canadian shoppers come and stay for a week. With a new 18-hole golf course, The Fortress, the big, resort-style Bavarian Inn Lodge, and an ever-increasing number of visitor attractions, the area is growing well beyond being just a day-trip destination.

Little in the commercial district still resembles Frankenmuth before it became a tourist mecca. It was a plain, sober Lutheran farm town, like many others in the Saginaw Valley and the Thumb today. It was founded in 1845 by a band of 14 young Lutherans from the town of Neudettelsau near Nuremberg. They followed their pastor's call to become missionaries in America. Their plan was to minister to the many Germans already in the Saginaw Valley and to the area's Chippewa Indians. Not surprisingly, the settlers' efforts to Germanize local Indians failed.

Once the forest was logged off, Frankenmuth's German settlers, like their countrymen throughout the Saginaw Valley, settled into farming, which they continue to pursue with characteristic industry and devotion. If you look, you'll see that Frankenmuth remains closely linked with the surrounding farm producers. Star of the West milling company is one of Michigan's largest flour mills. The brewery, the Zeilinger Wool Company, and the sausagemakers all use products from local farms.

The interstate highway program of the 1950s was what caused Alpine Bavarian architecture to be taken up with such enthusiasm in Frankenmuth. The new I-75 missed Frankenmuth by seven miles. Worried that their big chicken-dinner restaurants might be bypassed, the Zehnder family decided upon a dramatic theme to help business. They remodeled their Fischer Hotel in the picturesque Bavarian style. As the new Bavarian Inn, it offered waitresses dressed in dirndls, and German specialties like sauerbraten and schnitzel. (Zehnder's, the family's first restaurant styled after Mount Vernon, retains its Early American decor and emphasis on fried chicken.)

Tips for Enjoying Frankenmuth

Certainly Frankenmuth today is in the great American tradition of too much of everything. The best way to enjoy it is to stick to a short list of sights and not allow yourself to drift into too many, too-similar shops.

Park in the big lots behind the Bavarian Inn or Zehnder's. (Overflow parking is across the wooden bridge.) At the Bavarian-

One of hundreds of richly
evocative details from the
entrancing northern Italian
Christmas village scene at
Zeesenagel Italian Alpine
Village.

style **Visitor's Information Center** north of the Bavarian Inn,
pick up a helpful map and well-organized advertising **guide**.
Take a **snack and rest break** in the park at Main and Tuscola,
at the Main Street Tavern, at the Tiffany Biergarten with its original turn-of-the-century decor, or the Riverboat Cruise. Finish
with a trip to Bronner's to see the lights. Remarkably, **all visitor
attractions in Frankenmuth are handicapped-accessible**
except for the second floor of Schoolhaus Square.

To get to know the town, stay in a local bed and breakfast.
Here B&Bs are typically the homestay kind, where guests have a
spare bedroom in a plain, comfortable brick ranch house.

MUST-SEE SIGHTS

◆ **Zeesenagel Italian Alpine Village.** This wonderful miniature
re-creation of everyday Italian life, and the simple Christmas legend told with it, is alone worth a trip to Frankenmuth. Interior
designers David Zeese and Don Nagel were so inspired by the
18th-century *presepio* or nativity scene they saw in a Roman
church 25 years ago that they decided to create figures for a permanent diorama of their own. It was first displayed at Comerica

bank in downtown Detroit. Later they decided to move to Frankenmuth and install the tableau, which they enlarge every year, in a dramatic permanent setting that imitates a town nestled into the mossy slopes of a steep hillside.

Traditional Italian *presepio* were commissioned by wealthy nobles. They often included representations of entire villages or estates, with realistic individual portraits of loyal retainers or productive farmers they wished to honor.

Zeesenagel's 1/6 scale scenes have come to fill over ten scenes with 550 realistic figures. Their Alpine village includes all segments of society — dignitaries with their noses in the air, beggars (a reminder to others to share), and a fool, ignored by all, who in the end delivers the message about the true spirit of Christmas. On the guided tour, each of Zeesenagel's longtime staffers tells the story in his or her own way. Special lighting effects and music add to the drama and magic. You could enjoy seeing and hearing this several times.

Colorful scenes of Italian street life are everywhere — a customer sniffing a fishmonger's wares, a fruit vendor arguing with a customer, a puppet theater, a lacemaker. The figures Zeese and Nagel create with much feeling are highly individualized. Facial expressions and gestures are so vivid, you can almost hear the figures talk.

A delight in itself is the eclectic Zeesenagel **gift shop** of international crafts and Christmas figures, from dollar novelties to French *santons* (counterparts to presepio figures) and beautiful Orthodox icons. *780 Mill, at the bottom of the hill south of Zehnder's. (517) 652-2591. May 1-Jan. 6: open daily 10-6. Otherwise: weekdays 12-5, weekends 10-6. Tours ($2 adults, $1 12 and under) on the half-hour between 10:30 and 5:30 (last tour).* **Winter tours only on weekends.**

◆ **Bronner's CHRISTmas Wonderland.** For years it's been the world's largest Christmas store. In 1991 it became twice as big — 200,000 square feet in all, including warehousing. It's as big as four football fields.

Bronner's is a phenomenon. The year-round illuminated **outdoor display** is extensive. Indoors there are 260 decorated Christmas trees and 800 animated figures. In many categories — Advent calendars, nutcrackers, 6,000 kinds of glass ornaments, 500 styles of Nativity scenes from 75 countries — Bronner's selection is stupendous. Much is from Germany, Italy, and the former Czechoslovakia. But Bronner's goes to great lengths to emphasize the international aspect of Christmas. Bibles come in 33 languages, and ornaments and banners in 70. Children's books and Christmas stories in world languages are on hand. Chanukah and Kwanzaa are also included. Inclusiveness, in fact, is a Bronner's hallmark and a key secret of its success. Nativity scenes of all sizes come in versions with brown skin, and so do some Santas. Bronner's is not a discount store. But it imports in such quantity that some prices — for instance, on glass ornaments ordered direct from German factories — are very attractive.

Not everything relates to Christmas. Decorations for other seasons and holidays are on hand, along with gifts and souvenirs from around the world. Collectibles like Hummel and Precious Moments attract post-Christmas shoppers.

The place is so big *it's easy to become disoriented.* Take note of which entrance you used (there are four) so you can find your car. Refer to the store directory to find what you're especially interested in. And break up your visit by going to the new **refreshment area** (it's near the west exit by the nativities, books, and nutcrackers) or by seeing **"The World of Bronner's,"** an 18-minute, multi-projector slide show that tells the Bronner's story with folksy family photos. It's shown every hour or so, from 10 or 11 until 4 or 7 (more frequent showings over a longer time period from June through December). The store's own 500-figure **Hummel collection,** complete **Precious Moments collection** and other interesting displays are in the auditorium room.

A 1993 addition at the south end of the parking lot was the **Silent Night Memorial Chapel**. It's an exact replica of the chapel that replaced the church in Oberndorf, Austria, where the world's favorite Christmas hymn was written. Plaques with "Silent Night" in a hundred languages line a walkway to the chapel, which is open daily for visiting and meditating. *On S. Main at Weiss on the south end of Frankenmuth. Events line: 1-800-ALL-YEAR. Open 361 days. June thru Dec: Mon-Sat 9-9, Sun 12-7. Jan thru May: Mon-Sat 9-5:30, Fri until 9, Sun 12-5:30.*

CRAFTS AND MANUFACTURING DEMOS & TOURS

Fudgemaking, cheesemaking, woodcarving, wool-carding, milling, beermaking, taffypulling — a visit to Frankenmuth has become a great place to see a variety of free crafts demonstrations. Now the city has started a new Agriculture Tourism Park on Weiss Street behind Bronner's. Only agricultural production facilities can locate there, and only if they offer public tours of the entire manufacturing process.

The following demonstrations and tours stand out:

◆ **Frankenmuth Brewery.** Now that Heileman's has closed its big Frankenmuth brewery, this small brewery is the state's largest. It's the same size as local German breweries, with a capacity of 50,000 barrels a year. Its German brewmaster makes distinctive, flavorful German-style beers using state-of-the-art German equipment. Frankenmuth Pilsener, Frankenmuth Dark, and Frankenmuth Bock (a dark, rich, beer traditionally brewed only in springtime) have won awards; Old Detroit Amber Ale won the Chicago Beer Society's best of show two years in a row. They sell for under $7 a six-pack at stores like Meijer. Frankenmuth's motto: "Brewed in Michigan, where quality doesn't have to be imported." Freshness improves the taste of beer, so it's a real advantage to buy quality beers locally. Half-hour **tours**, given on the hour, include a video on brewing and a short tour of the tanks and bottling line, followed by two beers of your choice in the hospitality room. The **gift shop** sells many logo items, glassware, and beer-related gifts. *425 S. Main, just south of Tuscola. (517) 652-6183. Jan-Mar: Thurs-Mon noon-5. Mid-May thru Dec: Mon-Fri 11-5, Sat 11-6, Sun 12-5. $1.75/person. For tour info, call (810) 652-2088.*

◆ **St. Julian Winery.** This facility includes not only a free tasting room for the many noteworthy wines and sparkling fruit juices from the mid-range St. Julian Winery (Michigan's largest), but an actual small winery where solera cream sherry is aged from wine made in the main winery in Paw Paw. *127 S. Main, 1 block north of School Haus Square. (517) 652-3281. Tasting room open Mon-Sat 10-6, Sunday 12-6, closes at 5 daily Jan thru April. Free winery tours weekends at 1 and 3.*

◆ **Frankenmuth Woodcarving Studio.** You can watch noted German sculptor Georg Keilhofer execute commissions for churches and individuals. Instruction in wood-carving is offered in once-a-week nine-week courses and intensive one- and two-week summer seminars. Most of Keilhofer's work is for commissions, but his shop sells many wood carvings from Europe, both religious and secular. He carries a large selection of top-quality woodcarving tools and supplies.

In the little park next door, a delightful gazebo commemorates the Brothers Grimm with fairy tale scenes carved on oak panels. *976 S. Main, south of the river but north of Jefferson. (517) 652-2975.Mon-Sat 9-5.*

◆ **Zeilinger Wool Company.** For over 80 years Zeilinger's has processed raw wool, straight off the sheep, and used it as batting in custom comforters. A **self-guided tour** shows visitors all steps of the process, from washing and air-drying wool to carding it and making hand-stitched quilts and comforters. On weekends, however, manufacturing employees are off. Quilting supplies and fabrics are here, too. *1130 Weiss (north of Bronner's). (517) 652-2920. Mon-Sat 9-5:30, Sun 12-5.*

◆ **Frankenmuth's Historic Woolen Mill.** Today this old mill is more of an upscale sweater store, though you can see wool-filled comforters being made in a large workroom, and see how wool is processed — right on Frankenmuth's main pedestrian drag. *570 S. Main between Cass and Tuscola. (517) 652-8121. Open daily. June thru Labor Day: 9-9. Otherwise: 9-5.*

FRANKENMUTH HISTORY

◆ **Frankenmuth Historical Museum.** At this superior local-history museum, light is shed on everything from chicken dinners to Frankenmuth's origins near Nuremberg. Strong visuals and lots of letters convey the immigration experience, the life left behind in Franconia, and the unusually strong ethnic community they created here. One gallery is for special exhibits that change yearly. *613 S. Main. (517) 652-9701. June-Dec: Mon-Sat 10:30-5, Sun 12:30-5. Jan-May: Mon-Fri 12-5, Sat 10:30-5, Sun 11-5. April: Wed-Sun. Admission by donation.*

◆ **St. Lorenz Church and Log Cabin Church.** This much-enlarged 1880 brick Gothic-style church houses the largest congregation east of the Mississippi — 4,300 strong — in the conservative Missouri Synod of the Lutheran Church. You can stop in any weekday for a **self-guided tour** of the sanctuary, where splendid contemporary stained-glass windows show scenes of Lutheran history, from St. Paul to Luther to Frankenmuth's missionary ministers on horseback. If you call in advance, volunteer Sharon Bickell will give you a most interesting look back at the settlement's early days. You'll visit a **reconstruction of the original log church** and parsonage, complete with packing-case pulpit. St. Lorenz still holds a **German-language service** with hymns each Sunday at 9:15 and on Wednesdays in Lent and Advent at 9:30. *On Tuscola at Mayer, about a mile west of downtown. Park in rear and go in back door. Call (517) 652-6141 for tour.*

PLACES TO TAKE A REST

◆ **Willkommen Park.** A pleasant, shady spot on downtown Frankenmuth's main intersection at Main and Tuscola. Benches, drinking fountain, but no restrooms. Carryout food from Willi's, Main Street Tavern, or Satow's.

◆ The historic **Tiffany Biergarten** saloon at 656 S. Main, the unpretentious **Main Street Tavern** at 310 S. Main up the hill, or the **Riverview Cafe,** 445 S. Main are nice places to sit and rest and have refreshments. The cafe has shady decks going down to the Cass River.

◆ **Frankenmuth Riverboat Tour.** Festive Dixieland music and informative commentary by a Frankenmuth native make this 45-minute cruise up the pretty Cass River especially enjoyable. The boat is a diesel-powered, two-deck paddlewheeler. A fine way to rest your feet while learning more about Frankenmuth. *Leaves from the Riverview Cafe, 445 S. Main. (517) 652-8844. Runs May thru Oct. Leaves at 12:30, 3:30, 4:30, 7 (6 in May, Sept & Oct). $5/adult, $2.50 12 & under. Tip: buy tickets early. $10 cocktail cruise July & August includes minstrel, hors d'oeuvres.*

◆ **Fischer Platz.** This pretty, popular Bavarian-style "town square" with many benches was created as part of the Bavarian theme campaign circa 1960. The Pied Piper tale is enacted on the Glockenspiel several times a day (check sign in front) but it's a disappointment compared to the wonderful antique German moving clocks it was modeled on. Restrooms, visitor information kiosks. *Just north of the Bavarian Inn, next to the Visitors' Center.*

◆ **Picnic facilities in public parks.** Picnic tables and barbeque grills are in tip-top shape at both convenient city parks. **Heritage Park** at the north end of Weiss has long, scenic frontage along the Cass River, and more playground equipment. **Memorial Park** on East Tuscola, 1/4 mile east of downtown, is a hilly area with a creek running through it. (Tobogganing here is the best around.) Amenities include a **swimming pool** open to all, **rose gardens**, and an **exercise trail.** Get good bratwurst and franks, rolls, pota-to salad, and cole slaw at Willi's Sausage Haus (page 374

OLD FRANKENMUTH

Beneath the thick icing of tourism, there's still a very German small town in downtown Frankenmuth. Here's where to find it.

◆ **Satow's Drug Store.** The lunch counter is a popular local hangout where you can get an earful of German, and of the distinctive Frankenmuth dialect of English, in which "just" may be "chust" and nearly every sentence sounds like a question. The soups are homemade, and the prices can't be beat; lunch specials are $3 or so. *308 S. Main, just north of Tuscola. Mon-Fri 8-9, Sat until 7, Sun until 4.*

◆ **Main Street Tavern.** An utterly plain German-American gasthaus where the food's as important as the beer. Owner Keith Boesnecker, who was Zehnder's baker for years, spotlights local products whenever possible. And he makes all the bread and buns on the premises. That all makes for quality bar food. The $2.10 quarter-pound cheeseburger is made from local beef and cheese. Willi's next door supplies the excellent bratwurst ($2.50) and the beef stix and Italian sausage used on the Willi Pizza. (Square pizzas are a house specialty.) Frankenmuth Pilsner and Dark are $1.25 on draft, while Carling's (still a local favorite even if no longer locally made) is 75¢, or 50¢ on darts night (Wednesday). *310 S. Main, just north of Tuscola. (517) 652-2222. Mon-Sat 9 a.m.-2 a.m., Sun noon-2 a.m.*

◆ **Willi's Sausage Haus.** As soon as you walk in the door, the smell and the plain, super-clean appearance tell you how German Willi's is. The main decoration consists of photos of Willi playing his accordion. A master sausagemaker, he turns out sausages, hams, and bacon — 95 items in all — here in his shop and smokehouse, and in his new wholesale plant in Vassar. Locals shop here for their traditional favorites from bratwurst and weisswurst to head cheese and a famous beef jerky made from carefully trimmed top round. Non-traditional innovations include many turkey products, made without fatty skin,

One of many worthwhile demonstrations in Frankenmuth is at master woodcarver Georg Keilhofer's shop on Main Street.

such as turkey pepper loaf and smoked turkey bratwurst. Prices compare favorably with suburban delis.

A sausage of your choice can be grilled to eat at the Schnellimbiss stand-up counter or in the park across the street. A line of imported German specialties is on hand: chocolates, mustards, cookies (good holiday gifts) and Rudolph's excellent rye bread from Toronto. Small-group tours may be arranged. *316 S. Main, just north of Tuscola. (517) 652-9041. Mon-Sat 8-6, Sun 11-5.*

◆ **Star of the West Milling Company.** Michigan's wheat fields once made it a breadbasket of America, but Michigan wheat has been relegated to niche markets since Minneapolis became America's milling center at the turn of the century. That niche is strong, because Michigan soft winter wheat has the lowest protein of any east of the Rockies. Low protein means low viscosity, and a flour that's good for cookies and pie crust. The Star of the West is one of only six commercial mills left in Michigan, all enormous. Its big silos are right downtown. Customers include commercial bakers and Battle Creek's cereal makers, who buy bran. At its interesting store across the street, 25-pound sacks of Nightingale brand pastry-type flour — white, graham, wheat germ, and bran — are sold for under $5/bag. This is also a sporty work clothes shop, and a garden shop with bird feeders, seed, and the like and a farm-supply store where you can get (among other things) numbers to put on cows' ears. *121 E. Tuscola. (517) 652-9971. Mon-Fri 7 5.*

GIFT AND SPECIALTY SHOPS

Competition has made for a very broad market. Many shops focus on high-ticket collectible lines, character dolls, wood carvings, German beer steins and cuckoo clocks. There's some good stuff here, if you focus on finding what really interests you. Here are some highlights:

◆ **Rau's Country Store.** A rambling, appealing mix of many gift categories and price levels. Hard candies, tin boxes, reproduction Victorian lamps and glassware carry out the old-fashioned country store theme up front, but there's lots more further back and downstairs, including cassettes of polkas and German folk songs, a nice selection of Chinese baskets, die-cast toys, oak shelves, miniature cottages, and, in the basement, loads of inexpensive scrapbook cutouts. **Doll house miniatures**, displayed in well over a hundred room settings, are fabulous here and across the street at Pinocchio's. *656 S. Main. (517) 652-8388. Mon-Fri*

10-8, Sat 9-10, Sun 12-7. Longer summer hours.

◆ **Kite Kraft.** It's mostly kites — over 100 kinds, plus windsocks and other flying toys — but it's also activity-oriented toys, from Brio trains to funny wind-ups and cheap, entertaining novelties like the $1.25 balloonocopter (helicopter blades powered by balloons) and a $2 blugle (a bright plastic tube that plays different notes when you swing it). Toys are demonstrated all the time. The owner, a longtime elementary teacher, follows up customers' suggestions. *In School Haus Square, 245 S. Main north of Tuscola at the north end of the visitor area. June-Christmas: Mon-Thurs 10-6, Fri & Sat 10-8, Sun 11-6. Otherwise: closes weekdays at 6, Sun at 5.*

COLLECTORS' MUSEUMS

Frankenmuth's huge flow of customer traffic makes possible some wonderful displays of serious collectors' stuff. Highlights include:

◆ **Rau's Country Store.** In a basement gallery is a really charming collection of 19th-century **German souvenir glassware** — mementoes of stays at spas and resorts. Some glasses are painted, most are cut in two-layered cranberry glass. (See page 375). *Free.*

◆ **Memory Lane Arcade.** Kiss-O-Meter, The Egyptian Mummy Answers Your Question — here are favorite coin-operated games and music from amusement parks and saloons going back 90 years. They're playable, though you don't always get enough time for your quarter. Still, it's magical to go back in time and play all these evocative devices: Play Golf, the Mystic Swami, a 1933 Personality Indicator, player pianos, pinball games. The big attraction is Laughing Sal's Funhouse: a 1930-vintage automated woman who stood in front of funhouses and drew people inside with her laugh. She is joined on a stage by two automated clowns who laugh or hum along with her. *626 S. Main. (517) 652-8881. Open daily 12-9 in summer, until dark in fall, after Xmas weekends only, weather permitting. Free admission.*

◆ **Main Street Tavern.** (See page 374). Collection of **breweriana** about Frankenmuth beers, plus a history of brewing in Frankenmuth written by the owner.

◆ **Michigan's Own Military Museum.** Highly regarded new exhibits show off state veterans' memorabilia. Permanent exhibits display 15 Medals of Honor (the largest collection anywhere) and uniforms of all ten Michigan astronauts. Exhibits in the World Wars Room are changed every three to six months.

1250 Weiss (the road that parallels Main Street on the other side of Bronner's). (517) 652-8005. 10-5 Mon-Sat 11-5 Sun. $2.50 adults, $2 seniors, $1 Children 6-18. Under 6 free.

DISCOUNT SHOPPING AT BIRCH RUN . . . . . Before 1986 it was an obscure village at the I-75 Frankenmuth exit. Now Birch Run is Michigan's discount shopping capital. With 150 stores, its **Manufacturers Market Place** (517-624-4868; 1-800-866-5900) is bigger than its sister malls at Holland, Monroe, and Traverse City. Now it has been joined by **Village Shops at Birch Run**, with over 30 designer outlets.

Manufacturers Market Place features mostly brand-name outlets, including Gitano, Oshkosh, Bugle Boy, Van Heusen, Corning, Eddie Bauer, Esprit, Oshkosh, Guess?, Woolrich, and American Tourister. It has a multi-outlet food court. Village Shops at Birch Run's roster of designer outlets includes Liz Claiborne, Anne Klein, Evan-Picone, Capezio, J. Crew, Adolfo II, and Villeroy & Boch. It has a food vendor outside in good weather and umbrellaed tables on a terrace. Its indoor "relaxation room" offers TVs with sports events (to placate male companions of relentless shoppers), vending machines, tables, even couches for naps.

Both malls deal mostly in manufacturers' overruns not bought by non-discount retailers. Fashions typically show up six to eight weeks later than in department stores, though some are last year's models. Prices range from 20% to 70% off, which often can be beat by special sales at department stores, but the selection of discounted goods in one place is so far unparalleled in Michigan. *At I-75 exit 136; go west on Birch Run Rd. Village Shops are just west of Manufacturers Market Place. Both malls have similar hours. Mon-Sat 10-9, Sun 11-6.*

Dow Chemical Tour
and Visitor Center;
H.H. Dow Historical Museum

*Top-notch industrial history at a primitive brine well
and a sprawling modern chemical complex*

Good museums of industrial history are a new and unusual phenomenon. Industrial tours of any kind have become increasingly rare because of widespread liability and industrial espionage concerns. Visitors to Midland can be treated to not one but *two* exceptionally interesting looks at Dow Chemical, the world's sixth-biggest chemical firm. Dow was founded here in 1897, and out-of-the-way Midland (population 38,000) remains its headquarters today.

The **H. H. Dow Museum** tells the dramatic story of Dow's origins at a replica of the simple old grist mill and brine well where founder Herbert Dow started out in 1890. **Dow's plant tour** shows visitors parts of its Michigan Division, one of the world's largest and most diversified chemical complexes. At the 19,000-acre complex along the Tittabawassee River just east of downtown Midland, 5,400 people work, including Dow's world-wide research and development staff. Finally, there's the **Dow Visitor Center,** open weekdays, which shows interested visitors an overview of Dow consumer products and an interesting illustrated summary of its history.

These are probably the most intelligent exhibits of corporate industrial history in Michigan. They're made even more interesting by exploring the character and motivation of its founder, a remarkably persistent, independent, and creative man. Herbert Dow was more than a good scientist and collaborator with others. As a hard-headed businessman, he was able to break the lock German cartels had on the American market for chemicals, thus paving the way for a strong American chemical industry.

Still, you won't get the *whole* Dow story at the museum or visitor center. There's little official mention of "Crazy Dow." That's what skeptical Midlanders called 24-year-old Herbert Dow shortly after he arrived in town with a suitcase, a few hundred dollars, and an idea for extracting the valuable chemical bromine from the bromine-rich brine deposits under Midland. His studies at the Case School of Applied Science in Cleveland had convinced him that he could use electricity to extract commercial quantities of bromine from such salt deposits. Its use in photo processing and pharmaceuticals had made bromine valuable.

Nor are visitors reminded of the numerous campus protests against Dow on American college campuses in the 1960s and 1970s for Dow's role in making napalm used by the U.S. military against Vietnamese troops and villagers. There's no mention of a much-publicized chemical spill in nearby Freeland. (People left their homes for a week, according to rigorous emergency guidelines, but no one was hurt.) Or of the controversial plans for the ill-fated Midland nuclear power plant. Or of how Greenpeace environmental activists in canoes plugged the plant's outlets into the Tittabawassee River to dramatize the environmental impact of Dow discharges. Or how irate Dow administrators had activists spied on for years.

You *do* hear a lot on the tour about good walleye fishing in the Tittabawassee River and about Dow's ingenious uses for turning waste into new products, its advanced methods of waste treatment, and its generally outstanding safety and occupational health record.

Dow Chemical Tours. Dow's Midland operation, like many chemical facilities, is an amazing-looking labyrinth of buildings, industrial equipment, and pipes. Just driving by is impressive. Forty independent plants, each with its own production facility, quality control analysis lab, and warehouse, are joined by a network of insulated overhead pipes that carry steam, water, and raw materials to each plant. This open-air plant design differs from conventional plants enclosed in huge buildings. It allows for good ventilation, easy maintenance access, and great flexibility. Buildings and equipment are constantly being changed.

Visitors who make tour reservations are driven through this interesting complex in a van or bus for an up-close (if selective) view of operations. Your guide is an amiable, well-informed veteran foreman. He displays the upbeat enthusiasm and faith in better living through chemistry that mark Dow's corporate culture.

Tour stops include the Saran wrap plant and a state-of-the-art analytical lab. If everything is presented with an ideal, picture-perfect glow, down to happy-looking workers viewed on break in a snack room with a giant, deer-in-forest photo mural — well, that's more or less the way working at Dow really is, to

hear most locals talk about it. Layoffs are unheard of. Dow workers are well paid. Its big research staff gives Midland the educational and income demographics and international population of
a university town. Midland residents enjoy fabulous sports and
cultural facilities. And Midland is one of a dwindling number of
places where good jobs are still available to high school graduates. No other company town we've seen in Michigan — not Ann
Arbor or Battle Creek, Dearborn or Flint — thinks anywhere near
as highly of its reigning presence. *Reservations required for free
public tours, held Mon 9:30-11:30. (517) 636-8658. Call early;
availability limited, especially for spring and summer tours.*

DOW VISITORS CENTER. Many of the 500 products made in
Midland are displayed here — including Saran Wrap (introduced
in 1953), Ziploc bags (1972), Spray 'n' Wash (1970), Cepacol
mouthwash, Dursban insecticide, and Styrofoam (along with lots
of free ideas for holiday crafts using it). Less famous products
include plastics, agricultural products, and specialties like Latex
and Methocel. To move away from producing mainly bulk chemicals with lower profit margins and big price swings, Dow is
increasingly stressing consumer products, both through new
research and through acquiring makers of personal care products and pharmaceuticals.

An engineering model of the Midland aspirin plant, which
makes a third of the aspirin used in the U.S., will appeal mainly
to the technical-minded, as will many free educational publications. There's a touch-screen program on plastics recycling. The
interesting panels of photographs and text on company history
are of considerable general interest. *500 E. Lyon Rd. at Bayliss,
in the Dow complex just east of downtown Midland. From I-75,
take U.S. 10 into town. After you've passed Washington Street
and much of the Dow complex, look for Bayliss and turn left.
Center is on the next block. (517) 636-8658. Open Mon-Fri 8-4:30.*

H. H. DOW HISTORICAL MUSEUM. The life and accomplishments of Herbert Dow are engagingly presented in replicas of the
rough wood buildings where he launched Dow Chemical. These
include a primitive grist mill, brine well and derrick with hand-
made wooden pumping machinery, and pegged wood brine storage tank. The museum, owned and operated by the Midland
Historical Society, uses some slick presentational techniques —
voiceovers of actors who play family members and associates, a
worthwhile 12-minute film on Midland shown in a nifty little
1890s theater, and a spectral image of Dow himself, fancifully

revisiting Midland 60 years after his death and talking about an exhibit of products he developed. (Family members say it sounds like Dow, informal and down-to-earth.)

This isn't the pompous puffery you might expect, and it's not only for chemists and engineers, though they will be especially interested in the big display on the great Corliss steam engine exhibited at the 1876 Centennial Exhibition in Philadelphia (it fascinated the young Dow and a generation of nascent American inventors and technobuffs) and the reconstructed 1890 lab/manufacturing plant showing the bromine-extracting process on which Dow Chemical was built. There is a recreation of the workshop where, in his youth, Dow happily spent hours working on the inventions and projects of his mentor father, who was a master mechanic for a Cleveland shovel works. In a ghostly life-size tableau, early Dow scientists, recruited by Herbert Dow from his old alma mater, Case, sit around in shirtsleeves late at night brainstorming to solve a problem. *From downtown Midland, take Main Street west about 1 1/4 miles to Cook Road, turn left, and you're there. (517) 832-5319. Wed-Sat 10-4, Sun 1-5. Adults $2, $1 children, $5 family.*

🌲🌳🌲

CANOEING ON MIDLAND'S THREE RIVERS . . . . . is made easy with the **City of Midland canoe livery** (517-832-8438). It's at the foot of Ashman, which crosses Main in the very center of downtown Midland. You can paddle up the Chippewa to the Chippewa Nature Center, and from there up the Pine and back. They flow into the Tittabawassee, which is lined by city parks and golf courses northwest of downtown and by Dow Chemical to the southeast. But don't think you can get a duck's-eye view of the giant chemical complex. Canoeists will be met by Dow security who will transport them and their canoe around the plant and deposit them by the Mapleton boat launch to the east.

TUBING DOWN THE RIVER . . . . . is a popular recreation in these parts. Mount Pleasant, 30 miles west of Midland, has so little industry and such a modern sewage treatment plant that Central Michigan students like to float on inner tubes all the way through town. Tube and canoe rentals and transportation are available through **Chippewa Valley Canoe Livery and Campground** 13 miles west of Midland. (800) 686-2447.

Dow Gardens

A place of year-round beauty and harmony,
it fosters exploring and playful creativity
and shows what's possible in your own yard.

As soon as you enter the Dow Gardens, you're aware of how unusual they are. Signs and brochures invite you to explore the gardens by walking anywhere, including the grass. (But don't climb rocks and waterfalls.) One of the first things you see is not flower beds or a striking vista but a stand of tall pines with remarkable chunky bark — a clear hint that texture, form, and contrasts are as important here as more obvious displays of colorful blooms. Some staffers even like the gardens best of all after a fresh snow without any flowers whatsoever.

The design of the place beckons and draws you in, to explore an unfolding array of environments. Past the pine grove, the trail squeezes between massive boulders crossed by a splashing waterfall, then opens out to the annual flower beds and rose garden on your left. To your right is a maze formed by viburnums. Beyond that, an Oriental-looking red bridge draws your eye up a meandering creek.

In the rarefied ranks of great American gardens, the Dow Gardens are *most* unusual — fresh and creative. They owe little to the European gardens imitated by typical American industrialists of great wealth. Coached in imitative connoisseurship by art dealers, architects, and their own aspiring wives, industrialists typically built Italian palazzi or Norman French castles and installed formal gardens to go with them. The Dow family were never followers or imitators. Dow Chemical founder Herbert Dow and his architect son, the late Alden Dow, were broadly creative people. They shaped these gardens for over 70 years.

Visitors often call the Dow Gardens Japanese or Oriental because of the striking red bridge, the emphasis on textures and rocks, and the design principle of inviting you to explore without showing an overview of the entire place. Director Doug Chapman bristles at the idea that these gardens are Japanese. He wastes no time in explaining that these are *American* gardens and nothing else. Japanese gardens are small and very, very controlled miniature environments of highly selected plant materials, he

The beautiful studio-home of the late architect Alden Dow, son of the
Dow Chemical founder, overlooks the gardens which he and his father
painstakingly developed over 70 years.

explains. They are fussily maintained, pruned, and raked down
to the last detail.

The Dow Gardens are big — 100 acres, quite enormous when
compared with gardens that seem large but are really just half a
dozen acres. Yet the staff of gardeners here is quite small.
Maintenance is relaxed. Occasional weeds are allowed to invade
the lawn. Sprays and pruning are minimized. This is no minimal,
sparse, symbolic landscape like a Japanese garden. The famous
red bridge here is red because red is the natural complement of
green, not because it's supposed to look Oriental.

A broad range of plants, not just choice specimens, are
allowed to grow here, but only if they do well in Midland's cold
winters and sandy soils, and only if they help create a sense of
balanced harmony. "There is no such thing as a bad plant, just a
bad place" is an operating principle, illustrated by the presence
of a big silver maple, commonly considered a weed tree for its
messy habits.

The gardens are really Herbert Dow's extended back yard.
Creative and questioning by nature, he had always been interested in shaping his surroundings. When he arrived in Midland (see
page 377), a landscape of stumps surrounded the declining lum-

bering town. Beginning in 1899, he landscaped his house here to show what fellow townspeople could do with their own yards. He kept the grounds open to the public. Dow's forest green house, facing West Main, can be seen from the far side of the gardens.

An enthusiastic traveler, Herbert Dow became friends with a noted designer of Tokyo parks, who visited Midland frequently and shared landscaping ideas with Dow and other Midlanders. Lack of money early in his life prevented Dow from studying architecture. It was no surprise when his youngest son, Alden, forsook engineering and a Dow Chemical career for architecture.

Alden Dow became one of Frank Lloyd Wright's original Taliesin fellows. In his own long (1934-1973) architectural career, based in Midland, he remained absorbed in harmoniously joining architecture and nature — a clear debt to Wright, and to the Japanese. "Gardens never end, and buildings never begin," he liked to say. He found many ways to bring the outdoors inside and extend architecture out, via retaining walls, paving, bridges, and other garden structures.

No better example exists than these gardens and **Alden Dow's own studio-home**, one of the most celebrated of all 20th-century houses. You glimpse it from the gardens beyond the red bridge, a long, low house with extending copper-green eaves. It seems to float on the pond that surrounds most of the house.

Renewing the Dow Gardens, which had fallen into disrepair, and extending them became Alden Dow's retirement project in the 1970s. Working with director Doug Chapman, a former Michigan State University extension horticulturist, he refined favorite design ideas, added over a thousand different trees and shrubs, and built new greenhouses, a maintenance building, and a visitors' center with classrooms. The reorganized gardens extended Herbert Dow's original philosophy of helping and inspiring the backyard gardener.

In the gardens Alden Dow developed smaller fantasy environments that bring out the playful child in visitors. (The Dow family — Herbert, Alden, and others — considered creative play an important part of adult life.) Stepping stones cross the creek. A **"jungle walk"** through a hilly thicket leads to a hidden pool and wildflower garden. There's an irregular **maze** through viburnums, and a **land sculpture** of rounded miniature mountains.

Visit the gardens in the gentle, playful spirit of Alden Dow. Follow your instincts and explore. Don't stay on the main path. Don't let the map guide you. And don't pay much attention to the plant labels. Instead, follow the sound of plashing water or the

Even before spring leaf-out, the Dow Gardens offer striking vistas with
pine groves, waterfalls, and boulders. The first gardener was Japanese.
The gardens' Asian influence is apparent, but the scale and relaxed
informality is American.

scent of wet pine needles. If a distant object beckons, go there.

If you only have a little time, visit the interesting **sensory
trail** (designed with blind visitors in mind) by the main entrance
and the nearby **boulders and waterfall**. If you have longer, you
can check out the special areas like the **herb garden**, or **All-
America display garden** of annual flowers, or the **rose garden**
or **perennial garden**. The sizable, attractive **gift shop** emphasizes books on horticulture, garden planning, and nature, with
some plant-related gift items and cards.

*The Gardens are next to the Midland Center for the Arts on
Eastman Rd. (Bus. Rte. 10) at West St. Andrew's, just northwest
of downtown Midland. (517) 631-2677. Open 7 days a week at 10
a.m., closes at sunset. Closed Thanksgiving, Christmas Eve and
Day, New Year's Eve and Day. $2 daily admission fee. Children 5
and under free. Ask about the **folk festival** and other events held
in the Gardens.*

MORE OF ALDEN DOW'S BEST WORKS . . . . . including Dow's studio, are
part of an interesting, worthwhile **Midland Architectural Tour** on cassette
tape, meant for your car's tape deck. It may be rented for $5 at the Midland
Center for the Arts, right next to the Dow Gardens. (The center is open from
10 a.m. until performances and classes are over at night). The homes Dow

designed in the 1930s and 1940s are a must for anyone interested in his teacher, Frank Lloyd Wright. The narrated tour takes you through Midland's most elite neighborhoods and surveys noteworthy historic architecture from the 19th century to a 1957 space-age dome, insulated with Dow Chemical's Styrofoam. The tour takes at least an hour and a half — with options, two hours or more. It's like having a well-informed local resident show you around. An **annual tour of Dow designs** always includes a visit inside his studio-house — a fascinating place, full of playful surprises including a toy train collection and the so-called "Submarine Conference Room." (The pond outside comes up to its windows.) Call 1-800-678-1961 for information.

A LAVISH COMMUNITY CENTER FOR THE ARTS . . . . . is one of Alden Dow's ugliest buildings, the **Midland Center for the Arts,** next to the Dow Gardens. The interior space is much nicer, something like Wright's Guggenheim Museum. It includes a splendid performance space, changing **art and history exhibits** (on the 4th floor), and an attractive **gift shop** with handmade and ethnic gifts and jewelry. The unusual **Hall of Ideas** (levels 1-3) closes through September of 1994 for a total renovation of the exhibits, which start with geological eras in Michigan and a Foucault pendulum and end with *you* and your possibilities for contributing to the future. It's a typically dynamic, Dow approach that joins art and history, business and science in an idiosyncratic synthesis. The hands-on exhibits are unusual and stimulating if you're fresh. (This is serious stuff with a lot of reading, big on science and technology, and overwhelming if you're tired.) *On Eastman Rd. (Bus. Rte. 10) at St. Andrew's, just northwest of downtown Midland. Call (517) 631-5930 for performance and exhibit information. Hall of Ideas open 10-6 weekdays, 1-5 weekends. No fee; donation appreciated.*

PICNICKING . . . . . is encouraged in the **park by the Tridge**, architect Alden Dow's unique three-legged arched footbridge at the confluence of the Chippewa and Tittawabasse rivers in downtown Midland. There are picnic tables and grills, and you can walk across the Tittabawasse to a playground in Chippewassee Park. Take Ashman from Business Route 10 west into the heart of downtown all the way down to the river. The Tridge is right there, along with a lively **farmers' market**, open Wednesdays and Saturdays from spring through fall.

A BLEND OF MUSIC, ART AND SCIENCE THAT'S QUINTESSENTIALLY MIDLAND . . . . . is the 17-day **Matrix: Midland Festival** held each June in the Midland Center for the Arts. As science columnist Nancy Ross-Flanigan wrote in the *Detroit Free Press*, "Where else would the whimsical Chenille Sisters share the spotlight with a lecture on the future of nuclear power?" For info on the mix of dance, jazz, film, classical music, science, and more, call (517) 631-8250 weekdays and Saturdays.

Chippewa Nature Center

*Michigan's best all-around nature center
has a good natural history museum, interpreted trails,
and an authentic 1870s log homestead.*

Midland's Chippewa Nature Center clearly stands out from the rest of Michigan's many fine nature centers. First, it has a fabulous classroom and museum building. A comfortable lounge, shaped like a riverboat pilot house, seems suspended over the Pine River. Long views look upstream and down to the nearby confluence of the Pine and Chippewa. Using the bird-watchers' telescope provided, you can look out and see birds patrolling the river, hoping to catch a fish. The Center's architect, Midland's creative Alden Dow (see pages 383-385), learned from his teacher, Frank Lloyd Wright, how to design buildings that, when you're inside, seem to melt into the living world around them.

Displays, trails, and programs are all intelligently planned and user-friendly, with good signage to help you understand what you're looking at. Finally, Chippewa offers an unusually rich mix of things to do and see, including an authentic log homestead and displays of items as old as 7,000 years from on-site archaeological digs. Other nature centers have more interesting sites than this flat riverside bottomland of second-growth woods. But Chippewa provides the best all-around introduction to the natural history of its area, outdoors and in, and man's use of the environment. (The Gillette Sand Dunes Interpretive Center at Hoffmaster State Park near Muskegon is more dramatically situated, comparable in many ways, but more tightly focused.)

Highlights include:

◆ **Outstanding indoor wildlife observation areas** that look out onto feeders, shrubs, and flowers busy with birds and chipmunks. Bright annuals attract hummingbirds to the river window. The museum's wildlife window is busy year-round. Even the most infirm visitors could sit here and enjoy nature for hours.

◆ **A museum** of colorful, well-done **dioramas** show **Michigan geology** and scenes from **Saginaw Valley Indian cultures** of different eras. The geology exhibits nicely illustrate the notion that,

Perched in part over the Pine River, the nature center's fine museum illuminates Michigan geology and the everyday lives of Indian peoples who settled the Saginaw Valley.

seen in geological cross-section, Michigan is like a set of nesting bowls formed during different eras, mostly overlaid by a heavy layer of glacial till. Shown with each diorama are rocks or artifacts that go with that geological age. Unusually vivid displays on Indian cultures show scenes from everyday life in the Saginaw Valley at different periods, together with objects excavated from the nature center's **archaeological sites** and the archaeological methods used to uncover and identify them. The Saginaw River system, abundant with game and fish, has been one of Michigan's most important centers of Indian life.

The museum displays are intelligent and clear but dense and best absorbed a little at a time. Easier to enjoy are Indian naturalist **Smokey Joe Jackson's wonderful painted carvings** of birds and animals, and a scene with a giant beaver. Just after the last ice age, Michigan was home to beavers 3 1/2 feet tall.

◆ **"The Naturalist's Challenge,"** a nifty exercise in slowing down and making observations of natural objects. It starts with an indoor hands-on display, followed up with outdoor observations made with the help of a borrowed bird whistle, magnifying glass, and bug box. Parents are well advised to try this out first to get the hang of it.

◆ The expanded **River's Edge Gift Shop** is strong on the natural and cultural history of the Great Lakes area, and on native study accessories. Also on hand: gifts and souvenirs.

◆ **A 13-mile trail system** on flat terrain often parallels the Chippewa River. Highlights are the .4 mile **Arbury Trail**, handicapped-accessible and planned for blind people, and a wooded, fern-filled **oxbow** where nesting waterfowl and muskrats can be seen from a wildlife blind. In winter the trails are used for **cross-**

country skiing and **hiking**; they're ungroomed and sometimes rough.

♦ A **man-made wetlands** begun in 1990 as a replacement for wetlands destroyed to build a shopping mall north of Midland. Already the marsh vegetation is lush and wetland wildlife plentiful. Trails circle two basins; a boardwalk/dock lets you walk out over the water. *It's on Badour Road South of the Visitor Center, with its own parking area. Open roughly dawn to dusk.*

♦ An **1870s log homestead** from Midland County. The house is well crafted, not a temporary cabin, and authentically furnished. (The nature center staff includes an historian.) Other log buildings moved here are a **barn**, a **log schoolhouse**, and a **sugarhouse** used every weekend in March for very popular maple syrup-making demonstrations. *The homestead buildings are open for special events and on Sunday afternoons, 1-4, May through October. Walkers are otherwise welcome to look in the windows.*

♦ **Weekend programs**, usually free and geared to families, are usually on Saturday and Sunday afternoons. Early October's **Fall Harvest Festival** and March's **Maple Syrup Festival** are big annual events.

The Nature Center is southwest of downtown Midland on Badour Rd. at the Chippewa River. From downtown, take Poseyville Rd. across the bridge, turn right immediately onto St. Charles, turn left onto Whitman. In 3 miles, turn right at sign for nature center. (517) 631-0830. Mon-Fri 8-5, Sat 9-5, Sun and holidays (except Thanksgiving and Christmas) 1-5. Free.

Historic Huron City

*A look at the civilized, relaxed summer life of Yale's
Billy Phelps, "America's favorite college professor"*

Time moves slowly in Michigan's Thumb. The landscape is
utterly flat, and the Lake Huron scenery is pleasant but
unspectacular, no match for the Grand Traverse region
or West Michigan's sand dunes. So even vacation development is
blessedly low-key. In the absence of pressure to sell and develop
property, old households have often survived intact, with all their
everyday furnishings. They are natural museums maintained by
heirs over the decades, until, sometimes, they emerge as organized museums with public hours. Examples are the Sanilac
Historical Museum in Port Sanilac (which includes the local doctor's home, furnishings, records, and library) and the Harbor
Beach law office of Frank Murphy, Michigan's most illustrious
leader of the Depression era.

But the **House of the Seven Gables** in the historic **Huron
City** museum village is the most wonderful survivor of all. The
big, comfortable Italianate house built by lumberman Langdon
Hubbard sits behind a picket fence atop a long hill overlooking
Lake Huron. When you enter this informal house and walk into
the cozy, memento-filled library, the tea cart by the fire is set for
afternoon tea. Books are piled on the center table waiting to be
read and reviewed by Hubbard's son-in-law, William Lyon
Phelps, called "America's favorite college professor" in a 1930s
Life magazine feature. Classic Adirondack chairs look out across
to the lake. It's easy to imagine that it's 1932 and Billy Phelps is
about to come back from his afternoon game of golf.

Visitors immediately feel that this interior is no historical reconstruction. It's simply an old house that had been lived in by
the same family ever since it was built in 1881 — and a very interesting family at that, sure of themselves and unconcerned
with fashion. Langdon Hubbard had come to Michigan from
Connecticut as a young, high-minded, and ambitious young man
hoping to make his fortune in the West. He bought 29,000 acres
of timberland and an old sawmill, which he developed into a lake
port with a half mile-long dock.

By 1880 Hubbard's two sawmills produced 20,000 feet of
lumber a day. But the great Thumb fire of 1881 burned up the

The phenomenally popular Yale professor, William Lyons Phelps, summered at his wife's family place at Huron City. Phelps was also a dynamic Baptist preacher. His summer sermons attracted enormous crowds.

area's remaining timber. Such fires were common in logging regions. Loggers left treetops and other waste/wood behind in the ravaged stumplands. Dried over the years, they caught fire easily. The 1881 fire hastened the growth of inland towns like Bad Axe and Sandusky. The area's burned-over forests proved excellent for growing navy beans, potatoes, and, later, sugar beets. Old lumber ports like Huron City, however, were destined to languish except as modest resorts. In this area brine wells and salt making had been a byproduct of lumbering, and the process ended up contaminating well water with salt. The only sources of fresh water for port communities were Lake Huron and shallow, easily polluted wells. That limited their development.

After the fire, Hubbard rebuilt his big Italianate house and sold off his timberland to prospective German and Polish farmers. He didn't rebuild his sawmills, which could have salvaged the dead trees and provided some local employment. A general store, inn, church, and school were built for the farm village Hubbard hoped would prosper on the site. Today they survive, fully furnished, as components of Historic Huron City. Hubbard provided unusual amenities for villagers — a social parlor in the inn, a roller rink near the store and books from his personal library to borrow. But by 1883 Huron City had less than two dozen residents, down from 1,500 before the fire.

Huron City did prove an ideal summer retreat for the
Hubbard descendants, who moved to Grosse Pointe, and their
friends. The daughter, Annabel, married William Lyon Phelps, a
phenomenally popular English professor at Yale. He was Billy
Phelps to generations of Yale students who flocked to his interesting, easy-to-take lectures. Phelps was also an American Baptist
preacher and a prolific writer of book reviews and literary appreci-
ations for the general reading public. He and Annabel summered
in the House of the Seven Gables. So many vacationers showed
up at his non-denominational, Sunday-afternoon sermons that
the little church was expanded to hold 600. Seven Gables
remained in use through the death of the Phelps's heir in 1987.

Physical evidence of the Hubbards' and Phelpses' affluent,
civilized, and relaxed lifestyle is everywhere. There's an ornate
1886 pool table in the double parlors, and above it a print of a
Raphael Madonna. Parlor amusements range from a music box
with huge discs, circa 1885, to Mah-Jong tiles from that craze.
There are portraits of favorite dogs and cats, and racks of croquet
mallets and tennis rackets in the study. The ladies' fancy work,
seed pictures, twig shelves, and Annabel Phelps's almost Expres-
sionistic landscape paintings are all interesting. The books and
magazines in Phelps's large, airy upstairs study give a good idea
of the literary fare of well-read people in the 1920s and 1930s.

A house like this required an upstairs maid and a parlor
maid. Also, a cook and a kitchen maid worked in a cheerful,
practical kitchen, state-of-the-art in 1915 and hardly changed
since. Enthusiasts for authentic period decor won't be disap-
pointed by things like the 1915 dishwasher or the series of bedrooms from different decades.

The genial Billy Phelps stuck to a productive daily routine in
summer, beginning with calisthenics at six a.m. (All guests were
awakened to join in.) He then retired to his study to write until
noon. After lunch, he played golf. Grazing sheep clipped the golf
course between the house and Lake Huron, but were rounded up
at game time and herded under the old roller rink. Edgar Guest,
the *Detroit Free Press* columnist famed for his light verse, was a
frequent golfing buddy, and eventually built a summer cottage in
nearby Pointe aux Barques.

After Billy and Annabel Phelps's deaths, the property came
into the hands of Annabel's niece, Carolyn Hubbard Parcells
Lucas. The dynamic personality of Billy Phelps and the public's
great interest in him inspired her to furnish and preserve Huron
City's church, inn, and general store, and to build a trim brick

museum building to house exhibits on local history and Phelps's career. All the buildings are simple and attractive, painted white with green trim, giving them a neat New England look.

Huron City's buildings are more fully and authentically furnished than most museums'. That's a result of local people's long memories and many contributions. Much of the merchandise in the **general store** was left over from Langdon Hubbard's stock. The original **post office** and **lumbering office** remain in back of the store, while a large room is given over to displays of tools for lumbering and cutting ice.

The **lifesaving station** from nearby Pointe aux Barques has been moved onto the site. Here a breeches buoy and other life-saving equipment can be seen, along with displays on local marine history. Teenage tour guides are pleasant and competent.

The buildings of Huron City make up one tour; the summer house is a separate tour. Seen alone, Huron City is impressive. But it is overwhelmed by the compelling intimacy of the House of the Seven Gables, which seems too real to be a museum. Each 1 1/2-hour tour would probably be more enjoyable if taken on a separate day, or if separated by a trip to the beach. Just 2 1/2 miles east of Huron City on Lighthouse Road is the **Pointe aux Barques lighthouse** (1848) and a **county park** with campground, picnic area, and lawn down to the **beach**. If you do take both tours on the same day, bring a snack or lunch to eat at a picnic table. No refreshments except soft drinks are nearby, and each tour lasts 1 1/2 hours.

Huron City is on M-25 8 miles south of Port Austin and 8 miles north of Port Hope. (517) 428-4123. Open July 1 through Labor Day, every day but Tuesday, 10-5. Group tours available in June through Sept. Admission to each tour (Huron City or Seven Gables): $6/adult, $5 seniors, $3 12-18, under 12 free. $1 discount if you take both tours.

ANOTHER TRIP BACK IN TIME TO THE 1920s AND 1930s. . . . . is the **Frank Murphy Birthplace** in Harbor Beach. Murphy was the Michigan governor who refused to use the National Guard to quash the 1937 Flint Sit-Down Strike. By initiating collective bargaining, he paved the way for the United Auto Workers union. This is a very simple frame house, to which the storefront law office of Murphy's father is attached. Walk in and you feel like you're in 1910, what with the potbelly stove, kerosene lamps, and plain wood chairs.

Murphy's father made enough money to move into the impressive Gothic Revival house next door, where the children grew up. His famous son, a true labor hero, started his career in Detroit, became mayor (no Depression-era mayor did more to alleviate hunger among the jobless), governor (1936-38), U.S. Attorney General, and U.S. Supreme Court judge (1940 to his death in 1949). Murphy seems to have used the little house as a home base and repository for books and gifts, souvenirs and snapshots.

The houses are treasure troves of interesting historical objects. A resolution pending in the state legislature will turn the site over to the city of Harbor Beach to operate as a museum and memorial to Frank Murphy; plans are underway for a special opening ceremony in June, 1994. Everything in the houses has been kept the same as it was the day Murphy died. You can learn a lot about Murphy's character from the things he left here, and from talking to the UAW retirees who, as true keepers of the flame, run the museum. Inspirational books, pairs of riding boots, crucifixes and religious statues, countless autographed photos of Murphy with celebrities and labor leaders — all add up to a picture of his political ambition and concern for achievement and high principles, his Catholic faith, and his love of challenge and hard work. While governor of the Philippines from 1933 to 1935, he received some most unusual gifts displayed here. *142 S. Huron in central Harbor Beach, across from Norm's Place. (517) 479-9664. Open mid-June thru Labor Day, Mon-Sat 10-5:30, Sun 11-5. Free admission; donations welcome.*

A NICE PLACE TO LINGER AND WATCH BOATS. . . . . is shady **Harbor Park** overlooking the busy transient marina at Port Sanilac (population 650), some 33 miles north of Port Huron on M-25. Get the feeling of being out on Lake Huron by walking out to the long **breakwater** past the pretty Victorian **lighthouse** and the **Old Bark Shanty** (a favorite local landmark from pioneer days, not open to the public). Mornings and evenings the breakwater is usually well populated by fishermen, and for the October salmon run it's packed.

THE FINE ITALIANATE HOME OF A PIONEER DOCTOR . . . . . and most all his things, from a massive curio case full of bird's nests, Indian pipes, and coral specimens to medical books and his original medicines, make the **Sanilac Historical Museum** special. The doctor's grandson and only heir became a ship's captain, and never threw anything out or modernized much, since he only stayed here occasionally. Some rooms are given over to museum displays: a first-rate **quilt collection**, a Victorian display of stuffed birds with a painted backdrop, a good **marine history room** about the area's famous shipwrecks, and odd donations like a Mexican bullfrog mariachi band of stuffed bullfrogs wearing sombreros. There's a lot of high-quality stuff to see here (carriages, an old log cabin, a display on the fishing industry, a general store, a little dairy museum — Sanilac is Michigan's #1 milk-producing county). Pleasant **picnic area** and grounds, too. *On the west side of M-25 at the south edge of Sanilac. (616) 622-9946. Open from Memorial to Labor Day, Tues-Sun noon-4:30. Modest admission fee.*

Port Huron

*Striking views of freighters and water
in one of America's earliest inland outposts*

Strategically sited where Lake Huron pours into the St. Clair River, this city of around 34,000 offers several striking scenic and historic sights. It's a grand place to watch freighters and a good jumping off place for exploring the bucolic charms of the Thumb and the Lake Huron Shore. It became one of the earliest outposts in the American interior when the French built Fort St. Joseph here in 1686 to seal off the upper Great Lakes from the English. Later the Americans built Fort Gratiot in 1814 on the same site as Fort St. Joseph, also to keep the British out of Lake Huron and Lake Superior. American friction with British-controlled Canada had changed to cooperation by 1891 when the two-mile-long underground St. Clair Railroad Tunnel was built beneath the St. Clair River to join Sarnia with Port Huron. Located just south of John Street, the tunnel is still quite active. For the high railroad cars which can't fit through the tunnel, ferry service is in operation 24 hours a day to get them across the St. Clair River. The line's owner, Grand Trunk, has its big railroad car repair shops at 25th and Minnie streets. The Canadian National Railroad is building a second tunnel beneath the river; plans call for an observation area to be set up sometime during 1994 so that people can watch when the tunnel breaks through to Port Huron.

Despite its strategic position, Port Huron has been something of a backwater in this century. Military concerns disappeared after the Civil War, and no industrial giants sprang up here as they did in Midland or Battle Creek or Kalamazoo. For environmental reasons the city rejected the bids of chemical companies to build plants here; they settled on the laxer Canadian side of the river instead. Port Huron's main claim to fame is as the hometown of Thomas Edison. The one big event which attracts thousands is the **Mackinac Race Day** in late July, when a flotilla of sailing boats races to Mackinac Island.

Highlights of Port Huron are:

◆ **Blue Water Bridge.** This imposing structure rises 152 feet over the St. Clair River to allow freighters to pass underneath. It

Port Huron is one of the very best places to watch big Great Lakes freighters. Downbound traffic originating in lakes Michigan, Superior, and Huron all pass by. There are plenty of good parkside locations, and the river's narrow width brings the boats up close. This photo was taken at the Blue Water Bridge decades ago.

is 1.4 miles long, with a main span of 871 feet. Completed in 1938, it connects Port Huron with Sarnia, Ontario. Its height gives you a splendid view of Lake Huron to the north and the St. Clair River to the south. Also interesting are the bird's-eye views of Port Huron neighborhoods. Just to the north you see the Dunn Paper facilities. You can also walk across the bridge. *U.S. entrance is the northern terminus of I-94. Toll: $1.25 per car.*

◆ **1858 Grand Trunk Depot.** Port Huron's strategic location where Lake Huron flows into the St. Clair River provides an exceptional visual setting in this new park by the historic train station. To the left, facing Canada, looms the enormous **Blue Water Bridge**, and beyond that, the great expanse of **Lake Huron**. Directly ahead, the river is quite narrow, less than a quarter mile wide. It therefore flows quite swiftly, seven or eight miles an hour. The river's narrow width brings the big freighters up close.

Standing starkly near the railroad tracks is the recently restored 1858 **Grand Trunk Depot**. From here in 1859 Thomas Edison, a Port Huron boy of 12, embarked to sell fruits, nuts, magazines, and newspapers on the train to Detroit and back. He used much of his earnings to buy chemicals for the small laboratory he set up in the train's baggage car. Just south of the old depot is the new Thomas Edison Inn, a pricey 150-suite dining/hotel complex built by the owners of the popular St. Clair

Inn downriver. Just south of the inn's parking lot is where **Fort Gratiot** (1814-1879) stood. *Just south of the Blue Water Bridge. From Pine Grove Ave. take Thomas Edison Parkway just north of the tracks. Parking spaces and boardwalk by the river.*

◆ **Sarnia, Canada.** Port Huron's neighbor across the St. Clair River is a pleasant, if rather unexciting, place to visit. No longer are there great buys on Commonwealth products to lure Americans across the border. The flow is now reversed, and Canadians flock to Port Huron's malls for good deals. The economy of Sarnia (population 80,000) is based on the petrochemical industry, whose fascinating-looking plants sprawl for some 20 miles below the city along the St. Clair River. At night, the spaghetti-like complex of lights and tubing are quite a sight from the American side. An elaborate government-run information center is just to the south of the Canadian side of the bridge. *Take I-94 to the Blue Water Bridge. No passport necessary for American citizens.*

◆ **Lighthouse Park.** This park, next to the oldest surviving lighthouse in Michigan, is another good vantage point from which to enjoy the splendid view of Lake Huron as it enters the St. Clair River. Lights illuminate an asphalt path leading to the sandy beach. On foggy days, it's an eerie sight to see giant northbound freighters quietly churning past and becoming quickly engulfed in the mist on the Lake. On the short path to the beach, you pass a small Coast Guard complex, complete with an 1874 light keeper's dwelling of red brick and a white clapboard Coast Guard station. Also in the complex is the 86-foot-tall **Fort Gratiot Light**. It still flashes a warning to freighters coming south from Lake Huron into the river, a tricky maneuver because of the river's narrow width and swift current. *Off Omar St. between Robinson and Riverview 5 blocks north of the Blue Water Bridge. From Pine Grove north of I-94, take Garfield east to the park.*

◆ **Pinegrove Park.** This city park also fronts the St. Clair River and provides a wonderful view of the big bridge, the Canadian shoreline, and boat traffic. On the concrete walk right at the riverbank, fishermen with big landing nets fish for walleye and steelhead. At the park's northeastern edge, embedded in the riverbank, is the **Lightship Huron,** a retired floating lighthouse whose light could be seen for 14 miles. The 97-foot-long ship served six miles north of Port Huron from 1935 until 1970. After 17 years of being trashed by vandals who left hardly a porthole intact, the lightship has been lovingly restored over the past five years by retired sailors and Coast Guarders. It is open to the public on weekends from 1 to 4:30 p.m. Group tours can be arranged through the Port Huron Museum (313-982-0891). The lightship's high main deck is also a great outpost for watching freighters, although there is no predicting when or how often ships will come by. Since the 1993 completion of the Edison Parkway, which carries traffic right along the waterfront, the lightship has become a highly visible attraction. From I-94, take the Water Street exit and continue east, following the signs to Pinegrove Park; the lightship is just three blocks from the business section and only a couple of miles off the expressway.

North of the lightship you can see a red **pilot house,** quarters for the American freighter pilots who take the wheels of foreign vessels heading into U.S. waters. The vacant lot behind the pilot house was where Thomas Edison's family home stood.

Looking south across the river, you can see the beginning of Canada's 20-mile-long **"chemical valley,"** Canada's greatest concentration of chemical factories and a spectacular nightime sight reflected in the water. They are responsible for creating most of the pollution in the lower St. Clair River. *East off Pine Grove between Prospect and Lincoln, north of downtown.*

◆ **Diana Sweet Shop.** Fine woodwork abounds in this beautifully preserved 1926 sweet shop. The ornate tapestry, the lighting, the pressed metal ceiling, the pictures — all combine to create an extraordinary atmosphere. It is still owned and operated by the sons of the founder. Sweet shops flourished in the 1920s as the tempo of American urban life sped up and people stopped going home for lunch. Elegant interiors were a mark of success. Diana's preserves not only the decor but the menu: sandwiches, ice cream, pastries, and fudge. Don't miss the original 1926 "Violano Virtuoso" up front as you enter. For 25¢ it will play one of five tunes, plucking at a violin and hammering on strings. *307 Huron between Grand River and McMorran downtown. (313) 985-6933. Mon-Sat 7:15 a.m.-6 p.m. Fri to 8 p.m. Sat 7:30-6. MC, Visa, Am Ex. No alcohol.*

◆ **Port Huron Museum**. Formerly called the Museum of Arts and History, this sizable museum in the impressive 1904 Carnegie library building has a little bit of everything, from 7,000 B.C. Indian artifacts to recent paintings for sale by local artists. There is a remarkable array of Indian stone points and tools from the region. Archeological digs have recovered objects from Edison's boyhood home (which burned down), including evidence of his boyhood laboratory. In the McMorran Room are turn-of-the-century furnishings that illuminate Port Huron life in that era. The biggest attraction in the Cooper's Marine Gallery on the second floor is the freighter pilot house, restored piece by piece over a two-year period by the same volunteers who have rebuilt the Lightship Huron. Most haunting are the objects brought up by divers from wrecks. Among the items available in the **gift shop** arc books written by Thomas Edison and a history of Port Huron, *The Reflection* ($18.50). *1115 Sixth St. between Wall and Court, south of the Black River and downtown. Sixth is one block west of M-25, the main artery. (313) 982-0891. Wed-Sun 1-4:30. $1.50/adults, $1/seniors, 50¢/students, children under 6 free.*

Chapter 5
Mid-Michigan

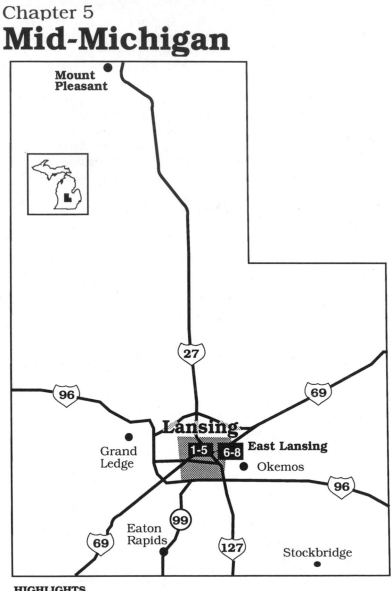

HIGHLIGHTS

For restaurants & Lodgings, see *Hunts' Restaurants & Lodgings of Michigan*

INTRODUCTION

Mid-Michigan

The wilderness hamlet of Lansing was chosen as state capital purely for its central location. None of the bigger, older Michigan cities could get a majority vote from the state legislature for the honor. Today its status as the seat of state government defines Lansing, along with another perk won by default. In the 1850s Michigan farmers successfully lobbied to start a college of scientific agriculture, one of America's very first. The tiny college that became Michigan State University was carved out of the woods east of Lansing. Today it's the state's largest university, a vast center of education and applied research.

No other Michigan city has such good freeway access. Major highways converge on the capitol's elongated dome from six directions. Easy access has made it very easy to commute to surrounding towns, draining vital energy from the central city. Very little historic preservation or gentrification has occurred in central Lansing, leaving generally dull streetscapes and an uninspiring downtown.

Lansing is also a center of auto manufacturing, the headquarters of GM's Oldsmobile division. It shares the characteristics of auto boom towns: rapid growth and low-density sprawl from 1905 to 1930, considerable ethnic variety, and economic decline since 1970.

Lansing puts its worst foot forward visually. Pretty spots are tucked away, while big parking lots and garages, blocky state office buildings, and aging commercial and industrial corridors are immediately evident. But as the following highlights reveal, Lansing has more than a few interesting and attractive places to visit.

❶ State Capitol. Masterpiece of Victorian decorating. See politicians in action Tuesday through Thursday.

❷ Michigan Historical Museum. Fine visuals present history with flair. Lumbering, mining, & prehistory stand out.

❸ Washington Street. Daytime-only downtown. Architecture makes it worth a look.

❹ Riverfront Park and River Trail. 5 1/2 mile pedestrian/bike path along the Grand and Red Cedar rivers connect lively destinations

❺ City Market. Fresh produce, baked goods, cheese, meat, and more, sold indoors year-round.

❻ Elderly Instruments. America's headquarters for folk recordings & instruments is a category killer with amazing selection and savvy staff.

❼ Three unusual museums. Impressions 5: Michigan's best hands-on museum. A car museum featuring Lansing's Ransom Olds. Plus the only U.S. surveying museum.

❽ Potter Park and Zoo. Riverside picnic grove, playground, canoe rentals. Pleasant small zoo perfect for brief visits. (Map shows entrance only. Park is to east.)

Highlights of
Lansing

0   1/4   1/2
     mile

Michigan State Capitol

*A tour de force of rich Victorian decorating
that's intense with political energy*

Michigan's state capitol is an exciting place to visit for the spectacle it presents of seeing lawmakers in action in a richly decorated Victorian setting. The high-domed exterior looks like a state capitol ought to look: formal and impressive. Finished in 1879, it was one of the first state capitols modeled after the nation's Capitol, which had itself been remodeled during the Civil War. Lincoln insisted that capitol construction continue despite the war because the Capitol stood for the union. The tall central dome was made possible by using cast iron, a new and relatively inexpensive building material. A Michigan soldier's letters home mentioned that the unfinished dome was the first thing he saw coming into Washington to join the fight, and that the finished dome was the last thing he saw leaving Washington finally to return home. The capitol with the finished dome, he said, represented everything he had fought for.

Before Michigan's capitol was built, state capitols had come in many styles, including Greek temples and Gothic castles. Michigan's use of the national Capitol as a model established that building form as the very symbol of the democratic form of government. The central dome stands for the executive branch and the balanced wings for the senate and house of representatives. This form set the standard for virtually all state capitols to come.

Even on the exterior, details like the oval windows in the dome hint that this building is no stern exercise in Roman dignity, but a product of the Gilded Age. The interior is rich in vivid colors, with contrasting decorative textures and patterns (including plaster swirled like tight waves, and lots of gold leaf). Ornamental details include chandeliers embellished with stags. It was a tour de force for its cost-conscious architect, Elijah Myers, who called for very little marble, expensive stone, or cabinet-grade wood. Most of the opulent effect was achieved with elaborate painted designs on plaster, and with pine that was grained to resemble walnut. Myers' success with Michigan's capitol enabled him to win later commissions for capitols in Texas,

In 1847, contentious legislators placed the state capital in the central-
ly-located wilderness settlement of Lansing after futile fights in favor of
established cities. The state capitol remains Lansing's defining landmark. Now, after a spectacular restoration, it is a nationally important
example of Victorian painted decoration.

Idaho, and Colorado. The capitol was designated a National
Historic Landmark in 1992, in part for its remarkable decorative
paint, over nine *acres* in all. It is the preeminent example of
Victorian decorative paint in the nation.

A careful restoration, begun in 1987, is now complete. The
beautiful painted wall decorations and the elaborate ceilings in
the **Senate and House chambers** have shed the subdued color
schemes deemed dignified enough to use in past redecorations.
The Senate walls, no longer a cautious, conservative forest green,
have returned to their original colors, predominantly a rich
Prussian blue, several shades of warm yellows, gold, and rose
used for the elaborate plasterwork. (An electronic display board
is concealed in the wall until the board's lights are turned on. It
shows proposed legislation and records the legislators' votes on
it.) Ceiling panels of white and ruby glass etched with seals of all
the states can again be seen — a favorite with visitors. The
House has received a similar treatment in its original color
scheme: vibrant corals, teals, and metallic silver, bronze, copper,
and pewter.

Now that the scaffolding is gone from the restored **rotunda,**
you can again get the spectacular full effect of looking up at the
richly patterned dome with its starry inner eye, you can also look
way down from the upper galleries. The governors' full-length

portraits are back, and so are the flags carried in battle by
Michigan Civil War regiments. (Replicas now stand in for the
badly deteriorated originals.)

The monumental capitol restoration job was awarded the
1992 Honor award by the National Trust for Historic Preservation — the nation's highest preservation award — for its challenge, complexity, and accuracy.

The capitol building is merely a magnificent stage set for the
drama of everyday government. Controversies are played out and
laws are made right here. When important legislation is being
voted on, the entrance lobbies to the house and senate chambers
really are filled with lobbyists — so-called because they must
wait in lobbies. Barred from the legislative floor, they send messages to legislators via pages and confer with them in the lobby.

The capitol and all its public meeting rooms are open to all
Michigan citizens. As the memorable late tour guide, Tony
Dodos, loved to point out, "Everyone here — the governor, your
representative, me — works for *you*. You pay us every time you
pay a state tax." Some retirees attend legislative sessions regularly and keep scorecards of the proceedings as if they were at a
ball game.

Here's what you need to know to be able to observe the
legislature in action and figure out what's going on:

◆ Call the **Capitol Tour Guide and Information Service** at
(517) 373-2353 to find out if the legislature is in session and to
find out who your representatives are if you don't know.
Normally the legislature is in session Tuesdays through
Thursdays, occasionally well on into the evening and early morning. Breaks are at Christmas (3-4 weeks), Easter (2 weeks), and
summer (from June or July into September).

◆ Your representative will be happy to phone or mail you information on what's happening on a given day, or when action is
scheduled on particular bills, or the dates of hearings on subjects that concern you.

◆ Bring your binoculars. Otherwise you probably won't be able
to read the nameplates on each legislator's desk.

◆ If at all possible, go on a free **capitol tour** when the legislature
is in session. Tours leave every half hour from the tour desk in
the ground floor, east (front) wing. Call (517) 373-2353 for
groups of 10 or more. From March through May, you'll probably
be with an elementary school group, but you'll still learn a lot

you didn't know. When the tour group is on the gallery, your guide can show you how to figure out what's going on.

Tours generally last about 45 minutes. You'll get an overview of Michigan history as it relates to the Capitol, information on the decorative painting techniques, and a participative story of the legislative process.

◆ Stop by your senator or representative's office for a look around and to pick up interesting free material, including a capitol walking tour, a coloring book for kids, and an introduction to state government. Especially helpful for your visit and for having input on legislation is *A Citizen's Guide to State Government*, with lobbying tips and legislators' photos and addresses.

◆ At the ground-floor **tour guide desk** in the east (front) wing, get a **map**. The printed journal of yesterday's legislative proceedings and **today's agenda** can be had for no charge at the Documents Room in the ground floor north wing, off Ottawa Street. (You can also ask for copies of any state laws.)

◆ Visitors are free to sit in the balconies in the rear of the senate or house, and in the senate and house fourth-floor conference rooms during any **public proceedings**. In the house, speakers' voices come over a p.a. system, so it's hard to tell who's talking. Look for the microphones on the side aisles, where representatives come to speak. A light goes on by the speaker's microphone. What's being considered on the floor is displayed on the electronic display board; refer to your agenda to learn more about it.

*On Capitol Avenue at the head of Michigan Avenue in downtown Lansing. From I-496, take Grand or Walnut exits and go north. The capitol is open weekdays from 8:30 to 5 (first tour at 9, last tour at 4); Sat & Sun from noon to 4. All tours are every half hour. Last tour is at 3:30. Free admission. For **group tours** and **questions** on state government, contact the Capitol Tour Guide and Information Service, ground floor, east (front) wing, (517) 373-2353. Convenient **parking** is in structures at S. Capitol and Allegan (just south of the Capitol), at Capitol and Kalamazoo, and at Grand north of Ottawa.*

BEFORE YOUR GROUP VISIT TO THE CAPITOL . . . . . you can see a **video** about its construction, history, and the renovation process. The Michigan Capitol Committee will mail it to you free of charge. Sign up early, especially in spring. Call (517) 373-5527, or write the committee in care of Capitol Tour Guide Service, Box 30036, Lansing, MI 48909.

Michigan Historical Museum

Michigan history through the 19th century,
told with visual pizzazz and architectural drama

After a century of being relegated to makeshift quarters, the state historical museum now enjoys a stunning new space and has become a major Michigan tourist destination. The combined museum/state library/archives complex, opened in 1989, is a real architectural and artistic show-stopper. Detroit architect William Kessler has brilliantly played off contrasts between polished and rough surfaces and natural elements associated with Michigan. These include limestone, copper, granite, and a 60-foot white pine, Michigan's state tree, dramatically planted in the central court. The museum only covers up to 1900. The 20th century exhibits open on the third floor in 1995.

Many of the expensive, expertly made displays are visually memorable: an Indian canoe pulled into a stretch of marsh and cattails in front of a realistic diorama of a lake; a lumberman's big wheel, 12 feet in diameter, used to move logs easily out of stump-filled forests; a two-story replica of the front part of Muskegon lumber baron Charles Hackley's elaborate Queen Anne home (see page 506), which unfortunately duplicates the old and historically inaccurate brown and yellow paint scheme, not the rich, complex original paint being duplicated in Muskegon. "Growing Up in Michigan: 1880-1895" in the mezzanine, which is entered up the house's stairs, uses diaries and reminiscences of five children who grew up in various kinds of homes throughout the state. (One was Della Lutes, author of the delightful *Country Kitchen* cookbook memoir, recently republished.)

The historical narrative itself is honest and intelligent. No punches are pulled. Within a few generations of contact with Europeans, it says, Native American culture was nearly destroyed and their self-sufficient way of life changed to dependence on manufactured goods. "Give the least to get the most" was the business motto of John Jacob Astor, whose fur empire dominated the Michigan wilderness's economy in the first part of the 19th century.

Striking sculpture and murals relating to Michigan's natural features are an extra bonus on visits to the impressive state history complex. It contains the state history museum plus its archives and library — both treasure troves of local and regional history. Michigan residents are welcome to use all three free of charge.

For those who take the time to read and look, many basics — especially in geology, Indian cultures, and mining — are clearly explained and interestingly illustrated. The mining exhibit is particularly detailed and satisfying (better than anything found in Copper Country today), down to specifics and samples of rock types and diagrams of the mining and smelting process. Visitors walk through a life-size passage of a **copper mine**, supported by leaning timbers, to see miners and carts and hear the boom of a distant blast. Interesting **video shows on lumbering and mining** by the state Bureau of Michigan History illuminate life in camps. Small sit-down theaters give your feet a rest.

However, the advice of prestigious and well-trained museum professionals from someplace else seems to have had too much influence on the exhibits, especially on the text. Missing are the telling details, the heart, and the intelligent hometown touch that the very best history can convey without being parochial or boosterish. The chief shapers of Michigan never come to life as the fascinating, often contradictory people they really were. Specific locations of photographs could be inconspicuously identified for those who appreciate detail and geography without attracting from the main point. Many visitor centers at Michigan state parks do far better in combining ideas with in-depth illustrative details for a powerful, one-two punch. Maybe that's because they are designed and written by interpreters who have fielded questions for years and draw upon a lot of experience.

The museum staff is aware of these shortcomings. "We are working very hard to 'humanize' all of our exhibits," states a staff member. Some staff on the floor do seem to welcome constructive criticism from the general public. Helpful volunteer **docents** are on hand to field visitors' questions and expand on exhibits. The museum staff has collected visitor feedback to improve the forthcoming exhibits after 1900 by including personal stories and quotes from Michigan people.

On the lower level there's an **exhibit gallery** for changing shows, a large **snack area** with sandwiches (weekdays only) and vending machines, and an attractive small **museum store** (closed Mondays) with books and gifts which relate directly to the exhibits. The museum store has one of Michigan's best selections of books on the history of African-Americans in Michigan. Occasional special activity days and programs usually relate to the changing exhibits in the lower-level gallery by the entrance.

The center is between Washtenaw and Allegan southwest of the capitol and east of Logan. See p. 402 for directional map. Park (free on weekends) just south of the building. (517) 373-3559. To schedule free tours of the Library and Historical Center for 10 or more, call (517) 335-1483. Mon-Fri 9-4:30, Sat 10-4, Sun 1-5. Free.

WHILE YOU'RE IN THE LIBRARY AND HISTORICAL CENTER . . . . pick up a pamphlet about the striking, unusually powerful **art works** in the building, and take a look around. . . . . **Michigan residents** can easily get **library cards** for the **Library of Michigan,** Michigan's version of the Library of Congress, in the west wing. (Materials may be checked out for a month and mailed back.) Collections of this beautiful and very user-friendly library focus on all areas of government, from social services to highways and sewers, and on local history and Michigan authors. *(517) 373-5400. Mon-Fri 9-6, Sat 9-5, Sun 1-5, closed state holidays.*

LUNCH WHERE THE MOVERS AND SHAKERS HANG OUT. . . . . at the **Parthenon** restaurant at 227 S. Washington in downtown Lansing. The food — Greek and American, meat and vegetarian — is pretty good, and at the noon hour the place is packed with politicians and state employees. Political meetings and receptions are often held here, too.

Riverfront Park and Trail

*A 5 1/2-mile riverside path and bike trail
through Lansing connects museums and market,
fishing spots and zoo.*

Lansing is one of those cities that puts its worst foot forward. Casual visitors see its less attractive side right
away. Parking structures and empty spaces dominate
much of a downtown that comes to life only at weekday with
office workers on their lunch hours. Major entrances to town are
dominated by low warehouses and factories or by modest, plain
neighborhoods from the great auto boom of the 1920s, led by the
two firms here founded by Ransom E. Olds.

Lansing's real beauty spots are a number of distinctive parks
along the Red Cedar and Grand rivers, which join in Lansing.
These places are so hidden away, you have to already know
about them to see them. Riverfront Park, an award-winning linear park along the Grand, is a marvelous rarity in the Midwest:
an urban park and pathway that dramatizes a natural feature
and connects interesting destinations.Accents enliven the route
for walkers, joggers, and bicyclists. The path is so well used,
night and day, that the park has been virtually crime-free since
it opened in 1976. Fishermen and canoeists enjoy it, too.

Here, as in most American cities, rivers attracted early
industries and railroads. They became sewers and dumps.
Warehouses and factories blocked them from public view as long
as industrial activity remained centered downtown. The notion of
an urban greenway in Lansing, discussed since the 1920s, was
finally realized as a Bicentennial project in 1976.

You could start the walk near Michigan Avenue, two blocks
east of the Capitol. Parking by the museums or city market is
easiest to find and usually plentiful. (Sometimes, however, these
lots are completely full in nice weather when there are events.)
But it's a more dramatic walk to start by the north end at the
dam and head toward the market and city center, with Lansing's
surprisingly impressive skyline ahead of you. A vivid landscape
really comes together here. There's the wide river and, behind it,
the skyline, dominated by the capitol dome, some new glass
buildings, and the warm orange and yellow bricks of two fine Art

Walkers, rollerbladers, and bicyclists enjoy Lansing's path along
the Grand and Red Cedar rivers. It
passes interesting industrial landmarks like the municipal power
plant (in the background) as well
as serene natural areas, the North
Lansing fish ladder, three museums, the city market, and the
Potter Park Zoo.

Deco buildings, the Michigan
National Bank tower and the
Board of Water and Light,
Lansing's city-owned utility,
with its landmark stack.
Though many old warehouses
were demolished for the park,
enough industrial relics remain
to give the walk some character. There are **coal silos** by the
dam and the frame and girders
of the old **salt sheds** by
Lansing Community College.
    North of Shiawassee Street the Grand's riverbanks haven't
been artificially straightened and channeled. Here they have
grown up wild with small, moisture-loving poplars, willows, and
maples. This accidental landscaping softens the urban views and
creates some lovely seasonal effects that look wonderful against
the river's sparkling surface on sunny days: the spring-green of
buds, bright yellows in fall, snow-traced branches in winter.
    Highlights along the 5 1/2 mile riverwalk include:
◆ **The North Lansing dam, canoe and fishing platform, and
fish ladder**. Some fishermen can nearly always be found at this
beautiful spot, where a water-level platform provides easy access
for canoeists and fishermen. The Grand's natural species here
include catfish, suckers, carp, bass, bluegill, and perch. Walleye,
coho, and steelhead have been planted. Fine organic sediments
in runoff make for water that's typically murky, but the
Department of Natural Resources says without reservation that
fish caught here are edible. **Grand River Bait and Tackle** (517-
482-4461) is a block away at 1201 Turner, at the corner of

Turner and E. Grand River.

Off to one side, by the stone generator built to power Lansing's street lights, an elaborate sculptural **fish ladder** is on the very site of the cabin and dam built by Lansing's first settler in 1843. During the fall salmon run from late September to mid or late October, it's usually crowded with people scrutinizing the roiling waters of the fish ladder steps to get a glimpse of a big fish heroically struggling upstream to return to where she was hatched and deposit her eggs. **Benches and picnic tables** make this a nice place to linger. Park off of Race, which goes south off Grand River Avenue just east of the river itself.

◆ The famous **Elderly Instruments** (page 418) makes a good destination if you're walking north along the park from the market and museum area. It's just west of the river on Washington just south of Grand River Avenue. For a return trip downtown through what was Lansing's most elegant neighborhood circa 1900, go south on Washington.

◆ **A pedestrian and train bridge** are just south of the Saginaw Street bridge, near the tennis courts. Here you can cross the river to the busy **Lansing Community College campus** and the outdoor performing space by the salt sheds. For upcoming LCC **performances, lectures, and exhibits,** call 517-483-1880 weekdays.

◆ For delicious, spicy, quick **Thai food**, eat in or take out from **Bangkok House**, on the south side of Saginaw in Riverfront Mall just east of the park. Benches (but no tables) overlook the river.

◆ The **Lansing City Market** occupies two enclosed market halls built in 1938. A smaller, enclosed version of Detroit's fabled Eastern Market, it also continues the tradition of big-city markets as places where a broad spectrum of social classes and ethnic groups come together to shop. The market operates year-round, so even in winter there's fresh produce brought in from the south, along with locally produced maple syrup, eggs, apples, root vegetables, baked goods, and such. A cheese shop, meat market, and florist are more like stores than stalls. A good bakery features cookies, breads, and a number of meat, vegetable, and cheese pies. There's a snack bar and lunch deli. Sit down and eat at indoor picnic tables or the **picnic/restroom/playground area** by the river across the parking lot.

From spring through fall, the colors and smells of the plants and farm produce are wonderful. The number of agricultural growers and producers is increasing. Only juried handcrafted

crafts are now allowed. Women from Lansing's Hmong community of Laotian refugees sometimes sell their intricate geometric
and storytelling embroideries and appliques here, usually
around Christmas and in summer. *On Cedar (one-way southbound) at Shiawassee. From Michigan Avenue, go north on Larch,
and west on Shiawassee, then south on Cedar. (517) 483-4300.
Free parking on market days. Tues-Sat 8-6 p.m.*

◆ **A picnic area and small playground** are between the market
and the river. For takeout food, try the market itself or **Roma
Bakery and Imported Foods**, a longtime Italian grocery at 428
North Cedar across from the market.

◆ **The Lansing Center** convention facility has been built
between the market and Michigan Avenue. The Riverfront Trail
squeezes alongside it by the river to get to the museums.
Walkers can cross the river to the Radisson Hotel and Grand
parking garage on a handy **skywalk**, reached by stairs or elevator in the Lansing Center parking garage.

◆ **Impression 5, the REO Museum, and the Michigan
Museum of Surveying** — see p. 415 for all three — are just off
the riverwalk south of the Michigan Avenue bridge. This cluster
ends the intensely developed section of the riverwalk with many
destinations. Stop in at the upper foyer of Impression 5 for no
charge and see a delightful soft-sculpture **underwater scene of
the Grand River**, complete with channel catfish, a school of
shiners, and an old tire.

◆ **Potter Park** (see page 414), 1¹⁄₂ miles southeast of downtown
along the riverwalk, has a big playground, a **picnic area** and
nifty small **zoo** in a grove of large oaks, and **canoeing** on the
river.

◆ Getting to **East Lansing** via the Riverfront Trail is easy as long
as you're in the City of Lansing. East of Potter Park is a wild natural area. But the nicely paved bike trail ends at the city limits.
For a half mile or so going east on Kalamazoo you have to share
the road with cars. Then you get to the M.S.U. campus, with an
excellent bike path system. (See page 421-431.)

◆ **Rental canoes** and **information on canoeing** can be obtained
from the Potter Park canoe livery (517-374-1022). As they flow
through Lansing, the Red Cedar and Grand are good beginner's
rivers, shallow enough that most adults could stand up in them.
You lose sight of the city along much of the waterway. Fall color
along the riverbanks is good.

Riverfront Park's current **northern terminus** *is at the Fish Ladder and dam. Park in the lot off Race or Factory just south of Grand River Ave. and east of the river. In the* **market area,** *park at the market, the Lansing Center lot ($2/ all day) or in the Grand garage just west of the river and north of the Radisson. The riverwalk enters* **Potter Park** *at Pennsylvania Avenue south of the Olds Freeway and the Grand Trunk tracks and goes all the way to the East Lansing city limits at Clippert, for 5 1/2 miles of paved riverfront bike path separate from streets.*

CAPITOL CITY RIVERFEST . . . . . over the Labor Day weekend is a wonderful, free four-day event held on both sides of Riverfront Park between the City Market and Lansing Community College. It features a carnival, all kinds of live music, waterskiing, fishing, canoeing contests and river exhibits, a Sunday-night lighted **pontoon parade**, and Monday-night **fireworks**. (517) 483-4499.

A NIFTY PARK AND ZOO FOR AN OUTING WITH KIDS . . . . . is Lansing's **Potter Park** and its fine small zoo. They're a perfect place for a picnic lunch and letting off steam. The park's pleasant setting is in a large grove of big oaks alongside the Red Cedar River. There's plenty of **playground equipment** and space for games, along with **picnic tables** and grills, and food concessions. **Canoes** can be rented here, too (517-374-1022).

The **Potter Park Zoo** has a tropical bird and reptile house, many monkeys and larger primates, big cats that look comfortable in natural-looking outdoor displays, and a farmyard. Kids can take camel and pony rides and go in a big enclosure and feed friendly goats. There are 400 animals in all, enough variety to please most kids, and the cost is low. Especially fun to watch are the penguins in their pool; many playful, cat-like lemurs with long, ringed tails; raccoon-like red pandas; and spider monkeys. Somehow the animals look happier under the leafy canopy, with chipmunks and squirrels scampering around. Pick up a self-guided tour and **map** (25¢) at the Zoovenir shop. *Park entrance is on Pennsylvania just north of the Red Cedar River. From the Olds Freeway (I-496) or Michigan Ave., take Pennsylvania south 1/2 mile. (517) 483-4222. Zoo open 365 days/year: 9-7 during daylight time, 9-5 standard time. $1.50/car parking for park & zoo. $2/adult, $1/child.*

Museum Drive

The state's best hands-on museum is next to two other interesting museums, all on the Grand River.

On a bank of the Grand River just east of the state capitol and downtown Lansing are three noteworthy museums all in a row. This was an old warehouse district, and the mill district before that. The museums have made use of the roomy old brick warehouses for their displays. Visitors can also embark on the interesting riverwalk from here (see page 410).

The three museums are:

IMPRESSION 5. Hands-on museums are difficult to do well. Especially when the emphasis is science, as is the case here, the tendency is to allow corporate benefactors to influence the displays and activities, too often destroying the interest value for kids. Impression 5 has successfully blended meaningful instruction with absorbing activities.

There's a lot of space here — 40,000 square feet, and it's full of interesting, informative things to do. There are classics found in many hands-on museums such as the giant soap bubble maker and a bicycle wheel gyroscope, along with uniquely ambitious projects. A room-sized **electronic circuit** lets kids plug in various components to create different effects. In an impressive **chemistry lab**, kids make slime and other concoctions. Big satellite dishes allow one person to communicate by whispers with another person 50 feet away. A state-of-the-art **computer lab** puts technology at your fingertips. Some of the exhibits, like pulleys lifting 30-lb. weights, demonstrate important principles with elegant simplicity. Others, such as one on fiber optics, are much more complex but still engaging. *200 Museum Drive, south off Michigan Ave. just east of the Grand River and downtown. (517) 485-8116. Mon-Sat 10-5, Sun 12-5. Adults $4.50, seniors and children 4-18 $3, children 3 and under free. Group rates are available.*

R.E. OLDS TRANSPORTATION MUSEUM. Not many people realize that Lansing native Ransom E. Olds was one of the towering pioneers of the auto industry. The Oldsmobile curved-dash

Ransom E. Olds' pioneering Oldsmobile (shown here in 1904) was the first mass-produced car that could reliably climb hills — a feature that made it the country's best-selling auto from 1901 to 1907. Olds' second automotive venture, REO, is now defunct. Even its famous trucks are no longer made. But Lansing remains Oldsmobile headquarters today. Olds and his auto ventures star in the R. E. Olds Museum.

runabout was the world's first mass-produced car. From 1901 to 1907, it sold more than all other models combined. Although Olds is responsible for Oldsmobile's headquarters remaining in Lansing to this day, he left after disagreements in 1904 and formed the REO Motor Car Company (named after his initials), also in Lansing. The REO automobile proved fabulously success-ful, too, but succumbed during the Depression.

The recently expanded museum displays up to 50 Oldsmobiles, REOs, and less well known automobiles built in Lansing. Here are the 1897 Oldsmobile (the very first production Oldsmobile); a concourse-class 1931 REO Royale convertible; and a super-rare concourse-class 1911 Olds Limited. Also on hand: a jaunty yellow REO Speedwagon truck, once viewed here by the popular rock group REO Speedwagon, which had not been aware of the source of its name. Also featured: Lansing aviation and fire-fighting history; motoring clothes and race suits; and advertising, PR, and photos in the archives. *240 Museum Drive. (517) 372-0422. Mon-Sat 10-5, Sun noon-5. Adults $2.50, students/seniors $1.50.*

MICHIGAN MUSEUM OF SURVEYING. This, the only surveying museum in the country, shows what a feat it was to survey Michigan by foot in the 19th century and what hardships surveyors endured. From 1815 to 1857, surveyors plotted out the state's 1,900 townships, each 36 square miles. At the museum is the rock which marked the spot southeast of Lansing from which all other measurements for the state are taken. Surveyors back then were paid $3 a day, with which they had to buy equipment and supplies and pay a field cook, hunter, rod man, chain man, and brush cutter. Historical photos show some of these intrepid men, who had to push straight through dense swamps to follow lines.

Michigan's famous surveyor, William Burt, was first alerted to the presence of huge iron lodes in the Upper Peninsula by deflections in his compass. His solar compass, invented in 1835, is on display here. It was a revolutionary improvement in the accuracy of field surveying, allowing much more accurate meridian measurements just by sighting the sun. *220 Museum Drive. (517) 484-6605. Tues-Fri noon-4. Donations welcome.*

***Directions:** Museum Drive is just east of the Grand River and downtown Lansing, south off Michigan Avenue. Quickest, easiest freeway directions: from U.S. 127, I-96, or I-69, take I-496 to downtown Lansing. Take Washington Ave. exit north to Michigan Ave., then east (right), then right again after you cross the river.*

Elderly Instruments

*America's mail-order center for traditional music
is also the retail hub of a lively local folk scene.*

The square brick Oddfellows' Hall in North Lansing has been reborn as a folkies' heaven — 14,000 square feet where you can find obscure recordings of bluegrass, blues, country, folk, jazz, and music with traditional roots from many countries and cultures. There's Tex-Mex and Celtic, African and Arab, and many more. Even more remarkable is the fact that musicians can try out almost any kind of acoustic instrument that exists, from the complete line of legendary Martin guitars to pennywhistles and concertinas, zydeco washboards and musical saws, simple rhythm instruments and kazoos. Gift items include related postcards, rubber stamps, trading cards, musical toys, dozens of T-shirts featuring blues masters, and bumper stickers with sayings like "String band music is a social disease" and "Hammer dulcimists never fret." The five-person repair shop is nationally known.

Though acoustic and traditional music have always been the major focus at Elderly, the musician/staffers are no strangers to rock 'n roll or gospel or jazz. They sell more electric guitars than any other music store in Michigan.

Bulletin boards and literature racks in the front hall put you in touch with folk-related festivals and workshops throughout the region. Early evenings the place is busy with lessons.

Some customers drive a long way just to visit Elderly. It may seem improbable to find the world's largest dealer in stringed instruments in a medium-sized Midwestern city. In fact, much of Elderly's business comes from catalog sales. Its **four catalogs** (recordings, acoustic instruments and accessories, books and videos, and amplified instruments) are themselves full of interesting reading on such topics as recommended recordings or ukuleles (billed as *the* instrument of the 90s). A more frequent publication lists Elderly's current supply of used instruments, their prices, and descriptions. Ask for the latest catalogs by calling (517) 372-7890.

The idea for this extraordinary institution occurred in Ann

The staff of Elderly Instruments, all musicians, pose out front with a collection of vintage Gibson guitars, made in Kalamazoo. Elderly slowly built a national reputation for traditional acoustic instruments and recorded music and instructional materials. 1993 photo.

Arbor, at the open-mike nights at The Ark, the now-legendary folk-music coffeehouse. There Sharon McInturff met graduate student and banjo player Stan Werbin. A chance purchase of a guitar at a yard sale prompted them to think about starting a business selling used acoustic instruments (hence the "Elderly" name). But a store already occupied that niche in Ann Arbor, so they moved to East Lansing and, in 1972, set up shop in a tiny space across from the Michigan State University campus. They couldn't afford to stock much, but they would order anything — and at a discount. Werbin hailed from the aggressive business environment of New York City, so discounts were natural to him.

Although the popularity of folk music had waned just about everywhere since the boom years of the late '50s and early '60s, a solid core of folk fans and performers still existed, thanks to a number of popular festivals and a small but active coffeehouse circuit. Many local performers like Sally Rogers and Joel Mabus, M.S.U. undergraduates who went on to become well-known folk singers and musicians, inspired enthusiasm by teaching at Elderly and performing on or near campus.

Without a big local market, members of Lansing's growing folk community had to organize for themselves volunteer-run coffeehouses in churches and on campus. Thus developed an active folk community, less vulnerable to shifting mass-market taste than audiences attracted by big trends in entertainment.

Interest in folk music increased in the Lansing area as the boom ceased nationally. Elderly grew in its own grassroots way. By 1975, the big folk-oriented music stores were fading, and Elderly was well positioned to introduce a mail-order catalog and become a dominant force in the shrunken field of folk.

1100 N. Washington one block south of Grand River and a mile north of downtown Lansing. (517) 372-7880. Mail order phone (Mon-Fri 9-5): (517) 372-7890. Store hours: Mon-Wed 11-7, Thurs 11-9, Fri & Sat 10-6.

ANOTHER ENTREE TO LANSING'S LIVELY ALTERNATIVE CULTURE . . . . . can be found at some of the shops on the friendly block of **East Michigan Avenue between Clemens and Fairview**, about 1 1/2 miles east of the capitol. In the early 20th century, these small storefronts were geared around a streetcar stop on the busy car line between Lansing and East Lansing. Today their attractive off-campus rents and convenient location have attracted an interesting variety of stores. They make for great browsing. Many are open daily, including Sundays, and evenings: the **Hearthstone Community Bakery**/restaurant. **Wolf Moon Food Co-op**, the delightfully old-fashioned **Gnome Sweet Shoppe**, and **Capital City Comics and Books** (good prices on good books). Stores with shorter hours include several worthwhile resale shops, Raupp Campfitters, and a women's bookstore.

Michigan State University museums and more

Natural history, art, Michigan history, folklife, astronomy – all are presented to the general public with intelligence and enthusiasm.

Compared with universities that have had over a century's worth of archaeological and natural history expeditions, Michigan State hasn't received the rare artifacts, unusual specimens, donations of art, or bequests that build up the most prestigious museum collections over generations. Up through World War II, Michigan State's alumni body was made up mainly of farmers, teachers, and such — not lines of work likely to result in gifts of magnificent buildings or choice libraries of rare books to the old alma mater.

But what M.S.U.'s museums lack in accumulations of rare and costly possessions, they usually make up in spirit — a real excitement about teaching and an enthusiasm for reaching out and connecting up with the everyday experience of the general public. M.S.U. museums are unusually well suited for family outings with children.

MICHIGAN STATE UNIVERSITY MUSEUM is M.S.U.'s many-sided museum of natural science, history, folk life, paleontology, and anthropology. Some of its over 2 million objects and specimens are stored in an entire sub-basement beneath Spartan Stadium, while the museum building itself is relatively small. Museum exhibits are rigorously selected to pack a lot of interesting material into a compact space. No other museum in Michigan has quite its knack for choosing themes and details that put visitors in touch with who we are in Michigan, where we are in the world, and where we come from.

On the first floor, **Heritage Hall** has small dioramas of Michigan logging camps and locks, a fishing wharf, forts and copper mines, along with appealing, authentically detailed life-sized recreations of a country kitchen, a general store, and a fur-trading post. A shed houses a 1904 Oldsmobile curved-dash runabout, the world's first popular-priced car, which turned

Lansing into a center of the auto industry. The interesting **Special Exhibits Gallery** generally highlights folk culture: the likes of African-American quilts, or Finnish saunas, or duck blinds and decoys.There's a good, small **gift shop**.

Upstairs, seven North American habitats, from forests to grasslands, tropics to tundra, are wonderfully represented in huge dioramas in **Habitat Hall**. Sweeping scenes with large animal specimens, and tiny insects and plants make it fun to examine these in detail. The hall's central area has two complete skeletons of the North American dinosaurs, allosaurus and stegosaurus. Changing major exhibits in the **East and West Galleries** include natural and cultural history topics related to Michigan.

On the lower level, the **Discovery Theater** offers well-chosen films, often on nature or Michigan history. **The Hall of Evolution** does a good job of illustrating every geological time period with scenes and samples of animal and plant fossils formed in that time. **The Hall of World Cultures** has colorful, interesting displays of artifacts from different cultures: shadow puppets from Java, swords from many cultures, the ritual uses of African masks, and South American clothing. The **Great Lakes Indians Gallery** features changing exhibits on woodlands Indian culture. *On West Circle Drive on the old part of the campus. Call (517) 355-2370 for directions, information on classes, activities, exhibits. Open Mon-Fri 9-5, Thurs until 9, Sat 10-5, Sun 1-5. Handicapped accessible. Free; donations welcome. Metered visitor parking in front, sometimes scarce.*

THE KRESGE ART MUSEUM, select and intimate, makes up in clever presentation what its collection lacks in depth. Highlights are wide-ranging: Zurbaran's dramatic "Vision of St. Anthony," G. Mennen and Nancy Williams' collection of African art, and a gigantic 1967 color-field canvas by Morris Louis. The introductory gallery of Greek through medieval art has a wonderful way of getting you to really look at individual small objects. *Just east of Collingwood and Farm Lane on the old part of the M.S.U. campus. Call (517) 355-7631 for directions, changing exhibits, special events. School-year hours: weekdays except Thurs 9:30-4:30, Thurs 12-8, weekends 1-4. Summer hours: weekdays 11-4, weekends 1-4. Closed Thanksgiving vacation, mid-Dec.-early Jan., Easter, Mem. Day and July 4 weekend, and for a month during the summer (call the museum to check dates; in*

1994, closed mid-June thru mid-July). Handicapped accessible. Free admission, donations appreciated. Limited visitor parking in front of museum.

ABRAMS PLANETARIUM. Enthusiastic presenters and top-notch projectors in the 150-seat auditorium make planetarium shows a popular form of entertainment for area families. Astronomy exhibits in the black light gallery are open weekdays (8:30-4:30), and before regular weekend shows. *Call (517) 355-4672 for this week's* **program**, *directions. At the corner of Shaw Lane and Science, south of the Red Cedar River.Look for the dome just east of Farm Lane. Show times: Fri & Sat 8 p.m., Sun 4 p.m. Special shows for children at 2:30 Sun. Adults $3, students $2.50, kids 12 and under $2. Starline (star-gazing info on this week's skies): (517) 332-STAR.*

THE DAIRY STORE. Students in the M.S.U. dairy program manufacture and sell their own ice cream, yogurt, and cheeses right here. If you come by at the right time, you can look through the plate-glass window and watch. Students love the generous cones of rich ice cream; black cherry is a special favorite. Wierdest item: chocolate cheese (it's something like a dairy-based fudge), developed for kids who won't drink their milk. Major renovations for plant and store start in September, 1994. *On the west side of Farm Lane just south of Shaw Lane and the Abrams Planetarium. (517) 353-1663 (info line), (517) 355-8466 (dairy store). Mon-Fri 10-6, Sat noon-5. Free group tours need 2 weeks' notice, minimum of 10.*

CANOE THE RED CEDAR THROUGH CAMPUS . . . . . and up to the dam at Okemos or (if you portage around a dam) down to Potter Park. The **M.S.U. canoe livery,** also known as the Red Cedar Yacht Club, is behind Bessey Hall at Farm Lane. (517) 355-3397.

VISITOR PARKING ON CAMPUS. . . . . is easy if you're willing to walk from two convenient **visitor lots** just south of the Red Cedar River. The Spartan Stadium lot at the very east end of Kalamazoo Street has a manned booth. It's a short, pretty walk to the Beal Garden across a foot bridge or the Kalamazoo Street bridge. Another lot is on Farm Lane at Shaw, in front of the Planetarium. On weekends, spaces along the circle drives can often be found.

GOOD BOOKS, FINE CRAFTS, AND GREAT PINBALL . . . . . are in downtown East Lansing across from Michigan State University, along Grand River and Albert, one block behind it. M.A.C. Avenue (it stands for "Michigan Agricultural College") is a connecting spine. Though still overwhelmingly oriented to undergraduates, with the predictable CD stores, fast food and ice cream shops, and bars, downtown is more interesting than it was five years ago. In comparison with hubs of sophistication like Birmingham and Ann Arbor, there's a "we try harder" friendliness about East Lansing that's refreshing, but high rents have hurt the area's interest value, pushing more creative businesses to areas like East Michigan Avenue (page 420).

Retail standouts along M.A.C. include **Brother Gambit** (leather and wood crafts and jewelry, 517-351-0825), **Campbell's Smoke Shop** (an old-fashioned tobacco shop with candy, knives, and gadgets, too, 517-332-4269), the original **Pinball Pete's** (Michigan's biggest and best games arcade, also with lovingly maintained pinball machines and bargain pop; the entrance is around the corner on Albert, 517-337-2544), and **Mackerel Sky Gallery of Contemporary Craft** in the diagonal row of stores facing Albert (517-351-2211).

Just east of M.A.C. in the 300 block of East Grand River, the **Curious Used Book Shop** (517-332-0112) appealingly blends serious reading, comics, science fiction, sports memorabilia, and all sorts of old magazines and printed ephemera; **Jacobson's** department store at 333 E. Grand River (517-351-2550) has a second-floor restaurant overlooking the campus. . . . . . **In Flight** at 507 E. Grand River (517-351-8100) combines Hackey Sacks and Frisbees with alternative clothing and Grateful Dead stuff. . . . . At 515 East Grand River, **Grand River Books** has moved in the big space where Jocundry's Books used to be. Upstairs, in greatly expanded gallery quarters, **Prints Ancient and Modern** has moved from its small space on M.A.C. 517-336-6366. . . . . Still farther south, near Taco Bell, the second-story space of 541 East Grand River houses a changing but interesting collection of offbeat businesses. The mainstay here is **FBC** (formerly Flat, Black & Circular), an excellent used CD store (517-351-0838). *A great deal of attended parking in ramps and lots along Albert means you needn't worry about getting a ticket. Many downtown stores open Sunday afternoons and Thurs & Fri evenings.*

FIRST SUNDAYS IN EAST LANSING . . . . . are something of an **arts open house** at various stores, museums, and restaurants. It's featured in a handy monthly **cultural calendar** available at Brother Gambit, Mackerel Sky, and elsewhere.

ANIMAL BARNS ARE OPEN TO THE PUBLIC. . . . . Involving the public is a tradition that goes back to M.S.U.'s roots as Michigan Agricultural College and the oldest land-grant college. South of Mount Hope Road, much of the vast campus is devoted to animal husbandry. Visitors are welcome to stop by the barns any day, look at the animals, and ask questions of the staff.

W.J. Beal Botanical Gardens and M.S.U. campus plantings

At America's first college of scientific agriculture,
a gorgeous campus combines beauty and learning
in a demonstration landscape.

Curving drives and Collegiate Gothic buildings in a park-like setting full of stately trees and flowering shrubs — the older part of Michigan State University's campus fits the popular image of what a college should look like. Huge beeches and some gnarled white oaks over 200 years old are between the Student Union and Beaumont Tower, just south of Grand River Avenue along West Circle Drive. Students walk to class through what has become a true arboretum over the years, with some 8,000 varieties of woody plants. Among M.S.U.'s huge, 42,000-student undergraduate population, appreciation of the gardens, the majestic trees, and the beautiful displays of lilacs, azaleas, and viburnum is surprisingly widespread — partly because the tucked-away nooks of the Beal Botanical Garden and the winding paths along the Red Cedar River are popular trysting spots.

Campus plantings here have been a central part of the institution's mission for well over a hundred years. Michigan State started in 1857 as the first U.S. agricultural college to teach scientific agriculture. The campus has long been regarded as a great outdoor laboratory for teaching, research, and observation. Horticulture, botany, and landscape architecture classes take advantage of the campus display of the widest possible variety of trees, shrubs, and woody vines suited to this climate. Very few planted environments in the Middle West have enjoyed such sustained commitment by faculty and staff, over almost a century and a half.

Highlights of campus plantings include:

◆ **The Beal Botanical Garden**, an outdoor museum of living plants arranged by family and by use. See plants used for dyes, flavorings, and perfumes, along with flowering plants good for honeybees, and select landscaping and vegetable species.

Exotic flowering landscape specimens have been planted on slopes descending from the gazebo entrance on West Circle Drive. Brick clay for the campus's first buildings was dug from this bank. Below is a flat, sunken expanse of the garden, where specimen plants and signs march like columns of soldiers in rows of regular squares of soil. The signs, well written and informative, are a big part of what makes visiting the garden so enjoyable.

One section focuses on plants that are common weeds — weeds that invade field crops, plants that foul up agricultural machinery, even poison ivy, neatly staked and marked with a red sign of warning. There are plants used in modern pharmaceuticals; cotton, flax, hemp, and other fiber plants; and plants used as food by Indians — all described as to origin, use, and culture.

By a charming **goldfish pond** around behind the library, there are benches and a plaque commemorating botany professor William James Beal, his 50 years of service to Michigan

The Beal Botanical Garden is an outdoor museum of plants, neatly arranged and labeled according to use (pharmaceuticals, herbs, dyes, etc.), family, or, in the case of noxious weeds, according to problem. The beautifully landscaped valley setting by the Red Cedar River attracts many non-botanists, too.

Agricultural College (as M.S.U was known into the 1920s), and his pioneering experiments in hybridizing corn. In 1873 Beal established this garden. According to the staff, the Beal Garden is "the oldest continuously operating botanical garden" in the U.S. *Look for the entrance **gazebo** by the IM Sports Building on West Circle Drive, not too far from the Beal Entrance off Michigan Avenue. A box along the walk usually contains a **free brochure** about the gardens, with map and botanical lists. (517) 355-9582. No charge. Guided group tours ($1/adults; 50¢/child) can be arranged in advance.*

◆ **The azalea and rhododendron garden** has soil adapted to acid-loving plants. Its displays are spectacular from late April through May and even into June. *By the music school just north of the Beal Garden across West Circle Drive.*

◆ **Landscaping groupings and collections of dogwoods, viburnums, and clematis.** These beautiful paths with their secret nooks show the lush, sensuous effects that can be achieved with screens and ground covers in narrow, shady spaces. The display of spring bulbs and early-blooming woody plants begins in March and gets into high gear from mid-April through May and early June. *Behind and alongside the IM Sports Building just west of the Beal Garden.*

◆ **The old Horticulture Gardens** are gorgeous in spring because of all the lilacs and flowering crabs around the pool. But the expanding Horticulture Department has moved everything else to a new location that's nearly three times as large. *On East Circle Drive at the northern end of Farm Lane.*

◆ **The Botany Teaching Greenhouses** contain plants used to teach M.S.U. botany classes. Inside are a **tropical rainforest room**, complete with mountain waterfall and stream; a **desert house**; and a **butterfly house** aflutter with activity. Interpretive labels tell you a lot about what you're looking at.

◆ **The new Horticulture Demonstration Gardens** are so extensive and so spectacular, even in fall and winter, that they deserve their own chapter. See page 429.

The campus has been planted to be attractive at all seasons, and it is. Early bulbs and flowering witch hazel are out in March, followed by a panoply of flowering shrubs and vines, plus annuals, that extend the season up to frost. The dramatic grasses in the new Horticulture Demonstration Gardens look good well into winter. Fall color and winter bark textures and branch forms are important considerations in plant selection.

Plant-lovers could get a good horticultural education just by studying campus plantings on a series of fine days throughout the year. Many campus plants are labeled; some have excellent explanatory signs for gardeners about which varieties to choose and what plant materials go well together. **"Campus Plantings,"** a map and complete guide to 15 shrub and tree collections and 200 individual specimens, is available from Campus Park and Planning, 412 Olds Hall, M.S.U., East Lansing, MI 48824.

Michigan State has such a splendid campus because it has long been one of the nation's premiere colleges of agriculture. Credit goes to the enlightened Michigan farmers who in 1849 began lobbying for a state college to promote modern agriculture. The University of Michigan in Ann Arbor and Michigan Normal in Ypsilanti both wanted the new agriculture school, but its farmer backers insisted on an autonomous college. They chose as its site 677 acres of forest five miles east of the new state capital in Lansing, conveniently located just south of the old plank road to Detroit (now Grand River Avenue).

Michigan's agriculture leaders became important backers of the 1862 Morrill Act. It established land-grant colleges to be funded by sales of federal lands and geared toward broad-based, practical education and public service for all levels of society. Michigan State and Pennsylvania State share honors as the first land-grant colleges.

For many decades, manual labor, three hours a day, was expected of all students — part of the hands-on laboratory approach which also enabled poor students to afford a college education.

A BEAUTIFUL, LEAFY PATH . . . . . for walking, biking, and jogging runs along the south side of the Red Cedar River almost the entire length of the campus, from the Kellogg Center on Harrison Road past the statue of "Sparty," the M.S.U. Spartan, to Hagadorn Road.

M.S.U. Horticultural Demonstration Gardens

Plants and designers work their magic
to create a delightful floral environment
and a fun introduction for kids to the world of plants.

Many people who loved Michigan State University's old Horticultural Gardens were concerned that brand-new gardens would lack the wonderful mood and atmosphere of the ones on East Circle Drive among picturesque Collegiate Gothic buildings. However, charming as they were, the old gardens were crammed into just three acres, and too far from the bleak-looking Plant and Soil Sciences Building and labs that house most horticulture and landscape classes.

Even after a killing frost, with most of the flowers gone and with many perennials and woody plants far from mature, the new gardens create a striking environment, thanks largely to the great sprays of ornamental grasses, by fall turned golden and reddish, and to the verticality and dramatic background texture they had grown to provide in just two and a half years. Up to 10 and 12 feet tall and four feet across, they are planted in islands as large-scale background foils for detailed, small foreground plantings. Michigan gardeners will find lots of ideas for new plants and plant combinations here.

A good deal of garden architecture – pergolas, gazebos, arbors, topiary frames, even an artificial hill – is required to enliven a part of the M.S.U. campus that is flat and rectilinear.

There's so much to see here, repeat visits, and at different times in the growing season, are in order. To help plan your visits so you won't miss tucked-away areas, here's a checklist and brief description of the garden complex.

◆ **Parking** and **entrance pavilion** off Bogue south of Wilson Road. Parking surrounds the **floral peacock**, 14 feet high. The body, built on a frame stuffed with packaging peanuts and eight to 12 inches of dirt, is planted in begonias and ageratum. Colorful annuals make up the 35-foot tail along the ground.

First, get your useful gardens map (and your weekday parking token) at the **Visitor Information Center** just inside the side wing of the Plant and Soil Sciences Building to the right of the round entrance pavilion. A select garden bookshop is inside, with free information on special **gardening programs** and classes for the general public. **Sparty's Greenhouse** (517-353-3770), run by horticulture students and open Mondays through Fridays from 8:30 to 5:30, is in this building; ask for directions.

◆ The **4-H Children's Garden**, alongside the parking area, is such a novelty it seems sure to become a popular regional attraction. Gardens relate to plant themes – 55 in all – designed with kids' interests and questions in mind. The **Pizza Garden** shows the herbs used in America's favorite school lunch. The **Sense-a-tional Garden** appeals to all the senses, with plants like aromatic ginger and luffa sponges. There's a **pharmacy garden**, a **perfume garden**, and a "small world" globe around which radiate gardens growing important foods for various parts of the world. An **African-American garden** grows plants used in Africa and plants introduced from Africa to America (including hibiscus, okra, black-eyed peas, watermelon, and cucumbers).

Everything is sized for children, and there are no "NO" signs. This type of children's garden is a first on any college campus. Children can wind through a maze, dance on chimes, and swing a gate that makes frogs in a pond spit water. Topiary teddy bears grow on frames designed by the topiary maker for the movie *Edward Scissorhands*. Group tours and workshops are most welcome. Call (517) 355-0348. *Open April through October. Free.*

◆ The **Idea Gardens** are another small area of specialty gardens, just west of the 4-H Children's Garden on the south edge of the main perennial garden. Volunteer master gardeners tend themed plots: vegetables, companion planting, cacti, herbs, plants for special needs children, and butterfly-attracting herbs.

◆ The **DeLapa Perennial Garden**, already described, is behind the large, round entrance pavilion. Don't miss the water lilies by the pond. In back, to the west, **Frank's Nursery and Crafts Rose Garden** includes the latest All-America Rose selections and hundreds of other roses. (Outside financial support from individuals and institutions has permitted the Horticultural Gardens' grand expansion by drawing on additional funds.)

◆ The large and impressive **Carter Annual Trial Garden** is easy to miss. From the rose gardens, take the axial path north between the Teaching Greenhouses and the Pesticide Research

Center. Past the houses, you'll come to a fountain and sunken garden. From here to the distant pool, over a thousand varieties of bedding plants are at their best in July and August. Among them are the **All-American Selection Trial Garden**, part of a nationwide program to test seed companies' new flowers in different climates, and **Fleuro Select**, European selections on trial.

Visitors are welcome to look inside the **teaching greenhouses,** full of student horticulture projects. They're open weekdays, 8 a.m.-4:30 p.m.

Gardeners are well advised to bring cameras and notebooks; these gardens are full of examples of plant varieties and planting combinations that will work well in many Michigan yards.

On the southeast side of the Michigan State campus, south of Wilson Rd. off Bogue St., one street east of Farm Lane. Enter off Bogue just north of the railroad tracks to find inexpensive visitor parking. Open from April through October, dawn to dusk. Free admission. Guided tours $1/adult, 50¢/student. Call (517) 355-0348 to arrange.

A SURPRISING ALL-SEASONS WORLD OF TEXTURES AND SHAPES . . . . . can be explored just south and across the railroad tracks from the Horticultural Demonstration Gardens. On the site of the old campus nursery, the **Clarence E. Lewis Landscape Arboretum** creates some wonderful effects. "In springtime the redolent trail through the flowering magnolias, viburnums, and witch hazels accentuates a spectacle of pastels," writes Victoria McArec. "Dogwoods, crabapples, and spireas offer their characteristic white, pink, or purple blooms. During summer, compare and contrast foliar textures and numerous shades of green. Yellow, red and russet tones abound in the fall. . . . . In the wintertime, the prominent forms of deciduous trees and shrubs stand out against a backdrop of snow-laden evergreens."

Bring a headset tape player to replace the sounds of auto traffic with classical music, and the arboretum can seem like a little piece of heaven. *Park off Bogue just south of the tracks.*

Chapter 6
West Michigan

HIGHLIGHTS

For restaurants and lodgings, see *Hunts' Restaurants & Lodgings of Michigan*

INTRODUCTION

West Michigan

While West Michigan is best known for its sand dunes and sugar-sand beaches, its history and development have been greatly influenced by a strong Dutch subculture. Holland and Grand Rapids form the center of the conservative Dutch-American subculture, which has a strong work ethic and a deep streak of cleanliness and environmentalism. Unlike the auto plants' history of bitter labor relations on the other side of the state, labor relations around here are generally quite good. Before participatory work practices were in vogue, they were already being practiced here.

Locally-owned companies have prospered and grown into internationally-known firms. Steelcase and Herman Miller have two of the most respected management cultures in the country. A Holland High School shop teacher founded Haworth in his basement and developed it into a major office furniture manufacturer. The Meijer family has successfully pioneered the dual grocery/discount store business. Donnelly and Prince have become major auto parts suppliers. Amway took direct sales to a new worldwide level. All have contributed much in the way of civic improvements to their home towns.

Ethical principles are discussed more here than most other places because many people have had a rigorous religious education. Many business leaders come from Holland's Hope College (affiliated with the Reformed Church of America) or Grand Rapids' Calvin College (run by the Christian Reformed Church). Grand Rapids is also the U.S. center of religious publishing. Its four religious publishers include Zondervaan, the world's largest.

❶ Gerald Ford Museum. Lavish, superbly executed tribute to Grand Rapids' native son. Reformer Ford defeated a GOP party boss in 1948.

❷ Amway Grand Plaza. Posh union of old and new, West Michigan's top hotel has several excellent restaurants, two floors of fine shops.

❸ John Ball Zoo. Dramatic hilly setting gives this splendid zoo an inviting atmosphere. See mirthful otters, monkey hill from above.

❹ Ed's Breads. Marvelous East European breads. Stands out in a state with many good ethnic bakeries.

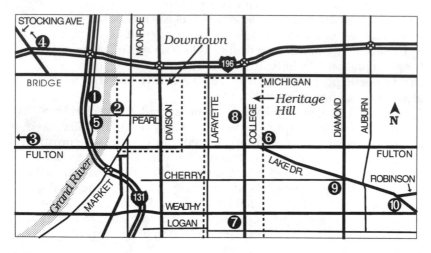

❺ Public Museum. Impressive building; all-new exhibits.

❻ Heritage Hill. Grand Rapids' elite residential area from 1840s to 1920s. Many architectural styles and detailing for the city's style- and craftsmanship-conscious business leaders.

❼ Meyer May House. Frank Lloyd Wright architecture at its best. Meticulous restoration makes this a must see.

❽ Voigt House. Victorian house with all the trappings

❾ Gaia Coffeehouse. The real thing, where the spirit of the counterculture lives on. Nearby **Heartwood antiques** has select furniture from Arts & Crafts and 1950s modernist eras.

❿ Eastown.

Highlights of
Grand Rapids

0   1/2   1
          mile

Gerald R. Ford Museum

*This superb museum vividly shows
the highs and lows of the short, eventful presidency
of Grand Rapids' native son.*

This is one of Michigan's very most interesting museums, and it also has a striking setting — on the western bank of the wide Grand River across from downtown Grand Rapids. The building is effectively monumental. The many permanent displays about Ford are outstanding. They're visually arresting, informative without being taxing.

Gerald Ford was only president for two and a half years, but he enjoyed a rich political career and confronted a number of important challenges as president. The display on Ford's fateful 1974 decision to pardon Nixon includes some of the many letters of outrage Ford subsequently received. Another fine exhibit uses once-classified intelligence reports to give a detailed account of the dramatic Mayaguez incident, during which Ford ordered Marines to recapture a pirated U.S. vessel. Ford's 1976 loss to Jimmy Carter, when he came from 20 percentage points behind and almost beat the Georgia governor, is colorfully documented. Betty Ford's courage and candor as First Lady is also nicely captured on a wall filled with photos, text, and memorabilia.

The quonset hut that served as Gerald Ford's campaign headquarters in 1948 reflects the modest means of the young candidate for Congress. Ford staged an upset victory over the entrenched machine-backed incumbent.

The museum's most popular display is the full-size **replica of the Oval Office** in the White House, just as it looked while Ford was president. It effectively gives the visitor a sense of what it's like to be in that room, known to intimidate even seasoned politicians. Just as arresting are the **showcases of gifts** from visiting dignitaries. There are big, brightly painted floor vases from the Chinese, a diamond-crested bird of solid gold on a silver tree from the Sultan of Oman, a dazzling ivory and gold bejeweled sword from General Suharto of Indonesia, and many other gifts.

Changing exhibits deal with topics related to the presidency. A sampling: Gifts from Russia (through Oct. 24, 1994), Presidential Portraits (Nov. 1-Jan. 16) and First Ladies' Gowns (Jan. 23-April 30, 1995).

Every hour, a **28-minute film** on Gerald Ford's life and presidency is presented in the comfortable auditorium. A small **gift shop** is tightly focused on presidential items, including real campaign buttons ($3 each, both parties), postcards of past presidents and their wives, lots of inexpensive souvenirs for kids, and many books (some autographed) by and about Ford.

North side of Pearl Street on the west bank of the Grand River; another entrance is off Bridge. From U.S. 131, take Pearl St exit 31B. Less than 1/2 mile by foot from downtown via a pedestrian bridge behind Welsh Auditorium and the Amway Grand Plaza. By car, take the Pearl Street bridge west and turn right, or take the Michigan Ave./ Bridge St. bridge and turn left. (616) 451-9263; Mon-Sat 9-4:45; Sun 12-4:45. adults $2, seniors $1.50, children under 16 free.

NEAR THE FORD MUSEUM . . . . . Ah-Nab-Awen Bicentennial Park in front of the Gerald Ford Museum is pleasantly open to the sky and cityscape. It's studded with interesting landscape features and sculptures, including a fountain and a giant button children can climb through. The interconnected, curved walkways are favored by strollers, dog-walkers, and joggers. A **pedestrian bridge** (a former interurban trestle, actually) lets you cross the Grand in leisure, look down at the water, and walk over to downtown and the Riverwalk behind the Grand Center complex. . . . . . Nearly every summer weekend the park hosts an **ethnic festival** with food and performances, or some other event. Call (616) 459-8629 for this week's events. *Along the west bank of the Grand from Bridge St. to Pearl. Park in Ford Museum's Pearl St. parking lot.*

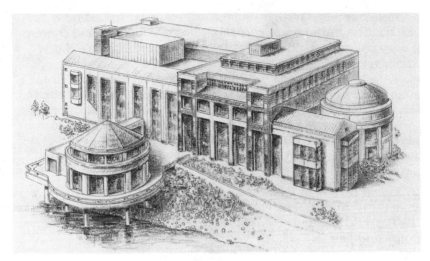

Van Andel Museum Center/ Public Museum of Grand Rapids

Grand Rapids has a fancy new home for its 150-year-old museum. It's billed as "a $35 million world-class education/entertainment center" and named after Amway's co-founder.

It's impossible to say much about the new version of Grand Rapids' excellent and venerable Public Museum because the exhibits are said to be "all new" and the museum isn't open yet. The projected opening date is November 19, 1994. All our guidebook can do is to quote a museum PR person on the new museum's exhibits and mention that the museum has 150 years worth of great stuff to use in its new exhibits. It has prepared many exceptionally intelligent and interesting exhibits in the past few decades.

"Exhibits exploring and celebrating West Michigan's history and natural environment" are featured in the new museum. "'The Furniture City' tells the story of the furniture industry. A re-creation of an early line-drive factory shows the working conditions of furnituremakers. **'Grand Rapids 1890s'** recreates Grand Rapids before the turn of the century. The horse and trolley from our [old] Gaslight Village will reappear in this new exhibit. The **'Anishinabek'** exhibit displays historic and contemporary objects depicting the culture of West Michigan's Native Americans.

"Also on exhibit will be a dramatic 76-foot whale skeleton suspended from the ceiling of the galleria, reminiscent of the way it was presented in the lobby of the old museum until the early 1970s. A fully restored, operating **1928 Spillman Carousel** makes its debut in the pavilion built out over the river."

The museum center will have a **gift shop** and a museum **cafe**.

272 Pearl St. NW at Front Avenue, on the Grand River across Pearl from the Gerald R. Ford Presidential Museum. From U.S. 131, take the Pearl St. exit and go east a block. (616) 456-3966. Call for hours and fees.

TAKEOUT FOR A PICNIC in Ah-Nab-Awen or John Ball parks . . . . . Get sandwiches and soups from the Choo-Choo Grill, Plainfield at Leonard,, fried fish and coleslaw from the Flying Bridge fish store across Leonard from the Choo-Choo, or Mexican sandwiches from Maggie's Kitchen (page 441).

MINOR LEAGUE BASEBALL HAS COME TO WEST MICHIGAN . . . . . A Class A affiliate of the Oakland Athletics, the **West Michigan Whitecaps** play at Old Kent Park in Comstock Park just north of Grand Rapids. Tickets ($3-$6) are available through Ticketmaster or at the park, off U.S. 131 on West River Drive. Call (800) 227-7946 (within area code 616 only) or (616) 451-6166.

FOR EVENTS IN AND AROUND GRAND RAPIDS . . . . . call the Convention and Visitors' Bureau **Funline,** (616) 459-8629. It covers one week at a time. An **events calendar** for a six-month period can be requested along with other visitor information from the Convention & Visitors Bureau, (616) 459-8287. . . . . . For monthly arts events and news, look for a copy of *On-the-Town* magazine at hotels and nightspots.

Ed's Breads and ethnic westside Grand Rapids

Good food and good deals if you know where to look

Hardly anyone thinks of Grand Rapids as a rich multi-ethnic city, so strong is its image as the epicenter of America's conservative Dutch Reformed subculture. But it is, and people who know where to look will be rewarded with good, authentic ethnic food at popular prices. Mexican-Americans live in many parts of the city. There are substantial Asian communities. African-Americans dominate the near southeast side, and west of the Grand is the home turf of Lithuanians, Ukrainians, Germans, Latvians, more than a few American Indians, and enough Poles to pay for St. Adalbert's, a splendid domed, multi towered basilica church as big as many European cathedrals. Seen from the freeway coming over the Grand's east bluff, it's a memorable sight.

The commercial district around Bridge and Stocking is the most obvious ethnic area, home to Polish and Mexican bakeries, two Mexican groceries, and Mexican and Polish restaurants. But the place with the widest following – the *only* place on the west side besides the zoo that attracts many suburbanites from Cascade and Ada – is a small bakery on Leonard Street on the northwest side.

◆ **Ed's Breads.** Ed's outstanding traditional East European breads are dense and flavorful, especially the sourer doughs, like the fabulous Latvian rye. At $1.75 to $2.50 for a big loaf, the breads here are a terrific value, and very good. So are the cookies, sweet-rolls, and rolls. Basics here, baked daily, are the huge, 2 1/4-pound loaf of Polish rye ($2.50), a staple with the German, Polish, and Lithuanian westsiders, and a 2 1/2-pound whole wheat loaf, popular with the co-op buyers. These are heavy, nutritious breads, truly the staff of life. A loaf of Ed's Bread "passes the bam test," a baker said with pride. "You lay it down on the counter and it goes, 'Bam!'"

Customers from all walks of life, from all over Grand Rapids and as far as Muskegon and Holland, come here regularly for their favorites like cream cheese-raisin bread (baked on Wednesdays in limited quantities) and bacon-onion rolls called bundukies (Saturdays).

Founder Ed Parauka first baked and improved his Lithuanian and Polish grandmothers' recipes in his basement. When he got them right, he opened this shop. Eventually a baker's long hours got to Ed, and he quit for a career installing industrial waste-water treatment systems. His onetime assistant and successor, Kathryn Kelly, has continued and improved on his tradition. Now that she is the mother of two, the baking staff has expanded to include her husband, John, and Marci Frace and Barb Rankin. Their hand-rolled loaves are made without preservatives, rolling machines, yeast stabilizers, or any of the modern inventions that enable bakers to easily turn out consistent products despite variations in temperature and humidity. Traditional baking is "more by instinct and experience — more alchemy," Kelly says cheerfully. It's more time-consuming but more challenging, almost an art.

Here, for your convenience, is Ed's weekly schedule of specialty breads. *Come early in the day for best selection.* Load up on bread for your freezer on your way home. You won't be sorry.

Tuesday: health bread, sourdough French bread.
Wednesday: cream cheese-raisin, Latvian rye, oatmeal-honey bread.
Thursday: pumpernickel, sourdough French, health and potato bread.
Friday: Lithuanian rye, oatmeal-honey, hotdog and hamburger buns, Parker House rolls.
Saturday: bundukies, buns, Parker House rolls.

1204 Leonard on Grand Rapids' northwest side, just west of Garfield across from Burger King. Leonard is a major east-west artery on the north side. From U.S. 131, take the Leonard St. exit and go west one mile. From downtown, take Division to Leonard, then west. (616) 451-9100. Tues-Fri 8 a.m.-5:30 p.m., Sat 8-noon. (Customers welcome before 8, but baking may not be finished.)

◆ **Lewandoski Market**, *1107 Walker at Powers.* In a plain, inconspicuous neighborhood grocery, butcher-owner Vic Hill makes widely admired sausages: smoked kielbasa ($2.69/lb.); delicious, super-spicy pepperoni ($3.99); German-style wieners ($2.69); ring bologna ($2.39); and kiska (a Polish sausage made of buckwheat, pork, and blood; $2.29). From Ed's, go south on Garfield to Walker (the diagonal street), then left for two blocks. *(616) 454-2281. Tues-Fri 8-6, Sat to 5.*

Continue into town (southeast) on Walker, which turns into

Stocking. Where it intersects with Bridge is an aging commercial district busy with small-scale entrepreneurial activity. Turn right onto Bridge and stop at two Mexican markets.

◆ **El Matador Mercado,** *653 Stocking,* is a small retail outlet of El Matador Tortilla Company, now moved out of the neighborhood into a $3 million factory. Its corn chips are sold here in quantity, along with basics like masa (corn meal), salsa, many sizes of canned refried beans, chorizo, and a half-gallon of picante sauce for around $5. Hispanics are the fastest-growing segment of Grand Rapids' population, and Hispanic businesses have flourished. El Matador's founding family, Mike and Isabel Navarro, are among a dozen Mexican-American millionaires in the area. They came to western Michigan to pick celery after World War II. *(616) 454-2163.*

◆ **Moctezuma Mexican Food Products** and **Maggie's Kitchen,** *636 Bridge,* share a very large, bright space. It has all the basic Mexican groceries and exotic canned juices and Mexican soda pop. Frozen tamales come from Chicago. A full line of spices for Mexican cooking in institutional sizes is imported and distributed. The basement is full of Spanish-language videos and recordings and lots of bright piñatas. Maggie makes pastries (the sweet rolls look great on a plate and go well with coffee for breakfast) and a range of **tortas,** authentic Mexican sandwiches, for $3. Many are meal-size. Table seating now lets customers eat in. *(616) 458-8583. Open daily 9-7, Sunday 9-4.*

A nerve center of the West Side's huge Polish community is **American Bread,** a popular bakery (good enough, but no equal to Ed's) and lunch counter at 712 Bridge. While you're in the area, you might want to check out the **Bridge Street Antique Center** at 445 Bridge, a pleasant, well-organized mall with 15 to 20 dealers. (Closed Mondays.)

NEXT TO ED'S ON LEONARD STREET . . . . . a large, well-stocked used book shop, **The Book Gallery,** carries a general line that includes magazines. *(616) 459-4944. Open Tues-Fri 10-8, Sat 10-4.* . . . . . . Clean and well-organized, the **Tried and True Consignment Shop** on the corner is strong on women's and men's career and casual clothes. Now also carries furniture. *(616) 774-9052. Tues-Fri 10-6, Sat 10-4.*

John Ball Zoo

A gem of a zoo with a lush setting
and wonderful views of playful otters and monkeys.

What gives this medium-size zoo its powerful and memorable sense of place is the way it winds up the steep glacial hill that rises abruptly from the adjoining level park on the flat valley floor of Grand Rapids' west side. Most zoos are flat. This one is vertical. Animal exhibits are tucked into grotto-like areas built of rocky shelves, some natural, some artificial. The rest of the hillside is in a semi-wild, natural state, covered by shrubby growth and shaded by trees. A 60-foot waterfall emerges from the hillside. On a summer day, the place seems like a lush oasis rising above nearby streets of closely-spaced bungalows.

The zoo has been here for a hundred years. Its effect on visitors is dramatic, as if they are entering an enchanted realm as they wind their way up the hill.

The zoo has over 600 animals. There are black bears and zebras and exotic birds. Two sights stand out. There's a wonderful **display of otters** whose playful antics can be seen from above and below water, thanks to a glass-walled tank. At **Monkey Island,** an elevated boardwalk gives a spectacular view down onto a rocky hill over which a big band of monkeys cavorts.

The darkened **herpetarium** lets you see nocturnal animals like foxes, jungle cats, and bush babies, under conditions in which they are naturally active. Spaces for lions and tigers seem depressingly small to some visitors. Zoo director Brenda Stringer points out that lions in the wild "don't budge an inch unless they're hunting. They sleep 22 hours a day. A lot of what you do in zoo exhibits is for the visitor. Animals don't demand a natural setting. Our exhibit sizes are approved — we are an accredited zoo. We have been especially successful as far as health, breeding, and temperament of the big cats."

For the next several years the zoo is being expanded. Most construction is in 1994. The walkways have been reconfigured with more frequent rest areas and wheelchair turnouts. The first round of new exhibits are due to open in spring, 1995. A **Michigan northwoods stream**, visible indoors and out, will empty into the new bald eagle aviary. (Only hurt birds are confined to zoos.) Fish in the stream can be seen from all angles. In one place, zoo-goers are below the fish, looking up. The former greenhouse/aquarium/penguinarium has been demolished.

Also to open in spring of '95, the new **habitat immersion aquarium** will simulate the environment of the coastal Pacific northwest. Colorful saltwater fish, including leopard sharks, swim through an underwater kelp forest. Other parts have octopus, and a crashing wave creates a tidal pool where anemone and starfish can be seen.

The new **aquarium/penguinarium**, a concession/visitor plaza and an outdoor amphitheater are also due to open in spring, 1995. Then construction on the African exhibit starts, to be finished in 1996, followed by the great ape area in 1996-1997.

John Ball, pioneer, legislator, and lawyer, was one of the many people who came west to Michigan in the last century to speculate in land. A delightful bronze statue at the zoo entrance shows him as an old man with his children at his knees. It commemorates his gift of 40 acres to the city for a park. Today the **park** part of the 100-acre complex is a large, shady, flat expanse with **picnic facilities**, ball diamonds, playground, tennis courts, and some playful contemporary sculptures.

Fulton St. and Valley Ave., 1¹/₄ miles west of the Grand River. From U.S. 131, take the Fulton Street exit and go west. (616) 336-4300 (recording); (616) 336-4301 (office). Open daily 10 a.m.- 4 p.m. ('til 6 in summer), year-round, including holidays. Adults $3, children 5-13 and seniors $1.50, under 5 free. Strollers and wheelchairs available.

Built into a steep, wooded hillside, the John Ball Zoo even has a waterfall in its children's zoo.

SUMMER THEATER IN JOHN BALL PARK. . . . . is next door to the zoo at the **Circle Theatre.** Five **mainstage shows** (usually three musicals and two plays; tickets $10-$12.50) run from May through September, Wednesdays through Saturdays at 8, Sundays at 7. Three **children's shows** (tickets $3) run from June through August, Tuesday through Saturday at 10 a.m. and 12:30 p.m. Call (616) 456-6656 for program and ticket information.

Meyer May House

Serene and sublime, it's a remarkably complete example of Frank Lloyd Wright's famous Prairie Style.

Seeing photos of Wright interiors — or seeing objects he designed taken out of context — leaves people unprepared for the emotional impact of the places he designed. Wright was famed for designing total environments, including leaded glass and furniture. He worked with favorite craftspeople and dictated to his clients just what kind of pictures and ceramics his rooms should have.

The May House was designed for the owner of a Grand Rapids menswear store in 1908, the same year as Wright's famous Robie House in Chicago. Famed architectural historian Vincent Scully has called it the most beautifully and completely restored of any of Wright's Prairie houses; serene, and suffused by a gentle unity. "To come suddenly into that interior environment is an overwhelming experience. It is to be wholly caught up and carried along by something rarely experienced: absolute peace, integral order, deep quiet grandeur and calm — all of it achieved in a house of no more than moderate size, ... set in the typical grid pattern of the American town." It's a vivid testament to Wright's originality to see this house in the context of its more conventional Heritage Hill neighbors in their late Queen Anne, Craftsman, and Classical Revival styles.

The quiet generosity of Steelcase, the big Grand Rapids office furniture manufacturer, made this amazing restoration possible. Except for the kitchen, it almost duplicates the house's 1916 appearance. The ambitious project employed scholars and top local and national conservators and restoration craftsmen in everything from furniture and art glass to pottery and linen. With typical modesty, Steelcase officials never mention the cost. They say the restoration is honoring a debt to Wright. In his celebrated Johnson Wax Administration Building, Wright insisted on designing a total work environment, which was the beginning of the modern workstation, the bread and butter of today's office furniture manufacturers centered in and near Grand Rapids. Wright contracted with Steelcase to manufacture desks and chairs for Johnson Wax.

The Meyer May House may be unequaled in giving visitors a sense of the total environment designed by America's greatest architect. Meticulously restored by Steelcase, the 1908 house features the original Wright-designed furniture, leaded-glass windows, and lighting, plus the textiles, mural, and other accessories he chose.

Visitors on the 1¹/₂-hour tour first come to the visitor center in the house next door and watch an interesting **video** showing the Meyer May house before, during, and after restoration. It focuses on techniques and puts the house in historical context.

The top-notch **tour** effectively illuminates the rationale for Wright's design idiosyncrasies. He designed each house as a private family refuge. This house has a hidden entrance to the side. The deep balcony overhangs let occupants sit on porches in privacy. The bedroom ceilings, like little tents, work to promote a settled feeling of enclosed security. In contrast, downstairs ceiling and molding details emphasize the flow from room to room, and a sense of richly expansive vistas.

The **perennial flower garden** — a striking geometric design in bloom spring through fall — is behind the house off Logan. People are welcome to look at it any time.

450 Madison S.E. at Logan southeast of downtown Grand Rapids in the Heritage Hill historic district. Take Fulton, Cherry or Wealthy to Madison, turn south. From U.S. 131, take Wealthy St. (616) 246-4821. Tues & Thurs 10-2 (last tour begins at 1), Sun 1-5 (last tour begins at 4). Closed some Sundays; call ahead. Reservations required for groups of 10 or more. Free.

🌲🌲🌲

PUT TOGETHER A FRANK LLOYD WRIGHT TOUR . . . . . over four or five days, and you'll see a lot of interesting places along with the Master's own architecture. Grand Rapids is well situated for making a pleasant loop, via the relaxing Lake Michigan Carferry (see page 533). You'll meet Wright fans who have come from around the world to make this pilgrimage. Here are leading stops, and phone numbers so you can call for a brochure:

◆ **Taliesin** (608-588-7024). Wright's famous summer office/residence in his family's home turf at bucolic Spring Green on the Wisconsin River, an hour west of Madison in Wisconsin's beautiful Driftless Region. There, no glaciers filled up the deep valleys with glacial till, as they did in most of the Upper Midwest, including Michigan.

◆ The **Johnson Wax Building** and **Wingspread** (414-631-2154) in Racine, Wisconsin, an architecturally rich and underappreciated old industrial city on Lake Michigan. Call the local convention and visitor bureau at (414) 634-3293 for more on historic Racine. Its 19th-century density didn't suit Wright, who designed his masterpiece office building to ignore the handsome nearby factories of Milwaukee cream brick. The Wingspread conference center is in the former home of the Johnson CEO.

◆ **Oak Park, Illinois** offers many tours of Wright's buildings (including the Unity Temple and the studio/residence he used until 1909), Ernest Hemingway's boyhood home and museum, and other noteworthy buildings in this turn-of-the-century suburb just west of Chicago. Call (708) 848-1500 for a helpful brochure summarizing tour information.

Heritage Hill

Grand Rapids' historic neighborhood of superbly detailed homes is probably the richest and most varied in the U.S.

Heritage Hill is one of America's most extraordinary historic districts. It numbers hundreds of uniquely detailed houses in an amazing variety of styles — over 60, from Greek Revival and Gothic Revival of the 1840s to Arts and Crafts and Spanish Revival of the 1920s. As a manufacturing city with many locally owned businesses, Grand Rapids generated considerable wealth and wasn't shy about displaying it. Prominent families, including design-conscious owners of the city's famous furniture factories, built these hillside homes up and away from their factories' smoke.

The historic district is six blocks wide and nearly one and a half miles long. It rises up and along the crest of the hill east of downtown Grand Rapids. Nearly every street has uncommon and rare architecture to dazzle old-house fans: unusually heavy and ornately detailed Italianate doors and window caps; unaltered Stick Style cottages; rambling Shingle Style lodges; Chauteau-esque castles; and a most peculiar Queen Anne house constructed of logs for a rustic effect. The Hill has two **Frank Lloyd Wright houses** and one adapted from one of his *Ladies' Home Journal* plans for small, moderate-priced houses. Wright's Meyer May House (page 445) is one of the most authentically furnished Wright designs in existence.

From the 1840s into the 1920s, "the hill" remained Grand Rapids' residential area of choice — a long period for any prosperous American city. In many cities, the elite neighborhood of choice changed every generation — even more often in fast-growing boom towns like Detroit. By the time people could afford to build on the prestigious hill, they were already middle-aged and wealthy. Families competed in devising unusual details to distinguish their big residences. Grand Tours in Europe acquainted them with many prototypes, which were seldom literally copied. Especially on the hill's south end, developed after 1885 or so, you can see strange blends of architectural styles.

In the 1920s the Hill was supplanted as Grand Rapids' best

address by East Grand Rapids — part of the nation-wide retreat of the upper classes to less public life in the suburbs. By the 1950s the Hill had become an aging neighborhood. Here and in other similar neighborhoods in older cities elsewhere, historic streetscapes were being chewed away by urban renewal and neighboring hospitals, churches, and schools eager for parking and new building sites. Much of the prime block of College Avenue was wiped out. The threat to this nationally significant neighborhood prompted the Grand Rapids city council in 1970 to create one of the country's earliest and largest historic districts and a neighborhood support agency. For awhile, an innovative revolving fund enabled many houses to be renovated and sold without use of any public grant money.

Exploring any Heritage Hill street by foot is rewarding.

Houses of special historic or architectural interest are listed from northwest to southeast. * means you can look inside during business hours.

◆ **Rowe House.** *226 Prospect north of Lyon.* Prairie Style. Built from a 1907 Frank Lloyd Wright *Ladies' Home Journal* design as "A Fireproof House for $5,000."

◆ **230 Fountain** *just west of Lafayette.* 1872, Italianate, with 1894 Classic Revival modifications. The onion-domed garage (visible from Lafayette) shows the kind of detail lavished even on fences and accessory buildings on Heritage Hill. From 1907 to 1964 Edmund Booth of Booth Newspapers fame lived here.

◆ **Holt House.** *50 Lafayette.* 1886. Unusual house in fieldstone and shingles, with many inventive touches. Reminiscent of rambling Shingle Style summer cottages in New England.

◆ * **T. Stewart White House.** *427 E. Fulton.* 1907, Tudor Revival. A lumber baron built this house and installed a gold leaf dining room ceiling by Tiffany. Three sons became famous: Roderick White as a concert violinist, Gilbert White as a sculptor in Paris, and Stewart Edward White as a popular, nationally known writer of adventure stories. Drawing on his father's experiences, Stewart White chronicled Michigan lumberjacks and the early West. Gilbert painted murals in the house's library with scenes from King Arthur's court, using faces of family members. As Warren Hall, the building now houses **Davenport College of Business** offices. Call ahead (616-451-3511) to look at the murals.

◆ **264 College.** 1889 Queen Anne with eccentric log construction. Built by an architect as his own home.

One of the most remarkable collections of historic architectural styles in a single neighborhood, Heritage Hill might have been eaten away by demolition from land-hungry institutions if it weren't for the white-gloved efforts of Republican ladies like Barbara Roelofs (right) and Linda DeJong. They lobbied successfully for a historic district. A revolving fund restored this stately house, which had had an addition wrapped around it while it was a synagogue.

◆ **Gay House.** *422-426 E. Fulton.* 1883. Built for the co-founder of Berkey & Gay, Grand Rapids' leading furniture manufacturer in the early decades of its furniture boom, for $50,000 — then an astounding sum.

◆ **Sweet House/Women's City Club.** *254 Fulton.* The cast-iron fence and drooping camperdown elm in front of this 1860 Italian villa-style house were popular Victorian lawn accents. Its builder, lumberman Martin Sweet, was long the richest man in town, until the financial panic of 1893 ruined him. He died here in near poverty. Later the house became a music school attended by young Arnold Gingrich, who became *Esquire* magazine's brilliant founding editor. He set his 1935 novel, *Cast Down the Laurel*, in this house. Today it's a private women's club.

◆ * **Voigt House.** Overstuffed Victorian chateau with original furnishings, now a house museum. A rare look at all the accoutrements of a grand, public lifestyle. Its suffocating decor helps you understand what modernism was all about. See page 453.

♦ **Byrne/Hanchett House.** *125 College.* Circa 1891. Attractive landscaping complements the rose stone and ornate detailing of this beautiful English manor house, built for a single woman. Private chapel has sumptuous stained glass windows.

♦ **The Castle.** *455 Cherry at College.* 1884. This rugged granite Norman chateau is a neighborhood landmark. It was built by bachelor brothers who got rich selling lumber for railroad ties.

♦ * **Sanford House.** *540 Cherry,* 1847. Greek Revival. This imposing house was once a country estate on the outskirts of town. Now it's a counseling office, and visitors can see the stair hall's splendid handpainted mural of a tropical scene.

♦ **McKay House.** *411 Morris.* 1924. Plain but impressive tile-roofed house built by banker and Republican boss Frank McKay. His control of the state Republican party was finally broken in 1948, when a progressive reform candidate, the young Gerald Ford, defeated his candidate for Congress.

♦ **Amberg House.** *505 College at Logan.* 1910, Prairie Style. Frank Lloyd Wright started design work on it, but Marion Mahoney, his first apprentice, finished after Wright abruptly left his practice in Oak Park and his wife and six children to spend a year in Europe with a client's wife.

♦ **Meyer May House.** *1908.* Most completely furnished and restored Frank Lloyd Wright house in existence. See page 445.

*See Grand Rapids map. Get a **free walking tour map** from the Heritage Hill Association office, 126 College (in rear) S.E., Grand Rapids 54903. Office open Mon-Fri 9-5. (616) 459-8950. **Homes tour:** first full weekend in Oct. $10, $8 in advance.*

PROMOTING URBAN LIVING . . . . . is a tough row to hoe in Grand Rapids, where an insular suburban mindset is especially prevalent. Here people who seem to be intelligent, functioning adults are afraid to visit friends who live in city neighborhoods south of Fulton and believe that there's nothing of interest or value on the west side except for the zoo. Chicagoans who drool over the fabulous deals on outstanding houses find such attitudes hilariously provincial. Fortunately the city has enough people of all ages who appreciate

Heritage Hill's exceptional environment to keep the area in demand and improving. Prices for very large multi-unit homes are often in the $90,000 to $150,000 range. . . . . . The **Heritage Hill Association** has volunteer ambassadors who sell their neighborhood, which is racially and economically quite mixed. The group works with residents to lobby for the neighborhood and resolve concerns and problems with crime, land use, housing maintenance, and preservation. Reach them at (616) 459-8950, or stop by weekdays at 126 College (in rear), Grand Rapids, MI 49503.

SEE INSIDE HERITAGE HILL HOMES . . . . . Stay at one of the beautiful **bed and breakfasts** on the hill. Call (616) 458-6621 for info on the Italianate Fountain Hill B&B, (616) 454-8000 for Peaches, a Georgian country manor at 29 Gay, and (616) 451-4849 for the Shingle Style house at 455 College, the Georgian Revival at 516 College, and the Arts & Crafts house (with period furnishings) at 243 Morris. . . . . . Attend the annual **fall homes tour** on the first weekend in October. Tickets are $9 in advance from the Heritage Hill Association (see above), or $12 on tour day. Meet at Davenport College, 415 E. Fulton between Prospect and College. . . . . . **Group tours** of the area can be arranged by calling Joyce Makinen at (616) 456-7121.

GETTING TO HERITAGE HILL . . . . . From U.S. 131, take the Wealthy Street exit and go east. From I-196, take College Avenue exit and go south. . . . . . For boundaries of the **National Register Historic District**, see the dotted line on the map to central Grand Rapids, page 434. . . . . . Call or write the Heritage Hill Association (above) for a **detailed neighborhood map** with notes to 76 houses.

OPENING IN EARLY 1995. . . . . . Michigan's largest **tropical conservatory** and several specialty greenhouses. They make up the first phase of the **Frederik Meijer Gardens** under development. It will eventually include the Michigan Botanic Garden and Meijer Sculpture Park that promise to be unique in the Midwest.. . . . . The five-story conservatory includes a 14' waterfall and many paths. Adjacent themed greenhouses include an arid desert house, a furnished Victorian fernhouse, and a children's maze, and an explorers' room interpreting the energetic plant-hunters of the past who have so greatly altered our yards and gardens. . . . . . A **cafe** and **gift shop** that sells plants are on the premises. . . . . The gardens are on 70 acres of mostly undeveloped woods and wetlands three miles east of downtown Grand Rapids, at *3411 Bradford NE a block northeast of East Beltline. From I-96, go a block north on East Beltline, then right on Bradford. Gardens are on left in 2,000 feet. (616) 957-1580. Call for hours. $3/adult, $1.50 children.*

Voigt House

On Grand Rapids' Heritage Hill, a complete Victorian mansion — from the velvet scarf on the library table to the pills and tonics in the medicine chest.

Here, remarkably preserved, is a Victorian household in a big, turreted 1895 chateau, complete down to the last fringed piano scarf. It brims with the excess that epitomized Victorian decor. A table with carved lion legs is diagonally draped with a fringed velvet cloth. Antimacassars decorate the tops of every upholstered chair. Oriental carpets rest on parquet floors with elaborate inlaid borders. Doorways and windows are draped or festooned with heavy multi-layered window treatments and portieres. Patterns on patterns are everywhere. Rich reds and greens predominate.

Some visitors love the Voigt House's richness. Others experience it as claustrophobic and stifling, and feel like running out into the sunshine and fresh air.

This fascinating place is a monument to family prosperity. It's a gem of a historic house because of the authenticity of its furnishings. The two generations of Voigts who lived here until 1971 saved just about everything: letters, receipts, dresses, the entire contents of medicine chests. Everything is here the way it was. Most of the elaborately styled furniture is from Grand Rapids. It's the conventional best that America's Furniture City had to offer. There's a heavy, masculine library and hallway accented with exotica like an Arabian figure holding calling cards; a delicate French parlor; a rather Germanic dining room with loads of Bavarian china; and a comfortable, casual music room. In the basement is the original laundry, fully furnished with soap, along with interesting Voigt flour mill memorabilia.

The German-American Voigts made their fortune milling flour. They were supremely fussy, according to accounts from a former housekeeper. Cotton wads at the corners of pictures protected the walls. Except for cleaning, servants never used the main staircase to avoid unnecessary wear on the carpet.

The possessions of Ralph Voigt, the son and heir to the family flour mills, extend the house into the 20th century. They in-

A Victorian chateau with all the original furnishings, the Voigt House realistically conveys the atmosphere of a wealthy bourgeois American household. Rich and solid, or suffocating? See for yourself!

clude a banjo and a simple bedroom suite with mementos of his years at Yale. The yard is planted and landscaped with plants of the Victorian era, a rose bower, and an iron geranium stand.

115 College between Fulton and Cherry. (616) 456-4600. Tues 11-3, 2nd and 4th Sundays 1-3. Admission includes guided tour: $3/adults, $2/seniors and children.

FOR A MEMORABLE CONTRAST . . . . . plan to visit Frank Lloyd Wright's serene Meyer May house after seeing the Voigt House. The Voigt House is just the kind of architecture Wright detested: a mock European chateau encrusted with ornament borrowed from the past. His own architecture reacted to that revivalist esthetic in every way. Both homes are fully furnished — a rare treat. It's hard to believe that they were built and furnished just 11 years apart. They're both open at the same time on Tuesdays and alternate Sundays.

OTHER RECOMMENDED ATTRACTIONS NEAR HERITAGE HILL. . . .
Take Fulton or Cherry east to diagonal Lake Street, turn southeast (right),
and you'll soon reach two interesting commercial subdistricts. Turn south
(right) onto Diamond and you'll be at the **Gaia Coffeehouse**, a pleasantly
laid-back counterculture hangout. Take a harder right onto Cherry to find
the exceptional **Heartwood** antiques, known for its Arts and Crafts, Art
Deco, and moderne furniture and accessories. Farther out Lake Street, at
Robinson Road and Wealthy, is **Eastown**, an offbeat collection of snack
shops, offbeat shops, and bookstores. Especially worth checking out: the
quality hot dogs and amusing soda shoppe atmosphere at **Yesterdog** (1505
Wealthy); **Argos** used books (1405 Robinson just east of Wealthy; 616-454-
1999); **Tim's Pantry** (1507 Wealthy; 616-451-4421), with fresh-brewed specialty coffee, teas, brewing devices, and such a range of unusual beans that
it has a big mail-order business without advertising; the user-friendly
Eastown Co-op (1450 Wealthy; 616-454-8820); and **McKendree** hand-crafted jewelry (1443 Wealthy; 616-458-0267), in a fascinating woodsman's
baroque building where Grand Rapids' fabled wood craftsmanship took off on
a wildly organic, 1960s bent. Be sure to see the bone-like interior staircase.

Jerry's Diner Village

Vintage diners, moved and restored by a diner fan and ceramics artist, now sell art and diner food.

Jerry Berta still marvels at how he, a ceramics artist, has become the savior and owner of three vintage diners — and a successful restaurateur to boot. This strange little diner village sits on a busy stretch of M-57 just north of Rockford, 15 minutes north of Grand Rapids and half a mile east of the U.S. 131 superhighway that heads north to Big Rapids and Cadillac.

If you've only seen pictures and video images of diners, it's a thrill to experience the stainless steel sunburst surfaces, cozy booths and counter, and classic accouterments (thick china mugs, ketchup bottles, menu boards, etc.) of the real thing. It all started with **The Diner Store**, a 1947 diner known for the better part of three decades as Uncle Bob's Diner in Flint. Now it's Berta's ceramics studio and gallery. The original Formica counter and booths and the pie shelf now display Berta's porcelain diner night lights ($150 and up), gas stations, salt-and-pepper sets ($45-$75), fantasy diners shaped like hotdogs and hamburgers ($200-$2,000), and diners with neon "EAT" signs. In a similarly playful vein are patterned teapots and slab vases by Berta's wife, Madeleine Kaczmarczk, neon clocks and signs by his friend, Ian McCartney, and souvenir mugs and pins.

For years Jerry and Madeleine have been familiar artists in regional and national art fairs. Berta's specialties are playful, cartoon-like porcelain diners, tail-finned cars, movie theaters, gas stations, and tiny blue plate specials, worn as pins. The popular miniature diners are what precipitated Berta's unexpected debut in the restaurant and tourism world. Looking up old diners to study and draw as sources of design details, he came upon Uncle Bob's in Flint, derelict and awaiting destruction. It seemed an ideal studio on account of its unusually large size (74 seats), so Berta bought it for $2,000. Construction work is second nature to him; he grew up helping his dad, a Detroit-area autoworker, build a house a year on weekends and model-changeover time. He found a highway lot a half a mile from his studio/home in the woods. For another $14,000 he moved the diner's four sections to Rockford and went about remodeling it. "NO FOOD — JUST ART," proclaims the neon window sign.

Berta's second diner is the celebrated **Rosie's Diner**, known to generations of TV viewers from the Bounty paper towel commercials starring Nancy Walker as Rosie the waitress. When Berta revisited Rosie's in New Jersey, owner Ralph Carrado asked him if he wanted to buy it. Carrado had already sold the lot to a neighbor and had unsuccessfully offered the diner to the Smithsonian. He was thrilled that the landmark diner would survive in good hands.

Rosie's Farmland Diner, manufactured in 1946, gained its present name after TV stardom. It's an unusually large diner — the long camera angles made it a favorite with ad directors for many products — and in excellent condition. The Paramount Dining Car Company included in this diner most of the design hallmarks of the best of the golden age of diners, that period shortly after World War II when America took to the road and returning GIs found diners attractive investments. Rosie's has curved glass-brick corners, a rounded Pullman-style roof, and an interior full of reflecting stainless steel sunbursts and a jazzy combination of ceramic tile, vintage Formica, and leatherette in red, pink, light blue, and black.

Berta was thrilled and captivated with the idea of adding real food to the diner concept. Never lacking in self-confidence, he plunged into the totally new restaurant business, despite his wife's apprehension.

The results are remarkable. The classic diner food is far better than that found in most diners, from the roll to the fresh green beans and fresh strawberries for pie in season. Just like Rosie's in its original location, on Route 46 in Little Ferry, New Jersey, Rosie's opens at 6 a.m. and serves burgers, meat loaf, pies and puddings, and blue plate specials. The clientele is a real cross-section of society, just like diners were. Many are the same people who patronized diners after World War II. And the price is right – $5.75 for a meat loaf dinner with potato, vegetable, salad, and roll. (This is West Michigan, after all, home of famously thrifty folks.)

Old diners are now very hot commodities, far from the white elephants they recently were. They're in demand here and abroad as symbols of the American spirit, forward-looking, streamlined, and egalitarian; intimate places where bankers and

Dusk shows off the full impact of the neon and reflective surfaces of Jerry Berta's beautiful diners. A longtime diner fan, he moved his first diner to be a studio/gallery near his home in Rockford. Later he acquired a second vintage diner and started a restaurant.

construction workers rub elbows and everyone is treated the same. Buoyed by Rosie's success, Berta has bought yet another diner for his complex. This one is for his envisioned **Delux Diner**, an "upscale, fine dining special-occasion restaurant in a classic diner setting," in his words, patterned along the lines of San Francisco's Fog City Diner. He found it in a 50-seat diner in Fulton, New York, named the Garden of Eatin'. A late diner, it dates from the 1950s and combines porcelain with the more common stainless steel exterior, and maroon and cream interior tiles, for a softer, less reflective look. Berta's Delux Diner (expected to open in fall, 1994) has a beer and wine license (with private-label wines!), a daily changing menu, and Art Deco wood booths of his own design, reminiscent of the earlier style of Worcester oak diners before streamlining took hold in the 1930s.

The diners are at 450014 Mile Rd. (M-57) 5 miles north of Rockford. 1/2 mile east of U.S. 131, 1/2 mile west of Beltline.

*Rosie's is open Sun-Thurs 6 a.m.-9 p.m., Fri & Sat to 10. (616) 866-FOOD. V, MC. The **Diner Store** is generally open 10-6 daily, later in summer. (616) 866-ARTS. **Minigolf** is open in good weather 10:30 a.m.-10 p.m. For **Delux Diner** hours, call (616) 866-FOOD.*

SPECIALTY SHOPPING IN A MOST SCENIC SPOT. . . . . is the big attraction of the **Squires Street Shops** in downtown Rockford, a pleasant place that's the world headquarters of Wolverine Worldwide shoe manufacturers (see p. 461). An old mill, now the **Arnie's Old Mill Restaurant** (one of the popular, upbeat, affordable Grand Rapids chain of Arnie's Bakery Restaurants), is at the center of an informal group of a couple dozen stores, mostly gift shops. *Shops are one block east of Main on Squires between Bridge and Courtland. If parking's tight, try the lot across from the Factory outlets or the lot off Monroe, one block east of the principal business block on Main. Typical hours are 10-5 daily, to 8 Fridays, and 12-5 Sundays, with summer weekdays to 8.*

Behind the shops by the Rogue River and dam is an attractive little **park**. Just east of Squires Street is Rockford's main business block, with a great old hardware store and **The Corner Bar** with its well-known Hot Dog Hall of Fame (see *Hunts' Restaurants and Lodgings of Michigan*). Connecting them is Courtland Street. The **post office** there has a WPA mural, "Along the Furrows," with an unusual, cubist-tinged version of Midwestern farm life.

The Melting Pot, 63 Courtland, resembles a fudge, cookware, and gourmet shop like many others, but its owners are committed to doing things right — and not for maximum profit, either. They're extremely knowledgeable about coffee. You may see snapshots from their recent trip to a supplier plantation in Costa Rica, for instance. As a wholesaler, they roast a day's supply of many kinds of beans fresh each day. (Freshness is paramount for great coffee.) Retail prices are unusually low — typically $4.75 and $7.95 a pound. Mail-order (616-866-2900) is available. Good fudge and chocolates are also made fresh daily, as are bagels — a boon to transplanted urbanites in the area. Open at 8 a.m. except Sundays, 12-5.

Baskets in the Belfry at 46 East Bridge (616-866-2890) has evolved from a basket shop into the ultimate, all-round feminine gift shop that makes the most of the familiar Victorian-country genre and expands it without ever seeming slavishly imitative or hackneyed. The romantic tone is set by grapevines and flowers, potpourri and soaps, lace and cutwork (an outstanding selection, from collars to valences, and not terribly expensive). But if you take the time to explore the many rooms of this former print shop, each with its own personality, you'll also find African and South American stone and wood carvings, nature books, a great all-around garden tool, afghans, an extensive selection of picnic baskets, and many surprises.

THE ATTRACTIVE ROGUE RIVER DAM . . . . . is where many things come together. It's a very popular **fishing spot**. There are spring steelhead runs and fall salmon runs below the dam. Above the dam are pike, bass, and panfish. A big **platform for handicapped fishermen** is on the west bank. The Rogue is clean enough for swimming and tubing. Canoe and tubing trips can be arranged through AAA Rogue River Canoe Rentals at 8 West Bridge, (616) 866-9264. (Warning: there's not much current, and you have to do a lot of paddling even downstream.)

You can enjoy the scenery and activity from a park bench behind the old mill and Squires Street shops, or take a cloth for a regular picnic. Takeout recommendations: coffee and bagels from The Melting Pot, or hot dogs or burgers from the famous Corner Bar downtown on Main at Court. The **Rockford Historical Museum** (open May through October, Tues-Sun 1:30-3:30) fills the former powerhouse on East Bridge with a more-interesting-than-usual mix of old stuff.

A SEPARATE BIKE PATH FROM ROCKFORD TO CEDAR SPRINGS . . . . . is part of an eventual **rails-to-trails bike path** from Grand Rapids to Cadillac. The Rockford segment, which starts between the dam and the depot near Squires Street, is hard-packed dirt, good cycling for all but the narrowest tires.

Hush-Puppy Tour

*An informative factory tour in Rockford
shows how Hush-Puppies are made.*

The factory tour at Hush-Puppy shoes is one of the best in the state. It offers a slice-of-life glimpse of an interesting manufacturing process from start to finish. (Many tours just show the packaging process.) And it's delivered by a veteran employee familiar with all aspects of plant operation. Here you see already-cut shoe uppers being shaped on a last (a form that's sized for different lengths and widths of feet). "Shoes are made with a lot of heat, steam, and pressure," explains human resources manager/tour guide Jackie McIntyre Heat softens the leather. Steam shapes it on the last. And pressure applies the cement and tacks that hold the shoe together. Then you see the shoes polished, inspected for quality, and packaged.

Wolverine World Wide began as the Krause tannery here in Rockford and remains headquartered here today. It's one of the leading U.S. shoe companies, with factories in the U. S., Puerto Rico, and the Dominican Republic. The firm's big breakthrough came when it invented a new process for getting skin off pigs sent to slaughterhouses. The old method immersed them in boiling water, thereby ruining the pigskin for any other use.

Pigskin, with its bristle pores, breathes more than cowhide. Pigskin's extra comfort prompted the Hush-Puppies name and the well-known logo. "People who know wear pigskin work shoes in summer," McIntyre says. As soon as you walk into this busy, noisy factory and see the degree of hand work in the 14-step shoemaking process, it's clear why so much U.S. shoe manufacturing has been relocated to countries with cheaper labor. Workers in this factory are highly competitive piece-rate workers who earn approximately $8 an hour. Each worker can perform at least two jobs and knows the basic procedure on 40 different shoe patterns at a time.

Wolverine World Wide employs a thousand people in Rockford, including 300 in the tannery, one of the world's largest. **Tannery tours** may be arranged for appropriate groups well in advance by calling Jim Wilcox or Kirk Spencer at (616)

866-5500. It's a messy process in which raw pigskins straight from slaughterhouses are tanned and colored — not for the squeamish, and not for children.

Many employees commute from towns like Greenville and Belding, which have been badly hurt by plant closings. It's logical that labor-intensive, relatively low-paying factory work like this could survive in this part of western Michigan, where the cost of living is much lower than in high-wage areas like Detroit.

Recently Wolverine World Wide has taken great strides to freshen its image among younger buyers. A talented designer updated favorite styles, added new ones, and introduced them in a "Shoes You Can Live In" ad campaign.

To schedule a free tour, call Human Resources Manager Jackie McIntyre at least a few weeks ahead of time, weekdays at (616) 866-5602, ext. 5354. Young children must be very well supervised (2 adults for every child).

SHOE FACTORY OUTLETS . . . . . occupy the old Wolverine World Wide buildings along Main Street just north of downtown Rockford. A large building now contains the Rockford Factory Outlet Mall and Shoe Museum. Now that the huge Manufacturers' Marketplace has opened in Holland, the mall has lost many stores, but bargains on shoes are still to be found. The **Little Red Shoe House** here is enormous, the biggest by far in the chain of WWW's off-price shoe stores. Prices average 25% off suggested retail, and, in the clearance loft to the back, an additional 25% to 50% less. Stock includes seconds, irregulars, overruns, closeouts of discontinued styles, and some regular styles of WWW brands (Hush-Puppies, Town and Country, Brooks) and others (Naturalizer, LA Gear). Special promotions on work shoes, athletic shoes, etc. change frequently. What makes this special are the discounts on all kinds of shoes for men, women, and children. There's an excellent supply of everyday athletic shoes and sandals, plus $15-$20 basic leather handbags. The **Brooks** retail store has discounts on the full line of Brooks athletic shoes. In the north end basement, the **shoe museum** has displays of Wolverine shoes, from 1900 to modern times. Here are big historical photos (one shows flesh being scraped off horsehide in the tannery) and a step-by-step explanation of how shoes are made today. *(616) 866-9100. Mon-Fri 9-8, Sat 9-6, Sun 12-5.*

Saugatuck

One of the state's most picturesque resort towns, with interesting shops and galleries, outstanding bed and breakfasts, and a lively street scene.

Saugatuck is one of the state's jewels, a little resort town blessed with a combination of natural and man-made beauty. Too small to handle large crowds gracefully, it can strike a dissonant note when jammed with tourists and boaters on summer weekends. On less crowded days and in the off-season, it is relaxed and pleasant.

The town is nestled along the Kalamazoo River on a half-mile-long plain between hills and Lake Michigan dunes to both east and west. South of the Kalamazoo River lies Saugatuck's sister community of Douglas. It too has about 1,000 year-round residents but lacks Saugatuck's gift shops and intensity. Douglas has some pretty old buildings in and around the town center just across the bridge, and a peaceful shore drive lined with turn-of-the-century summer houses. Because both villages were bypassed by railroads and late-19th-century commerce, they have the quaint look of pre-industrial Michigan, like parts of New England. Small-scale clapboard buildings are often embellished with Victorian gingerbread trim. Paths lead to tucked-away shops, patios, and balconies set back from the sidewalk activity. The public gardens and parks are delightful.

Here is probably the densest concentration of top-notch bed-and-breakfast inns in Michigan, ranging from elegant to country relaxed. The area has been invigorated by gays and other talented urban refugees, even as Saugatuck's reputation as an art colony has diminished somewhat. (But there are still plenty of artists here.) Saugatuck also functions as a magnet for free spirits who find nearby Holland and Ottawa County too confining.

Saugatuck is unusual in having a town common, deeded by town founder William Gay Butler, a Connecticut Yankee. Today these three corner parks on Butler at Main continue to have a small-scale New England charm. The temple-like facade of the Christian Science church is an attractive backdrop for the delightful little garden in the southwest park. A bronze statue of a

❶ Saugatuck Dunes State Park. Wild, pristine dune country, 2 mi. of uncrowded beach, 14 mi. of hiking trails. Dune tops offer nice lake views.

❷ Downtown Saugatuck. Lively mix of quality galleries, gift & clothing shops along with delightful town common and gardens.

❸ Queen of Saugatuck. Informative cruise on fake steamboat highlights marine geography of Kalamazoo Lake and Lake Michigan shoreline.

❹ Wicks Park & boardwalk. Civilized little park with benches looks across river to Mt. Baldhead. Evening concerts with dance orchestra in gazebo.

Lake Michigan

Saugatuck

FRANCIS

HOFFMAN

RICHMOND

Kalamazoo Lake

Kalamazoo R.

CENTER

RANDOLPH **Douglas**

N

❺ S.S. Keewatin. Bygone glories of elegant Great Lakes cruise ships live on in this 336-foot steamship, now a museum.

❻ Oval Beach. Costs $5 a car on weekends to join the crowd at this popular beach. Well-stocked concession stand.

❼ Mt. Baldhead. Reward of short but strenuous climb is splendid views of city and lakes. Pleasant picnic site below on river.

Bed and breakfast inns. Outstanding quality & variety; over 12 in area, from elegant to casual.

Highlights of
Saugatuck

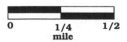

0   1/4   1/2
            mile

girl with a puppet commemorates the late Burr Tillstrom, creator of 1950s TV puppets "Kukla, Fran and Ollie." He was a beloved Saugatuck summer resident. Across Main Street is a pleasant children's playground. **Tennis courts**, a **basketball court**, and a gaily painted **restroom** building are on the other side of Butler.

Peaceful **Wicks Park,** on Water Street at Main, offers some lovely views over the river and across to the old cottage colony clustered around Mount Baldhead. **Riverside benches,** away from the summer crowds in downtown Saugatuck, make this a nice spot for a takeout picnic. Occasional evenings of **romantic dancing** or **concerts** take place around the **gazebo.**

On the Kalamazoo River in downtown Saugatuck is the **Coral Gables**, a vast, rambling dance hall/restaurant, reminiscent of the big old nightspots built up and down the coast to attract Chicago summer visitors. The hottest action within the complex is at the **Crow Bar**, a rock 'n' roll dance hall featuring live bands. Friday and Saturday nights from 8 to 2, it packs in a young crowd of hundreds. In the **Rathskeller** below, a trio entertains a more sedate, smaller crowd of dancers. The **El Forno** dining room (lunch and dinner) has the best water view. **The Bootlegger** bar features shrimp and oysters.

Art made Saugatuck nationally known. **Ox-Bow**, a summer school of art connected with the Chicago Institute of Art, operates at the picturesque remote tip of the peninsula across the river from downtown. It opened back in 1910 and still attracts serious students of art. Visitors are welcome to look around. The town's most visible artistic presence today is its unusually interesting art galleries.

Saugatuck's downtown on Butler and Water streets has a strong mix of gift shops, resortwear, and traditional casual clothing. **Saugatuck Drugs** on Butler at Mason is the town hub — a vast old drugstore with soda fountain and video arcade, art supplies, kites, costumes, and all kinds of diverting things.

Here are some shopping highlights, arranged along Butler from its south end at Culver to its north end, followed by outlying locations. It's always worthwhile to explore Saugatuck's nooks and crannies, since new shops open every year and some of the town's most charming spots are its odd corners.

◆ **Tuck's of Saugatuck.** Delightful shop devoted to fine Christmas ornaments and accessories, many designed especially for the shop. Each year Tuck dramatically changes the decor, which alone is worth a look. *249 Culver. Open all year. May-Dec: open*

Saugatuck's unusual site on a bend of the Kalamazoo River is shown in
this 1910 view from Mount Baldhead near the river's mouth. Across the
river on Water Street are a roller rink (since removed). At the far right
was the landmark Big Pavilion that burned in 1960; above it, the sister
village of Douglas, linked to Saugatuck by a bridge across the wide river.
Two churches and a school can be seen on the steep, wooded hill above
downtown to the left.

daily 11-5, in summer 10-8. Jan-April: Sat & Sun only, 11-5.

◆ **The Butler Pantry.** A kitchen accessory shop of unusual qual-
ity, the Pantry was created by ex-Chicagoans Fritz Helman and
Ron Aure. Upstairs the owners have fashioned a beguiling little
mini-mall looking out onto a delightful alleyway courtyard. *121
Butler. (616) 857-4875. Open year around. Memorial Day thru
Labor Day: Mon-Thurs 10-6, Fri-Sat 10-9, Sun 10-5. Off-season:
Sun-Thurs 10-5, Fri & Sat until 6.*

◆ **2nd Home.** Simple things with a highly refined sense of style
— that's the idea behind this distinctive new flower shop and
interior accessories store. The fabulous cut flowers look like
they're arranged for a photo shoot. More plants are in the charming rear courtyard. Things like rough cocoa mats contrast with
the subtle iridescent effects of seashells and glassware. The
owner specializes in selling store display design work here and in
Europe; the manager is a horticulturist and floral designer. Ask

to see their quarterly newsletter and annex across the street. *146 Butler. (616) 857-2353. Open year-round. May thru Oct. open 10-6 daily, to 10 in summer. Call for winter hours.*

◆ **Hoopdee Scootee.** This outrageous, amusing shop does a booming business in unisex clothing, Art Deco reproductions, T-shirts, sculpture, and adult cards. Custom-designed neon sells for $150 to $400. The checkout counter is made out of the front of a 1 1/2 ton truck. A car door shields the dressing room. *133 Mason, a few doors west of Butler. Open April 15-Halloween.*

◆ **Good Goods.** "Global art and artifacts" from traditional ethnic craftspeople and American artists. Everything from $5 Chinese papercuttings to fine contemporary gold and silver jewelry to wearable art and handblown glass perfume bottles. Many interesting textiles: caps with a Laplander look ($20-$30 or so), elegantly draped ikat coats ($650), chenille scarves ($20-$30), African stringed instruments and drums, pottery flutes and ocarinas. In summer has an outdoor cafe with cappuccino, espresso, pastries, and cookies. *106 Mason at Water, a short block west of Butler. (616) 857-1557. Memorial Day thru Labor Day: 10-10 daily. Off-season: 10-6 daily.*

◆ **Old Post Office.** A card shop extraordinaire (plus some puzzles, bags and boxes, giftwrap, rubber stamps, stationery, etc.) in the former post office, complete with antique mail slots. *238*

Butler. (616) 857-4553.

◆ **Singapore Bank Bookstore.** Saugatuck's biggest bookstore, a cozy, personal place run by an avid sailor, is located in the old Singapore Bank building. Moving the structure here from the buried town of Singapore saved it from entombment by dune sands. *317 Butler (2nd floor). May through Dec: Sun-Thurs 10-6. Fri & Sat 10-8. Winter: may close Tues-Thurs. Call first.*

◆ **Cain Gallery.** The summer home of a gallery in suburban Oak Park, Illinois, Cain shows paintings and prints, jewelry, sculpture, and art glass by living artists with national reputations. *322 Butler. Open Mother's Day thru color season. June 1 through Labor Day: 11-5 daily. Weekends only in May and fall. (616) 857-4353.*

◆ **Water Street Galleries.** Big upstairs gallery with a stimulating mix of contemporary art from artists throughout the U.S. Paintings by William Aiken of San Francisco, prints by Tony Saladino of Texas, bronze sculpture by Jean Jacques Porret of Chicago, and glass by Craig Campbell of Minnesota. *403 Water. (616) 857-8485. Mon-Sat 10-5, Sun noon-5. Closed Thanksgiving, Christmas, and New Year's Day.*

◆ **DeGraaf Fine Arts.** Sophisticated one- and two-person shows highlight works by artists including Bill Barrett (sculpture), G. Elyane Bick (tapestries), Charlie Brouwer (wood sculptures), and Stefan Davidek (paintings), For the many people who enjoyed Dan DeGraaf's Ann Arbor gallery in the 1970s and early 1980s, it's like coming upon an old friend. After years in the gallery business in Chicago, he has returned to his native West Michigan. A nice addition to Saugatuck's art scene. *403 Water Street on Main (enter around the corner on Main). (616) 857-1882. April thru December, Mon-Sat 11-5, Sun 1-5. Closed January thru March.*

◆ **Open Door Bookstore.** A little bit of many relaxing things, reflecting owner Ron Elmore's outlook on life. The books are strong on metaphysics and relationships, also on regional history, boating, American Indians, and children's. Cassettes and CDs of all forms of unusual piano music, from classical to jazz and New Age, have become a mail-order specialty. "They call me the music physician — I prescribe," Elmore jokes. Jewelry, wearable art, and supplies for massage and aroma therapy are also on hand. Visitors are welcome to sit and examine "story stones" — mixes of calcite and hematite found in beachside banks. They suggest stories and characters, viewed in some ways. *403 Water*

St. (616) 857-4565. Call to check seasonal hours. Summer hours are generally 10:30-5:30 daily, open weekend evenings.

◆ **Polka Gallery.** Genial, European-trained oil painter John Polka has been a Saugatuck fixture since 1964. In his studio/ gallery you can see him at work on his own dreamily romantic, impressionist paintings of flowers, landscapes, and figures ($100 to $5,000). Many scenes are local. Polka also does commission portraits and teaches classes in his studio. *731 Water. (616) 857-2430. Year-round, daily 9-8.*

◆ **Joyce Petter Gallery.** Often humorous or richly decorative, this art is meant to be "a delight to live with," as manager Mary Driscoll says. Eclectic, accessible, and interesting, the Petter Gallery showcases some five dozen high-quality American painters, printmakers, sculptors, glassmakers, and ceramicists. Landscapes often show ordinary subjects, urban and rural, in fresh new ways. The gallery's new home in a beautifully remodeled onetime lumberyard by the Kalamazoo River bridge in Douglas is three times as big as its charming, crowded warren of spaces on Butler Street. That means more room to show off the art, plus space for a fireplace, sofa and chairs, a coffeemaker and antiques to show how the art would suit a traditional home. Windows frame beautiful real-life views: a garden, a pretty street of old houses. Weather permitting, croquet can be played on the gallery green.

From May through September, the gallery hosts **bi-weekly openings** on Sunday afternoons from 12-5:30 p.m., with the artists present from 2-4. Recent additions are the huge floral watercolors of Cathleen Daly (they measure 7 feet by 4 1/2 feet) and joyful figurative oils on shaped canvas by Joyce Paul. Prices range from $300-$8,000. The staff enjoys explaining processes of printmaking, ceramics, and such. *161 Blue Star Highway at the bridge in Douglas/Saugatuck. (616) 857-7861. May thru December Mon-Sat 10-5:30, Sun noon-5:30. January thru March: weekends and by appointment.*

◆ **Button Galleries.** The site alone is so attractive, it's worth the drive to Douglas's leafy area of summer homes along Lake Michigan. Visitors can walk through the garden filled with rhododendrons and azaleas. Features contemporary oils and watercolors by national and regional artists. *955 Center in Douglas, one block east of Lake Michigan. Turn west from Blue Star Hwy. onto Center at the light, proceed toward lake. (616) 857-2175. Usually open* *daily 11-5 between mid-May and mid-Oct. In winter, Sat hours are noon-5. Call first.*

EVENTS IN SAUGATUCK . . . . . are dominated by the arts. There is ballroom dancing in Wicks Park, chamber music concerts, a summer music festival (usually jazz, but reggae is planned for 1994), and art exhibits. . . . . For an **events calendar,** call (616) 857-5801 or stop by the Chamber of Commerce office in the lower level of Citizens Bank on Butler at Mason. On weekends stop at the kiosk on Butler at Culver, across from Town Hall. . . . . $5 a day introductory **drop-in art lessons** are offered at Ox-Bow for a week in July by well-known Michigan painter Ellen Wilt and potter Vivian Vandenberg. Call Ox-Bow at (616) 857-5811 for details, or check out the posters around town.

ONE OF THE VERY BEST LAKE MICHIGAN BOAT CRUISES. . . . . Interestingly varied scenery makes the **Star of Saugatuck** an enjoyable $1^1/_2$-hour voyage. The 67-foot, 82-passenger boat goes out on Lake Michigan when the waves aren't too high. The informative guide comments colorfully on passing sights. He explains how the little flags on charter fishing boats tell how many fish were caught on the last outing, how the Lake Michigan shoreline has eroded 300 feet over the past 88 years, how the soft-sounding foghorn at the end of the channel going into Lake Michigan sounds much louder in a fog. It's best to take this pleasant voyage when it isn't too windy; then the boat can go farther out into Lake Michigan. In general, the earlier in the day, the calmer the water. There are restrooms, food and drinks, beer, and wine on board. *716 Water near Spear next to Gleason's Party Store, in downtown Saugatuck on the Kalamazoo River. (616) 857-4261. Daily early May thru Sept; weekends thru mid-Oct., weather permitting. $7 adults, $4 children.*

Mt. Baldhead & Oval Beach

A fine panorama, a great picnic spot, dune trails,
and a well-equipped beach –
just across the river from Saugatuck.

Named for its sandy crown before trees were planted on top, this 262-foot dune is the tallest in the region. It provides a superb view of Saugatuck, Lake Kalamazoo, and Douglas. The climb by wooden stairway is short but steep.

You can easily get here from downtown Saugatuck by taking the **chain ferry**, which runs from Mary and Water in downtown Saugatuck to Ferry Street, across the Kalamazoo River. *Mem.- Labor Day 9-9. Adults $1; children 50¢ one way. Call (616) 857-4243 to verify hours of operation.*

For a **delightful car-free picnic**, pick up tasty sandwiches at Loaf & Mug, 236 Culver, or at Pumpernickel's, 202 Butler. Take the chain ferry across the river and head north along Park Street to the foot of Mt. Baldhead. You can picnic either on the top or on the pleasant deck overlooking the river and downtown Saugatuck across the river.

On top of Mt. Baldhead is a **radar dome**, installed in 1957 as part of the DEW line stretching across northern America to warn of Soviet attack from the north. Shut down years ago, the dome now holds a ship-to-shore antenna. From the top, two interesting **trails,** one to the north and one to the south, lead to **scenic views** of the lake and forested surroundings.

The popular city-owned **Oval Beach** is just west of Mt. Baldhead. There are restrooms, changing rooms, a **snack stand,** a **game arcade**, a big parking lot, and a place to buy beach paraphernalia. You can rent **giant tubes** for $1 an hour, and also chairs and cabanas. The beach gets increasingly crowded around the third week in June, when Chicago schools let out and urban vacationers arrive in high numbers, especially on weekends.

Just above the beach, signs point to some quite nice **walks up on the dunes**. The one heading north along the ridge is especially recommended for its view over the lake.

To climb Mt. Baldhead, take the chain ferry from downtown Saugatuck on Water at Mary. See directions above. OR drive by car through Douglas and park at the Mt. Baldhead parking lot on Park St., 2 blocks north of Perryman St. **To reach Oval Beach**, *take the chain ferry across the river, head south on Park St. and turn left onto Perryman for a leisurely hike that takes you through scenic dunes. OR arrive by car through Douglas. Ferry St. in Douglas becomes Park St. in Saugatuck; Park St. intersects with Perryman; turn left onto Perryman, which takes you through the dunes directly to Oval Beach. (616) 857-1121. Season officially runs Memorial thru Labor Day; lifeguard and concession stand hours vary according to crowds, but are generally 11 a.m.-6 p.m. $5 per car. Season pass $25. Walk-ins free.*

AN EXCEPTIONALLY NATURAL AND PEACEFUL BEACH . . . . . the **Saugatuck Dunes State Park** is protected from hoards of beachgoers by its remote location. It's one of western Michigan's most beautiful yet uncrowded nature spots. The 866 acres include over two miles of Lake Michigan **beach** and 18 miles of groomed **cross-country skiing trails** (from beginning to expert levels) through the wild, pristine dune country to wonderful dune-top views of the lake. There are a few picnic tables, but no restrooms or changing areas. The parking lot is a mile from the beach, and the sandy, hilly path makes it seem even longer. *3 1/2 miles north of Saugatuck. Take Blue Star Highway to 64th St., go north 1 1/2 miles to 138th Ave., west 1 mile to park. (616) 399-9390. 8 a.m.-10 p.m. daily. $4/car/day, $18 annual state park sticker.* **No camping.**

THE SAUGATUCK DUNE RIDES . . . . plunge you through shifting sands in a converted 3/4 ton Dodge pickup. The 35-minute ride emphasizes amusement, not nature appreciation. Roaring up and down steep slopes, the driver is likely to suddenly shout things like, "No brakes! We've lost the brakes!" Even without the histrionics, the journey is rather harrowing. The 16-seat open-air vehicles have no rollbars. *Blue Star Highway, 1/2 mile west of I-196 on exit 41, 1 mile northeast of Saugatuck. (616) 857-2253. Open May 1 thru mid-October. Through September Mon-Sat 10-6, Sun 12-6. In July & Aug. open until 8. In October weekends only. $9 adults; $6 children ten and under.*

S.S. Keewatin ship museum

A huge steamer by Saugatuck evokes the elegant era of Great Lakes cruise ships.

The 336-foot *Keewatin*, permanently moored here, is a rare vestige of the wonderful era of Great Lakes steamship travel. It was one of the last of the big boats, in service until 1965. The *Keewatin* sailed from eastern Lake Huron to Thunder Bay on western Lake Superior. The six-day round trip cost $30 in 1908, including meals.

An admirably knowledgeable tour guide gives visitors a thorough look at the Scottish-built vessel: the ornately carved mahogany interiors, the compact staterooms, the forward lounge for female passengers only, and the Edwardian dining room. The spartan galley had Chinese chefs. (The original French cooks drank too much.) On top is the great 50-foot funnel. Fired by coal, the boat's 3,300 horsepower engine took 150 tons of coal a week.

Alongside the *Keewatin* is the last of the coal-fired Great Lakes steam tugs, the *Reiss*.

On Blue Star Highway at the Kalamazoo River. See map. (616) 857-2107. Guided tours 10-4:30 daily, Mem. Day thru Labor Day. Adults $3, children 6-12 $1.50.

Holland

Not just tulips and wooden shoes,
Holland has a lively, picture-perfect new downtown
and a pretty, old-fashioned park.

It's the city's Dutch heritage that brings visitors to Holland – that and the beaches at the very popular state park just north of town. The big draw is Tulip Time in May, when Holland is jammed with half a million tourists who have come to see millions of tulips. Other Dutch attractions are in high gear all summer. **Windmill Island**, a sort of mini-theme park, has the only authentic old Dutch windmills allowed to leave the Netherlands. **Dutch Village** (a recreated village out on U.S. 31 by the new Manufacturers' Marketplace) and the **Holland Museum** offer some interesting glimpses of Dutch culture. Even the two **wooden shoe factories** – tourist traps in the nostalgic style of several decades ago – have a certain charm and sincerity.

Holland's downtown, one of the state's most pleasant, has reoriented itself to feature appealing specialty shops in the face of mall competition. Architectural details from the Northern Renaissance are in evidence as you walk around the downtown business district. You can take nice downtown walks to Centennial Park, the Holland Museum, the attractive Hope College campus, and the lovely historic neighborhood along Twelfth Street west of River. It's especially nice in spring, when block after block is lined with tulips.

Few American industrial towns remained as ethnically pure for so long as Holland. Founded by Dutch religious dissenters in 1847, it remained 90% Dutch for over a century.

Holland's founding Separatists were rural artisans and farmers. They had resisted the 19th-century Dutch movement to modernize the state-controlled church. Some were actually jailed by the Dutch government for their belief in a more literal interpretation of the Bible. The opportunity in the 1840s to form their own self-run community in America had the same appeal it had for the Puritans two centuries earlier. Times were hard in the Netherlands then, and the success of the industrial revolution in

❶ Kirk Park. Area's best beach combines natural scenery, pretty picnic spots, good playground, splendid beach backed by high dunes and dark beech woods. Bike path from Holland.

❷ Veldheer Tulip Gardens. Costs $2 in May to enter the formal garden, but the 30-acre tulip field out back is more magical. Visit at dusk, when tulips glow. Next door is only Delftware factory outside Netherlands.

❸ Dekker Huis. Splendid small local museum in Zeeland illuminates lives of impoverished rural Dutch immigrants of 1847. Vivid displays of early austerity, eventual prosperity.

❹ Dutch Village. Beguiling mix of history, nostalgia, and storybook kitsch. Small theme park; 18th-19th c. village theme. Wonderful antique carnival rides, street organs. klompen dancers.

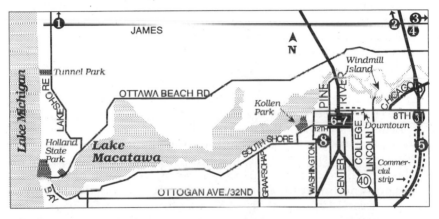

❺ Wooden Shoe Factory. Fun, old-timey tourist trap has Holland's best demonstrations of wooden shoe making. See antique French sabots and Dutch klompen; sample Dutch sweets and cheese.

❻ Centennial Park. Old-fashioned park with lighted fountain, rock grotto, windmill-shaped flower beds, potted palms from city greenhouse, all beneath canopy of century-old trees.

❼ The Holland Museum. Dutch bourgeoisie were the Western World's first to create cozy, private homes. See their cheerful sitting rooms. Learn about Holland's Tex-Mex community.

❽ Pereddies. Authentic Italian bakery-deli started by transplants from metro Detroit. Typifies the new Holland: easygoing, pleasant, and multiethnic. Mexican neighborhood just southwest of here.

Highlights of
Holland

0   1   2
miles

England had weakened the Dutch economy.

Hard times and religious oppression in the Netherlands led increasing numbers of pious rural folk, an estimated 250,000 in all, to emigrate to the U.S., mainly in an arc around southern Lake Michigan. Often whole congregations or neighborhood units arrived together and established their own communities. By 1849, new arrivals had founded the nearby villages of Zeeland, Vriesland, Groningen, Overisel, and Drenthe, named after the newcomers' place of origin.

Loyalty to home and neighborhood are characteristic of the Dutch. In Holland, Michigan, this was reinforced by the immigrants' strong religious convictions and by intentional isolation in their own small, self-contained city. As a result, Holland remained unusually homogeneous four and five generations after the first immigrants arrived. Natural blondes were the rule.

Prosperity and suburbanization are now eroding Holland's Dutch complexion as outsiders move here to fill the growing number of job openings. West Michigan's Dutch have an enviable work ethic reinforced by their Calvinist religion, and a long history of self-employment in farms, small manufacturing shops, stores, and services rather than working in factories or large organizations. Now some of Holland's many home-grown industries have become spectacularly successful: Haworth office panel systems and furniture, Prince automotive accessories, Donnelly auto mirrors, Herman Miller office furniture of nearby Zeeland. They created a boom in the late 1980s that drew many outsiders to the city for the first time in its history.

As more people come to the area to fill jobs, the Dutch may actually become a minority of Holland's residents. The hundreds of high school kids who practice for months to perform as klompen dancers at Tulip Time now come in a very broad range of hair colors and skin tones. Most noticeable are the Mexican-Americans, who now make up a quarter of all public school students.

DUTCH ATTRACTIONS

◆ **Dutch Village.** Evocative, appealing interpretation of a 19th-century village. A real highlight. See page 487.

◆ **Holland Museum.** What used to be the Netherlands Museum has now moved into Holland's grand old post office. It now goes beyond Dutch culture to tell the story of the entire city of Holland, including its Mexican-American and Asian residents.

Rare sight: a 200-year-old operating Dutch windmill, the only one allowed to leave the Netherlands. It's a majestic sight at dusk from the Black River causeway and park on North River north of downtown. Five stories high, it grinds flour sold at Windmill Island. Windmills and wooden shoes symbolize Dutch ingenuity and hard work that made a difficult, wet environment productive.

Exhibits focus on Holland's remarkable economic development and the cultural values that created the climate for growth.

Many of the charming artifacts from the old museum are on display: a quaint tiled Dutch living room first recreated in the Cincinnati apartment of a Dutch immigrant; a large doll house, furnished down to inkwells and cookie cutters; and many things shown in the Dutch exhibit of the 1939 World's Fair, including an 11-foot clock surmounted by the Queen and her ministers. Press a button and it plays the Dutch national anthem.

Downtown at Tenth at River in the old post office facing Centennial Park. (616) 392-9084. Mon, Wed, Fri & Sat 10-5, Thurs 10-8, Sun 2-5. Closed major holidays. $3 general admission, $2 seniors and students, family rate $7.

◆ **Windmill Island Municipal Park.** This city park, built for tourists, features De Zwaan ("The Swan"), five stories high, the only **working Dutch windmill** outside the Netherlands. It grinds whole wheat flour sold at the park, but only when supplies are low and the wind is between 15 and 20 knots. Call before coming to find out whether it's in operation. The park's other unique highlight is **"Little Netherlands,"** a delightful folk art model of a canal-laced Dutch town in 1847, the year Holland's settlers left for America. Local artisans built and carved it as a Tulip Time project in the 1930s and put in lots of jokey scenes and corny comments.

Windmill Island has loads of tulip beds, **klompen dancers**, a 1910 **carousel**, a pleasant **terrace** by the cafe. But a lot of tacky merchandise and dated displays spoil the effect. More rigorous quality standards would help a lot. On the whole, the privately owned Dutch Village, where more attention has been paid to details, is a better family entertainment value. *Just northeast of downtown Holland at Seventh and Lincoln. (616) 396-5433. Open May into late October. May, July & August: Mon-Sat 9-6, Sun 11:30-6. June: Mon-Fri 10-5, Sat 9-6, Sun 11:30-6. Sept & Oct: weekdays 10-4, Sun 11:30-4. Adults $5, children 5-12 $2.50.*

◆ **Veldheer Tulip Gardens.** See page 484 for description and why it's nicest at dusk.

◆ **DeKlomp Wooden Shoe and Delftware factory.** See artisans hand-paint traditional Delft designs. Page 484.

◆ **Wooden Shoe Factory.** Fun tourist trap. See page 486.

DOWNTOWN POINTS OF INTEREST

◆ **Retailing on and off of Eighth Street.** Holland's main street, Eighth, is today a picture-perfect scene of unusually handsome and distinctive turn-of-the-century buildings. For years downtown Holland was the only major shopping area within 25 miles. In a foresighted response to two shopping malls that opened in 1988, the city launched a massive streetscape improvement project involving pleasant benches, beautiful flower beds, attractive street lamps and paving, and Snowmelt, a costly underground heating system to keep sidewalks clear of snow.

For awhile it looked as if downtown was being kept alive by good intentions and money from automotive accessory maker Ed Prince. Today it's remarkably lively, with many interesting and creative new businesses. It's designed for browsing, with book and CD stores, galleries and upscale specialty apparel shops, lots of places to eat and snack, two excellent bakeries, a furniture museum, and four little parks. For restaurants, consult *Hunts' Restaurants and Lodgings of Michigan.* There's even an art movie theater, the Dutch-style **Knickerbocker Theater** at 86 E. Eighth (616-395-4950) and a downtown bowling alley, the **Holland Bowling Center** (616-392-1425). Pick up a store location map at area stores to get the full picture. And remember, *virtually everything is closed on Sunday. A growing core of stores are staying open until 9 p.m. at least on Mon, Thurs, and Fri.*

Five **parking lots along Ninth** make it a handy place to park. The good shopping starts on River at Ninth, a block south of Eighth. Selected shopping highlights, arranged from west to east, include:

Black River Gallery. An attractive artists' cooperative with some fabulous, fresh watercolor and pastel landscapes and flower pictures. *213 S. River. (616) 392-7479.*

The Shaker Messenger of Shaker and Folk Art. Country crafts of very high quality from makers individually known to the proprietors. For do-it-yourselfers, there are books and plenty of inspiration and encouragement. Pick up a newsletter featuring special talks, demonstrations, workshops, and artists' receptions. *210 S. River. (616) 396-4588. Open Mon, Thurs, & Fri 10-9; Tues, Wed, & Sat 10-5:30.*

Reader's World. An exceptionally well managed and attractive newsstand with a good selection of books, including local and regional titles. *194 River at Eighth. Mon-Fri 9-9, Sat & Sun 9-6. (616) 396-8548.*

Tower Clock Accents. Beautiful, wide-ranging gift, china, and stemware store in downtown Holland's most striking building, made of blue-gray local Waverly stone in 1891. *190 S. River. (616) 393-0305.*

Holland Arts Council. The **gallery** typically shows work by several Michigan artists in one medium at a time. The **shop** is crammed with unusual jewelry, cards, and art-related toys and gifts. Pick up the **newsletter** with upcoming workshops, performances, and dances visitors can join in. *25 West Eighth. (616) 396-3278.*

The Bridge. Self-help crafts store supplied by artisans from 40 developing countries. Textiles, wall hangings, rugs, and jackets especially stand out. Merchandise is reasonably priced and attractively displayed. The store is run by a volunteer ministry of Western Theological Seminary, the Reformed Church in America school connected with Hope College. *18 West Eighth. (616) 392-3977.*

Booksellers on Main Street. Good browsing and an attractive mix of books, cards, and gifts. *49 East Eighth. (616) 396-0043.*

Downtown Holland: Eighth Street has been transformed from a pre-mall downtown into specialty shopping with streetscaping of mini-parks, benches, flowers, and a sidewalk snow melt system.

Alpen Rose. A genuine Austrian konditorei in front of a large restaurant. The co-owner is an Austrian who came to the U.S. to work as pastry chef on Mackinac Island's Grand Hotel. The whipped cream pastries and European-style breads are terrific. *4 East Eighth at Central. (616) 393-2111.*

Tikal. Alternative and ethnic women's clothing from many countries, including Mexico, Guatemala, Indonesia, Thailand, and Nepal. Also sterling silver jewelry. *6 E. Eighth. (616) 396-6828. Tues, Wed, & Sat 10-5:30; Thurs & Fri 10-9.*

Castle Park Gallery. After spending many summers in Holland, owner Tom Stevens moved his gallery of fine arts and crafts up from the Carolinas in June, 1993, and began adding western Michigan artists to the over 100 artists represented. The gallery is becoming especially known for its art glass from Michigan, Santa Fe, Seattle, and elsewhere. Oils, watercolors, sculpture, pottery, and jewelry are in all price ranges up to around $4,000. Hand-made cards start at $2. *8 E. Eighth. (616) 395-0077. Mon & Fri 10-9; Tues thru Thurs & Sat 10-5:30.*

The Tin Ceiling. Cooperating owners pool their resources to create 5 shops under one roof. Folk art and traditional, Victorian and Scandinavian crafts, with a little touch of country. *10 E. Eighth. (616) 395-2623. Mon & Fri 10-9; Tues thru Thurs & Sat 10-5:30.*

Waalke's Butcher & Deli. Big, bustling place with lots of seating, good breads, many imported cheeses and other foods, deli salads, frozen takeout entrees that could be a boon to vacationers. *44 E. Eighth. (616) 395-0998.*

Tewlews Gallery. Joan Van Leeuw and Jane Van Loo (that makes the two lews in the name) have assembled interesting, bright works by some 50 Midwestern artists in various media, including lots of jewelry. Their gallery occupies the back half of the storefront; to reach it, you pass through **Gudruns**, a shop specializing in cosmetics imported from Europe, perfumes, and accessories. *54 East Eighth (616) 396-0855. Mon-Sat 10-5, except Fri until 9.*

Moynihan Gallery and Framing. Artist-in-residence Kathleen Moynihan and her husband, Larry Weller, who specializes in custom framing, offer original art, posters, hand-crafted cards, books and artistic gifts. *78 E. Eighth until August/September, 1994: then new location at 48 E. Eighth. (616) 394-0093. Mon-Sat 10-8.*

Till Midnight. Bakery arm of Holland's creative and very popular cafe/restaurant. Especially known for French, sourdough, and herb breads. The sidewalk cafe is a nice place for dessert and coffee. *208 College just south of Eighth. (616) 392-6883.*

Jacob's Ladder. Comes close to being a New Age/Late Punk/Christian CD store. It's truly unusual, says a social historian of music, who's on the lookout for such things. In West Michigan, where so many people are steeped in the Christian Reformed subculture, you come to expect occasional offbeat twists on conventional Christianity. *214 College. (616) 392-3303.*

Baker Furniture Museum. The study collection of original-state European antique furniture that Hollis Baker assembled in the 1920s is on view for the public as well as for top-of-the-market Baker Furniture designers. A 15-minute **video** shows Baker craftspeople at work. For people already knowledgeable about furniture, the museum is quite interesting. Examples of the originals sit alongside the exacting Baker copies. Often it's hard to tell them apart, so cleverly executed is the new "antique" finish. Hollis Baker, the founder's son who launched Baker's quality antique reproductions, collected mostly 18th-century English, French, and Italian furniture, with some freely painted folk baroque pieces. *100 East Eighth east of College. Enter through middle door, take elevator to lower level. (616) 392-8761. Open April thru Oct, Mon-Fri 10-5, Sat 9-12. Closed Sundays and holidays. Adults $2, children 12-16 $1, children under 12 free.*

◆ **Centennial Park.** This old-fashioned, leisurely downtown square beneath a canopy of trees planted for the nation's centennial in 1876 occupies Holland's original market square. Over the years numerous picturesque adornments have been installed: a rock grotto, central fountain (illuminated at night), old-fashioned carpet beds of flowers in the shapes of a windmill and wooden shoe, and palm trees brought out each summer from the city's Victorian greenhouse. A walk down West Twelfth takes you to Holland's most beautiful historic homes and churches. Pick up **walking tour guide** at the Herrick Public Library on River at Twelfth. *Between South River and Central between Tenth and Twelfth streets.*

◆ **Hope College campus** and **De Pree Art Center and Gallery.** Small (2,500 students) liberal-arts college founded by and affiliated with the Reformed Church of America. The campus is an attractive architectural hodge-podge dating from 1857. See the campus by walking along the Van Raalte Commons, a part of Twelfth Street converted to a mall connecting College and Columbia streets. The DeWitt Center off Columbia has a cafeteria, student bookstore, and game arcade. The De Pree Gallery, named in honor of former Herman Miller furniture chairman and Hope alum Hugh De Pree, mounts occasional shows of nationally known artists and leading Dutch artists. *The art center is behind the visitor parking lot off Columbia between Eleventh and Twelfth. Summer hours: Mon-Fri 9-5. evening and weekend hours in winter. Call (616) 394-7500 for gallery exhibits.*

WHICH LAKE MICHIGAN BEACH? . . . . . All have playgrounds for small children and concessions in summer. . . . . .On the north side of Lake Macatawa at Lake Michigan, **Holland State Park** is probably the most crowded, and there's nothing but asphalt behind the sandy beach, but the big red lighthouse and channel with boat traffic is a highlight. You can fish off the pier by the light. . . . . **Tunnel Park**, so-called because a tunnel under a dune goes to the beach, is favored by local families. It's a mile north of the state park on Lake Shore Drive. . . . . Some 10 miles north of the state park and channel, **Kirk Park** has the most beautiful natural setting. The beach is backed by high dunes; a dune stairway affords a good view of the lake. A shady picnic area is behind the dunes.

BIKE RENTALS AND FREE BIKE MAPS. . . . . of several recommended bike paths and routes can be had at **The Highwheeler**, 76 E. Eighth. (616) 396-6084. . . . . . An **off-road bike path now goes from Holland to Grand Haven**, passing three popular beaches (Holland State Park, Tunnel Park, and Kirk Park). There are no Lake Michigan views along the path itself, but the shady back dunes and huge beech trees are beautiful. A marshy estuary at Port Sheldon is a good place to see waterfowl. See page 498.

FOR A YEAR-ROUND VISITOR PACKET . . . . . contact **Holland Convention & Visitors Bureau**, 171 Lincoln, Holland, MI 49423 in the renovated depot on Eighth at Lincoln, just east of downtown. (616) 396-4221. Open Mon thru Fri 9-5.

HIGH-CALIBER SUMMER THEATER . . . . . **Hope Summer Repertory Theatre** is a favorite vacation highlight, with its popular and interesting plays and musicals. Single tickets cost $12-$17; a 4-show coupon is $48 (seniors $44). Early reservations are advised. Call (616) 394-7890.

Veldheer Tulip Gardens/ DeKlomp Wooden Shoe & Delftware Factory

The acres of spring tulip fields are spectacular, especially when the sun is low.

Veldheer's spectacular mass of tulips attracts throngs of tourists in May. The longtime Holland tulip-grower has a very pleasant **formal garden**, complete with drawbridges and the inevitable ornamental windmills, which are also sold in the adjoining garden shop. The large windmill is an authentic copy of a traditional Dutch drainage windmill. In summer the gardens are filled with many varieties of lilies, peonies, and Dutch iris that Veldheer's is propagating and selling here.

But the truly spectacular sight is the 30-acre **tulip field** behind the warehouses. Evenings, when the tour buses are gone, the locals come out after work to enjoy the tulips. At dusk, the sweeping masses of flowers, almost as far as you can see, seem to glow and shimmer with their own light, especially on overcast days. This striking phenomenon, known as the Purkinje Shift, comes just at sunset, when the receptors in your eye's retina shift from using cones (for color vision) to the more accurate, black and white rods at the retina's periphery. For a brief time, you still perceive color, but differently, more toward the red end of the spectrum.

Beds in the formal gardens are numbered to correspond with Veldheer's mail-order catalog, so you can place orders for fall bulbs after seeing the real thing in bloom (about April 20 through May). Veldheer claims to grow the world's largest selection of tulips, over 100 varieties in all, plus various daffodils, hyacinths, crocus, fritillaria, and the new peonies and lilies. Prices average $4.85 for 10 tulip bulbs.

Next door, under the same ownership and management, is the **DeKlomp wooden shoe and Delftware factory**. It's the only place outside the Netherlands where earthenware is hand-painted in the Dutch style using genuine Delft glaze. In the 17th-century, during the short but glorious time of Dutch dominance at sea, blue-and-white Delft imitating expensive Chinese porcelains was manufactured for middle-class Hollanders. Painters here are happy to answer questions and explain the difference between real, handpainted Delft and much cheaper lookalikes with print-ed decal transfers. Popular items include personalized wedding and retirement plates ($80 and up when completely hand-painted), tiny shoes and figurines ($8), house portraits, and wedding or baby tiles.

De Klomp also has a **wooden shoe demonstration work-shop** with picture windows. The large stock of plain and decorat-ed wooden shoes ("klompen" in Dutch, "sabots" in French) is made in the Netherlands; prices here ($16.45 for a women's size 7) are somewhat cheaper than at other outlets. The usual Dutch sweets and souvenirs are also for sale.

On Quincy just east of U.S. 31, 4 miles north of Holland. Clearly visible from the highway. (616) 399-1900. Open year-round. May: daily 8-dusk. June thru December: Mon-Fri 8-6, Sat-Sun 9-5. January thru April: Mon-Fri 9-5. Admission to formal gardens: $2.50 adults, $1 children 6-16.

WORTHWHILE IF YOU LIKE OLD CARS. . . . . An unpretentious museum with an interesting assortment of vintage American vehicles, the **Poll Museum of Transportation** was started by a retired tool-and-die manufac-turer. His collection is continually being upgraded. Favorites include a rare 1904 Cadillac, 1908 and 1910 Buicks, a 1931 Packard, and the big, wood-sided 1948 Chrysler Town and Country convertible in mint condition. Col-lections of toy trucks, model trains, seashells, and bottles, plus a large gift shop, broaden the appeal. *On U.S. 31 at New Holland Rd., a mile north of Veldheer's. Open Mon-Sat May 1 thru Labor Day. Adults $1, children 10-12 50¢, under 10 free. Call (616) 399-1955 for hours and to confirm admission prices.*

THE GRANDMOTHER OF LOCAL FESTIVALS . . . . . was started in the 1930s by a Holland schoolteacher who wasn't Dutch, is **Tulip Time**, begin-ning on the Wednesday closest to May 14. It draws some half-million visitors, largely seniors in tour busses. The opening **parade of street scrubbers** and bands goes into action when the governor officially inspects the street and sees dirt. There are loads of **shows** (from Lawrence Welk and Christian music to barbershop, vaudeville, and 50s songs), displays, **folk dancing in wooden shoes**, historic **tours**, etc. The biggest crowds are Saturday. It's impeccably organized, a real volunteer-powered community event locals go all-out for. Call 1-800-822-2770 or (616) 396-4221 for information.

TULIPS WITHOUT TOURISTS . . . . . Consider visiting Holland the week before crowds jam the town for Tulip Time. Flowers are likely already in bloom all over town. (Bulb varieties are planned to bloom during Tulip Time no matter how the weather may vary.) **Tulip Lane**, 8 miles of clearly designated tulip-lined streets, starts at 12th and River, by the Herrick Public Library, and winds through historic and suburban neighborhoods. You can hear **klompen dancers** being told how to smile at the 6 p.m. dress rehearsals at Centennial Park (Thurs, Fri, Mon & Tues before Wed's kick-off parade). Dancers are recruited from Holland High. It's fun to see so many Mexican-Americans in wooden shoes.

HOLLAND'S BEST WOODEN SHOEMAKING DEMONSTRATIONS . . . . . The only American member of the Dutch guild of klompenmakers works in a sawdusty, sneezy wood shop at the **Wooden Shoe Factory**, a giant, old-timey tourist trap that's lots of fun. The specialized wood-turning equipment used here in making wooden shoes was manufactured in the Netherlands and France at the turn of the century. An interesting display shows many kind of wooden shoes worn in damp, low-lying areas of France, Holland, and Belgium. *On U.S. 31 just south of 16th St. 8 a.m.-6 p.m. daily. Demonstrations run from 8 a.m. to 4:30 daily except Sunday.*

Dutch Village

*The charm and music of an old Dutch street carnival
in a recreated 19th-century village*

If you go to only one tourist sight in Holland, Dutch
Village should be it. This recreation of a 19th-century
Dutch village is a beguiling combination of fantasy, nostalgia, education, and gentle kitsch. A private, family-fun attraction that grew out of a tulip farm, it does a good job of entertaining visitors while illuminating the 18th- and 19th-century village
life Holland's immigrants left behind — a better job, in fact, than
Holland's municipally owned Windmill Island.

The brick buildings that line Dutch Village's four canals look
authentic, with their careful detailing and imported tile roofs.
They are sandwiched between truck-filled U.S. 31 (noise buffers
would be a nice improvement) and the sprawling Manufacturers'
Marketplace outlet mall. Despite the busy location, an illusion of
leaving the 20th century behind is effectively created by the big
willows and cheery brick houses. New perennial gardens with
over 250 varieties make the grounds even more attractive
throughout the growing season.

The best part of Dutch Village is the operating, antique street
carnival, free for the cost of admission to the grounds. There's a
carousel, two splendid, ornately carved Dutch **street organs**,
and the **Zweefmolen**, a swing something like an antique
carousel. It's just scary enough for older kids to want to ride it
again and again — conveniently allowing adults to look longer at
interesting exhibits and shops. For little children, there's a wavy
slide descending from a wooden-shoe house. **Ducks** can be fed
on the pond, and **goats** and **sheep** in the half- scale barn.

High-kicking, adept **klompen dancers** perform at 10:30, 12,
2, 4, and 6 to waltzes and gallops played on the **Gauen Engel
organ**, an oversize 1880 Amsterdam street organ restored by the
famous Carl Frey in 1960. For organ-lovers, this alone is worth
the cost of admission. Visitors can go behind the organ to see
the bellows, wood pipes, and punched music paper (much like a
player piano's) in action. Recordings of street-organ classics are
for sale in one of the gift shops. Attached to the barn is a typical

Music from this ornate antique street organ, one of two at Dutch Village, adds to the mood of a turn-of-the-century Dutch street carnival. Rides on an antique carousel and giant swing and klompen dancers performing in wooden shoes are included in the admission price.

18th-century **farmhouse**, realistically furnished, with an alcove bed in the stairwell, and a root cellar down below. The nearby garden area has a European-style grape arbor, roses, loads of tulips in season, and a giant stork holding a diaper. Visitors can sit and pose for photos — one of many such planned photo opportunities.

Tucked away and easy to miss are old-fashioned displays of **Dutch regional costumes** and a well-done **windmill diorama** in a building across the way, along with a **cheese-making exhibit.** Next to it, in a grisly allusion to medieval superstitions that survived in 17th-century Holland, is a scale where suspected witches were weighed. If they were unusually light, they were suspected of being able to fly. Near the entrance, the **Bioscoop** (movie theater) shows a free movie on the Netherlands.

The gift shops at Dutch Village cover an enormous range. The **Souvenir Shop** covers the low end, including the usual Dutchware plus costume dolls, God Bless Our Camper plaques, and some attractive tulip posters. The **Arts and Crafts Building** goes upscale with lead crystal, Dutch lace valences, a lot of pricey English and French collectibles (interesting carved figures, quaint porcelain villages), beer steins, Delft-trimmed

Dutch copper and brass cookware, and cases of stunning Royal Delft, including a $900 plate after a Rembrandt painting. In the same building is a small **wooden shoe factory** (for demonstration only) and shop.

Imported cheeses, Belgian chocolates, Dutch cookies, and jams are for sale in the **Gourmet Food Shop** and **terrace** overlooking the Manufacturers' Marketplace pond.

Holland's only restaurant serving Dutch food is the attached **Queen's Inn**. Don't miss the section of real thatched roof. It comes down to near eye-level so you can see just how thick and tight-bundled it is.

Every year, starting the day after Thanksgiving and ending Christmas Day, Dutch Village has a free display of 50,000 Christmas lights daily from dusk until around 9. Running concurrently with the Christmas lighting display is a special Dutch Dinner Theater Christmas program Wednesday through Sunday. For adults, lunch is $15.95 and dinner is $17.95. The cost for children through age 12 is $8.95 for either dinner or lunch. Both dinner and theater are included in the price. The Christmas program without dinner is $6 for adults and $5 for children. Times vary, so call for information.

*James at U.S. 31, 2 miles northeast of downtown Holland. (616) 396-1475. **Shops** open year-round 9-5:30, in summer until 8. (No entrance fee for shops.) **Grounds** are open from the last weekend of April through mid-October. Gates open at 9 a.m. and close at 6. Admission: $5 adults, $3 children 3-11.*

50 OUTLET STORES . . . . . are next door to Dutch Village at **Manufacturers Marketplace**, open Mon-Sat 10-9, Sun 11-6, closed Thanksgiving, Christmas, and Easter. In addition to name-brand outlets like Bass Shoes, Van Heusen, Eddie Bauer, Carter Childrenswear, Evan Picone, and Black and Decker, some stores offer deeper discounts on miscellaneous closeouts. Outlets offer wide selection on discounts you might have to wait for sales to find locally. But everything's a trade-off. How do your purchases at outlets affect local businesses you care about? If we don't support our local merchants, we won't have any!

Dekker Huis

*Where Dutch immigrants' faith, early poverty,
and hard-won success come to life*

When it comes to conveying the life experiences of ordinary people, this small museum, run by the Zeeland Historical Society, is exceptional. The historical society members who show visitors around are apt to be lifelong Zeelanders who are part of the history themselves. Their museum brilliantly uses objects to convey ideas. There's a trunk — a very small trunk — displayed with everything the typical Zeeland pioneering immigrant family took to America. These Dutch Secessionists were simple country people, among the poorest of all the American emigrants from Northern Europe. When they first arrived in western Michigan in the late 1840s, they lived very simply indeed.

The museum consists of a furnished house built by a grocer next to his store and, in the store, exhibit space including a

The home and store of a Dutch-American grocer is now Zeeland's insightful local museum. The town of Zeeland (population 5,500) is still thoroughly Dutch, the way more cosmopolitan Holland was 20 or 30 years ago.

gallery for changing shows. The founders of Zeeland all belonged
to the same Secessionist congregation in the farm town of Goes
(pronounced "Hoos") in Zeeland, a northern province of the
Netherlands. Like most of the first wave of Dutch settlers to
western Michigan, the congregation emigrated together, in 1847.
Drenthe, Overisel, Vriesland, Zeeland – the map around Holland
is dotted with the names of the places Dutch pioneers came
from. Zeelanders left their cozy Dutch kitchens for harsh conditions on the Michigan frontier. For awhile, the whole village
shared a single hand-made shovel. (It's here in the museum.)

When you step inside the grocer's small but comfortable dining
room and parlor, furnished roughly as it was about 1920, you
experience the material success the immigrants were so proud
of, and the bourgeois domesticity for which the Dutch are famous. Lace curtains, dark wood trim, imitation Oriental carpets
— it feels cozy but a little stuffy, like the living rooms of millions
of Americans' grandmothers' houses. So does the master bedroom, with its made-in-Zeeland bedroom suite and blue-and-
white linoleum imitating tile. The laundry is set up for wash day
on the house's side porch — complete with washtubs, mops in
the corner, underwear drying, and blueing in a jar.

*37 E. Main in Zeeland, about half a block west of the downtown
business district. (616) 772-4079. Thurs 10-4, Sat 10-1. Also open
by appointment. Closed Nov.-early March. Free.*

ALSO RECOMMENDED . . . . . A brief look at the rest of **Zeeland,** a most
distinctive American town that bans the sale of liquor, almost entirely shuts
down on Sunday, and has more jobs (over 8,000) than people (5,500). The
Zeeland Bakery on Main Street bakes Dutch butter cookies and Holland
rusk, which locals eat soaked in milk.

Nowhere is the vaunted Dutch-American work ethic more pronounced
than in Zeeland, the headquarters of three large and famous home-grown
industries: **Bil Mar Foods** ("Mr. Turkey"), **Herman Miller** furniture (a leader in
functional design with one of the most admired corporate cultures in America),
and **Howard Miller** clocks. (The latter two are seen east of town out Main.)
Poultry farming and vegetable-raising, two traditional occupations, are still in
evidence. On **Church Street**, one street south of Main, are huge Dutch
Reformed churches, impressive homes from the early 20th century, and old-
fashioned corner parks at Church and Central. The street's air of well-built
solidity suggests the Calvinist attitude that worldly prosperity is a natural sign
of devout Christian faith. **Paul de Kruif**, Dutch-American author of *Microbe
Hunters*, grew up in the Queen Anne house just east of the largest park.

Grand Haven's Boardwalk

*At the mouth of the Grand River, Michigan's liveliest
pedestrian promenade connects a marina,
a fine historical museum, the famous musical fountain,
and the dramatic Lake Michigan light and pier.*

From early morning until late evening, both visitors and
townspeople stroll along this interesting waterfront walkway. It extends along the Grand River's mouth over a
mile, terminating at the Lake Michigan pier and light by Grand
Haven State Park. Active boat traffic on this part of the Grand
ranges from large freighters to million-dollar yachts. The boardwalk (actually it's mostly asphalt) makes a terrific walk because
it's punctuated with pleasant places to sit and many interesting
sights, from an extraordinary variety of expensive pleasure boats
to ice cream stands to a good museum and the drama of going
out on the pier. Lake Michigan piers are grand places to get in
touch with the incoming weather, the big lake, and the wide variety of people who come to fish for perch. Piers can be fatally dangerous in storms, however.

Large crowds descend on the town of Grand Haven (population of 18,000) because it has the closest Lake Michigan beach to
Grand Rapids, Michigan's second largest city. On summer weekend evenings, especially on a holiday, the scene on the boardwalk can be intense, not just with pedestrians but with the low
throbbing of powerboats in the adjoining channel and cruising
cars along Harbor Drive. Towards sunset, crowds gather to see
and hear the illuminated Musical Fountain. For some, it's great
fun to be where the action so clearly is. For others, it can seem
like the All-American nightmare. They're advised to visit the
boardwalk in midweek, in the off-season, or in the morning.

Many highlights accent this pleasant walk. They are
arranged from east to west, starting at the boardwalk's east end
on Jackson at Second Street and ending at the pier. You can
park at the lot by the Farmers' Market off Jackson. (See page
496 for more parking hints.)

♦ A striking **historic railroad display** on North Harbor Drive
just north of Chinook Pier includes a huge coaling tower and a
1941 steam locomotive, with tender and two old cabooses.

❶ North Beach Park. Nice, less crowded beach and terrific dune to climb, with splendid view of town and lake.

❷ Arboreal Inn. Out of the way, but worth the drive. Excellent food, great atmosphere in quaint, rustic setting.

❸ Boardwalk. Lively and scenic, with lots of boats, views, strollers, snacks, Snug Harbor Restaurant.

❹ South Pier. Dramatic walk out to two old lighthouses. As popular with strollers as fishermen.

❺ Lake Michigan beaches. Trees are scarce, but these beachside parks are packed with swimmers, kites, and RVs.

❻ Highland Park. Haunting Victorian summer colony in wooded dunes. Scenic boardwalk winds through it.

❼ Lake Forest Cemetery & Duncan Park. Beautiful 19th-century setting with hills, dales, majestic beeches.

❽ Idyllic drive along the Grand to historic Eastmanville and Lamont, two mid-19th-century river villages.

Highlights of
Grand Haven

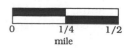

0   1/4   1/2
mile

◆ The **farmers' market** is off North Harbor just east of the city marina at Chinook Pier. Open Wednesdays and Saturdays June through October from 8 a.m. until everything's sold. Also on Mondays 1-7 p.m. in July and August.

◆ **Chinook Pier**, two blocks north of Washington at 101 North Harbor, is home of a large **charter fishing fleet** (616-842-2229), Grand Haven's municipal **transient marina** (616-847-3478), and a minigolf course (616-846-2445). Chinook Pier is also the departure point for two summer sightseeing tours, one by bus and the other by boat. (See notes on page 496-497.) Alongside popular Marina Mike's convenience store and sit-down snack bar are shops selling cookies and ice cream and some of the coolest T-shirts and beachwear to be found at any Michigan resort.

◆ The famous **Musical Fountain** across the Grand River is seen from a viewing stand by the boardwalk, behind the old depot and historical museum at the foot of Washington downtown. The sprays emanate from a plain fountain part-way up Dewey Hill on the other side of the river. Every evening at approximately 9:30 p.m. from mid-May through Labor Day, the half-hour display of changing colored lights and spray, and the recorded music concert (40,000 watts worth) attract crowds of pedestrians and flotillas of pleasure boats, for a coordinated half-hour concert of recorded music. The program of pop favorites changes each night; Sunday night is hymn night. Pleasure boats crowd together in the river to view the event. The fountain even speaks! "Good evening, ladies and gentlemen. I am the Grand Haven Musical Fountain." Built by volunteers, financed by donated funds, the fountain represents much that is near and dear to this community. To criticize the distant visual display as "insipid" and the sound quality as "fuzzy" is to experience the enduring wrath of local boosters.

◆ The **Tri-Cities Historical Museum** is on the river at the head of Washington Street in the old Grand Trunk Depot. It has a wonderfully rich assortment of local artifacts illuminating the area's colorful past, from trapping, lumbering, and shipping to manufacturing, railroading, and the Coast Guard past. Don't miss the tourism display in the basement, or Spring Lake folk artist Lewis Cross's huge, striking, and poignant painting of hunters and one of the vast flocks of now-extinct passenger pigeons that used to fly up the Lake Michigan shore. There's also some great reading, like this newspaper article about the arrival of Grand Haven's first railroad: "The railroad has put an end to our solitude. For twenty long, tedious, dreary winters we have been shut up in solitary confinement for no fault of ours . . . like bears in their hibernation. But now we believe we are on the high road to advancement. We see no reason why we should not become the Milwaukee of Michigan." The museum **shop** has a good selection of books and walking tours to the area. *(616) 842-0700. Open daily except Mon, Memorial Day thru Labor Day, 10-9:30, Sun noon-9. Open noon-4 on weekend afternoons September thru May. Adults $1, children 17 and under free.*

◆ The **Brass River Display** is between historical museum and the Chamber of Commerce on South Harbor Drive at Washington. It's a wonderful brass sidewalk map, 50 feet wide, of all the tributaries which feed into the Grand River. This splendid brass map vividly shows how the immense catchment area of the mighty Grand River extends all the way to the Irish Hills south of Jackson. It was made with volunteer help by employees of the local Grand Haven Brass Foundry.

◆ **Downtown Grand Haven** extends along Washington Street from Harbor Drive and has some of West Michigan's best specialty shopping. (See note, page 496.) The first two blocks are largely geared to visitors. The long building of cream-colored brick is **Harbourfront Place,** a shopping/restaurant/office complex in the converted 1906 Story & Clark piano factory.

◆ **The Coast Guard Search and Rescue Station** at 601 S. Harbor (616-847-4500) lacks the excitement it used to have, before the cutter *Acacia* was transferred to Charlevoix to replace its cutter, which ran aground and sank near Marquette. The small boats you're likely to see here are the Coast Guard's primary search-and-rescue boats, a 44-foot motor lifeboat and a 41-foot utility boat.

◆ The striking **South Pier** with its **catwalk** and **lighthouse** is at the end of the boardwalk, a mile from downtown and the historical museum. The long pier's catwalk, once used to get out to the lights during storms, has great nostalgic value to locals, who pitched in to pay for restoring it. The pier is a great place to stroll — except during storms, when it can be very dangerous. It's also popular with fishermen for perch in summer and for steelhead, salmon, and brown trout in fall and spring.

◆ **Grand Haven State Park.** Stunt kites from the Mackinaw Kite Company on Washington Street are often demonstrated on the popular **beach** next to the pier here. A concession stand, playground, and restrooms are nearby. The 187-site modern **camp-**

The crush of boats and jet skis in the water and the tanned bodies on shore make Grand Haven State Park and City Beach magnets for the exhibitionistic and the gregarious and a place to avoid for lovers of peace and quiet. This photo was taken during the summer's big event, the Coast Guard Festival.

ing area, pure asphalt and sand with hardly a tree in sight, is one of the most popular in Michigan. Come early to park here on weekends. The social meat market where tanned bodies are on display is farther south in front of the concession building of **City Beach.** *On South Harbor Drive a mile west of downtown. Also accessible from the south via Lake Ave. which goes west off Lake Shore/Sheldon/Fifth. (616) 842-6020.*

PARKING TIPS. . . . . Come early in the morning or just after noon to find a place in the two big lots along Franklin. The Grand Haven trolley (see below) transports people from downtown parking to the beach.

GRAND HAVEN'S HIDDEN INDUSTRIAL WATERFRONT COMES ALIVE. . .
. . if you take the relaxing and surprisingly interesting 1 1/2-hour narrated harbor cruise on the **Harbor Steamer.** (Actually it's a diesel-powered paddle-wheeler.) The scenery isn't much until the boat gets to Spring Lake, though the effects of the changing light and setting sun at the evening cruise are beautiful everywhere. At the trim suburb of Spring Lake you see pretty water-

front homes and parks and the beautiful red-roofed Tudor Robbins estate. But good historical narration makes the industrial harbor seem interesting, too. Grand Haven's lumber boom days are vividly recalled. Maritime fans will enjoy the knowledgeable commentary on hard-working ships and barges seen on the trip. There's good stuff for rail fans, too. Bring a jacket; it can get windy on the water. *Leaves Chinook Pier at 101 North Harbor Drive. Call (616) 842-8950 for schedule and price information.*

INEXPENSIVE BUS TOURS. . . . . on the **Grand Haven Harbor Trolley** line are far less interesting (the narration is slight and jokey) but enjoyable if you have the time and don't expect too much. You'll see some interesting parts of the Tri-Cities you'd probably miss. . . . . . From Memorial Day through Labor Day, Harbor Transit (616-842-3200) runs trolleys from Chinook Pier to Grand Haven, leaving on the hour and on the half-hour from 11 a.m. to 10 p.m. daily. From the pier, the trolley travels out Harbor Drive to the state park, turns around there and comes down Washington Street to center town, turns around in the Bookman municipal parking lot across from Eighth Street, and returns along Washington Street to Chinook Pier. The trolley can be flagged down. The regular fare is $1; seniors over 59, handicapped, and children 12 and under ride for 50¢.

DOWNTOWN GRAND HAVEN . . . . . has some of West Michigan's best specialty shopping. Closest to the boardwalk is **Harbourfront Place,** a shopping/restaurant/office complex in a big 1906 piano factory. Many other visitor-oriented gift and t-shirt shops are near the boardwalk. . . . . The town's top gourmet shop for good wines, cheeses, fancy foods, and freshly roasted peanuts is **Fortino's,** an old grocery store at 114 Washington with a been-there-forever atmosphere. Next door, the **Mackinaw Kite Company** (616-846-7501) has an awesome selection of kites and other wind toys, from indoor versions to traditional Chinese kites to stunt kites and power kites that lift the flier off the ground. You can get instructions for making your own kites, too. . . . . **G. Louise** (616-847-0045) is a fashion-forward women's boutique at 121 Washington. Don't miss the clever, eco-friendly, multicultural new fashion and accessory stores across the street from it, near Buffalo Bob's. . . . . The **Michigan Rag Company** at 121 Washington (616-846-1451) prints and sells colorful, sturdy beach and boating wear, screen-printed on cotton fabrics in bright, punchy repeat designs like fish, log cabins, Michigan lighthouses, umbrellas, and more. Designed here by Richard Sweet, they're sold in summer resorts throughout the U.S. Seconds are substantially marked down. Big windows let passersby see screenprinters at work. . . . . **Buffalo Bob's** at 126 Washington at Second (616-847-0019) has taken over the former downtown drugstore and come up with a really idiosyncratic retail mix: beach store, rollerblade store, novelty shop, Western wear store, and soda fountain with soups, sandwiches, ice cream sodas, and old-fashioned phosphates. **Bicycle and rollerblade rentals** are available. . . . . . An exceptional gift shop, **Ad Lib**, 218 Washington (616- 842-7300) carries quite a mix, currently crystal and silver, M. Hadley earthenware, paisley table linens, raku ceramics from Botswana, clay figures from Ecuador, Russian painted boxes and figures, Mexican painted earthenware. The new **Ad Lib antiques and garden store** is in a historic house across the rear alley. . . . . In the same interconnected complex as Ad Lib at 214-222 Washington, **Whims and Wishes** (616-842-9533) carries an original medley of contemporary and antique gifts and jewelry, and **Bach's Lunch** (616-846-2224) is a charming coffee and lunch spot looking onto a pretty landscaped courtyard.

GOOD VACATION READING . . . . . is on hand downtown at **Hostetter's News Agency**, 135 Washington at Second (magazines, mass paperbacks, some regional; open long hours) and at **The Bookman**, the West Michigan shore's biggest new and used bookstore, in the midtown shopping district at 715 Washington, a block west of Beacon Blvd./U.S. 31. *(616) 846-3520. Open Mon-Fri 9-9, Sat 9-6, Sun 8-5.*

FOR ART WORTH CHECKING OUT. . . . . A cooperative of area artists is in a large, attractive series of rooms upstairs over The Bookman (enter off the parking lot in back). **The Gallery Upstairs** (616-846-5460; open Tues-Fri 10:30-5:30, Sat 10:30-4) features over 30 participating artists, largely painters and jewelers. Flowers and landscapes are particularly strong here and elsewhere in West Michigan, where the area's passion for horticulture, linked with the Dutch, comes together with the resort art market.

BICYCLING AROUND GRAND HAVEN. . . . . Two beautiful off-road bike paths now make the Grand Haven area a good bicycling destination for family bicyclists. . . . . . A **bicycle path to Holland** (22 or 29 miles, depending on the route) along Sheldon Road/Lake Shore. Sheldon begins in downtown as Fifth Street, and eventually turns into Lake Shore Road. The path starts about half a mile south of the hospital on the east side of Sheldon. You pass big beech trees and attractive houses near the lake, then reach **Kirk Park** with its beautiful, wooded dunes and beach (see page 483) at 9 miles, **Pigeon Lake** (11 miles), Tunnel Park, and **Holland State Park** (21 miles). The Butternut turnoff leads from Pigeon Lake more directly to the city of Holland for a 22-mile trip (one-way). . . . . . A **bike path around Spring Lake** is some 16 miles long. Highlights include many water views, several bridges over bayous, and a stop at the pretty Fruitport city park. You can park at Central Park, half a block north of Savidge. . . . . . **Free bike maps** with these paths and suggestions for several loops over lightly traveled roads may be had at **Rock 'N' Road Cycle**, 300 North Seventh at Elliott. (616- 846-2800). Mon-Fri 11-7, Sat 10-5.

Highland Park

*Grand Haven's enchanting 19th-century cottage colony
has magical boardwalks through steep, forested hills
and shady valleys.*

This haunting summer colony of a hundred cottages sits among dunes overlooking Lake Michigan. Since 1886 Highland Park has been a summer retreat for well-to-do families. Many longtime cottagers come from as far away as St. Louis and Louisville, as well as Chicago and Grand Rapids. Today these cottages command fancy prices — from $100,000 to $250,000. Many family cottages, especially those in from the lake, retain a rather austere simplicity that hasn't changed for decades. What's special here are the quaint narrow roads, the striking dune environment with steep hills and shady valleys, and the old beech and maple forests.

The best look at Highland Park is from the rambling **boardwalks** that go back and dip through the steep, heavily wooded back dunes. It's dark and cool here, a nice respite from too much sun on the beach. The dunes drop off so dramatically, the boardwalks seem suspended in the treetops as they pass by the cottages' ample porches. From them you can look down on wildflowers and scampering chipmunks. The quaintest cottages are back away from the lake. Some are only approachable via the boardwalk and numerous steps.

The leisurely atmosphere of plain, rustic summer retreats lives on at Highland Park's Khardomah Lodge. The rooms are small and simple, the public spaces rambling and inviting — the opposite of most contemporary lodgings.

Finding Highland Park's boardwalks can be a trick. If you are on the beach, look for the stairs climbing the bluff just south of the busy Lake Avenue intersection. They lead to an **overlook** with benches, a popular place for viewing sunsets, in front of the pink Highland Park Hotel. (Actually this was the annex for the stately main hotel, which burned in 1967.) Walk briefly back along Lake Avenue; behind the hotel, you'll see Lover's Lane. Go down it a ways, and a little to your left you'll see the white painted railing to stairs that look like a private cottage entrance. This is actually part of the boardwalk, maintained by the Highland Park Association. The boardwalk winds around among the cottages, sometimes ending on a road. (The roads themselves are oriented to parking, not views, and much less interesting.)

To more fully experience the beauty of Highland Park, you may want to stay either in the **Khardomah Lodge**, which dates from 1873, or the **Highland Park Hotel**, a bed and breakfast.

Along and off of Highland Rd., south of Lake Ave., overlooking Lake Michigan. Just east of the Bil Mar Restaurant, which is at 1223 S. Harbor.

BEHIND HIGHLAND PARK . . . . . Duncan Park is a dark and mysterious-looking beech-maple climax forest on the back dunes about half a mile from Lake Michigan. It's for walking, cross-country skiing in winter, and picnicking. Entrances are on Lake Drive and Sheldon Avenue (the southern extension of Fifth). . . . . . Just west of the park's Lake Drive entrance, entered off Lake, is **Lake Forest Cemetery**, established in 1872 among the hills and dales of the forested back dunes. Few cemeteries can approach this one for the combination of beautiful setting, interesting plants and monuments, and varied strands of local history and American immigrants' experience represented in the dates and birthplaces of people buried here: Yankee, Scotch, and Irish pioneers, soon followed by numerous Dutch. The deep shade of majestic beeches contrasts with the play of light on their elephant-smooth trunks. The great trees anchor the winding paths and are effective natural foils to the elaborate post-Civil War monuments. To get a splendid **map and history** of Lake Forest Cemetery, complete with 35 identified sites, ask at the Tri-Cities Historical Museum (page 494).

Hoffmaster State Park and Gillette Visitors' Center

An inspired nature center expands your enjoyment and understanding of Lake Michigan's splendid dunes.

Part of the dunes' magic is their contrast of sun and sand with deep, dark shade. The beach and foredunes are sunny and windswept, with only dune grass and occasional shrubs and scrawny trees. The back dunes are dark and cool, mysterious beneath the canopy of huge maples and ancient looking, elephant-barked beeches. Hoffmaster State Park, more than most Lake Michigan parks, gets you interested in the complete dune environment, not just the beach and foredunes.

What makes Hoffmaster so very special is the top-notch nature center at the **Gillette Visitors' Center**. It provides one of the best views of Lake Michigan's dunes, which are the longest stretch of freshwater dunes in the world. And it tells their story in an unusually compelling way that makes you respect their fragile ecology and grandeur.

The best part of the story is told outdoors, on the dunes themselves, through excellent diagrams and explanations of the very view you are seeing. A **boardwalk** and 200-step **dune stairway** lead visitors up through a beech maple forest so towering, dark, and shady that it seems to have been there forever. There are frequent seats for resting and looking down on the trees. At the summit is a spectacular 180-foot-high overlook with a bird's-eye view of a vast landscape. To the west and north you see Lake Michigan and the two lines of dunes paralleling it. East you see sandy, low-lying blueberry farms and pretty Little Black Lake.

On the walk up the stairway and back down and out to the beach, you see how the back dunes vary from desert-like conditions on their west-facing slopes to virtual rain forests of perpetual dampness in the troughs and east slopes, where moist winds off the lake drop their moisture as they hit land. These diverse biologic zones fascinate naturalists; the basic principles of plant succession were, in fact, based on observations of Lake Michigan sand dunes by University of Chicago biologists.

The nature center here is one of the two or three best in

**The long dune stairway behind Gillette Visitor Center offers a spectacu-
lar panoramic view and interpretive signs that give a good, on-the-scene
idea of sand dune formation and ecology.**

Michigan. If you're short on time, pass over the elaborate but jar-
gon-filled displays of the Exhibit Hall, prepared by an outside
firm of museum professionals. (One exception is the impressive
new, interactive Spinning Cube that tells how sand dunes are
formed and shows samples of different kinds of sand.) Opt
instead for the outstanding multi-image slide show, **"Michigan
Sand Dunes and Hoffmaster State Park,"** shown in the comfortable, 82-seat theater. Written and produced by the center's own
talented naturalists, Earl Wolf and the late Sandy McBeath, it
tells Lake Michigan's sand dune story through the 19th-century
logging and resort eras, up into the present time. They were
formed by prevailing westerlies some 3,000 years ago, piling up
sand deposited by glacial meltwaters. Every hour on the hour, a
second beautifully photographed slide show features seasonal
wildflowers or other natural subjects in the park.

Downstairs, the well-thought-out **hands-on classroom** is a
great rainy-day destination. Kids seem fascinated cuddling a
stuffed owl to see how soft and plumped-up its layers of feathers
are. Visitors can request to see **videos** on shoreline erosion and
on moose, loons, and bluebirds — all species at risk due to
increased development of their natural habitats. Here from late
spring through Labor Day are numerous live cold-blooded animals and fish to watch.

The excellent **bookstore**, run by an enthusiastic volunteer organization, focuses on nature publications for all ages. It has a fine array of posters, notecards, and nature-related gifts, too.

Spring wildflower displays in backdune forests like these are spectacular. On Mother's Day each year the **Trillium Festival** offers many guided walks and more. Call (616) 798-3573 for a schedule of **special programs** and guided walks at Gillette; group tours are by appointment. In summer there's a guided walk or program every day.

Adjoining the visitors' center are 10 miles of wonderful **hiking trails** through beech-maple forests, up dunes and down onto fairly remote beaches. In winter, three miles of intermediate cross-country **ski trails** through the forests begin by the picnic shelter at the end of the drive past the Visitors' Center.

Hoffmaster has 2 1/2 miles of **beach** with beautiful dunes as a backdrop. The beach is most crowded by the concession stand and bathhouse, close to large parking lots and an unshaded **picnic area**. But if you walk south down the beach, in 10 minutes you can be away from the crowds and close to the beautiful boardwalk that leads back to the spectacular dune overlook connected to the Gillette Visitors' Center. Much nicer **picnic areas**, deeply shaded and relatively private, are along the main road past the beach turnoff.

The 333-space modern **campground** ($14/night) is one of the nicest in Michigan, despite its large size. It's in a separate part of the park to the north, off Lake Harbor Road, beneath a shady canopy of pines and hardwoods. Its beautiful setting and proximity to a campers-only beach make it quite popular. Half the spaces are reservable, and reservations are advised on all summer weekends. Weekdays there's usually space except during special events. The campground is open all year, but water and showers are turned off from mid-October through mid-April.

See map for location of Hoffmaster State Park. It's 6 miles south of Muskegon and 7 miles north of Grand Haven. From U.S. 31, take the Pontaluna Rd. exit and go west. (616) 798-3711. State park sticker required: $4/day, $18/year. **Gillette Visitor Center:** *(616) 798-3573. Open all year 10-5 daily, closed Mon. No extra fee.*

Pleasure Island and Michigan's Adventure

Two good water parks near Muskegon — one with roller coasters, too

leasure Island and Michigan's Adventure are both near Muskegon. Both have water parks, and both give unlimited rides for one entrance fee.

PLEASURE ISLAND, Michigan's largest water park, is quite different from an urban water park, where concrete and chlorine seem to dominate. It's built on Little Black Lake around three lagoons, not far from Lake Michigan and Hoffmaster State Park. It's really a park, nicely landscaped, with lots of flowers — a place where families come to spend the day. There's something for everyone — thrills for older kids and teens, and gentle river rides for grandparents and small children who don't meet the 48" height requirement for many rides. In the newer, River Country part of the park, the **Lazy River ride** is slow and relaxing, like a miniature float trip in innertubes, while **Thunder Falls** is like going over a cliff in an innertube. At the **Runaway River** family inner tube slide, tubes with one or two riders (little kids can sit on laps) go down a long, winding slide.

The 10 waterslides are the park's big attraction. They range from two long, gentle **Corkscrews** (410 feet long, they start from Michigan's tallest slide tower) to the terrifying **Black Hole**. In it, a green translucent tube goes through the side of a hill, where it's all black, makes several harrowing loops, and emerges, depositing its victims at high speed into a bank of water. Almost as scary is the **Rampage**, which hurtles you in a small sled steeply down a slide and sends you skidding across a pond. In the **Twister**, two slides spiral around each other, enclosed at the top, then opening up. It's fun, not scary. There are also two speed slides and three kiddie water slides. A **sandy beach** is for picnicking and swimming. Other attractions include 18 holes of **miniature golf**, a kiddie **water play area**, and pedal boats.

Two attractions feature combat roles. **Water cannons** are personal giant squirt guns, used in a confined area. The **bumper boat ride** gives you your own little rubber boat, complete with small outboard motor. For five minutes you can bash into other boats in the pond to your heart's content.

Advice: this place is an especially enjoyable and uncrowded if you visit in the morning or after 4 on a weekday, when rates go down. Summer weekends between July 4 and the middle of August are busiest, and Saturday is busiest of all.

Pleasure Island is on Pontaluna road on the way to Hoffmaster State Park, between Grand Haven and Muskegon. From U.S. 31, take the Pontaluna Rd. exit, go 1 1/2 miles west. (616) 798-7857. Open daily from Mem. Day to Labor Day. In the first half of June: open weekday 10:30-3:30, weekends 10:30-6. After that, closes at 8:30 p.m. $14.95 admission and all rides for anyone over 48" tall. $10.95 for kids under 48" or kids 2 to 4. Discounts after 4 p.m.: $8.95, or $6.95 for kids 2 to 4. Senior saver: $6.95 admission for age 60 and up.

MICHIGAN ADVENTURE has fewer crowds, shorter lines, and two scary roller coasters in addition to water park attractions. On the other hand, the setting isn't as attractive. It's less of an all-day family destination. But area teens and preteens prefer it. Sixth-grader Colin Wolf likes the water slides at Pleasure Island but says Michigan's Adventure is "110 times better" because "it's a water park *and* an amusement park. Everybody I know who goes to Michigan's Adventure always goes back."

The **water park** has a wave pool with six-foot waves; a kiddie water play area; the Lazy River and the Action River (inner-tube rides on streams of different speeds); and 11 water slides: speed slides, inner-tube slides, and body slides.

The **amusement park** has 20 rides, including six kiddie rides and two roller coasters. The **Wolverine**, the big, wooden coaster, takes you on a long ride, lulls you into a false sense of security, then drops you by surprise. The **Corkscrew**, Colin's favorite, turns you upside-down twice and has other sudden turns.

To him, the **Log Ride** stands out among the other rides. "You get in a log and drop really fast down a waterfall by surprise." In addition, there's a giant gondola wheel similar to a Ferris wheel; a Tilt-a-Whirl; a Scrambler; the Flying Trapeze swing ride; a Falling Star; a carousel; and Muttley's Putt-Putt car rides.

Michigan's Adventure is 8 miles north of Muskegon. From U.S. 31, take the Russell Rd. exit, follow signs. (616) 766-3377. Open weekends in May, daily beginning in June thru Labor Day. Hours are 11 a.m.-7 p.m., to 8 p.m. from late June thru Labor Day. $15/person; children 2 and under free. Season pass $50.

❶ Muskegon S.P./Scenic Dr. Beautiful park, uncrowded 3 miles of beach, dunes, inland beach & campgrounds.

❷ Winter Sports Complex. Learn to use 40 mph luge sled. Scenic lighted x-c ski trails, warming lodge. In beautiful state park.

❸ Museum of Art. Outstanding small museum geared to a refreshingly broad public. Don't miss Curry's "Tornado over Kansas."

❹ Hackley House. Exuberant, spare-no-expense Queen Anne fantasy, top-notch restoration.

❺ S. S. Silversides. Tour big WWII sub that sank 23 Japanese ships. Looks ready to head out again to sea.

❻ Gillette Visitor Center. Compelling slide show of Michigan's dunes. Sensuous walk thru damp dune woods to spectacular overlook.

❼ Pleasure Island Water Fun Park. Scary "Rampage" Water Slide & "Black Hole"; kiddie water play area; plus attractive picnic area, sandy beach.

Highlights of
Muskegon

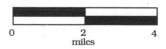

0   2   4
        miles

Hackley & Hume Houses

Gems of Victorian architecture — the exuberant legacy of Muskegon's richest and most generous lumber baron

Victorian love of ornament may have reached a new height in the 1888 home of Muskegon's great benefactor and richest lumber baron, Charles Hackley. When the restoration now underway is finished, it will be the finest restored Queen Anne house in North America. That's the belief of Muskegon County Museum director John McGarry, who oversees the project. "When it's done, it will be Charles Hackley's house in 1890, restored down to the cigar in the ashtray," he says. The complex Victorian paint scheme involves 28 shades of paint, mostly in the green-yellow green-gold-brown spectrum, with some red accents.

The Hackley House shares an elaborate carriage house with the impressive but more modest next door home of Hackley's business partner, Thomas Hume. The three buildings form a remarkable urban ensemble. Their many towers give it the

The Hackley House (left) and Hume House, photographed not long after their completion. These quintessential lumbermen's mansions are being restored with unusual accuracy, thanks to an enormous amount of original documentation about them.

many-turreted silhouette of a romantic walled town, rich in colors and textures. Inside it is almost completely restored and fully furnished, often with the Hackleys' own furniture. Noted architectural historian Wayne Andrews called the Hackley and Hume houses "peerless specimens of the flamboyant style" and devoted nine pages and the cover photo to them in his fascinating *Architecture in Michigan.*

Houses of this size and splendor were usually made of brick or stone, but Hackley and Hume built in wood, the material that made their fortunes. Surfaces are alive with carved and tiled ornament. Stained glass filters outside light for a dreamy interior look in the elaborately carved entry hall. Correspondence between the architect and Hackley reveals the hall's theme of welcome and the architect's little architectural jokes and comments. Carved figures of the Victorians' five races of man greet the visitor. Less obvious are caryatid portraits of Hackley and the architect. Over them all squats Darwin's monkey, looking down from the stairway.

The dining room is another highlight. Plain peach walls enlivened with simple stenciling play up the elaborate decorative detail of the tile fireplace and buffet, carved with widely used Victorian dining room motifs of hunting, fishing, and fruit. Deer, hunting dogs, fishing creels, and apples can all be spotted.

Hackley (1837-1905) refused to take his money and run from the stump-scarred north country when its timber ran out. In Muskegon's greatest boom year of 1886, Hackley and Hume were among the few who already realized that Michigan's timber would soon be gone. To perpetuate their fortune, they bought vast acreages of timberland in the West and South. Hackley apparently regarded his great wealth as a trust fund to be administered for society's benefit — though some small-town cynics attributed his generosity to vanity and a wish to rename Muskegon "Hackleyville." At any rate, Hackley decided to invest in Muskegon and try to develop it as a modern, enlightened industrial city.

A retiring and enigmatic personality, Hackley often deferred to the advice of a trusted circle of friends. He started by giving the city a superb library, park, hospital, and new industrial arts school, then promoted the city as a superior place to live and do business. He and his friends used those model institutions to attract industrial companies that could, and did, turn Muskegon into an important industrial city, the biggest on Lake Michigan's

Muskegon's great benefactor, Charles Hackley, withdrew from the public eye. But he made a ceremony of personally issuing to Muskegon residents library cards to his grand library. To get a card, citizens were ushered to his second-story office (shown above) to see Hackley.

eastern shore. Modern-day Muskegon's leading employers – Sealed Power (now SPX), Brunswick bowling, S. D. Warren paper, and Shaw-Walker office furniture — all originally located in Muskegon because of the Muskegon Improvement Company started by Hackley and his friends.

In all, Hackley's gifts to Muskegon between 1888 and 1912 totaled nearly $6 million — a stunning testimony to the wealth of successful capitalists before income tax. In appreciation, Muskegon has celebrated Hackley Day (May 25) as a school and city holiday since 1888. (Generations of Muskegon natives can still sing the Hackley Day Song!) Hackley's monumental legacies dominate central Muskegon.

Now, when restoration of the two houses is in progress, is an especially interesting time to view the houses. Exposed layers of wall treatments reveal the houses' decorating history. Work on restoring rotted wood ornament continues outside and in the Hume House basement. The Hume House is being restored to 1915 to take advantage of a wonderful resource found in the MSU archives: an insurance inventory taken in that year which lists every piece in every room.

Volunteer guides include details of the restoration process and everyday life in the big Hume family and for the retiring Hackleys. Charles Hackley usually preferred to take a behind-the-scenes role in local affairs. A limp from an old logging accident made it hard to get around. But he did assume one idiosyncratic public role. He asked everyone who applied for a free library card to his splendid public library (see page 514) to come to the second-floor study of his house and get it from him in person.

An especially lovely time to visit the Hackley and Hume houses is on late-afternoon and evening tours in the holiday season. (Call for dates.) Gas lighting and the shadows it casts make the Hackley House's rich colors glow. The houses are authentically decorated for the holidays. Free carriage rides around the block are offered on evening tours.

484 W. Webster at Sixth, in downtown Muskegon, 2 blocks west of Hackley Park. From U. S. 31, take the Muskegon exit for Bus. U.S. 31 (Seaway) to Sixth. Follow signs. (616) 722-7578. Open late May through September, Wed, Sat & Sun 1-4. Group tours by appointment at other times. $2/adults. 12 and under free.

FOR MUSKEGON'S FASCINATING LUMBERING HISTORY. . . . . go to the **Muskegon County Museum** (page 515). In the Lumber Queen gallery, first request to see the outstanding half-hour **tape/slide show.** It clearly conveys the lumber barons' business strategy, along with the colorful, dangerous life in lumber camps. Then look at the dioramas of lumbering scenes in Muskegon.

WALKING TOURS THAT INCLUDE THE HACKLEY AND HUME HOUSES, ... and an English garden, and end with free refreshments are held Wednesday and Sunday by appointment only. Call **Muskegon Heritage Tours**, (616) 728-4393. Adults $7, children 5-18 $2. Group rates are available.

BIG CHANGES NEAR THE HACKLEY HOUSE. . . . . After decades of suffering under a negative self-image as a declining foundry town, Muskegon has waked up to its positives: West Michigan's most extensive lakeshore parks, less expensive boat slips, historic gems and tremendous cultural resources, a downtown that is reorienting itself to Muskegon Lake now that key foundries are gone, and a multiethnic lumbertown populace that likes to party and drink beer. That can be refreshing when so much of West Michigan is dominated by the Dutch, who mainly only drink at home. The new SPX headquarters and gorgeous **Rafferty's restaurant** offer a grand sunset view looking west down Muskegon Lake. . . . . **Heritage Village,** the neighborhood around the Hackley House, is coming back after years of devolving into low-rent apartments. Two pleasant bed and breakfasts are on the same block as the Hackley House. Houses are being moved onto vacant lots. The historic **Fire Barn Museum** at 510 W. Clay is open the same hours as the Hackley House. Retired firefighters can show kids how to use replica equipment. And in 1994 Business Route 31 will be rerouted near the lake, so high-speed traffic won't tear through the historic neighborhood. . . . . . The historic buildings remaining along **Western Avenue,** down the hill from the Hackley House toward the lake, are showing signs of life. **Seeback's Deli** and coffeehouse (616-722-4362) at 477 W. Western Avenue is delightful. It's open Mon through Thurs 9 a.m.-6 p.m., Fri & Sat 9 a.m.-10:30 p.m., and Sun 9 a.m.-1 p.m. The handsome Romanesque Revival **Union Depot** (1895) becomes the Chamber of Commerce/Visitors' Bureau new home as of fall, 1994. And the twin-towered Amazon Building is being developed as condos and shops.

CHEAP SIGHTSEEING TOURS OF THE MUSKEGON AREA. . . . . are available via the **Muskegon Trolley Company.** All major destinations are connected by trolley buses. For 25¢ a person, you can get an hour's tour. Most weeks it's daily including Sunday. You can flag down the trolley. One route goes around Muskegon Lake from the state park on the north to downtown, the Hackley-Hume houses, and Pere Marquette State Park. Another goes south to Hoffmaster State Park and Pere Marquette. Call (616) 724-6420, or stop by the bus kiosk in Muskegon Mall. An informative brochure/map tells you want you're looking at.

EVENTS IN AND AROUND MUSKEGON. . . . . include the **Cherry County Playhouse** in its new home in the superb Frauenthal Theater, Friday-evening summer parties in Hackley Park, concerts by the **West Shore Symphony** and the summertime Blue Lake Fine Arts Camp special guests, a top-notch civic theater, the Muskegon Fury professional hockey team, a big air show, and more. . . . . . Call the **Convention and Visitors Bureau** at 1-800-235-FUNN or (616) 722-3751 for events info. After fall, 1994, it's in the Union Depot at 586 W. Western at Sixth, down the hill from the Hackley House. . . . . . For **films, plays, exhibits, lectures,** etc., call the Hackley Library (616-722-7276).

Muskegon Museum of Art

Western Michigan's top art museum —
small, stimulating, geared to a broad audience

Thanks to the beneficence of museum founder Charles Hackley (page 506) and two astute early directors, Muskegon has long had the finest art museum in western Michigan. It's a very pleasant place, accessible and stimulating. The Hackley Gallery contains the permanent collection, strong on realistic paintings that are interesting and complex. The Walker Gallery is a big, open space well suited to changing shows, sometimes very large in scale and quite powerful.

Some choice paintings are here, mostly purchased many decades ago. The best-known is the dramatic "Tornado over Kansas" by John Steuart Curry, a prominent proponent of the regionalism that dominated American art in the 1930s. Whistler's famous "A Study in Rose and Brown," a simplified, unpretty portrait of a young woman, created such a controversy in Muskegon that the museum's talented first director, Raymond Wyer, quit in a huff. He then went to Worcester, Massachusetts, and also built its museum into one of national prominence. The extraordinary "Tea Time," by Whistler's contemporary William Merritt Chase, was also avant-garde in its day. Winslow Homer, Edward Hopper, and Andrew Wyeth, are among the other prominent American painters represented here.

The European holdings, not as extensive, also include some choice works. The most important is "St. Jerome in Penitence," painted circa 1516 by Joos Van Cleve. The saint, in a fascinating, vivid landscape, is surrounded by symbolic and anthropomorphic forms. Don't miss another important Dutch painting, Jan van der Heyden's haunting "The Moat of a Castle with Drawbridge." Portraits of Martin Luther and his wife, Katharina von Bora, were painted by their friend, Cranach the Elder.

Unusual treasures for a small museum on the geographical periphery of the art world include a set of Rembrandt etchings and the largest collection of works of **Françoise Gilot**, both generous gifts. Gilot was part of a circle including Matisse (who influenced her style), Braque, and Picasso, with whom she lived

for years. (Paloma Picasso is their daughter.) In "Gods of Greece,"
all her works with classical mythology themes are shown in
Muskegon (Sept. 8-Nov. 27, 1994). Another good show is "Clearly
Art: Pilchuk's Glass Legacy" (Dec. 9, 1994-Jan. 29, 1995), featuring works from the preeminent Seattle glassblowing school,
including Dale Chihuly and cohorts. Some two dozen **changing
exhibits** a year cover topics from printmaking to children's book
illustration to porcelain and cross-fertilization between Asian
and Western art. They make it worthwhile to stop in when you're
in the vicinity. (Access and parking are easy.)

**Today the Hackley Gallery has been restored to look much as it did in
1912: paintings hang over one another, brilliantly set off against walls
of dark green and cranberry. Astute purchases by its first director
formed the nucleus of this outstanding small museum.**

"We've always been a cutting-edge, open museum, geared to a broader public but ahead of the crowd," said former director Al Kochka with pride. Recently the Hackley Gallery has been restored to its original 1912 appearance. Dark, rich green and cranberry fabrics cover main gallery walls and set off the paintings like vivid jewels. The deep, saturated colors are a radical departure from the white walls that became de rigueur for museums in the 1950s. Over the past 15 years, museums have gradually introduced colors (mostly pastels) on gallery walls. Muskegon museum staff thought long and hard before returning to the dark colors, but everyone is pleased with the stunning results and the way they make the marble wainscoting stand out. By comparison, the one light gray gallery seems dull. The renovation also included installing state-of-the-art climate control systems and removing drop ceilings to reveal the English box-style ceiling system for skylights.

The lower-level **gift shop** has a nice selection of notecards, books, posters, jewelry, and inexpensive gifts for children.

On West Webster just east of Third and Hackley Park in downtown Muskegon. Park alongside the towered building on Third. (616) 722-2600. Handicapped accessible. Tues-Fri 10-5, Sat & Sun 12-5. Free; donations appreciated.

FABULOUS VICTORIANA NEAR THE ART MUSEUM . . . . . Right next door on Webster at Third is the first and most splendid of all Charles Hackley's gifts to Muskegon, the **Hackley Public Library**, a Romanesque Revival castle from 1890. Don't miss the impressive main reading room sparkling with leaded glass; the huge oil painting of the library's dedication (a hundred deft portraits
traits of Muskegon society at the twilight of the lumbering era); four stone fireplaces with Art Nouveau touches; and the upstairs children's room mural of a parade of colorful literary characters from around the world. . . . . Across Webster is the **Torrent House**, a massive stone chateau built in 1892 for the then-astonishing sum of $250,000. Lumberman and mayor John Torrent located his magnificent pile here to show up his rival, Hackley. Visitors are welcome to look in. . . . . At Webster and Third is shady **Hackley Park**, Hackley's entry in the competition among aspiring cities of the late 19th century to erect monumental public sculptures honoring the veterans who served their country. At the corners, bronze figures of Lincoln, Grant, Sherman, and Admiral David Farragut were radical for their day because of their realistic

poses. Popular **Parties in the Park** with live music, food, and beer are held here Fridays from 5 to 9, from early June through early September.

A CURIOUS DOWNTOWN MALL. . . . . A block down Third at Clay is one of the nation's most unusual malls. In the 1970s **Muskegon Mall** put a roof over four principal downtown retail blocks. It incorporated several large office buildings and the stately old Century Club and tore down 96 surrounding buildings to provide free parking in the heart of downtown. The only trouble is, there's not much of downtown left except for parking lots and large institutional buildings. It was a dramatic — or desperate — solution for a depressed industrial city. Unlike many such cities, downtown Muskegon is not deserted at night. Nearby frontage along Muskegon Lake has finally been developed for recreation and entertainment, and the mall is being expanded to stay competitive.

AN AMBITIOUS AND CREATIVE LOCAL HISTORY MUSEUM. . . . . New directions make downtown's **Muskegon County Museum** an outstanding rainy-day destination. An ambitious new **multimedia gallery** opening in 1994 deals with local history in terms of the **changing environment** and ecological issues. It starts with geology, rocks and minerals, and mastodon bones found by the salt in northern Muskegon County, and ends with zebra mussels, otters at play on an old foundry site, and the nature in a typical backyard. "The Powers of Ten" film puts **geological time in perspective.** Upcoming permanent galleries deal with human history and recreate a factory setting. The museum can do a lot because it produces its own exhibits in-house, then recycles many to out-county sites. Every two months there's a new **changing exhibit,** often devoted to collectors with delightfully folksy captions: Your Favorite Christmas Gift, Tiny Objects You Saved, yo-yos, etc. , ... Other highlights include the lumber exhibits (see above) and the poignant display on the extinct **passenger pigeons** that once darkened the skies here along the Lake Michigan shore, and the successful **BodyWorks hands-on gallery** of the human body. Its food and calories game is a hit. A dramatic, oversized painting by folk artist Lewis Cross of nearby Spring Lake shows a swirl of the docile birds being shot at by farmers. Also, on the lower level, Victor Casenelli's 19 dreamily impressionistic **murals of Muskegon's history,** done for Lumberman's Bank in 1929. *430 W. Clay at Fourth in downtown Muskegon, 1 block west of Hackley Park. Barrier-free entrance on Fourth St. side; phone ahead to have it open. (616) 722-0278. Mon-Fri 9:30-4:30, Sat & Sun 12:30-4:30. Free.*

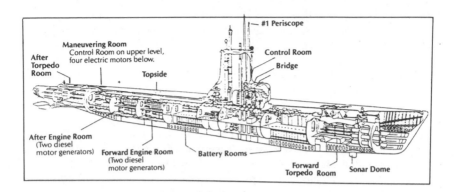

U. S. S. Silversides

In Muskegon, tour one of World War II's fightingest subs, which looks much as it did back then.

For anyone interested in World War II or naval warfare, this is a major attraction in western Michigan. Military equipment that survives a war has usually seen little action, but this big sub was a Pacific workhorse. Completed just after the attack on Pearl Harbor in 1942, the Silversides went on to sink 23 ships. It went on 14 patrols in all, losing only one man while sinking over 90,000 tons. During one reconnaissance mission, crew members even watched a Japanese horse race by periscope.

The excellent condition of the ship and the fact that its furnishings are nearly complete make the tour worthwhile. As you go below and walk from bow to stern, it looks very much as it did during World War II, with the same bunks, sonar equipment, brass torpedo doors, radios, and charting table. The tour gives a good feel of what it was like in those very cramped spaces to go out on a 45-day tour deep into enemy territory.

1346 Bluff, in Pere Marquette Park on the channel wall's south side. Call to confirm location for 1995. Take U.S. 31 to the Sherman Rd. exit; turn west onto Sherman, which becomes Beach St; follow Beach St. to Pere Marquette Park. Ticket booth (616) 755-1230. Jun-Aug daily 10-5:30. April and Oct Sat & Sun 10-5:30; May & Sept weekdays 1-5; Adults $3.50, seniors 62 and older $2, children 5-11 $1.50. **Overnight camping program** *6 p.m.-9:30 a.m. Mon-Thurs $10 per person, Fri-Sun $15 per person.*

Muskegon State Park & Winter Sports Park

*A quarter-mile of Olympic sledding thrills,
delightful cross-country skiing even at night,
and wonderfully uncrowded beaches in summer*

Large snowfalls and beautiful, forested scenery make Muskegon State Park ideal for winter sports. Due to nearby Lake Michigan, it commonly has at least some snow when most of southern Michigan is completely snowless. In a dark, snowy evergreen forest, the golden glow of dots from the lighted ski trails and the big golden beacon of the warming house's huge windows are enchanting. The low lampposts make intimate pools of light – much more beautiful than the floodlit effect of high parking lot-style lights. A family-oriented ice rink is also maintained, weather permitting.

Centerpieces of the beautiful Muskegon Winter Sports Complex in Muskegon State Park are a **luge run** (the only other one in the U.S. is at Lake Placid) and some of the longest lighted cross-country ski trails in Michigan. In the luge, an Olympic sport, a small, one-person sled of wood, metal, and canvas is steered down an iced chute that has wooden walls. The side walls are contoured with snowy slush, and the luge run is iced nightly after each day's use with a mix of snow and water, then misted for a slick, even surface.

The helmeted driver lies down facing up on the sled and steers it by bending one flexible front wood runner support and raising the opposite shoulder. Everything goes by in a blur. On the Muskegon course, sleds can go up to 40 m.p.h. And that seems even faster when you're four inches from the ground. Anybody can experience the thrill of luging. Some people have more of a knack for steering to achieve the maximum possible speed, without costly overcorrections on turns.

A volunteer group of outdoors enthusiasts started and developed this remarkably attractive facility in order to develop interest in the sport in the Midwest. Among them was Mark Grimette from North Muskegon, whose team's fourth-place finish in the

1994 Winter Olympics was the best an American team has ever done in the luge.

Anyone can buy a day's pass, which includes a sled, helmet, and coach. You don't need reservations. Just show up in lightweight shoes or boots, gloves, and clothes that are warm but not fancy. First-timers are fully supervised; they start at the base of the starting ramp of the shorter, slower lower track, so they can become accustomed to the sensation and gradually build-up speed without being terrified. Careful volunteer coaches observe and instruct all lugers and decide when they can advance to a higher level. Waits are not long. By the end of the day beginners will be completing the entire lower run in 10 seconds, a speed of about 25 m.p.h. The faster (40 m.p.h.), twisting upper track has far more turns and banks.

"It was an incredible experience – the speed!" said one happy novice who traveled from Jackson to learn to luge. "As long as you felt comfortable, they moved you right along! We did the [lighted] 5k ski trail as it was getting dark. The trail was really nice; it goes into pockets of trees."

The **ski trails** were laid out specifically for skiing. Many state park ski trails are really hiking trails, with turns too sudden for all but the best skiers. The trails here are ideal for novices, because they combine easy turns and interesting scenery. The 2 1/2 kilometer trail is flat to rolling; the 5k trail has three hills that provide a challenge for better skiers. (A bypass lets less skillful skiers avoid the short, steep hill.) Trails are tracked for both ski-skaters and conventional skiers. Sheltering pines protect skiers from the wind and preserve the snow from the sun. Design details have been better thought out on this volunteer project than on many professional jobs. **Ski rentals** are available for adults and children.

The Winter Sports Park is at the north end of Muskegon State Park, off Scenic Dr. across from the Lakeshore Campground, around the curve north of the landmark blockhouse. (616) 744-9629. Season from mid-Dec. to mid-March, depending on weather. Park hours: Mon-Fri 3-10, Sat & Sun 10-10. Luge open hours: Fri 5-9, Sat 12-9 & Sun 10-6. Competitions and meets held on Sat. a.m.; public welcome. State park sticker required: $4/day, $18/year. Ski trail fee: Mon-Fri $3 adults, $1.50 children; Sat-Sun $4 adults, $2 children. Luge fee (including equipment rental): lower track, $12 adults, $8 age 17 and under; upper track, $17 adults, $13 age 17 and under.

BEAUTIFUL BEACHES THAT ARE NEVER CROWDED . . . . . are what **Muskegon State Park** is known for. When Holland and Grand Haven are packed, this is the place to reliably find waves, sand, and solitude. There are three miles of Lake Michigan beach along Scenic Drive, plus **Snug Harbor**, a pleasant, quiet bay of Muskegon Lake, with warmer water. Off Memorial Drive, Snug Harbor is a perfect place for small children to swim, swing, and fish. Boaters and fishermen favor the 177-site, modern **Muskegon Lake Campground** by the boat launch on the channel's Muskegon Lake side. The 180-site **Lake Michigan Campground** (also modern) is among the most scenic state park campgrounds, nestled in a grove of towering maples and beaches, an easy walk across the dunes from a campers-only beach. Campgrounds fill on summer weekends, often by Wednesday night. *On the north side of the Muskegon Lake channel. From U.S. 31, take M-120 southwest and follow the signs through North Muskegon onto Memorial Drive (the park's south entrance). Or take Scenic Dr. from Whitehall. (616) 744-3480. State park sticker required: $4/day, $18/year.*

THE PERFECT PLACE FOR A SNACK AFTER SKIING . . . . . is the cozy **Bear Lake Tavern** in North Muskegon. *360 Ruddiman at the Bear Lake channel. (616) 744-1161. It's about three miles east of Lake Michigan on the shore road along Muskegon Lake.*

White River Lighthouse Museum

An unspoiled and picturesque setting — amid the relaxed, old-fashioned resort life of the White Lake area

Tucked away behind huge beech trees at the channel from Lake Michigan to White Lake, this old limestone and brick lighthouse looks so simple and homey, it seems the lighthouse-keeper could still be there. Today this delightful little museum owned by Fruitland Township is still a home — of the curator. Maybe the lived-in feel, and having a small boy around, is part of what gives this place its special aura. Part of the magic is getting there: taking the winding lane out through the old summer houses, and walking through the deep shade of the beeches into the lighthouse's sunny yard, where you see the big lake for the first time.

Tightly spiraled in the narrow tower is a beautiful wrought iron stairway. After a somewhat spooky, claustrophobic ascent, it leads you to a fine view of Lake Michigan.

Low-key displays include photographs, maps, ships' models, and nautical artifacts, mainly about White Lake's maritime history. The curator is happy to explain how the museum's navigational devices are used. The first boats in the area were Indian fishing canoes, followed by fur-traders' canoes, lumber schooners, and the resort-era steamers beginning in the 1880s. Big steamers brought summer people from Chicago, Indiana, and St. Louis to White Lake's summer hotels and cottages. A **changing exhibit,** based on the curator's ongoing research and new historical resources, is mounted each season. For 1994 it features photos of lighthouse life, taken by a keeper's daughter.

A museum highlight is the station's original Fresnel lens, which reflected and magnified the oil lamp in the tower. These beautiful big crystal lenses, handmade in France, were the lighthouse keepers' crown jewels, kept clean and polished, along with the brass mountings. A Fourth Order Fresnel lens like this magnified the oil lamp so it could be seen 14 miles away. Today an electric light has been installed. When it's turned on at dusk, as it is on fall afternoons when the museum is open, the lens pro-

This detail of a late 19th-century painting shows the White River light-house and a lumber schooner at the channel between White Lake and Lake Michigan. Several of Frederick Norman's on-the-scene paintings of the White River logging era can be seen at the Whitehall branch of First of America Bank at 119 S. Mears.

jects beautiful rainbows around the room

A **shop** goes well beyond mass-produced souvenirs. It offers watercolors and prints of the lighthouse by various artists, and popular ties handpainted with the lighthouse and other nautical designs. **Lee Murdock**, singer of old and new Great Lakes sailing songs, comes yearly for a day of afternoon storytelling and evening concerts. (For 1994 it's August 6.)

Year-round, people come to the lighthouse to walk along the channel wall and get to Lake Michigan. (The beach up to the water line is privately owned.) This "Government Channel" was created in 1871, during the lumber boom. Lumber schooners leaving Lake Michigan's lumber ports had become so numerous that the federal government financed many navigational improve-ments, including this lighthouse, erected in 1875.

Civilized simplicity still sets the tone for White Lake resort life, which feels far away from today's harried pace. Cottages here are likely painted brown, or classic white with green trim, *never* mauve and pink. Trees and green are everywhere. These charms are showcased on the drive out South Shore Drive from Whitehall to the lighthouse.

The direct channel here bypassed the White River's cir-cuitous old channel north of here. Today the **Old Channel Trail** starting in Montague and going west along White Lake, then north near Lake Michigan, makes for an exceptionally scenic drive. To get to little **Medbury Park** and the beach across the channel from the lighthouse here, take Old Channel Trail, but turn west at Lau Road when the main road turns north.

The lighthouse is at the south side of the White Lake channel, at the end of Murray Rd. Murray Rd. goes west from the junction of Scenic Dr. (along Lake Michigan from Muskegon) and South Shore Rd. (along White Lake from Whitehall). Or come from U.S. 31 via Duck Lake State Park (see below). (616) 894-8265. **Museum** *open Mem. Day through Labor Day Tues-Fri 11-5, Sat & Sun noon-6. In Sept.: weekends only. $1 admission ages 19 and over. Ages 10-18: 50¢. Tours of museum and dune ecology are available by arrangement.* **Grounds and channel walk** *are a* **public park** *open year-round.*

A SCENIC DRIVE AND NICE BEACHES . . . . . To get to the beaches, go south along the aptly named Scenic Drive to **Duck Lake State Park**, an old scout camp. It has beach frontage on both Lake Michigan (park along Scenic) and on pretty Duck Lake, which is unspoiled by development and good for fishing. Take Michillinda Road to the main park entrance on Duck Lake. The picnic area is beneath big oaks. The park has no camping at this time. . . . . All the major east-west roads lead to **Scenic Drive**, which parallels Lake Michigan from Muskegon State Park in North Muskegon to White Lake. For a pretty, winding way to Muskegon, continue south on Scenic from Duck Lake State Park through the wooded dunes of Muskegon State Park into the beautiful lakefront suburb of North Muskegon. *To get to Duck Lake State Park from U.S. 31,, take the Lakewood Club exit 10 miles north of Muskegon and follow signs. (616) 744-3480. No camping.*

THE LOW-KEY CHARMS OF WHITEHALL AND MONTAGUE. . . . . Friendly and unfussy, the twin towns at the head of White Lake offer two rival weathervane manufacturers (both on Water Street in downtown Montague), two drugstores with soda fountains (**Lipka's** and the bustling **Todd Pharmacy**), both on Ferry in Montague, and two good eat-in bakeries, both in Whitehall. **Morat's Bakery** on North Mears overlooks the White River marsh, and **Robinson's Bakery** at 1019 S. Mears makes outstanding, authentic Swedish breads and cookies.

There's the weird, wonderful **Montague Historical Museum**, a community attic in a church on Meade and Church up the hill in Montague. It's open summer weekends 1-5. Also worth checking out in central Whitehall: the **Timekeepers' Clock Shop**, 303 S. Mears, a shop for clock restoration and repair inside a handsome historic house used as a bed and breakfast;

American Sampler gift shop at 124 S. Mears; and, inside the First of America Muskegon Bank at 119 S. Mears, the remarkable, accurate **paintings chronicling White Lake's lumbering industry**, done from life by an area signpainter in the 1870s. . . . . . The local claim to fame, the **world's largest weather vane**, is less appealing than its setting on **Ellenwood Landing.** That new marina is on the causeway between Whitehall and Montague that separates White Lake from the sweeping marsh of the White River. It offers fine sunset views. Sailboats set the tone of boating here. Fast motor boats don't like to contend with these pokey vessels, so they gravitate elsewhere. . . . . . Take in the views and the marsh's many swans from the asphalt boardwalk or the **Dog and Suds** parking lot, across the causeway from Ellenwood Landing.

FOR MORE INFORMATION ABOUT THE WHITE LAKE AREA. . . . . stop by the **Chamber of Commerce**, in the old depot on the causeway, for more information about this attractive, unspoiled resort area. Or call (616) 893-4585. . . . Summer events include **concerts** at **Blue Lake Fine Arts Camp** (616-894-1966) on Twin Lake, outside Whitehall, and summer theater at the **Howmet Playhouse** (616 894-2540) in Whitehall, affiliated with Blue Lake. . . . . For info on the pretty **Hart-Montague Trail** for bicycles, rollerblades, and wheelchairs, see page 526.

AN ACCESSIBLE TREASURE FOR CANOEISTS. . . . Famous as a logging river, the **White River** today is less canoed, less fished, and more remote in feel than some better-known, longer rivers up north. A quiet river trip here puts you in touch with wildlife that usually flees at the sound of hikers. Especially in the early morning and late afternoon, you can see blue heron, sandhill cranes, many kinds of ducks, and occasionally beaver.

The narrow White winds across a floodplain that's a half-mile to a mile wide. Sometimes it's up against a steep, forested bank. Sometimes it's surrounded by marshy flats. Other times it flows through hardwood and conifer forest that hasn't been logged in this century. Within the Manistee National Forest, it's a designated **wild-scenic river**, which means that timber on the floodplain can't be cut. Fishing is good for bass, northern pike, and salmon and steelhead runs.

There aren't many public access points to the river. By far the easiest way to canoe it is to use the **Happy Mohawk Canoe Livery**, which rents canoes, tubes, rafts, and kayaks. Sample prices, including all equipment and transportation: $11.25/person for a canoe trip of four hours paddling time; $7/person for a 2 or 3-hour tubing expedition.

The Happy Mohawk owners also own and operate the exceptionally picturesque **White River Campground**. It's in the heavily wooded valley of pretty little Sand Creek where it joins the White River. *735 E. Fruitvale Rd., 5 miles east of U.S. 31 northeast of Montague. From U.S. 31, take Fruitvale Rd. exit, go 5 miles east. (616) 894-4209. Campground open May through October.*

Chapter 7

Northern Michigan

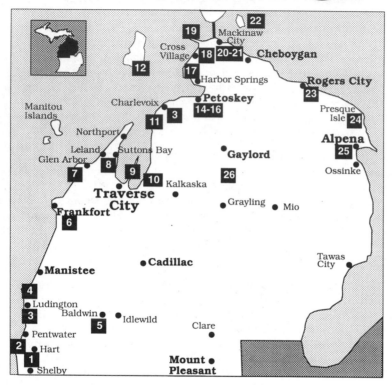

HIGHLIGHTS

For restaurants & lodgings, see *Hunts' Restaurants & Lodgings of Michigan*

INTRODUCTION

Northern Michigan

Tourists and resorters have flocked to northern Michigan to escape the summer heat ever since loggers left the region in the 1880s. Once the logs gave out, the same railroads and Great Lakes shipping lines that hauled the lumber south began advertising the region as a vacation paradise and started transporting vacationers to the region. Wealthy families from St. Louis, Indianapolis, and other Midwestern cities built big summer cottages up here, some quite large. Most of these fine old homes are still in use, many enjoyed by descendants of their original owners.

Driving north, you can often feel the temperature drop as you enter the upper third of the Lower Peninsula. Accompanying this delightful change is the changing landscape: farms become farther apart and forests thicker. The fresh, cool air and the abundance of shoreline have made this region a growing tourism area. In no other part of Michigan does tourism so dominate the local economy.. With interstates, the North has become accessible for getaway weekends and year-round second homes. (Locals regard hurried weekend "trunk-slammers" with far more disdain than established summer people with cottages.)

Other economies up here have failed to thrive. Significant agriculture is limited to the fruit belt along Lake Michigan and potatoes near Rogers City. With a few exceptions, industry didn't develop, either. But tourism continues to grow, with more and more resort developments and golf courses being built. The fate of most of those living in the north is to work like crazy and endure crowds for short, intense tourism seasons (July and August, and for some the ski season from January into March). The fall color season bustles briefly. Outstanding destination golf courses draw golfers from May through October. September is the real sleeper season for people who want nice weather and no crowds.

There's a lot of poverty and illiteracy that's hidden from visitors who stick near the water. But it's quite obvious along inland highways, where you see a lot of weather-worn trailers and shacks with huge woodpiles. Love of the outdoor environment and shared scenery is the universal common denominator for everybody up here. "A view of the bay and half the pay" are the bywords of every urban refugee who tries to establish a professional career in Traverse City of Petoskey.

Hart-Montague Trail

A beautiful, easy bike path
through woods and orchards, hills and villages.

This 22 1/2-mile asphalt path leads bicyclists (roller rollerbladers and wheelchair users, too) past a variety of rural scenery and small-town sights that are really surprising to anyone not familiar with the high sandy hills and orchards of Oceana County, between Muskegon and Ludington. (Horses are also permitted on the trail, but not on the 10-foot-wide asphalt strip.) In the northern reaches of Michigan's fabulously diversified fruit belt (see page 47), Oceana County is a top U.S. producer of apples, tart cherries, asparagus, and Christmas trees.

Along the trail, farming is much in evidence. There's the sight and smell of cherry and apple blossoms in mid-May; the wind-sown wild asparagus along the trail, hidden and succulent in spring, feathery and gold in fall; the ripe red fruit in July and September; and the stacks of fruit crates by the long brick canneries.

Contrasted to these orderly fields are stretches where trees and shrubs have grown up along the trail. They harbor wildlife, which is fun to see while bicycling. And they buffer road noise along the trail's southern third, where it parallels Oceana Drive (Old U.S. 31). In the north, between Mears and Shelby, the trail goes through a high oak forest and looks down on a lake.

Starting in the 1870s, the area's agricultural economy developed in conjunction with the very railroad line that has been converted into the Hart-Montague Trail. Today the string of five small market centers spawned by the railroad remain no more than villages. Hart, the county seat and biggest town, has a population of just under 2,000. Their small, simple scale makes these towns ideal for bicyclists to explore. The entire landscape has the nostalgic simplicity of rural America in the 1940s and 1950s, a time before sprawl and rural decay, when the countryside looked like the pictures of Dick and Jane visiting their friendly, apple-checked grandparents down on the farm.

Scattered along the linear park are four picnic shelters and

Bicyclists pass lots of asparagus fields and orchards on the way from Montague to Hart. Five villages on the way and four picnic shelters offer plenty of opportunities for rest and refreshment.

three unsheltered tables for trail users. There are no restrooms or phones along the trail, but every town has a restaurant. Bikes can be rented at several places along the trail. (See note below.)

Which direction to start in? None of the bike rental places currently offers shuttles, so unless you have two cars, you'll have to make a round trip. The views from the north to the south are definitely the best. The distant hills are so dramatic and striking, it hardly seems like Michigan. The grade on the trail's northern third is slightly downhill from north to south—so you might want to save that for a boost when you're tired. South from Rothbury, it's flatter and less interesting.

If you've been on rails-to-trails bikeways before, you're aware of how easy, almost effortless, the bicycling is, thanks to the gentle railroad grade. The only exception is when there's a strong wind in the wrong direction. Even a 10-year-old in not very good shape could accomplish a round trip with an overnight. Hart, at the northern trailhead, is a pleasant town with a beautiful, wooded park and campground overlooking a small lake and swimming beach. At the south trailhead, the twin towns of Montague and Whitehall sit at the east end of White Lake, a drowned river mouth that empties into Lake Michigan, just seven miles away. (The best bike route to a Lake Michigan beach is following Garfield Road due west out of New Era to the Stony Lake area.) Both Hart and Whitehall/Montague have motels and bed and breakfast inns.

Two helpful **map-guides** may be requested by calling (616) 873-3083 weekdays. A little booklet with ads has lots of tips, ads for most area bed and breakfasts, and a trail map. An area map for bicyclists shows the best bike routes to area attractions like Silver Lake and Stony Lake. These routes are quite busy in summer and are for experienced cyclists accustomed to auto traffic.

Here are points of interest in each town along the trail. Every town has at least one cafe. Many establishments are closed on Sundays.

HART. John Gurney Park offers roomy camping with all the amenities (electricity, water and sewer, showers; $12-14/night, less for rustic sites), in a beautiful wooded setting overlooking a lake with fishing and a wading beach. (It is a bit weedy.) There's tennis and a playground. *Northeast of downtown Hart at 407 State. (616) 873-4959 or (616) 873-2488 (in winter). Camping reservations taken; only fills on holiday weekends.*

Hart has a pleasant downtown with La Fiesta Mexican restaurant and some fine old houses.

MEARS. Smallest of the trailside towns, and home of the **Oceana Co. Historical Museum** with changing displays of local history, two blocks west of the blinker light on Fox Road. *It's open between Memorial Day and Labor Day weekends, on week-ends from 2 to 5 and on July and August Wednesdays, also 2-5. (616) 873-2600/(616) 861-2965. Donations appreciated.*

SHELBY. Right by the trail, **Shelby Gemstones** makes "the ulti-mate simulated diamond" and shows visitors how it's done (except for certain secret chemicals) in hourly shows in a 50-seat auditorium. Simulated rubies, emeralds, and sapphires are also made here, and set, like the diamonds, in 600 styles of 14K gold jewelry, displayed in the showroom. *On Industrial Dr. northeast of downtown Shelby. (616) 861-2165. Open year-round, Mon-Fri 9-5:30, Sat noon-4.*

Downtown Shelby, along a north-south street just east of the trail, is a lively little place. More businesses are along Oceana Dr. (Old U.S. 31), another north-south road farther east. There on the northeast side of town, across from the high school, the **Shelby Pavilion** (616-861-2300) is a nifty, old-fashioned roller rink and ice cream parlor. It includes the **Fireplug Restaurant**.

MONTAGUE. See pages 520-521.

*Hart trailhead is just east of the U.S. 31 Polk Rd. exit at the parking lot to Hansen's supermarket. **Montague trailhead** is on Eilers Rd. just east of Bus. Route 31 at the northeast edge of Montague. Administered by Silver Lake State Park; call (616) 873-3083 for information. Trail pass: $2/day, $10/year, or $5/day, $25/year family pass, available at vendors in each town: in Hart, the Country Store Dollar Store, next to Hansen's; in Mears, at The Woodshed; in Shelby at the Shelby Pharmacy; in New Era at the Country Variety gas station; in Rothbury at the Shop N Go; in Montague at the Bicycle Depot.*

BIKE RENTALS ALONG THE TRAIL are . . . . .

◆ in **Hart** at the Wells 602 House Bed & Breakfast, 602 State Street. (616) 873-3834.

◆ in **Rothbury** at Rothbury Hardware & Farm Supply. (616) 861-2418 or (616) 894-8590. Closed Sunday.

◆ in **Montague** at the **Bicycle Depot** on Bus. U.S. 31 on the northeast side of town.

WINTER ON THE TRAIL . . . . . **cross-country skiers** and snowmobilers are both permitted on the trail. Because of the railroad right-of way's long sight lines, the snowmobilers can't come upon the skiers by surprise. The trail parallels nearby Lake Michigan, so snow is plentiful, thanks to the lake effect.

Mac Woods' Dune Rides and Silver Lake State Park

Thrills and insight on the ghostly dunes,
with sunset's pinks and purple shadows

This 35-minute ride up and down the sand dunes at Silver Lake offers thrills, hauntingly eerie scenery, and surprisingly intelligent commentary. It's actually worth the money, unlike most of the overpriced go-kart rides, water slides, and family attractions that could make a Silver Lake vacation a thrifty parent's nightmare.

The eight-mile tour conveys the drama of these unusual dunes west and north of Silver Lake. They are *live* dunes, constantly moved by the wind. On a windy day you can feel the dunes in action as you're peppered with wind-borne sand. When the shoreline timber was logged off in the 19th century, hardy dune grass restabilized most denuded sand dunes enough that new vegetation eventually stopped most wind erosion and created "dead" dunes. But in a few places the dunes were so high and windblown that dune grasses couldn't get established.

Crescent-shaped Silver Lake itself is filling in with windblown sand about four feet a year. It's really becoming "Sliver Lake," the tour guide jokes. Eventually the wind will cut down the high dunes that separate Silver Lake from Lake Michigan to a more typical height. A few sandblasted pine stumps remain from the logging era. Treetops buried by shifting dunes look like bushes. The buried jack pines die, but poplars survive by sending out additional root systems from their trunks. Mostly, though, what you see is a treeless desert, more like the Sahara than normal Michigan dunes with their diverse plant life.

Courteous well-informed drivers take visitors in safe, fat-tired trucks that have been modified as long, open-air vehicles. The ride includes some moderately thrilling dips and climbs, stops for picture taking, and a pause at the beach to wade in Lake Michigan. Towards sunset is by far the best time to go on the ride. The flaming sky and blue lake are dramatic behind the rosy dunes, and the slanting light delineates the dunes' shapes and patterns. Oddly, crowds are smaller at this spectacular time.

Old-fashioned tourism prevails here. The dune rides' gift shop is a classic, genial tourist trap. The Burma-Shave-type signs as you enter the dunes have corny mother-in-law jokes. In the 1930s, resort operator Mac Woods bought a thousand acres of this duneland cheap. When the state of Michigan bought the land as part of an expanded Silver Lake State Park, the dune rides retained concession rights to continue operations. Since the dunes are already actively moving, the rides don't contribute to extra erosion.

On 16th Ave. at Scenic Drive just south of Silver Lake, Mears, MI. From U.S. 31, take Shelby or Hart exits, turn west, and follow the signs. (616) 873-2817. Open daily from mid-May thru mid-October. hours from mid-June thru Labor Day: 9:30-sundown. Shorter hours otherwise. Adults $9, children 3-11 $6, under 3 free.

THE MIDWEST'S ONLY DESIGNATED OFF-ROAD-VEHICLE AREA IN SAND DUNES . . . . . is at the north end of the dunes at **Silver Lake State Park**. Here the 300-space parking lot is frequently filled as four-wheelers, dune buggies, trucks, and motorcycles from all over the Midwest create a constant whine and roar that's heard for miles. This goes on from April 1 through October 31. Sandy Korners (616-873-5048) offers **ORV rentals**, lessons, and guided drives. . . . . For info on Michigan's two other **designated ORV areas** and hundreds of miles of marked trails, call (517) 373-1275, weekdays 8-5.

WALKING THROUGH THE DUNES . . . . . is permitted in a third section of Silver Lake State Park. But the distant roar of off-road vehicles is omnipresent. Wilderness-seekers will prefer the undeveloped **Nordhouse Dunes** north of **Ludington State Park** (page 535).

THE SILVER LAKE SCENE . . . . . involves commercial tourism of an intensity seldom found in Michigan. Minigolf, go-kart rides, Jellystone Park, waterslides, trout farms, frozen yogurt stands, and such are everywhere, and hardly anything is cheap. But when the sun is low and the sky illuminated, it is lovely to look across the genuinely silver lake to the ghostly bare, dunes. Blue shadows are cast on the pink dunes. . . . . **Pontoons, sailboards, jet skis, and more can be rented** from the Wave Club, (616-873-3700) . . . . The **Silver Lake State Park beach** along Silver Lake takes advantage of the beautiful dune view and provides an island of some serenity. It's a kempt, suburban little park with grassy lawns. Some good-sized pines provide up-north vacation atmosphere and shade. The **lakeshore campground** of 102 small lots is typically jammed with campers' boats. The 146-lot **campground** across the road is roomier and more private. Both have electricity and showers, and both are likely to be full. Reservations are advisable; nearby private campgrounds can handle overflow. *From U.S. 31, take Hart/Mears exit at Polk Rd., go west on Polk through Mears, follow signs to Silver Lake State Park beach. (616) 873-3083. State park sticker required: $4/day $18/year.*

A LOVELY, SECLUDED LAKE MICHIGAN BEACH . . . . . away from the hubbub of Silver Lake, but nearby, is **the Little Sable Point Beach** section of the state park. (Sable is pronounced "SAH-bel" and means sand.) It's a long beach with an open landscape of poplars, beachgrass, and low dunes, dominated by the tall red brick shaft of the handsome **Little Sable Point Lighthouse**. Get there by taking Scenic Drive along the south shore of Silver Lake. Past the Mac Woods Dune Rides building and many cottages, it becomes Channel Drive. The paved road stops by Silver Creek. Look for the signs and the narrow dirt road at the left. It goes alongside the creek, through a heavily wooded area of surprisingly dramatic cottages, to **Golden Township Park** and then on to Little Sable Point. In the peak summer season, plan on arriving by 10 a.m. to find a spot in the smallish lot of this attractive beach. *State park sticker required. $4/day, $18/year.*

PRETTY PENTWATER . . . . . a resort village of charming clapboard storefronts and pleasant houses, looks a lot like Saugatuck without so many shops. It's about 15 miles north of Silver Lake, just off U.S. 31. There's a nice **park** for picnics by the marina on Pentwater Lake. The sugar-sand Lake Michigan beach at **Charles Mears State Park** is an easy walk to downtown shops and a nifty ice cream bar with minigolf. A **double-decker bus** goes to Ludington. For particulars on Pentwater, call (616) 869-4150.

The S.S. *Badger*
Lake Michigan carferry

*The only scheduled cross-lake passenger ship offers
a relaxing mini-cruise between Ludington, Michigan,
and Manitowoc, Wisconsin.*

For anyone who wants to get a taste of what the Great
Lakes passenger cruises of the first half of our century
were like, a four-hour, 60-mile trip on the refurbished
S.S. Badger, the carferry between the ports of Ludington,
Michigan, and Manitowoc, Wisconsin, is in order. There's noth-
ing else like it on the lakes today.

Crossing Lake Michigan, even at one of its narrower points,
makes you realize just how *big* the Great Lakes are. Sailing at an
average speed of 18 knots an hour, it takes anywhere from 45
minutes to an hour to lose sight of land. Then for another 45 to
60 minutes there's no land to be seen in any direction.

Granted, the Badger has no white-tablecloth dining room or
luxury lounge – to see that, you'll want to visit the S.S. Keewatin,
the 336-foot passenger ship permanently docked in Saugatuck.
But the Badger has enough well-done amenities aboard ship that
it completely lives up to its billing as "a unique and affordable
travel experience with many of the features and amenities of an
ocean cruise," from the **cafeteria** and upper-deck **snack bar** to
the intelligent **mini-museum** on carferry history and the ship-
board **theater** with free G-rated family films. In keeping with the
"family fun" theme, there are also board games on loan and a video arcade. **Badger Bingo** is played on each daytime and early
evening trip, also at no extra charge, with prizes. There's a **bar**
with beer, wine, and cocktails, and singalongs led by crew members.

Still, the main attractions are the views from the deck. Large
groups gather on the bow of the promenade deck, where there's
an old-fashioned holiday air that comes from the pleasure of
having nothing to do. Along the sides, there's lots of space for
anyone who wants a railside seat. Crew members enjoy showing
passengers around the ship. Forty-two staterooms, arranged like

The renovated carferry S. S. Badger comes closer to being a Great Lakes cruise ship than anything else on the lakes today. Staterooms, bingo, movies, meals, and other amenities are offered on the four-hour, 60-mile trip. The ferry makes easier travel between southern Michigan and the far western Upper Peninsula.

Pullman cars with two berths each, can be rented for $25 extra. (That's per stateroom, not per person.) They're especially in demand for the nighttime Manitowoc-to-Ludington run. More comfortable seating, especially important for late-night cruises, was added for 1994. A helpful on-board travel service advises passengers of what there is to see and do on each side of the lake, and gives out lots of maps and brochures.

The atmosphere is completely different from the latter years of the Badger's operation by the Chesapeake & Ohio Railroad. The interior is bright and fresh, and the crew is uniformly cheerful and enthusiastic. The railroad company built the Badger and its sister ship, the Spartan, in 1952. At that time they were the largest car ferries ever built, and their passenger accommodations were equal to the first-rate train service of the day. But by the 1970s, the car ferries' main emphasis had become hauling freight cars across. Bad service and dingy surroundings were part of a plan to discourage passengers and justify discontinuing passenger service altogether. The C&O abandoned service between Muskegon and Milwaukee in 1980 and between Ludington and Manitowoc at the end of 1981. From 1983 through 1990 Ludington investors operated the Ludington run but went bankrupt and stopped operations. 1991 was a sad year for Ludington. After a hundred years of local pride centered on its carferry, the town lost its daily morning and evening bustle, as the crowds gathered by the dock and the beautiful boat steamed out of the harbor. (In many ways watching the Badger sail off is more dramatic than any single aspect of the cruise itself. If you're around Ludington when it sails, by all means plan to see it.)

It took a man with a dream and a lot of money to make the Badger into the pleasant experience it is today. Of course he was a Ludington native – a good number of kids who grow up around the big Great Lakes boats are emotionally imprinted for life and go to great lengths just to be around them. Charles Conrad made his money by founding and developing Thermotron Industries in Holland, Michigan, makers of ultra-cold test chambers for environmental simulation, largely in aviation and space programs. In retirement Conrad bought and upgraded several Ludington-area resorts. When the ferry stopped, he was aghast, like most of Ludington. His father had been a chief engineer on the carferry trains, and he had gone along on many cross-lake trips. Now, after two successful seasons, there's talk of reconditioning one of the two other car ferries Conrad bought and reviving the Muskegon-to-Milwaukee route. There's also talk of competitors doing the same thing, so Conrad's company no longer makes passenger figures public.

Ludington dock: *at the east end of downtown Ludington, a few blocks south of U.S. 10 at the foot of William Street.* **Manitowoc dock:** *in downtown Manitowoc, south of the river. From I-43, take U.S. 151 east from Exit 149, turn right on 10th St., then left onto Madison. Follow signs to dock.* **1994 schedule: May 20-June 23:** *depart Ludington 8:30 a.m. EST, depart Manitowoc 2 p.m. CST.* **June 24-August 28:** *depart Ludington 7:30 a.m. EST and 8 p.m. EST, depart Manitowoc 1 p.m. CST, 12:30 a.m. CST (this trip has fewer amenities and 20% reduced fare). Call for 1995 schedule.* **Passenger fares:** *adults $33 one-way, $55 round trip; seniors 65 & up $30/$50; children 5-15 $15/$25. Under 5 free. Staterooms $25. Badger mini-cruise (round-trip without vehicle in 2-day period): adult $40, child $20.* **One-way vehicle fares:** *autos, vans, pickups $40. RVs, trailers: $3/foot (under 7' wide), $5/foot (7'-8'6" wide). Motorcycle $30, with sidecar or trailer $40. Bicycle $5.* **Reservations & info:** *(800) 841-4243 or (616) 845-5555.*

HOW MUCH TIME AND STRESS IS SAVED BY TAKING THE carferry? . . .
. . It all depends on where you're coming from and where you're going. One
thing is certain: it's a most relaxing trip. You'll feel 1000% better getting off
the ferry than driving through Chicago, with its constant traffic and construction. The boat trip lasts four hours, and it's at least an extra half hour
on either end to load and pick up your car. Bicycles are simpler and cost $5
each way. To help calculate, it's 7 1/2 hours driving time from Ludington to
Manitowoc around Chicago under optimum conditions. Drive times to
Ludington (at the speed limit) are 4 1/2 hours from Detroit, 1 hour 40 minutes from Grand Rapids, 3 1/2 hours from South Bend. Drive times from
Manitowoc are 2 hours to Madison and Milwaukee, 4 1/2 hours to
Minneapolis, 3 1/2 hours to Chicago. For drivers from metro Detroit and
southern Michigan, the carferry *really* pays off if you're going to Door County,
Minneapolis, the western Upper Peninsula, or the Apostle Islands. For North
Shore Chicagoans and Wisconsinites going to northern Michigan, the carferry
is 1 hour to Cadillac, 1 1/2 hours to Leland or Traverse City, and 2 1/2
hours to Charlevoix.

IN MANITOWOC AND TWO RIVERS . . . . . there are the excellent, large
Manitowoc Maritime Museum with WWII sub to tour (28 subs were built in
Manitowoc); a historic fishing village/museum with tug; a coast guard museum; and much more. Phone 1-800-542-4600 or (616) 845-0324 for info
packet.

FOR MORE ON LUDINGTON & VICINITY . . . . . call (800) 542-4600 or
(616) 845-0324. Ludington has one of Michigan's nicest in-town beaches
and, just five miles north of the ferry, Michigan's biggest, most diverse sand
dune state park and natural area. (See page 537.)

BICYCLING FROM THE carferry . . . . . works well in both Michigan and
Wisconsin. Ludington is a small town free of the noose of high-traffic arteries
and freeways that make larger places so hard for bicyclists. Call the
Trailhead Bike Shop (616-845-0545) for advice on good bike routes. The
northern trailhead of one of Michigan's few rails-to-trails bike paths is in
Hart, just 15 miles away. (See page 526.) . . . . . Wisconsin is justifiably
famous as a bicycling paradise, with far more rails-to-trails paths than any
other state, sometimes linked for great distances. Also, the dairying industry
means virtually all back roads in dairy areas are paved for year-round reliable daily access by milk trucks. Good, low-traffic roads for bicycling are
clearly marked on a super-detailed map published by the state. Call (800)
432-TRIP to ask for it and any other information on Wisconsin. 2-3 week
delivery time. . . . . . Bike info is available aboard the carferry, too.

Ludington State Park and Nordhouse Dunes

The best all-rounded of Michigan's many state parks, with a long Lake Michigan beach, a large inland lake, a river, extensive trails, a nature center, and more.

Ludington State Park offers the most satisfying mix of natural scenery and popular activities — swimming, boating, hiking, fishing — of any single state park. The 5,300 acre park has six miles of sandy, dune-backed Lake Michigan beach with a handsome lighthouse, an outstanding fishing lake, an inland beach, a fine nature center, and 18 miles of hiking trails. For people who really want to get away from it all, it joins the 3,400-acre Nordhouse Dunes, where cars are not permitted.

With so many fine outdoor features together in one park, it's no wonder you have to make summer reservations for Ludington State Park's 391 campsites early. But you don't have to camp here to enjoy the park. The town of Ludington has a big variety of motels, and nearby campgrounds don't usually fill up. Backpackers can camp along any of the Nordhouse Dunes' trails.

Of special interest here:

◆ The park's six-mile **Lake Michigan beach,** backed by low to high dunes, is longer than any other in Michigan's state park system. The designated swimming area stands out because of a handsome shingle **bathhouse** and **concession** building built by the Civilian Conservation Corps during the Depression. Beach-goers can pull over, park anywhere along the 3 1/2-mile main entry road and walk over to the beach, or walk another mile and a half up the beach from the bath house to the beautiful **Big Point Sable Lighthouse.**

◆ An **inland beach,** good for swimming on days when Lake Michigan is too cool, is by the dam at the west end of **Hamlin Lake.**

◆ The mile-long **Big Sable River** joins Hamlin Lake and Lake Michigan right at the main swimming beach. It's shallow and clear, ideal for **tubing.** A **bike and jogging path** parallels it and

At Ludington State Park, miles of accessible sandy beach mean there's plenty of room to spread out.

the road to Hamlin Lake. A pretty **picnic area** is midway.

◆ **Hamlin Lake** is a 4,000-acre lake, 10 miles long, with excellent **fishing** (panfish, some walleye and pike), with lots of coves and inlets that make for interesting boating, too.

◆ **Canoes and boats** can be rented at Hamlin Beach.

◆ The **trail system** is one of the very best in the state parks system. It's long — 18 miles altogether. It's varied, passing through dunes, by Hamlin Lake, and along the river. Interconnected trails go to all the park's major activity centers, for hikes of 1 to 8 hours. Trails are dotted with occasional **scenic lookouts**, shelters, and toilets. Designated cross-country ski trails include a 6-mile beginner/intermediate trail and an 11-mile advanced trail.

◆ The attractive small **nature center** is tucked between deeply shady back dunes and the south bank of the Big Sable River, behind the windswept entry area of scrubby jack pines. Its highlight is an outstanding multi-screen **slide/tape show** that puts Ludington State Park and Michigan's sand dunes (the world's longest stretch of freshwater dunes) into geological and historical perspective, from the dunes' formation some 3,000 years ago to logging and tourism in the late 19th century. If you see the sand dune show, you will look at Lake Michigan's lakeshore in a new, more understanding way.

Exhibits include live snakes, other reptiles, amphibians, and fish common to the region. Detailed three-dimensional maps of the bottoms of all the Great Lakes are of special interest to sailors. The one-mile **Skyline Loop** starts with a dune stair by the parking area and climbs the dune ridge for views clear to the Ludington lighthouse and down into the treetops below. A small **gift shop** is well-stocked with nature books. Call for times of scheduled **nature walks** and **interpretive programs**, at which children can hold reptiles, under the naturalist's supervision. *Easy to miss; look for the sign three miles into the park, shortly before you come to the river. Typically open May-Sept, daily 10-5:30. Call to confirm spring & fall hours.*

◆ **391 modern campsites** and three rustic mini-cabins on three mostly shady campgrounds, offer little privacy but are always full in July and August

Ludington State Park is 7 miles north of Ludington on M-116. (616) 843-8671. State park sticker required: $4/day, $18/year. Camping fees: $14/night in season, $8 otherwise.

A DUNELAND WILDERNESS . . . . . where wheeled vehicles are forbidden is the 4,300-acre **Nordhouse Dunes**, just north of Ludington State Park. Naturalists appreciate dune country for its many kinds of habitats, from damp to desert-like. Ten miles of **trails** here go through areas rich in wildlife and wildflowers. A long, sandy **beach** is fine for swimming. **Back country camping** is permitted along the trails. The **Lake Michigan Recreation Area** operated by the U.S. Forest Service has 100 of the nicest campsites in the U.S.: very large, shady, and close to the beach. No electricity or showers; two of the four loops have flush toilets. $9/night. Reserve well in advance for peak summer season, or plan on staying in overflow space until a spot opens up. *Lake Mich. Rec. Area and the trailhead for Nordhouse Dunes trails are about 10 miles south of Manistee, then west off U.S. 31. Lake Mich. Rec. Area Rd. leads to campground in about 12 miles. Call (616) 723-6716 or (616) 723 2211 for information on the dunes and recreation area. Call (800) 283-CAMP for reservations.*

Shrine of the Pines

Overlooking the Pere Marquette River, an idiosyncratic memorial to the forest's ravaged grandeur and to the beauty of the wood itself.

The North Woods of Michigan and Wisconsin are dotted with heartfelt rustic architectural tributes to the inspiring power of nature and the beauty of wood. One of the most striking is the Shrine of the Pines, just south of Baldwin. Here Raymond "Bud" Overholzer, a small-town farm boy who fell in love with the North and became a hunting and fishing guide, decided to build his own personal shrine. He had seen the aftermath of the logging era's terrible destruction. Logging companies left the cutover forests littered with vast amounts of unusable wood. Stumps, treetops, and bard slabs, left for decades, became vast, dry tinderboxes for forest fires.

Making amazingly organic furniture from the leftover roots and stumps was Overholzer's passion, which he pursued from the 1930s into the 1950s. He worked in the same vein as Stanley Smolak, the creator of Legs Inn north of Harbor Springs, and drew on the same Central European traditions of withdrawing from society into the peace of the woods, and of a woodworking style which sometimes blended the rustic and picturesque with touches of the grotesque.

Overholzer, with the help of builder Louis Merrill, had a natural feel for designing a total environment where the site, buildings, and interior furnishings complement each other. The area around the hunting-lodge "shrine" is a delightful place to walk and linger. The lodge takes in the view of a beautiful bend in the Pere Marquette River from its site on a high bank. The first American stocking of the German brown trout *(Bachforelle)*, in 1884, helped turn the Pere Marquette into a noted fishing stream. Today it has been designated a National Scenic River. The stand of pines around the lodge, planted by Overholzer, are not yet majestic, but they do contribute a pleasantly piney smell. **Trails** lead along the top of the bank, off to a small **gift shop**, and down to the river.

Set in the symmetrical log lodge are freeform windows and

From the 1930s into the 1950s, Bud Overholzer made freeform, organic furniture from tree trunks and roots, in trib ute to the great pines fallen during the logging era. Here a tree trunk serves as a cabinet and base of a gun rack.

dormers. They give the place the look of organic 1960s back-to-nature architecture, though actually it's much older.

The enjoyable guided tour that takes visitors into the lodge to see the sensuously handcrafted furniture is a form of folk art itself. It encourages visitors to admire Overholzer's enduring vision, painstaking craftsmanship, and ingenuity in using only materials of the forest (he avoided nails and glue). Pieces of root form door handles. Hand-rubbed like all the furniture, they are smooth and sensuous to the touch. Other roots, carefully selected, form a balustrade on the stairway that spells out "REST."

There's a huge, 12-seat dinner table formed from a single root. And there's the poker table with little shelves for each player to set cards and a drink. None of this apparently was ever used except for his wife's rocking chair and one other piece of furniture. Woven into the tour is the story of a persistent individualist with a dream, and an unusual and enduring romance whose surprising secret is revealed at the tour's end.

By the parking area are a **concession stand** with hot dogs and pop, and **picnic tables** for visitors to use.

On M-37, 2 miles south of Baldwin, 35 miles east of Ludington on Lake Michigan and 20 miles west of Reed City on U.S. 31. ((616) 745-7892. Open May thru October, 10 a.m.-6 p.m. $2.50/adult, $1.50 for ages 55 and over, $1 ages 6-12.

FOR MORE NORTHWOODS MYSTIQUE . . . . . stop at the interesting **Newaygo County Historical Museum** in Newaygo, 41 miles south of Baldwin on M-37 on the way to Grand Rapids. It's in the powerhouse to the dam on the south side of town, and it's open daily from June until school starts (September). In May and September-October, regular hours on weekends; weekday tours available on request. Hours: 8:30-5, Mon-Sat and 1-5 Sun. (616) 652-9281. There's lots of material on the late **Earnest Jack Sharpe**, popular versifier and creator of Newaygo Newt. A sample of Sharpe's appreciative verse is this tribute to the Shrine of the Pines:

> *Near the forest's edge the temple stands*
> *Upon a grassy bank, where it commands*
> *A gorgeous view of swiftly flowing stream,*
> *Where tired souls may sit awhile and dream.*
> *Dreams of the past in keeping with this shrine*
> *Created in honor of the pine.*

Newaygo is an old logging center on the Muskegon River. Just east of town on the river's south side, the **High Rollway Scenic Panorama** offers wonderful views in fall color season. Rollways were where loggers rolled logs down to the river, to float down to the many lumber mills at the river's mouth.

CANOEING THE PERE MARQUETTE . . . . . Baldwin has two canoe liveries. **Ivan's Canoe Rental** (616-745-3361) is at the Pere Marquette bridge three miles south of town. **Baldwin Canoe Rental** (616-745-4669) offers canoeing and rafting on the Pere Marquette and Pine rivers and weekday Christian retreats at its campgrounds. The entire river is very beautiful. It has been designated a National Scenic River by both the National Forest Service and the State Forest Service. It is one of the cleanest rivers in the state. You can see the gravel bottom. It has a good current — it's not boring, nor is it dangerous. The Pine is faster and more exciting but requires a more experienced canoeist.

A FAMOUS RESORT AND ENTERTAINMENT MECCA . . . . . was developed four miles east of Baldwin at **Idlewild** for middle-class black Americans who were barred from owning vacation property at most resorts. One of many land developments started to make money from cutover timberland, Idlewild was marketed with testimonials from respected black professionals who already owned property there. Simple vacation cottages and a few stores developed around four lakes, but the resort's wide fame was based on the big-name black entertainers who performed at Idlewild, especially after World War II. Segregation caused the resort to flourish. The civil rights movement of the 1960s offered black people more options and helped send Idlewild into decline. Today longtime residents, however, have helped stabilize it as a low-key vacation and retirement community.

A HAVEN FOR WILDFLOWERS OFF M 37 . . . . . An unusual variety of habitats around Loda Lake north of White Cloud led the Federated Garden Clubs and the U. S. Forest Service to develop the **Loda Lake Wildflower Sanctuary** in 1938. Native Michigan wildflowers have been encouraged and transplanted to this thousand-acre preserve. A brochure interprets plants at numbered posts along the one-mile trail. The wildflower display begins with the usual woodland wildflowers in early May and continues until early June. Orchids and carnivorous plants may be viewed on special marked stops along the trail at this time. Many kinds of ferns can be seen throughout the growing season. **Picnic tables** overlooking the lake are by the parking area at the trailhead. Bring your binoculars and you can see a variety of songbirds and waterfowl, too. *From M-37 six miles north of White Cloud, turn west onto Five Mile Road. In one mile, turn north onto Felch Ave. (dirt). Entrance is in a mile, on right side of road. Brown signs for sanctuary are on M-37. Request the brochure that goes with the numbered trail from the Manistee National Forest White Cloud Ranger District, 12 N. Charles/M-37 in White Cloud. Brochures are also available outside the ranger office at this same address 24 hours a day, 7 days a week or at the sanctuary itself. (616) 689-6696.*

CAMPING ON PUBLIC LANDS AROUND BALDWIN . . . . . falls under three jurisdictions. The **Manistee National Forest Baldwin Ranger District** can provide information on 20-site Bowman Bridge Campground on the North Country Trail and the 4-site Gleason's Landing (both on the Pere Marquette National Scenic River), and three other campgrounds. They're at 650 N. Michigan Ave., Baldwin 49304. (616) 745-4631. The 24-site Benton Lake Campground and the 28-site Nichols Lake Campground, both 4 1/2 miles off M-37, are managed by the **Manistee National Forest White Cloud Ranger District**, 12 N. Charles/M-37, White Cloud 49349. (616) 689-6696. Three campgrounds northeast of Baldwin are part of the **Pere Marquette State Forest**, Route 1, Cadillac, MI 49601. (616) 775-9727.

The Gwen Frostic Studio

*In a workshop/store that seems to grow out of riverbank
and woods, a crusty artist-philosopher-entrepreneur
has created a domain based on nature.*

Gwen Frostic's remarkable business is an extremely successful studio/shop that mass-produces original
linoleum block prints of simple natural subjects. It's run,
hands-on, every day, by Gwen Frostic, pithy 88-year-old artist-
entrepreneur-philosopher-printer who was a feminist long before
the current movement emerged. Her domain is her studio-
salesroom-home, built into the side of a riverbank hill in a completely organic style that reminds many people of Frank Lloyd
Wright.

In summer up to 1,200 people a day come here to buy Gwen
Frostic's line of note cards, giftwrap, napkins, blank books,
prints, and books written and illustrated by Frostic – at prices so
low they seem like wholesale.

Many visitors see only the setting and products. The studio
overlooks the valley of the Betsie River, just south of Crystal Lake
and west of Benzonia. Built of the earth, it has a sod roof and
walls made of local stones and boulders, contrasted with rustic
wood. Plashing water from fountains sets a peaceful mood. Freeform rock pillars add to the inventive, natural atmosphere. Look
down at the concrete floor, and you'll see deer tracks and leaf
impressions in the floor surface.

Most retail shops are designed to make the merchandise pop
out and take center stage. In Gwen Frostic's studio, the cards,
arranged by color (the papers are soft pinks, yellows, beiges, and
blues) become a completely integrated part of the overall design,
functioning like a pattern of wallpaper or carpet.

A set of large windows by the sales counter lets visitors look
down on 13 old Heidelberg presses that print all Frostic's cards
and papers. The air is filled with the smell of ink when the sheet-
fed presses are in action between 9 and 4:30, Monday through
Friday.

Big windows look down on a pond and nature trails from the
Round House, added in a wing by the entrance to handle crowds

at peak seasons. Down from the entrance is Frostic's library, where visitors are welcome to sit and read. Or they can go out from here onto the trails by the pond and the Betsie River.

It's the ultimate in an integrated, values-based system of life, art, and livelihood, which fits right into Frostic's grand theme, a holistic view of life that ultimately revolves around nature and its many kinds of power. "All things are part of the whole," she summarizes her philosophy. "Nothing can exist alone. I have never felt any separation between my business and me."

Nature never goes out of style. "Keep it simple" is another business principle. No UPS or no credit cards in her mail-order business, and no wholesale prices, either. (Frostic cards sold elsewhere are simply marked up from prices at her store.)

"She's a genius in her art and business," says a longtime admirer. "Nature has always been her theme. She's faithful to her principles. She's studied people and knows what they like. All her prints are technically originals; she gets 40,000 reprints from her linoleum blocks. Everybody else in her line of work depends on outside offset printers to print their images. In her poetry, she really gets down to the essence of life. She's her own publisher and printer. I don't know any other artist who's doing all that." Such rare independence and persistence in pursuit of a goal could well stem from Frostic's determination to overcome early childhood handicaps.

After spending childhood summers on Crystal Lake, Frostic moved north in 1955, developed her successful business in a Frankfort storefront before building the studio in the

Printmaker Gwen Frostic has used her many design talents to create an autonomous fiefdom — her home, studio, shop, and manufacturing facility built into the valley wall of the Betsie River near Frankfurt. Nature has always provided her inspiration and her raw materials.

early 1960s. Today, with a staff of 30, Frostic is able to spend a good deal of her energy in writing books about her philosophy of life – books that, she says with a smile, hardly anybody reads. But they're for sale at the studio, along with the cocktail napkins and gift enclosures. If you visit the studio, take time to walk the nature trails where she studied her subjects. And read a few pages of her philosophic musings.

River Rd, 2 miles west of U.S. 31 between Benzonia and Frank-fort. Drive down to studio is just west of Higgins Rd. intersection. Open daily from 1st Sun of May to 1st Sun of Nov, 9-5:30. Otherwise open Mon-Sat 9-4:30. (616) 882-5505.

A CITY UPON THE HILL . . . . . in the Biblical sense of a holy place elevated above crass trading and sensuality. That's what the idealistic Congregational founders of **Benzonia** hoped to build. Their plans to develop Northern Michigan's version of Oberlin College failed, however, as famed Civil War historian Bruce Catton told the story in **Waiting for the Morning Train**, his compelling personal history of his hometown and region at the end of the lumber boom. Today Benzonia is a backwater compared with Leelanau County resorts not far to the north. The charming cluster of **art galleries** and **Northern Delights** bakery/restaurant, just west of U.S. 31 by the main four corners, is worth a visit. Ferries, Bruce Catton, gliding, and other Benzie County history is told in the **Benzie Area Historical Museum** that now occupies the large old Congregational Church on River Road/Homestead Road, across from the onetime college campus. Don't miss Lou McConnell's wonderful sawmill model in the basement – a fine piece of folk art with engaging figures. *Open April thru Oct at least Fri & Sat 10 a.m.-4 p.m. June thru Sept: open Tues-Sat 10-4. (616) 882-5539. $1/adult, 50¢/children.*

DOWNTOWN FRANKFORT IS BOUNCING BACK . . . . from hard times that began with the loss of the Ann Arbor Railroad carferries in 1982. A grass-roots economic development group purchased the closed Pet cherry pie plant and has its products in many supermarkets. New Main Street shops along the Betsie Bay and a large antique mall are worth checking out. **The Bookstore** is a pleasant spot for browsing. It's fun to walk out on the **pier** leading to the breakwater light. Just north of it are a nice **beach** and playground. Inside the **post office**, a WPA mural dramatically depicts a carferry caught in a fierce storm. . . . . . Across the bay in Elberta, one of the last remaining railroad carferries, **The City of Milwaukee**, awaits restoration as a museum ship.

Sleeping Bear Dunes National Lakeshore

Beaches and trails with splendid views,
maritime and lumbering history,
and two uninhabited islands to explore

Centerpiece of this sprawling national park is the most famous of Great Lakes dunes, Sleeping Bear. The national lakeshore, visited by some 1.25 million people a year, is a varied 35-mile stretch of scenic shoreline extending some two miles inland. It includes:

◆ a scenic drive
◆ a variety of good swimming beaches
◆ a dozen hiking trails to many outstanding overlooks
◆ smaller lakes
◆ rivers
◆ an attractively woodsy rustic campground
◆ a state-of-the-art modern campground
◆ two large islands, North and South Manitou.

Sleeping Bear once was larger, looming 600 feet above Lake Michigan. Topped by trees, the dune did look like a bear. It sat back from the shore, protected by a peninsula of sand. But dunes and shorelines are marked by alternating periods of stability and change. Since the early part of this century, wave action has devoured the sand peninsula and begun to erode the glacial plateau beneath Sleeping Bear itself. Its front is now a bluff sliding into Lake Michigan. Winds, having destroyed the plant cover on top, send sands sailing over to the Dune Climb, an area so volatile that human footsteps can do no additional harm. By 1980 Sleeping Bear was down to 400 feet.

The area offers a hard-to-match blend of outstanding natural areas and civilized amenities. No matter how crowded the towns are, there's plenty of room to spread out in the national lakeshore. To acquaint yourself with the area, start with the following:

◆ Begin your visit with a stop at the **Sleeping Bear Dunes Visitor Center** just outside the village of Empire. Its **book shop** is excellent. The array of **free literature** includes several pamphlets well worth reading carefully to kick off your stay here: "Sleeping Bear Dunes," "The Story of the Sand Dunes" (a fine introduction to local geology), "Sleeping Bear Point Coast Guard Station," and pieces on North and South Manitou Islands and Pierce Stocking Scenic Drive. "Hiking Trails" summarizes all 12 trails. (These can also be requested by mail.) The free **hiking trail maps** don't give elevations; to really know what hills you're in for, buy a topo map ($2.50/area) at the visitor center. Visitor maps from the Empire and Glen Lake chambers of commerce include a lot of helpful information. **Free daily programs** and **guided walks** about the area's natural and human history have been dropped because of a budget crisis for 1994. Rangers hope they'll be back for 1995. Walks include a visit to the ghost town of Aral and a shipwreck walk along the notoriously dangerous Manitou Passage. *Off M-72 at M-22 just east of Empire. (616) 326-5134. Open daily except Thanksgiving and Christmas, at least from 9:30 to 4. Inquire for possibly longer summer hours. Free.*

◆ Next, take a short, marvelous hike along the **Empire Bluff Trail.** This highly recommended 1 1/2-mile round trip goes up into a deeply shady beech-maple climax forest, out into the high, perched dunes, and to an observation platform some 400 feet above the lake. The **trail guide**, free from the visitors' center, makes it even more enjoyable. Your reward is a view that includes two-thirds of the entire National Lakeshore, from Platte Bay on the south to Sleeping Bear itself on the north, out to South Manitou Island. *From M-22 about 1 1/2 miles south of Empire, turn northwest onto Wilco Road and look for the sign.*

◆ A third good introduction is the 7.4-mile-long **Pierce Stocking Scenic Drive**, named after the area lumberman who developed it as a private visitor attraction in the 1960s. An excellent interpretive brochure is available at the entrance. The first dune overlook and picnic spot looks down on Glen Lake and a three-mile stretch of duneland leading up to Sleeping Bear itself. The second and third overlook/picnic areas offer closer views of the vanishing big dune, a mile away; the second Lake Michigan Overlook also has a fine view of the shoreline down to the Empire Bluffs and Platte Bay. *From M-22 2 miles north of Empire, turn north onto M-109. Drive entrance is in 1 mile. Open 9 a.m. to 1 hour after sunset. For early-morning walks, park by the entrance. Free.*

Michigan's most famous dune, Sleeping Bear, towers 400 feet above Lake Michigan. The splendid Sleeping Bear National Lakeshore incorporates many hiking trails, beaches, and scenic vistas.

Here are highlights of the Sleeping Bear Dunes area. All noteworthy attractions are arranged by activity category.

BEACHES (arranged from south to north)

◆ **Platte River Point Beach.** Kids enjoy this beach because the Platte River winds around behind Lake Michigan to make a shallow, warm-water area for wading and making sand architecture. There's a **picnic area**, flush toilets, and drinking water available. *From M-22 just east of the Platte River bridge, about 10 miles south of Empire and 14 or 15 miles north of Frankfort, take Lake Michigan Rd. about 2 miles to Lake Michigan. Free.*

◆ **Esch Road Beach.** A simple, hardly-developed beach in a pretty, natural setting. Pit toilets. *From M-22 4 miles south of Empire, take Esch Rd. a little over a mile to Lake Michigan. Free.*

◆ **Empire Beach.** This pleasant village beach with grassy lawns offers a fine view of Sleeping Bear, the Manitou Islands, and passing freighters. Sandy beach frontage is on both Lake Michigan and South Bar Lake, for a nice cool-weather swimming alternative. There's a **picnic area** with grills, gazebo, restrooms, volleyball net, basketball court, and **playgrounds** on both beach-front areas, plus a **boat launch** and shore fishing. A historical marker fills you in on Empire's boom years as a lumbering center, 1873-1917. The trim little Manning Memorial Light was erected in 1991 in memory of an avid fisherman and lifelong Empire resident who always wanted a light to guide his fishing boat home. *From the west end of Front Street in downtown Empire (the westward extension of M-72), turn north onto Lake to reach the beach. No charge. Beach parking can fill up on nice summer days; come by noon.*

◆ **Glen Lake Beach.** This sandy beach has a fine view of Little Glen Lake, with hills in the background and the Dune Climb across the road. No lifeguards are on duty. **Picnic tables**, grills, changing house. *Take M-109 from M-22 at either central Glen Arbor or 3 miles north of Empire. Beach is about 4 miles from either end. Free.*

◆ **Glen Haven Beach.** By the now-deserted piers of the Glen Lake Canning Company, this extremely simple little beach at Sleeping Bear Point has good swimming and nice views of the Manitou Islands. It's a favorite **sunset walk**, year-in and year-out, for many area residents. The distant islands are striking, set against the rosy sunset sky. **Picnic tables**, pit toilets. The entire village of Glen Haven is now boarded up, awaiting possible future restoration by the National Park Service. *From central Glen Arbor, take M-109 west to Glen Haven, turn in by the parking area by the old cannery. Free.*

◆ **Good Harbor Bay Beach.** Lots of surrounding natural vegetation and striking views of the bluffs of Pyramid Point and North Manitou Island make this very simple, uncrowded beach attractive. Before you come to the **picnic area**, look for the trailhead to the **Good Harbor Bay Hiking Trail**, a 2.8 mile loop. It goes past low dunes and across low ridges into a forest along a creek. *Take M-22 about 8 miles northeast of Glen Arbor or 9 miles southwest of the intersection with M-204. Turn north at County Road 669 (you'll see the sign to Cedar; go in the opposite direction). When you get to the lake, turn right. Free.*

◆ **Good Harbor Beach.** Like Good Harbor Bay Beach, but on the east end of Good Harbor Bay. Pit toilets. *At the end of County Road 651, a mile west of M-22, 7 miles due north of Cedar and 4 miles southwest of the intersection of M-204 and M-22 near Leland. Free.*

ADVENTURES

◆ **Dune Climb.** Sleeping Bear today is a live dune. As the wind cuts down its top, sand spills over the back here. This 150-foot wall of sand is a strenuous climb, more so for adults than light-weight kids, but climbers are rewarded with a view of Glen Lake and the surrounding countryside. To see Lake Michigan from the top of Sleeping Bear, however, it's a two-mile walk across hot sand, and two miles back. Water, hats, and sun protection are advised. **Picnic tables** and a **refreshment and souvenir stand** are near the parking lot at the dune climb's base. The Warnes family, souvenir stand proprietors, have been in the area for generations. They're a fine source of local history. *Take M-109 from M-22 at either central Glen Arbor or 3 miles north of Empire. Dune Climb is about 4 miles from either end. Free.*

◆ **South Manitou Island.** In the early days of Great Lakes shipping, this small island (about 3 1/2 by 3 1/2 miles) bustled with activity. Woodcutters supplied fuel for steamers. (On each trip through the Great Lakes a ship consumed from 100 to 300 cords of wood). South Manitou farms supplied provisions for ship crews. The island had a village with stores, a busy harbor, and a lighthouse to mark the entrance to the Manitou Passage, a much-used but potentially dangerous shortcut. By 1960 the last farms were gone and the Coast Guard station had been closed Some old-timers remained and catered to the summer people and boaters who came to the island. In 1970 the National Parks Service began condemning and buying the island as part of the Sleeping Bear National Lakeshore, and its natural life slowly came to an end as property owners sold out and life lessees died. Today abandoned farm buildings, a school, and a cemetery remain as evocative testimony to changing times.

As part of the National Lakeshore, the island has been open since 1970 to primitive, low-impact campers, to hikers, to boaters (who must anchor offshore and come in by dinghy), and to day-trippers who take the 1 1/2-hour voyage over, spend three hours on the island, and return to Leland. Manitou Island Transit, the ferry service, is owned and operated by the Grosvenors, whose family lived for generations on the island. They know it well and offer a 1 1/2 hour **island tour** in an open-air vehicle that can be customized for special interests. It focuses on everyday details of bygone island life, then ends with a cemetery visit about the real people who lived it. Sign up for the tour on the boat; it's $7 for adults, $4 for children.

Near the docks, rangers give **talks** about the **lighthouse** and shipping (currently at 1 p.m.) that include a trip up the unusually tall, 100-foot lighthouse tower. The **Visitor Center** in the old village post office tells the island's natural and human history.

Day-trippers can also choose to explore the island on their

own. If you don't plan your time carefully, you'll find yourself running to catch the ferry, or faced with the prospect of spending the night in the open. Three hours enables you to see the grove of **virgin white cedars** (ask rangers how to find the world record-holder, 17 1/2 feet around), get to the huge **perched dunes** overlooking the rocky coast on the island's west side, and see **the wreck of the Francisco Morazon**, run aground in 1960 off the island's south tip. On a sunny day, seen from a bluff, its rusty hulk is dramatic against the blue waters of the Manitou Passage, a tempting but treacherous shortcut for ships. If you're inclined to hike along the beach, wear wading shoes or consider the time you'll spend detouring around stream inlets to avoid getting your feet wet. All-day **natural history tours** of South Manitou ($35 including ferry) are led every other Thursday in summer by the Leelanau Conservancy. Call (616) 256-9665 for info.

No food is available on the island; bring your own. Ten miles of marked **hiking trails** go through dense, mature forests and old fields. Some forests, far from the harbor, have never been cut. Wildflower colonies there have grown undisturbed, so you can see jack-in-the-pulpit and trillium of enormous size. Sandy **beaches** are plentiful; the protected east bay is especially popular. The island's small size makes it hard to get lost for long; South Manitou is a good place for families' first big backpacking adventure. Careful planning and disposal of waste is imperative, to avoid trashing the island. Camping is permitted at three main **campgrounds** (from one to four miles from the dock; campers hike there), at scattered **backcountry campsites** for up to 6 people, and at a few larger group campsites. No reservations are taken; get a permit at the visitor center. Try to go on a sunny day when the scenery shows to best advantage. **To help plan a trip** to either Manitou island, call the National Lakeshore at (616) 326-5134 for free handouts or to order one of two helpful visitor guides: Steve Harrington's *Visitor's Guide to South Manitou Island* (24 pp., $1.50) or Robert Ruchhoft's *Exploring North Manitou, South Manitou, High and Garden Islands of the Lake Michigan Archipelago* (362 pp., $14.95). Ask about various historical books on the Manitous. *Manitou Island Transit leaves from Fishtown in downtown Leland. Daily service June thru August; no Tues. or Thurs. trips in May, Sept., Oct. 9:30 a.m. check-in, 10 a.m. departure. Reservations recommended. (616) 256-9061 or (616) 271-4217. Day trip: $18 adults, $13 children 12 and under. No bicycles.*

◆ **North Manitou Island.** Logging, farming, cherry-raising, and the Coast Guard have all vanished from North Manitou, where two towns once were. All that remains are abandoned and ruined buildings, a few private camps, and a small visitor staging area in the east village with a ranger station for emergency assistance. Most of the island was a private hunting preserve; seven deer introduced in 1927 have proliferated into a herd as high as two thousand. Their overbrowsing has destroyed young trees and shrubs and made the island look like a park — pretty now, but ultimately ruinous. Liberal hunting seasons in recent years have reduced the deer herd, and vegetation is showing signs of recovery. Topography varies from low, open dunes to rugged bluffs.

Since the National Parks Service bought the hunting preserve in 1984, it is managing the island as "a primitive experience emphasizing solitude, a feeling of self-reliance, and a sense of exploration." That means: no cars or wheeled vehicles; water at only one place; two outhouses; one campground; fires only at two fire rings. Low-impact camping (burying human waste, packing out trash) is required. Thirty miles of **marked trails** make three interconnecting loops around the island. To go elsewhere, a compass is essential. Campers are free to choose backcountry sites under certain limitations. *Manitou Island Transit leaves Leland at 10 on Sunday, Wednesday, and Friday, June thru August and returns immediately, without a layover. Call (616) 256-9061 or (616) 271-4217 for other times and for **hunting information**. Round-trip fares: $18 adults, $13 children 12 and under. No bicycles*

◆ **Canoeing or kayaking on the Crystal River.** Short, 2 1/2 hour trip on the beautiful Crystal River as it goes from Fisher Lake through cedar and balsam forests on state land with lots of wildlife. A good family trip. Lots of places to get out and swim or wade. *Crystal River Canoe Livery, at the Glen Arbor Shell Station on M-22 just northeast of Glen Arbor. (616) 334-3090 or (616) 334-3831. 9-5 daily in season.*

◆ **Canoeing on the Platte River.** A delightful, easy 1 1/2-hour trip through hardwood forests, wetlands, sand dunes, and Loon Lake. Much animal and bird life can be seen if you go before noon or after 6 p.m. The gentle current of this shallow river makes it ideal for canoeing novices; the wildlife makes it attractive to veteran naturalists. Start by the M-22 bridge at the Platte River between Empire and Frankfort. **Canoe rentals** from the

Riverside Canoe Livery (same location), (616) 325-5622. Parking is scarce; come early.

◆ **Hiking.** The 12 hiking trails lead through distinctive environments to scenic overlooks. The Parks Service's "Hiking Trails" brochure summarizes the special features of each trail; separate hiking and cross-country skiing maps are available for each. Three trails are especially recommended. The 1 1/2-mile **Empire Bluffs Trail** (page 548) gives the best overview of the entire shoreline. The 4-mile Otter Creek loop of the 15-mile **Platte Plains Trail** goes alongside a stream full of wildlife, including beavers, and through a fragrant cedar swamp. The **Dunes Trail**, a strenuous 2.8 mile loop, starts near the Glen Haven Maritime Museum. It explores the spooky, desolate dunescape atop Sleeping Bear, including a ghost forest of trees that flourished before being buried in sand. Wind-sculpted patterns in the sand are striking. (Water, a hat, sunscreen, and shoes are recommended for hot dune hikes.)

Two easy, 1 1/2-mile, one-hour hikes come with interpretive brochures to put you in touch with sand dune ecology (**Cottonwood Trail**) and the rich variety of species found where forests meet fields (**Windy Moraine Trail**).

INDOOR ACTIVITIES

◆ **Empire Area Historical Museum.** A vast collection of interesting things has been built up by an energetic group of summer folk and Empire natives (a mix of Belgians, Frenchmen, and Norwegians recruited by logging companies). The museum displays antique vehicles, a nifty model of the big Empire Lumber Company where the public beach now is, and a turkey feather Christmas tree. Centerpiece of the museum is the splendid back and front bar from Andrew Roen's saloon that flourished during Empire's logging heyday, along with a coin-operated music box and horse race game. Headlines from newspapers across the nation tell the story of the discovery, after the old man died, of $125,000 in cash, plus this disassembled bar and "a lot of great stuff that belonged in Empire," according to the museum's founder, service station owner Dave Taghon. Many unusually interesting old photos of everyday life in these parts help make this a fine place to spend a rainy day. An inexpensive **gift shop** features local history and reproductions of antique books and cardboard ornaments. Museum publications include several

Rod Conklin is one of many
artists in the vicinity of the
national lakeshore who makes
and sells work inspired by the
natural beauty of northwestern
Michigan. His delightfully simple studio home is between
Glen Lake and Honor.

photo albums and a new book of 1860 letters between a soldier
and his wife in Glen Arbor, discovered as a house was being
demolished. They illuminate early life in northern Michigan. *On
M-22 at the intersection of La Core and Salisbury, on the north
edge of Empire. (616) 326-5316 or (616) 326-5181. Mem. Day thru
June: open Sat & Sun 1-4. July & August: daily except Wednesday 10-4. Sept. thru color season: Sat & Sun 1-4. Also open by
appt. Free admission; donations welcome.*

♦ **Sleeping Bear Point Coast Guard Station Maritime
Museum.** Worth a visit for the beautiful setting alone. The interesting brochure available at the Visitor Center (p. 547) makes
better reading than the exhibit text. "The [Coast Guard] surfmen
became folk heroes, greatly respected for their courage and skill,"
it points out. "Neighbors often came by to watch their drills." You
can see a **video** of the breeches buoy drill and relive the crew's
rigorous weekly schedule. The **Manitou Passage** off Sleeping
Bear was a favorite shipping shortcut, deep but narrow and
therefore the scene of many wrecks, recounted here. The big historic photos and spartan quarters of the lifesaving crew and
keeper are dramatic. There's no hint of the personal lives of these
self-sacrificing men except the intriguing audio reminiscence of a
Coast Guard admiral whose father was a lighthouse keeper.
Don't miss the boathouse, restored to about 1905, with a beach
cart, surf boats, and other rescue items. *West of Glen Haven.
Take M-109 to Glen Haven, 2 1/2 miles west of Glen Arbor, and
follow signs to the Museum on Sleeping Bear Point. (616)
326-5134. Limited 1994 hours due to budget crisis: open weekends only, 10-5, Memorial thru Labor Day. Call (616) 326-5314 for
1995 hours. Free.*

♦ **Shopping in Glen Arbor.** See page 573.

The National Parks Service will mail you requested information. Call (616) 326-5134 or write: Sleeping Bear Dunes National Lakeshore, National Parks Service, Box 277, Empire, Michigan 49630. For visitor center hours and location, see p. 546-547.

BEST STOPS FOR PICNIC FIXINGS . . . . . In Empire, **Deering's Market** on Front at La Rue has a big meat counter and produce section and its own smokehouse. . . . . In Glen Arbor, **Steffen's IGA** at M-22 and M-109 has the best selection and prices on groceries and meats. . . . . . Both are open year-round.

A TIME-TESTED BICYCLING GUIDE . . . . . to 6 counties from Leelanau and Benzie to the Straits is available for $5 from Monstrey's General Store (see page 561) and bike shops in Traverse City and Petoskey. Scenic back roads make for outstanding cycling, mostly fairly challenging, with some flat, easy shoreline routes.

LEELANAU NATURAL HISTORY ACTIVITIES . . . . . are held throughout the year by the **Leelanau Conservancy.** They include Wednesday **nature walks, workshops** on subjects from drawing to birdwatching, and field trips, including $35 all-day **excursions to South Manitou Island.** Call (616) 256-9665 weekdays, write the Leelanau Conservancy at 105 N. First, Leland, MI 49654, or stop by the office And pick up a flyer in the vestibule. (It's around the corner from the Bluebird restaurant.)

VISIT THE PEACEFUL, RURAL STUDIO . . . . . of watercolorist and wood-carver **Rod Conklin** not far from Empire and the Esch Road beach. Here in a trim, tidy outbuilding of a hillside farm, he carves charming smooth sumac birds, using both colors of the wood to good advantage. His framed prints ($25-$75) and paintings are clean, simplified distillations of nearby shoreline scenes and farm vignettes. *7339 Valley Rd./C.R. 677. First house south of C.R. 610. From M-22 by Esch Rd., go 4 miles east on C.R. 610. From M-72/Airport Rd., turn south at golf course, go south 4 miles. (616) 325-6482. Open regularly June thru color season, 11-5 daily. Stop in or call ahead any time.* . . . . . On summer weekend afternoons, the Benzie County Historical Society holds open the pretty brick **schoolhouse** at the corner of C.R. 610 and C.R. 677 just north of Rod Conklin's studio.

Leelanau Peninsula

One of the state's major attractions, this picturesque finger of land draws large number of visitors annually. Here's how to enjoy its many delights.

The little finger of lower Michigan's mitten, the Leelanau Peninsula extends 30 miles into Lake Michigan, forming the west arm of Grand Traverse Bay. Here history and geology have combined to create a most delightful landscape. The most recent glacier, as it retreated north, formed long, stream-lined hills called drumlins. "From every hillcrest, a panorama of carefully tilled farmlands and wooded slopes unfolds before the visitor's eye, with the ever present lake waters as a background," described the Michigan W.P.A. guide of 1940. "Off the western shore of the peninsula, the Manitou Islands rise, hazy green, above the horizon." Cherry orchards, joined more recently by a few vineyards, create a beautiful, orderly, highly cultivated landscape, dotted with nine pleasant villages.

The interior's striking hilliness is reminiscent of upper New England, lovely at every time of year. Fruit trees blossom in the early green of spring. Winter reveals the shapes of trees and buildings with great clarity. In fall, long views of distant barns and lakes are framed in hills glowing with color, with enough evergreens to set off the flaming reds and yellows. Summer, when the area is most crowded with visitors, may well be the least interesting season, when the landscape is reduced to vacation basics: lots of green, blue water, and sand. But the blue itself can be stunning. On sunny days it's a vivid turquoise, created by light reflecting from the white, sandy bottom of Grand Traverse Bay.

The area's diverse economic activities from the 1850s into the early 20th century created distinctive small towns and attracted many kinds of peoples that today make the peninsula more interesting and varied than many other areas dominated by resorts. The peninsula's first settlements were three separate Indian missions founded south of Northport around Omena between 1849 and 1852. Protestant missionaries brought Indian congregations here because they hoped, in vain, that the isolated area would remain free of white settlers, away from the corrupting influence of alcohol. Intermarried offspring of these Chippewa and Ottawa bands remain here today, largely in the reservation at Peshawbestown, between Suttons Bay and Omena.

Leland (the county seat) and Northport developed as ports for commercial fishermen and provisioners of Great Lakes vessels. Supplying cordwood and food to ships was the original livelihood for many remote ports. Suttons Bay first prospered with sawmills, then became a fruit-processing center. Many nationalities, including Bohemians, Norwegians, Belgians, and Poles, were recruited to work in lumber camps and mills, of which the Empire Lumber Company in Empire was by far the largest. Today the Polish town of Cedar is locally famous for its sausage and its Polish Festival each August.

What accounts for much of the peninsula's visual charm and its small-scale, small-town ambiance is the area's economic paralysis since 1910 in every sector but tourism and agriculture. The only non-agricultural industries were sawmills and, in Leland, 19th-century charcoal iron smelting. The transition to tourism occurred when Chicagoans came north to escape the pressures of city life and find cool weather and solace. Resort development was in full swing by 1890, well before the lumber ran out.

For most of the 20th century, Leelanau enjoyed a successful balance between local people and nature-loving cottagers and vacationers from big cities, who provided incomes for old

The hilly, high interior of the Leelanau Peninsula offers an unfolding
succession of delightful views: curving hills, often accented by orderly
rows of cherry trees marching across them; simple old farms and barns;
occasional country churches and cemeteries; and often the blue, blue
water of Lake Leelanau in the peninsula's heart or Lake Michigan at its
edges. This sketch by water colorist Suzanne Stupka Wilson looks across
to Stoney Point and Grand Traverse Bay near Suttons Bay.

Leelanau families. The 1970s saw a new influx of outsiders —
urbanites seeking a simple life in tune with nature. These
included writers, artists, and craftspeople, whose studio/shops
add greatly to the pleasure of drives in the country.

At the same time, the seeds of change were planted that now
disrupt the old balance. Second homes, long an important part
of the local mix, began to change in character from leisurely
summer cottages to condos for people driving up for the weekend, mostly from metro Detroit. These so-called "trunk-slammers" don't have the old-time cottage-owners' concern and commitment to the area, engendered by years of personal ties. The
resort economy, which had been on a ma-and-pa level, started
attracting big-time developers with large projects like The Homestead and Sugar Loaf resorts and condo complexes. Establishing
the Sleeping Bear Dunes National Lakeshore in 1970 helped promote the change to more intense development. So did the booms
in downhill skiing and boating.

Today Suttons Bay, with easy access to Traverse City via
M-22, has become a virtual suburb. Leland, long an attractive
mix of pleasant but modest houses and old summer homes, has
become so slicked up and gentrified, with so many shops geared
to traditional decor and upscale resortwear, that many year-

round Leelanau residents consider it ruined and avoid it altogether, especially in summer. Zoning policies as far away as Northport are now set by exurbanites intent on fending off threats of development, with the ironic result that cherry farmers attempting to survive by running produce stands are thwarted by strict township regulation of signs.

To the casual visitor, the results of all this development are mixed. There are a lot more shops everywhere, and some are quite interesting. Most cater to visitors and second homeowners. (Everybody else depends on a weekly trip to the Meijer supermarket/discount store in Traverse City.) Leland, Suttons Bay, and Glen Arbor are outstanding places to see the latest ingenious trends in interior design for second homes. Artists' studio-shops are now plentiful; at any one, pick up a free copy of *Arts and Crafts Trails in Northern Michigan*, a listing and map of various studios. There are two fabulous restaurants — Hattie's in Suttons Bay and La Becasse in tiny Burdickville, on Glen Lake — and numerous good ones, all fairly expensive.

The negatives are the traffic in towns and on much of M-22 in summer, and the anger and depressed resignation you encounter among people who love this place. Pick up a copy of the interesting weekly newspaper, the *Leelanau Enterprise*, and you'll realize how intense the local political battles are. It's full of letters by concerned local residents, including novelist Jim Harrison, a persistent critic, about the perils brought by development and tourism to a precious, vulnerable rural way of life.

Still, Leelanau remains a place with no fast food restaurants, no tanning booths, no traffic lights (except for a new one near Traverse City), and three bookstores – a point of local pride.

You can enjoy the Leelanau's beauty without the crowds by seeking out less convenient beaches (see below and page 549), by hiking, by biking on scenic roads in the morning, and — perhaps best of all — by planning a visit in May or June or October or January. Winter is beautiful here, and the **skiing** is excellent – downhill at **Sugar Loaf Resort** (616-228-5461), with a 500-foot vertical drop, and cross-country in the Sleeping Bear National Lakeshore and Leelanau State Park. A lot of interesting people live up here and get into retailing to make a living. The people, in many ways, are what make Leelanau special, in fact. When you visit in the off-season, they have plenty of time to talk.

Travel brochures that suggest a 93-mile driving tour of Leelanau to be done in a day (or a half day!) miss the charms of the area entirely. This is a special blend of nature and simple man-made diversions, best enjoyed slowly — by lingering and walking, swimming and bicycling.

Here are some of the peninsula's highlights, arranged along M-22 from Traverse City north through Suttons Bay to Northport and south from Northport to Leland and Glen Arbor.

BETWEEN TRAVERSE CITY AND SUTTONS BAY

◆ **Monstrey's General Store and Sport Shop.** Ideal first stop for lots of free printed information and advice on the area. Bicyclists will find a $5 **bicycling guide** to six counties of northwestern Michigan invaluable. Just finding this shop is an adventure that gets you off the beaten path of M-22 and into the hilly, scenic interior overlooking Lake Leelanau. There are **rentals** of bicycles, tandem bikes, bike carts for small children, sailboards, tubes, and small boats. Amish furniture and classic toys, books on the region and on bicycling and adventure travel. *8332 Bingham Rd./C.R. 618 in the hamlet of Bingham. From M-22, about 10 miles north of Traverse City, turn west on 618. Store is between 633 and 641. (616) 946-0018. From mid-April to Christmas. Hours at least Tues-Sat 10-6. From Mem. to Labor Day Mon-Sat 10-6, Sun noon-5. Other times by appointment.*

◆ **Bellwether Herbs.** Gail Ingraham was an investment banker in Traverse City until eight years ago, when she decided what she really wanted to do was grow things. Now she has quite an extensive set-up – three acres of herbs and perennials. You can buy over 350 varieties of potted herbs and perennials, plus everlasting annuals and dried everlastings ready to arrange. "We consider our gardens a living picturebook of ideas for our customer," says Ingraham, who is happy to advise customers about garden design. *On northwest corner of Shady Lane and Elm Valley Rd. toward Suttons Bay. Take M-22 north 8 miles from Traverse City. Turn left (west) on Shady Lane and head 1/3 mile west. Northwest of Traverse City south of Suttons Bay. Open from May to Christmas. May 1 to Labor Day: Tues thru Sat 10-5, Sun 10-3. After Labor Day to Christmas: Fri-Sun, same hours. (616) 271-3004.*

◆ **Nature's Gifts.** Wide-ranging rock shop, from inexpensive mineral specimens and rough rocks to polished agate slabs, handcrafted jewelry, bookends, and belt buckles. With gemstones and semi-precious beads, you can design or make your own jewelry. An extra bonus: spectacular view of Grand Traverse Bay from the patio. *On Hilltop Rd. 1/4 mile west of M-22, 10 miles north of Traverse City and 5 miles south of Suttons Bay. (616) 271-6826. Open May thru Dec., Mon-Sat noon-5 p.m. or by appointment.*

♦ **L. Mawby Vineyards.** At this unpretentious, highly regarded small winery, the owner-winemaker-publicist-poet will give you a personal tour. Larry Mawby, an original in all respects, believes that the eventual reputation of this wine region, still in the early stage, will rest on blends of the French hybrid grapes found best suited to the soil, and on its Vignoles — wine made from that specific type of white hybrid grape. L. Mawby is known for rich, full-bodied dry Vignoles, fermented and aged in oak, like all his wines, and the fanciful proprietary names of its blends, like Shard O'Neigh (a red blend) and P.G.W. Pun. Lately he's also excited about his newer sparkling wines. Striking wine labels, prints and poems, designed by his wife, Peggy Core, are also for sale at the tasting room, along with her drawings, cards, baskets, and jewelry. *4519 Elm Valley Rd. 5 miles south of Suttons Bay. From M-22 2 miles north of 618, turn west on Hill Top Rd., then north on Elm Valley. (616) 271-3522. Tastings and tours from May through October, Thurs-Sat 1-6 and by appointment.*

♦ **Boskydel Vineyard.** The wine is good, the view is terrific, and the atmosphere – Old World in flavor but not in the least imitative – is unequalled at the winery of retired Northern Michigan College librarian and pioneer winemaker Bernie Rink. He was the first to grow wine grapes anywhere in the Grand Traverse region, when his family began testing French hybrid grapes (see page 37) here in 1965. "Such Boskydel varietals as Vignoles, Seyval Blanc, and De Chaunac will have a magic all their own," he states. "Boskydel Red, White, and Rose blends will approximate and many times exceed good ordinaires from France." *On C.R. 641 about 2 miles south of the town of Lake Leelanau, on the east shore of the lake. From Traverse City and M-22, take C.R. 633 west at Greilickville, turn north in 3-4 miles onto C.R. 641. (616) 256-7272. Open daily year-round 1-6 p.m.*

SUTTONS BAY

This village of 560 was not so long ago considered the slummier part of the toney Leelanau Peninsula. Here is where migrant cherry-pickers would hang out on summer evenings. Then mechanical pickers displaced the migrants, and Suttons Bay became gentrified to the point where it is now a fashionable address. The refurbished row of main street storefronts, in a color-coordinated pastel paint scheme by local architect Larry Graves, looks like "a set from a Hollywood movie," as one shop-keeper puts it. Professionals living here appreciate the conve-nient commute to Traverse City. Locals who decry the transfor-mation of Leland into "the most pretentious kind of tourist trap" still consider Suttons Bay a nice, friendly town. Don't miss the big old trees and substantial Victorian houses in the picturesque neighborhood just west of downtown on St. Mary's and Lincoln avenues.

The pleasant **municipal beach** and park is north of down-town. Two exceptionally enjoyable events take place here: the **Jazzfest** (fourth Saturday of July, featuring musicians who played with bands of the Big Band Era) and the **Suttons Bay Art Fair** (first weekend of August) with very good food booths and superior arts and crafts.

For access to the bay in a less busy setting, go out to Stony Point, reached by taking M-22 south of town but staying near the bay and going east onto Stony Point Road when M-22 goes south. Soon you'll come to **Sutton Park**, a nice, shady small suburban park with a sandy **beach** and good views of boats in the harbor. Three more miles and you're at the point, where **Vic Steimel Township Park** looks across to the tip of the Old Mission Peninsula. The shore is stony, and poison ivy grows in the rocks, but the natural setting beneath cedars and birches makes this a fine destination for a **picnic** at the tables here. Light traffic and interesting houses along the road make this a good, easy **bicycle ride**.

Suttons Bay is a year-round town, more of a suburb than a resort, and many of its stores are open all year. Here are some highlights (arranged from south to north on St. Josephs Street/M-22). Most stores are open daily from mid-June through Labor Day.

◆ **Suttons Bay Bookstore.** Now has used books, CDs and cas-settes, and lots of Native American books and posters, along with the usual good personal service, unusual cards, and rainy-day activities. Also new: art featuring local subjects. *On the south end of St. Joseph south of Broadway, across from the stone RR depot. (616) 271-3923. Open Mon-Sat 10-5 at least. From mid-June to Labor Day open Sun noon-4.*

◆ **Sew Central** fabric store also houses the mezzanine workshop where Kate Fiebig creates **Leelanau People**, nifty soft sculptures and puppets of Leelanau folks like her grandfather. Hand-puppets begin at $12; 36" figures run $200-$350. Call (616) 271-6774 to find out when she's there. *117 Broadway, west of St. Joseph.*

◆ **Enerdyne Nature and Science Playthings**, owned and run by a former teacher, is based on the premise that science is fun — and that educational toys aren't just for children. This large and recently expanded store has bird houses and feeders, garden furnishings, water rockets, butterfly nets, unpolished rocks and rock tumblers, good nature books, CDs and cassettes with nature sounds, games, a new Northwoods Lodge area, wood-stoves, and more. *212 St. Joseph St. (616) 271-6033.*

◆ **Bay Theater.** First-run and foreign/art films and occasional concerts and live dramatic performances. *216 St. Joseph. (616) 271-3772.*

◆ **The Painted Bird.** Unusual contemporary crafts, art by talented local artists, and wearable art. When the staff isn't busy with customers or stock, they're likely weaving at the big loom.

◆ **Suttons Bay Galleries.** Original antique prints (birds, architectural, botanicals, maps, and Japanese woodblock prints), along with Russell Chatham's original lithographs. *102 Jefferson, one door down from St. Joseph on the way to the harbor. (616) 271-4444.*

◆ **Danbury Antiques** is widely known for English "smalls": boxes, candlesticks, brass, and porcelain, purchased by the owner in England. It anchors an interesting cluster of shops. *305 St. Joseph. (616) 271-3211.*

◆ **Will Case-Daniel Jewelry.** Tucked off a courtyard behind the main street shops, silversmith Will Case-Daniel has created an idiosyncratic world that spills out of his diverting shop (it sells cards and accessories plus jewelry made by himself and others) into the charming courtyard. Look up to see his weathervanes. Also displayed here: moody, simplified Leelanau landscapes by David Grath. *305 St. Joseph St. (rear). (616) 271-3876.*

◆ **Suttons Bay-kery.** Fresh bread, including sourdough, oatmeal, and seven grain whole wheat, as well as morning sweet rolls, croissants, and turnovers, reasonably priced. Sofas and easy chairs make this place seem like home, and lots of good reading furthers the effect. *318 St. Joseph. (616) 271-6540.*

◆ **Inter-Arts Studio** was the first of some two dozen gift and interiors shops in Suttons Bay. Owner Ken Krantz, an architect by training and admittedly fussy, sells his own drawings of Leelanau scenes along with only things he likes: colorful Polish rugs, many other area rugs, glassware, lots of bedspreads and fabrics (including hard-to-find India print bedspreads, those cheap, multipurpose classics of the 1960s), and other classics of contemporary design. *326 St. Joseph, across from the Total station. (616) 271-3891.*

BETWEEN SUTTONS BAY AND NORTHPORT

◆ **County Road 637.** For a scenic interior drive to Northport with less traffic and wonderful vistas, turn west on 204 from Suttons Bay. In about two miles turn north onto 637. You see fieldstone houses and cherry orchards, especially delightful in blossomtime in mid-May and in late June and early July when the fruit is ripening. When you come to the striking **Saint Wenceslas Catholic Church** at the T intersection with C.R. 626, get out to look at the beautiful scrolled markers in the Bohemian cemetery. 637 rejoins M-22 at the popular **Happy Hour Tavern.**

◆ **Leelanau Sands Casino and Super Bingo Palace.** A 1991 expansion briefly made this the largest of Michigan's casinos on Indian reservations, with space for 500. The Grand Traverse band runs it to create jobs, fund tribal government, and promote economic development. It advertises "Las Vegas-style gambling." But don't expect bright lights and glamorous shows. This is pretty sedate stuff, geared to conservative Midwestern tourists. The right to gamble on Indian reservations is based on tribal rights to self-government. The adjacent **Peshawbestown Indian Art Store** (616-271-3318) has some interesting art and crafts made by Woodland Indians. *On M-22 in Peshawbestown, about 4 mi. north of Suttons Bay. 1-800-962-4646. Open 7 days a week, year-round.*

◆ **Omena.** This picturesque small hamlet at the head of Omena Bay was first settled in 1852. The name means "Is it so?" in Indian, a phrase often used by an early white settler when talking with the local Indians. Steamers made use of the bay to take on cordwood, potatoes, beans and apples from the region. The first dock was built in 1868. Later, hotels and resorts, long since gone, were built to accommodate vacationers. Old photos are displayed in a case in front of the combined post office and general store. In an old gas station at the bend, the Von Holt Farm Market offers a luscious and tempting array of local fruit and produce, jams and smoked fish, and the inevitable cherry products.

The **Tamarack Craftsmen Gallery** occupies the old Omena general store, perched on a hill surveying the beach and bay. The building was what inspired owners David and Sally Viskochil to start their extraordinary gallery of American crafts over 20 years ago when they got out of the Peace Corps. They are committed to displaying work by artists they believe in. Much of it is interestingly strange. The place has a vivid, imaginative look, with lots of handblown glass. They were the first to show the twig furniture of Clifton Monteith. Dewey Blocksma, who is gaining a national reputation for his outsider art, is another longtime artist. So is Catherine Baldwin, the last quill basket-maker in the area. Though prices go into the thousands of dollars, there are plenty of little things like earrings and mugs for $20 and under. *On M-22 in Omena. (616) 386-5529. Mem.-Labor Day: Mon-Sat 10-6, Sun 12-5. Otherwise: Tues-Sat 11-5, Sun 12-5.*

NORTHPORT

This pretty village has long attracted interesting summer people. Being so far from Traverse City (25 miles) thins the traffic in summer and keeps the atmosphere less suburban, more like a number of galleries and antique shops, mostly seasonal, and two unusually attractive picnic spots. **Bay Front Park**, a couple of blocks away from the commercial district, is right on Grand Traverse Bay, with a good view of tiny Bellow Island in the distance. It has a pleasant **beach** and **playground**. The adjacent **marina** is lined with pleasure boats and charter boats. The tall ship Manitou, a 114-foot two-masted topsail schooner, is berthed here when it's not out on three- and six-day windjammer **cruises**. Call (616) 941-2000 for info on sailing/hiking cruises to nearby islands. Free summer **concerts** are held at the marina every Friday at 7 from July 4 weekend through August.

Two wonderful old-timey souvenir shops with a beguiling dime-store atmosphere have been at the marina for decades. **Nature Gems** sells rocks and seashells, minerals and Petoskey stone jewelry at all price levels. (616) 386-7471. **The Shipwreck** has gotten into upscale collectibles, but nautical decor, from tiny treasures to dramatic objects to do-it-yourself craft kits, remains its strong suit. (616) 386-5878. In the next block, next to the post office, the **Northport Pedaler** (616-386-5644) rents many kinds of bicycles and dispenses information on recommended routes. (Note: there's too much traffic for families to bike to the state park.)

Northport is where Great Lakes sport trolling was pioneered in the early 1920s by George Ruff. Methods he and his wife developed for catching trout and other gamefish set the pattern for other charter services. A few blocks north up from downtown at Third Street and Fourth is a serene, picturesque **mill pond and park**, shaded by a big old apple tree. A picnic table and short footpath are here. Beyond the pond is the charmingly eccentric Old Mill Pond Inn.

At the tip of the Leelanau Peninsula, the Grand Traverse or Cat's Head lighthouse, part of Leelanau State Park, has been turned into a museum. From its tower you can see east across to the top of the Old Mission Peninsula, north to Medusa's cement silos in Charlevoix, and west to the Fox Islands.

Tucked in a neighborhood north of the town center, **Joppich's Bay Street Gallery** has been focussing on Michigan artists long before regional art became a popular cause. Owner Edee Joppich, a painter herself, travels throughout the state during the off season searching out 50 artists to participate in the coming year's exhibit. Most have never been shown here before. Typically a third of the participants are on college or university faculties. Paintings, sculpture, original prints, and fine art crafts are displayed in airy galleries inside a remodeled house. Prices range from $20 to $10,000 and up. *109 N. Rose (also called Bay). one street over from M-201. Northport's main street. and a block north of the marina. (616) 386-7428. Open from 11-6. weekends in June and Sept thru mid-Oct. daily from July 4 weekend thru Aug.*

Anchoring a lively collection of downtown gift and antique shops is the new **North Country Gardens**, now in the former grocery store. Its selection of dishes, jewelry, birdhouses, and garden ornaments features colorful, strong graphics, often based on vegetables and flowers. They are rustic and contemporary, eclectic and vibrant – "quite wonderful," says one artist. *On Waukazoo at Nagonaba, where M-22 turns. (616) 386-5031.*

In a Victorian cottage a block south on Waukazoo, **The Beech Tree Gallery and Cafe** is a wonderful spot to enjoy lunch (soups, sandwiches, salads) or dessert beneath a huge copper beech. Inside are fiber and ceramics, furniture, clothing, and jewelry, often with a contemporary, updated, sophisticated country theme. Quilts are featured. *202 Waukazoo. (616) 386-5200.*

Most Northport shops are right along M-22 and easy to check out. Two interesting artists' studio/shops might be missed, however. **Village Arts**, on the south side of Nagonaba just west of Waukazoo, is a collective of artists working in a polished, avant-garde contemporary vein: Larry Fox (furniture), Martha Eldredge (jewelry), and more other artists than in their old spot. *(616) 386-5510. June weekends, daily in July & August.* **ZO:ON Gallery** shows Char Bickel's shadowbox collages and soft sculpture of angels, bears, fish, and animals of mythological inspiration, alive with shimmery color and pattern hand-painted on silk. They have a fresh but mysterious appeal. *122 W. Naganoba next to City Hall. (616) 386-5937. Open weekends from mid-May through mid-Sept. or by appointment. In July & August open daily except Wed. Hours 11-6.*

BEYOND NORTHPORT

◆ **Woolsey Airport.** Aviation with a Fred Flintstone look. This small, picturesque fieldstone airport from the 1930s is fun to explore. There's a picnic table outside. *About 4 miles north of Northport on C.R. 629.*

◆ **Leelanau State Park (south section).** Here the beautiful sandy **beach** and spectacular views of the Fox and Manitou islands are blissfully peaceful and uncrowded – because a mile hike through a dark beech-maple forest is required to get there. It's an easy, pretty walk – well worth it. You can climb the **Lake Michigan Overlook** first for an even better view – especially memorable at sunset. Eight miles of **trail loops** through low dunes and hardwood forests are well marked with colored posts, and with maps at major intersections. But other confusing trails have been informally made. *Only turn where you see a post!* The hilly, 2-mile **Mud Lake Loop** reaches a platform for viewing migratory waterfowl in spring and fall. **Cross-country skiing**

The stony beach by the lighthouse at Leelanau State Park offers good pickings for rockhounds and fine views at sunset and, on the east-facing campground side, at sunrise.

here is very popular. Beachgoers here will be rewarded with an astonishing number of Petoskey stones from the ancient coral seas. *Just past Woolsey Airport on C.R. 629, turn north on Densmore Road. Trailhead is in about 1 1/2 miles. State park sticker required; $4/day, $18/year.*

◆ **Leelanau State Park.** At the tip of the Leelanau Peninsula, this 1,200-acre state park offers some of the most picturesque **campsites** in the entire state parks system. You can get a relatively secluded spot overlooking Grand Traverse Bay and a rocky beach (unpleasant for swimming or wading unless you bring wading shoes). The 52 campsites ($6/night) are rustic (pit toilets, no showers) but so beautiful that they're always full in good weather from July to Labor Day. Over half are reservable, and some vacancies open up daily, especially in mid-week. They are assigned on a first-come, first-serve basis.

A beautiful **picnic area** with a playground is by the large lighthouse at the peninsula's very northernmost point. A former lightkeeper's son, who grew up here, is now a retiree and the curator of the **lighthouse museum**. From the tower you can see across to the tip of the Old Mission Peninsula and out to the

Manitou and Fox islands. You can even see the Medusa cement plant in Charlevoix (page 597). The curator's father made some of the remarkable **pebble lawn ornaments**, which include an elaborate flower bed in the shape of a crown and a miniature lighthouse that's a purple martin house. *Open from May thru October. 12-5 weekends at least. In July & August. open 11-7 daily. (616) 386-7553. Free admission: donations welcome.*

Lighthouse and campground are at the end of C.R. 629. 8 miles north of Northport. From town. take 201 north to 629. State park sticker required: $4/day. $18/season.

◆ **Kilcherman's Christmas Cove Farm.** Third-generation fruit farmer John Kilcherman has become intensely interested in the history of old apple varieties. He grows 170 varieties of antique apples and sells many of them at this attractive farm stand. For special occasions he makes up sampler boxes of antique apples, complete with a brochure he has written. His wife, Phyllis, sells objects decorated with Scandinavian *rosemaling* — folk art flowers and such. It's a pretty place to stop and sample good apples, and to hear about the travails of fruit farming. *On Christmas Cove Rd. (also called De Long Rd.) off 201 n. of Northport. (616) 386-5637. Call before making a special trip.*

◆ **Peterson Park.** A remote, pretty park — a big, grassy area on a bluff, from which the Manitou and Fox islands can be seen. An amazingly large maple is the park's focal point; there are picnic tables, a small play area, and restrooms tucked away in a woods. Stairs lead down a long ways to a stony **beach** with lots of Petoskey stones. *From 201 in Northport. take either the North or South Peterson Park Rd. No fee.*

◆ **Woodland Herb Farm.** A delightful enclosed garden and a first-rate herb shop are the attractions of Jon and Pat Bourdo's simple farm, the oldest of a number of herb growers in northern Michigan. The small fragrance garden, enclosed in high shrubbery, includes a tiny pool and a fountain surrounded by plants. Visitors are welcome to sit on a bench and take in this serene little cosmos. On one side is a wonderfully weather-worn shed. Inside the crowded shop are products made with over 200 varieties of herbs grown on the premises — potpourris and sachets, pesto mixes, and unusual vinegars, dressings, relishes, chilis, and chutneys. *7741 North Manitou Trail (M-22). a mile or so west of Northport. (616) 386-5081. Open May-November. Monday through Saturday 11-5.*

LELAND

The chief draw in this popular, often crowded old fishing village is **Fishtown**, a picturesque group of weathered old fishermen's shanties along the Carp River, where Lake Leelanau empties into Lake Michigan by the ferry dock to the Manitou islands. Its transformation into tourist shops around 1970 changed this pretty resort village into Leelanau's first and most intensely developed tourist shopping hub. With enough old boats, fishnets, and fishy smells to seem authentic, Fishtown is still an interesting place when it's not packed with people – in the early morning or the off-season. People come not just to shop or sightsee but to fish by a dramatic little waterfall and dam. Some commercial fishing continues. (Its peak was during the first three decades of the 20th century.) **Carlson's Fishery** (616-256-9801) sells smoked whitefish and fresh whitefish fillets. Interesting photos on the wall show Bill Carlson's forbears at work. Next door, another Carlson runs the **Village Cheese Shanty** (616-256-9141), a friendly gourmet and coffee shop with lots of local products to sample and a thoughtful selection of American and imported cheeses at all price levels. The harbor is a lively place, what with a charter fleet and Manitou Transit's boats to the

The **Woodland Herb Farm** near Northport is the oldest of several herb farms in northern Michigan. Its small fragrance garden is an especially serene spot.

Manitou Islands. (See page 549-551.) The municipal **beach** is just north of the harbor. *From M-22 just north of the bridge in Leland, turn west onto River or Pearl. Come early; parking is limited.*

Since the early part of this century, Leland has been the summer retreat for many old-money Midwestern families – and some Easterners, too, but especially people from northern Indiana. A sudden family illness on vacation forced one of the Ball brothers of the Muncie canning jar company to stay here awhile. His family was so taken with Leland, they spread the word to friends and family. Compared with Harbor Springs, the tone here is not at all grand, but quite low-key and unpretentious in a traditional sort of way. Now, after several generations, summers are like a big reunion of farflung kith and kin who see each other picking up mail at the post office, shopping at the Merc (the **Leland Mercantile** grocery on Main at River), meeting with townspeople for morning coffee at the volunteer fire department, going to weekly sings at the rather simple golf club, and having dinner and drinks at the Leland Lodge.

Perhaps that heritage and image are what led Leland shops to adopt their generally traditional, rather preppy tone compared with other Leelanau towns. Most shops are open daily in summer. Shopping standouts include **Tampico** (southwestern sterling silver jewelry, Mexican folk art and glassware; 616-256-7747) and **Inland Passage** (regional gifts; 616-256-9900) sharing a rear courtyard location at 104 North Main. Across the street, at 109, **Leelanau Books** (616-256-7111) is a fine place for browsing and getting local information. Closed Sundays. South on Main Street, the **Main Street Gallery** features original work by local favorite Nell Revel Smith (a sort of latter-day Marcel Prendergast with brighter colors), flowery painted furniture by Molly Phinney, and works by other area artists, plus antique paintings and prints. *307 S. Main/M-22, 3 blocks south of the bridge. (616) 256-7787.*

Tucked away on a side street off M-22 just south of the Carp River, the little **Leelanau Historical Museum** is not to be missed. Well-done permanent exhibits tell the story of Leelanau's settlement and development from the first lighthouse on South Manitou Island. There's a hands-on display of old-fashioned toys, and interpretive material on the Manitou Passage State Underwater Preserve. (Divers can get additional shipwreck information here.) A significant **changing exhibit** is mounted each year: in 1994, "World War II – Leelanau Remembers," and in 1995, folk art of Hans W. Anderson, a Northport fisherman. The excellent small **shop** offers local history books, old-fashioned toys, and locally produced needlework kits and crafts, many not to be found elsewhere. *From M-22, 203 East Cedar, next to the library, turn east just before the bridge. (616) 256-7475. Open year-round. Mid-June thru Labor Day: 10-4 daily except closed Wed., 1-4 Sun. Otherwise: Fri-Sun 1-4. $1/adult, 50¢/student.*

SOUTH OF LELAND

◆ **Good Harbor Vineyards.** If you show up at the tasting room for the instructive self-guided tour of this small winery, you may be talking to the owner and winemaker, Bruce Simpson, himself. His Trillium, a semi-dry mix of Seyval, Vignoles, and Vidal grapes, is Michigan's most successful blended, proprietary wine. *On M-22, 1/2 mi. s. of the intersection with 204. On a hill behind Manitou Market. (616) 256-7165. Open mid-May thru Oct., Mon-Sat 11-6, Sun 12 6 and by appt.*

◆ **Sleeping Bear Dunes National Lakeshore.** See chapter beginning page 547.

GLEN ARBOR

This crossroads in the middle of the national lakeshore and Glen Lake residential area has become a center for year-round artists, who love walking the beaches and dunes all year long. The relative isolation of Leelanau's southwest corner, about 20 miles from Suttons Bay and Leland and an hour from Traverse City, means kindred spirits have collaborated more in joint projects. Here, for the time being, anyway, shops and studios that reflect the artist-proprietors' creative spirits are holding their own against more ordinarily upscale resort gift shops.

Another continuing influence is the old Christian Science summer community that founded the private, secondary Leelanau School. Its original location has developed into **The Homestead**, a condo resort worth visiting to see how well much of it fits into the beautiful natural site. Its developer, Bob Kuras, has stirred up an enduring political hornet's nest with his plans to build a golf course involving some wetlands along the Crystal River. Original work by area artists is shown at the **Glen Lake Artists Gallery** cooperative, next door to **Arbor Lights** general gift store. Both preserve the classic general store setting. *On Lake Street across from the Lake Street Studios. (616) 334-4230.*

Open daily 10-5 in summer.

The Totem Shop on M-22 in "downtown" Glen Arbor is the ultimate resort-area general store, with something for everybody. Fun for kids. Art and crafts materials are a hidden strength. *Open daily in season. (616) 334-3533.* On Lake Street toward the beach, **Becky Thatcher Designs** is the friendly studio/shop of jewelry designer Becky Thatcher. After spending childhood summers in Glen Arbor, she developed this successful business, largely based on translating Sleeping Bear memories of sunsets, islands, and lakes, into jewelry. She likes to use beach stones, often carved into bears, beavers, birds, and fish. Custom designs and unusual colored gemstones like tourmalines and opals are another specialty. *5975 Lake. Turn onto Lake toward the lake. (616) 334-3826. Open year-round, daily in summer.* Furniture-maker Paul May and his wife, who illustrates the beautiful American Spoon Foods catalogs, show their work at a gallery behind their home. Look for the sign **Kristin Hurlin Illustration/ Manitou Woodworks**. A quiet, contemplative appreciation of nature and wood pervades both their work. Hurlin's pen-and-ink drawings and watercolors of Leelanau landscapes and botanicals are for sale as originals and as cards, T-shirts, and limited edition prints. May's custom furniture, cabinetry, lamps, and clocks are mainly Shaker- and Mission-inspired designs. *On M-22 just east of the shore road in Glen Arbor. (616) 334-3128. Open May thru Oct. daily 11-4 or by appointment.*

On Lake Street just east of Art's Tavern, the **Lake Street Studios/Center Gallery** is an artists' working/teaching studio coordinated by resident watercolorist Suzanne Stupka Wilson. Classes for children and adults are offered in various media, with workshops up to a week long. Weekly one-person painting shows are mounted throughout the summer; visitors are welcome at Friday-evening openings. Other artists include silversmith Ben Bricker and fiber artist Majel Obata. *6023 Lake, just east of Art's Tavern on M-22 at Lake. (616) 334-6112. 10-5 daily in summer. Otherwise by chance or appointment.*

On M-109 on the south end of Glen Arbor, are a cluster of interesting shops around the **Cottage Book Shop** (616- 334-4223), open seasonally, run by Molly Weeks, an area native and wife of the *Detroit Free Press* political columnist George Weeks. Nearby are studio/shops of photographer **Ken Scott** (616-334-6101), who specializes in evocative area landscapes, and printmaker **Ruth Conklin** (616-334-3880), whose woodcuts incorporate simplified northwoods subjects.

◆ **Amanda Bricker Wildflowers.** The artist's studio shows her three-dimensional sculptures of porcelain flowers and oxidized copper leaves on a wood base, as seen in the Smithsonian catalog. *6847 S. Dune Highway/M-109, across from the Dune Climb on Little Glen Lake. (616) 334-4603.*

BEACHES AND BOOKS . . . . . They go together, especially in Leelanau County where beaches are generally quiet and natural, and three good bookstores (pages 563, 572, and 574) do a good business in local history and lore. Especially recommended: Kathleen Stocking's *Letters from the Leelanau* ($5.95 paper) and *Lake Country* ($15.95 paper), essays of blended personal reflection and portraits. They capture in great depth the worlds (rooted and rural, exurban seekers and artists) and issues that make this area so fascinating. An in-depth Leelanau guide that combines places and shops with vignettes of people is *Seasons of the Leelanau* by Sandra G. Bradshaw ($9.95 paper). Also recommended is *Ghost Towns of Michigan* ($16.95 paper) by another local author, Larry Wakefield.

A SUMMER OF CHAMBER MUSIC, FOLK, AND RAGTIME . . . . . takes place in over a dozen concerts at various Leelanau locations. Cost per concert: $7 or so. The **Manitou Music Festival** was founded by an Interlochen faculty member and a summer resident. Call (616) 334-6112 to get a brochure. Folksinger Claudia Schmidt seems to be a regular favorite.

NOT JUST A BIG-NAME CONCERT VENUE, ... the summer music school at **Interlochen National Arts Camp** south of Leelanau and west of Traverse City is worth visiting in daytime. It's a pleasant and even inspiring atmosphere to see and hear high schoolers playing music and socializing in this relaxed, creative setting. Visitors are welcome to stop by, and to spend the night in the parents' "hotel." Call (616) 276-9221 for information on **free daily events** and student and faculty concerts. Have a bite at the **snack shop** near the **camp store**, full of interesting music T-shirts and souvenirs. Call the box office at (616) 276-6230 for info on big-name classical and pops concerts. *From Traverse City/Suttons Bay take U.S. 31 west to M-137 at the village of Interlochen, follow signs south to camp. From Glen Arbor and Empire, take C.R. 677 south (it's the southern continuation of the road across Glen Lake) to U.S. 31, then east (left) to Interlochen.* . . . . . Tip: at **Interlochen State Park** (616-276-9511), if you use the rustic campground at Green Lake, you'll wake up to Interlochen campers' reveille and be treated to concerts and music practice throughout the day and evening.

Old Mission Peninsula

Perfectly suited for growing cherries, Old Mission
is one of the most scenic areas in the state.

This thin, high ridge of a peninsula, 18 miles long, bisects Grand Traverse Bay. It's more intimate than its neighbor to the west, the Leelanau Peninsula. The scenery on a drive to the tip is spectacular, as each rise in the road offers new, panoramic views of hilly vines and orchards dropping down to the blue bay. The hilly land is some of the finest in the country for growing cherries and grapes. The bay moderates temperatures and prevents early spring warming that endangers fruit buds. So suitable is the soil and climate for cherries that once there was no denser concentration of cherry trees in the country. Now wine grapes are proving more profitable and increasing in acreage.

The orchards and vineyards are a pleasant foreground for the hilltop vistas of the bay to the east and west. A white sandy bottom makes the water so turquoise that it would seem artificially enhanced if seen in a photograph. The roads hugging the east shore — East Shore Road, Bluff Road, and Smokey Hollow Road — are less developed and more scenic than those on the west shore. Highway M-37 follows the central spine to the northern tip and provides plenty of spectacular panoramas.

The peninsula is named for the first settlement in the Grand Traverse region, a Presbyterian mission started in a log cabin in 1839. A replica of the cabin is now a small museum (see below).

The peninsula is today experiencing a fierce, drawn-out struggle between developers and those who want to preserve the rural landscape. Cherries have been the major crop for well over a century, but overproduction has made the orchards' economic viability tenuous. Every year over 50 new homes are built on the peninsula, and the population has jumped to nearly 5,000 from just over 2,500 in 1970. Underwood Orchards, long a popular tourist spot at the peninsula's base, is now a housing development. Thanks to vigilant township planners, the views from the hillcrest will remain unobstructed.

Recommended stops on the peninsula, arranged from south

Chateau Chantal, sited on the hill crest of a former cherry orchard, brings an elegant form of agritourism to Michigan. It functions as the a wine tasting room (the view of both arms of the Grand Traverse Bay is exceptional), a winery, the co-owners' home, and a bed and breakfast.

to north, include:

◆ **Chateau Grand Traverse.** This 80-acre winery makes some of the finest domestic Rieslings to be found. Owner Ed O'Keefe was for many years the only Michigan vintner to grow exclusively vinifera grapes — prestigious Old World varieties that are more susceptible to frost and disease than hybrid or native grapes. Current wines include five Rieslings (from $8 to $50/bottle), three Chardonnays, four red wines (Gamay, Merlot, Syrah, and Pinot Noir), and Mission Blush ($4.99). Chateau Grand Traverse is now sold in 23 states. Try some at their tasting room. The vineyard's much-praised cherry wines ($4.99) are a tasty novelty and good Michigan gift item. Spicy cherry makes a good hot winter drink; the new cherry Riesling is a terrific picnic wine. 25-minute winery tours are held on the hour from Memorial Day through Labor Day; weekends only in spring and fall; by appointment only in winter. Complimentary tastings are year-round. Call to schedule large groups. Mail order available. *M-37 at Island View Rd. 8 miles out of Traverse City. (616) 223-7355; (800) 283-0247. Open regularly April thru Dec. April & May: 10-5. June-Dec: 10-6. No Sunday sales before noon.*

◆ **Bowers Harbor.** Midway up the western shore of the peninsula, Neah-Ta-Wanta Point creates this well-protected harbor. One of the better restaurants in the Traverse City area, the Bowers Harbor Inn, is in an old summer home here. There's also a **public beach**, a marina, and a picnic area. The old summer hotel at the point has become a bed and breakfast and the Neahtawanta Center for Peace Research and Education. *Reached by Peninsula*

Dr. on the west shore, or turn west off M-37 at Bowers Harbor Road, then right onto Peninsula.

◆ **Bowers Harbor Vineyards.** This new, small, family-run operation grows a few grapes but mainly markets Chardonnay, Riesling and sparkling wines made for them at nearby Chateau Grand Traverse. Linda Stegenga says their wines aren't the same as Chateau Grand Traverse's, and urges visitors to taste and compare. The drive from M-37 to the tasting room offers some grand views. *2896 Bowers Harbor Road a ways east of the bay. From M-37/Center Rd., go 8 1/2 miles north of Traverse City to Seven Hills Rd. Turn left, go 1/2 mile, turn left on Bowers Harbor. Winery is on left. (616) 223-7615. Open daily 11-6. Jan-March, open weekends only or by appointment.*

◆ **Chateau Chantal.** Michigan's first taste of California-style wine tourism on a grand scale. This big brick French Provincial-style winery, conspicuously perched like a castle on the hillcrest of a former cherry farm, combines production facilities, wine cellars, a luxurious tasting room, the co-owners' large apartment, and three bed and breakfast rooms. Principal partners are winemaker Mark Johnson, the former winemaker at nearby Chateau Grand Traverse, and financial backer Bob Begin, a former Catholic priest. Both have loved living in European wine regions. (Johnson is a graduate of the prestigious wine institute in Geisenheim, Germany.) Chateau Chantal grows only vinifera grapes. Riesling, Chardonnay, Gewurztraminer, and Pinot Noir are currently in production. They also make an ice wine, a sparkling wine, and a cherry wine. Their first vintage was 1990. Most wines run $7-$12. Sweet Harvest Riesling and 1990 Gewurztraminer have won gold medals at the Michigan State Fair.

The tasting room is furnished like a sunny, elegant living room, with sofas and a piano. Visitors are welcome to sit and enjoy the spectacular views of *both* arms of Grand Traverse Bay. Visitors are given escorted tours of the entire facility. In July and August, the winery offers **"Sunset on the Terrace"** evenings ($6/person), enjoying wine, cheese, bread, and fruit while listening to the Jeff Haas Jazz Quartet. Call for info on wine seminars. *On Center Rd./M-37, 2 miles north of Mapleton, (616) 223-4110. Open daily year-round, noon to 5. In summer open 11-5.*

◆ The **Old Mission Church.** This little historical museum is a replica of a log church built in 1839 by the Presbyterian missionary to the Chippewa Indians. Its original bell is in this belfry. The informative historical displays inside were done by the Old Mission Women's Club — another example of how enthusiastic amateurs can outdo professional museum curators.

Visitors learn that until 1900, many residents of the peninsula's eastern shore would get two or three months' provisions at a time by boating across the bay to Elk Rapids. A brief history of local cherry farming points out that because the soil here is so perfect for cherries, that's what everyone grew. So when an early frost occasionally wiped out the cherry crop, the peninsula was thrown into a profound depression. Another disadvantage of a single-crop economy was having to pick all the cherries at the same time, straining the available labor supply. At first local Indians were used as pickers, then Jamaicans, then Japanese, then Mexicans. First the Mexican migrants lived in old cars and tents, then in permanent huts along the roadside. By 1965 cherry-picking machines were becoming widespread and migrants were no longer needed. *On Old Mission Rd. in the hamlet of Old Mission. 18 miles out on M-37, turn right onto Old Mission Rd. Open daily from 8 or 9 a.m. to 6 p.m. or so, from Mem. Day through color season.*

◆ **Haserot Beach.** A local calls this 250-foot public beach the best swimming in northern Michigan. A lifeguard is provided by the township. The beach is protected from chilly winds by the cove. *North of Old Mission. From M-37, take Swaney Rd. east to shore.*

◆ **Old Mission Point and Light.** This quaint old lighthouse, not open to the public, dates from 1870. The original frame light keeper's dwelling remains. The 45th parallel of latitude intersects here, halfway from the North Pole to the Equator. At the peninsula's rocky point is a swimming **beach** (really more of a wading beach), a simple, pretty spot. There's a fine view west across to Omena on the Leelanau Peninsula, and east to Eastport at the outlet of Torch Lake. The state has acquired the surrounding 513 acres, but it remains a day-use facility with no camping.

A REAL DOWNTOWN IN A RESORT AREA . . . . . downtown Traverse City is well worth exploring. Expanding cultural establishments are filling up the vacant space caused by the new mall. Horizons Books took over the vacant Penney's at 243 E. Front between Park and Cass. It's open daily from 7 a.m. to 10 p.m., and to 11 p.m. Friday and Saturday. Entertainment is another downtown strength. As Northern Michigan's biggest city, and the hub of the increasingly affluent Grand Traverse region, Traverse City has a range of specialties, services, and arts organizations found nowhere else in the region. It looks a lot like Ann Arbor on a bay. . . . . . In addition to the four principal shopping blocks of Front Street between Pine and Boardman, explore West Front on the way to U.S. 31/Division and take Union Street from downtown across the Boardman River into "Old Town."

LOCALS ARE EXCITED ABOUT . . . . . Northwestern Michigan College's new exhibit and auditorium space, the **Dennos Museum Center**. The displays are unusually interesting, and the building is open, airy, and beautiful. The three permanent displays are the **sculpture gallery**, the **Inuit Gallery**, showing a selection from former NMC librarian (and winemaker) Bernie Rink's collection of contemporary Eskimo art, one of the nation's largest; and the hands-on **Discovery Gallery**. (See the colors of your on-screen image change; make sounds by touching different colors on a wall.) Call also for lecture and performance schedule. . . . . . In summer, the Dennos Center is home to the **Michigan Ensemble Theater**, nonprofit professional summer stock. Its comedies and revues run from mid June through early October. Individual tickets: $19. Call (616) 922-1552. *On the campus of Northwestern Michigan University, off U.S. 31 roughly two miles east of downtown Traverse City, and follow signs. (616) 922-1055. Open Mon-Sat 10-5 (to 8 in summer), Sun 1-5. $2/adults, $1 under 18.*

The Music House

From music boxes to nickelodeons and giant organs,
take in the nostalgic sounds and visual glamor
of mechanical music-makers at a top-notch museum.

The story of the automation of music, from the elaborate music boxes of the 1870s to the Victrola and talking movies of 1929, is told — and better yet, played — in this impressive, intelligent museum created by two collectors. The two-hour guided tour includes satisfying demonstrations of music on 12 instruments. Guides are the same people who work restoring music-makers. The giant Regina music box has interchangeable punched metal discs and a delicate, tinkling sound. There's a reproducing player piano, briefly popular in the 1920s. Its piano roll was punched to exactly recreate, for example, George Gershwin performing *Rhapsody in Blue*. Musicologists come here to hear just how Grieg and Rachmaninoff really played the music they wrote.

It's a thrill to see and hear these instruments in action. Many are lavish with carved ornament and gilt. The music conjures up scenes in shoebox theaters, saloons, and dance halls. Some music is meant to blow you away with a throbbing bass and penetrating, clear melody. It's fascinating to see the bellows and hammers working inside these clever mechanical devices.

The magnificent and rare Amaryllis organ — a great, gilded confection of pipes, carved foliage, and moving louvers — imitates a dance orchestra and vibrates the floor with its bass notes. Built for a big Belgian dance hall, it looks like it belongs in an 18th-century Baroque church. A similar instrument in a less elaborate case was once strategically positioned on a rooftop at an amusement park in New Jersey to provide background music throughout the park.

One co-founder of this museum is an architect who has recreated antique room settings for some instruments. The electric player piano (known by many names, including nickelodeon) is in an elaborate saloon from the 1890s, all mahogany and mirrors. The tiny, make-believe Little Lyric Theater showcases a Reproduco piano-organ combination, used as a popular and inexpensive accompaniment for silent movies.

Restoration of additional instruments is ongoing. Work is underway on a large Wurlitzer theater organ, soon to be enjoyed from the museum lobby. Eventually 20 vintage jukeboxes will appear in a "Big Band Era Gallery." Six are now on display.

Before or after the tour, visitors can examine extensive **displays** on the evolution of the Victrola, the radio, and early TVs. (No audio demonstrations go with them.) The **gift shop** carries many tapes of music played on music boxes, chapel bells, player pianos, and street organs.

The Music House occupies the hay barn and granary of the cherry and dairy farm where one founder grew up. That's been the story of Grand Traverse, he points out — cherries and agriculture replaced by tourism, condos, and golf.

The Music House is in a complex of barns on the west side of U.S. 31 about 8 miles northeast of Traverse City and 1 1/2 miles north of M-72. (616) 938-9300. Open May through October, Mon-Sat 10 a.m.-4 p.m., Sun 1-5. Open weekends from Thanksgiving thru New Year's Day. Call or write for details on holiday program. $6.50/ adults, $2/children 6-16, children under 6 free. Allow 2 hours per tour.

A FINE CHERRY ORCHARD TOUR. . . . . . is just north of the Music House at **Amon's Orchards and U-Pick.** Here in the center of U.S. tart cherry production, overproduction perennially depresses wholesale cherry prices. To stay profitable, orchards have had to turn to marketing their cherries and cherry products direct to visitors. Amon's has reoriented itself to tourism while retaining a pleasantly farmy flavor. It's family-run, and less slick than other heavily advertised orchards. Half-hour **wagon tours** by knowledgeable employees cover area cherry history and how cherries are grown and marketed. There's also a **petting zoo** of common farm animals kids can feed. In the sales room and bakery, you can buy sweet and tart cherries, apples, and plums. Plenty of knowledgeable people are around to field questions about cherry cookery and cherry agriculture. Amon's offers **free samples** of some fairly exotic cherry products like cherry pepper meat sauce and cherry barbecue sauce. Cherry-fudge sauce is the best-seller, and cherry mustard is awfully good, too. Splendid views of the East Arm of Grand Traverse Bay make this an outstanding place for an afternoon of cherry-picking. *On the east side of U.S. 31, 2 1/2 miles north of M-72. (616) 938-9160. Open daily May thru Oct. from 10-6. Free admission to u-pick orchards and sales room. Call for tour times and rates. Tours ($1-$3) on request during May.*

Fisherman's Island State Park

An uncrowded up-north Eden
just south of bustling Charlevoix

This relatively new, little-developed state park is a stunning bit of pure, unmessed-with natural beauty that occupies a prime spot along six miles of Lake Michigan shore south of Charlevoix. Although this region has become uncomfortably developed, this park manages to be uncrowded. Of the 90 rustic campsites, 14 directly overlook the beach. The others are across a road but a very short walk to the beach.

As at many beaches in the Charlevoix-Petoskey area, stretches of rocky piles of limestone gravel alternate with pockets and little bays of sand. Rocky limestone outcrops make for a more rugged shoreline than vacationers expect. Occasional boulders are dramatic accents. This area south of Charlevoix is actually better for finding **Petoskey stones** than the Petoskey area itself. (Hint: the distinctive markings show up much better when the stones are held under water.)

What you gain in scenery and privacy, you give up in convenience. What keeps away the hordes in this popular vacation area is the lack of plumbing (pit toilets are the rule), no showers, and no bathhouse. There isn't much of an official trail system, either. But in from the shore there are plenty of paths through the dense woods of birch and aspen, along with spruce, balsam fir, and occasional hardwoods. The many low, swampy areas are full of tamaracks and cedars.

Most everywhere around here are the simple, beautiful basics conveyed in the romantic image of northern Michigan: the big blue lake and long beaches, accented with birches, aspens, and pines. You have it all to yourself, the way it would have been in Hemingway's time — actually better, since then the North Country had been recently logged over. The trees are much taller today. Twenty miles of unmarked paths wind through the forest, and alongside fragrant cedar swamps.

The main day-use beach and **designated swimming area** is at the end of a two-mile drive past the two campgrounds. Its parking area is very seldom full. People are welcome to pull over anywhere along the road and get out and swim. The park's northern section off Bell's Bay Road contains the two sections of **campsites** and a simple **scenic overlook** near the entrance. The **southern part of the park** is a secret treasure, undeveloped and unmarked by signs. But it's a trick to reach. Thirteen miles southwest of downtown Charlevoix on U.S. 31, go west on Barnard Road until you get to the Norwood Township Park in the village of Norwood. The two-track road behind the park goes north along the shore. Conditions are rough; check ahead at the park office. You may be able to drive 2.3 miles north along the beach to Whiskey Creek. Or you may want to pull over and walk the rest of the way.

In his *Michigan State and National Parks* guide, outdoorsman Tom Powers says this lovely, isolated stretch of creek and beach is among his very favorite places in all of northern Michigan. He suggests planning on spending at least the better part of a day here. If you're very lucky, you may come upon what was perhaps the Woodland Indians' most important source of chert stone, used in weapons and tools. The quarry, consisting of holes the size of bushel baskets, is almost impossible to find in the heavy forest with its fern-covered floor.

*The **main entrance** to Fisherman's Island State Park is off Bell's Bay Road, which joins U.S. 31 two miles south of Charlevoix, almost across from the Brumm Showroom (616) 547-6641. State parks sticker required: $4/day or $18/year. Park open May thru November. 90 rustic campsites (no electricity or running water) fill up on weekends and occasional weekdays in season (mid-June through late August), when reservations are advised. $6/night.*

ARTS AND CRAFTS FROM NATURAL MATERIALS . . . . . are the focus of the **Norman Brumm Showroom** on U. S. 31 southwest of Charlevoix. Brumm is well known for copper enamel bird and wildflower sculptures, and suncatchers made of sliced agate in black metal frames, often shaped like birds. The large and handsome store also carries a very wide range of jewelry, notecards, prints, baskets, pottery, and other decorative gift items, all with natural themes. Generally simple and good-looking, occasionally they verge on the cute. Even people who aren't drawn to the gift items may well enjoy looking through drawers upon drawers of mineral and shell specimens plus books and drawings on natural subjects. It's like nature's dime store — kids and craftspeople can get a lot of treasures for little money. *On U.S. 31 at Bells Bay Rd., 2 miles west of Charlevoix. Open daily, April through Christmas 9:30-5:30, until 9 Fri. (616) 547-4084.*

Beaver Island ·

A two-hour ferry ride from the mainland,
life here is still pure and simple.

Of all Michigan's permanently inhabited islands, Beaver Island (53 square miles, population 400) is the only one that's over five miles from the mainland. Eighteen miles from the nearest Lower Peninsula shore, it has much more of an island feeling than islands connected by a bridge or a short ferry ride. It's completely different from summertime Mackinac Island with its huge and stylish Victorian summer "cottages" and hotels, though both are inhabited largely by the descendants of Irish fisherfolk.

How you feel about Beaver Island depends a lot on how you feel about the pace and huge variety of choices of contemporary life — how much you like things slowed down and simplified. Beaver Island has cars, but not very many. It costs $75 to take them over and back on the ferry. There's TV, but few stations and no cable. You have to plan ahead to get here. The ferry from Charlevoix takes two hours and costs $27 round-trip. The plane is $50 round-trip and only flies in decent weather. The ferry vibrates and sometimes tosses unpleasantly. From late December through March it doesn't run at all.

Beaver Island is occasionally promoted as something of a natural wonder on account of its isolation. But really it's a plain, pleasant piece of Michigan's north country — flat and sandy, covered with second-growth pines and hardwoods. Only in the past 30 years have the beaches gained the inevitable rim of cottages, and those are mostly quite simple, more like Upper Peninsula "camps" than the stylish waterfront second homes near

The Beaver Islander takes two hours to go from Charlevoix to the island.

Charlevoix.

What you see when you finally arrive at St. James, Beaver Island's port and only town, is a collection of very plain, small buildings — either clapboard houses and storefronts built over the years by the descendants of Irish fishermen who first settled in the 1840s, or a few aluminum-sided motels and ranch houses of the 1960s. That's when the man who had been buying property at tax sales over the years divided some of it into vacation lots and sold them.

All that's left of the island's brief, bizarre period as the only kingdom in the United States — the self-proclaimed kingdom of breakaway Mormon leader King James Jesse Strang — are a few old frame buildings (the Mormons' print shop is the local museum) and the name St. James, after Strang himself. Most of the names you see — Erin Motel, O'Donough Grocery, Donegal Bay on the island's northwest end — reflect the island's strongly Irish past and present.

Beaver Island is a subtle place that needs a personal guide, an insider who knows the little, everyday things that make island

Don't look for spectacular scenery on flat, unassuming Beaver Island. But it's a wooded, peaceful place to get away from it all, with little traffic, few shops, and uncrowded campgrounds and beaches. This old boathouse is now a museum about the island's once-active role as a fishing and boat-building center.

living special, not just the island's geography and exotic history. Nothing you visit is in any way amazing in and of itself — not the scenery, not the architecture, not the island's few summertime restaurants, shops, and resorts. (Only the sizable, modern supermarket and the Shamrock Tavern are open year-round.)

First-time visitors are lucky to have such a guide in Jim Willis, a crusty but amiable retiree. He is the only full-time employee of **Beaver Island Tours**. He'll meet you at the dock and take you to all the major sights. Later you can make longer, more leisurely expeditions to those places that interest you the most. You'll see the Old Mormon Print Shop and Marine Museum, the lighthouse, the old convent, Barney's Lake, the fateful dock former Tiger star Norm Cash fell off of after a night of drinking and drowned. He'll fill you in on Beaver Island's peculiar history, about how the charismatic Strang (by all accounts a gifted and intelligent leader) moved his band of some 2,000 followers to Beaver Island in the 1850s. The Mormons soon took over the fledgling county government by virtue of their numbers, moved the county seat to St. James, and drove off the Irish fishermen from their "kingdom" before Strang was killed by a rebel of his own group. The Mormons were then driven out by earlier fishermen residents who wanted their island home back.

Best of all, Willis tells you, in a laconic, philosophical sing-song, about island life today. How the bank is open from 9 to 1 Tuesday mornings, except during the summer season. How Charlevoix County won't give the two island townships a full-time deputy sheriff, so islanders have to make up a living wage for him by paying him to mow the lawns of the two township campgrounds. "The current deputy comes from Battle Crick," Willis says. "Likes it quite well here — and he should. There's no crime here. Most of his problems come when someone has too much to drink at the Shamrock Bar."

Beaver Island was long the center of northern Lake Michigan's profitable fishery, Willis explains, but overfishing and alewives killed off the industry, and the island's population dropped dramatically. A declining population is always a concern in isolated small communities. If it drops too low, important institutions (school, church, having a doctor) are threatened. Beaver Island lost its doctor, and when its resident nurse practitioner left for Operation Desert Storm, it made national headlines.

Today building vacation homes keeps the island economy going. Development battles are intensifying between "islanders" (natives who grew up here and who need jobs to stay) and "off-islanders" (people from somewhere else, who usually favor limiting development to preserve the island's natural environment). The islanders have the majority vote in St. James and the northern fourth of the island, but in the southern three-fourths, Peaine Township, off-islanders now outnumber islanders.

Don't plan to come to Beaver Island unless you want to relax. There's very little in the way of entertainment, except for the local bands that play Saturday nights in summer at the Shamrock Pub. Transportation for visitors consists of a few taxis and rental cars, bikes (the interior trails are ideal for mountain biking), and their feet. Summer people bring their old cars to the island, but in the off-season, cars aren't a common sight. With so few cars, it looks like the 1930s.

If you just want to look around Beaver Island, you can make a $27 day trip and have 7 1/2 hours on the island. But spending four hours on the ferry to see a few low-key sights on the run doesn't really add up. You're better off to stay a few days, or at least overnight, and unwind. Any of the island's half dozen lodgings or its rental houses are pleasant if simple. You can bring a **bike** on the ferry for $10 round-trip or rent one from **Beaver Island Sports** (616-448-2266). Then you can pick up a picnic from O'Donough's Grocery or Clarkston's Deli next to the Shamrock, and explore the island at your leisure.

It's about 14 miles long and almost seven miles wide, shaped like a teardrop. The only town is St. James, at the harbor on the northeast side. Much of the island's northern third is a pretty rural landscape of log farms and abandoned barns, with seven inland lakes. Fishing in them isn't too good, but it's awfully pretty. The rest of the island's interior is public land administered by the Mackinaw State Forest, crisscrossed by hiking trails and some faint two-tracks. (Mountain bikes are also allowed.) Several lakes and ponds are here, and good berry-picking. A perimeter road goes around the island, though on the less developed west side it's often a mile from the shore. It goes by the old convent (now the Circle M restaurant), the nine-hole public **golf course**; the 25-site **state forest campground** with its sandy beach, seven miles south of St. James; the Central Michigan University research station and conference center; and a mile-long sandy **public beach**. Look for the "public access" sign near Cable Creek, some 12 or 13 miles south of St. James. Then go through the forest to the parking lot and be prepared to walk a mile to the beach.

A trip to the **Beaver Head Light** on the island's south tip is the highlight of a round-the-island trip. Youth groups are restoring the large brick keepers' residences. The tower, open to visitors daily from 10 a.m. to 9 p.m. in summer, offers a fine view of the island interior and shore. Just west of the lighthouse, the road borders beautiful Iron Ore Bay and its sandy, easy-to-reach swimming **beach**.

In a mile, the perimeter road turns north and stays a mile inland. Several roads and two-tracks lead west toward the lake, bordered on the west shore by a bluff. Take any of these roads or the trails that lead west from the road ends, and you'll be almost sure to have the beach all to yourself.

Bicycles, sailboards, and fishing boats can also be rented at Beaver Island Sports. Local history becomes an avocation for many summer people; the grocery store, museums, and attractive island library (donated by the summer resident who owns the Lands End mail-order company) have many books about the island. Browsing in shops could last a couple of hours, if you stretched it. Boats to smaller islands in the Beaver Archipelago can be chartered. There are enough restaurants to be interesting. The Shamrock has good BBQ, and the Circle M, in the old convent outside town, is a pretty place to spend an evening. (Call and management will provide transportation.)

The two **museums** of the Beaver Island Historical Society do a good job of illuminating the island's history and the lives of the people who have lived on the island — Indians, fishermen, Mormons, and "interesting characters who have sought seclusion," like a beloved Russian refugee physician. Historical society members have tracked down descendants of the Mormons who lived here and invited them back to reunions; their stories are part of **Old Mormon Print Shop** museum. The **Marine Museum** offers displays about fishing and boat-building on the island. *The museums are open from mid-June to Labor Day daily from 11-4, Sundays 12-3. Combined admission: $1.50/adult, 75¢/children.*

Whatever you do, don't leave the island without visiting the **Beaver Island Toy Museum and Store**, overlooking Paradise Bay a little past the Marine Museum. Inside this simple bungalow, the golden age of dime stores lives on. You'll find charms like tiny coppery baseball mitts, cheap plastic necklaces, magic tricks, cowboy stuff — it's like returning to the 1950s, with bits of the 1960s and 1930s thrown in. Most things are for sale, but some are for display only. The deadly categorizing of the typical serious collector is altogether absent. The owner has avoided any sense of real-world monetary value and make her cache of warehouse finds into a fantasy realm. Explore the little creations that line the outdoor paths and gardens, and you may be tempted to create some backyard fantasies of your own. Local artists' works, including owner Mary Rose's watercolors, are now offered in a separate room. *Open in season, 11-4 daily, noon-3 on Sundays. In the off-season, inquire in the residence in the barn out back.*

PLANNING A STAY AT BEAVER ISLAND . . . . . The **Chamber of Commerce** is an excellent clearinghouse for any inquiries, including cottage rentals. (616) 448-2505. Box 5, St. James, Beaver Island, MI 49782. Get a **free map** when you get off the boat; the complete **$4 map** is worthwhile if you intend to bike or hike. . . . . For the ferry schedule and reservations, call the **Beaver Island Boat Company**, (616) 547-2311. The ferry runs from April thru December and costs $27 round trip ($13.50 for kids 5 to 12). From late June through August boats leave Charlevoix at 8:30 a.m. and 2:30 p.m. at least. Inquire about the very attractive spring and fall package ($140 per couple for a night's lodging, ferry, breakfast, dinner, tour, and museum fee). The $38 day-trip summer package includes ferry, lunch, tour, and two museums. . . . . . . **Island Airways** makes frequent, non-scheduled flights from Charlevoix. Call (616) 448-2326. . . . . . **Beaver Island Tours'** excellent 1-hour tour is available daily at the dock as the ferry disembarks. $7/adult, $4/children 5-12. Package tours and custom tours are also available. Arranged through Beaver Island Boat Company.

IRISH TRADITIONS LIVE ON . . . . . at Beaver Island, where many islanders are descended from fishermen who came from the islands of Aran in County Donegal in 1856. The island's St. Patrick's celebration lasts for days. Irish country dancing is done at the church. And an Irish Fest is being started. Irish music is much in evidence at the annual homecoming on the second weekend of August. Call the Chamber of Commerce for details – (616) 448-2505.

RESERVING A RENTAL CAR . . . . . Although bicycling is more in the pure and simple spirit of Beaver Island, rental cars are available from Armstrong Car (616-448-2513), Gordon's Auto Service (616-448-2438), and Beaver Island Jeep (616-448-2200).

GATHERINGS ON BEAVER ISLAND . . . . . A traditional small-town **homecoming** is held the second week of every August. . . . . . **Museum Week**, around the third weekend in July, involves nature walks, often a talk by Central Michigan University's summer resident reptile expert, drum-making workshops, a tour of the Russian Dr. Prother's home, and music on the porch with resident folksingers Claudia Schmidt, Kevin White, and others. . . . . . The **Shamrock Pub** and the **Catholic church** are the main social centers. Look for posters around town advertising events.

CRAFTS AND WRITING WORKSHOPS . . . . . are offered by some of the growing number of artists and writers who live on Beaver Island. Celebrated quilter **Gwen Marston** (616-448-2565) offers occasional **quilting workshops**. Nonfiction writer **Mary Blocksma**, author of *Naming Nature* and the soon-to-be-published *Fourth Coast*, is leading workshops on nature identification and "finding your writing voice." Cost: $325/week, including dorm-style accommodations. Call (616) 448-2876. During the summer, **Cheryl Podgorski** leads **crafts workshops** on potpourri/herbal crafts and a variety of other subjects that can be arranged in response to people's requests. You can write her at Box 151, Beaver Island 49782, or call (616) 448-2930.

RUSTIC CAMPING . . . . . is available at the St. James Township Campground, a half mile from St. James on the island's north tip, and the state forest camp ground on the East Side Road. Both have pit toilets and hand pumps. Even in busy summers they don't fill up. No reservations; first-come, first-served.

Earl Young Houses

Charlevoix's beguiling "Mushroom Houses"
look like they were designed by gnomes or Smurfs.

It has been called "Charlevoix the Beautiful" ever since the dawn of Charlevoix's resort era in 1879, when the humble lumber port of Pine River was renamed to honor a Jesuit priest. Rampant overdevelopment has spoiled the nice little resort town on three beautiful lakes. Today it's condo city along many stretches of central waterfront. Downtown is such a zoo in summer that locals and longtime summer people try to avoid it altogether. The drawbridge on the busy channel to Round Lake raises every half hour, adding to the traffic.

Fortunately, the look of Charlevoix's leisurely, lovely past survives in places. The private **Belvedere Club** occupies a prominent hill at the southwest edge of Lake Charlevoix. Its old-fashioned Victorian houses are ample and gracious. The winding paths along immaculately trimmed lawns and trees make it special. Inspired by the success of Bay View (page 607) as a Methodist camp meeting and resort, local developers successfully approached a Kalamazoo Baptist group to launch the resort in 1878. Summer colonies like this seem untouched by the hectic, hurried lifestyle ushered in after World War II; so does the **Grey Gables** restaurant in a big Victorian house at 308 Belvedere on the north edge of the Belvedere Club. The club is closed to the public in July and August, but you can see some of it east of U.S. 31/Bridge Street just at the south

Houses designed and built by Charlevoix's Earl Young seem to grow organically of their own accord, built of local stones and boulders.

Irene Young

❶ Fisherman's Island State Park. Outstanding scenery along 5-mile rocky beach, good for finding Petoskey stones. Sandy swimming area. 90 idyllic rustic campsites in pines, some right on lake.

❷ Brumm Show-room. Huge variety of nature-related jewelry and gifts by Norman Brumm and others. Big area with drawers of specimen shells, polished rocks for collectors and craftsmen.

❸❹ Earl Young gnome homes. Inspired, eccentric rustic architecture. Smurf-like roofs, huge stones, fascinating details. Self-taught architect/ realtor Young built clusters in Boulder Park (❸) & on Park St. (❹),

❺ Channel walkway. Very pleasant path leads from busy Bridge St. to Michigan. Ave. Beach. Wooded park and Earl Young homes above it. Good for viewing boats, drawbridge, sunsets.

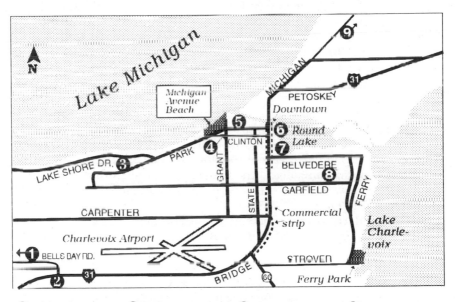

❻ East Park/ City Dock. Colorfully diverse harbor. See Beaver Island ferries, Coast Guard cutter *Acacia*, commercial fishing boats, many sailboats, power boats, big yachts.

❼ John Cross Fisheries. Picturesque landmark famed for good fresh and smoked whitefish, trout, perch, salmon, all locally caught. Fishing boats dock here.

❽ Belvedere Club. Stately row of Victorian cottages on Ferry St. overlook Lake Charlevoix and Yacht Club. Impeccable old resort. Interior closed to public in summer.

❾ Mount Mc-Sauba. Highest dune in area. Scenic downhill and cross-country skiing. Hiking trails, viewing platforms, wonderful beach with wild, natural, open feel.

Highlights of
Charlevoix

0   1/2
                     mile

end of downtown. Turn east onto Belvedere and follow it around
the corner onto Ferry. A similar summer resort development
established by Congregationalists from Chicago is the **Chicago
Club**, on the north side of Round Lake west of the little Pere
Marquette Depot on Lake Charlevoix. It too is off-limits to the
general public, but some houses can be seen at the end of East
Dixon Ave., the first through street to the east on the north side
of the drawbridge.

What makes Charlevoix worth a trip today are some beautiful
waterfront parks, the most interesting harbor in northern Lower
Michigan, and the wonderfully strange stone homes designed by
Earl Young, a real estate broker and self-taught architect. He
built them from the 1920s through the 1950s. These are the
most surprising and original of all the wonderful northwoods
architecture inspired by northern Michigan's natural beauty and
encouraged by the 1920s' quest for the picturesque.

Young used natural materials — mostly different kinds of
local limestone and glacial fieldstone, with cedar shake roofs.
Rather than relying on variations of typical rustic style — log
hunting lodges, for instance, or Shingle Style blends — he took
popular vernacular styles of the day and fitted them so inge-
niously and organically to the materials and sites that they look
like they grew of their own accord, following rules devised by
gnomes and elves.

Irregularly curving roofs mark all Young's homes. He must
have had accomplished craftsmen — maybe boatbuilders accustomed to curving hulls — to make these amazing roofs. The
smallish, medievally picturesque 1920s houses in Boulder Park
are off Park Street along Lake Michigan on the west side of town,
just past the hospital. They are made of oversized rose and gray
fieldstone boulders, sometimes fully three and four feet long. The
stones' great size gives the houses a fairytale, dollhouse look.
Don't miss the tiny bungalows along Park at Clinton, across from
the beautiful woods of shady Lake Michigan Park. Park Street
can be reached by taking Bridge or the parallel residential streets
of State or Grant north almost to the channel, then turning west
onto Park.

By the entrance to Boulder Park are two much later Young
ranch houses, faced with long, thin pieces of local white limestone. Young's flowing roofs and sinuous retaining walls give
them a sensuous, romantic appeal that's rare in ranch houses.

To appreciate the details — the roofs, the playful chimneys, the quaint doorways, the inventive retaining walls — plan on parking your car and walking by each group of houses.

Young's only public buildings are the **Appletree** gift shop at 224 Bridge (next to the movie theater), with an unusual stone interior, and two hotels overlooking the Pine River Channel — the **Weathervane Terrace** and **The Lodge**. The lobby interiors are worth a look for their almost incredibly massive fireplaces, but they lack the intimate charm of the house interiors.

For a **free map and brochure** on many of Earl Young's homes, stop at the **Charlevoix Chamber of Commerce** at 408 Bridge, corner of Belvedere; or call (616) 547-2101. The most magical houses of all aren't indicated on the map, however. Here's how to discover them for yourself. Go north on Bridge Street (U.S 131) across the channel. At the Y, stay left and go onto Michigan, a settled old residential street that backs up to Lake Michigan. In about 2 1/2 blocks, look for a small, wooded pullover that goes down by the public walkway to the beach. Park there. Two delightful houses are tucked in the woods to your right. A third, with a crazily constructed gatehouse that confounds conventional building methods, is away from the lake around the corner on Burns.

A CONVENIENT LAKE MICHIGAN BEACH AND SCENIC WALKWAY . . . . . is the **Lake Michigan Beach** on Grant north of Park. The beach has chang ing rooms, a concession stand, playground, picnic area No fee. Plenty of parking. The hillside park behind it provides a lovely backdrop of pine woods, nice for a picnic or a stroll to see the Earl Young homes on Park Street (page 593). A waterside **walkway** curves around along the channel for a good view of the busy boat traffic. The **pier** gives a good view of the activity at the big **Medusa Cement** port a mile west at South Point. This is a fine spot to watch the sun set over Lake Michigan.

ONE OF LAKE MICHIGAN'S LAST FISHERIES. . . . . is the **John Cross Fishery**. This simple, highly regarded Charlevoix landmark gives an idea of what fishing was like in the days before World War II, when Northern Michigan's economy was more balanced with non-tourist enterprises like commercial fishing. Overfishing and then alewives brought an end to most commercial fishing, except for Indian fishing boats permitted by treaty. Indians own and operate the tugs docked here. They catch the fish that John Cross supplies to leading area restaurants. *John Cross Fishery is down off a drive at 209 Belvedere just east of Bridge. (616) 547-2532. Summer hours:*

daily 9-5. Winter hours vary with availability; call.

OF CHARLEVOIX'S MANY SHOPS. . . . . only the Koucky Gallery can't be
found elsewhere. Most Charlevoix shops here are branches of shops from
other northern Michigan resorts: **Mettler's** upscale, updated traditional
clothing; **Tom's Mom's Cookies**; **Northern Possessions'** handcrafted contemporary furniture, clothing, and gifts; **American Spoon Foods'** intensely
flavored fruit preserves and condiments; the worthwhile **Rocking Horse Toy
Company**; too many fudge shops; and a host of other stores. Specialty shopping is compressed in three busy blocks of Bridge St./U.S. 31 south of the
channel. The **Koucky Gallery** features decorative art — mostly playful, fun,
and accessible — from some 300 artists and craftspeople: ceramics, sculpture, weaving, furniture, jewelry, painting, and prints. About a third of them
live around Charlevoix, which has long been a favorite base for artists who do
the circuit of better art fairs. Some pieces here are huge, like local favorite
Todd Warner's earthy four-foot llamas and chickens. Many pieces use odd
materials and techniques, like jewelry made of rubber and glass beads. These
are things you don't see everywhere, and not necessarily expensive. Jewelry
and mugs begin at around $20. *The Koucky Gallery is at 319 Bridge in down-
town Charlevoix. (616) 547-2228. Closes in late March thru much of April.
Open Mon-Sat 9:30-5:30, Sun 10-4. In summer open until 9.*

CHARLEVOIX'S BUSY HARBOR . . . . . is one of the most diverse and interesting in Michigan. It's home port to the Beaver Island ferry, a commercial
fishing boat, the Coast Guard buoy tender *Acacia,* and a dazzling array of
sailboats and some yachts. To get to the **City Dock**, just south of the U.S. 31
drawbridge, turn east and go behind downtown stores. Benches and tables
make **East Park** a nice place to sit and observe the action. For frequent
summer band concerts at the park, look for posters or ask at the Chamber
of Commerce. A **walkway** along the south side of the Pine River channel connects the harbor with Lake Michigan Beach. Once a month a huge freighter,
the *Myron C. Taylor,* goes through the channel and up to the head of Lake
Charlevoix taking coal to a power plant. It's quite a spectacle; the Coast
Guard can tell you when it's scheduled. Call (616) 547-2541. . . . . . The
Coast Guard cutter *Acacia* welcomes visitors whenever it's in port, which is
often from July into October. A seaman is always on watch. Call (616)
547-4447 to make sure it's not out on a buoy-tending run (in fall or spring)
or being repaired, or gone to a summer festival.

A LOOK AT OLD CHARLEVOIX . . . . . and the present-day beauty spots
remaining from the old resort days is presented in the chatty, beautifully
illustrated little booklet, **Historic Charlevoix: A Guide to Walking and
Driving Tours of the Charlevoix Area's Most Historic Sights**. It's available at the Chamber of Commerce (see below).

FOR VISITOR INFO ON THE CHARLEVOIX AREA, ... on the prestigious Waterfront Art Fair and the popular Apple Festival, call the Chamber of Commerce at (616) 547-2101, or write them at 408 Bridge, Charlevoix, MI 49720. Hours: Mon-Fri 9-5, also Saturdays in summer.

BOAT RENTALS . . . . . allow anyone to spend a few hours or more on beautiful Lake Charlevoix. Rates at **Ward Brothers' Boats** (616-547-2371) are from $30 for two hours on a 13-foot 4-person Boston whaler to $250 a day for the 19' Larson Bowrider that holds 10 for a day of waterskiing and sport. A 12-person pontoon boat rents for $110 an afternoon. The dock and boat shop are at the harbor on the foot of Antrim, off Belvedere.

SAILING CRUISES ON THE TOPSAIL SCHOONER APPLEDORE . . . leave the City Dock in Charlevoix at noon, 3 p.m., and 7:30 p.m. in July and August. The 85' sailboat goes as far down Lake Charlevoix's north arm as time and winds permit – no farther than Hemingway Point. Rates $20/adult, $11/child. $5/$3 extra for wine and cheese sunset cruise. Call (616) 547-0024 for reservations and information.

WHAT MEDUSA CEMENT DOES AT CHARLEVOIX . . . . . Limestone and shale are quarried here, then crushed, blended with much smaller amounts of sand and iron ore, ground fine, and baked in a 2,800° F. kiln. The resulting clinker is stored and eventually ground here so fine that it passes through a sieve that's able to hold water. Pneumatic pipelines take this cement powder to storage silos where it awaits shipment on the *Medusa Challenger* or the *Medusa Conquest*. These freighters take cement to Cleveland (Medusa's headquarters), Milwaukee, Manitowoc, and Detroit, 32 hours away. The Medusa silos and ships are familiar sights to Detroit's Rivertown entertainment district, next to St Aubin Park. To find out when the *Challenger* or *Conquest* is in Charlevoix, call (616) 547-9971.
 Cement shipment by lake boats is an important factor in concrete's low cost. (Cement is concrete's basic ingredient.)

❶ Gaslight District. Over 75 mostly upperend resort shops in attractive old storefronts.

❷ Bayfront Park. Lively waterfront park with marina, refreshments. West of the museum is a historic mineral spring, scenic Bear River valley & iron bridge.

❸ Little Traverse Museum. Handsome depot now home of stimulating historical museum. Splendid display on passenger pigeons, Ottawa quill boxes.

❹ Crafts shops One mile west on U.S. 31 is cluster of crafts shops, fine bay view. Quality affordable crafts at Artidio/galleries nearby.

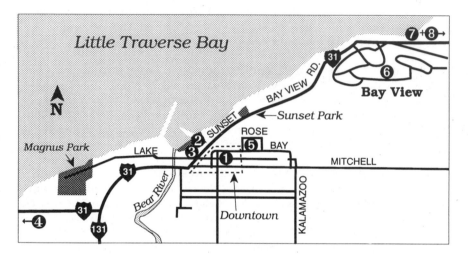

❺ Perry Hotel. 81-room, 1899 brick hotel/restaurant, jazzed up Victorian-style by famed innkeeper Stafford Smith. Long, old-fashioned porch, great Gaslight District location.

❻ Bay View. Peaceful, well-preserved 1875 Methodist summer retreat for relaxation, spiritual and moral uplift. Wonderful old cottages. Eat and stay at Bay View Inn or Terrace Inn.

❼ Petoskey State Park. Delightful view of bay from 1.25-mile beach with occasional Petoskey stones at south end. Scenic campsites and picnic sites among pines, boardwalk atop wooded dunes.

❽ Indian Hills Trading Co. Choice array of Indian crafts. Southwest, Eskimo, plus local Ottawa specialties like sweet grass boxes, quality quill boxes & ash baskets. 1681 Harbor Springs Rd.

Highlights of
Petoskey

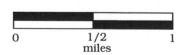

Petoskey and its Gaslight District

Many good shops, a landmark museum, and a splendid chain of waterfront parks give Petoskey one of Michigan's most enjoyable downtowns.

The old resort town of Petoskey is one of the jewels of northern Michigan. Like Saugatuck or Marquette, it's a place that has retained its charming character in spite of being a major tourist spot. Here are the highlights:

LITTLE TRAVERSE HISTORICAL MUSEUM. The handsome, impressive Shingle Style depot that houses this large, interesting local museum is an eye-catching reminder of the importance of railroads in developing Petoskey and other fashionable northern Michigan resorts for Midwesterners who grew rich in the post-Civil War era. The museum, just north of U.S. 31 and below the busy road on the waterfront, is a good introduction to the area.

In the mid-1870s, as the timber on which the local economy depended was running out, railroads teamed up with lumbermen and local business leaders to promote the Little Traverse Bay area as a resort. The museum commemorates Petoskey's

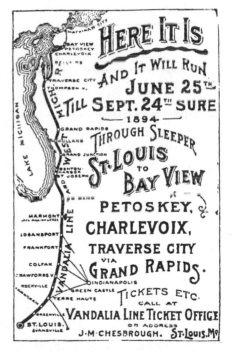

1894 advertisement. Railroads companies, seeking to replace lost lumber business, played an active part in developing major Michigan resorts like Petoskey and Mackinac Island.

railroad era with a reconstructed railroad station manager's office, complete with clicking telegraph key.

Virtually all the giant white pines in the region were logged. A museum display suggests their grandeur with a cross-section of a 225-year-old tree that's almost four feet across. A 300-pound Petoskey stone, one of the largest known, is here. Beautifully patterned when polished, it is fossilized coral, a remnant of the Devonian seas that covered Michigan some 250 million years ago.

A vivid old mural depicts passenger pigeon hunting, so popular and lucrative here before the turn of the century that farmers neglected their crops to pursue it. The meat was a delicacy in fancy big-city restaurants, and the feathers were used to make pillows and mattresses. An estimated three billion to five billion of these plump birds were here before settlers arrived. One flock was 240 miles long and a mile wide. The birds were so docile that hunters simply clubbed them to death. By 1878 whole boatloads were being shipped from Petoskey. The last flock was seen in 1900. The last passenger pigeon died in 1914 in a Cincinnati zoo.

Probably the most important collection here is the **quill boxes** made by Ottawa in the area over a hundred years ago. These small boxes of birchbark are completely covered with beautiful patterns and images of animals and flowers, made of dyed porcupine quills punched into the bark. Boxes of this quality predate the era of commercial Indian crafts made for tourists. It took an immense amount of time to make them (one small box uses ten porcupines' worth of quills). They were bestowed as important gifts for people the makers especially wished to honor.

But what draws the most visitors here is an extensive collection of material on **Ernest Hemingway**, who spent each of his first 18 summers at his family's cottage on Walloon Lake south of town. Later, after Hemingway was wounded as an ambulance driver in World War I, he spent the winter in Petoskey, writing *The Torrents of Spring* and collecting materials for the famous Nick Adams stories that appeared in *In Our Time*. Hemingway met his first wife, St. Louisan Hadley Richardson, in this area; they were married in the little church in Horton Bay. An interesting **gift shop** with many good regional books adds to visitors' enjoyment of the area. *Located on the waterfront of downtown Petoskey, west of the marina. (616) 347-2620. Ample parking by museum. Open May 1, Tues-Sat 10-4; also open on Mondays between Memorial Day and Labor Day. $1 donation. Research material available in winter by appointment.*

BAYFRONT PARK. For an enjoyable stroll on the waterfront and up the leafy banks of the rushing **Bear River**, park in the public lot at the mouth of the river on West Lake Street. **Bayfront Park**, the dazzlingly transformed waterfront that once was an industrial eyesore, extends from the limestone cliff by Sunset Park to the east all the way west past the marina to the Little Traverse Museum and beyond, connecting to walkways along the Bear River valley. Start at the **Bayfront Park Resource Center**, where a short **video** tells about the park's past and present. In front of you are the 90-slip marina and sailboats on the bay. An unusual **playground** is tucked in a sunken sand pit near the marina.

Go east to reach the shady **picnic area** with the 35-foot **waterfall**. The stairs by the waterfall lead up to a scenic overlook that connects to **Sunset Park**, with a gazebo and telescopes.

Go west along the shore and you'll come to the Little Traverse Museum (page 599), City Hall, and the mouth of the Bear River, often lined with fishermen. The river is stocked with brook trout and steelhead. Across the drive is picturesque **Mineral Well Park**, a shady, old-fashioned gazebo and **picnic area** built so that health-conscious Victorian resorters could take in the foul-smelling sulfur waters. The Bear River rushes dramatically, dropping 75 feet within a mile, through a natural area that's wild with otter, beaver, minks, and waterfowl. It's hard to imagine that it once was an industrial mill district. **Trails** on either side of the river extend back a mile and a half; hikers can make a loop by using the Bridge Street bridge at the inland end. The east bank can be used by cross-country skis and mountain bikes.

GASLIGHT DISTRICT. For people who choose to spend their vacation time doing resort-area shopping, the Gaslight District in downtown Petoskey stands out for its size (almost 80 stores in a six-block area geared to visitors), for setting (well preserved two-story Victorian brick storefronts and a pleasant park), and for tradition.

This shopping district has catered to the Midwest's wealthiest resorters since the turn of the century, when steamers took Harbor Springs summer people across the bay to Petoskey stores to be fitted for fall suits and dresses. You don't see as many independent boutiques with "Petoskey and Naples" on their signs as you might have 25 years ago, and there's more ordinary gifty stuff, but a good deal of the old flavor of serving the carriage trade remains. Fudge shops haven't taken over.

The Gaslight District is a concentration of shops still oriented more to well-heeled summer people and those who want to look and live like them, than to tourists. The area is geared to browsing. Prices are high because rents are high and the season is short, but there are some terrific markdowns at the end of the season in October. Shops now stay open year-round. This is a good place to find fashionable skiwear and after-ski wear, as well as other sports gear and clothing.

Antique shops are clustered around Bay at Howard, at the district's north (bayside) end. Interior furnishings are more likely to be looser and more contemporary, sometimes in a folkish vein, in keeping with a relaxed, summer cottage feel. Updated traditional clothes for women are the area's strength, in shops like **Mettler's** (400 Bay) and **Pappagallo** (402 E. Lake). This is where to find things like oiled thornproof country jackets imported from England (over $260) and top-quality blue blazers for small boys (over $150), in addition to handknit sweaters, print sundresses,

Mineral Well Park on the Bear River near downtown Petoskey. Now fishermen come for spring and fall steelhead runs, and hikers enjoy the leafy trails on both high riverbanks. In the late 19th century, tourists came to the mineral well to take in the foul-smelling sulphur waters.

polo shirts, Benetton, Ralph Lauren, etc. Gifts and collectibles
are becoming a bigger deal here, especially if they have ducks
and fish on them, or if they have an Up North flavor (Petoskey
stones, moccasins, birch boxes). For toys and novelties, **Games
Imported** (206 Howard), **The Rocking Horse Toy Company**
(325 E. Lake), and **Grandpa Shorter's** (301 E. Lake) all carry
things you're not likely to find at your local mall.

Caution: the famous cherry berry pie at Jesperson's
Restaurant on Howard Street, which Hemingway is said to have
liked, is over-priced and over-rated (too sweet). The restaurant
began in 1903 but today lacks any historic charm.

A handy Gaslight shopping guide is available at the helpful
Chamber of Commerce in the little office with columns on the
corner of Mitchell and Howard. Or call (616) 347-4150 for a visitor packet. **Store hours** are open 9:30-5, Monday through
Saturday. Only about 20 stores are open Sunday; hours vary.

Stores worth special mention include:

♦ **Grandpa Shorter's**. The consummate, old-fashioned Northern
Michigan souvenir shop: big selection of moccasins, Petoskey
stones, rubber tomahawks for kids — all the classics, plus well-
chosen new novelties and some quality gifts. Lots of inexpensive
toys and games for kids. Incorporates junk without being junky.
All the fun of a good old-time dime store. *301 E. Lake at
Petoskey. (616) 347-2603.*

♦ **McLean & Eakin Booksellers**. General bookstore focused on
customer service, amenities like free coffee, chairs for browsing.
Call for special events, held monthly at least; regular singles
night with music, refreshments on second Fridays. Best children's section in the area. *307 E. Lake. (616) 347-1180. Extended
hours: to 8 weekdays, Sundays noon to 4.*

♦ **Ward & Eis Gallery**. Works by top leather craftspeople from
across the U.S. include practical, beautiful handbags from 30
individual craftspeople, many kinds of calendars and organizers,
and amazing decorative masks. Handbags run from $30 to $200,
with many in the $50-$80 range. All come with lifetime guaran-
tee. There's a growing array of leather jewelry, including realistic,
life-size leather feathers of birds of prey. Another new addition:
leather and pottery from various Indian craftspeople who have
become friends of the owners. There are Lakota (Sioux) beaded
leather rattles and axes, things from Huichol artists living in the
Sierra Madre, and pottery from Steve and Leigh Smith of the

Mohawk Six Nations. Co-owner Don Ward loves to talk about crafts of Native American peoples and the workplaces and methods he has seen. The one store in Petoskey not to miss. Beautiful bay view from rear window. *315 E. Lake. (616) 347-2750.*

◆ **Gattles**. Custom linens for the carriage trade — for instance, here you could have pillowcases embroidered to match your wallpaper. Big mail-order clientele for unusual merchandise and services. *331 E. Lake. (616) 347-3982.*

◆ **Symons General Store**. A friendly gourmet grocery in a charmingly cluttered old storefront with high tin ceilings. The best wine and cheese selection in town, plus breads, muffins, deli items, and imports and Michigan products for gift baskets. *401 E. Lake at Howard. (616) 347-2438. Open daily; in summer, open evenings.*

◆ **Great Lakes Design**. Geared to informal summer residences. A good deal of hand-decorated furniture. Each year a changing array of unusual accents hand-painted in Mexico in folk art styles is featured such as colorful flower and fruit designs on large plates, blue and white bathroom ceramics in a loose, informal pattern, from a $20 toothbrush and towel holders to a lavatory basin. *406 Bay (also in Harbor Springs). (616) 347-9831.*

Native Detroiter Justin Rashid has built American Spoon Foods into a highly regarded maker of gourmet sauces, condiments, and fruit toppings, based largely on Michigan-grown fruit, herbs, and mushrooms.

◆ **American Spoon Foods.** Justin Rashid's highly regarded company is Michigan's biggest culinary success story. Its nationally famed fruit preserves and all-fruit, no-sugar spreads concentrate the natural-fruit taste by using top ingredients and minimizing sugar. It's on the pricey side (roughly $5.25 for a 9-ounce jar), but it's a souvenir gift with cachet. Until a few years ago, the shop here doubled as the kitchen, where everything was produced. A greatly expanded product line now includes condiments, pasta sauces, salad dressings, and more, devised by chef/co-owner Larry Forgione, in addition to Michigan-grown fruit toppings. On the counter: a vast array of opened jars for sampling. If there's anything you'd like to try and it's not open, just ask. Most popular: sugar-free sour cherry spoon fruit. Other big sellers: dried cherries, strawberry preserves, and smoky Southwest Salsa, rated in the *New York Times* top four salsas. Also for sale: pretty birchbark gift baskets, evocative prints of Northern Michigan scenes by artist Kristin Hurlin. *411 E. Lake, almost at Park Avenue. (616) 347-1739. Open weekdays 10-5:30, Sat 10-6.*

◆ **Northern Possessions.** Bright, often primitive-sophisticated or whimsical American crafts — cabinets painted with bears and fishes, $300 soft suede boots, colorfully embroidered, looking like something a Cossack might wear, furniture, lots of jewelry. Looks more original if you haven't checked out the Chicago gallery scene. *222 Park Ave. (616) 348-3334.*

◆ **Horizon Books.** Large branch of the Traverse City bookstore also has a good selection of better magazines. *319 E. Mitchell. (616) 347-2590. Open daily 9 a.m.-9 p.m.*

To get to the Gaslight District, follow signs from U.S. 31 to downtown. Large parking lots are at the foot of Bay Street and between Bay and Lake just east of the tracks. But come by 10 in summer for easy parking. Later, look for a uniformed teen to direct you to long-term parking or a free 1/2 hour space. Shops are open 9:30 to 5, Mon-Sat. Only 20 or so shops stay open summer evenings and Sundays.

FOR A PLEASANT LUNCH BREAK . . . . . treat yourself to a meal in the elegant bayview dining room of the **Perry Hotel** on Bay at Lewis. The big old brick building, directly across from the old train station and the tracks, has been beautifully restored by area restaurateur Stafford Smith. Its new exterior paint scheme brings out its architectural detail. . . . . . Or you could make up a picnic lunch from the imported cheeses, deli items, and fresh-baked muffins and sourdough bread at **Symons General Store**, Lake at Howard. (See page 604) . . . . . Picnic spots: the **waterfront park** (get there safely by finding the tunnel under U.S. 31 down from the intersection of Bay and

Petoskey streets) or **Pennsylvania Park** (see below).

A SHADY DOWNTOWN PARK . . . . . is alongside the railroad tracks that define the Gaslight District's eastern edge. **Pennsylvania Park** runs between Mitchell and Lake. It has benches, picnic tables, and a gazebo where **summer band concerts** are held Tuesdays and Fridays at 12:15 and Tuesdays at 7 p.m. between June thru late August. Restrooms and pay phones are across the tracks at the Chamber of Commerce, Mitchell at Howard.

MOVIES IN PETOSKEY . . . . The **Gaslight Cinema** at 302 Petoskey has not only been reopened and refurbished, it has added three more screens for a total of five first-run movies. Call (616) 347-3480 for program information. **Children's Saturday matinees** are at 3 p.m., and in summer at 1 and 4. . . . . . The **Petoskey Film Theatre** screens art films two or four nights a month at the McCune Arts Center, 461 E. Mitchell. (616) 347-4337.

A SCENIC DRIVE TO HORTON BAY . . . . . takes in crafts galleries and Hemingway lore. Take U.S. 31 west out of Petoskey toward Charlevoix along Little Traverse Bay. A mile out on the right, at 2666 Charlevoix Road, is **Artisans** (616-347-6466), a large shop with an extensive selection of quality American contemporary crafts at moderate prices. If you have time, it's fun to stop and see the working jewelry and pottery studios across the road, too. In three or four miles, look for Horton Bay Road (C-71), which goes due south to the old lumbering village of **Horton Bay** (population 49) on Lake Charlevoix. Just after the lumbering era's end, young Ernest Hemingway used to walk from his family's cottage on Walloon Lake to fish and hunt near the Point at Horton Bay. The classic **Horton Bay General Store** (616-582-7827), where he sometimes stopped, is well supplied with Hemingway memorabilia along with groceries and a lunch counter. Several of the Nick Adams stories are set in and around Horton Bay. Its little church was where Hemingway married Hadley Richardson of St. Louis, another resorter. Three popular restaurants kept Horton Bay alive when lumbering was gone. Today it owes its fame to its weird and wonderful **Fourth of July** parade, a totally home-made affair that attracts some 14,000 spectators.

A BEAUTIFUL FARM STAND WITH A GORGEOUS VIEW . . . . . Take Petoskey's main drag, Mitchell Street, up the hill and east about three miles to **Bill's Farm Market**. (This is a great low-traffic way to I-75; just stay on C-58 until the Wolverine exit.) Here, arranged with an artist's eye, are all the basics and a lot more – miniature vegetables grown for restaurants like Stafford's inns and Tapawingo; 25 kinds of squash, including the delicious Sweet Dumpling; and finger-size ears of sweet corn that are edible. *445 Mitchell Road. (616) 347-6735. Open mid-June through mid-December, Mon-Sat 9-6, Sun 12-5.*

Bay View

*A charming, peaceful 19th-century religious resort
that keeps its special atmosphere.*

This remarkable colony of 438 cottages and 28 public
buildings overlooks Traverse Bay just east of Petoskey.
Most of the cottages were built before 1900, and the village, with its big trees and winding lanes, retains the aura of an
earlier era. Michigan Methodists organized Bay View in 1875 as a
place for summer camp meetings. Initially a tent camp, it grew
within 20 years to included elaborate cottages, a hotel, chapel,
and eventually a fine library. Famous speakers at Bay View have
included William Jennings Bryan and Booker T. Washington.

Camp meetings came out of the Second Great Awakening of
early 19th century America which ignited the fires of religious fer-
vor and swept across much of the new nation. Methodists and
other groups encouraged camp meetings, often in the woods, as
ways "to come together for religious refreshment and revival."
They were especially concerned about establishing an atmosphere
conductive for their children to have conversion experiences.

Earlier Methodist summer camps had been established in
the East. Bay View was the very first formally organized summer
colony in the logged-off North Woods of Michigan. As such, its
influence was enormous. When later associations planned
Wequetonsing and Harbor Point in nearby Harbor Springs, for
instance, they carefully studied the Bay View model — its common spaces and community buildings and its paths and roads.

Bay View cottages were built on a series of natural terraces
— ancient beach lines created by higher lake levels in eras when
glacial meltwaters were gradually receding. The founding
Methodists were not wealthy people. The first houses were tents
and simple 12' by 16' cabins. By the 1890s these cabins were
being enlarged in style, with big front additions. The Queen Anne
style is dominant, with lots of gingerbread trim on wide porches
across the front, and on small second-story porches above. All
cottages originally had views of the bay, now blocked by trees.
Many of them face away from the drives, so to really experience
Bay View, you should get out and walk across the campus.

Jean Lau

Evelyn Hall, one of Bay View's meeting areas, was built in 1890 by the Women's Christian Temperance Union. Bay View today continues the extensive summer programming that started in the Chautauqua tradition of spiritual uplift and educational enlightenment.

(Parking spaces are plentiful along most drives.) Don't miss the wonderfully complex **Evelyn Hall** from 1891.

"The spiritual atmosphere of Bay View has always been highly moralistic, with a stern interdiction of Demon Rum, cardplaying, dancing, and other fleshly pursuits," wrote the late John Rauch, a longtime observer and chronicler of the area's resort history. Sundays were dedicated to worship and everyone attended three services. . . . As late as 1910, no deliveries in Bay View or other traffic was permitted to disturb the pious Sabbath. There was much hymn singing and prayer meetings on weekday nights."

Today's Bay View is considerably more relaxed. Just about half of the current residents are Methodists, some of them the sixth- generation of Bay View summer residents. Members of the Bay View Association have taken great care to preserve the community's Victorian look. Cottage owners are required to get association approval for even minor exterior changes. Residents own their own cottages (costing at least from $40,000 to $200,000) but lease their land from the association. Bay View is occupied only from May through October, although two inns are open year-round.

Days are filled with courses, sports, lectures, plays, and concerts, just as they were in the colony's early years. A small but select summer school of music attracts gifted musicians from around the country. The 2,000-seat auditorium is where **concerts** are held at 8 p.m Wednesday and Sunday. To receive a free program of services, vespers, concerts, and events open to the public, call (616) 347-6225. Daily events schedules are published in each day's *Petoskey News-Review.* A **museum** on the main campus in the two oldest buildings is open beginning in July and August from noon to 1 on Sundays, and 2:30-4:30 Wednesdays.

A popular place for visitors to stay and eat is **Stafford's Bay View Inn** close to Little Traverse Bay. Less fancy, quieter, and more in the original spirit of Bay View is the relatively austere **Terrace Inn**, facing the central campus. Two bed-and-breakfasts are in vintage cottages.

The main part of Bay View is just south of U.S. 31 on the eastern edge of Petoskey. Encampment Drive takes you to the central campus. To reach the Bay View main campus from Petoskey, take U.S. 31 past the S curve by the train tracks and turn south (right) on Fairview Avenue. Take it to the T intersection. The campus is just ahead of you. Park anywhere. For information on summer concerts, plays, or events, call the Bay View business office at (616) 347-6225.

RENT MOUNTAIN BIKES, CROSS COUNTRY SKIS, SNOWSHOES, AND MORE . . . . at **Adventure Sports**, 1100 Bay View Road east of Bay View. Prices are reasonable ($15/day for a mountain bike and helmet), and the staff can advise you on the many good trails and routes in the area. Open daily in summer and ski season. (616) 347-3041.

Petoskey State Park

Convenient to upscale resort towns, it has a woodsy setting, scenic beach, dunes, and a wonderful bay view.

Many of Michigan's smaller, older state parks up north don't have much more natural atmosphere than suburbanized lake lots. They have grassy lawns, rows of planted trees, a beach, and boat launch. A lot of the campgrounds resemble miniature subdivisions of RVs.

Petoskey State Park is different. It manages to combine convenience of location and facilities with a wonderful natural atmosphere in only 305 acres. The park enjoys a choice site in and behind the dunes at the funnel-like end of Little Traverse Bay. The mile-long **beach** not only has soft sand but a fabulous view of Harbor Springs and Petoskey in the distance. The shoreline frames the setting sun for spectacular sunsets, followed by the twinkling town lights reflected in the water.

There's a **concession stand**, **bathhouse**, and **playground**. The parking lot is big enough to handle demand on all but the hottest days of the year. There's plenty of room to walk down the beach and get away from crowds. If you're lucky, you may be able to find a Petoskey stone along the south end of the beach, among the stones and gravel. Wooded dunes provide a natural setting for the beach, unlike some popular parks near resort towns, where the beach environment consists of sand, water, sky, and shimmering row after row of parked cars.

Petoskey State Park is gorgeous in fall. A mix of hardwoods makes for especially rich colors contrasting with the conifers' dark green and the white paper bark of birch trees

Be forewarned that sometimes west winds across the funnel-shaped bay concentrate all sorts of floating refuse from boats right here. Parks employees clean up regularly, but it can occasionally be a problem.

A stand of big pines gives the **picnic area** in a hollow behind the dunes its own special aura. It's deeply shady, unlike the open beach, and filled with piney scents and scampering chipmunks.

The two **campgrounds** nestled in wooded dunes behind the

beach manage to offer 190 sites with modern amenities (electrical hookups and showers) while retaining a good deal of privacy and a wonderful, woodsy feel. They typically fill up from mid-June through late August. Reservations for half the sites are taken starting January 1; the other half are first-come, first-serve. They may fill up before noon. You can camp in Petoskey's nearby Magnus Park (on the bay but far less scenic) and take a priority slip that keeps your place in line when the next day's spaces are doled out at 8 a.m.

Petoskey State Park is just off busy M-119, less than 10 miles southeast of Harbor Springs and four miles east of Petoskey. Each resort has bustling, upscale downtowns of charming late 19th-century buildings loaded with all the most refined material diversions of late 20th-century consumerism. Sometimes all that stuff and stimulation demands an antidote in exercise and nature. Two trail loops start by the campground registration office. At the .7-mile **Old Baldy Trail**, a stairway climbs steeply up into heavily wooded dunes for a spectacular view of the bay through the trees. When you climb the dunewalk stairs into the rustling, dark, cool forest of pines and maples, you feel remote from the traffic along 119's commercial strip half a mile away. The much easier 2.7-mile **Portage Trail** goes through lower dunes to Lake Michigan and a little inland lake. It's recommended for **cross-country skiing** in winter. (The campground stays open in winter, too, but without running water or showers.)

For more of a real wilderness experience, Wilderness State Park (page 625) and the Bliss Township beach (page 626) are not too terribly far away — about 35 miles north on county road 81. But for combining natural beauty and convenience to two of northern Michigan's most attractive old resort communities, Petoskey State Park is tops.

The park is at 2475 Harbor-Petoskey Rd. (U.S. 119) about 1 1/2 miles north of U.S. 31. (616) 347-2311. It's open year-round but running water and flush toilets are shut off between Nov. 1 and May 1. State park sticker required: $4/day or $18/year. Camping $13/night.

❶ Bluff Gardens. Fancy farm market with choice tiny vegetables, jams and jellies & a huge stock of peasanty, gay Quimper earthenware.

❷ East Bluff Drive. Best view of the charming downtown and harbor is from this stairway between the high school on bluff and Spring St. down below.

❸ Downtown shops. Attractive retail area with pricey resortwear. Creative surprises in crafts and home accessories.

❹ Hoover Flower Shop. Cut flowers, plants, and dried arrangements for stately summer homes come from these colorful fields and greenhouses.

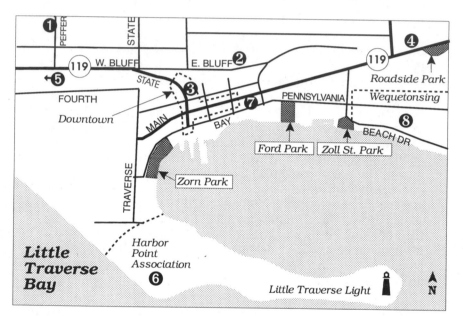

❺ Tunnel of Trees. Twisting highway along Lake Michigan is one of the state's most scenic drives.

❻ Harbor Point. No outsiders allowed at this elite summer colony. Only horses provide summer transportation.

❼ Blackbird Museum. The Indian postmaster built this post office in 1876. Tells about the traditional life of local Ottawa.

❽ Wequetonsing. Glimpse traditional resort life of the affluent. There's sailing, golf, flowers, drinks on the veranda at this grand old cottage colony.

Highlights of
Harbor Springs

0   miles   1/4

Harbor Springs

*The Midwest's most exclusive old resort area
has an interesting downtown, lovely resort colonies,
and wonderful views of bay, town, and woods.*

This famous old resort town — "the Newport of the Middle West" — still manages to hold onto its great physical beauty and small-town charm. This remains true despite the vastly increased development, in the 1970s and 1980s, of nearby second homes, golf and ski resorts and the resulting new intensity of retail activity. Harbor Springs lacks the disturbing sense of development gone rampant. It has avoided the four-story condo complexes in Charlevoix and the busy fast-food strips abutting Bay View and Petoskey.

East Bluff Drive still has a stunningly picturesque view. Overlooking the turn-of-the-century downtown, you see a crescent harbor full of sailboats and, on the point, a leafy, lovely summer cottage colony and lighthouse. To the east, in the century-old resort association of Wequetonsing, a stately parade of large, picture-perfect summer homes have gracious verandas looking out across flower-bordered lawns and paths to the sailboats on Little Traverse Bay. There are extensive areas of golf course, woods, and wetlands along the main entrance to Harbor Springs from Petoskey, buffering the east edge of town from development. Many of the wooded areas are now public preserves that have been donated to the **Little Traverse Conservancy** (see page 622) by individual landowners, or bought with Conservancy funds.

At the height of the season in July and August, downtown traffic and crowds can spoil the tranquil aura of the place. Some people prefer the quieter times — midweek in summer, or in the morning, or any time in the lovely spring and fall. Winter bustles again with skiers who come to the two ski slopes built on the dramatic, steep hills north of town the **Boyne Highlands** ski resort (616-526-2171) on Highlands Drive or **Nub's Nob Ski Area** (616-526-2131) on Pleasantview Road.

Downtown Harbor Springs still has enough old-timey places with character to maintain the leisurely, civilized sociability of an old resort town. To see it in action, stop for coffee and doughnuts

The block of summer shops in downtown Harbor Springs has some delightful, quirky nooks and crannies like the courtyard leading to Tom's Mom's Cookies.

between 9 and 10 a.m. at Mary Ellen's lunch counter and magazine stand on Main Street. The plywood magazine racks and general ambiance are straight out of the 1940s. Here you'll witness a congenial coffee klatsch that includes all spheres of permanent residents, from natives to "trust-fund babies."

Harbor Springs' identity as the Midwest's premiere resort community began just five years after the railroad first arrived at Petoskey in 1873. Lumber, the main freight of Northern Michigan railroads, was running out, and the railroads aggressively promoted the area's recreational virtues to hayfever sufferers and wealthy Midwestern families escaping hot summers at home.

The success of nearby Bay View (page 607) inspired the formation of two resort associations in Harbor Springs, Harbor Point and Wequetonsing. (Its local nickname is pronounced WEE-kwee.) Both were tonier and more fun-loving than earnest, education-minded Bay View. But both were patterned after the Methodist colony in that the associations own the land and approve the cottage owners. That control gives resort colonies like these a century-old visual and social continuity that's almost unheard of in fast-changing American society, where suburbs can boom and decline within a generation.

A much earlier group of residents are the Ottawa (Odawa) Indians, who moved into the area between Harbor Springs and

Cross Village in the 1700s and remain here, in diminished numbers, today. The Odawa were able to hold on to these villages while Indians in the more desirable farmlands of southern Michigan were forcibly moved west by the U.S. government in the 1840s. Wealthy Harbor Springs resorters and tourists actually helped maintain the local Odawa community during the early 20th century by buying the famous quillwork and crafts.

The old resort families hailed from big Midwestern cities where technical know-how of German immigrants had combined with Yankee enterprise to create great manufacturing fortunes in the decades during and after the Civil War. Townspeople protect the privacy of the famous old families who come here — they include some automotive Fords, some glass-making Fords of Toledo, and some Gambles of Proctor & Gamble — while they readily divulge the presence of newcomers like Detroit Piston Bill Laimbeer, rock star Bob Seger, and radio personality J. P. McCarthy, all of whom have second homes in the newer areas just outside Harbor Springs.

Highlights of the Harbor Spring area include:

◆ **Downtown shopping.** *Downtown is centered along two blocks of Main St. between State and Gardner, with an increasing number of shops on Bay and on the adjoining three blocks of State.* **Parking lots** *along Third and Bay.* **Seasonal hours.** *Summer hours: daily from 9 or 10 a.m. to 5 or 5:30 p.m. Some stores are open evenings. Many stores stay open Sundays through fall color season. Winter hours Mon-Sat from 9 or 10 a.m. to 5 p.m.*

The delightful, small-scale historic storefronts and cottages, combined with the choice merchandise and some fresh ideas, make for pleasant browsing in Harbor Springs. Many of the familiar, upper-end resort retailers in Northern Michigan have shops here, but what makes Harbor Springs stand out are an unusual number of individualistic gallery/shops. These change from summer to summer; high rents and a short season make for high turnover.

Several unusual shops you might miss are on North State near the bend at the bluff. At the nonsensically named **Pooter Olooms** *(339 N. State; 616-526-6101)*, owner Jenny Feldman and manager Anne-Gaelle Maizeray buy bare pine and colorfully painted country antique furniture in France, Austria, and Scandinavia. These pieces form the basis of an inspired assemblage of collector quilts, garden sculpture, and folk art, antique and contemporary. The folk art, both naive and sophisticated, often has a spiritual aspect and occasionally verges on the darkly mysterious. It includes a lot of tramp art purchased in Europe, idiosyncratic one-of-a-kind pieces, and work from a dozen gallery regulars. This includes Kim Nicolas's vases and candlesticks and lamps made of Michigan stones, embellished with woven willow or hickory; Kelli Sniveley's muted paintings incorporating postage stamps like religious icons; Liz Galbraith's elegant lamp-shades of Japanese-style paper she makes; and North Creek Creations — fish, birdhouses, and other primitives made by a family that home schools in Northern Michigan. *Open daily year-round. From Mem. to Labor Day Mon-Sat 10-6, Sun 11-4. Otherwise Mon-Sat 10-5, Sun 11-3.*

Just opened next door, **Primitive Images** showcases the owner-made birch and twig furniture and interesting lamps with woven shades. Toward town, **Boyer Glassworks** *(207 N. State; 616-526-6359)* features Harry Boyer's handblown glass vases, paperweights, and ornaments, plus less expensive crafts and jewelry. (Boyer's glass earrings are striking.) Harry Boyer was close to the 1970s beginnings of the contemporary art glass movement in Toledo. Visitors can watch him at work.

Main Street's year-round businesses are centered in the main business block east of the major intersection with State. Farther east, small single-story storefronts and converted houses are more likely to house summer-only businesses. **Huzza** *(136 E. Main; 616-526-6914)* creates an eclectic contemporary style that plays off good contemporary design with antiques in its mix of interior decor, tabletop accessories, expensive women's clothing, and gifts. In the sale room, the same top-quality clothes are more affordable. **The Coyote Woman** gallery *(160 E. Main; 616-526-5889)* makes nearly every list of noteworthy shops with its mix of Southwest and contemporary art, jewelry (in sterling silver and 14-karat gold, often with semi-precious stones), and accessories like pottery, Navajo rugs, and sculpture in stone, bronze, and raku. Along with the strong Southwest element are local artists like Chuck Parsons, well-known for his scenes and abstract images. Stop in for a brochure of Harbor Springs' seven other year-round galleries.

Between the Covers *(152 E. Main; 616-526-6658)* is a book store that offers good browsing, a cozy, literate atmosphere, an excellent regional section, and even a backyard terrace with seats. Service is informed and personal, and the selection is much more discriminating than the usual resort bookshop. *Open* *daily 10-6 in July & August; otherwise open Mon-Sat 10-5.*

In the 200 block of East Main, most stores are summer-only, from June through August — too bad, because fall is such a pleasant time to visit the area, and many of these shops are delightful. A standout is **The Real Nancy Drew** (616-526-9857), open daily in summer. The real Nancy Drew, who lives in Niles, Michigan, grew up in Bloomfield Hills, went to Catholic schools, spent summers in Harbor Springs, and is the mother of three. Her popular cartoons, in a colorful style somewhere between a freewheeling kid's and Picasso's, draw on that background as well as funny, realistic insights on mothers, daughters, and shoppers. They appear in the *Chicago Tribune* and on T-shirts, totes, shirts, sundresses, and furniture for sale in her store and in several little books about Catholic memories, interesting women, and "resort life in dreamy northern Michigan. . . too good to be true?" The entire interior is painted with lots of zig-zags and squiggles, creating an intensely wacky environment.

A core of old-line Harbor Springs institutions have managed to escape escalating rents by owning their buildings. **Cassidy Hardware** *(135 E. Main)* is a classic, with wood fixtures, squeaky floors, and all sorts of paraphernalia for wild birds. **Hovey's Pharmacy** *(205 E. Main)* displays interesting historic photos by its entrance. **Gurney's Harbor Bottle Shop** *(215 E. Main; 616-526-5472)* is known for its wonderful sandwiches, thick stacks of roast beef or ham with a distinctive sauce on a fresh homemade bun. Order a half-sandwich (with half the meat) so you can get your mouth around it. **Mary Ellen's Place** at 145 E. Main (formerly Linehan's) is a newsstand and soda fountain that's the premiere local institution for keeping up with everyone in town and a fine spot for an inexpensive snack in this pricey town. Summer residents have their personal cubbyholes for their hometown papers. The **Harbor Springs Library** is upstairs on Main at Spring; enter around the corner at 206 Spring. It's open daily in summer, otherwise most afternoons and Saturday mornings. This light-filled, comfortable, old-fashioned space has a fine view of the harbor. There you can browse through back copies of the *Harbor Light* weekly newspaper, a literate, leisurely chronicle of town and resort life. It's an all-too-rare continuation of the tradition of serious small-town journalism.

◆ **Holy Childhood Catholic Church and School.** This striking complex — a simple, Gothic clapboard church and adjacent three-story brick school — is the direct descendant of the

Catholic Indian mission that was the basis of the first permanent settlement at Harbor Springs. French Catholic missionaries had converted area Indians in the 1700s. In 1823, residents in the nearby Ottawa village of L'Arbre Croche asked the U.S. government to send them a Catholic missionary. By 1833 the mission had become the largest Indian mission in the northern U.S. Franciscans took over in 1886 and built a large school and dormitory for Indian students. Indians today resent such institutions because they weakened Indian families. *150 W. Main. 616-526-2017. Masses at 8 a.m. weekdays, 5:30 & 7 p.m. Sat., 9:30 and 11 a.m. Sun, year-round.*

◆ **Andrew Blackbird Museum.** Odawa chief Andrew Blackbird started Harbor Springs' first post office in his kitchen here in 1862. Indians held the paid government jobs in Harbor Springs' early years. But as whites moved in, they took over the Indians' positions. When they claimed Blackbird's house couldn't handle the volume of mail, he built the adjoining storefront. But he lost his job anyway. Blackbird continued his career as a writer and lecturer. His works and some possessions are on display, along with various stone points, baskets, and Indian clothing from here and elsewhere. Now the local Odawa tribe has taken over the museum. The collection of beautiful Odawa birchbark boxes

Holy Childhood Church at the head of Main Street was erected by the Indian mission that was the basis of the first permanent settlement at Harbor Springs. The present church was intentionally sited as the street's focal point, getting around the wishes of resorters to straighten the street and reduce the Catholics' visual impact on the town.

covered with dyed porcupine quills is a point of pride. *368 E.
Main, next to the Shay hexagon house. 616-526-7731. Mem.-Labor
Day: Mon-Sat 1-5. Otherwise by appt.*

◆ **Shay House.** This odd hexagonal house with projecting
hexagonal wings (1892) illustrates the inventive mind of its
owner and designer, Ephraim Shay. In 1881 he had invented a
revolutionary new locomotive. Small and versatile, it enabled
narrow-gauge track to be laid easily to remote mines and stands
of timber. The Shay locomotive made logging much more efficient
— so efficient, in fact, that Northern Michigan's forests, considered so vast they would last a thousand years, were nearly gone
by 1910.

In his adopted home town of Harbor Springs, Shay devised
an early household water system and experimented with steel-
hulled boats. The pleasant, light-filled house, sheathed inside
and out with embossed metal in many patterns, is now used as
offices. Visitors are welcome in the lobby. *373 E. Main.*

◆ **Harbor area.** Many sailboats and a grand view of the Harbor
Point lighthouse and Little Traverse Bay behind it make this harbor exceptionally picturesque. The waterfront park has many
benches, a small **local museum** with limited hours, restrooms,
and a small **swimming beach** west of the piers and State Street.
A boat ramp is just east of the **Irish Boat Shop**, which even has
a staff sailmaker. A board sail ramp is at the foot of Zoll Street,
east almost at Wequetonsing.

◆ **Wequetonsing.** Unlike many other exclusive summer colonies,
Wequetonsing (pronounced WEE-kwee-TON-sing) isn't a gated
enclave that's off-limits to the public in summer. It gives you a
rare glimpse of the living continuation of a very leisurely, very private, very privileged summer world. Routines for some are generations old. One older banker habitually enjoys a newspaper with
breakfast, then spends an hour on the phone with his private sec-
retary back home. Backgammon is at 10, then lunch at the club,
followed by golf and bridge, shopping, or a fashion show for his
wife. Cocktails on the veranda are followed by dinner, often at the
club, and then to bed.

For townspeople and retirees, it can be an education to work
for these old guard families, usually so charming and considerate
in their private lives. Teams of summer workers start opening the
vacation homes in May and June, painting and repairing, groom-
ing the perfect lawns, installing bedding plants. Then eight hectic

The pretty summer resort of Wequetonsing, just east of Harbor Springs, was established by Presbyterians from Allegan, Michigan, and Elkhart, Indiana, so that "worn-out and sweltering humanity could repair to recover health and enjoy rational recreations." The most impressive houses (left) face Little Traverse Bay, while smaller cottages line pedestrian walks (right).

weeks in the service of the resorters: cleaning, cooking, shopping, and serving. After Labor Day, a deep collective sigh — of relief and regret that the whole magical show is over for another season.

Wequetonsing was laid out on the Bay View plan, with a common activity building (the casino), playgrounds, and tennis courts clustered along Second Avenue between Pennsylvania and Central. The golf course is across the Petoskey Road. The bayside houses grew grand and showy, but simpler places, closely spaced, line the pedestrian walkways that lead back from the water. Just to the west is town. To the east and north of Wequetonsing, along Beach Road, are a series of wooded **nature preserves**, open to the public, interlaced with paths and boardwalks. The spring wildflowers are beautiful, but the trails are often wet. Parking is by the A.C. Fischer Preserve sign. *To reach the nature preserves and Wequetonsing from town, take Main or Bay east to Zoll, go south to the shore and turn left onto Beach Drive. To take a scenic, slow alternate route from 119 and Petoskey, look for Powell Road to your right about 2 miles north of U.S. 31. As soon as you pass it, look for the inconspicuous Beach Drive to your left. Turn onto it and take it into town.*

◆ **Hoover Flower Shop.** Fresh-cut and dried flowers, bedding plants, and shrubs for the carriage trade are supplied from these five greenhouses and five acres of fields. Fields are filled with color in July and August. You can buy dried flowers and grasses by the piece. The color range of dried sweetheart roses (75¢/stem, reduced in spring) may be unequaled. *M-119 (Petoskey Rd.) just east of Harbor Springs. (616) 526-2992. Open May through mid-October and Thanksgiving to Christmas.*

◆ **East Bluff Drive.** This part of Bluff Drive boasts a splendid view of town and bay, along with Harbor Springs' most elaborate non-resort Victorian houses. A stairway descends from the high school up on the bluff down to Spring Street. *State east to Arbor.*

◆ **Bluff Gardens.** A produce stand catering to the entertaining needs of Harbor Point and Wequetonsing resorters has evolved into a purveyor of homemade fancy foods, sold at this glorified farm market and by catalog. There are jams, dressings, and relishes (about $4 an 8-ounce jar). Even the tiny carrots and beets are displayed like jewels in the carpeted sales area. Bluff Gardens' pride is its stock of Quimper, the French earthenware famous for its peasanty motifs in blue, yellow, and red-orange. *721 W. Lake. From downtown Harbor Springs, take State up the hill to West Bluff (M-119). In about a mile turn right onto Peffer, then left onto Lake. (616) 526-5571.*

◆ **"Tunnel of Trees"** (M-119) to Bliss Township Park and Wilderness State Park. *See page 625.*

◆ **Thorne Swift Nature Preserve and Beach.** These 30 acres of beautiful beach, dunes, and fragrant cedar swamp have been donated for use as a park and nature center. A **dune stair and overlook** offer close-up looks at pioneer dune plants, and a panoramic view of the bay. The small swimming **beach**, seldom crowded, is reached by a 1/4-mile trail. **Boardwalks** pass shallow-rooted cedars leaning crazily in the swamp for a surreal effect. The wonderful cedar aroma makes this a special destination. So do the outstanding interpretive signs and pamphlets for three short nature trails. Naturalist-rangers give **scheduled guided tours** and are often around to field casual questions. Call to arrange a nature walk anytime in summer. *Lower Shore Dr. 3 1/2 miles west of Harbor Springs. Take M-119 to Lower Shore Dr. (616) 526-6401. Open daily Mem.-Labor Day 10 a.m.-sunset; weekends Sept. & Oct. Call for permission to enter other times. $2/car for non-residents.*

FOR A MINI-GUIDE TO NATURE PRESERVES . . . . . some dozen in all,
stop by or call the **Little Traverse Conservancy** outside Harbor Springs.
(616) 347-0991. The office is open weekdays 8-5. It's just off the Harbor
Springs-Petoskey Road (M-119) at 3264 Powell Road on the north shore of
Round Lake, at the headwaters of the Inland Water Route to Lake Huron.
There's a self-guided brochure to a short trail near the lake, a good area for
spring wildflowers, birds — and mosquitoes. Other good-size preserves are
near Harbor Springs, on Burt Lake, on the lower Pigeon River (where a cabin
can be rented by groups), and near Lake Charlevoix. . . . . A **complete directory** to all Conservancy preserves — all open to the public — is $10 at the
office, $12 by mail.

THE BEST BEACHES. . . . . if you like the away-from-it-all mood and natural, windswept dune environment, are at **Bliss Township Park** and
Wilderness State Park on Sturgeon Bay, north of Cross Village. See page
623. The beach at **Thorne-Swift Nature Preserve** (page 621) is natural, close
to Harbor Springs, but small.

FOR A DOWN-TO-EARTH CONTRAST TO HARBOR SPRINGS. . . . . take
U.S. 31 to Alanson on the Inland Waterway, visit **Bob's Place** restaurant (it
draws folks from all around), the excellent **Dutch Oven** bakery and yarn
shop, or **Spanky's** snack bar, with a nice deck overlooking the waterway at
the swing bridge. To see the waterway, turn east onto River in the center of
Alanson. A little park with a dock is across from Spanky's. You can come
upon some interesting, offbeat shops in and around Alanson. . . . . West of
Alanson, the **Oden State Fish Hatchery** in Oden is right off U.S. 31 across
from Crooked Lake. Interpretive signs tell about what fish are being reared
there. . . . . Going to Mackinaw City, U.S. 31 shows you a slice of life in the
real northern Michigan that is as much trailers and roadside bars and welfare as it is condos and marinas and art galleries.

THE INLAND WATERWAY. . . . . Indians used the Inland Water Route
through interconnected Crooked Lake, Burt Lake, and Mullet Lake to get
from Little Traverse Bay to Lake Huron. Later, little steamers took resorters
to their summer cottages on the lakes. Today navigation ends at Crooked
Lake, just a few miles from Lake Michigan. It's a popular route for power
boaters — often *too* popular, if you enjoy quiet — and most of the route is
lined with cottages. . . . . A good deal of the way between Crooked Lake and
Burt Lake is pretty and natural, full of wildlife, especially in the morning,
before the boaters are out in force. Rentals of fishing boats, pontoons, and
a mile south of Alanson off U.S. 31. Look for the sign. They can point out visitor highlights on Burt Lake or sell you a little guide.

Legs Inn

The pinnacle of rustic folk architecture in Michigan is also a warm Polish restaurant north of Harbor Springs.

The North Woods is full of inspired folk-art creations. None is more improbable than Legs Inn in Cross Village, along the Lake Michigan shore 20 miles north of Harbor Springs. It's a Polish restaurant and bar created by Stanley Smolak, who came to America as a young man to work in a Detroit auto factory. He got to know the Ottawa Indians in Cross Village, which in the 1920s was still a living center of the Ottawa culture. What fascinated him was the Ottawas' close connection with nature, and the intimate linking of the material and spiritual worlds.

In the late 1920s Smolak started work on the inn, which grew in stages to encompass many moods and environments. What's seen from the road verges on ugly. There's no landscaping to soften the busy exterior façade of small, irregular fieldstones, accented by totem poles and a fanciful row of curved upside-down furniture legs on the roof (hence the "Legs" of the name). Hand-painted lettering on piled-up boulders advertises "BEER, LIQUORS, SOUVENIRS, DRIftWOOD."

The interior is far more compelling. The barroom is dark and grotto-like, easy to pass over on your way to the restaurant in the rear. The restaurant's picture windows overlook a beautiful rear terrace with outside dining, pines, and a flower-filled rock garden. In the distance is Lake Michigan. It's a popular spot on summer evenings at sunset. Children can run around the extensive grounds and play while their parents linger over dinner and dessert.

The restaurant's atmosphere is cheerful and warm. There's a big stone fireplace and interlacing rafters of sticks. Dining areas are separated by screens of intertwined driftwood, glistening with shellac. Here and there primitive, pixyish faces painted on the driftwood peek out.

The food is Polish home cooking, the equal of Hamtramck or Chicago's favorite Polish restaurants. The cabbage rolls are outstanding. Whitefish is also available, along with European dishes like goulash and chicken in wine. Dinners (with soup or salad, bread and potato) are around $9 to $15, sandwiches and lunch entrees $4 to $7. A world-wide selection of over 50 beers is on hand.

If you time your dinner visit right, you can stroll outside to enjoy the sunset over the lake, and then linger in that amazing grotto of a barroom. After your eyes are acclimated to the dark, you'll make all sorts of discoveries. Phone booths are made of hollowed-out trees. A lacey, tangled lattice of shellacked roots above the balcony disappears into the dark. Faces and figures seem like spirits emerging from branches and roots.

Smolak's Depression-era art is based on found materials, inspiration, and persistence.. "He claims that any man can do what he did if he only keeps his eyes open and his hands busy," states one appreciative article. "For the world is filled with fine and great wonders, things which people take no notice of because they have eyes yet do not see and hands that lie idle."

After Smolak's death, Legs Inn devolved into something of a dive. Today it has been rejuvenated into a family restaurant and local meeting place that's a refreshing change from the carefully traditional interiors so evident in nearby Harbor Springs and Petoskey. There's a variety of **live music** on weekends and during the week July through August; Sunday afternoons feature music in the garden. The **gift shop** offers Indian-made arts and crafts as well as items imported from Poland.

Legs Inn is on 119 just north of Levering Road, 22 miles from Mackinaw City and 20 miles along the lakeshore route from Harbor Springs. (616) 526-2281. Open the weekend before Mem. Day through 3rd weekend in Oct. Summer dining-room hours 11-10, Sun. noon-10. Fall hours noon-9. Bar open until 2 a.m. Full bar. Visa, MC.

A LOVELY DRIVE TO LEGS INN . . . . . is along the lake, through the celebrated **Tunnel of Trees**, narrow M-119 that twists above the shoreline. The overarching trees, the glimpses of Lake Michigan from the bluff, the aroma of cedars and pines — all combine to make this very special. Bicyclists favor the drive in morning, but traffic is rarely heavy or fast. Colonies of trillium cover the woods around Memorial Day for a spectacular show. After dark, you're better off avoiding the twists and turns and taking the inland route back to Petoskey. Take 66 (Levering Road) east from Cross Village; in 9 miles turn south at 81. It eventually ends at Harbor Springs-Petoskey Road.

Wilderness State Park

30 miles of unspoiled coast, picturesque cabins,
sandy beaches with no crowds,
and rugged backcountry trails for skiing and hiking

Wilderness State Park is a world apart from Mackinaw City's motel-land, yet barely 15 minutes away. It combines a location near major destinations around Petoskey and the Straits with an exceptional expanse of varied natural beauty: rocky limestone shores facing the straits and backed by cedars and birches that can sustain themselves on these thin, rocky soils; a series of islets stretching out into Lake Michigan; a long crescent of a sandy beach facing west; and a remote, forested back country, laced with trails. At a little over 8,000 acres, Wilderness ranks as one of the Lower Peninsula's largest, most complex, and least developed parks.

Wilderness Park Road leads from Mackinaw City past the campgrounds and main beach to Waugoshance Point. Along the shore and point are **five lighthouses**, some abandoned, some still functioning, all erected to warn vessels away from the shallow shoals as they turn into the straits. The point and the two long offshore islands near it extend almost five miles out into Lake Michigan, just 15 miles from the Upper Peninsula. A newly improved gravel road enables you to drive out to the point. You can even walk to the islands in low water. The point is a favorite spot for birders because over 100 species either nest here or migrate through. The point is closed during the rare Piping Plover's nesting season.

Lakeshore Campground (150 large modern sites) is an open, suburban-style campground with lake views. Across the road, the 100 large modern sites in the **Pines Campground** are shaded and private. Both fill up in summer and cost $14/night. Make reservations, or arrive before 2 p.m. to get a site. Five rustic 4- to 6-person **log cabins** in scenic beach spots are for rent, along with three 24-person cabins near the campgrounds. Reservations are needed well ahead for all cabins.

A beach that's sandy, even less crowded, and more natural, backed by dunes, is reached at the park's southwest corner, where M-119 joins Lakeview Road. Look for the sign to **Sturgeon**

Bay Picnic Area. It has grills, tables, and pit toilets. An overnight cabin is nearby. The sandy beach along Sturgeon Bay stretches five miles north within the park.

In the rugged interior backcountry, many paths and old logging roads cross a glacial landscape of wetlands and high hills like Mount Nebo. Check with park staff for tips on combining trail segments to suit your requirements, and to be sure that the popular trail to Waugoshance Point (2 miles each way) is open. The park has over six miles of groomed **cross-country ski trails** and 12 miles of separate **snowmobile trails**.

Main entrance and booth are on Wilderness Park Rd. (C-81), 12 miles west of Mackinaw City. Write: Wilderness State Park, Carp Lake, MI 49718. (616) 436-5381. State park sticker required: $4/day, $18/year.

A SURPRISING, QUIET, NATURAL SIDE TO MACKINAW CITY . . . . . can be seen by taking the **shore route** from town to Wilderness State Park and avoiding Trail's End Road. To see the quaint, rustic cottages of the Wawatam Association, follow the south perimeter of Colonial Michilimackinac west to Straits Avenue and Lakeside Drive. This old Indian trail is today a charming but bumpy drive by back doors of cottages. Turn left at Cedar to avoid a long detour, and go right (west) out Central. At the T, the right (north) road end out to McGulpin Point offers a terrific view of the Mackinac Bridge. Then go back (south) and turn right (west) briefly onto Trail's End. A beautiful, simple **public beach** lies ahead where the road turns; another similarly sandy public beach is in a couple of miles. Both have toilets. Follow the signs from here to Wilderness.

A DELIGHTFULLY REMOTE BEACH . . . . . with a backdrop of wild-looking dunes, is at **Bliss Township Park** on M-119 about 10 miles north of Legs Inn on Sturgeon Bay. It's not fancy — amenities consist of two outhouses — but it's a favorite choice of many Petoskey people. From Mackinaw City, take County Road 81 southwest, but keep going west on Lakeview when 81 turns south. See also **Sturgeon Bay Picnic Area** at **Wilderness State Park**, p.625.

Colonial Michilimackinac

Living glimpses of frontier life of the French, Indians and British at this reconstructed 18th-century fort, built to control the lucrative fur trade.

By 1779-1781, the British had abandoned and burned this old stockaded fur-trading post and fort overlooking the Straits of Mackinac. But so many bits and pieces of everyday life and military armament were left buried in the sand and so many accounts of life at the old fort had been written, that it has been possible to reconstruct the fort's buildings with great accuracy and to recreate the life here.

The fort has been restored to the 1770s, when British soldiers were garrisoned here but the traders continued to be a polyglot mix of British, French, several Indian peoples, mixed-blood descendants of them all, and even some Jews, the first to live in Michigan. Millions of artifacts have been excavated here since 1959, along with the foundations of the burned buildings, in the oldest ongoing archaeological site in the U.S.

New interpretive exhibits and recreated events are continual-

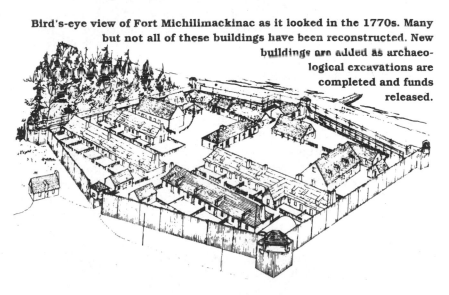

Bird's-eye view of Fort Michilimackinac as it looked in the 1770s. Many but not all of these buildings have been reconstructed. New buildings are added as archaeological excavations are completed and funds released.

Interpreter Annette Naganashe at the encampment of native peoples outside the fort. Interpreters here work at various traditional everyday tasks: weaving mats, cooking, and (here) making a rope.

ly being added, thanks to the fort's favorable position as one of the three Mackinac State Historic Parks. These parks are well funded by the ample gate receipts at these popular tourist attractions. Even if you have been here before, return visits can be worthwhile. The past five years have seen the reconstruction of the rowhouse home of 18th-century fur-trader Ezekiel Solomon, the addition of a recreated French colonial wedding to the fort's scheduled daily events, and a unique new underground archeological exhibit, "Treasures from the Sand."

Most interesting is the Indian encampment outside the palisades. Here visitors can go inside a wauginogan (a tipi with a rounded top) and a nasaogan (a tipi with a pointed top), simply furnished with a few bowls and utensils, furs, and a cradle board, all of which visitors are welcome to examine. Costumed interpreters who are Michigan Indians are busy at assigned tasks.

All the re-enactors have jobs like preparing food, cooking, and making and fixing things. It's fascinating to watch them and ask questions. Though they may have scripted demonstrations, these interpreters are broadly informed, often longtime students of their subject matter, and they can field many kinds of questions. Other costumed re-enactors play actual people such as fur trader Peter Pond, who summered at the fort after spending winters in Minnesota, and a representative British wife who gives a most interesting talk about the 18th-century vegetables she grows in her garden.

Plan on starting your visit with a 30-minute **guided walking tour** to familiarize yourself with the village inside the palisades of the fort. Then explore it at your leisure, taking in the re-enactments and talks that interest you the most. The **cannon-firing and muzzle-loading demonstration** is a great favorite with kids. The fort is fully staffed and presents its full schedule of re-enactments from mid-June through Labor Day.

Fur-trading in the upper Great Lakes caused competitive friction between France and Great Britain through much of the 18th century. A small fort at the northern tip of Michigan's Lower Peninsula was built here in 1715, part of France's ongoing efforts to keep the British out of this lucrative trade zone. There was never a big military force here, usually about 20 soldiers. Still, as the present reconstruction of the old site shows, it was a typical fort of the day, surrounded by an 18-foot-high stockade. As many traders as soldiers lived in the community, which was cut off from the outside world six months a year.

The French finally surrendered their northern territories to Great Britain in 1760, and the British occupied Fort Michilimackinac for another 20 years until they built a more defensible fort on Mackinac Island. The most notable event during their stay was the 1763 massacre of most of the fort's British soldiers by the local Indians, part of Chief Pontiac's ultimately unsuccessful plan to repulse the British.

Like many historical reconstructions, Colonial Michimilimackinac focuses on the details of daily living, military history and technology, and trade networks, rather than on ideas and the social consequences of historical events. Little mention is made of the fur trade's vast impact on the Indians it touched, who quickly became dependent on useful trade goods, and on the alcohol which too many traders used as a trade good.

An excellent array of books on the area and on the fur trade are in the **museum shop**, along with crafts and souvenirs that reflect the fort's history and the culture of Straits Indian peoples. The shop, in the Visitor Center under the Mackinac Bridge approach, is also open to people without museum tickets.

Take northbound I-75 to exit 339 just before the bridge, follow signs to fort. (616) 436-5563. Information pack mailed upon request. Open daily from mid-May to mid-Oct. Hours: May 11 thru 27 10-4. May 28 thru June 14 9-5. June 15 thru Sept 4 9-6. Sept 5 thru Oct 16 10-4. Adults $6.50, children 6-12 $4, family $20. **Mackinac State Park combination ticket** *(for here, fort on island, mill): adults $12.50, children $7.50, family $38 (unlimited admission throughout the year).*

▲🌲▲

TWO PLEASANT PARKS FOR WATCHING BOATS AND THE BIG BRIDGE
. . . . A shady park stretches east along the shore from Colonial Michilimackinac, which is on the west side of the Mackinac Bridge, to the **Old
Mackinac Point Lighthouse** and along the shore past a few motels. Plenty of
benches and **picnic tables** make this a fine place to sit and enjoy the bridge
and Straits view, or walk along the beach (the white limestone rocks are full
of fossils), or read a book about the area's rich history. Regional books are at
the Sign of the Copper Lantern at 215 East Central or at the Colonial
Michilimackinac museum shop at the visitor center under the bridge
approach. You can see the sunrise and sunset from this park because of its
unusual location at the tip of a peninsula. The effect of the bridge lights
reflected in the water is memorable. . . . . If you walk east down Huron
Avenue from the lighthouse towards the docks, you will pass the less tour-
isty, older neighborhoods of Mackinaw City. Little public areas at the ends of
streets offer changing perspectives on the big bridge. **Wawatam Park** at the
foot of Jamet and Etherington east of Huron has some play equipment and
interesting outdoor exhibits about fishing history and the Mackinaw boat.

SHOPPING IN MACKINAW CITY . . . . . is a lot more interesting than it used
to be. There are still lots of general gift shops that could be just anywhere,
and more than enough rubber tomahawks and T-shirts and fudge shops, but
several places have their own distinctive personalities. Standouts include:
◆ **Sign of the Copper Lantern**, *215 East Central. (616) 436-5121.* Part
nature store, part rock shop, part gallery of Michigan artists and craftspeople. Book department is strong on nature, regional, and activity books for
kids and grown-ups.
◆ **Tundra Outfitters**, *301 E. Central. (616) 436-5243.* Gifts and limited edition prints related to Alaska and wolves, plus Alaskan-style clothing designed
for serious cold weather. Owners sponsor a sled in the Iditarod race.
◆ **Sandpiper Alley**, *105 N. Huron (another entrance is on Langlade). (616)
436-5309.* Michigan gifts and crafts.
◆ **Mackinaw Kite**, *105 N. Huron. (616) 436-8051.* Inspired and inspiring
array of kites, from fun toys to stunt kites that can do amazing loops and lift
a person off the ground. Also: wind-powered toys, windsocks, and books on
kite-flying and kite-making through the ages.
◆ **Mackinaw Bakery**, *110 Langlade (near McDonald's). (616) 436-5525.* Old-
fashioned, full-line bakery with tables to sit down at for coffee and soup.
◆ **Traverse Bay Woolens**, *312 S. Huron. (616) 436-5402.* This up-north
tourist center chain has switched to natural fibers and greatly upgraded the
quality of its blankets, sweaters, and sportswear.

Mill Creek State Historic Park

A beautiful trail overlooks a reconstructed
1790 sawmill powered by a working waterwheel.

A reconstructed 18th-century sawmill in an unusually scenic location means that this park is an extraordinary place to visit. The original mill was built by a Scottish trader in 1790 to supply lumber for the British fort on Mackinac Island. It was powered by Mill Creek, which flows into the nearby Straits of Mackinac linking Lake Huron and Lake Michigan.

The mill has been rebuilt to duplicate the original, complete with a big wooden waterwheel. **Demonstrations** show what noisy, shaking contraptions water-powered mills were. A **visitor center/museum** by the entrance and parking lot puts the site in historical context and displays items uncovered on the site by archaeologists. The excellent **museum shop** features books, activities, and gifts related to nature and to logging.

A highlight is a 15-minute walk on **Mill Pond Trail**. It forms a loop from the visitor center to the sawmill and around the mill pond. On the way are two

Perched over picturesque Mill Creek, this replica of a 1790 lumber mill gives visitors a dramatic and noisy view of how sawmills worked before steam power. A bonus is the beautiful location in a hilly area close to Lake Huron.

delightful **overlooks** from which you can look down on the sylvan scene and even see the Straits and Mackinac Island. Another 25-minute **trail**, also a loop, takes you through a forest along the top of the bluff paralleling the mill stream. An hour-long **trail** follows the stream farther back to some beaver dams.

This point of entry to the natural world of northern Michigan is an excellent complement to the bustle and crowds nearby.

On U.S. 23 1/2 mile southeast of Mackinaw City. (616) 436-7301. Open mid-May to mid-Oct. Summer hours (June 15-Labor Day) 9-6. Otherwise 10-4. Adults $4.50, children 6-12 $3, 5 & under free, family (two adults and children under 14) $14. See page 00 for information on combination tickets.

TWO OUTSTANDING PRIVATE MUSEUMS IN MACKINAW CITY. . . . .
Teysen's **Woodland Indian Museum**, over Teysen's cafeteria restaurant at 416 N. Huron, across from the docks, features gorgeous beaded leather clothing, baskets, and other artifacts in a very interesting, to-the-point display done by Michigan State University museum specialists. It tells you a lot more about Michigan Indian cultures than many bigger, more tedious museums. Displays periodically changed. *(616) 436-7011. Open from early May through color season, 7 a.m - 9 p.m. Adults $2, students free, group rates available. Guided tours can be arranged.* . . . . . The **Mackinac Bridge Museum** was started by an ironworker who helped build the bridge. It's over his pizzeria. The displays aren't professional or slick, but the project has both intelligence and the heart of grassroots history. There are hundreds of workers' personalized hardhats, photos of the ferries and huge lines at the Straits during hunting season, and an excellent half-hour film about designing and building the bridge. Not to be missed. *Over Mama Mia's Pizzeria, 231 E. Central at Henry. (616) 436-5534. Free.*

Mackinac Island

This celebrated resort features an 18th-century fort, the famous Grand Hotel, striking rock formations, wonderful bike and carriage rides, and no cars.

An 18-minute boat ride from either the Upper or Lower Peninsula, this three-mile-long island is a major Midwestern travel destination for several reasons. Its interestingly rugged terrain provides many pleasant panoramas and views of striking limestone formations.

The island's military and economic history is equally colorful. Various Indian peoples met there to trade. The British built a big fort here in 1781, and American and British forces fought a battle in 1812. For 50 years it was the center of the North American fur-trading network. The legendary fur trading tycoon John Jacob Astor had his main trading office from 1817 to 1834. One of the world's most famous Victorian hotels, Grand Hotel, is perched on the side of a bluff, visible from the mainland.

The absence of autos and the use of horses and bicycles for transportation give the island the aura of another age. The decision to ban autos was made for practical, not aesthetic, reasons in the 1920s, when the automobile's potential destructive impact on the island environment was becoming apparent. Even inexperienced cyclists enjoy the scenic but undemanding trip on the paved road that hugs the lakeshore all the way around. There's the additional adventure of having to take one of the many ferries from St. Ignace or Mackinaw City to the island's harbor and resort town at its southern end, giving passengers a striking view of the large Victorian summer houses, the big fort, and the majestic Grand Hotel, all situated on steep limestone slopes.

Most of the island is a park, laced with roads, bike trails, and foot trails that are clearly signed. The free visitor map identifies them all. Because the island is mostly limestone, with only a thin layer of topsoil, it has been little farmed. The rocky terrain, eroded by wave action from earlier, high lake levels, includes many interesting formations such as Arch Rock, Devil's Kitchen, Sugar Loaf Rock, and Chimney Rock.

The island was a popular meeting and trading place for

Ojibway, Odawa, and Huron people. They called it the great turtle (Michilimackinac), because of its humped, oval shape. French missionaries began setting up missions in the Straits area to convert the Indians in the 17th century. At the same time, exporting Great Lakes furs to Europe became a highly profitable enterprise, pursued by both the British and French. In 1781 the British moved their mainland fort here, and the island became the center of Great Lakes fur trading until the beaver population was decimated by the 1830s.

Tourists escaping the summer heat began visiting the picturesque island in 1838. By the 1870s Mackinac Island had become a three-day steamer trip from Detroit and a two-day train trip from Chicago. Congress made the island the country's second national park in 1875. Tourism boomed along with the Midwest's industrial economy, which developed greatly during the Civil War. Fort Mackinac was closed in 1894, and a year later over 80% of the island was designated Michigan's first state park. That protected it from further development.

Under 400 of the island's 2,300 acres remain privately owned. The handsome huge, Victorian summer "cottages" just to the east and west of the harbor now sell for up to $700,000. Even some of the modest workers' homes in Harrisonville, toward the center of the island, sell for over $100,000, forcing some of the 500 year-round residents to leave the island for cheaper housing elsewhere. The biggest issue now facing the island is overdevelopment as new shops and housing have created low water pressure, power outages, and landfill problems.

Some 900,000 "fudgies," the locals' sardonic term for visitors, come to the island each year. Getting off a ferry in the harbor, they are confronted with a bustling street full of carriages and tourists, fudge and souvenir shops. It's easy to get drawn into the tourist shuffle, going from sight to sight and shop to shop. But that's not what makes the island special.

Follow this advice for a really enjoyable trip:

1. Read up on the island ahead so you have a rough itinerary worked out when you arrive. Call or write ahead for a map and information packet from the Mackinac Island Chamber of Commerce (906-847-6418 or 906-847-3783) and from the Mackinac State Historic Park (616-436-5563). *Mackinac Connection: An Insider's Guide* by longtime summer person Amy McVeigh is a chatty, informative 160-page book with many helpful tips and candid info on all lodgings, restaurants, shops, outings, events, walks, bike rides, and much more. Highly recom-

Mackinac Island's unusual limestone formations led late 19th-century tourists to explore the island's interior. Here two boys have climbed Sugar Loaf Rock. Fresh, cool air and outdoor activity contributed to the island's reputation for invigorating refreshment.

mended pre-trip reading. It's available at many bookstores, or see our mail-order book section in the back of this book.

2. Consider spending a night on the island so you can have two days of activities and time to relax and explore the island's natural interior. Many people have the mistaken idea that Grand Hotel, where a special deal is $120 per person, is the only hotel on the island. That's far from the case. Most hotel rooms are $80 to $100 and up, but there are simple tourist homes with rates of $40 and $50 for two. Get a lodgings list from the Chamber, an annotated list from *Mackinac Connection,* or recommended lodgings from *Hunts' Restaurants and Lodgings of Michigan.*

3. Take a carriage tour first to see what you most want to visit.

4. Get a free Mackinac Island map at the **Chamber of Commerce** across the way. Walk right on Main Street a block from the docks and stop at the foot of Fort, beneath the fort. The **Visitor Center of the Mackinac State Historic Park** shows a good introductory video and offers more info. *(Open 9 a.m. to 7 p.m. in summer, to 4 or 5 otherwise.)* Note, too, the handy public restrooms behind the Chamber and here.

5. Walks are a real delight. Figure out how to alternate walks and rest periods where you can sit and take in the many splendid views. Walks through the village along Market Street and the east end of Main are exceptionally enjoyable; so are walks along East Bluff and West Bluff. *Mackinac Connection* outlines several walks.Wear good walking shoes!

6. Take a break. Good spots for rest and relaxation: benches scattered many places; Marquette Park, on Main Street below the fort; the terrace restaurant at the fort; the porch and gardens of Grand Hotel (anyone can use them for $5); the garden next to St. Anne's Church on East Main; church sanctuaries, held open for visitors; the Chippewa Hotel's Harbor View dining room, inside and out, at Main and Fort; at the other end of Main at French Lane, the Iroquois Hotel's Carriage House, with a grand Straits view.

7. Get a good book to read about island history, nature, or architecture from the Island Bookstore in the Lilac Hotel on Main Street, or at the gift shop at the fort. Reading breaks get you planted in a place and slows you down from the numbing tourist pace.

8. Take the bike ride around the island and, if you're in shape for the hills, explore the interior. The nature center and snack at British Landing makes a good break half-way round the island.

9. Early mornings and evenings are especially beautiful, and less crowded in peak seasons — another good reason for spending the night.

10. Consider a visit in fall or spring. (Before mid-June the wildflowers are wonderful.) The pace then is slower and things are less crowded. Most shops stay open all season. The only thing you'll miss is the Market Street historic buildings, open only from mid-June thru Labor Day. From the last week or so of August through Labor Day the crowds drop off considerably.

11. Have a picnic. Prices for island food are on the high side, restaurants can be crowded, and sometimes the food isn't very good. If sticker shock gets you upset, pick up a sandwich at Doud's Mercantile, the island's only grocery, at Main and Fort, or bring food from the mainland. Mackinaw City's Mackinaw Bakery, next to McDonald's on Langlade just north of Central, has good pasties and bread.

Highlights for visitors to the island are:

◆ **Carriage tour.** Thirty local families pooled forces over 40 years ago to start this cooperative company. Today they operate about 75 carriages, using some 300 horses, to transport visitors around the island. The narrated tour, approved by the city and the state park, lasts one hour 45 minutes. It's a pleasant, informative, slow-paced drive which takes you by most sights. Stops at Fort Mackinac and Arch Rock let you get out and enjoy the wonderful view. You can be dropped off at Grand Hotel at the tour's end. (It's a pleasant half-mile walk back to town.) *Begins downtown at the Mackinac Island Carriage ticket office on Main Street opposite the Arnold docks, next to Chamber of Commerce. Open from mid May through mid Oct. Summer hours (from mid June thru-Labor Day) 8:30-5:30 or so. Otherwise 9 3. Adults $11.50, children 4-11 $6.*

◆ **Fort Mackinac.** Perched on a bluff overlooking the harbor, this historic fort is well worth visiting. Its views of town and harbor below are delightful. The well-preserved fort has been restored to look as it did in the 1880s, when the army garrison's main duties were to take care of the national park. Seen from that perspective, the fort's military significance seems trivial. But that wasn't the case in 1780-1781, when the British built the fort to protect their fur trade interests west of their breakaway colonies, or in the War of 1812, when the British captured it from the Americans.

A short **slide/tape show** is a good introduction to the fort. The views from the blockhouses and parapets are wonderful. Of the scheduled **historical demonstrations and recreations**, the cannon firing by an enthusiastic and expert costumed guide is always a hit. Audience questions are encouraged. The military music concert/talk is a lot more interesting than the court martial. Musicians played important roles in signaling. Skilled buglers were often recruited from immigrants at Ellis Island. On the **children's tour**, kids roll hoops and play other games from the 1880s. In the Children's Discovery Room in the Officers'

The parapets of Fort Mackinac offer splendid views of the town below and the Straits of Mackinac and freighter traffic in the distance. Some interpreters wear the uniforms of the soldiers stationed here in the 1880s, when Prussian spiked helmets were adopted by the U.S. Army.

Stone Quarters, children can try on military hats and coats and period costumes and pose for photos in them. Other hands-on displays introduce what things associated with the fort's history sounded like and felt like (beaver pelts, for instance). Down below, in the same Officers' Stone Quarters from the 1780s, is a delightful **tearoom.** The tapered masonry walls are from two to four feet thick, so the windows are like little niches. Food is also served on the terrace, which has a fabulous view. The excellent food, prepared by Grand Hotel cooks, includes soup, salads (Greek salad is under $6, rotini and vegetables about $7), personal pizzas (around $5), and sandwiches ($7 and under). The $4 pecan fudge ice cream ball is enough for two.

You can go inside 14 original buildings, furnished as they were in 1880, including barracks, blockhouses, a canteen, and a post commissary. The **officers' quarters**, quite a contrast to the enlisted men's spartan rooms, are the most interesting, appointed with a good deal of Victorian bric-a-brac to make families feel at home. The social niceties among military wives are explained in fascinating detail. *Same hours, prices as Fort Michilmackinac.*

(page 627). The joint pass to all three historic parks is a good deal. The helpful **visitor center** *to the fort is below the fort on Main at Fort, opposite the park. It's open 9 a.m. to 7 p.m. in summer, to 5 in the first part of June, to 4 at other times.*

◆ **Market Street** parallels Main a block inland. While Main Street's dense storefronts and hotels were built for the busy Victorian tourist trade, Market Street's detached houses reflect the much simpler Mackinac Island of fishermen and fur-traders before the Civil War paved the way for the industrial boom of northeast America. Many buildings on Market Street are furnished as museums today, though there are tourist homes, a few shops, and public buildings. It's a refreshing summer contrast to the throngs on Main Streets.

The ticket for the fort also admits you to several historic or reconstructed Market Street buildings, open from June 15 through Labor Day from 11-5. The **McGulpin House** is a French-Canadian log house from the 1780s. At the **Beaumont Memorial**, dioramas show the startling investigations of Dr. William Beaumont, the first doctor to observe how the stomach functions, thanks to a gunshot wound of Alexis St. Martin that left a hole that never healed. Spinning and baking are demonstrated at the 1780 **Edward Biddle House**. Behind it, a blacksmith is at work at the **Benjamin Blacksmith Shop**. Many demonstrators at the Mackinac State Historic Parks have made lifetime avocations of these summer jobs and are extremely knowledgeable about their subjects. Don't miss the **Robert Stuart House**, the local museum of the city of Mackinac Island. It's full of photos and memorabilia, with a knowledgeable staff of local people who love to talk about island life.

◆ **Huron Street and East Bluff.** One of Mackinac's most delightful walks goes past Marquette Park, at the fort's foot, where Main turns into Huron Street and goes to Mission Point. Prim, simple pre-Victorian houses are mixed with later summer places, often used to house the island's legions of summer workers. The yards and gardens are beautiful. **St. Anne's Catholic Church**, the island's biggest and most active church, has a delightful public garden and little basement museum with lots of island photos and some St. Anne's artifacts going back to when the parish was at Michilimackinac. A marker commemorates Magdelaine De La Framboise, a prominent and generous Michigan French-Indian fur trader whose legacy helped build the church.

Cut through St. Anne's garden path to get back to McGulpin Street and visit **The Mackinac Island Butterfly House**, in a greenhouse that still supplies many of the island's bedding plants and geraniums. Visitors pass through antechambers with two curtains to enter the large greenhouse, a magical place where butterflies fly freely around, pausing to munch on fennel, cabbage, and other favorite plants. If you sit still awhile, they'll land on you! Proprietor Doug Beardsley views the butterfly house as a livelihood and a mission that capitalize on the butterfly's natural charm to get an ecological message across. "The butterfly is a spokesman for the insect world," he maintains. "People may wonder why there aren't as many as there used to be. Today you can buy enough chemicals at the hardware store to kill the whole town's insects. If you interrupt the food chain by eliminating the insect biomass, you've got trouble. We have to get away from the mindset that everything ought to be perfect, without insects on it." There's also a terrific **butterfly gift shop.** *Open daily from Mem. Day thru Sept., about 9 to 8; butterflies are more active when it's warmer, from 9:30 or 10 to 7 or so. Admission is $3 for adults, $2 for children. (906) 847-3972.*

Come back out onto Huron Street and continue east at least to stop inside at **Mission Church**, a New England colonial church with a pretty octagonal belfry. It was built by the United Foreign Missionary Society in 1829-30 as part of the mission established in 1822 to "civilize and educate" Indians who came to the island to trade, and to uplift the soldiers at the fort and the local people. A few blocks farther (skip this if you're tiring) is the **Mission Point Resort** (906-847-3312), a sprawling family-oriented resort that enjoys a fine view of the shipping lanes. Contemporary buildings of natural materials, erected by Moral

If you take a seat at The Mackinac Island Butterfly House, like proprietor Doug Beardsley here, chances are a butterfly will light on you, too.

Rearmament, a murkily patriotic crusade, in the 1950s and 1960s, have been improved by the resort. The library and public areas are fine for relaxing, and the restaurant has a good view of freighter traffic.

Return by taking the back streets (Mission or Truscott) to Mission Hill at the top of Truscott, so you can get a closer look at the massive late 19th-century "cottages" on East Bluff and enjoy the view looking down at the Huron Street buildings you've just passed. Go west and take the second stairway down to go past the tourist homes on Bogan Lane, which leads you to Huron Street again. Or continue walking along the bluff to the fort and governor's summer house (see page 640) and return on Fort Street.

◆ **Grand Hotel**. This is a living American vestige of the late-19th-century European tradition of elegant summer resorts. When a consortium of railroads and steamship companies finished the hotel in 1887, it became the world's largest summer hotel and the world's largest pine building, with the world's largest porch — 660 feet. It still holds those records today.

The formalities of a bygone era live on here. The hotel still requires dresses or skirts for women and jackets and ties for men at and after dinner. The $5 fee charged non-guests to visit the hotel and grounds is a reasonable cost for spending the better part of a day here, exploring the lovely Victorian gardens, enjoying the lobby and porch with their splendid views of the Straits, and having lunch in the varied restaurants and bars (all top-notch). A swim in the pretty but small pool is $8 extra. But the overpriced ground-floor shops, gussied up with Anglophile status symbols and self-important Grand Hotel souvenirs, with little pertaining to the rest of the island, can leave a bad taste in your mouth. Enter upstairs at the central entrance for a better first impression of the hotel and its busy, courteous desk staff.

Small rooms start at around $120 per person, double occupancy, modified American plan, including breakfast and dinner; an extra 18% gratuity is added. To get the most out of a Grand Hotel stay, guests should take advantage of all the **special facilities** and **daily events** that were part of resort life in the grand tradition. There's the big breakfast and five-course dinner, the **parlor and porch** (popular for late-afternoon and evening cocktails and just sitting), golf at the recently expanded **18-hole public course** (the first nine has wonderful views and some challenging holes; the second nine, reached by a carriage ride, is in the woods), **tennis**, swimming in a beautifully landscaped **pool**, a 4 o'clock **tea concert** with champagne, sandwiches, and pastries, **dancing** at dinner, and nightly entertainment in the intimate **Audubon Bar**, the vintage Art Deco **Terrace Room** (dancing with a seven-piece swing orchestra), and the **Cupola Bar** (dancing to a jazz trio in a rooftop room with a dazzling view).

Grand Hotel has long had a mystique as a summer locus of fashion, power, and political activity. Hotel history, chiefly photos of famous guests and important conferences, is displayed in a two-room **museum** on the lower level. (Having the **Governor's summer mansion** on Mackinac Island adds to the power mystique. The 1902 summer house, reached by heading up Fort Street around the bend from the fort, is open for public tours on Wednesday mornings from 9:30 to 11:30 a.m.)

The updated decor of Grand Hotel was created by famed decorator Carleton Varney, who drew on his own memories of seaside summers in Massachusetts to emphasize the mood of a Victorian summer resort. He uses motifs like the hotel's signature red geranium, repeated boldly on black carpets; trellis wallpapers; and vibrant summer colors for guest rooms: daffodil yellow, sky blue, deep green, and geranium pink. The effect of all this clever decorating is cheerful — the interiors feel warm and lively even on rainy days.

◆ **Bicycle tour around the island.** Rent either single or tandem bikes for this delightful, easy eight-mile trip.

The Governor's summer home: one of the many large and interesting "cottages" built on the east and west bluffs overlooking the island village was this post-1900 variant on the Shingle Style. The state of Michigan bought it for $15,000 in 1945 to use as the governor's summer residence. Visitors can tour it Wednesday mornings.

Roughly half way around the island on the western shore is **British Landing**, the place where Indians and British soldiers landed in 1812 in their successful surprise attack on Fort Mackinac. You can get a bite to eat at the well-equipped snack shop here. There are also **restrooms**, a **picnic area**, and **nature center** staffed in summer by a naturalist who's happy to answer questions. A half-mile **nature trail** with many interesting explanatory markers and nature displays goes through forests and up a bluff formed when lake levels were much higher. The bluff here has a good view of the Mackinac Bridge. The trail then goes on to the beautiful Croghan Water wetland area.

British Landing is where, during the winter, an ice bridge forms to St. Ignace, allowing year-round residents to snowmobile off the island. *For bike rental information, see page 646.*

◆ **Bicycle tour into the island's interior.** Island-lovers agree that to really get to know the island, you need to explore its natural areas and appreciate their beauty. The interior has some steep bluffs, and bicycling may be a challenge. Don't be embarrassed to push your rental bike up some hills.

Here's a short but challenging tour to the island's highest point, not too far from town. Start behind the fort where several trails come together. Take the South Bicycle Trail, not the road, to the dramatic limestone **Arch Rock**. (That way you'll avoid the carriage tours). From there, take Rifle Range Road inland, turn right onto Garrison Road, and you'll come to **Skull Cave**. The island's caves were formed when water from higher lake levels thousands of years ago eroded parts of the limestone. Continue on Garrison Road past the **cemeteries** (always interesting for amateur historians). Turn right onto Fort Holmes Road and you'll soon reach **Fort Holmes**, on the spot where the British, having landed unnoticed on the island's north end, surprised the American fort during a bloodless battle in the War of 1812. When the British got their cannon on this high point aimed at the big American fort below, the Americans didn't even consider defending it. They surrendered without a shot. The British built a small stockade and blockhouse here. The spectacular Straits view from the reconstructed stockade is worth the arduous trip.

Now go back to Garrison Road. When you reach it, you can go right and end up at British Landing (close to two miles north), or turn left and go back to town. Consult your free map for other options. Wherever you go, it's downhill!

◆ **Shopping.** *Mostly along Main, with some shops on Market.*
Mackinac shopping is improving. Many visitors' impressions of
the island are unfortunately dominated by the fudge and ice
cream shops and generally ordinary souvenir stores that line
Main Street. Sidewalks are crowded in season; service mostly
depends on untrained summer help. For generations, shopkeepers did well enough appealing to the captive market of passive
day-trippers who visit the fort and Grand Hotel, then browse in
the shops by the ferry docks. Time-honored souvenirs like rubber tomahawks and moccasins, humorous wood plaques and
souvenir teacups are fun and nostalgic but get tiring fast, as do
suncatchers and T-shirts.

The 1980s' boom in upscale island inns and mainland
motels has brought some new and tony shops, mostly big on
updated traditional clothing and accessories that run heavily in
the direction of traditional duck prints and decoys, dolls for collectors, Victorian-styled luxuries, and fancy soaps. But better
stores of this kind can be found elsewhere in northwest
Michigan, especially in Petoskey and Leland. The short season
and high rents necessarily tend to increase already high prices.
Consider limiting shopping time in favor of the taking advantage
of the island's unique scenery and hiking and bicycling
opportunities. Or save it for a rainy day.

Four shopping highlights are:

Maeve's Arts & Antiques. Contemporary American handcrafts
in a whimsical, folkish vein mix well with colorful handcrafted
artifacts from many cultures. New: ethnic musical instruments
and bells. Clothing includes Guatemalan Indian clothing and
hand-dyed batik from Indonesia. The outstanding jewelry selection is strong on handmade silver from Mexico, Bali, and India.
Pam Finkle's original paintings of island scenes take souvenir art
to a high level. Shop owner Maeve Croghan has spent many
summers on the island where her Irish ancestors lived and
worked. *Main Street near Astor, between the Arnold and Shepler
docks. (906) 847-3755.*

Island Scrimshander. The proprietor is one of three brothers
who are the only craftspeople to make a living at the ancient
whalers' craft of engraving ivory. Sometimes you can see him at
work. *Opposite Maeve's, on Main west of Astor. (906) 847-3792.*

Island Books. Personal, complete bookstore, with everything
from vacation reading and regional titles about Mackinac and

much of northern Michigan to books on computers, investments, and gardening. *Main between Astor and Hoban, closer to Astor, in the Lilac Tree Shops. (906) 847-6202. Open from May thru Oct. from 10 to 5 at least. Summer hours 10-10.*

Fort Mackinac Museum Shop. One of three very good museum shops of the Mackinac State Historic Parks. All go way beyond the usual gift shop in their efforts to illuminate chosen themes and historic periods with a choice selection of books and authentic historic-reproduction artifacts. Specialties here are pre-industrial cooking and crafts, along with military, Civil War, and Indian history and popular culture of the Victorian era, when the fort was still in operation. Excellent regional selections. Out-of-the-ordinary items include replicas of Indian trade silver pendants ($10-12), tin fifes and harmonicas with instructions, hooked rugs in colorful scenes ($170-$350), and tiny birch boxes with quill turtles ($10-$20). Many toys and gifts are $2 and under.

GETTING THERE. . . . . The many highway billboards show how competitive the **ferry** lines to Mackinac Island are. The three ferry companies have similar prices (adult round-trip $11.50, children 5 to 11 $6.50, bikes $4). All offer valet parking for $3 or less. But their schedules vary. If you anticipate a tight schedule or want to get on or off the island early or late, compare schedules before buying your ticket. (The schedules are at virtually every motel, restaurant, or visitor information center in the area.) Other variables are atmosphere and speed. A 14- to 18-minute trip from Mackinaw City is the rule. Local commuters often use all three ferries, depending on the circumstances. In all cases, be sure your luggage gets on the boat.

Arnold Transit (906-847-3351) is the biggest line, and its catamarans are newest and fastest. They make the trip from Mackinaw City (they depart from the southern of Arnold's two Mackinaw docks) in 14 minutes, from St. Ignace in 9. One veteran island commuter prefers the stable catamarans when winds and waves are high but avoids Arnold in peak summer season because of the crush of daytrippers. A lot of people who really enjoy leisurely boat rides prefer Arnold's slow boats that take 40 minutes from Mackinaw City's State dock and 30 from St. Ignace. Overnight parking is $1 a day, valet parking $3.

Shepler's (616-436-5023) is the second ferry in size, with a 16-minute ride from Mackinaw. Service is a passion for owner Bill Shepler, who also organizes service seminars for Mackinaw City businesses. Shepler's parking and loading systems are streamlined, and there's free overnight parking up to 5 days. Shepler's Car Care will fill up and wash your car while you're on the

island and even change the oil and do minor repairs.
Star Line (616-436-5044) is the newest and smallest ferry line, with a more
laid-back atmosphere and less of a crush. That can be refreshing in midsummer. Its boats are the ones with rooster-tails of water behind them. Valet
parking is cheaper, but overnight parking is from $2 (guarded, at the dock) to
$4 (indoors).

RENTING BIKES . . . . . If you plan on doing a fair amount of bicycling, it's
better to take your own bike and lock to the island. (Take off flags; they scare
the horses.) Take your own helmet, in any case. They can't be rented for san-
itary reasons. Bike rental businesses are at several points along Main Street
and at the Iroquois and Mission Point hotels. Standard rates are pretty much
the same ($4/hour for single-speed or three-speeds, $5-$5.50 for mountain
bikes, $5-6 for tandems), but the equipment can vary considerably. Calling
around can help you find what you want. **Ryba's** (906-847-6261) is the
biggest, with three locations. It also offers mountain bikes and 18-speed
bikes. **Orr-Kids** (906-847-3211) is on Main across from the Haunted Theater.
They offer Visa and Mastercard and have Burley carts for 1 or 2 kids (up to
90 lbs.), mountain bikes, and adult strollers. **Island Bicycle Livery** (906-
847-6288) is near the Shepler Dock on the lake side. It's is the only place to
offer all-day rates, which begin at $15, children's bikes, and baby seats.

HOW TO SAY IT. . . . . . "Mackinac" and "Mackinaw" are pronounced the
same way. The letter "c" is silent, so the last syllable is "naw." "Mackinac" is
the way the French spelled the Indian word, "Mackinaw" the way the English
spelled it. It's *never* right to say "MACK-i-NACK" when you're talking about
Mackinac Island.

INTELLIGENT SMALL-TOWN JOURNALISM SURVIVES. . . . . in the
Mackinac Island Town Crier and the *St. Ignace News*, the weekly newspapers of retired University of Michigan journalism professor Wes Maurer, Sr.,
now in his 90s, and his son, Wes Maurer, Jr. The Maurers and their staff
serve up an intelligent mix of local news and sports, weddings, events, and
national and international political news, told with perspective and flair.
Numerous nationally known journalists got their start interning for the
Maurers' papers. . . . . Pick up a copy to see what intelligent, aggressive
small-town reporting is like.

TO LEARN MORE ABOUT MACKINAC'S GRAND COTTAGES. . . . . . their
architecture (often Shingle Style, Stick Style, or Queen Anne), their owners
(who numbered many Midwestern movers and shakers), and cottage life, get
View from the Veranda, by State Historic Parks director Phil Porter at the
fort's bookshop or Island Bookstore on Main Street near the Lilac Hotel. The
historic photographs are wonderful.

Rogers City

A spectacular quarry, freshly caught whitefish, fabulous smoked pork loin, and miles of uncrowded beaches at this unpretentious Lake Huron port

This town of 4,000 is home to the largest limestone quarry in the world. Despite the abundance of beautiful Lake Huron beaches both in and around the city, few tourists come here compared to the northwestern coast of the Lower Peninsula. The conservative Polish, German, and Italian residents attend the thousand-member-plus Catholic and Lutheran churches in town. Some 300,000 acres of commercially harvested timberlands here in Presque Isle County create the biggest employment sector. German and Polish farmers raise huge quantities of beans. Eight per cent of the U.S. crop of kidney beans comes from this county. The cool, moist climate is also excellent for potatoes.

Over the years, so many Rogers City men have become sailors in Michigan Limestone's big fleet of carriers, based here, that Rogers City has styled itself as "The Nautical City" and called its downtown mall "Mariners Mall."

Highlights of Rogers City and vicinity include:

◆ **Michigan Limestone & Chemical Company quarry.** It can be viewed from two strategic locations (see map). The **viewing stand off Business 23** south of town reveals the vast expanse of the 5,000-acre quarry. Over the decades the company has dug down over 250 feet to mine the almost-pure limestone. View huge shovels scooping up blasted chunks of limestone and loading large dump trucks. From the **harbor view**, open daylight hours, you can better see the screen house, where the chunks are sorted by size, and the harbor, where up to two freighters at a time can be loaded. Some 400 freighter trips haul away the 10 million tons excavated annually. The limestone costs just $3.50 a ton wholesale, less than the cost of shipping. Call (517) 734-2117 to find out when freighters will be in port.

◆ **Lakeside Park/Rogers City Harbor.** A pleasant, long lakefront park has a nice, sandy beach and many amenities: playground, concession stand, picnic tables, basketball, a bandstand

❶ Seagull Pt. Nature Area. Picturesque setting on Lake Huron with nature trail and beach.

❷ Gauthier & Spaulding Fisheries. Buy cheap whitefish fresh from Lake Huron at one of the few remaining Great Lakes fisheries.

❸ Plath's Meats. Famous for smoked pork loin, made in the smokehouse back of the 78-year-old German shop.

❹ Historical Museum. Striking old bungalow where presidents of the quarry lived for over 5 decades. 1920s flappers' hats a highlight.

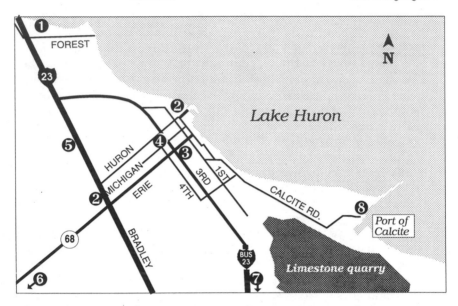

❺ Kortman's Restaurant. Terrific family eatery with good, modestly-priced homemade dishes and plain, down-home atmosphere.

❻ 12 miles to Ocqueoc Falls. Erosion has leveled these waters to a frisky rapids, but it's a pretty picnic site with a 7-mile hiking trail.

❼ Quarry view. 1 mile south. Dramatic bird's-eye view of 5,000-acre, 200-feet-deep limestone quarry, the world's largest. Bring binoculars.

❽ Harbor View. See big freighters load up with limestone at this 5,000-acre quarry. Big brick strcture sorts stones by size.

Highlights of
Rogers City

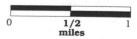

0   1/2   1
miles

where summer concerts are held. It overlooks the busy marina and fishing pier.

◆ **Gauthier & Spaulding Fisheries.** On the front of G&S's Bradley Highway/U.S. 23 retail outlet is a colorful painting of the boat used to catch the whitefish sold here. From April to the end of October, the 46-foot *Viking* pulls up a 1,500-foot trapnet from 90 feet of Lake Huron water. A good haul is a ton of fish. Either smoked or filleted, the fish are around $3 a pound.

Third-generation fisherman John Gauthier says northern Lake Huron has the cleanest water in the Great Lakes. On Lake Huron just west of the city harbor is the firm's dock and wholesale office. Around noon daily the *Viking* returns with its haul. Buy fish right off the boat for about $1 pound. Tucked behind their shack-like office loom the decaying remains of the *Catherine*, an old gillnet tug. Looking like a small submarine, these wooden fishing boats are totally enclosed with no deck, so the crew never has to be exposed to the often hazardous, frigid waters of the upper Great Lakes. *103 S. Bradley Hwy/U.S. 23 (retail outlet). 360 E. Huron Ave. (fishery). (517) 734-3474.*

◆ **Presque Isle County Historical Museum.** This handsome bungalow, built in 1914, was occupied until 1957 by Carl Bradley, first president of Michigan Limestone & Chemical, and his successors. Some rooms are now furnished with period furniture and accessories. Others have selected local artifacts. Don't miss the flamboyantly colorful 1920s flapper hats discovered decades later in the back of a local clothing shop. In the basement is a beautiful, authentic Indian birchbark canoe. *176 W. Michigan Ave. at Fourth St. Open June through Oct., 12-4 weekdays. (517) 734-4121. No admission charge; donations appreciated.*

◆ **Plath's Meats.** A modest-looking meat market on Rogers City's main street, Plath's is famous for the smoked pork loin prepared in the smokehouse behind the retail shop; it's also served at the Buoy Restaurant and Lounge in town. Third-generation Plaths use the same recipe for preparing the smoked pork that Emil Plath brought over from Germany in 1913. *Open Mon thru Sat 9-5. 116 South Third. (517) 734-2232.*

◆ **Three beautiful beaches north of Rogers City along U.S. 23.** Gently sloping, sandy beaches and some low dunes mark much of the Lake Huron shore north of Rogers City, in contrast with the broken, fossil-rich limestone rubble that predominates to the south. Going north along U.S. 23 from Rogers City, at the edge of town you come to **Seagull Point Park**, an uncrowded beach backed by low dunes with an interesting variety of tough little shrubs. A two-mile **interpretive trail** close to the lake explains the area's natural history. Soft sand here can make walking slow going. Across the road, the **Herman Volger Nature Preserve** is a quiet, vehicle-free foot travel area along the impounded Trout River. There's **cross-country skiing** here in winter.

About three miles northwest of here, **P.H. Hoeft State Park** offers not only 144 shady, modern **campsites**, a picnic area, playground, and CCC-era shelter, but a mile-long **beach**, again backed by low dunes. One **trail loop** (1.2 miles) passes behind the dunes and then goes along a creek in a .75 mile loop, revealing quite a variety of wildflowers. Another trail loop (1.5 miles) crosses U.S. 23 and goes into a forest. Both are groomed for **cross-country skiing** in winter. *On U.S. 23, 5 miles northwest of Rogers City. (517) 734-2543. Campsites are $8/night; reservations advised in July and August. State park sticker required. $4/day, $18/year.*

Two miles north of Hoeft State Park, the **Presque Isle County Lighthouse Park** is a delightful picnic spot, with tables and grills in the birches and pines overlooking the sandy beach. The Forty Mile Point Lighthouse and tower, though not open to the public, are a nice focal point for the park. *Look for the brown park sign between Hoeft State Park and Manitou Beach Road.*

THE POSEN POTATO FESTIVAL . . . . . Posen (population 260), a Polish farming village 15 miles southeast of Rogers City, enjoys a reputation for growing exceptionally tasty potatoes on its rocky limestone soil. On the first weekend after Labor Day each year, it hosts a delightful festival. Polka and country bands play continuously from noon to 1 a.m. Saturday and to 9 p.m. Sunday. As many as 25,000 watch a mile-long parade at 1:30 Sunday. But the big draw is the potato pancake smorgasbord beginning Sunday morning at 10:30. Signs lead visitors to local farmers who sell 100-pound bags of their potatoes for about $7.

'THE LARGEST WATERFALL IN THE LOWER PENINSULA" . . . . . is the title bestowed on **Ocqueoc Falls** — testament to how little competition for the honor there is. It looks more like a rapids than a waterfall, but despite its puny drop, it's a fine place for a picnic because of the picturesque site. A seven-mile **hiking and cross-country skiing trail** starts next to the falls. *On M-68 at Ocqueoc Falls Highway, 12 miles west of Rogers City.*

LIMESTONE IN NORTHEASTERN MICHIGAN . . . . . Cartographer David Brown tells the story in one of the information-packed city map notes in his fascinating, useful *Atlas of Northern Michigan Cities.* (See books by mail at the end of this book.) "For millions of years, ancient seas covered most of Michigan. In parts of these seas were many coral-forming organisms. By long accumulation and compression they formed large limestone deposits. One of these formations, called the Dundee, comes to the surface at Rogers City [and also Alpena and its namesake, Dundee, in extreme southeastern Michigan]. It took 300 million years for this 250-foot stratum to form."

Rogers City limestone that had been too crumbly to be a construction material was discovered, in tests in 1907, to be unusually pure, - a great asset as a key agent in making steel and many chemicals. The **Michigan Limestone and Chemical Company** which began operating in Rogers City in 1910, was bought by **Carl D. Bradley** and **U.S. Steel**, and eventually owned entirely by U.S. Steel. The Bradley Transportation Line it founded is a major Great Lakes carrier.

Presque Isle lighthouses

*Two of the Great Lakes' most unusual lighthouses
are tucked away on an unusually scenic stretch
of Lake Huron shore.*

Presque Isle — "almost an island" — is a beautiful, old, and almost completely undiscovered resort area way off the beaten track between Alpena and Rogers City. You could pass near it on U.S. 23 and never know it was there. It's wedged between Grand Lake (seven miles long) and the Lake Huron shore, which here consists of picturesque points and beaches of broken, fossil-rich limestone. A large limestone quarry at Stoneport inconspicuously occupies a third of the area.

Two delightful and distinctive lighthouse museums are Presque Isle's chief public attractions, along with the new, 84-sl. transient **marina** at Presque Isle Harbor, open May 15 through September 15 (517-595-3069). Both lighthouses are at the edge c cedar forests on the two-mile spit of land that forms the Presque Isle Harbor, one of Lake Huron's best natural harbors. The lights here were important parts of the federal government's early system of navigational aids in the Upper Great Lakes.

Two unusual natural areas add to the area's appeal for more

The Old Presque Isle Lighthouse and Museum overlooks the entrance to Presque Isle Harbor, shown here with winter's eerie lake ice formations.

adventurous explorers. The Besser-Bell Natural Area has trails around a ghost town, and a sandy beach. Thompson's Harbor State Park is an undeveloped state park with seven and a half miles of Lake Huron shore and an unusually large concentration of the threatened dwarf lake iris.

THE OLD PRESQUE ISLE LIGHTHOUSE AND MUSEUM goes all the way back to 1840. Its thick, squat stone tower served for 30 years before being replaced by the "new" and much taller Presque Isle Light farther out on the spit, which developed into a Lifesaving Station and later a Coast Guard Station. The Stebbins family of Lansing purchased the property in the early 1900s, fixed up the light tower and reconstructed the simple stone and stucco house as a vacation home and repository for their many antiques. For the past two decades they have opened it to the public.

There's a storybook mood about this place, beginning with the old front range light that has been moved to the road to mark the entrance. After going along a dirt road through a dark cedar forest, visitors park and emerge from the trees to the sunny, grassy keeper's cottage surrounded by a trim stone wall. A flagstone porch overlooks a rocky coast and the Presque Isle Harbor. Picturesque additions and improvements inside have made the place a reflection of its owners' tastes and collecting interests more than anything authentic, but it's completely charming in its own way. Slate floors, leaded glass, a big stone fireplace, and exposed timbers salvaged from Lansing's old post office give the place an almost medieval English look. Wood doors come from a shipwreck. A mounted Portuguese sawfish decorates a wall.

The Stebbinses collected a lot of interesting old stuff, but it was museum manager Lorraine Parris's inspiration to make the little museum hands-on. "You tell kids they can't do something and they do it anyway," she says. She got tired of watching out for all the antiques. "When I made it a hands-on museum, the artifacts more or less stayed." She shows visitors how to use the old brass sextant. She lets them play the pump organ, and ring the cowbell. She encourages questions and likes to tell local shipwreck stories. And she delights in describing the mystery of how the light in the tower can be seen from the walkway of the harbor lately, even when there's no bulb and no power to the light.

Scattered throughout the yard are various other antiques: fake stocks, an old cannon, anchors, and the ton-and-a-half bronze bell from the old Lansing City Hall, which visitors are

At the New Presque Isle Lighthouse, enterprising museum manager Dan McGee plays the part of lightkeeper for special occasions. He will demonstrate his collection of ship steam whistles for interested visitors.

welcome to ring. But the real highlight is a trip up the winding stone steps of the two-story tower. Visitors can walk out on the parapet surrounding the lantern room for a beautiful and thrilling view.

Off U.S. 23, 23 miles north of Alpena and 20 miles south of Rogers City. There should be signs to the lighthouses. From Rogers City, turn left onto Hwy. 638 before you reach Grand Lake and turn left again at the harbor. From Alpena, take the right Y at the Hideaway Inn onto Hwy. 405 and continue north past the harbor to lighthouse. (517) 595-2787. Open in early May thru Oct. 15. 7 days, 9 a.m.-5 p.m. Open to 6 p.m. between Mem. and Labor Day. $1.50/adult, 50¢ ages 6-12.

THE NEW PRESQUE ISLE LIGHTHOUSE AND MUSEUM sits amid a hundred-acre township park with **picnic tables, restrooms** and **nature trails** through the woods of pines and cedars. On the limy soil here and at the nearby state park, the endangered blue pitcher thistle and dwarf lake iris flourish.

This is another delightful spot, which another enterprising museum manager has developed into something original. Dan McGee, the son and grandson of Great Lakes sailors, was hired as a caretaker by the group who took over the abandoned light and Coast Guard station here. Now he convincingly plays the part of a turn of the century lightkeeper for group tours and special occasions. He has collected **steam whistles** from many different Great Lakes boats and assembled them under a gazebo. He'll demonstrate them for interested visitors.

The 100-foot lighthouse **tower** is the tallest on the Great Lakes. It's open to the public from noon until 5 during two special events: the Fourth of July picnic and barbecue and the Labor Day pig roast. Both events are held on Saturday of the holiday weekend. Restoring and stabilizing the lighthouse here has been a successful community project. The **museum shop** is unusually good. *The New Presque Isle Light is a mile beyond the Old Light (see above). (517) 595-2059. Open May 1 thru Oct 15, daily 9-6. Free; donations appreciated.*

GRAND LAKE . . . . . has four public fishing sites, three picnic areas, and abundant perch, bass, pike, walleye, and muskies. For an area **brochure**, write Presque Isle Area Commerce Committee, Box 74, Presque Isle, MI 49777, or request it at either lighthouse museum.

VIRGIN WHITE PINE, A SANDY BEACH, AND THE GHOST TOWN OF BELL. . . . . . are part of the **Besser-Bell Natural Area.** Trails go through a dark cedar forest, soon to emerge on Lake Huron's shore. It makes for a pleasant hour's walk and a nice afternoon at a remote beach. A house is used as a clubhouse for local functions. It's best reached from U.S. 23 south of Grand Lake. Turn east at the Hideaway Inn onto Grand Lake Rd. At the Township Hall, turn right (you're still on Hwy. 405) and look for the signs in about a mile. Park at the main parking area.

WET MEADOWS, INLAND DUNES, AND ROCKY BEACHES. . . . . . make undeveloped **Thompson's Harbor State Park** a naturalist's delight. Its four miles of hiking trails are marked, although a compass might be well-advised, and the hiking is not strenuous. The trailhead is one mile inside the park entrance, which is twelve miles southeast of Rogers City or five miles from the junction of U.S. 23 and M-65. The park, which awaits future development, is the last legacy of Genevieve Gillette, ardent parks promoter and landscape architect. The state bought it with money she left to the people of Michigan. Thompson's Harbor is administered by managers at P. H. Hoeft State Park in Rogers City. (517) 734-2543.

The Alpena area and the Jesse Besser Museum

*An old lumber and cement town
with unusual architecture, a fine museum,
excellent diving, and a Lake Huron shoreline
of great natural beauty.*

For enjoying the natural beauty of the Great Lakes with nary a trace of trendy gentrification, there's no place else in the Lower Peninsula that comes close to the Alpena area, overlooking Lake Huron's Thunder Bay. Two undeveloped state parks nearby (Negwegon to the south and Thompson's Harbor to the north) have 14 miles of completely undeveloped Lake Huron shoreline between them.

Alpena is not easy to get to. It's 74 miles from the nearest interstate, and 104 miles up the two-lane U.S. 23 from Standish on Saginaw Bay. The atmosphere, like that of most old lumber towns, is definitely unpretentious, working-class, and friendly, with lots of corner bars in the Polish north end along U.S. 23. There is a surprisingly lively cultural scene, thanks to spirited local arts advocates.

After the turn of the century, lumbering was in decline in this region when a group of lumbermen realized that Alpena had all the necessary ingredients for making portland cement: pure limestone, marl, shale, and clay. They formed the first portland cement plant. A local competitor eventually became the largest cement plant in the world. Herman Besser and his son, Jesse, invented and manufactured an enormously successful machine for making concrete blocks. The Besser Company remains the world's leading producer of such machinery.

Jesse Besser became an active area philanthropist; his gifts of buildings and land always stipulated that buildings on the site be erected of concrete. As a result, many 20th-century public buildings and houses are made of concrete, often with unusual finishes. The 1930s concrete courthouse at First and Water, for instance, was sand-blasted and treated with "Resto-crete" for an enriched color. Herman Besser's bungalow home at 403 South

Second was the first to use Bes-Stone Split Block that resembled long, narrow blocks of rough-faced limestone.

Buoyed by the big cement industry, paper mills, and also by Wurtsmith Air Force Base 35 miles south in Oscoda, the local economy perked along into the 1970s without having to develop the tourism that most of northern Michigan had to rely on much earlier. But Wurtsmith closed in 1992, and the big cement plant, under its new owners, La Farge, today employs a fifth of what it once did. Visitors can get a terrific value in the Alpena area and feel like they're making a valuable contribution to local economic development.

Major attractions of the Alpena area include:

◆ **Bay View Park and the Thunder Bay Marina,** downtown just south of the Thunder Bay River. Both have been handsomely redone. The marina (800-332-9204) has 77 transient slips, a boat launch, charter boat service, a fish-cleaning station, and restrooms and showers. Just south of it is Bay View Park with tennis courts, a bandshell (**summer concerts** are Tuesdays at 7 and Thursdays at 8 in July and August), a playground, and a swimming beach.

◆ **Historic homes on State Avenue/U.S. 23,** the main entry into town from the south. Built along the shore are impressive and often unusually elaborate homes of lumbermen, bankers, lawyers, and other business leaders who promoted Alpena and profited from its prosperous decades around the turn of the century. Fans of historic architecture will enjoy walking down State from Bay View Park to Richardson Street, then heading inland a block and returning along First. Cement block king Jesse Besser's own Moderne house, a 1939 testament to the durability and versatility of concrete block, is at 232 South First. Today it's the Besser House bed and breakfast. Three more lakefront parks are to the south, in the older part of town.

◆ **Old Town,** north of the river across the Second Avenue bridge, has many handsome old commercial buildings. Entrepreneurs John and Connie Van Schoik have invested in renovating some and developing the noteworthy **John A. Lau Saloon** and restaurant at 414 North Second and the **Display Case** (517-356-2758), a gift/gourmet/import store at 428 North Second, next to the unusual floral creations of **Lasting Expressions** (517-356-9372). You can watch candles being made at **Sonlight Candles**, at 309 North Second. Another popular visitor stop is **Jeannie's Sweet**

Shop, an ice cream parlor with homemade chocolates. It's downtown – south across the Second Street bridge and up half a block at 109 West Chisholm. (517) 356-6541.

The Thunder Bay Theatre at 400 N. Second (517-354-2267) is northern Michigan's only year-round professional theater company. It also hosts many shows and performances. The three-screen **Royal Knight Cinema** is at Second and Chisholm (517-356-3333). Under renovation is the **State Theater**, with two screens, 204 North Second Avenue at Park Place (517-354-3500).

◆ **Jesse Besser Museum and Planetarium.** One of Michigan's most impressive museums, Besser combines historical, scientific, and art exhibits on two levels. A striking three-story-high Foucault pendulum greets entering visitors, vividly showing the effect of the Earth's rotation.

The museum's highlight is its spectacular collection of artifacts from **Great Lakes Indians**, particularly in the historic era. It's one of the finest in the country. A local state highway employee and his son, now a museum curator, gathered the 20,000-item Haltiner Collection. Their most remarkable discoveries were found right across the street: copper artifacts dating back 7,000 years, made by a still-mysterious people known only as the "copper culture."

Local history highlights include a recreated avenue of Alpena shops from the 1890s, a popular diorama with mounted indigenous birds and animals, and a room devoted to Jesse Besser and his roles in concrete technology and Alpena-area philanthropy.

Changing exhibits, 25 a year, showcase widely varied subjects. Call for information on related **lectures.** Some examples: contemporary Great Lakes Native American artists (Aug/Sept 1994); maps of the Great Lakes, drawn from the museum's own outstanding collection (Sept/Oct 1994), Christmas shows of dolls and quilts; and a commemoration of the end of World War II, highlighting area contributions to the war effort. Many exhibits showcase emerging Michigan artists.

The **Sky Theater Planetarium** (75¢ additional admission) has shows at 1 and 3 p.m. Sundays and in July and August Thursdays at 7:30. *On the north edge of Alpena, 1 block east of U.S. 23 North, at 491 Johnson. East of Holiday Inn, next to the Alpena Community College campus. (517) 356-2202. Open Mon-Fri 10-5, Thurs to 9, Sat & Sun noon-5. $2/adult, $1 students & seniors, maximum $5/family.*

◆ **Sportsmen's Island** is in a bay of the Thunder Bay River, right in town by the Holiday Inn across from the Besser Museum and the Chamber of Commerce. It's a handy place to fish from platforms, bird-watch, and see wildlife from a canoe or along a one-mile perimeter **nature trail**. *Parking is on roadside park at U.S. 23 and Long Rapids/Johnson.* The **Washington Street Park** off M-32 just west of downtown offers another good view of the river, with lots of geese who greet people, hoping to be fed.

◆ **Presque Isle Lighthouses.** See page 652.

◆ **Squaw Bay.** U.S. 23 goes right through a big marsh south of town. You can pull over and get out to watch some beautiful water birds.

◆ **Dinosaur Gardens.** This roadside attraction is no kitschy tourist trap but a moody, eerie place, a sensitively executed folk art installation that was the life work of self-taught artist and sculptor Paul Domke. Through a dark, primordial, ferny cedar swamp wind built-up trails. A plashing creek bisects the forty acres. Every so often a huge, life-size dinosaur is seen around a bend. The creatures are realistically fashioned of concrete, Alpena's favorite building material, here mixed with gravel and deer hair and applied on substructures of metal and lathe.

Domke had a fine feel for creating a complete environment, taking best advantage of the natural setting that evokes the imagined mood of dinosaur time, a part of creation deeply bound up with his own religious beliefs. Occasionally he combined images of dinosaurs and Christ — "as a testimonial to his belief that Christ was the master planner of an Earth that included dinosaurs," according to an explanatory sign. The Gardens' effect is greatest toward dusk. *Dinosaur Gardens are north of the center of Ossineke on U.S. 23, 10 miles south of Alpena. (517) 471-5477. Open May 15 thru Oct 15, 10-6 daily (9-6 during peak season). $3/adult, $2/children 6-12, $1/children under 6. Funds go to maintaining the concrete sculptures.*

◆ **Negwegon State Park.** This undeveloped gem of a state park is, so far, the delightful secret of local people and a limited number of outdoors lovers who eschew the crowds and conveniences of developed parks. "Many believe the most beautiful and possibly the most isolated beaches on Lake Huron lie [here]," writes Jim Du Fresne in his comprehensive and useful guide, *Michigan State Parks.* "Words like 'paradise' are often used . . . to describe the park's shoreline, a string of bays and coves stretching 6.5

miles." Rocky points separate the coves; the interior is pine, cedar, and white birch. Ten miles of **trails** in three loops go along the shoreline and through the interior. They start at the parking lot. There are pit toilets. No camping. *Park is off U.S. 23 (but not signed), 12 miles north of Harrisville and 18 miles or so south of Alpena. From U.S. 23, turn east onto Black River Road. In 1.5 miles you'll see a cemetery on the left. Just past it, turn north (left) onto Sand Hill Trail.* **Warning:** *this sandy, unimproved road can be difficult in very dry or very wet weather. In about 2 1/2 miles, watch at your right for a good gravel road with park entrance signs. Go east 1 1/4 miles to parking lot. No fee.*

GOOD INFORMATION SOURCES FOR THE ALPENA AREA . . . . . The **Alpena Chamber of Commerce** (1-800-582-1906) is on U.S. 23 North at Johnson St., just south of the Holiday Inn, in the Alpena Civic Center Building. Ask here for info on **cross-country skiing** in nearby state forests. **24-hour visitor information centers** are at principal entries to town: on U.S. 23 South at Dawn Donuts; on U.S. 23 North at Kurvan's Restaurant and Mini-Mart; and on M-32 West at the Bagley Marathon Station. Call for a helpful visitor's packet. The Northern Radio Network puts out the handy **Sunrise Side Vacation Guide** of some 50 pages, widely available at chambers of commerce and participating businesses in Lake Huron communities.

A POPULAR PLACE FOR DIVERS . . . . . because of its clear waters and interesting underwater limestone formations, the **Thunder Bay Underwater Preserve** contains 80 shipwrecks in a protected area of 288 square miles just off Alpena. Fourteen of these are moored shipwrecks that can be explored by charter wreck-diving service. The unusually dense concentration of shipwrecks is due to the number of hazardous shoals and rocky islands here. Also, at this point in Lake Huron, upbound ships must turn to the northwest. "If captains overestimated their ships's capabilities during northwestern gales, they sometimes found themselves in trouble," writes Steve Harrington in his useful *Divers Guide to Michigan.* In 1981 the state made the area a preserve, prohibiting divers from taking artifacts from wrecks.

Right on the Thunder Bay River is **Thunder Bay Divers**, offering charter wreck-diving service at a cost of around $60 per day, per diver (call them at 517-356-9336 to verify price). Located at 160 East Fletcher in Alpena, they have rental equipment, dive store facilities, and an air station. Group boat tours are available if arranged in advance. July and August are the best months for diving. A favorite dive is the 550-foot German freighter Nordmeer in 40 feet of water, which sank in 1966 with a load of coiled steel bound for Chicago. Divers can swim through the cargo hold of the upright wreck.

Hartwick Pines State Park & Michigan Forest Visitor Center

See a rare, majestic stand of 200-year-old pines,
a remnant of the awesome forests
that once covered a third of the state.

Before the rush of settlers to Michigan in the 1830s, over 13 million of the state's 38 million acres were covered with white pine. Thriving in poor, sandy soil, these majestic trees grow up to 200 feet tall and could live 500 years. They were prized because the tall, straight trunks make excellent building lumber and are light enough to float down rivers to lumber mills.

It took the white man half a century to transform these forests into the lumber that built towns from Michigan to the treeless Great Plains and rebuilt Chicago after the fire of 1871. By the 1920s the once-huge forests were cutover wastelands. One of the very few virgin white pine forests remaining is the 49-acre stand at this state park. Actually it's a mix of white pine, red pine, and eastern hemlock. Taking advantage of the park's handy location on the main highway for vacationers heading up north, Hartwick Pines has long been a place where visitors can learn about lumbering days, more with an emphasis on camp

The majestic white pine, Michigan's state tree, provided much of the capital invested in the automotive industry and other important early-20th-century businesses.

life and wood-harvesting technologies than on the environmental and social consequences of the dramatic changes brought by the destruction of the north woods. Now the popular state park has been revamped and reconfigured, with a single entrance, new campground, big new **visitor center** building and 100-seat **auditorium** open for the 1994 season.

Introducing the whole range of indoor and outdoor destinations is a 15-minute, nine-projector audiovisual show, "**Logging in Michigan: 1860-1900**," shown throughout the day. The **exhibit hall** deals with Michigan forests and forest management. A cutaway view of an artifical tree shows how its vascular system works. Hands-on computer games present the choices of various forest management scenarios in game form. The **museum shop** features books and educational materials on logging, Michigan flora and fauna, and state parks.

If at all possible, visitors should plan to take advantage of the remarkable **guided tour** offered by veteran interpreter Wendell Hoover and his new colleague, Ann Stevens. Hoover has spent his career immersed in the logging lore and lingo he learned from his grandfather and other former woodsmen or shanty boys. (Never were they called lumberjacks.) The tour takes up to two hours to visit the Big Pines. It tells about the ecology of the north woods and the kinds of trees it was made of. But it really comes alive in conveying life in the logging camps where a highly organized 75-man crew cleared an acre of forest a day. Hoover plays different roles. As the walking boss, he snaps to his crew, "I don't care about you, but protect those horses. Know what they're worth? Five hundred to eight hundred dollars!" You'll learn synonyms for lice – "seam squirrels" or "crotch crickets" – and tips like "Sleep with your boots on. That keeps 'em soft." Free tours are offered, usually from mid-June through Labor Day. Call (517) 348-2537 after Mondays at 11 a.m. for that week's schedule. Off-season, "special request" tours can be arranged for groups of any size. $25 minimum, $50 maximum.

New, handicap-accessible blacktop trails lead from the visitor center to the Big Pines, home of the dying Monarch and two white pines that are even taller. The **Logging Camp**, with its life-size, compellingly realistic recreations of a mess hall, kitchen, bunkhouse, and office, remains through 1994. After that, the fate of the old buildings, constructed by the CCC in the 1930s, is uncertain. A **big wheel**, used to haul logs over rough ground, can be seen in the woods; a team of horses and a driver with a log-driver's excellent sense of balance put the big wheel to use on Black Iron Days on the last weekend in August. Everything but the logging camp interiors and the inside of the log **Chapel in the Pines** is easily handicap-accessible.

The logging camp area, blacksmith shop, and the outdoor **steam sawmill** come to life four weekends a year. Centered around various handcrafts demonstrations and old-time string music, these events have developed into friendly social gatherings of kindred spirits who camp and share stories in the evening and look forward eagerly to next year's event. Crafts demonstrators are apt to be experienced professionals; their works are for sale at wholesale prices. Call (517) 348-2537 to confirm dates. The two-day events, held from 10 a.m. to 4 p.m., include **Sawdust Days** (4th weekend in June, a new event focused on spinning, weaving, and dyeing); **Wood Shaving Days** (3rd weekend in July, features woodcarving); **Black Iron Days** (4th weekend of August; blacksmithing); and **Old-Time Days** (3 days around the 4th weekend of September, with a little of everything).

These virgin pines were saved by the national panic of 1893, which so depressed demand for lumber that the logging outfit cutting it suspended operations. When the economy improved, it wasn't worth the trouble to set up a new camp for so little acreage. In 1927 Karen Hartwick purchased 8,236 acres from the Salling Hanson Lumber Company and donated it to the state for a state park.

The imposing parcel at Hartwick Pines is preserved as an authentic white pine forest looking very much like a typical stand half a millennium ago. It's a big enough area to give the visitor a sense what awesome forests covered the state. The white pines are so tall that their wide, dark trunks dominate a walker's view. You have to crane your neck to look high up and see where the trees' branches begin eight or nine stories in the air.

A one-mile **Virgin Pines Foot Trail** takes visitors on a loop through the woods to a reconstructed **19th-century logging camp** with bunkhouse, sawmill, and dining room. At the parking lot, an **interpretive center** illuminates Michigan's logging history and tells about Michigan forests. This park is an excellent place to learn about Michigan's forests and colorful, important logging era. (The Muskegon County Museum, page 515, and the fabulous Hackley House lumber baron's mansion in Muskegon, page 507, are other must-see destinations for anyone interested in lumber history.)

The Big Pines and interesting interpretive displays are such a heavily used draw that they overshadow the rest of the park, which itself is exceptional. At 9,672 acres, Hartwick Pines State Park is the largest state park in the Lower Peninsula and the best place where an extensive and typical stretch of prime north woods habitats— forest, three stocked fishing lakes, and streams —is coupled with the conveniences of a modern state park campground (showers, electricity, and full trailer hookups).

A good look at the park's less obvious charms is provided by the **Au Sable River Trail**, an easy three-mile loop that begins on the south side of M-93, opposite the main vehicle entrance. It crosses the East Branch of that legendary river twice. Famous for trout fishing, the Au Sable was originally full of grayling until they were fished to extinction in the late 19th century. Stocked trout thrived so well that fishing parties earlier this century would often catch over 500 fish an outing. Today the North Branch and main stream of that famous stream are so heavily canoed that only the shallow and uncanoeable East Branch and the upper reaches of the North Branch retain the mystique of yesteryear. About three miles of the East Branch passes through the park. "Here the river is a crystal-clear stream that gurgles over gravel banks and undercuts the banks around deadheads and trees," says veteran outdoorsman Jim Du Fresne in his highly recommended *Michigan State Parks: A Complete Recreation Guide for Campers, Boaters, Anglers, Hikers & Skiers.* It's an excellent but overlooked stream for rainbow and brook trout, he says, fished with flies and short, six- to seven-foot rods, or with worms or spinners.

The Au Sable River Trail also passes a rare forest of virgin hemlock trees 80 to 90 feet tall, saved from the saw by a sudden drop in the price of its bark, which was used for tanning leather. An optional, steep **scenic overlook** at the northwest extreme of the walk gives a panoramic view of the area.

Another hiking loop, the easy two-mile **Mertz Grade Nature Trail**, passes through a variety of forests, on part of an old logging railroad grade. It links up with the Big Pines trails behind the visitor center.

For motorists, a good way to see the rest of the park is along the eight-mile **Scenic Drive**, entered from M-93 some two miles north of the main park entrance. Here interpretive signs and turnouts encourage visitors to get out of their cars and take in the natural world. The drive crosses the Au Sable River and

Prime habitat for the rare little blue-gray Kirtland's warbler is in young
jack pine forests in and near Hartwick Pines State Park in Crawford and
Oscoda counties. Breeding grounds are off-limits except for free guided
tours led by Forest Service naturalists from mid-May through July 4.

passes an area with some individual white pine that are now
over 200 years old but were considered too small by early loggers. A stand of virgin jack pine – an unusual group of elderly
members of that short-lived species – is along the Scenic Drive.
Cross-country skiers are finding Hartwick Pines State Park a
superior destination. On the north side of M-93, some 17 miles
of intermediate loops are groomed. (These are open to **mountain
bikes** in summer.) Narrow bridges make it impossible to groom
the Au Sable Trail and Mertz Grade Trail, but skiers use them,
too. **Ski maps** are available at the main entrance contact station,
open year-round.

The new, 100-site **campground** combines all the modern
amenities (blacktop sites, showers, flush toilets, electricity;
$12/night) with unusually large and private sites. Most are
shady. Full sewer and water hookup is available at 36 sites
($16/night). Water is on from May through October.
Reservations advised for summer and holiday weekends.

Two especially nice times to visit Hartwick Pines are mid-May
into mid-June when the variety of **wild flowers** in bloom is great-

est, and at the end of September, when **fall color** is usually at its peak. There's a good mix of colorful hardwoods through most of the state park: maple, beech, oak, aspen, and birch, which makes for a full range of reds and yellows, especially near the river. In the winter there is almost always snow on the ground, and a visit then shows what it was like during the logging season.

Hartwick Pines State Park is off I-75 at Exit 259, a little north of Grayling. Go north on M-93 three miles to park entrance. Or take M-93 7 1/2 miles north of Grayling. The park and campground are open year-round. (517) 348-7068. The **Michigan Forest Visitor Center** *is likely to be open year-round, too. Hours from mid-June thru Labor Day are from 8 or 9 a.m. to 7 or 8 p.m. Call (517) 348-2537 to confirm hours or arrange tours. State park sticker required: $4/day or $18 year.*

CANOE THE MANISTEE . . . . . to avoid the crowds on the popular Au Sable and have an equivalent canoeing experience. Both rivers pass through Grayling and are well served by area liveries. Call the **Grayling Area Visitors' Council** at (800) 937-8837 for a Grayling area information packet.

FOR OTHER, LESS DEVELOPED CAMPGROUNDS NEAR GRAYLING . . . . . ask for maps and information from these state and national forest offices:
♦ **Au Sable State Forest**, Route 1, Box 146, Mio, MI 48647. (517) 826-3211. 10 campgrounds with 260 campsites in Crawford County.
♦ **Huron National Forest, Mio Ranger District**, 401 S. Court St., Mio, MI 48647. (517) 826-3252. Two campgrounds with 36 campsites between Grayling and Mio. Request the large and elaborate map/guide of all facilities and trails (hiking, snowmobiling, horseback riding, cross-country skiing, and more) in the Huron National Forest and adjacent state forests between Grayling and Oscoda. It's a goldmine for outdoorsmen. Campgrounds are on the Manistee and Au Sable Rivers and on many nearby lakes.

FREE GUIDED TOURS TO SEE THE RARE KIRTLAND'S WARBLER . . . . . attract birders from all over the world to Grayling and tiny Mio, 30 miles east on M-72. The particular preferences of the little blue-gray bird with the yellow breast and male's beautiful song have made it an endangered species. The Kirtland's warbler will nest only in Jack Pines, between five and 15 feet tall, or roughly between eight and 20 years old. Each breeding pair requires at least 30 acres. Jack pines cones release their seeds only when burned. Modern fire control has allowed the Jack Pine to mature where it was once periodically burned and renewed through forest fires. No new habitats for

Kirtland's warblers are naturally created.

A section of northeast Michigan centered at Mio is the only place in the world where Kirtland's warblers breed today. Since 1975, 23 areas of public land have been managed to encourage Kirtland's warblers. A 1993 census identified 486 singing males (assumed to be half of a mating pair) – a big gain from the low of 167 in 1987, but hardly enough to put the little bird off the endangered list.

Kirtland's warbler breeding grounds are off-limits except for these free guided tours, led by U.S. Forest Service naturalists between May 15 and July 4. **From Grayling** at the Holiday Inn on I-75 Business Loop South, they leave daily at 7 a.m. and 11 a.m. (517) 337-6650. **From Mio**, they leave Wednesday through Sunday at 7 a.m., with an extra 11 a.m. tour on weekends. Meet at the Forest Service office, 401 South Court at the corner of M-33, across from the Mio Motel. (517) 826-3252. Reservations only necessary for groups.

IN NEARBY GAYLORD . . . . a convenient stop is the quarter-century-old **Call of the Wild Museum.** Here you can see dozens of scenes of stuffed wild animals native to the area. Interesting descriptions by each exhibit tell such things as how Michigan's wild turkeys disappeared in 1888 and weren't restocked until the 1950s, or how the American elk was hunted almost to extinction. A large gift shop sells everything from saddles to clothing. *850 S. Wisconsin. Take exit 282 from I-75, east 1/4 mile. (517) 732-4336. June 15-Sept 2: daily 8:30 a.m.-9 p.m. 9:30-6 rest of year. Adults $4, children 5-13 $2.50.*

A FALL COLOR SPECTACULAR BETWEEN GAYLORD AND CHARLEVOIX . . . . . if you're willing to huff and puff, can be had from the overlook at **Avalanche Park**, overlooking **Boyne City** and the length of Lake Charlevoix. A series of staircases – 460 steps in all – goes up from the park entrance, on the last block in town, up to an overlook platform with benches. It's a fabulous view, because the curving hills surround the long lake and the town is laid out like a toy in neat rectangles down below. Once you're up, other trails lead back into the high country. . . . . .You can cheat and enjoy some of the view from a car from Pleasant Valley Road, which enters Boyne City from the south and turns into Pleasant Street. . . . . . In winter, Avalanche Park is a **winter sports park**, with downhill skiing, sledding, skating, and toboggans.

Chapter 8
Upper Peninsula

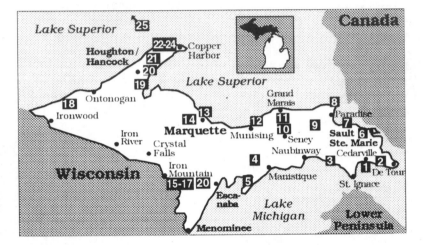

HIGHLIGHTS

For restaurants & lodgings. see *Hunts' Restaurants & Lodgings of Michigan*

Upper Peninsula

In many ways the U.P. is a world apart from the rest of Michigan. Separated by the Straits of Mackinac from the Lower Peninsula, it shares over a 200-mile border with Wisconsin. When Marquette residents take shopping trips, they don't go to the Lower Peninsula but to Green Bay, Wisconsin.

The winter up here is harsher than down below. Huge banks of snow aren't melted until summer has almost begun. The U.P. is so remote from the populous southern part of the state (Philadelphia is closer to Detroit than Ironwood) that a surprising number of Michiganians have never ventured north of the Mackinac Bridge.

The U.P. is big place — 300 miles across — with vast stretches of forest. Logging continues to be big business here, largely to supply pulp for papermills. Nothing has come along to even remotely approach the riches generated by the region's huge copper and iron mining industries in the 19th and early 20th century. Iron mining today is a pale shadow of bygone boom times. There's a generally depressed look to much of the U.P. Yet there's a fierce loyalty to the place, and surprising number of the descendants of the immigrants who came from Italy and Scandinavia, Cornwall and Croatia have stayed on. There's a shared sense of this being a place, not unlike Alaska, where one can live a freer, more independent life, away from the pressures of careers and status. Hunting and fishing are serious, lifelong pursuits for many. There's a great deal of pride in being a Yooper.

Les Cheneaux Islands

Off Hessel and Cedarville, a maze of channels between rocky limestone isles and peninsulas make a low-key, unhurried paradise for sailors, boaters, and fishermen.

Les Cheneaux Islands and the rocky peninsulas, wildflower meadows, and old resort area around them are an untrumpeted treasure of the Eastern Upper Peninsula. Within just 45 minutes of the Mackinac Bridge and Sault Ste. Marie, they make a fine base for a week of relaxation with some sightseeing as far away as Tahquamenon Falls and Whitefish Point.

Except for the second Saturday of August, when the Antique Wooden Boat Show at Hessel puts the area in the news, the area is *way* off the beaten tourist track. There's not a big golf resort or shopping district to be found — and that's the way the old-money families who have summered here for a hundred years want things to stay. Though increasing numbers of retirees and urban refugees are making their permanent homes here and the school population is increasing, about the only signs of recent development are a nice new supermarket and a two-story Comfort Inn in Cedarville.

Pronounced "Lay SHEN o" and known as "the snows," Les Cheneaux means "the channels" in French. Here rocky fingers of limestone, sand, and gravel stretch out southeast into Lake Huron's most northwestern waters and break up into a series of 36 islands along 12 miles of shore. Some islands are quite large, others big enough for just a few cottages. Tiny Dollar Island in the Snows Channel, is just a big enough perch for a single fantastic Arabian-inspired house that extends its verandas and docks out into the water and seems to float without terrestrial support.

The sheltered bays and channels make for ideal sailing and boating — protected from the Great Lakes' winds and waves. (Waves are typically ten feet higher out on the lake than within the Snows.) Constantly changing vistas created by the complex shorelines of many islands and inlets make for interesting boating even at very slow speeds — in a rented fishing boat with an

Les Cheneaux Islands Antique Wooden Boat Show on the second Saturday of August at Hessel celebrates the area's tradition of building, maintaining, and restoring wooden boats. Island cottagers depended on boats for transportation and fishing. That kept local boat shops busy long after commercial fishing declined. This 1906 photograph shows photographer Andrew Tanner, his wife, and son in their Mackinaw boat.

outboard motor, or even a canoe. (A fit paddler can canoe from Hessel to Cedarville in two hours.)

The area's idiosyncratic shoreline architecture adds interest to cruising. Along Les Cheneaux Club and Snows Channel are wonderful old boathouses, weathered gray or painted brown or dark green, elaborately rustic like the big summer houses they are connected with.

The Snows has been a favorite summer retreat since the late 19th century. Then, at the end of the logging era, older Middle Western cities were establishing themselves as industrial and commercial powerhouses and centers of great wealth. Wealthy Ohioans built their rambling summer houses, modestly referred to as "cottages," on 6 1/2 mile by 3 1/2 mile Marquette Island, off the onetime fishing port of Hessel, and 4-mile La Salle Island off Cedarville. Tucked away on wooded islands, these summer homes aren't as ostentatious as their counterparts on Mackinac

Island or Harbor Springs. Les Cheneaux has always enjoyed a very low-key charm.

Boats have always been, of necessity, the primary form of transportation here. Through the 1930s, summer people arrived by D&C steamer from Detroit or Cleveland. Into the early 1960s M-134 from St. Ignace was a gravel road. Today, there are no cars on the islands, even the big islands. Summer islanders use runabouts to get to the mainland, where marinas park their cars.

The area has the largest number of restored wood-hulled boats in the United States. Cottagers' boats are in storage nine or ten months a year, so they're spared a lot of wear and tear. Thanks to the natural conservatism of the old-money ethos, it's de rigueur in these parts to keep that poky old mahogany Chris-Craft for 40 years and to maintain it in excellent condition. (Mertaugh's Boat Works in Hessel is the oldest Chris-Craft dealer in the U.S., since 1925, though new owners have given it a contemporary look.) Another source of vintage wood boats is the local boat-building trade, which developed to serve fishermen and was kept alive by purchases from summer visitors.

It all makes for a pleasant little paradise for environmentally-conscious boaters and sailors who hate the noise and posturing of macho powerboats and the boaters who go with them. At the municipal marinas at Cedarville and Hessel during July and August, wooden boats can be seen in all directions, with more and more sailboats all the time. The attractively designed marinas have plenty of benches that make them nice places to linger.

Viewed from water or from land, the shoreline of Les Cheneaux makes for a tranquil landscape. (See page 675 for the drive along beautiful M-134 from Cedarville to Detour.) White boulders and mostly gravelly beaches are played off against a blue summer sky, the bright greens of poplars and birches, and the contrasting dark cedars and hemlocks. In late summer, splashes of goldenrod and purple asters make for a simple beauty that's an ideal antidote to overstimulated lives. Fall colors, more yellow than red, stand out against the evergreen and water.

This sense of sweet simplicity and harmony with the natural world is captured in *Hollyhocks and Radishes*, the delightful and hugely successful cookbook inspired by author Bonnie Mickelson's many summers in the Snows and by the generous, life-loving spirit of Julia Chard. For years she dispensed fresh vegetables, coffee, cooking tips, and country wisdom from her front-yard produce stand near Hessel. Her observations on life

Seeing beautiful old boathouses like this, photographed in 1906, adds to the joy of boating in Les Cheneaux. Picnic tables and campsites on picturesque Government Island may be used at no charge.

and the world around her give the book a wonderful depth.

Nowhere else in Michigan have summer people and longtime residents so intelligently and observantly showcased their favorite place as here — with the possible exception of Beaver Island. The two museums of Les Cheneaux Historical Society are well worth a close look by anyone interested in their subject areas.

◆ **Les Cheneaux Historical Museum** offers a remarkable range and quality of projects on the area's social and natural history. The **videos** really stand out; many are also for sale for $28. Ask to see videos on the area's natural history and **unusual glacial geology**, and on its long history of **building wooden boats**. The simple joys of resort life circa 1906 — fishing and boating, picnics, and fish fries — are recorded in detail in the Tanner Collection of historic photographs. Local boatbuilders have been interviewed, local limestone fossils of unusual interest collected. It's all here: lumber camps, commercial fishing, native peoples (and dugout and bark canoes), old summer hotels, beautiful boat models. Disgusted with academia, historian Philip Pittman has devoted himself to capturing the sweep of history of this small place in the massive — and surprisingly engaging — *Les Cheneaux Chronicles: Anatomy of a Community*. Real students of natural and human history could spend a rainy day here without the least regret. (Kids are likely to last about 10 minutes, however.) The **gift shop** is strong on books and notecards of local interest. Inquire about occasional Monday-evening programs. *On*

Meridian Rd. in Cedarville, one block south of light at M-134 and M-129. (906) 484-2821. Open from Memorial Day thru September. In June & September, Tues-Sat 11-4. In July & August, daily 10-4, Sun 1-4. Donations appreciated.

◆ **Les Cheneaux Maritime Museum.** A relocated boathouse contains boats and boat-related items from the 1920s to the present. *In Cedarville, on M-134 two blocks east of the light and just east of the high school. Same hours as main museum, but call (906) 484-3354 to confirm. Donations appreciated.*

RENTING BOATS . . . . . Most resorts and cottages rent boats to guests. Otherwise, go to Paul's Waterfront Cottages in the heart of Cedarville. Paul Sjoberg has fished here since 1957. He rents boats and tackle and sells bait. (906) 484-2868. . . . . To rent a small sailboat in July or August, try Frank Ingram. (906-484-3493.) He keeps it at his place on Marquette Island.

BOATING IN LES CHENEAUX . . . . . can be fun, but tricky navigating. Is that an island ahead, or a point? A channel or a bay? You have to keep track or where you are! Every motel and resort has a map. . . . . . **Picnicking** and **camping** are encouraged on beautiful **Government Island** just off La Salle Island and an easy 4 1/2 miles straight out of Cedarville. The shore is surprisingly rocky and steep, though there are some flat picnic sites and campsites with fire rings and beat-up picnic tables. Birch and conifers dominate the two mile island; its southeastern tip overlooks Lake Huron and the yacht entrance to Cedarville Bay. *No charge.*

GOLFING . . . . . at the golf course of **Les Cheneaux Club,** founded by original resorters, is open to the public. The course is on the mainland. On Four Mile Road south off M-134 between Hessel and Cedarville. (906) 484-3606.

FOR A GOOD SWIMMING BEACH . . . . . go east on M-134 past M-48. See page 676. Or stay at a resort that has developed its own swimming beach.

FOR GOOD EATING . . . . . there are several recommended restaurants (see *Hunts' Restaurants and Lodgings of Michigan)* plus the seasonal **Hessel Home Bakery** on M-134 in Hessel (906-484-3680) and the delightful **Nye Vegetable Farm** half a mile north of Hessel. Take 3 Mile Road half a mile north from M-134, turn left on Nye Road. Farm is on corner.

M-134 from Cedarville to De Tour

An idyllic stretch of beaches, dunes, rocky points, and woods makes for a pleasant drive or bike ride.

Just east of Les Cheneaux, the 24 miles of M-134 from Cedarville to De Tour pass a series of rocky points and little bays, some with sandy beaches and low dunes, others with marshes full of wildlife. The tiny (population 400) village of De Tour overlooks the De Tour Passage, where the St. Marys River that leads from Lake Superior and Sault Ste. Marie empties into Lake Huron. ("De Tour" means the turning place. The word is pronounced correctly in the French way, with the accent on the second syllable — "de-TOUR.") Two parks along the passage are ideal for watching up-close the big freighters that come by every hour or so. (See page 276 for background about Great Lakes shipping today, and why there are fewer but bigger freighters on the lakes today.)

So much state land abuts M-134 (it's part of the Lake Superior State Forest) that the highway seems part of a beautiful, magically under-used park. Frequent pulloffs make it easy to stop and watch birds, or swim or beachcomb for the area's plentiful limestone fossils, or walk into the low natural areas of birch, cedar, and hemlock.

Although there's no separate bicycle path, M-134 has extra-wide, two-foot paved shoulders that make for good bicycling. There's still not very much traffic here, and summer residents are often seen walking along the shoulders enjoying the pristine scenery. Another plus for out-of-shape cyclists: it's quite flat. Mountain bikes would allow additional adventures: taking the often rough, unimproved roads south off M-134 out to the points.

For a delightful, lazy day, wear your swimsuit or shorts and good wading shoes, and bring binoculars for watching birds and boats. Take a picnic lunch, and stop often along the way. Recommended provisioning points on M-134: the Hessel Home Bakery (the pasties are excellent) or the big Cedarville Foods supermarket.

From the blinker light at M-134 and M-129 in Cedarville, here are points of interest and approximate mileage:

◆ **Les Cheneaux Historical Museum.** (One block south on M-129.) See page 673.

◆ **Les Cheneaux Maritime Museum.** (1/4 mile, just east of the high school.) See page 674.

◆ **Michigan Limestone**, Cedarville Plant. (4 miles.) If you're lucky, you may see a freighter being loaded and pulling out of Port Dolomite at McKay Bay, on the eastern edge of Les Cheneaux.

◆ **Prentiss Bay marsh.** Here Prentiss Creek forms a wide marsh. The scores of nesting boxes are for tree swallows. They are among some 300 in the area made from scrap by longtime resident Harry Harris, a former gunsmith, a birdwatcher, and dedicated ecologist. Each spring he deploys the boxes from his boat; each fall he takes them in. (Every year or so Les Cheneaux Historical Society presents his bird slide program.)

◆ **Highway department roadside park** (18 miles; 1 mile east of M-148). Much more than a typical roadside park. There's a beautiful, sandy **beach**; a shady, grassy **picnic area** with lots of pleasant picnic tables and grills; plus pit toilets and a water pump. Through some birches and cedars and over some low dunes is the beach. The view is accented by occasional offshore rocks and the square Martin Reef Light seven miles to the southwest. It warns boaters away from shallow water.

◆ **De Tour State Forest Campground**, formerly De Tour State Park (17 1/2 miles; 3 1/2 miles east of M-48). A real find for picnickers, swimmers, and campers who don't require a lot of conveniences. Out of sight of the highway towards St. Vital Point are a nice, sandy **beach**, a few picnic tables, a hand pump, pit toilets, and 25 large, private campsites in a mature coniferous forest. *$6 camping fee. Self-registration.*

◆ **Boat launch.** (At the outskirts of De Tour village.) Parking area, pit toilets, and launch are well off from the highway in a woods.

◆ **Picnic area and dock.** (At the outskirts of De Tour.) A pleasant, shady natural area with a grand view of the De Tour Passage. Pit toilets.

◆ **Dr. Shula F. Giddens Memorial Gardens.** (10 miles east of M-148 on west edge of De Tour village.) Sunny park and gazebo overlook the De Tour Passage and resemble an ambitiously landscaped front yard that's colorful with flowers. Benches let you sit and enjoy the view.

◆ **Ferry landing** and **museum** in De Tour village. The big back windows of the Fogcutter restaurant look out directly at the passing parade of small boats and the occasional Lake Superior freighter entering and leaving the North Channel. Gull's Landing, east by the new public marina, has a similar view and better food. The **De Tour Passage Historical Museum** across the road has exhibits, a very helpful volunteer staff, and lots of free publications about the area. *It's open most days and Friday nights in season.* Best source for local information: the **Point De Tour Cafe** (906-297-5165) on Elizabeth (the street by the ferry) at Ontario (the main street up the hill). It's the only year-round restaurant, with good food and big portions.

ABOUT DRUMMOND ISLAND . . . . . At De Tour, the ferry crosses the one-mile channel to Drummond Island, yet another stretch of low-key northwoods vacationland where inland lakes, protected bays, a state forest campground, and extensive state lands laced with trails make for boater's and outdoor lover's paradise. It's the largest U.S. island in the Great Lakes. Ferries run about every hour. The round-trip is $8 for car and driver. Call or write the Chamber of Commerce, Box 200, Drummond Island, Mi 49726; (906) 493-5245. It's a misconception that Tom Monaghan's Domino's Lodge (a 3,000-acre golf resort now sold and renamed **Woodmor**) wrecked the island. For more info on Woodmor, call (906) 493-1000. The 18-site **state forest campground** ($6/night, primitive) is on beautiful Maxton Bay. No reservations. A mile north of Woodmor.

SPRING FISHING . . . . . is famous around Les Cheneaux and Drummond Island. The perch and smelt run roughly the last week in April and the first part of May . . . . . Summer and fall fishing off Drummond Island is for northern pike, walleye, perch, and small-mouth bass . . . . . Summer fishing at Les Cheneaux includes salmon, pike, and herring.

FOSSILS ARE PLENTIFUL . . . . . in the dolomite limestone that forms the bedrock and much of the beach gravel here. Fossil coral and shellfish are common.

U.S. 2 from St. Ignace to Naubinway

*See 17th-century sites in St. Ignace,
followed by long stretches of beach and dunes
and beautiful, convenient campgrounds*

For most of the 42 miles west from the Mackinac Bridge to Naubinway, a onetime fishing village at Lake Michigan's northernmost tip, U.S. 2 parallels Lake Michigan. The highway passes right alongside long, sandy beaches and low dunes alternating with forests and marshes. It's punctuated with some high overlooks and dramatic vistas. Some outstanding campgrounds invite visitors to linger and make this their base camp.

An Upper Peninsula trip will be off to a mellow start if you plan to slow down here, take time out from driving, and resist the urge to keep hurrying. If you don't learn to slow down and stop, much of your trip is likely to disappear in a blur.

This delightful stretch of U.S. 2 is ideal for switching gears, getting out of your car, and observing a fuller way, using all your senses, that can't be done on windshield tours. Bring binoculars to see offshore islands and lighthouses.

A short stop in St. Ignace can help tune you in to the over 350-year recorded history of this still-sparsely populated part of Michigan, where a substantial portion

Father Jacques Marquette, the Jesuit missionary who was one of the first Europeans to see the Mississippi, founded a Jesuit mission at St. Ignace in 1671. Two St. Ignace museums deal with the impact of the French on Straits history, from the French and Ojibway points of view.

of the native-born locals are descended from a mix of native Ojibway, French trappers and voyageurs, and Irish fishermen.

Recorded history of the Straits area goes back to 1634, when Jean Nicolet passed through the Straits trying to find a route to the Orient. Soon French fur-traders had superimposed a far-flung fur-trading system on the preexisting Native American trade network. Its center was at the straits, first at Michilimackinac (Mackinaw City), then on Mackinac Island. Jesuit priests were troubled about the harm done to native peoples by the fur trade and by trade goods (especially alcohol, which Indians couldn't tolerate). They established a mission here in 1671 and named it after their order's founder, St. Ignatius Loyola.

Here's a recommended itinerary that can be compressed to a couple of hours or expanded to last a day or more.

◆ **Museum of Ojibway Culture/Marquette Mission Park.** This intelligent, small museum in a former Catholic church focuses on the simple, subsistence culture of the Ojibwa (Chippewa) people, the original residents of the upper Great Lakes. Exhibits depict their ingenuity in deriving from the water and land around them all the necessities of life in a cold, harsh climate. In the back room, "Currents of Change in the Straits" deals with the arrival of the Hurons, Odawa, and French, and their political alliance against their common British enemy. The point of view is that of native peoples.

The museum and church occupy the very site of the Jesuit mission (1671-1701) where Father Jacques Marquette served. Here in this vicinity too were villages of Huron and Odawa (Ottawa) people, driven from their homelands in southern Ontario in the 1640s by the hostile and expansionistic Iroquois.

A memorial to Father Marquette occupies the park by the museum, where significant archaeological digs have occurred. An authentic Huron longhouse and other outdoor exhibits describe how Huron and Odawa refugees adapted their culture to this new land, just when French traders and voyageurs were introducing changes that would forever destroy the native peoples' difficult but ecologically balanced way of life. On Labor Day weekend here the Sault Ste. Marie Chippewa tribe holds a well-regarded traditional **pow-pow**. Without competitions, it's more like a big family reunion attended mostly by Indians. An expanded **museum shop** in the former restaurant next door features area Woodland Indian handcrafts and a good selection of books on Indians and French history of the Straits area. *500 N. State at the north end of downtown St. Ignace. (906) 643-9161. Open from Memorial Day thru September. From mid June thru Labor Day open daily 10-9. Otherwise open Tues-Sat 1-5. $2/adults, $1/student, $5/family.*

◆ **Father Marquette National Memorial and Museum.** This simple, spare museum focuses on the achievements and spiritual motivation of Jacques Marquette (1637-1675), who founded Sault Ste. Marie and discovered and mapped the Mississippi River in his nine short years in North America. Here the perspective on the vitally important 17th-century Straits history is that of the French. **French Heritage Days** are celebrated here on the second weekend of August.

Across I-75 **Straits State Park** (906-643-8620) offers 322 modern campsites with hot showers, but why put up with small sites and highway noise when you can enjoy a much quieter, more natural campsite on water a few miles west on U.S. 2? (See page 670.) *The memorial/museum is south off U.S. 2 just west of I-75 and St. Ignace. (906) 643-8620. Open May-October. State park sticker required: $3/day, $18/year.*

◆ **Boulevard Drive/Point Labarbe Road.** For many visitors, St. Ignace goes by in a blur of pasty shops and older motels that sprawl west for miles on U.S. 2. To avoid most of these distractions, take the shore road out of town. You'll see sweeping views of Lake Michigan, with an occasional freighter and the most dramatic **views of the Mackinac Bridge** bridge from the parking area at the foot of Boulevard Drive. (Telescopes are available there.) In a few miles the shore road joins U.S. 2.

About a mile west of where Point Labarbe Road joins U.S. 2, you can turn south onto **Gros Cap Road** and follow the shore for another four miles or so. *To reach the shore road from U.S. 2 just west of I-75, turn south onto Boulevard Drive at the Howard Johnson's/Marquette Memorial Drive. Boulevard Drive is gravel for a mile or so. To continue onto Point Labarbe Road, turn right before you get to the parking lot and stay along the shore.*

◆ **Riverside Park and Helena Island overlook.** This blufftop park and picnic spot takes in a grand view of St. Helena Island two miles offshore. French fishermen from Gros Cap (the shoreline village once below the bluff here) established a prosperous town on St. Helena in the 19th century. The natural harbor on this beautiful island's north shore made it an ideal fueling stop

Visitors are welcome to visit the Coast Guard icebreaker Biscayne Bay in summer at the station on the southwest end of St. Ignace. It belongs to an improved class of more efficient icebreaking tugs. The curved hull, wider on top, breaks ice by applying pressure from above.

for wood-fired steamships, and a pleasant destination for outings by boat or sleigh. The classic, tapered 1873 light tower and the brick keeper's house on the south shore, abandoned for 60 years, have been stabilized and renovated in a noteworthy Boy Scout service project. The island makes a fine destination for small boats, provided the water is calm. With rocky and sandy shorelines, forests and wetlands, meadows and sandbars, it offers much variety in a small (1 mile by 1/2 mile) space. Drawbacks for adventurers: snakes and poison ivy.

◆ **Point aux Chenes River Marsh.** Just east of Point aux Chenes, this river's many twists between Round Lake and Lake Michigan form an unusally large and undisturbed marsh (also inaccessible, except by canoe during high water), home to loons, osprey, eagles, and terns. An osprey nest is visible from the road near the river bridge.

◆ **Lake CCC Camp Round Interpretive Site/Sand Dunes Cross-Country Ski Trail.** Half a mile north of U.S. 2 on H-57/ Brevort Lake Road, this trail-laced forest within the Hiawatha

National Forest offers 15 miles of **trails** and an excellent outdoor **exhibit** about the Civilian Conservation Corps and its camp that was here in the 1930s — one of 2,650 camps across the U.S. that employed 600,000 men in 1935. Flat gravel walks connect large, engraved metal signboards marking the sites of various camp buildings. Signs convey what camp life was like for jobless young men working on CCC reforestation projects, making trails, and building many of Michigan State parks' most beautiful rustic buildings — all for $30/month plus food and clothing. "City boys surrounded by trees," says one heading describing typical CCC crews as "boys that didn't know an ax from a baseball bat." At Round Lake some 200 young men built roads, planted trees, made the dam and campgrounds at Brevort Lake, and cleared logging debris to prevent fires.The site is now a meadow filled with wildflowers in late summer. The philosophy and politics behind the CCC are clearly conveyed through excellent writing and graphics. This is an inspiring place, in a very quiet way.

Six **trail loops** (each a couple of miles) go through open areas and wooded old oak forests on the backs of dunes. In summer, loops A, B, and C offer more stable footing; D, E, and F go through more bare sand. The **ski season** here usually lasts from early December through March. Trails are **groomed** on Mondays and Fridays, and there's firewood for building a fire at the **warming cabin** by the entrance. Call (906) 643-7900 for trail conditions.

◆ **Lake Michigan beach between Point aux Chenes and Brevort.** Between H-57/Brevort Lake Road and Ozark Road in Brevort, U.S. 2 passes right along eight miles of beautiful, sandy, wide beach. Low dunes lead back from the north side of the highway and invite exploration by nature-lovers. Wide shoulders make it easy to pull over and stop anywhere. No facilities here — maybe that's why this fabulous beach is so reliably uncrowded.

◆ **Michigan Beach Lake Campground and picnic area** (Hiawatha National Forest). Perched on low dunes, 35 large, quite private campsites in a shady, mature forest have flush toilets, no showers. $8/night. Sites fill up on summer weekends. Come by Wednesday or Thursday. *On U.S. 2 about 6 miles west of Brevoort Lake Road and about 3 miles east of Ozark Road. (906) 643-7900.*

◆ **Brevoort Lake Campgrounds** (Hiawatha National Forest). The National Forest campground here strikes a good balance between privacy, community, and convenience. A seasonal camp host's trailer is at the entrance; frequent patrols ensure the desired quiet, family atmosphere. Large, shady, private campsites with no showers or electricity characterize the 50-site main campground along a little peninsula and the 20 sites on the west edge of Brevoort Lake. Two-thirds of the campsites are directly on the beach. ($8/night.) **Spencer's Landing**, an extraordinarily helpful camp store before the main campground, sells reasonably priced frozen meat and vegetables, milk, groceries, and every kind of camper's necessity, and bait. It rents **canoes** and **fishing boats** ($10/day, but bring your own motor) and **kayaks** ($3/hour). (906) 292-5471. Open from second weekend of May thru first snowfall or second weekend of October. Hours: 8 a.m.-10 p.m. Nearby is the lakeside **picnic area** with tables and grills.

Big **Brevoort Lake** (4,233 acres) has a man-made spawning reef that has helped create a good walleye fishery. *20 miles north west of St. Ignace off U.S. 2. Turn north onto Brevoort Camp Road for 1 mile to park. (906) 643-7900.*

♦ **Cut River Bridge and picnic area.** Even the most oblivious motorists notice the striking, deep limestone gorge formed by the Cut River as it empties into Lake Michigan. But it's easy not to know about the attractive, shady picnic area at the bridge's east end, from which a paved path and stairway descend 160 feet to the river. From the bottom, it's an easy walk to the sandy beach. You can also walk across the bridge on a pedestrian walkway. The view down is terrific. Be advised that the sway and vibration from big trucks may be thrilling or alarming. *On U.S. 2 about 4 miles west of Brevoort.*

♦ **Hog Island Point State Forest.** Just off U.S. 2, 58 private rustic campsites (vault toilets, hand pump) enjoy easy access to a sandy Lake Michigan **beach.** *Half-way between Epoufette and Naubinway on U.S. 2. (906) 293-5131. Campsites are $6 per night; seniors $3. No more than 4 people at a campsite.*

♦ **Prinski Roadside Park.** This pleasant picnic spot beneath the pines looks out onto a sandy beach and a point of rocks that march out into Lake Michigan like a series of stepping stones. *2-3 miles east of Naubinway off U.S. 2.*

♠♣♠

FOR PEOPLE WHO LIKE BEACHES THAT ARE REALLY OFF THE BEATEN PATH . . . . . try these two west of Naubinway, off U.S. 2 about 14 miles southwest of town. Look for the sign to the **Big Knob Campground** of Lake

Superior State Forest. The 23-site rustic campground is at the end of a road that winds at least six miles through forest and wetlands, to emerge on a **beach** overlooking Lake Michigan. . . . . . **Scott's Point** is the closest mainland point on either peninsula to the Beaver Archipelago. Squaw Island and its light are barely 10 miles offshore, and Beaver Island is another six. The wide, sandy **beach** descends so gradually into the water that even adults can wade out for a hundred feet without getting their knees wet. Shore birds are abundant. *From U.S. 2 at Gould City, go south 9 miles on Gould City Rd. Park is at road's end.*

ANTIQUARIAN BOOKS NEAR BREVORT . . . . . Mary and Eugene run an interesting used bookstore, **First Edition**, and the Black Letter Press from their country home on 461 Worth Road. From Brevoort, go north on Ozark Road for half a mile until you reach Worth Road. Their main specialty is Michigan and Great Lakes history, but there's lots of good general reading on hand. Open daily from Memorial to Labor Day. The rest of the year is by chance or by appointment. Hours are casual; when a customer knocks on the door in the morning, the bookshop is open and often stays open until 10 or so in the evening. (906) 643-7071.

LAS VEGAS-STYLE GAMBLING IN ST. IGNACE . . . . . takes place in a converted motel north of town, now the **Kewadin Shores Casino**, run by the Soo Tribe of the Chippewa Indians. It offers the usual slot machines, black jack, keno, roulette, and big-six in a facility that's smaller than the band's original spread outside Sault Ste. Marie. Call (906) 643-7071 for information.

DIVING IN THE STRAITS AREA . . . . . Almost a dozen wrecks are buoyed for divers. Still more are described in Chuck and Jeri Feltner's authoritative, interesting *Shipwrecks of the Straits of Mackinac* . . . . .For a **dive brochure**, call (906) 643-8717. For more info and for reservations on the 42-foot Rec Diver, call Straits Diving, (906) 643-7009.

FOR PROOF THAT INFORMED AND INFORMATIVE SMALL-TOWN WEEKLIES ARE STILL POSSIBLE . . . . . pick up a copy of **The St. Ignace News**, published by retired University of Michigan journalism professor and nonagenarian Wesley Maurer, Sr. and his son Wesley Maurer, Jr. Its principles: "upbuilder of the Home — Nourisher of the Community Spirit — Arts, Letters and Science of the Common People."

VISITORS ARE WELCOME . . . . . to tour the **U.S. Coast Guard's Cutter Biscayne Bay**, when it's docked at its home port in St. Ignace. The Coast Guard Station is at 1075 South Huron. This relatively new class of icebreaking tug uses a wider beam and greater horsepower to break more ice, and a "blubber" hull lubrication system to do it more efficiently. Air is slowly forced through ports in the hull, which makes water flow upward, reducing friction between the hull and ice. Call (906) 643-6435 to arrange a tour.

Kitch-iti-kipi (Big Spring)

An extraordinary sight: in a tranquil, sylvan setting,
10,000 gallons of water a minute
bubbling up in a deep, crystal-clear pool

Few natural sights in Michigan compare with the beauty and mystique of this enormous, bowl-like spring. Through a picturebook pine forest, you come upon an amazing, emerald-green spring, round and jewel-like, 200 feet wide. By pulling a simple raft, you get out to the middle and gaze down through 40 feet of crystal-clear water. Bubbling up from the bottom is a constant flow of 10,000 gallons of water a minute. Large trout swim lazily around, their movements readily visible even at a distance. Moss-covered logs fallen to the sandy bottom look like a pile of sticks so close you could almost touch them.

The water here stays 45° F. year around, so you can see the spring in any season. But the best time is during summer, when this cool glade is a delightful contrast to warm summer days. In the morning, when mist hangs over the water and turns the surrounding woods into abstract, mysterious shapes, the effect is especially powerful. Arrive either before mid-morning or towards dusk to experience the serenity of the place when few others are around. There's a pleasant **picnic area** and a **concession stand** with refreshments.

Kitch-iti-kipi (pronounced "KITCH-i-tee-KI-pee") is Michigan's biggest spring. Its name means "big cold water." No one knows for sure where this enormous volume of water comes from. Some say it's from the Seney area. Hydraulic pressure forces the groundwater to the surface. It empties into a stream leading to Indian Lake, which in turn empties into the Manistique River.

Palms Book State Park and Kitch-iti-kipi are northwest of Manistique. From U.S. 2, take M-149 8 miles north. (906) 341-2355. Open for day use, 8 a.m.-10 p.m.; no camping. State Park sticker required: $4/day, $18/year.

Fayette Historic Townsite

Once a filthy worksite for iron furnace laborers,
this 19th-century ghost town on the Garden Peninsula
is scenic today.

This picturesque industrial ghost town curves around pretty Snail Shell Harbor, on a bit of land jutting out into northern Lake Michigan. Its heart is the great limestone stacks and beehive charcoal furnaces of a charcoal iron-operation started in the 1860s. The weathered silvery frame buildings and the restored stone furnaces have been preserved as ghosts, not repainted and spiffed up as if they were new. A scenic limestone bluff in the background was used as a quarry for stone and for limestone flux which removed impurities in the smelting process. Fayette is a peaceful place today, all green with leaves and grass — a far cry from the mud and dirt and stockpiles of materials during its productive years in the 1870s and 1880s.

Fayette is near the tip of the Garden Peninsula, especially fertile because the moderating waters of Lake Michigan surround it. Isolated and remote, the 21-mile-long peninsula has become such a favorite with marijuana growers that the state carried out its largest-ever eradication program here and on the nearby Stonington Peninsula.

Fayette boomed after demand for high-quality iron escalated during the Civil War. The Jackson Iron Company chose this area for a new blast furnace because the site had limestone to purify the molten iron, and abundant hardwood forests to fuel the furnaces. A railroad took iron ore from the Negaunee Range near Marquette southeast to Escanaba, from which it was shipped 25 miles to the iron furnaces in Fayette.

Fayette set production records during its heyday, but by the mid-1880s, improved methods of making coke iron and steel were making charcoal iron too expensive to produce. The smelting operation here closed down in 1891. The hotel lived on as a resort for many decades.

You have to plan a visit to Fayette for it to be a real highlight. The scenery won't automatically carry the day. Lake Michigan is surprisingly seldom seen from most of the Garden Peninsula's roads. And the museum town can be off-putting if you see the wrong things first. Here's what to do:

1. Come early or late in the day when the slanted light is dramatic and there aren't many people. Sometimes a morning mist rising off the harbor gives a soft, romantic, ghostly look to the place. Evening sunsets are spectacular.

2. Get a free townsite map and buy *Fayette: A Visitor's Guide* at the visitors' center front desk for $3. Avoid the misleading visitor center displays, where an unctuous voice in a melodramatic recording proclaims, "It was a nice life" for Fayette's workers, who were "a happy, contented lot." Newer interpretive displays in the village are based on careful historical and archaeological research, and they're much more sophisticated and honest. A visitor's account of Fayette workers' housing in 1870 described mud, filth, horrible smells, and ragged children — much worse than anything she'd seen in Cleveland slums.

3. Wander around the buildings and look inside. The hotel, town hall and shops, and one supervisor's home are furnished with satisfying period accuracy. Other buildings, like the office, are full of interesting and detailed exhibit panels. Read them, and you'll learn about subjects as diverse as the butcher business, medicine before the acceptance of antiseptics, ladies' entertainments, traveling shows, and labor history. (When orders for iron were slow, workers didn't get paid — sometimes for weeks on end!)

4. After 11 a.m. the village will likely be filling up with tourists. You could take a 25-minute **guided tour** of Fayette's main street. Or take your booklet, sit down on a bench or at the picnic tables at the parking lot's edge, and read through it for a good overview of the charcoal iron-smelting process, the town, and the interesting ongoing archaeological investigations of the area. They reveal much about the lives of workers and their daily activities that hasn't been recorded in surviving letters and diaries.

5. Don't miss the **hiking trail up the limestone bluffs** east of the harbor. Four spots offer beautiful views clear across to the Stonington Peninsula to the west. The state park has **seven miles of hiking trails** in all.

Snail Shell Harbor offers a **transient marina** (there's no pump-out station but it is a scenic setting for overnights), a **boat ramp**, and **fishing** for perch and smallmouth bass. **Camping** at Fayette's semi-modern campsites ($8/night) is unusually secluded and uncrowded for a state park. Tall trees give each of the 80 campsites unusual privacy, but also block any water view. There's running water, electricity, pit toilets, and no showers, which means the campground fills up only for the park's two special events: the **Blessing of the Fleet** in mid-July and mid-August's **Heritage Days**. The beach is only a quarter-mile walk away.

Fayette State Park is 16 miles south on M-183 from Garden Corners and U.S. 2, between Escanaba and Manistique. (906) 644-2603. Open from mid-May through mid-October. Fayette Townsite is open from 8 a.m. to 5 p.m., until 9 in July & August. State park sticker required; $4/day, $18/year.

A 2,000-FOOT WHITE SAND BEACH . . . . . backed by low dunes is about a mile south of Fayette Townsite, in a different part of the state park, reached by another road off M-183. There's a large **picnic area** and a **changing house**. State park sticker required; $4/day, $18/year.

ANOTHER BEACH AND PICNIC AREA . . . . . even less crowded, is the **Sac Bay County Park** off 183 about five miles south of Fayette. Continue south to the end of M-183 and you'll be at **Fairport**, almost at the very tip of the Garden Peninsula. It's **a commercial fishing village**, one of the few left in Michigan. There's no store or restaurant, but you can stop by the fish shed and buy **fresh whitefish to cook out.** Some fishermen are Indians who fish with gill nets, once used by all commercial fishermen. By the 1940s overfishing had greatly reduced Lake Michigan's commercial catch. Laws today favor sport fishermen and prohibit gill nets, except for Indians who are protected by old treaties assuring their traditional means of livelihood.

A LITTLE FARMING AND FISHING VILLAGE . . . . . that's looking more and more like a ghost town itself is **Garden** (population 268), once the peninsula's commercial hub. As small farms and orchards decline, so does its year-round population. Quaint frame storefronts are increasingly empty. Cottagers and retirees bring some life to the place in summer. There's an attractive little crafts gallery and consignment shop, a small, summer-only **historical museum**, and two popular **restaurants** with good food.

CAMPING AND SWIMMING NEAR KITCH-ITI-KIPI . . . . . On the Upper Peninsula's fourth-biggest lake, **Indian Lake State Park** has two modern campgrounds and beaches, and good fishing for walleye and perch. **Indian Lake** is quite shallow and therefore warms up sooner than most Upper Peninsula lakes. **South Shore Campground** has 157 sites with little privacy but right on the lake; reserve in advance. The adjacent **Chippewa Trail** comes with a brochure about wild foods used by Indians. **West Shore Campground** has 144 secluded sites farther from the lake; it's rarely full. *A few miles west of Manistique. At Thompson, turn north off U. S. 2 onto M-149; park is in 3 miles. Follow signs to west unit. (906) 341-2355. State Park sticker required: $4/day, $18/year.*

Soo Locks

A key link between the Great Lakes
gives a close-up view of giant freighters.

For watching big boats up close, there's hardly a more dramatic place anywhere than the Soo Locks at Sault Ste. Marie. Here visitors may be a scant 20 feet or so from 800-foot-long freighters moving slowly into the MacArthur Lock, the closest to shore. The four locks enable vessels to bypass the falls (a 21-foot drop) of the St. Marys River. The river joins Lake Superior to the lower Great Lakes and ultimately to the Atlantic.

The locks, on the American side of the river, are operated by the U.S. Army's Corp of Engineers, The Corps runs an elaborate and interesting **Soo Locks Information Center**, open long hours. From 7 a.m. to 11 p.m. visitors can see a short **film** on the locks' history and operations. Also on view are a large working model of the locks, a large relief map of the Great Lakes, and many charts and photos about the history and operations of the locks. A sign on the wall tells which freighters are due the next two to three hours. The elevated **outside viewing platform** allows you to get a close-up, birds'-eye view of the big boats as they wait the few minutes it takes for a chamber to go 21 feet up to Superior level or 21 feet down to Huron level. The public address system announces the cargo, destination, and statistics of each ship. Don't fail to pick up the outstanding **free guide to Great Lakes shipping.** With it you can identify most Great Lakes shipping traffic by using its chart of vessel types and its colorful displays of international flags and Great Lakes shipping companies' stack markings.

Twelve thousand vessels pass through these locks each year. About one fourth are huge cargo vessels, some carrying as much as 70,000 tons. The principal cargo of the outgoing oceangoing vessels is grain from the American heartland, while downbound Great Lakes freighters are most likely to be carrying iron ore.

Alongside the locks, the **Soo Locks Park**, also maintained by the Engineers, is a beautiful place to linger, especially in the evening when lights reflect on the water and illuminate the trees. Benches and a colored fountain make it a peaceful, pleasant place, in contrast to the cluttered tourist shops on the other side

The Soo Locks give boatwatchers a good, close-up look at boats, and the visitor center provides lots of background about Great Lakes shipping. There are far fewer big bulk carriers on the lakes today, due to new vessels' huge capacities and currently decreased shipping tonnage.

of Portage Avenue. They continue to be the most dismal and uninspired tourist traps in Michigan.

Nowadays you should expect to wait a while to see a big boat pass through the locks. Only 120 U.S. and Canadian cargo vessels are registered on the Lakes — down from 300 just 10 years ago. That's largely because efficient high-volume thousand-foot bulk carriers are gradually replacing 600-footers with the same number of crew but less than half the capacity. Also, the collapse of Communism means much less Great Plains wheat is being shipped overseas.

One big cargo ship comes through the locks every hour and a half on the average, though ships sometimes bunch due to bad weather. Plan your visit to coincide with a big ship's arrival by calling the **Boat-Watchers Hotline**, (906) 632-0888.

To reach the locks, take the I-75 Ashmun Street exit and go to downtown Sault Ste. Marie. At the T intersection, turn left onto Portage. Locks are in one block. Dates of opening and closing the locks each year vary with the weather. Usually they open in mid-

March and close in mid-December. **Corps of Engineers informa-tion center** *open 7 a.m.-11 p.m. daily. Free.*

For a ship's perspective of the locks, take the interesting **Soo Locks Boat Tour**. Get seats at the front of the boat if possible. The two-hour excursion takes you through the locks up to the level of Lake Superior and a rather surrealistic view of Canada's huge riverfront Algoma Steel Mill, with its 10,000 employees and five blast furnaces. On the wharf are enormous piles of purplish taconite iron pellets from Lake Superior's iron-mining regions. You also pass the quarter-mile-long Edison Sault Electric Company. (See page 693.) Across the river, you see downtown Sault Ste. Marie, Canada, and its seaplane station for fighting forest fires. The planes swoop down onto lakes and in just seven seconds fill their two water tanks on the move. The tour boat also passes by the vast Algoma Steel Mill and under the 2.8-mile-long International Bridge to Canada. *Boat tour docks are along Portage east of Ashmun Bus. I-75 and the locks. One is next to the Museum Ship Valley Camp, half a mile east of Ashmun; another is 1.7 miles east of Ashmun, beyond the Edison Sault powerhouse. For the complex, changing* **schedule,** *call (800) 432-6301 or pick up a brochure — they're everywhere. Boats leave hourly or more often between 9 a.m. and 5:40 or 6:40 p.m. in July & August.* <u>Buy tickets ahead of time</u>.

The American and Canadian settlements at the Soo have always been strategic outposts. The recorded history of the area goes back to 1618. Father Jacques Marquette started a mission at the Soo in 1668. The Straits of Mackinac soon became the center of a vast fur-trading network. In 1855, the first canal around the rapids actually caused an economic tailspin by taking away local residents' livelihood portaging freight around the rapids.

In the late 19th century, there were plans for Michigan's Sault Ste. Marie to become a major northern metropolis by using the St. Mary's River as a power source. Francis Clergue from Maine pursued this dream but went bankrupt in developing the striking, quarter-mile-long **power plant** where the waterpower canal meets the river, on East Portage two-thirds of a mile east of Ashmun. The anticipated new industries never came. Despite Clergue's ultimate financial failure, deals and alliances he made with Canadian investors transformed Sault Ste. Marie, Canada, into a major industrial center. He helped create the Algoma Central Railroad (the famous but dull Snow Train), St. Mary's Paper, Algoma Steel, and Algoma Central Marine. Clergue's story is poignantly told at the Tower of History.

For a good overview of the area, take the Twin Sault Tour (see below), and then visit the weird but worthwhile **Tower of History**. This high concrete tower, in an architectural style of the 1960s known as Brutalism, was built as the bell tower for the planned new building of the church next door. In 1967, after the $660,000 tower was finished, the governing bishop said enough already to the grandiose local project. A local nonprofit historical society turned it into a museum — a very uneven museum. The best parts are the amazing **view** from its top of the locks, waterways, and hills and the poignant and dramatic **film** about Francis Clergue, the visionary developer of the area's industrial potential who eventually went bankrupt and left. (Algoma Steel and the Algoma Central Railroad are among his creations.) *326 E. Portage, 3 blocks east (right) from Ashmun/Bus. I-75. (906) 632-3658. Open mid-May thru mid-Oct. $2.95 adults; $1.75 ages 6-16.*

Don't leave without driving a few blocks east on Portage to see the monumental, quarter-mile-long **Edison Sault Power Plant**, Clergue's glory and downfall. It was built of reddish-brown sandstone excavated from the Power Canal that makes an island of downtown Sault Ste. Marie and powers the plant. But the project failed to attract enough industries to the area. Clergue went bust, and Sault Ste. Marie, Michigan, is today not another Minneapolis but a town of 15,000.

ENTERTAINING AND INFORMATIVE . . . . . but bumpy, the **Soo Locks Tour Trains** take you through both the U.S. and Canadian Sault Ste. Marie. In the U.S. the conveyances are open trailers pulled by a mock-train truck; in Canada it's a double-decker bus. Looking down at the river from the high 3-mile-long bridge is worth a trip in itself. You learn a lot about both cities. The American city (population 15,000) was larger until the turn of the century, but now is dwarfed by its Canadian neighbor (population 82,000). The Canadian guide explains how that country's high taxes on cigarettes, alcohol, and gasoline help pay for the country's universal health insurance and how even a modest home here costs well over $100,000. The Canadian Soo is heavily Italian; Giovanni's is a good Italian restaurant. The two-hour **Twin Sault Tour** is the one to take. It can give you time to shop and eat in Canada, if you choose. *Tour depot is at 315 W. Portage, across from Soo Locks Park and next to the Haunted Depot. (906) 653-5912. Opens June 15, closes Oct. 15, Leaves hourly between 10 and 4, June thru August. Call for fall times.*

A FREIGHTER AND A MUSEUM . . . . . The **Museum Ship Valley Camp** is an old Great Lakes freighter whose large cargo holds have been converted into a Great Lakes theme museum. In one cavernous space an **Edmund Fitzgerald display** effectively captures the eeriness with which that huge freighter disappeared suddenly from the view of a trailing freighter. A torn half of one of its lifeboats, one of the few remnants of the wreck to surface, is displayed. Especially interesting is the Valley Camp's **pilothouse,** which contains one of the lakes' first radar systems. Also on view are the captain's quarters, the quarters of the other officers and crew, the mess hall and galley. Exhibits are uneven, and some are dated. The place is so big, it's really a "find-it-yourself" museum that depends on the visitor's intuition, luck, or pre-existing interest and knowledge of the subject. It's a great place to visit on a rainy day. With more rigorously user-friendly interpretations, it could become an outstanding museum.

SIMILARLY UNEVEN . . . . . is the ambitious new **River of History Museum** in the old Beaux Arts post office building. Spoken stories at a few compelling life-size dioramas — including an Indian dwelling you can even go into — focus on key periods of area history. But in its first year, most displays either told too little or too much, with too much reading. Still, it's a good rainy-day destination, with a fine museum shop of educational materials and local crafts. *209 E. Portage, a block east (right) from Ashmun/Bus. I-75 downtown. (906) 632-1999. Open mid-May thru Dec. By appt. in winter. Basic hours: Mon-Sat 10-5, Sun 12-5. In July & Aug. open to 8. In Nov & Dec, closed Sun & Mon. $2.50/adult, $1.25 ages 5-18. $8 family.*

On the shores of Whitefish Bay

A drive with many points of interest and gorgeous views of Lake Superior and ships

Between Brimley near Sault Ste. Marie and Paradise is a shoreline road along Whitefish Bay that offers terrific Lake Superior views looking out onto shipping lanes, plus a lighthouse museum with a stunning view from its tower, a remarkable scenic overlook, a fish hatchery, a beautiful short section of the North Country Trail with a swinging bridge, and several picnic areas, campgrounds, and beaches.

It all makes for a lovely day's drive, especially magnificent in color season, when maples, birches, and dark green conifers make rich color contrasts. The area is a fine vacation base from which to explore the eastern Upper Peninsula and visit nearby Tahquamenon Falls.

If you're going between Tahquamenon Falls and Sault Ste. Marie, it's well worth the extra time to take this east-west scenic route instead of the direct but dull M-28. Here are directions and highlights, arranged from east (Sault Ste. Marie) to west (the mouth of the Tahquamenon River and Paradise).

♦ Take Bus. I-75/Ashmun/Mackinaw Trail out of Sault Ste. Marie. Stop to pick up brochures and information sheets at the helpful **Hiawatha National Forest office** on Bus. I-75 (906-635-5311). Do not turn onto I-75. Instead, continue south on Mackinaw Trail to Six Mile Road (at the cemetery) and turn left. In a few miles you might enjoy stopping at well-known Great Lakes marine artist Mary Damroske's **Mushroom Cap Studio**, where baskets, pottery, and her own prints and cards are for sale. Look for the blue garage on the north side of the road. After eight miles on Six Mile Road you will reach Lake Shore Road and Brimley.

♦ **Brimley**, a resort hamlet where the Waisko River empties into Lake Superior. Look for the "Cedar Shop" sign just before you reach the big lake, turn down a forested lane, and you'll come to the **Cedar Shop** home business, a charming little spread where lumber dealer Steve LePine sells classic and updated versions of rustic Adirondack furniture made of local white cedar. If he's not in the shop, just walk in. (906) 248-3392.

◆ **Brimley State Park**, right on Lake Superior, is a tidy, small, suburban-style state park with a **picnic area** that has an **outstanding view of freighters** heading to and from the Soo Locks. Modern camping. The **beach** here makes it one of the warmest places to swim in Lake Superior. (906) 248-3422.

◆ **Kings Club Casino** is a small place on the shore road just west of Brimley run by the Bay Mills Indian Community. (906) 248-3227.

◆ **Mission Hill/Spectacle Lake Overlook** offers one of the most memorable scenic panoramas of the entire Upper Peninsula, almost on a par with Brockway Mountain Drive. Here a steep sandstone shelf dramatically towers over the Lake Superior shore. To the left, the white tower of the Iroquois Point lighthouse stands out among the dark pines. If you're lucky, you can see some freighters heading in and out of the Soo Locks, visible to the far right. Call (906) 632-0888 to learn when upbound and downbound ships are due at the locks. Behind it are the Algoma Steel stacks and, blue in the distance, the rugged Laurentian hills of the Algoma Region of Ontario. Just below are Spectacle Lake and Monocle Lake. A plaque remembers Herman and Frances Cameron, an inspirational, community-minded Chippewa couple from Bay Mills who liked to come here "for contemplation and renewal." Follow their example and don't hurry from this serene spot. The inconspicuous turnoff is a little west of the Bay Mills Indian Cemetery. If you continue due west up on the hill, you will arrive at the Dollar Settlement on Whitefish Bay in five bumpy miles.

◆ **Monocle Lake Campground** of the Hiawatha National Forest offers 39 rustic sites (picnic tables, fire ring, pit toilets, hand pump) in a hardwood and birch forest, on 172-acre Monocle Lake, which is stocked with walleye, bass, pike, and perch. Lake Superior and the Point Iroquois light are just a mile away. A **picnic area**, beach, and boat launch are separate from the campsites. A two-mile **hiking trail loop** from the picnic area goes on a boardwalk across a beaver dam and wetland. When the trail comes to a bench in a quarter mile, a spur leads left up the bluff, with another grand **view** overlooking the shipping channel. *From M-28, take M-221 to Brimley, go west on lakeshore 7 miles. (906) 635-5311. Only fills on holiday weekends. $4-6/night.*

Fabulous views of shipping traffic entering
and leaving the St. Marys River near
the Soo Locks can be seen from the
tower of the Point Iroquois
Light Station or from an
even higher overlook
at Mission Hill.
Volunteers
have turned
the light-
house into
a museum.

◆ **The Point Iroquois Light Station and Museum** brings
together all the elements that create the lighthouse mystique for
so many people. The site is memorable. It's in a woods just back
from a beautiful beach with ample deposits of driftwood and colored rocks, including some agates. The 65-foot **tower** offers a
fine view of the shipping lanes at the St. Marys River entrance.
Call (906) 632-0888 to find out when freighters are expected.

The lighthouse has been furnished to give an idea of the life
the lightkeepers led, while other museum rooms show lighthouse
technology and the history of navigational aids. This important
light station housed three families. Betty Byrnes Bacon, who
grew up here, recalled her life at this self-sufficient homestead in
the 1920s in a delightful book, *Lighthouse Memories*. It's available here at the attractive small **museum shop** of the Bay Mills-
Brimley Historical Research Society, who have worked with the
Forest Service to develop this museum. *On Lake Shore Dr. 5
miles west of Brimley and east of Paradise. (906) 437-5272. Open
from Mem. Day thru October 15. Thru Labor Day it's open daily
from 10 a.m. to 5 p.m. and 7 p.m. to 9 p.m. Call for fall hours.
Donations appreciated.*

◆ **Big Pine Picnic Area.** Yet another beautiful **beach,** where
agates might be found, is beyond the pines of the picnic
grounds. Picnic tables, grills, and benches make this a fine place
to linger and see **sunsets.**

◆ **Bay View Campgrounds** of Hiawatha National Forest. Here 24
rustic, private campsites (**picnic tables,** fire ring, pit toilets,
hand pump) are steps away from the sandy Lake Superior
beach. A camp host lives here in summer. *From M-28 at Raco,*

take Forest Road 3154 to Dollar Settlement, turn west (left) 2 miles. (906) 635-5311. $6/night. Fills on many summer weekends and sometimes during the week in hot weather.

◆ **Pendills Creek National Fish Hatchery.** Two million Lake Trout stocked in the Great Lakes come from this hatchery and one nearby. Long tanks are covered with round plastic roofs. Here fry are reared for a year, until five to eight inches long. Then they are released. Visitors can enter the tank buildings and walk across metal catwalks to look down at the masses of little fish. More interesting is the pond of big, dark brood fish, from five to 19 or so years old, weighing four to 12 pounds. Eggs are taken from them in fall, fertilized, incubated for 40 days, and then shipped to the Jordan River Fish Hatchery near Gaylord to be raised to 2 1/2 inches before coming back here to be raised.

Displays and pamphlets show eggs developing into fish and tell the story of how parasitic sea lamprey from Lake Ontario nearly destroyed the Upper Great Lakes fishery in the 1930s before being controlled by a combination of lampricide chemicals and natural predators like the coho salmon. *On Lake Shore Rd. 4 miles west of Dollar Settlement and Forest Rd. 3154. (906) 437- 5231. Open Mon-Fri 8 a.m.-4:30 p.m. Free.*

◆ **Indian Fishing Historical Marker** and **Whitefish Bay roadside park**. A little west of the Pendills Creek Hatchery, this spot offers a sweeping view and an interesting story of how a 1981 Supreme Court case brought by Big Abe LeBlanc of Bay Mills, a leader of the Grand Traverse Band, ruled that Michigan Indians gave up their land in an 1836 treaty but not their right to fish.

◆ **North Country Trail Segment.** An especially scenic part of the long-distance hiking trail is clearly marked at a parking area by Lake Shore Road west of Menekaunce Point. From there it's a one-mile hike to the swinging bridge, and another half mile to Tahquamenon Bay.

◆ **Rivermouth Unit of Tahquamenon Falls State Park.** Good fishing, rustic and modern campgrounds, and a Lake Superior beach. See page 704.

◆ **Paradise** is a pleasant little resort community with several perfectly fine motels and restaurants strung along M-23, where it veers west to Tahquamenon Falls. Due north is the Great Lakes Shipwreck Museum at Whitefish Point (see page 699). Many motels overlook Whitefish Bay.

Great Lakes Shipwreck Historical Museum

Overlooking treacherous Whitefish Bay, it dramatically illuminates hundreds of Lake Superior sinkings.

O n a point of land that forms the entrance to Lake Superior's Whitefish Bay, this museum overlooks an expanse of water to the north called "the graveyard of the Great Lakes." Shipwrecks were common here, because the shipping lanes were congested with ships entering and leaving Lake Superior during the mining booms. High seas from 200 miles of open water to the west compounded the poor visibility from fog, fires, and snow. Most wrecks are from the 19th century, when over 3,000 commercial vessels plied the lakes, compared with just 120 today. Skippers were less experienced, and wood-burning steamers stayed close to the fueling stations on the shore, so they often ran up on rocks and shallows. In an 80-mile stretch from Whitefish Point to Pictured Rocks, there have been over 300 shipwrecks, killing 320 sailors. The first to go under was the *Invincible*, a British schooner which went down in

A museum occupies the former Coast Guard Whitefish Point Light Station complex.

The dramatic Shipwreck Museum grew out of Tom Farnquist's Lake Superior diving experiences. It has gathered outstanding photographs of the many wrecks off Whitefish Point, including the Edmund Fitzgerald.

an 1816 gale; the last was the *Edmund Fitzgerald* in 1975.

The view at the sandy point is beautiful. You can see the Canadian mainland, across water 600 feet deep. Along the beach are countless colored stones worn smooth by water. This was a stopping place for Indians, 17th-century French voyageurs, and Jesuit missionaries.

Whitefish Point is also a favorite flyway for migrating birds (see below). The original lighttower at Whitefish Point was the first on Lake Superior, dating from the early copper boom of 1849. That first light was replaced in 1861 by the unusual iron tower within a framework of triangulated metal supports. The keeper's house, under restoration, opens to visitors in 1995.

A sizable Coast Guard Station developed around the lighthouse. In 1985 it became the home of the Great Lakes Shipwreck Historical Museum, newly founded by Tom Farnquist. He was a Sault Ste. Marie junior high biology teacher and is a longtime diving enthusiast. He and other Great Lakes divers are concerned about the loss of shipwreck artifacts and wanted to share the excitement and history of shipwrecks with a wider public. He has also become expert at underwater photography. Mysterious, evocative photographs of dives, enlarged as backgrounds for exhibits, make this impressive small museum far more compelling than if it merely displayed artifacts.

The museum interior uses eerie, somber music and lights to convey the haunting world of underwater shipwrecks. Models of boats which have sunk in Superior are juxtaposed with items brought up form the depths, such as a ship's bell from the schooner *Niagara,* sunk in 1897, or a carved bird from the steamer *Vienna,* sunk in 1892. The centerpiece is a huge, gleaming lighthouse lens with 344 crystal prisms. An adjoining **theater** shows an entertaining 16-minute film on Great Lakes shipwrecks. For1994 it's about the Edmund Fitzgerald. The **museum shop** sells a well-chosen array of Great Lakes maritime books and gifts and Upper Peninsula souvenirs.

Take M-123 north to the end of Whitefish Rd. past Paradise. (906) 635-1742. Open May 15-Oct. 15, daily 10-6. Adults $4, children $3, families $14.

MICHIGAN'S BEST BIRDWATCHING FOR BIRDS OF PREY . . . . . is when the hawk migration peaks at **Whitefish Point** during late April and early May. Birds use the point poking out into Lake Superior to minimize flying over open water. Fifteen thousand to 25,000 hawks have been counted in a season. Some 7,000 loons come a little later, with ducks and grebes, followed by songbirds through May and early mild June. The Michigan Audubon Society's **Whitefish Point Bird Observatory** is open next to the old Coast Guard Station from March through June, conducting research and banding, especially of raptors (eagles, ospreys, hawks, falcons, etc.). During the last week of April and the first two weeks of May, bird-watchers book up area motels for miles around. Almost 300 species of birds in all have been counted here, including bald and golden eagles, merlin and peregrine falcons, and unusual Arctic birds. All summer long the point, almost surrounded by water, also attracts unusual numbers of water birds, such as Common Loons, Grebes, Cormorants, and Sandhill Cranes. Unusual shorebirds include the Whimbrel, Willet, Marbled and Hudsonian Godwits, and the endangered Piping Plover. Low, windswept dunes, miles of undeveloped beach, and the fun of watching ships make Whitefish Point a fine place to spend the day. *Call (616) 344-8648 for more information.*

MAGNIFICENT VIEWS OF WHITEFISH BAY . . . . . can be had from the **Point Iroquois lighttower** (page 697), 55 miles southeast of Whitefish Point on the scenic shore road to Sault Ste. Marie, and from the nearby **Spectacle Lake Overlook** (page 696). For information on ships approaching and passing through the locks, call the Corps of Engineers at the Soo Locks (906-632-0888).

Tahquamenon Falls

Spectacular views of Michigan's most majestic falls,
a tourist magnet in a huge wilderness park

Most Michigan waterfalls are attractive but puny affairs compared with the mighty falls of the world. Michigan's one really substantial waterfall is the **Upper Falls** here at Tahquamenon. The falls are nearly 200 feet across, and as much as 50,000 gallons of water a second plunge 48 feet into a canyon below. The state park has constructed an exciting platform that allows you to stand right at the lip of the falls, so you can take in the dramatic contrast between the serene meanderings of the upper Tahquamenon River and the roaring foam below the falls. The river is darkened by tannic acid from the many hemlocks, cedars, and spruces along its banks, which gives the initial spill of water an interesting brownish hue.

The stairway to this memorable vantage point is reached by turning right as you go from the parking lot to the falls. It's a .4 mile walk to the falls. From this same viewing platform you see, far downstream, the once-again peaceful river as it flows between reddish bluffs another 10 miles towards Lake Superior's Whitefish Bay south of Paradise. The left trail from the parking area leads to a less spectacular view of the falls from the lower river.

A .8 mile **interpretive nature trail** leads from the platform at the Upper Falls. Pick up a **brochure** at the trailhead.

In midday in July and August, the crowds and cars by the Upper Falls can be overwhelming. If you don't like being part of a herd, but you're here in July or the first half of August, try coming before 10 a.m. (the earlier the better) or after 6 p.m. Remember, it stays light until 10 p.m. up here. Another reason to go earlier or later: the light effects and wildlife are best in the early morning and evening.

Energetic and fit hikers might well prefer approaching the Upper Falls by foot, for maximum dramatic impact. An up-and-down riverside **trail** of medium difficulty follows the Tahquamenon River for four miles upstream from the trailhead at the Lower Falls to the Upper Falls, crossing smaller streams on boardwalks along the way. Once at the Upper Falls, of course, you need to walk four miles back.

At the Upper Falls visitors are greeted by an unusually striking log building, called **Camp 33** to recall the logging company that originally owned most of the state park. The high-ceilinged timberframe structure was built with oak posts and beams (no nails) which are exposed on the interior. It houses an unusually impressive souvenir shop with a good selection of regional books and materials about nature. The concessionaires who erected the building and run the store are descendants of the lumberman who donated the parkland to the state.

The buildings and seating of the **picnic area** and **restaurant** terrace outside Camp 33 are designed around a central fireplace, the way old logging camps had buildings clustered around a central fire pit. They look out into the surrounding forest of big trees, well separated from the massive parking area. The restaurant serves homemade pasties, cooked-to-order hamburgers, and similar fare.

The **Lower Falls**, four miles downstream, is smaller but in its own serene way equally delightful. Here the Tahquamenon River drops 22 feet in a series of cascades that surround a sizable island and a series of boulders. You can view the series of falls

At the Upper Tahquamenon Falls, the Tahquamenon River drops dramatically down from the sandstone cliff that underlies the glacial soils of the area. This is the same sandstone cliff or escarpment that forms the Pictured Rocks, only here it is inland.

from a high bluff, but for about $1 a person you can rent a row-boat which takes you much closer. A **footpath** goes right up to the falls. When it's warm enough, visitors enjoy wading in the cascading water at their own risk.

There's a **picnic area** along the river and an **Elias Brothers Big Boy** restaurant by the parking lot.

Spectacular **fall color** peaks here well into October, later than much of the U.P. A mix of maple, birch, and pine makes for rich yellows and reds contrasted with dark green. An easy, flat trail into the forest is the four-mile **Giant Pine Loop** that begins at the brink of the Upper Falls and passes by some very old white pines. This trail is groomed for **cross-country skiing** in winter.

Park visitors are concentrated so intensely at the two falls, it's easy to forget that this 40,000-acre park is Michigan's second-biggest state park, stretching 13 miles west from Whitefish Bay at the Tahquamenon River's mouth, and that most of it is a designated **wilderness area** where you won't see a powerline or hear a car.

Trails up to 13 miles long enable hikers to get away from the crowds. They pass by many habitats, including pine forests, sandy ridges, and boggy lakes typical of the eastern Upper Peninsula, and a **virgin beech-maple climax forest** some three centuries old. Avoid the swampy areas during black fly season, usually from May through most of June.

Don't expect too well-tended trails. Budget cutbacks have cut parks staff. "We try to at least keep the windfalls off," a park ranger said. Waterproof footgear is recommended. Twelve miles of the **North Country Trail** (see page 696) pass through the park. A series of three **wilderness lakes** with northern pike and perch can be reached by an access road to Clark Lake and a half-mile portage to Betsy Lake. Ask park staff for details.

Below the Lower Falls the Tahquamenon River offers the park's best **fishing**: northern pike, muskies, and walleye, plus a steelhead run in early spring and late October. **Swimming** can be done at the river's mouth in Paradise — if you can tolerate cold water.

Campgrounds here are modern (electricity, hot showers, the works) and wooded, but sites are not large (30 to 45 feet wide). At the Lower Falls, the 87-site **Riverbend Campground** has a few sites right on the river. The **Overlook Campground** has 100 sites. Both are modern. The **Rivermouth Campground** has 76 modern sites and 55 rustic sites (showers $2 extra).

*On M-123, 15 miles west of Paradise. Open year-round. State
park sticker required; $4/day, or $18/year. (906)
492-3415.*

TWO BOAT CRUISES TO THE UPPER FALLS . . . . . both come with recommendations. We prefer the **Toonerville Trolley and Riverboat Trip** because it uses a real narrow-gauge train over old logging track (like the Detroit Zoo's) drawn by a five-ton diesel locomotive originally used in mines. Third-generation tour operators, descended from the original loggers, provide live narration that focuses on Ojibway lore, logging history, and flora and fauna seen on the all-day trip. Corny jokes are rare. The train takes 35 minutes to reach the Tahquamenon River. There a 350-passenger boat with a cafeteria, restrooms, and enclosed, open, and covered decks takes passengers for two hours (21 miles) down a remote part of the river inaccessible by roads. Passengers get out before a rapids and walk 5/8 of a mile each way toward the thundering falls before they finally come into view. *Train leaves Soo Junction (about 2 miles north of M-28 and 12 miles east of Newberry) at 10:30 a.m., returns at 5. Come by 10 or so. Operates daily, June 15-October 6. (906) 876-2311; (906) 293-3806 (winter). Reservations recommended for holiday weekends. $15/adult, $7 children 6-15. Under 6 free.* . . . . . For information about the **Tom Sawyer Riverboat Cruise and Paul Bunyan Timber Train** leaving from Hulbert Corners, 12 miles north of M-28, call (906) 876-2331/(906) 632-3727. It involves a river cruise first, followed by a rubber-tired "train" and hike.

CANOEING THE TAHQUAMENON . . . . . The only canoe livery is just north of Newberry, at M-123 and CR 462. **Mark's Rod & Reel Repair and Canoe Livery** offers very beautiful, 2-hour paddles from the Dollarville Dam east to the Tahquamenon River Logging Museum in Newberry, and longer trips farther down the river into the gorgeous, wild country above the dam. A four-day or so trip to the falls, with camping anywhere you can find a clear spot, is for experienced canoeists. There's good fishing for pike, muskie, walleye, and panfish. Cost: $25 for spotting and taking you and your canoe to the put-in point, plus $15/day rental fee. (906) 293-5608.

A SURPRISING FIND . . . . . is the unassuming roadside **Tahquamenon River Logging Museum** and **Nature Study Area** just north of Newberry on M-123. Parts of it are typically dreary displays of tools and equipment without vitalizing ideas or stories. But the **local history displays** in the old house are excellent, and the **interpretive nature trail** leading back through a woods and swamp to a scenic river overlook gives a remarkably clear explanation of northwoods tree species. If you can see the top-notch logging **video**

done by Wendell Hoover, Hartwick Pines' logging historian, you'll gain a new appreciation of the social history of logging and the lives of shanty boys. (They never called themselves "lumberjacks.") Lively old-time **music jamborees** are held on the fourth weekends of July and August. The music starts about noon and lasts until everyone gets tired. *On M-123 at Tahquamenon River, 1 1/2 miles north of Newberry. (906) 293-3700. Open 9-5 daily from Memorial thru Labor Day. $3/adults includes tour of nature trail and buildings and slide show.*

GOOD CANOEING NOT FAR FROM THE FALLS . . . . . Two Hearted Canoe Trips can arrange a wonderful, easy four- to six-hour family canoe trip ($20/canoe) to its pleasantly rustic Rainbow Lodge and Campground at the river's mouth on Lake Superior, or two- and three-day trips for experienced canoeists. (906) 658-3357, or (906) 293-5533 in winter. Hemingway appropriated the Two-Hearted River's memorable name and gave it to the river Nick Adams fished in, but actually Hemingway fished the Fox, which flows through Seney into the Manistique River and Lake Michigan.

HIKE FROM MARQUETTE TO ST. IGNACE . . . . . , over 200 miles, along the completed sections of the **North Country Trail**. It goes from Marquette through the Pictured Rocks and Muskallonge State Park on Lake Superior and the Hiawatha National Forest, passing by the Lower Tahquamenon Falls along the way. For a big brochure, contact the National Parks/ National Forest Service visitor center, (906) 387-3700; 400 E. Munising Ave., Munising, MI 49862. Eventually the trail will extend from the Appalachian Trail in New York State to North Dakota.

Seney National Wildlife Refuge

For seeing a splendid range of northwoods wildlife,
little can match this vast domain.

Even for people with a casual interest in wildlife, the enormous 95,000-acre refuge southwest of Seney is a magic place where it's easy to get an intimate look at many different northwoods wildlife habitats. Even motorists driving along the wildlife drive may see eagles, trumpeter swans, and loons feeding. Bicyclists using the 80 miles of trails along dikes and back roads can stop and see an occasional black bear and signs of elusive wolves and moose who live in the refuge. Birders intent on expanding their lists of birds sometimes drive thousands of miles to spot the yellow rail or black backed three-toed woodpecker found here.

Hints for finding wildlife to watch are conveyed through excellent interpretive displays in the visitor center and through signs along the wildlife drive. Knowledgeable staff can direct visitors to unusual habitats such as recently burned areas and different types of bogs.

The story of the north woods is essentially many variations on one epic theme: exploiting natural resources, done by trapping from about 1650 into the 1830s and by logging in the 19th and early 20th centuries. There was the Big Cut and the boom that went with it, and then there was the inevitable bust — the cutover land and devastated local economies, and all the different ways various people responded, from local and state political leaders to railroads to agricultural researchers to early conservationists to loggers-turned-farmers to real estate promoters.

The story of the Seney National Wildlife Refuge, a huge (95,000 acres) and peaceful wetlands draining into the Manistique River between Newberry and Munising, is told through an orientation slide show and a well-written display at the refuge's visitor center. From 1881 to 1900 the area was logged off. Fires swept many cutover lands, including the Great Manistique Swamp here. A decade later, land speculators started to drain this marsh to develop it for farming. They failed, but waterfowl diminished because their habitat was lost. Most of this

Fish in the refuge's wetlands are managed to provide plenty of food for Bald Eagles and other fish-eating birds and mammals. Visitors have a very good chance of seeing eagles.

land — like much poor land across the U.S. — reverted to the government for nonpayment of taxes during the Depression. Such land, through farsighted parks and recreation plans of the 1930s, became the cores of many public parks.

Conservationists organized to try to protect the threatened waterfowl. The state of Michigan asked the Roosevelt administration to include the Seney land among the submarginal farmlands to be developed as waterfowl refuges. In 1935, using funds from duck stamps, and labor from the Civilian Conservation Corps and WPA, an intricate system of dikes and dams created thousands of acres of permanent marshes for waterfowl at Seney. They planted aquatic plants favored by ducks and geese: pondweed, bulrushes, duck weed, wild rice, wild celery, and more.

Today the refuge is managed to create wet and dry cycles that mimic nature by controlling water levels. (Because the pools are man-made, wet-dry cycles can't occur naturally.) Controlled fire imitates the beneficial effects of lightning-caused fires, for instance, clearing underbrush, creating tender young growth for deer, and heating jack pine cones until they burst and seed.

Though wildlife management is the refuge's main purpose, much has been done for visitors. The visitor center, 1.5-mile nature trail, and seven-mile marshland wildlife drive have become popular Upper Peninsula attractions. Recently the back roads and dikes have been opened to bicycles and hikers, making for nearly **80 miles of bike and hiking trails**, ideally suited for viewing wildlife, where mountain bikes are welcome. **Canoeing** is encouraged along the Manistique River. For information on canoe and mountain bike rentals, see page 710.

Plan your visit so you'll be able to view wildlife in the early morning or evening, when birds and mammals are most active. Hours at the outstanding visitor center are from 9 to 5, but the drive, trails, and paths are open from sunup to sundown. Over 200 species of birds and 50 species of mammals, including the Eastern timber wolf, have been recorded here. A bird list is available at the visitor center. A detailed **map and guide** to the entire refuge is available off-hours in the rack in front of the Visitor Center or, in the off-season, at the main office next door. As part of the refuge's "Watchable Wildlife Program," the map includes hints for seeing wildlife, and marks places and habitats where certain kinds of wildlife are often seen.

Main visitor attractions include:

◆ **Visitor Center.** Excellent displays, a knowledgeable staff, and the Seney Natural History Association's small **nature bookshop** make this a good first stop for orientation. A new multi-projector **slide/tape introduction to the refuge**, 15 minutes long, tells visitors what they can expect to do and see here. The loon exhibit invites visitors to hear the four main calls of the loon while seeing a beautiful diorama of a loon swimming with its offspring on its back. A short video shows loons in action. Loons are plentiful in the refuge because it meets their three main requirements: for clean water; quiet, undisturbed nesting islands; and a good supply of fish to eat.

Leaflets describe the refuge's policy and opportunities for hunting and fishing. Northern pike, bullheads, and perch are the most common fish caught on refuge pools. Get information on the nature trail, driving loop, and back roads (closed to vehicles). Visitors can **borrow binoculars**, a bird guide, and a flower guide at no cost. *Open daily May 15-October 15, 9 a.m. to 5 p.m. (906) 586-9851. Everything except the women's restroom is handicap-accessible. Free admission.*

◆ **Marshland Wildlife Drive.** This seven-mile self-guided auto tour on a one-way gravel road connects three observation decks (each with scopes provided) in favorite habitats where Trumpeter Swans; loons and osprey; and Bald Eagles can sometimes be seen. The speed limit is 15 mph. **Interpretive signs** are most informative. Deer, beaver, turtles, waterfowl, and wading birds are also plentiful. Motorists are encouraged to get out of their cars and walk along dikes and back roads to improve their chances of seeing more wildlife. Binoculars can be borrowed at the visitor center. An extra **fish loop** adds three more miles and three handicap-accessible **fishing platforms** to the drive. Narrow clearances and car traffic make it more enjoyable for bicyclists to use back roads, and they'll see more wildlife, too. *The wildlife drive starts near the visitor center and ends on M-77, just south of the main refuge entrance. It's open from May 15 through September 30, daylight hours only.*

◆ **Pine Ridge Nature Trail.** A 1.4 mile loop with interpretive signs takes visitors past many kinds of wildflowers. It's a peaceful experience except for the sound of nearby road noise.

◆ **Backcountry paths** along dikes and service roads offer hikers and bicyclists 80 miles of prime wildlife viewing. Intersections are clearly marked so users can easily plot their routes and see where they are on the detailed refuge map. Surfaces are varied. Hard-packed gravel and sand work fine for bikes with narrow tires in most conditions, but mountain bikes would be better, especially after rain.

◆ **Northern Hardwood Cross-Country Ski Area.** Ten miles of groomed trails, usually ski-able from mid or late December into March. Trails start at the parking lot off M-77, half a mile south of Germfask. For snow conditions, call (906) 586-9851.

◆ **Canoeing** can be done on several of the refuge's streams. The Manistique River is the only stream that can be easily canoed through the refuge during the allotted daylight hours. Canoeing is not allowed on the refuge pools or marshes. There are three

Nearly a hundred miles of back roads and dikes make it easy for mountain bikers to get away from road noise and traffic and increase their chances of seeing wildlife.

popular places to put in: at Northland Outfitters on the north edge of Germfask off M-77, at the Big Cedar Campground, a private campground in Germfask (906-586-6684), and at the pretty picnic area between M-77 and the Manistique River about a mile south of Germfask. Canoeists end up at the 10-campsite Mead Creek Campground of Lake Superior State Forest on County Road 436 south of the wildlife refuge.

The main entrance to the Visitor Center is on M-77, 2 miles north of Germfask and 5 miles south of Seney on M-28. Between May 15 and September 30 the Marshland Driving Tour is open between sundown and sunset. The Visitor Center is open from May 15 to Oct. 30 between 9 and 5. (906) 586-9856. Visitor use of the refuge is limited to daylight hours. In the off-season, the entrance to ski trailsstarts at the parking lot off M-77, half a mile south of Germfask. Admission is free.

CANOE, KAYAK AND MOUNTAIN BIKE RENTALS . . . . . are at **Northland Outfitters** on the north edge of Germfask just east off M-77, 1 1/2 miles south of the refuge entrance. (906) 586-9801. Its large, shady campgrounds for RVs and tents are near the river in a pretty spot. They can arrange for short two- and four-hour trips on the Manistique and long, multi-day canoe trips on the Manistique and Fox rivers and the Big Island Lake Complex. . . . Canoes may also be rented at the **Big Cedar Campground**, a private campground in Germfask. (906) 586-6684.

THE TOWN THAT WAS SOLD ALL AT ONCE . . . . . Twelve miles south of the Seney National Wildlife Refuge on M-77, the town of **Blaney Park** began as the company town of the Wisconsin Land and Lumber Company, which innovated the tongue-and-groove hardwood flooring still used today (page 00). Then it was the Blaney Park Resort, a popular outdoorsman's resort during the 1940s and 1950s. The resort declined and the town was sold at auction in the mid-1980s. Now the new owners of Blaney Park, a diverse crew largely of urban refugees, have breathed new life into the store, the Blaney Inn Restaurant, the Blaney Camp 9 cottages, and the Celibeth House inn (see *Hunts' Restaurants and Lodgings of Michigan*). The store, right on M-77, has aspects of a funny, funky museum.

Grand Marais and vicinity

A tranquil, picturesque refuge on Lake Superior

The simple little village of Grand Marais sits in splendid isolation on an unusually well protected Lake Superior harbor. West Bay offered such good protection to 17th-century French explorers that they gave it the name "marais," which means "harbor of refuge." The town sits up from the bay, giving most locations a splendid view of the water. This far north, the sun doesn't set until after 10 p.m. in June, and the beautiful afterglow on the lake can last until 11.

The older houses in Grand Marais date from its boom years between 1860 and 1910, when it was an active fishing and lumber port full of saloons and lumber mills. It then lay nearly dormant for over half a century until revived by resorters and tourists attracted to the quiet scenic beauty. Their aluminum-sided ranch homes now seem to outnumber the simple older homes.

Today Grand Marais makes for a tranquil, out-of-the way base from which to explore the unspoiled forests, dunes, and beaches that surround it. At the end of a single blacktop road, this village is really at the end of the line. And a surprising number of urban refugees are well aware of its special quality. Novelist and poet Jim Harrison escapes to his cabin near here when his Lake Leelanau home gets too busy with summer visitors. Ann Arbor songwriter Jay Stielstra set his popular North Country Opera in a fictionalized Grand Marais bar where the women's restroom is marked "Setters" and the men's room "Pointers."

Grand Marais has some 400 year-round residents today; its size triples in summer. From any of several downtown lodgings, you can walk a very short distance down to the city park on West Bay. Lake Superior's open water is less than a mile north on a sandy spit. The sand is less rocky in adjacent East Bay, but there aren't many days in the year when most visitors will want to brave the cold Lake Superior water. It's warmest when the wind blows in from the north, piling the warmer top water towards the shoreline.

You would expect Grand Marais to be at its most tranquil in winter. Ironically, snowmobiles make it a jarring time to visit.

The noisy machines converge here some weekends, when local merchants report doing as much business as during the height of the summer season. Winter weekends are the worst; weekdays arc likely to be a good deal quieter. One way to be sure to have peace and quite is to rent snowshoes from the Lakeview Inn ($7/day) and hike over the snow either east or west of town. Along the bluffs either east or west of town are pristine state forests and fine views of Lake Superior. If you head west toward Sable Falls, you'll likely run into sizable herds of nearly tame deer.

The short peninsula that forms West Bay leads to a lighthouse and Coast Guard station, home of the Grand Marais **Maritime Museum** (open weekends 10-6, July through Labor Day). Displays in the small museum are done in the minimalist style typical of the National Parks Service that spotlights a few objects: the third-order Fresnel Lens from the nearby Au Sable light tower, a breeches buoy used by lifesavers, some photos of local fishermen and the Lifesaving Station. The toilet in the ladies room is in almost the very place where the Coast Guard radioman last made contact with the Edmund Fitzgerald.

Nearby, a stone pier protecting the harbor entrance holds the front range light. A nearby bungalow houses the folksy museum of the **Grand Marais Historical Society** (906-494-2725), open Tuesday thru Sunday from 1-4 from late June thru Labor Day, weekends only in September, and by appointment. It's devoted to commercial fishermen, who "have seen the works of the Lord and its wonders in the deep."

Go west along the shore to come to another beach extending miles to the west: the famous **agate beach**, where even novices can find the variegated, translucent stones of quartz while strolling along the shoreline looking through the clear water. Banded agates are formed by liquid quartz in cavities of preexisting rock, which may have a pitted potato-skin texture. Most common are shattered pieces with distinctive agate banding. (The colors are formed by different impurities.) Some people find more where the bank meets the beach. A one-mile walk down the beach and you're at the mouth of Sable Creek. A short path along the creek leads up to the delightful **Sable Falls**.

Several highlights of the Pictured Rocks National Lakeshore (pages 717-721) are most accessible from Grand Sable Get information at nearby Grand Marais Visitor Center (page 715). Going west from town, these include:

◆ **Sable Falls** off H-58 about a mile west of Grand Marais. A delightful half-mile walk and stairway take you through a forest and reveal the falls and Lake Superior in tantalizing glimpses before letting you look down on the entire cascade from the rocky shelf that forms it. Continue down and along Sable Creek, then go right (east) to get to the **agate beach** (see above).

◆ **The Grand Sable Bank and Dunes** are best seen by taking the

The **Log Slide, 300 feet** above Lake Superior, offers distant views of the Au Sable Point Lighttower and the Grand Sable Banks. Decades ago, loggers rolled logs down from it to waiting lumber schooners.

footpath back from Sable Falls a ways and picking up another half-mile walk across the creek to the dunes. First you pass through a jack pine forest, then enter a bleak dunescape where only a few hardy plant pioneers like marram grass can take hold. Excellent interpretive displays explain the principles of plant succession in the beach's harsh, dry, hot/cold, nutrient-deficient environment. You can also see a small **ghost forest** of trees overwhelmed by sand.

The banks and dunes, seen from this vantage point midway up their 275-foot height, seem dramatic and overwhelming. They are entirely bare and blindingly blank on a sunny day, slanting into Lake Superior at the steep, 35 degree angle of repose common to all piles of dry sand. The banks stretch west for five miles, down to the Log Slide. Don't be tempted to walk down to the lake here; walking back up the sand would be very difficult.

♦ At its **Grand Sable Visitor Center**, on H-58 about five miles west of Grand Marais, you can find free information on the National Lakeshore, including campgrounds, day hikes, and backcountry camping along the 43-mile **Lakeshore Trail** along the entire shoreline. Displays and a small **bookstore** focus on the area's natural and human history. *On H-58 about 5 miles west of Grand Marais. (906) 494-2669. Open from late May thru mid September, from at least 9-5 daily. Open to 7 from mid June thru early September.*

♦ **Log Slide.** This high point of the ridge along Lake Superior is almost 300 feet above the water. In the late 19th century loggers rolled and slid logs down a 500-foot slide on the sharp incline, to be loaded on Great Lakes lumber schooners. It is well located for fine views of the Grand Sable Banks and Dunes to the east and the Au Sable Point lighthouse to the west. *Off H-58 about 8 miles west of Grand Marais and 24 miles east of Munising.*

♦ **Au Sable Point Light and Lighthouse**. The red brick lightkeeper's house and attached white cylinder of a tower sit atop picture-perfect red sandstone rocks. The lighthouse and tower are being restored but not yet open to the public, except on free **guided walks**. Call (906) 387-3700 for schedule. In any case, the easy 1 1/2-mile walk from the Hurricane River Campgrounds (3 miles round-trip) is worthwhile. Climb down the rocks from the lighthouse and go west a ways, and you'll come upon some shipwreck skeletons sticking out of the sand.

♦ **Twelvemile Beach.** This long sand and pebble beach is

approached from the road through a beautiful white birch forest. Swimming here is awfully cold, but the beach is fine for picnics and walks along the Lakeshore Trail. At the Twelvemile Beach campground, 38 shady, private rustic campsites with tent pads and hand pumps ($8 a night per car) sit on a bluff overlooking the lake. A two-mile interpretive **nature trail** takes you through the beautiful and unusual **White Birch Forest** of large birches. Sun-loving pioneers after forest fires and cutting, birches are normally soon shaded by more adaptable maples. Here they have thrived longer, thanks to moist soils and plenty of sunlight. (The birches can also be seen from H-58.) *Take H-58 (unpaved) about 15 miles west of Grand Marais or about 37 miles east of Munising.*

FOR PICNICS ALONG THE SHORE . . . . . you can pick up excellent smoked whitefish sausage, smoked turkey, cheese, and fresh baked bread at **Lefebvre's Fish Market & Bakery** on Harbor Street east of downtown.

CAMPING AT THE NATIONAL LAKESHORE . . . . . is at scenic, rustic campgrounds. **Campfire interpretive programs** make them special. Hurricane River and Twelvemile Beach are near Grand Marais, Little Beaver Lake is midway between it and Munising. The 67 spots are available on a first-come, first-serve basis. To get a spot in July and August, come early and wait for someone to leave. Self-registration at the site. $5 fee.

BEAUTIFUL U. P. CAMPGROUNDS WHERE YOU CAN ALMOST ALWAYS FIND A SPOT . . . . . are the rustic campgrounds on **U. S. Forest Service** national forest land. They don't have amenities (showers, electricity, pump-out stations), but they don't have the crowds, either. $5/night fee; self-registration at the site. Most are on lakes — either Lake Michigan, Lake Superior (by Tahquamenon Bay and also west of Munising), or a smaller lake. The 860,000-acre **Hiawatha National Forest** has 10 campgrounds near St. Ignace and Sault Ste. Marie, and 15 more from Munising and Escanaba to Manistique and Rapid River. For a map of all campgrounds, call (906) 387-3700, write USFS, 400 E. Munising Ave., Munising, MI 49862, or stop by the **Park Service/ Forest Service visitor center** in Munising at M-78 and H-58 in Munising.

Pictured Rocks National Lakeshore

Colorful cliffs meet clear, green Lake Superior in a series of memorable views, with many waterfalls and miles of wilderness hiking and canoe trails nearby

This extraordinary 43 miles of shoreline, extending from Munising to Grand Marais, contains some of Michigan's most remarkable scenery. Most famous are the **Pictured Rocks**, only visible from the water, and best seen toward sunset. Most see it by taking a three-hour boat cruise from Munising. Arrive early to get a seat on the top deck, the best place to view the scenery. The cruise begins by passing 14,600-acre **Grand Island**, once the private retreat of Cleveland-Cliffs Iron Company, today a primitive (i.e., unimproved) recreation area that recently became part of the National Lakeshore. It's soon to be developed. A delightful wooden lighthouse from 1869 is on its eastern shore.

Superior's beautiful blue-green water contrasts strikingly with the towering cliffs, over 200 feet high. The colors of the sandstone cliffs are subtle. Blues and greens result from the presence of copper, the reddish hues from iron. In mid-day on a glary day they can be washed out; the 5 p.m. cruise in July and

[Top photo] Shoreline erosion at different lake levels created these caves near Bridal Veil Falls. The Pictured Rocks boat cruise enters one of the caves if waters are calm enough.

August would be best.

Because the scenery is so striking, Pictured Rocks was designated the first National Lakeshore in the U.S. in 1966. That means it's administered by the National Park Service.

The **Hiawatha National Forest/Pictured Rocks National Lakeshore Visitor Information Center** is a highly recommended first stop for anyone planning to spend a day or more at Pictured Rocks or the Munising area in general. It is on M-28 and H-28 in Munising. Its staff is equipped with a wide range of information not only on the national lakeshore but on the less heavily used Munising District of the Hiawatha National Forest. Its campgrounds consist of easily accessible ones on Lake Superior at Bay Furnace and on Au Train Lake, as well as four more remote ones on lakes, accessible from Highway 13.

The Visitor Center has maps and handouts for the Hiawatha National Forest's remote, gorgeous **Big Island Lake Wilderness Area** south of Munising. There's no road access to these 23 small lakes, from 5 to 149 acres, which are linked by waterways or by marked portage trails. Motors are banned. Canoeists can camp in designated spaces or choose their own sites. Abundant wildlife includes eagles and many loons.

Maps to some 16 miles of groomed **cross-country ski trails** are available. A stimulating array of free **guided nature walks and programs** are held daily (often two times a day and around the campfire at night) from July 1 through Labor Day. Topics include "Shipwrecks and Lighthouses," stargazing, area farms and iron furnaces, black bear research and activity, and bird and nature walks. Call (906) 387-3700 to plan your trip around programs that interest you.

The Visitor Center has some displays and an excellent small bookstore of relevant nature books and area history, plus USGS maps and trail maps for hiking and canoeing in the national forest and national lakeshore. The helpful staff is happy to mail information sheets on many specific features of the national forest and lakeshore, upon request. *The Visitor Center is at M-28 and H-58. (906) 387-2512. Open year-round. From May thru Oct. 15, open 9-5 daily (to 6 from mid June thru mid September). Off-season: open Mon-Sat 9-4:30.*

Two routes connect Pictured Rocks' major sights and campgrounds. The 43-mile **Lakeshore Trail** is the only route that follows the shoreline. Several designated backcountry campsites are along the way. (Permits, available from either visitor center,

are necessary for this.) Trailheads are at Sand Point or Munising
Falls at the Munising end, and at the Grand Marais Visitor
Center. Typical hiking time: three nights and four days. The
Altran shuttle runs Monday and Friday with a 10 a.m. pickup
at Munising Falls and 11:30 a.m. at Grand Marais. It will drop
off hikers at any point along H-58. No bicycles are allowed on
trails. Hikers might well consider hiking part of the trail — say,
from the Munising trailhead to Sand Point and Miners Castle
(about 6 miles) and an additional mile through the woods to
Miners Falls, for a 12-to-14 mile round trip. Or time your hike so
the Altran trolley can take you back. (Call 906-387-4845.) You
might even ask them if they could drop you off somewhere else.

By car, **H-58** is a gravel road through the forest, some three
to six miles inland. Only for a mile between the Twelvemile
Beach and Hurricane River Campgrounds does it offer a Lake
Superior view. Jigging and jogging, it takes some 53 miles to get
from Munising to Grand Marais. Additional drives north to sights
along the lake only increase the tedious trip. By the time you've
bumped along for 15 or 20 miles on it, you'll be carsick and
bored with the forest's beauty. Plan carefully to minimize driving
and break it up with stops and walks along the way.

Sights of exceptional interest along the shore, arranged from
Munising to Grand Marais, are:

◆ **Munising Falls**. This slender, exceptionally attractive falls has
a dramatic 50-foot drop into a small, rocky canyon. In winter the
sight is equally spectacular when the column of water is frozen.
The pleasant, 800-foot path to the falls used to wind in a loop
just *behind* the falls, but the biggest rockfall in the lakeshore's
recent history has changed the path. The excellent **interpretive
center** at the parking lot gives historical perspective on the
region's geology and logging history. It's next to the site of an
1868 blast furnace which made 16 tons of pig iron a day. *On
H-58 about 2 miles east of downtown Munising and the intersection of M-28 and H-58. Unstaffed center is open May 1 through
Oct. 31, daily 8:30-4:30.*

◆ **Sand Point and beach.** From this point of land jutting out
toward Grand Island, you get a good view of the island and the
city of Munising. In the evening there is a distant **view of the
Pictured Rocks**. (They're shaded in the morning.) The beach just
south of the point is one of the warmer **swimming spots** in Lake
Superior. Local swimmers point out that once you get acclimated
to the chilly water, you don't feel the cold. *East of Munising a lit-*

*tle over a mile on H-58, then left on Washington St. 1/2 mile to
Sand Point Rd. North 2 miles.*

◆ **Miners Castle and Falls.** A spectacular view looks down at an
emerald-green Lake Superior cove from high upon a majestic,
castle-like cliff, a single great stone some nine stories tall. The
clearness of the water lets you see the rocky bottom even at considerable depths. The Pictured Rocks cliffs can be seen from land
here, but the orientation means the light is never right for a good
view. Another trail leads to a nice, long **beach** just northeast of
Miners Castle. Farther inland, off Miners Castle Road and accessible via a half-mile trail, is **Miners Falls**, one of the Upper
Peninsula's larger falls, with a 70-foot drop. Towards the end of
the trail to it is a panoramic view of Lake Superior in the distance. *Take H-58 east from Munising. In about 7 miles, turn north
on Miners Castle Rd. for 6 miles to Miners Castle, which is handicap-accessible.*

◆ **Au Sable Light, Hurricane River Campground, Log Slide,
Grand Sable Dunes, Sable Falls, and Maritime Museum** are all
most easily accessible from Grand Marais. See pages 712-717.

*Pictured Rock Boat Cruises leave from downtown Munising
from June thru early October. Call for times and reservations.
(906) 387-2379. Adults $18, children 12 and under $7, under 5
free. The 37-mile trip takes 2 hours and 40 minutes.*

*Pictured Rocks National Lakeshore's super-helpful **main visitor
center** is at the junction of M-28 and H-58 in Munising. See page
718 for hours. Open year-round. Call (906) 387-3700 to get a general or backpackers' visitor packet. The **Grand Sable visitor
center** is on H-58 about 5 miles west of Grand Marais. open from
late May thru mid September. See page 715 for hours. No fees for
national lakeshore except for developed campgrounds.*

TRIPS TO GRAND ISLAND . . . . . The same cruise service company taking
visitors to the Pictured Rocks also provides ferry service to Grand Island. The
island is 27 miles in circumference, bigger than Mackinac Island. Much of
its shoreline consists of dramatic, high sandstone cliffs. Two bays have
sandy **beaches** and pretty **campsites,** but you must bring your own water. It
has **hiking trails, mountain bike trails,** places to camp and fish, but few
other improvements. It was recently designated a national recreation area,
but improvements are still in the planning stages. *2 trips a day in June and*

September, 3 in July and August. Round-trip fares are about $10/adults, $5/children 5-12, under 5/free. Mountain bikes are $3 extra. (906) 387-2379.

10 MILES SOUTHEAST OF MUNISING . . . . . take a quick **tour of Iverson Snowshoes** in Shingleton. It's one of only two wood-frame snowshoe factories remaining in the U.S. You will see how workers take long strips of white ash, steam them to increase their flexibility, bend them around a form and dry them in a kiln overnight. The labor-intensive job includes hand-lacing with traditional rawhide or more durable neoprene. The handsome pairs cost $65 to $110, including harness. Snowshoes are easy to use and practical. Iverson's makes nine models for different purposes. *Turn north on Maple St., two blocks west of Shingleton's only blinker. (906) 452-6370.*

SHIPWRECK SIGHTSEEING AND DIVING . . . . . in the Alger Underwater Preserve off Munising is easily arranged through Capt. Pete Lindquist's **Grand Island Charters** (906-387-4477). **Shipwreck cruises** at 10 a.m. and 5 p.m. leave from the Munising dock and take visitors out to look down at three wrecks close to the surface, in clear water, and also offer views of sandstone bluffs on Grand Island and the Pictured Rocks. Reserve places on the 2 1/2-hour cruise the night before. $15 adults, $7.50 12 and under. Lindquist also takes divers out to wrecks (there are eight); a diving instructor is on his staff. . . . . . Clear waters and eroded underwater "caves" are other area attractions. Call the Alger Chamber of Commerce, (906) 387-2138, for a **dive brochure**.

Marquette

Blessed with beautiful views, imposing buildings,
a wonderful city park, and an interesting downtown

In contrast to the sleepy, depressed look of many Upper Peninsula towns, this city of 23,000 is an uncommonly attractive place to visit. Marquette has been an important port since the 1850s, when the Soo Locks opened up shipping throughout the Great Lakes. The city rises sharply from the lake, giving pleasant views of Presque Isle harbor and Marquette Bay. These are punctuated by dramatic landmarks: the ore docks, the old red lighthouse, and Presque Isle, a beautiful park jutting out into Lake Superior.

Marquette has more for visitors to see and do than any other single place north of the bridge. **Northern Michigan University**, with its 8,900 students, gives economic stability to the city, as does a large regional hospital complex and a maximum-security prison. Thanks to the area's logrolling former state representative, Dominic Jacobetti of Negaunee, the U.P.'s patron saint, the university campus now has the "Yooper Dome" (officially known as the Superior Dome), which hovers like a weird space station on the horizon from many vantage points. The 8,500-seat enclosed stadium is big enough for football games.

Marquette is one of those frontier boom towns found scattered throughout the Middle and Far West that developed because of the money and influence of Eastern investors — in this case, three men from Worcester, Massachusetts, who, in 1849 organized the second iron mining company in the Marquette Range.

In erecting public buildings, churches, industrial structures, and their own homes, Marquette's business powers chose many of the leading architects of Detroit, Chicago, Milwaukee, and Cleveland. Marquette attracts architecture buffs with its impressive stock of elaborate 19th-century buildings concentrated in a very small city (1990 population: 22,000). Many buildings are made of richly detailed Lake Superior sandstone, deep red in color — what's known as brownstone in New York City. (See page 725 for historic walking tours.)

The billions of tons of iron ore shipped from Marquette since the 1850s helped pay for many of these fancy buildings. In the second half of the 19th century, 40% of the world's iron ore came from here, fueling America's transition from an agricultural to an industrial society. From April through mid-December, two to three freighters a day still pick up enormous loads of ore at the north ore dock just below Presque Isle Park. You can watch the noisy process from Lakeshore Boulevard or Presque Isle.

For over a hundred years, Marquette has reigned as "Queen City of the North" – of the Upper Peninsula, at any rate. It feels more cosmopolitan – and less distinctively Yooperish; go to nearby Ishpeming or Negaunee for local color - than anyplace else in the U.P. With the September, 1995 closing of K. I. Sawyer Air Force Base south of town (the equivalent of the U.P.'s fourth largest city), Marquette faces a huge economic development challenge.

Marquette highlights include:

♦ Two **spectacular views** of the city. From the south, see the city, bay, and lake from **Marquette Mountain downhill ski area**. You can drive to the summit. *Marquette Mountain is 1 1/2 miles south of Marquette on CR 553. From BR 41, turn onto Furnace and go 1 block to Division (which is also CR 553), turn left and go 1 1/2 miles south. (800) 944-SNOW.* From the north, **Sugarloaf Mountain** offers an equally grand view. It's a 15- to 20-minute walk to the peak. The trail is well marked, right by the parking lot. Steps built by the Boy Scouts at various points as well as benches and a deck at the peak make this a non strenuous climb. *Sugarloaf Mountain is north of Marquette on CR 550. In town, BR 41 becomes Front Street. Take Front to Washington, turn west and go to Fourth Avenue; turn north onto Fourth, which becomes Presque Isle Avenue, and go to Wright; turn west to CR 550.*

♦ **Downtown**. Centered on Washington between Front and Third, downtown Marquette is well worth exploring for its interesting shops, striking architecture, and fine views down to the harbor. The elaborate 1883 **Vierling Saloon** on Front at Main has a great view of the bay from its back windows. In the historic Harlow Block at 102 W. Washington at Front, the **Italian Place and New York Deli** (906-226-3032) is a much-talked-about restaurant which arrived in 1994. **Sandpiper Books** (112 W. Washington) is a general bookstore with in-depth sections on U.P., Upper Great Lakes, and Native American topics. *(906) 225-0400. Open Mon thru Wed 10-6, Thurs thru Sat 10-8.* Next door, **Michigan Fare** (114 W. Washington; 906-226-3894) features a nice selection of Michigan products and Upper Peninsula handcrafts. **Wattsson & Wattsson** (118 W. Washington) draws visitors with a replica of the old Ropes Gold Mine in nearby Ishpeming, displays about the mine, and jewelry made of gold from that mine. **Snowbound Books**, around the corner and up the hill at 118 N. Third, is a large, well organized, and friendly used book shop with an excellent regional and maritime section. *(906) 228-4448.*

In the next block, **Babycakes** at 223 W. Washington is that U.P. anomaly — a trendy spot, in this case a cappuccino bar with a rotating selection of 80 kinds of muffins and many delicious specialty breads, all made on the premises. *Open Mon thru Fri 6 a.m.-6 p.m., Sat 7 a.m.-5:30 p.m. (906) 226-7744.* Marquette still has two downtown movie theaters, right across the street from each other: the **Delft** at 139 W. Washington (906-226-3741) and the **Nordic** at 136 W. Washington (906-226-6191).

Art and architecture fans might enjoy stopping in the 1936 **post office** at 202 W. Washington to see the WPA mural of Father Marquette exploring Lake Superior's shores; at the splendid, twin-towered 1890 **St. Peter's Catholic Church** two blocks south on S. Fourth at Baraga; and at the dignified, beautifully restored 1902 Beaux Arts **Marquette County Courthouse** on Third at Baraga. (Scenes from the 1959 classic *Anatomy of a Murder* were filmed here. Peek inside the second-floor courtroom if you can!) At Baraga and First, **Angeli's Bakery-Deli** (906-226-7335) still bakes cross-shaped, crusty cornetti - designed for dunking and sopping up pan juices. The south side of town was — and is — the immigrant, Catholic side, and the Catholic Church wanted to make a strong architectural statement to counterbalance the unusually large and elegant **St. Paul's Episcopal Church** on the northside hill at Ridge and High, amid the homes of its wealthy parishioners.

◆ The **Marquette County Historical Museum** focuses on the cultural development of Marquette County, including the social impact of fishing, shipping, logging, and mining. Its excellent collections are used to mount 1 that change twice a year. A new life-size diorama, made with help from area Chippewas, lets kids crawl inside an authentically furnished wigwam. Another realistic life-size diorama shows the Burt survey party, outfitted with a very early solar compass. Don't miss the huge 1881 bird's-eye view of Marquette and its busy harbor. There are good regional history books at the **gift shop**. Pick up easy-to-use **walking tour**

guides of downtown and the Ridge-Arch Historic District for $1 each. *213 N. Front at Ridge, 2 blocks north of Washington. (906) 226-3571. Mon thru Fri 10-4:30, open 3rd Thurs to 9 p.m. Adults $3, ages 12-18 $1.*

◆ **Fresh fish** from a downtown dock. **Thill's Fish House** (906-226-9851) is located just north of the downtown ore dock, at the foot of Main. It's the last commercial fishing operation in what was once a thriving fishery. Buy fresh whitefish fillets for anywhere from $3.65-$4/lb.; smoked whitefish sausage for $4.50/lb.

◆ **Maritime Museum**. Located in the big old Water Works Building not far from the lighthouse. Outboard engines were first developed in Marquette, and the museum has some very old ones. A typical Finnish fishing shanty has been reconstructed. Photos and exhibits explain how taconite pellets, a condensed form of iron ore, have made it more economical to ship iron. There's a well-stocked **gift shop**. Large, colorful ship flags hang from the high ceilings. *E. Ridge at Lakeshore Blvd. just north of downtown. Open daily June 1 thru September 30, 10-5. (906) 226-2006. $2.*

◆ **Marquette Harbor Light**. One of Michigan's most picturesque lighthouses perches atop a red stone bluff at the Coast Guard station at the foot of Ridge. Not open to the public, but worth viewing from nearby parks.

◆ **Lakeside bike path**. You can rent 5-speed bikes and take a pleasant 12-mile bike ride along a shoreline **bike path**. It extends 7 miles south of downtown and 5 miles north to Presque Isle. *Rent bikes at Lakeshore Bike & Kite, 505 Lakeshore Blvd. just west of the lighthouse. It's on the bike path, near the Lower Harbor just north of downtown. (906) 228-7547.*

◆ **Ridge and Arch Historic District**. East of High and Pine Streets, Marquette's mining and shipping magnates built their homes on a high bluff overlooking the harbor and Presque Isle. The dramatic site and the concentration of grand homes make this a fine place for a leisurely walk. Pick up a $1 printed walking tour at the historical museum (page 724), or call (906) 226-3571 to find out about guided $3 **walking tours** held three times a week. (Tour leaders are often district residents who invite the group home for interior tours.) Architectural highlights include: an elaborate 1880 Italian villa at **410 E. Ridge**; the elaborate Gothic Revival house at **450 E. Ridge** built for early Cleveland mining investor Henry Mather; the 1875 stone Gothic

Awesome sight and sound: at one of Marquette's long ore docks, railroad cars from Ishpeming's Tilden Mine empty iron-rich taconite pellets into the dock's 200 pockets. When a giant freighter pulls up to the dock, chutes are lowered from the dock into the boat's cargo hold. Loading is a noisy, interesting process to watch. Call (906) 226-6122 to find out when a freighter will be at the ore dock by Presque Isle Park.

Revival house at **430 E. Arch**; and the 1887 Shingle Style house at **425 Ohio**, one of the few surviving houses designed by the important Chicago architect John Wellborn Root. One of the grandest houses in the entire Upper Peninsula, John Longyear's house at Arch and Cedar, was dismantled and shipped to Brookline, Massachusetts, after other business leaders rebuffed his plan to donate all his bluffside property down to the shore as a memorial for his dead son.

◆ The **Cleveland-Cliffs Ore Dock** on Lakeshore Blvd., shortly before the entrance to Presque Isle Park, is a monumental sight to see and hear. The steel-framed dock juts out almost a quarter of a mile into Lake Superior, 75 feet above the water. The railroad approach is a mile-long earth embankment. Railroad cars from the taconite processing facility near the mines continually move out along the top of the ore dock and empty taconite pellets (a concentrated form of iron-bearing rock) down into the ore dock's 200 pockets. Usually once or twice a day, a bulk ore carrier comes to the dock to load. Chutes from each pocket are lowered into the cargo hold, and taconite thunders down into it. Then the ship shifts 20 or 30 feet (winches being tightened or loosened let it move), and new pockets empty into the hold. It's a noisy, impressive spectacle — a worthwhile opportunity to view giant 600- to 1,000-foot ships in action, at close range. This particular ore dock, built by a Cleveland-Cliffs subsidiary in 1912, revolutionized the shipping of iron ore. *To find out when an ore carrier will dock, call (902) 226-6122.* Nearby is the giant, coal-fired generating station of Wisconsin Electric Power, the main electrical plant in the Upper Peninsula.

◆ **Presque Isle Park.** This rocky, wooded, and extraordinarily picturesque peninsula just north of town is a splendid setting for an outing any time of year. A gazebo and picnic area on a promontory near the entrance looks out into the lake and back at the ore docks and harbor. A one-way, two-mile-long **interior road** has turnouts and footpaths at especially scenic points. Northwest of the peninsula are several craggy, dark islets and the Huron Mountains, blue in the distance — a grand view, especially at sunset. The high cliffs plunging into Lake Superior prove tempting — and sometimes fatal — for overadventurous rock climbers and divers. Five miles of **trails** go up and down through woods of hardy conifers kept small by wind and rock. From May through most of March, four miles of **groomed cross-country ski trails** that wind through the woods with occasional lake views are among the most beautiful imaginable. The most developed part of the park is to the west, where a shallow, protected bay makes Lake Superior tolerable for **swimming**. Here too are a small **zoo**, **tennis courts**, a **concession stand**, and another **picnic area**. (Marquette's huge **swimming pool** and a **water slide**, open to the general public, is a little outside the park entrance.) Summer **band concerts** are held on Thursday and Sunday evenings in the bandshell right across from the picnic area and playground. Presque Isle Park is at the end of Lakeshore Drive, about three miles from downtown. *(906) 226-3051. Open year-round. No fees except for pool admission.*

◆ **Jilbert's Dairy** provides dairy products for much of the U.P. Adjoining the dairy is its popular ice cream shop. A local favorite is "Moosetracks," vanilla with Reese's peanut butter cups mixed in. At any time you can look through glass windows at ice cream being made and milk being processed. Also on hand: a nifty collection of old milk bottles and an assortment of U.P. specialty foods from Baroni's spaghetti sauce to "squeaky cheese" (juustua), sweetish and soft. *(906) 225-1363. Corner of W. Ridge & Meeske Ave. where U.S. 41 business route splits off the highway.*

GUIDED TOURS OF THE AREA . . . . . Marquette native **Fred Huffman**, owner and operator of Marquette Country Tours, takes visitors on informative tours of the city and surrounding countryside. Sunrise and sunset tours of the city are given regularly. Other tours include scenic waterfalls, the historic Marquette Iron Range, and Marquette's rugged north country, Big Bay, and vicinity. *For an appointment and price information, call Fred at (906) 226-6167.*

A SPECTACULAR FALL COLOR TRIP from Marquette to the remote village of **Big Bay** is a circle tour along county road 510 and 550. You'll drive through thick forests and past **waterfalls** on the 35-mile dirt road. Colors are usually at their peak from late September to mid-October. . . . . . In Big Bay are the **Lumberjack Inn** restaurant and two of the U.P.'s most famous lodgings: the wonderfully isolated **Big Bay Lighthouse**, where you can watch awesome Lake Superior storms from the top of the tower, and the historic **Thunder Bay Inn**, once a general store for lumber companies in the region. Henry Ford bought the building in 1943 to use as a hotel for guests. Just down the hill was the lumber mill used to make panels for the famous Ford "woody" station wagons. In 1959 the popular bar here was the setting for parts of the movie *Anatomy of a Murder*. Locals still talk about it.

WINTER SPORTS IN AND AROUND MARQUETTE . . . . . have much to recommend them. The season is from mid-December or earlier through March. The settings are unusually attractive and varied. On the simple, rustic side are the backwoods former mining lands of the **Lucy Hill luge run** in Negaunee, and the quiet and remote **cross-country ski trails** (one flat, two challenging) near **Suicide Hill**, a **ski-flying hill** in the woods outside Ishpeming. In contrast, there's the rock-and-roll intensity of Marquette Mountain (800-944-SNOW), where incredibly adept ski addicts from N.M.U. and K.I. Sawyer are out in force on weekdays in mid-March. Marquette Mountain's 600-foot drop is the third highest vertical drop in the Midwest, and the Lake Superior view from the top is stunning.

The **cross-country loops at Presque Isle Park** (page 727) can't be beat for scenery. **Al Quaal**, a wild and natural 300-acre Ishpeming city park on the north edge of town, overlooks Teal Lake. It harkens back to the earlier, folksier, simpler style of winter sports of the area's many Scandinavian immigrants. Its 1200-foot iced **toboggan run** is great fun (rentals are $2/hour, including helmets; open weeknights 5-8, weekends 1-8). Adjacent **downhill**

ski runs and a **slalom run** with rope tows are also lighted, and the five kilometers of cross-country **ski loops** (some easy, some intermediate) are gorgeous. *Go north at the intersection of US 41 and Hickory, the corner where you'll see the Chamber of Commerce office. Best number to call for information: (906) 486-6181.*

Outstanding **snowmobiling** through many miles of off-road trails between Marquette, Ishpeming, and Big Bay is a magnet. **For information on winter sports,** call (800) 544-4321 or Country Inn (906) 485-6345,

SNOWSHOES . . . . . are quiet and easy to use - no learning required. A great way to enjoy Presque Isle Park or walks in the woods around Ishpeming and Negaunee. (Mining lands are open to the public.) . . . . . **Rent snowshoes** at Johnson Sport Shop, 1212 N. Third, (906) 226-2061.

A GOOD PLACE FOR PICNIC FIXINGS AND TRAIL MIX . . . . . is the friendly **Marquette Organic Food Co-op** at 325 W. Washington. *(906) 225-0671.*

Michigan Iron Industry Museum

Overlooking a picturesque river valley near Negaunee, this superb museum shows how the region's 19th-century iron mines and forges were central to the industrialization of America.

Situated in a rural area that overlooks the Carp River where an old iron forge operated, this impressive museum uses dramatic displays to illuminate the great historical importance of iron mining here in the Marquette Range. It's in the rugged, wooded hills just outside the old iron-mining center of Negaunee. The museum is at the place overlooking the Carp River where an iron forge was built just four years after surveyor William Burt's famous 1844 discovery of nearly pure iron deposits at the surface. That happened at Teal Lake, which you can see on the north side of U.S. 41 in Negaunee, just a few miles west of here. Burt's magnetic compass fluctuated so suspiciously that he sent his men out to investigate. They returned with iron ore from rock outcrops. The next year prospectors from Jackson, Michigan, were guided by native Ojibway to a place where iron ore was right at the surface, visible in the roots of a fallen tree. That site became the Jackson Mine on the south side of Negaunee, the first (1847) of the enormously important Lake Superior area mines that launched the great manufacturing industries and helped create the wealth of Great Lakes cities from Milwaukee to Buffalo.

The forge here converted ore directly into wrought iron used in things like nails, wire, and bolts. It took an acre of hardwoods to make five tons of iron. Little remains of the long-abandoned forge, but a pleasant **trail** leads from the museum past the 19th-century site. From this modest beginning blossomed 40 mines in the Marquette Range by 1872. They extracted a million tons a year of the richest iron ore in the world. But by the end of the 1870s the range's rich surface deposits were becoming exhausted and the Upper Peninsula's Menominee and Gogebic Ranges to the west were coming on strong.

Mine shafts and horizontal drifts lie under large areas of Ishpeming and Negaunee, sometimes requiring weakened streets to be abandoned. This view of Ishpeming shows a March snowbank. To the left, the skyline is punctuated by three monumental Cleveland-Cliffs headframes that house the hoist ropes which carry miners and ore up from the mines. Cliffs' president hired Prairie School architect George Maher to design monumental, Egyptian-inspired obelisks to house two headframes (1919) The tall, boxy headframe between them later replaced both older devices.

The museum does a good job of showing just how important the U.P.'s iron has been. Almost half of the nation's iron from 1850 to 1900 was mined from here. In the 150 years since 1833, the California gold rush produced less than a billion dollars of minerals. Michigan lumber has produced almost $4.5 million of wood. The Keweenaw copper ranges generated about twice that amount. But the riches from iron dwarf these, worth some *$48 billion.*

Today none of the miles of U.P. underground iron mine shafts are producing ore. The only two mines operating today are the Tilden and the Empire, both open-pit operations. They are within a few miles of each other, off County Road 35 right across from the community of Palmer, southeast of Ishpeming. To see mining operations up close, take a two-hour **tour** of the **Tilden mine** during the summer months. The tour bus stops at an overlook where you can watch the mining machines pulling rocks out of the earth and hauling them to the processing plant. Inside the plant, you see the huge blast furnaces in action. *One tour per day mid-June thru late August, Tues-Sat. Bus leaves the Marquette Chamber of Commerce (906-226-6591) at noon, the Ishpeming Chamber of Commerce (906-486-4841) at 12:30. Bus seating is limited; call either Chamber of Commerce for reservations and for tips on appropriate dress (for example, no sandals* *allowed). Restricted to adults and children age 10 and up. Cost per person: $5-$6.*

Today the U.P. iron industry excavates greatly diluted ore in huge, 300-ton blasts. Lake Superior iron mining remains competitive only because of a process that concentrates the ore into 64% pure iron pellets called taconite. These can then be shipped economically from the Michigan ports of Marquette and Escanaba to foundries around the Great Lakes.

Museum directions: *from U.S. 41, 3 miles east of Negaunee and 5 or 6 miles west of the outskirts of Marquette, turn south onto M-35 for 1 mile, turn west onto CR 492 for 2 miles, then turn north onto Forge Road. Signs are clear. For information about* **special events** *at the museum, call (906) 475-7857. Open daily May thru October, 9:30-4:30. Free.*

BLACK FLIES, RUSTY CARS, DEER-HUNTING, SEX, SAUNAS, BEER . . . . and other important aspects of U.P. life have been immortalized in the sympathetically satirical songs of **Da Yoopers** of Ishpeming, Mich. The group's "The Second Week of Deer Camp" got nationwide air play. Simple pleasures are extolled in songs like "Fishin' wit Fred": "It's a perfect day for fishin', drinking beer and telling lies. It's a little bit like Heaven when you're fishin' wit da guys." Da Yoopers have great Yooper accents and a variety of musical styles to suit each topic, from Finnish accordion polkas to heavy metal. Pick up their tapes at Holiday gas stations (*Culture Shock* is our favorite), or at **Da Yooper Shop** on U.S. 41 just west of Ishpeming. (Look for the billboard.) There you can also buy such things as a beer can holster or beer gut T-shirt. Check out the ingenious variations on outhouse yard art! Be advised: some listeners consider some of Da Yoopers' songs "too gross." It's blunt, it's earthy, it's far from tasteful, but it's not mean and not sexist, either. *Mail-order available. (906) 485-5595. Summer hours: Mon-Fri 9-9, Sat 10-6, Sun 11-4. Winter hours: Mon-Fri 9-5.*

ALSO IN ISHPEMING . . . . . exhibits of antique skis and other skiing equipment plus short biographies of leading U.S. skiers are on display at the **U.S. National Ski Hall of Fame**. Ski-jumping, introduced by the area's numerous Norwegians, got its start in Ishpeming, and the local ski club organized the hall many years ago. *On U.S. 41 look for the new building with a roof shaped like a ski jump. (906) 485-6323. Mid-May thru September: 10-8. October thru mid-May: 10-5. Closed major winter holidays. Adults $3, students $1, children under 10 free.*

EXPLORING ISHPEMING AND NEGAUNEE . . . . . is fun for people who like distinctive places. These towns are at once plain and stately, the results of booms and busts endured through a large measure of simple living. The depressed downtowns have many ornate sandstone-trimmed buildings. Near outlying mine headframes more houses cluster, some in amazingly picturesque spots. . . . . . Don't miss **Jasper Hill** on Ishpeming's southeast side, on Jasper one block south of its intersection with Bluff. The dramatic park, punctuated with piles of red rock from mining, has a splendid view from its summit; across the way is the 1891 Swiss-style guest cottage owned by Cleveland-Cliffs Iron Mining. . . . . . Another striking site: the vaguely Egyptian **headframes** of the Cliff Shafts Mine. From U.S. 41 on Ishpeming's west side, take Lakeshore Drive south to Lake Bancroft. . . . . . Both towns have operating downtown movie theaters: the **Butler**, "Showplace of the North," in Ishpeming (906-486-4661) and the **Vista** in Negaunee (906-475-7188), operated by the Peninsula Arts Council. . . . . . Potter Marilyn Mutch has turned Negaunee's freight depot into the **Depot Gallery and Studio** (906-475-4007), where she works and exhibits some noteworthy area artists. It's on Rail at Gold, a block south of downtown.

IMMIGRANT LABOR FOR THE IRON MINES . . . . , came largely from **Italy** and **Finland.** Conditions in those countries caused large-scale emigration in the very years of iron mining's greatest boom, from the 1890s into the early 1920s. 1919 was iron's peak production year; by 1929 large-scale production was over. A lasting result of iron mining is an unusual blend of genes (a Finn and an Italian produce dark-haired, pale-complected offspring), cultures, accents, and cuisines. **Cudighi** (COULD-uh-gi) is a spicy, fried pork sausage unique to the Ishpeming area, served in a sandwich with pizza fixings. Try it at **Ralph's Italian Delicatessen**, (906) 485-4557, on U.S. 41 right across from the U.S. National Ski Hall of Fame. Italian craftsmen made possible the area's outstanding stone architecture. Scandinavians developed winter sports and paid homage to Heikki Luunta (HEY-kee LOON-tuh), the Finnish snow god.

THE CULTURAL ICON OF THE U.P. . . . . . is the late **John Voelker**, former Michigan Supreme Court justice, who quit to come home to Ishpeming and devote himself to fishing after his *Anatomy of a Murder* novel struck Hollywood paydirt. *Trout Madness* and *Trout Magic* reflect his passion for fishing. The crusty, completely unpretentious author lived in an old house up the hill from Ishpeming's library and drank down the street at the Rainbow Bar on E. Canada at the intersection with First Street. His papers are at Northern Michigan University in Marquette.

IXL Museum

*At a remote site where hardwood flooring
was first perfected, this striking mill
headquarters building takes you back in time.*

Few historic sites are preserved so splendidly well as this remote old office of a U.P. hardwood lumber mill. It was here in the 1880s that the machinery to produce hardwood flooring was first perfected. Until then American homes used softer pine for wooden floors. Hardwoods like maple and oak were too difficult to work and tended to warp. Lumber mill manager George Earle perfected a kiln process here to remove the right amount of moisture from hardwood. He also created machinery to make tongue and groove hardwood sections, still the method for laying hardwood floors.

Located just south of the village of Hermansville, the Wisconsin Land & Lumber company grounds are in pristine condition. Except for the absence of a few original structures, things are little changed from decades ago. The kiln still operates, although the original company is defunct. The museum building was the business office, built in 1882. Earle's office was here. A medical doctor by training, he used the big table in the middle of his office for amputations and other emergency operations. This building is also where the 600 to 800 IXL workers came to receive their weekly scrip for pay, to spend in the company town. (The IXL name is a punning abbreviation for "I excel.")

The interior has not been reconstructed to look like an historic office; it simply has changed little in recent decades. Old Burroughs adding machines and inkwells adorn big oak desks. Dumbwaiters sent messages between the first and second floors. The original old mechanical clocks and crank telephones remain in place, as if the place had suddenly been vacated 75 years ago and left untouched.

Hermansville is on U.S. 2 26 miles west of Escanaba and 15 miles east of Norway. Turn at the sign for the IXL Museum and go 4 blocks south. (906) 498-2498 or (906) 498-2410. Open Memorial Day thru August, 1-4 daily. Adults $1, students 50¢.

Piers Gorge

Along the Wisconsin border south of Norway,
the big Menominee River cuts a deep trough
in a spectacular rush of water.

Here the Menominee River has cut a dramatic, deep gorge and created powerful rapids of foaming white water as it rushes towards Green Bay at Menominee and Marinette. The Michigan/Wisconsin border is formed by the Menominee River from west of Iron Mountain, and by its tributary, the Brule River. At Piers Gorge the river has created an extraordinarily beautiful place where steep-sided bedrock walls up to 70 feet high contain the rushing river as it roars over a series of stone shelves in four quite distinctive waterfalls.

Despite the drama, this isn't a big tourist spot. There are no cross-country ski trails or nearby camping sites. The area has kept a natural, unspoiled appearance. No park signs or steps have been constructed. The road to Piers Gorge is not plowed in the wintertime.

You can look down at the river and falls from an easy, level path that starts at the parking area, briefly passing through a fragrant cedar swamp. Short side trails branch off to the rim of the gorge, allowing visitors to look down at the rushing river with a minimum of effort. The round trip along the rim back to the parking lot is 1 1/2 miles. The most dramatic falls are a ways upstream.

The more adventurous can take trails that descend tortuously along the canyon walls to the river itself. In places it's possible to frolic in the gentler rapids – at your own risk, of course – or step across half the wide river on the many stones and boulders lying in the riverbed. The river banks are loaded with stones of all shapes and sizes, providing plenty of ammunition for stone-skippers. Argosy Adventures (715-251-3886) organizes **raft expeditions** through the rapids. The rafting season usually starts in June.

From U.S. 2 at Norway (that's 8 miles east of Iron Mountain and 43 miles west of Escanaba) turn south onto U.S. 8 and drive 2 miles. Look for Piers Gorge Road on your right. Drive 1/2 mile to parking lot. If you cross the bridge and get to Wisconsin, you have gone too far. Go back 1/4 mile and look for Piers Gorge Road on your left. Open from the time the snow melts through Labor Day.

A GOOD MUSEUM IN CASPIAN. . . . . . just south of Iron River is the notable **Iron County Museum**. Lots of mining exhibits are in the old engine house of the famous Caspian Mine (1903-1937). Over 6 million tons of iron ore were lifted by the **giant hoist** just east of the engine house. This was among the most productive of the Menominee Range mines. Miniature **models of mines** show how shafts in the region were as long as one mile and how huge buckets called "skips" hauled the ore up. Logging had also been important in the area. An 80-foot **diorama of a lumber camp** shows such things as the dining hall, where "the cook made sure that everyone ate and only ate, by standing with a butcher knife and threatening anyone who talked." There are also three authentic Indian **dugout canoes**. Among the 20 outbuildings is a **1930s Finnish sauna**.

Iron Mountain Iron Mine

*Travel far beneath the earth to see
how difficult and dangerous iron mining really was.*

Michigan's most interesting mine tour takes visitors through 2,600 feet of underground drifts and tunnels and shows what iron mining was really like. Led by a knowledgeable guide, visitors don raincoats and hard hats and ride the same railway system that took miners to their jobs until the mine closed down in 1945. Visitors experience the gloomy, difficult working conditions in a typical iron mine. There are also spectacular views of **large caverns** on the 35-minute trip. **Drilling demonstrations** show how loud, dirty, and dangerous the work was.

When the first tunnel here was dug in 1870, the incredibly rich ore was 85% iron. But it took three men 10 hours to dig just four feet by hand. The highest-paid miner was the blaster, who got 25¢ an hour. Each of the Iron Range's many ethnic groups had its own job in the mines. The Finnish specialty was the timbering – constructing the tamarack supports that held up the horizontal drifts. Deep shaft mines like this finally became obsolete when huge power shovels made open-pit mining much more economical. Wear a sweater; far underground it stays a constant 43° F. year around.

On U.S. 2 in Vulcan, 10 miles east of Iron Mountain and 2 miles east of Norway. (906) 563-8077. 35-minute tours June to mid-Oct, daily 9-6. Adults $5.50, children 6-12 $4.50, under 6 free.

IN NEARBY IRON MOUNTAIN . . . . . The **Cornish Pump and Mining Museum** has a 725-ton water pump, the nation's largest when built in 1890. It lifted 200 tons a minute from the shaft of the Chapin Iron Mine, the largest producer in the Menominee Range. Seeping water is a big problem for deep mines, which have to continuously pump out water to keep operating. It took 11,000 tons of coal a year just to operate the pump. Here as in many U.S. mining districts, experienced Cornish miners from Cornwall in the southwest of England took the lead in developing improved mining technologies. There are also lots of local mining artifacts and photos here, as well as a **World War II glider display**. The gliders were made in Kingsford, just south of Iron Mountain. *2 blocks west of U.S. 2 on Kent St. in Iron Mountain. (906) 774-1086. Open May thru October, Mon-Sat 9-4. $4 adults, $2 students, children 10 and under (with parents) free.* . . . . . The **Menominee Range Museum**, located in an old Carnegie library building, has many local historical items, including reconstructions of a dentist's office, trapper's cabin, and a 19th-century kitchen and bedroom. *300 E. Ludington, 1 block east of U.S. 2. (906) 774-4276. Open May thru October, Mon-Sat 9-4. $4 adults, $2 students, children 10 and under (with parents) free. Special rate available when you visit both the Cornish Pump and Mining and Menominee Range Museums.*. . . . .

Lake Antoine Park is a delightful county park on Lake Antoine, just northeast of Iron Mountain. (Locals pronounce it, "an-TWINE," not the French way.) There's a spacious, wooded **picnic area**, a wonderful swimming **beach** with a swimmers' dock well out in the lake, and a **boat launch**. A **concession stand** sells hot dogs, ice cream, popcorn, and camping supplies. Reservations for the 80 **campsites** are recommended around holidays. *Open Memorial thru Labor Day. (906) 774-8875.*

Porcupine Mountains

Huge virgin forests, wonderful waterfalls and views,
rugged hiking trails, and wild rivers
in a 65,000-acre park overlooking Lake Superior

This vast and rugged state park in the remote northwestern part of Michigan's Upper Peninsula contains some of
the Midwest's most extraordinary natural features. The
Porcupine Mountains are the only true mountains between the
Rockies and Alleghenies. The 65,000 acre park encompasses a
great deal of wilderness backcountry in addition to the spectacular
panoramas that are the main attraction for park visitors. **Whitewater canoeing** here is the most challenging in Michigan, and
downhill skiing is the very best in the Midwest. Thirteen slopes
have a vertical drop of 600 feet, and the lift ticket fees are bargain-
priced. (Kids 12 and under ski free!) Because this remote area was
so inaccessible, an astounding 36,000 acres escaped the lumberman's axe — the largest virgin forest east of the Mississippi. It is a
realm of towering hemlocks and hardwoods. There are **85 miles of
hiking trails** and dozens of waterfalls.

The **Presque Isle River** is as tumultuous as they come. For
many sightseers, the highlight of the Porkies is the river's final
half mile before it flows into Lake Superior. You can pull near it
by car, then take a half-mile elevated **boardwalk** up the side of
this rollicking river. Multiple waterfalls, powerful rapids, and
deep holes make for spectacular scenery and suicidal canoeing
here. Experienced canoeists and kayakers enjoy the challenging
whitewater of the Presque Isle from M-28 to South Boundary
Road, a 17 1/2-mile trip. Intermediate paddlers can deal with
the Presque Isle above M-28.

In complete contrast is the peaceful scene at the **Lake of the
Clouds Overlook,** at the end of M-107, one of the state's most
famous views. You can look down on it from overlooks near a
parking lot, or approach it by footpath another two miles east.
The park's most scenic trail is **Escarpment Trail**, four miles long
along a ridge. In addition to a great view of Lake of the Clouds, it
reveals interesting rock formations along the dramatic escarpment. A shorter trail connecting a number of high scenic view-

Most of the visitors to the Porcupine Mountains are concentrated at the campgrounds, roadways, the winter ski slopes, and the Lake of the Clouds Overlook (here), one of Michigan's most famous views. There's plenty of room to get away in the wilderness.

points is the **Overlook Trail**, a 3 1/2-mile loop. Both trails start at M-107 west of the Union Bay Campground. Another celebrated panoramic view is from a 40-foot observation tower on Michigan's second-highest point, **Summit Peak**.

Only the Superior shoreline and southern boundary of the park were ever logged, so large tracts of land are virgin pine and hemlock forests. There was serious copper mining here. Of nine abandoned copper mines, all but one are now capped. The **Mead Mine** along M-17 allows visitors to enter about 100 feet of the mineshaft. This is also a good place to **picnic;** get supplies at the general store in Silver City.

Serious **backpackers** can plan several-day adventures along the Porkies' 85 miles of trails, many of which have cabins and shelters for hikers. In this rugged wilderness, steep grades and unbridged stream crossings are common, according to outdoor writer Jim Du Fresne. His 159-page book, **Porcupine Mountains Wilderness State Park**, is recommended for anyone who plans any outdoor adventures in the park.

By all means begin your exploration of the Porcupines with a trip to the **Visitor Center**, less than three miles west of Silver City off M-107 on South Boundary Road. Helpful park rangers can give information about trails, backpacking, canoeing, fishing (for steelhead, salmon, and trout), and more. Call or write, and they'll mail you information. At the Visitor Center, there's a big, detailed relief map of the huge park. Topographical maps are for sale. Displays and a nine-projector **slide show** inform visitors about the area's history and natural features.

Campgrounds range from modern and semi-modern sites to rustic outposts — just over 200 sites in all, from $10 and $8 down to $6 per group of four. Reservations are recommended in July and early August. If you reserve one far enough in advance, you can rent well-equipped, drive-in **wilderness cabins**, complete (in some cases) with a rowboat to take out on a remote lake.

In winter, the park also features the most exciting place for **downhill skiing** in the Midwest from mid-December through March. Some 10 miles of alpine ski runs include seven intermediate trails, four expert trails, and three novice trails. Daily lift ticket: adults $18 weekdays, $20 weekends and holidays. Ages 13-17: $13 weekdays, $15 weekends and holidays. Half-day rate is $2 off regular rates. There are also 25 miles of groomed **cross-country ski trails**. A **warming shelter, concession**, and **rental facility** serves all skiers.

Headquarters/visitor center is about 4 miles west of Silver City on M-107. Write: Porcupine Mountains Wilderness State Park, 599 M-107, Ontonogan, MI 49953. (906) 885-5275. Visitor center open from late May through mid-October, daily 10-6. Ski season from mid-Dec. thru March. State parks sticker required: $4/day, $18/year.

Hanka Homestead

On a beautiful, remote hillside, take a trip back in time to a self-sufficient Finnish farm.

O n the western Upper Peninsula, Finns have intermarried for generations and so colored the regional culture and accent of the western U.P. that you can meet Yoopers without a drop of Finnish blood who speak with a strong Finnish-influenced accent. Some Finnish descendants whose families have been in this country for four generations sound like they learned English as a second language. Saunas are still commonly seen in back yards from Marquette to Copper Country on the Keweenaw Peninsula. The world's only Finnish-American college, Suomi College, is in Hancock. Dozens of co-op stores, a feature of many Finnish agricultural communities, survive in small places. Unfussy Scandinavian cleanliness sets the norm up here; it's hard to find a Copper Country motel, no matter how old or primitive, that isn't clean.

While many Finnish things have been incorporated into the distinctive Yooper culture, pure Finnish survivals are rare. Probably the most remarkable is the Hanka Homestead, a self-sufficient pioneer farmstead at the base of the Keweenaw Peninsula. Its farmhouse and nine outbuildings are carefully

crafted Scandinavian log construction. The Hanka farm has been restored to the way it was in its prime in 1920, when it was the home of Herman Hanka, a disabled miner, his wife, and their four adult children. On the farm they continued the Old World ways they had brought with them to the U.S.

By the time you get to the Hankas' place, you've gone down five miles of country road off U.S. 41; turned at a fire tower near the top of a long, high hill; and gone down a rugged gravel road through a mile of forest. It's quite remote from the outside world, just as the Finns were who homesteaded in this neighborhood in the 1890s. The log house, two-story log barn, and smaller out-buildings sit in an 18-acre clearing, surrounded by forest, with the Huron Mountains blue in the distance across nearby Keweenaw Bay. The scene looks like something you'd expect to find in a remote hollow of the Smokey Mountains.

One mainstay of self-sufficient local economies like these was that neighbors traded and shared harvest work and other skills and products. The disabled father, Herman, tanned hides and made shoes for neighbors. His son Jalmar tinkered and fixed things. The family boarded logging horses, which needed intermittent rest between periods of strenuous work. Jalmar and his brother Nik, the farm manager, worked in logging camps in the winter, where their sister Mary cooked. One neighbor went to town every Saturday to shop for the neighborhood. People raised their own grains and vegetables, kept chickens and sometimes a pig, depended on the Jersey cow and her rich milk for butter and cheese, and hunted rabbits, partridges, and deer. Such a short growing season (85 frost-free days) made cold-resistant root crops like turnips, rutabagas, and potatoes important. Pre-serving and preparing food took up an immense amount of time. Social life consisted of visiting, playing instruments (Nik played the kantele, a homemade Finnish guitar), occasional dances at a pavilion near where the fire tower is, church, and the weekly Saturday sauna.

Finland's shifting 19th-century economy had transformed many independent farmers into a class of industrial workers and landless tenants without opportunities. Only the oldest son could hope to farm his own land. Finns emigrated to the north-ern U.S., largely to work in mines. Between the peak years of 1899 and 1914, over 200,000 Finns came to the U.S., largely from two rural counties, Vaasa and Oulu. On the edges of U.P. mining towns, miners farmed smaller plots to support their large

families. It was considered a big step up from working in the dangerous mines to buy a 40-acre farm under the Homestead Act and become a full-time farmer.

Everything changed in the 1920s for farms like the Hankas'. New sanitation policies allowed the sale only of Grade A milk, produced and cooled under super-sanitary, refrigerated conditions. Grade B milk produced at farms like these could be sold only as cheese. Phone service in this remote neighborhood, unreliable to begin with, became so expensive that customers dropped it and lines were removed. Forests reclaimed many fields. Sons went into the army, saw a bigger world, and often ended up working in Detroit's auto factories like Mary's son, Arvo. They returned to the U. P. only to retire.

The farm stopped being improved in 1923, when Nik, its energetic manager, died. Gradually most of the Hankas died off, but easy-going Jalmar lived on until 1966. His needs were simple and he didn't have the ambition to modernize. The farm pretty much remained a time capsule of old Finnish folkways.

Scouts from Old World Wisconsin, a museum of ethnic farm buildings in southeastern Wisconsin, came up here to buy the barn and move it. But they were so impressed with the unaltered condition of the classic Finnish farm that they encouraged a local group to preserve it as a museum. The guide is likely to be descended from nearby Finnish farmers, and thus able to answer many questions and share personal experience. The **tour** is strong on explaining the how-tos of a subsistence lifestyle: how fish were smoked in the sauna, which was then prepared for the family's bath; how rag rugs were woven on neighborhood looms; how grain and food were stored. In the spirit of old-fashioned Finnish housewarmings, spontaneous demonstrations of crafts and music occur on occasions like the museum's opening day or

Finnish midsummer. A satisfying amount of information on the people who lived here is available to the patient reader in a somewhat tedious $6 book.

On U.S. 41 about 10 miles north of Baraga, turn west onto Arn-heim Road. As you pass the fire tower, continue straight onto the gravel (the blacktop turns west). Follow the gravel road left (east) to the farm. Open Mem.-Labor Day on weekends noon-6 or by appointment. Probably open daily in summer except on Wednesdays. Call (906) 353-7116. Admission by donation.

TO EXPERIENCE A WORKING FINNISH DAIRY FARM TODAY . . . . . stay at **Palosaari's Rolling Acres** (906-523-4947), a bed and breakfast on a third-generation farm not far from the Hanka Homestead. The 1940s Cape Cod farmhouse is a trim, efficient headquarters of the 200-acre farm. Cliff and Evy Palosaari are no part-time hobby farmers but the real thing. They're also warm, unpretentious hosts who enjoy sharing stories and down-to-earth Finnish philosophizing with their guests. They have seven grown children. One helps run the farm and intends to buy it from his father. The heavily mechanized operation milks three dozen cows; a farm tour explains the equipment, from plows to combines and large round balers. Evy, active in many farm organizations, is also an expert baker well versed in the old Finnish ways.

FRUIT, FLOWERS, AND A FULL -LINE RESTAURANT. . . . . are at the **Keweenaw Berry Farm** on U.S. 41 a few miles south of Chassell. It's the prettiest of all the produce-stands-turned-into-visitor-attractions we've seen. To get the full effect, you have to walk behind the big retail building through the grounds, colorful with flowers. You can pick or buy **strawberries** (small Keweenaw strawberries are unusually sweet) and raspberries. A **bakery** has pasties, sandwiches, hamburgers. ice cream. **cider** and doughnuts. The full-line **restaurant** specializes in Finnish and Scandinavian foods. Construction is underway on a **miniature village** showing Keweenaw life during the mining period of the 1880s-1920s. When finished, the village will cover five acres. *On U.S. 41 a few miles south of Chassell. (906) 523-6181. Open May 1 thru Christmas, Mon-Sat 8-9 , Sun 10-9.*

PREPARE YOURSELF TO SLOW DOWN AND ENTER THE NATURAL WORLD . . . . . by stopping at the **Sturgeon River Slough Natural Area** alongside U.S. 41 about 18 miles north of Baraga. The grueling drive to get to the Keweenaw Peninsula can leave you spinning. This is a good spot to start unwinding on the last leg of your trip. There's a **lookout tower** and **picnic**

tables by the roadside parking area. You could pick up a pasty and fresh fruit at the Keweenaw Berry farm just south of here and have a picnic. The **De Vriendt Nature Trail,** with interesting interpretive signs, makes a 1.75-mile loop through the slough, now a nesting site for Canada geese, mallards, wood ducks, black ducks, and blue-winged teal. The view of sweeping marshland and sky is relaxing. The slough had been pastureland so wet it could only by farmed by horses. Now channelization and flood control structures regulate the Sturgeon River to avoid spring flooding,. The slough of onetime farms is managed as a stopover spot for migrating waterfowl and a nesting spot. The aim is to increase the Upper Peninsula's resident goose population for hunting.

AN EXCEPTIONAL GIFT SHOP AND HERB GREENHOUSE . . . . . . where the accent is on nature and regional crafts is **Einerlei** on Route 41 in Chassell. This restful, resourceful place makes you want to slow down, enjoy your home, watch birds, and learn to do something useful and enjoyable like making lampshades or embroidering your own placemats. It has grown into a handsome, rambling series of spaces that feature sweaters that look hand-knit ($40-$75), books on decorating and gardening, a tabletop shop, a kitchen shop with fancy foods, a new North Country room, and an outstanding, well-stocked crafts room strong on how-to books and supplies, from paints and dyes to ribbons. The tightly planned rear **garden** of herbs, perennials, and scented geraniums (all for sale) centers on a **greenhouse** disguised as a summer house. *(906) 523-4612. Look for the green awnings on the west side of U.S. 41 in the center of Chassell. Mon-Sat 9-6 (Jan thru April 10-5), Sun 11-5.*

Quincy Hoist

A Keweenaw landmark outside Hancock shows how far mining companies went to extract copper.

This huge hoist shows what a big-time operation Keweenaw copper mining once was. The hoist was designed to haul ten tons of ore at a speed of 36 mph from a depth of almost two miles. It only operated during the 1920s and early 1930s, near the end of the Copper Country's heyday. The Quincy Mining Company had the resources to build this largest-ever steam-powered hoist because it had mined one billion pounds of copper since opening in 1856. Huge profits justified the enormous investment in this hoist. The big drum held 13,000 feet of 1 5/8 inch cable, and mine managers hoped that a much deeper shaft would be dug. But worldwide competition finally made the mile-deep copper in this part of the Keweenaw too expensive to extract. Much cheaper open-pit mining today supplies worldwide demand. The once-booming peninsula began its decline in the early 1920s.

Keweenaw diehards still dream of a day when the demand for copper will rise enough to reopen the mine. Only 10% of the copper has been removed. But so far underground, the temperature stays an uncomfortable 100° F. And the big hoist is no longer operable.

Tours of the hoist, shafthouse, and mine take visitors back to the 1860s. Educational and historical displays on the way into the mine set the stage for a journey 2,000 feet into a hillside actively mined during the Civil War. Tourists enter through an adit, or waterway, rather than through the headframe, the tall structure sided with corrugated steel where the miners began

The headframe outside Hancock (left) houses the huge Quincy steam hoist. Stamping mills in Ripley (right) processed copper ore to be shipped on the Portage Canal. These and other Copper Country landmarks will be in the Keweenaw National Historic Park.

their workshifts, traveling 30 at a time well over a mile down to their stations. It was also here at the headframe that copper ore — millions of tons — was pulled up and dumped. The ore was then taken downhill by rail car to be purified in a stamping plant at Ripley on the Portage Canal. An informative six-minute news-reel-type film shows poignant glimpses of the men as they take their seats to be plunged to a dark, hot, and dangerous place of work. Mining procedures of that era are explained as the tour carries you 500 feet below the surface.

Located 1 mile north of Hancock on U.S. 41. (906) 482-3101. Memorial Day thru fall color season, daily 9:30-6 with the last tour beginning at 5:30. Hoist & mine tour: $10 adults, $7 children 12 and under. Hoist tour only: $3.50 adults, $2.50 children. Mine tour only: $8 adults, $5 children.

ANOTHER COPPER MINE FARTHER NORTH . . . . . near Copper Harbor, is the **Delaware Copper Mine**, in operation from 1847 to 1887. You descend just 110-feet into the main shaft during the 40-minute tour. You can also see evidence of prehistoric mining pits and the ruins of 19th-century mining buildings. *Take U.S. 41 to Delaware, 34 miles north of the Houghton-Hancock bridge. It's 12 miles south of Copper Harbor. (906) 289-4688. Mid-May and Sept thru mid-Oct, 10-5; June thru Aug, 10-6; mid-Dec thru mid-March, noon-5 on Tues, Thurs, Fri, & Sat. Adults $6, children 6-12 $3.50, children under 5 free.*

STOCK UP ON PICNIC SUPPLIES . . . . . at the **Keweenaw Co-op** in Hancock. It's definitely the best specialty grocery on the peninsula, with good produce, cheese, Asian and Middle Eastern ingredients, even wine and a deli section with meat, in addition to the expected natural and bulk foods and gourmet specialty items. Stop by for trail mixes and quality deli items before heading out to Copper Harbor, and you'll be prepared for impromptu picnics. *As you drive north out of Hancock, U.S. 41 swings hard right at Santori's Tire. To get to the co-op, don't go right, go straight up onto Ethel. Co-op is in 2 blocks at Ethel and Ingot. (906) 482-2030. Daily 9-9.*

DISTINCTIVE YOOPER FOODS . . . . . are a mark of strong regional identi-ty, self-sufficient isolation, and the great distance from normal distribution channels. Some groceries and big supermarkets like Fraki's in Calumet (one street north of Fifth) have **"squeaky cheese"** (*nisula*, a pleasantly sweetish, somewhat Jello-y fresh cheese), **saffron rolls** (light dinner rolls, a Cornish introduction, flavored and colored with brilliant yellow saffron with raisins added), and local Vollwerth's sausage. **Thimbleberry jam** is sold at houses along main tourist routes, and **pasties**, that famous Cornish meat-potato-rutabaga pie eaten by miners for lunch, are everywhere. **Trenary toast** is a twice-baked cinnamon toast made in Trenary, south of Marquette, and dunked in coffee. Great for camping — it keeps forever.

DOWNTOWN HOUGHTON . . . . . along Shelden Avenue is distinctive and architecturally rich, a college town full of surprises to reward the perceptive pedestrian. Lavishly ornamented buildings from the mining boom climb a steep hillside; interconnecting walkways make it easy to go from store to store in winter. There's plenty of parking on decks entered off Shelden or from the street below it. . . . . . **Book World** at 507 Shelden has the area's best magazine selection and a good array of paperbacks and hardcovers. Strengths include mining, local history, and Finnish culture. . . . . . For gifts and accessories, **The Windingo** at 403 Shelden stands out. . . . .

ROCKHOUNDS WILL BE DAZZLED . . . . . by the **A.E. Seaman Mineral Museum** at Michigan Technological University, a onetime mining college. In 1990 an act of the state legislature made it the official mineralogical museum of Michigan. Highlights of this extensive collection include a complete collection of specimens from the mineral-rich Upper Peninsula, a cave of iron ores, and dramatic fluorescent minerals displayed under black light. *The campus is a mile east of downtown. 1400 Townsend Dr., on the 5th floor of the EERC building (adjacent to the university library and to Parking Lot 5) on the Michigan Tech campus. Handicap-accessible. (906) 487-2572. Metered parking available within 1 block of museum; on Sat you may park in Lot 5. Open year-round Mon-Fri 9-4:30; in July thru Oct, also open Sat. 12-4. Free.*

Calumet and Laurium

*The past lives on in multi-ethnic Copper Country —
once a rollicking boom region bustling night and day.*

During the copper boom in the early 1900s, the scene on
Calumet's main street was more like a leading metropolis than a remote mining town. It had brick streets,
movie theaters and a grand opera house, frequent trollies, electric lights, and impressive four-story buildings of brick and
sandstone. Evenings were as bright and busy as daytime,
because miners worked round-the-clock shifts and so many people had money to spend.

The Keweenaw's booming copper mines had recruited workers from most parts of Europe, and many languages could be
heard on the streets: Finnish, Italian, Croatian, Slovenian,
French, Polish, German, Swedish, Gaelic, Norwegian, Greek,
English (spoken in Cornish, Irish, and Scottish accents), Welsh,
and Yiddish. Each major ethnic group had its saloons, over 70
in all, where outsiders dared not venture as the evening wore on.
And virtually every nationality had its church, many of them
magnificent, paid for in part by the Boston-based Calumet and
Hecla mining company.

Starting in the 1870s, the copper mines around Calumet
proved the most profitable the world has known. Copper was an
increasingly vital component used in the booming electrical and
plumbing industries of a rapidly modernizing world. And in
those days these were the biggest copper mines anywhere.

"Everywhere I saw steeples, steeples for churches," writes a
fictitious visitor to Calumet in 1900, created by historian-
journalist David Marciniak in his interesting *Copper Country
History* magazine. "On a door one poster advertised a revival and
temperance meeting. Another extolled the virtues of an upcoming mandolin and harp concert. . . . Businesses abounded: a
candy kitchen, Madam Buddha — clairvoyant and trance medium straight from the World's Fair. Enameled iron beds, four dollars and up. Fishing tackle, lawn mowers, poultry screen and ice
cream freezers. A Chinese laundry. The Bosch Brewing
Company."

The Calumet and Hecla Mining Company was the richest and biggest mining company of them all. Its office, now used by its successor, the **Lake Superior Land Company**, isn't a tourist spot. But it is interesting, and open to the public during business hours. It's on Red Jacket Road, just west of U.S. 41 by the turnoff to Calumet, in what looks like an oversize Queen Anne house made of contrasting stones of red and grey.

Despite the changes in ownership, the interior of these once nationally famous offices, trimmed in varnished wood, remains very much as it must have looked when Calumet and Hecla reigned supreme in these parts: classic oak desks and map cases, cases of mineral specimens, and a big oil **portrait of Alexander Agassiz**, son of the famed Harvard botanist. Though he would rather have devoted himself full-time to the study of botany, Agassiz was persuaded to spend his most productive decades managing Calumet and Hecla in absentia. The company's Bostonian paternalism was widely resented here as controlling and condescending. East of the office building is a big piece of "**float copper**," pure copper formed in pockets created by volcanic bubbles. Outside is a seated bronze **statue of Agassiz.** He has a cold, analytical gaze that changes unsettlingly as you shift your point of view.

Finns, Italians, Poles, Swedes, Norwegians, Croatians, French-Canadians, Russian Jews, Greeks — substantial numbers of most major American immigrant groups circa 1900 found their way to the Keewenaw Peninsula, either as mine workers or as small businesspeople catering to miners. Traces of mining are everywhere, from the rusted headframes that dot the landscape to the stories of miners and their descendants.

Calumet and Hecla sold its mines and land to Universal Oil Products. A 1968 strike closed the long-declining mines altogether. Later Universal sold its property, which includes most of Keweenaw County, to Lake Superior Land. The firm leases land for mineral rights, logging, and recreation, develops it, and sells it, sometimes in small lakefront lots. These park-like lands are open to the public for hiking, berry-picking, and hunting. But control is moving far away. Lake Superior's new owner is a Californian of Lebanese descent.

Today Calumet and its more genteel sister community of Laurium are shadows of what they were in the decade after 1910, when 40,000 people lived in the area. Calumet now numbers 800, Laurium 2,200.

The glorious, boisterous past is felt everywhere, but muted by the years, and by the simple lifestyle of local residents. They're a special breed, composed of people who have hung on after the mines finally shut down in 1968; old-timers come back to retire; grown-up kids who went to school or visited grandparents here; and the nature-lovers and Michigan Tech faculty who have moved to these towns 12 miles north of Houghton.

There is an island atmosphere about this isolated place, akin to the gentle, faded mood of declining mining boom towns of the West — the kind of places populated by old hippies, artists, and retired miners. Many splendid red brick and red sandstone buildings of the boom years remain. They have been preserved by local pride and by the complete absence of development pressure since Keweenaw copper mining first began to sour after World War I.

The people remain, too, hanging on to memories and to dreams that some day, when the world price of copper rises high enough, the mining companies will pump and drain off the water that has filled up the mines, reopen them, and tunnel further south along the Keweenaw vein where much copper still lies deeply buried and untapped. (The Centennial Mine in nearby Kearsarge did reopen in 1990, but more as an adjunct to the timber industry. Its copper is used in a nearby facility that makes Wolmanized lumber.)

Recently the **Keweenaw National Historical Park** was established. Modeled after the historic urban industrial park in Lowell, Massachusetts, it will include historic landmarks in Calumet, plus the Quincy Hoist and the smelters in Lake Linden. National Parks signs mark various park components,

Splendid architecture, beauti-
fully detailed but earthy in red
Jacobsville sandstone, is the
legacy of mining wealth the
Keewenaw Peninsula and nearby
Marquette. The 1900 Calumet
Theater (here) can be toured in
July and August.

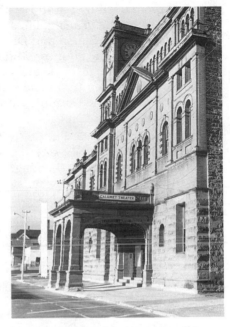

but nothing clsc has been
funded.

In the meantime,
Copper Country is a proud
backwater. "Living up here
is like living in the 1940s,"
says Lake Linden's dentist,
a University of Michigan
grad in his late 30s who
likes to boast that he has
the lowest income and best
lifestyle of anyone in his
dental school class. "The old
values are important. Most people are honest. But you have to
make your own activities — there's no entertainment here. A lot
of newcomers don't understand that."

It especially helps to have a local map in looking around
Calumet and Laurium because they are really collections of
smaller communities. Many consist of miners' houses clustered
around onetime mine shafts: Tamarack, Centennial, Osceola,
Red Jacket. Laurium has neighborhoods of more substantial
houses for managers and white-collar workers. A good map is in
the current year's edition of the always-interesting *Copper
Country History.* (As we go to press, it is uncertain whether this
magazine will be available free or by subscription; for information, call 906-337-5640.)

Noteworthy sights in the area include:

◆ The handsome red sandstone **Calumet Theater,** built at Elm
and Sixth in 1900, and paid for by taxes on Calumet's busy
saloons. **Tours** are held in July and August. The interior has
been faithfully restored to its original rich colors of gilt, red,
green, and cream. The old theater still creaks enough to seem
truly historic. You get to visit the dizzying upper balcony and
antiquated lights still in place. When you get to the backstage

dressing room used by Sarah Bernhardt, among others, it's not hard to imagine the grueling life of train travel that took the likes of John Philip Sousa and Douglas Fairbanks to such remote corners of the country. Today many kinds of events are held here, including local theater, visiting foreign bands and dance troupes; a country music series sponsored by a local radio station; and the Detroit Symphony Orchestra. *Call (906) 337-2610 for information.*

◆ Next to the theater at 322 Sixth, the landmark **Shute's 1890 Bar** remains closed as we go to press. It may reopen under new owners. Shute's still has the magnificent bar and all the trappings that marked boom town saloons. The bar itself has a splendid stained-glass canopy with vines; elaborate plaster caryatids frame the raised dance floor.

◆ Two blocks south on Sixth at Portland, the **post office** has a dramatic W.P.A. mural of broad-backed miners at work deep within the earth.

◆ Summer tours of the unusually elaborate **St. Paul the Apostle** church, built by Slovenian Catholics from 1903 to 1908, let you see the beautiful stained glass windows, altar, and paintings. Go north on Eighth from here and you'll be in Calumet's most attractive residential district. *Eighth and Oak. (906) 337-2044. The church is generally open as early as 7 a.m.; during summer, parishioners serve as guides from noon-3. Donations appreciated.*

◆ If you take Oak or Elm to Ninth and go south on Ninth until it turns into Osceola, you'll come to **Swedetown** in three-fourths of a mile. It's one of the little outlying mineshaft hamlets where some miners (especially Scandinavians) kept milk cows and chickens and big gardens out back, to help feed their large families and make ends meet. The mining companies built these standard, six-room houses; today they sell for around $20,000. The beautiful **Swedetown Ski Trails**, six miles of cross-country trails, wind through small, rolling hills. They're groomed for traditional cross-country and ski-skating, and they're skiable well into April, after the snow cover has melted on south-facing slopes up here.

◆ Retailing in Calumet isn't much, although the town is the trade center for all of Keweenaw County and the northern part of Houghton County. There's just not much money or many people here, and it's too easy to go to Houghton. **Copper World** and

Copper Art are two visitor-oriented stores together on Fifth at Portland, as you enter downtown from Red Jacket Road. The selection of copper items here is tremendous, and prices on items from copper teapots, plates, and molds to burnished sailboats and copper jewelry are lower than in Copper Harbor's more tasteful, less overwhelmingly coppery shops.

◆ **Coppertown**. This museum doesn't currently begin to approach the quality of the State of Michigan's iron-mining museum near Negaunee, but it does focus on copper mining and show how Calumet and Hecla produced usable copper from copper-bearing rock. Lots of mining equipment, old and new: drills, lamps, carts, and much more. *On Red Jacket Rd. between U.S. 41 and Calumet. (906) 337-4354. Open early June through Sept. Mon-Sat 10-4. Adults $2, children 12 & under 50¢. Coppertown may offer **Calumet historic trolley rides**, a 45-minute narrated tour along Fifth Street, Calumet's main street. Daily July through September, trolleys may leave Coppertown on the hour; adults $4, children $3.*

◆ Neighboring **Laurium** shows off Copper Country's more gracious side. Time has not been kind to the historic downtown along Hecla. But just east of it, along Tamarack, Pewabic, and Iroquois between Second and Fourth, is a lovely, settled, neighborhood of turn-of-the-century homes, built with style and comfort to compensate mine managers for the hardships of having to live in this remote place. Some houses are quite grand, with rear carriage houses, sweeping stairways, stained-glass windows, and low red sandstone walls along the street; some are merely pleasant. Yards feature flower gardens, very long wood piles, and occasional Italian shrines. Deep maple shade sets this part of Laurium apart from the sparse streetscapes of miners' homes. To get to Laurium from U.S. 41, turn southeast onto Lake Linden Rd. (M-26) at the visitor center.

Laurium Manor, a bed and breakfast inn at 320 Tamarack, in the 41-room antebellum mansion of mining magnate James Hoatson, is open for tours daily May through October at noon, 1, 2, and 3; $2/person. In November through April, tours can be arranged by calling (906) 337-2549.

At Third and Pewabic, there's a corner park with a **band shell**, where Thursday-evening summer concerts take place at 7 o'clock. You can get a good Jilbert's ice cream cone for your walk through historic Laurium at the **Honey Cone**, 224 Hecla at Depot. For a takeout picnic in the park, you can pick up pasties at **Toni's Country Kitchen**, nearby on Third at Kearsarge. It's reputed to have the best pasties around.

◆ **Jukuri's Sauna** is one of three public saunas left in the U.P. (Lots of homes have saunas out back, or inside the main house.) This plain tile building has 12 private, gas-fired saunas that rent for $3.50 an hour. They're fired up Wednesday and Friday from 2 to 10 and Saturday from noon to 10. For many families, a relaxing visit to Jukuri's is a Saturday-night tradition, especially in mid-winter. (No one wears swimsuits, but men and women usually bathe separately.) Eating and unwinding is part of the event, and a big selection of junk food is sold in the pine-paneled foyer along with Jukuri's sweatshirts and T-shirts. *Wed & Fri 2-10 p.m., Sat noon-10. 600 Lake Linden Rd. (M-26). (906) 337-4145.*

THE BEST DISPLAY OF COPPER-MINING HISTORY . . . . . . is in Lansing in the **State Historical Museum** (see page 406). Its **mining exhibits** include a life-size recreated passage within a copper mine. Currently it covers copper-mining far better than anything you'll find on location, although the establishment of the **Keweenaw National Historical Park** promises to change that.

GOING DOWN TO LAKE LINDEN . . . . . from Laurium on M-26 is a spectacularly steep and scenic drive, because you're descending from the tilted-up edge of volcanic crust that carries the vein of copper. . . . . The **Douglass Houghton Falls** drop over the sheer cliffs of this edge. From M-26 about 1 1/2 miles southeast of the outskirts of Laurium, look for a flat dirt parking area to the left (northeast) side of the road. A path along the hilltop offers splendid views and the pleasant sound of Hammell Creek plashing between grassy banks. Then it disappears. Suddenly, without warning signs, a canyon opens up before you, dangerous and dramatic, and you see the creek rushing over rocks, then down to the canyon floor far below. There's no railing at all; this worthwhile adventure is no jaunt for rambunctious children. . . . . **Lake Linden** is a French-Canadian town built alongside the Calumet and Hecla stamping mills. C&H's great innovation was to develop a process that utilized small amounts of copper deposits carried by much of the area's rock, and not just the pure pockets of "float copper" formed in volcanic gas bubbles. C & H carried quantities of copper-rich rock by narrow-gauge railway down to Lake Linden on Torch Lake. There the rocks were crushed and the metal smelted out of the rock. The onetime C&H office and medical dispensary now house the motley collections of the **Houghton County Historical Museum**, yet another collection of poorly explained local history so common in U.P. mining areas. *On M-26 south of downtown. Open early June thru Sept, Mon-Sat 10-4, Sun 1-4. Adults $2.50, seniors and students $2, children under 12 free, family $5.* . . . . . Far more evocative and interesting to the average visitor is the **Lindell Chocolate Shoppe** at 300 Calumet in downtown Lake Linden. It is an elaborate sweet shoppe from the 1920s, the glory days of that restaurant genre. Quick lunch counters and soda fountains like this thrived in newly industrialized areas, where workers had cash for inexpensive treats. Italian and especially Greek immigrants latched onto the sweet shoppe as a business opportunity where the whole family could work, making hand-dipped chocolates and ice cream, and where it didn't matter if their English was rudimentary. Here the Greek owners' names, Grammas and Pallis, are proudly spelled out in tiles on the entryway. Inside, the marble counter on the soda fountain has given way to Formica, but the back booths and paneling are perfectly preserved. The interior is all aglow with golden oak, accented with little fringed lamps. The food is ordinary lunch-counter fare.

M-26 from Phoenix to Copper Harbor

Something like Maine, something like Scandinavia — great natural beauty without any pretensions

About 15 miles north of Calumet begins one of the most idyllic and undeveloped landscapes in the United States. From Eagle River to Copper Harbor, the Lake Superior shoreline looks a lot like Maine. Rocky shores and islets are interrupted by occasional crescent bays and beaches — some sandy, some rocky. Few summer houses block the shoreline view from M-26; considerations of real estate values and money don't yet seem to come into play in this remote northwoods paradise. Frequent roadside parks have benches, picnic tables, and occasional gazebos. Tidy rustic signs hanging from brown cedar posts point out historic and scenic highlights. On the opposite side of the road, trails climb into ferny-floored forests of white pine, balsam, and hardwoods. Here, and on cutover sunny areas of birch and aspen, the landscape looks amazingly like Scandinavia. Thimbleberry bushes with velvety, maple-like leaves and bright red berries border many roads and cover open woods; occasional houses advertise "THIMBLEBERRY JAM FOR SALE." The intensely-flavored spread is locally prized.

Every few miles a sign points out the path to a waterfall, formed as short creeks and rivers come cascading down to Lake Superior from the peninsula's high spine. Past Eagle Harbor, you can choose to stay along the lovely shore. Or you can take the famous Brockway Mountain Drive (page 766) up to a spectacular panoramic view of the shoreline and inland lakes that leaves you feeling you're floating above the Earth's surface in a balloon.

When you drive out from Calumet on U.S. 41/M-26, you follow a high ridge and fault line that forms the spine of the Keweenaw Peninsula. The ridge is marked by a string of spare, plain mining settlements — Kearsarge, Allouez, Ahmeek, Mohawk, Phoenix, Delaware — that stretch much of the way to Copper Harbor. Here the ancient, mineral-rich volcanic crust, part of the Canadian Shield, tilts northwest down into Lake Superior. The ridge is the crust's edge. At the hamlet of Cliff, it

Waves crash against the rocks below the lighthouse at Eagle Harbor. Its museums and bookstore are fine places to spend a rainy day.

becomes a dramatic, sheer rocky precipice. It looms over the Eagle River, which cuts through the Cliff Range at Phoenix and tumbles down to Lake Superior. At Phoenix M-26 turns northwest off U.S. 41 and takes the scenic route along the Eagle River and Lake Superior shore to Copper Harbor.

From here to the Keweenaw's tip at Copper Harbor, copper deposits were closer to the surface, and in smaller amounts. Mining boomed early, in the 1840s, and played out soon. All of Keweenaw County, from Allouez and Mohawk to Copper Harbor, numbers only 1,700 year-round residents.

In 1844, the Cliff Mine became the Keweenaw's first mine to strike it rich and earn big profits. It and nearby mining villages and shipping ports toward the Keweenaw's tip are the oldest settlements in the western Upper Peninsula. Many houses and churches date from well before the Civil War and the ensuing industrial boom. They're simple frame buildings — sometimes you even see log houses — without any of the opulence of late 19th-century buildings in Calumet or Laurium, Houghton, or Marquette, with their sandstone ornament and stained glass.

Plan on stopping for a picnic along the way, perhaps in a secluded spot on the beach or in the woods, or in one of the two delightful little parks overlooking Lake Superior between Eagle Harbor and Copper Harbor. For best selection of fresh fruit and deli salads, you might want to plan ahead and stop at the food co-op (page 748) or the big supermarket in Calumet. Otherwise, there's a decent little grocery in Mohawk, simple general stores in Phoenix and Eagle Harbor, and bakeries in and near Copper Harbor.

Here are some interesting stops along M-26 between Calumet and Copper Harbor:

◆ **Superior Crafts** in Ahmeek. Resourceful locals make rustic cedar furniture and lawn swings in a former mine building, the "dry" where 300 to 400 miners used to clean up and change clothes. Signs about mine safety precautions are still on the walls. *(906) 337-0875. Mon-Fri 7:30-4:30, Sat 8-1.*

◆ **Keweenaw Handcrafts Shop** and the **snow gauge** just north of Ahmeek mark the entrance to Keweenaw County. The county is full of charming W.P.A. relief projects from the 1930s like these. Relief projects were widespread because of Keweenaw County's 85% unemployment rate during the Depression. The shop, now run by the Community Action Agency, sells things made by 260 craftspeople, mostly senior citizens, in three counties. Among the ordinary dolls and kit crafts are some attractive, reasonably priced traditional crafts like rag rugs ($23 for a 55" rug), folk art whirligigs ($32), and handmade children's sweaters under $20. *(906) 482-5528. Open Memorial Day thru mid-October.* The much-photographed **snow gauge** records annual cumulative snowfall, often 250 inches. Because the accumulated snow continually compacts and melts, there's rarely more than five feet at a time, except in drifts. (Snow removal is a major priority of local government. Locals don't usually have to wait long for the snow plow to come, but it's understood that all winter engagements are tentative, depending on the weather.)

◆ In **Phoenix**, stop at the **picnic table** by the **Church of the Assumption** or the general store and take in the view of river valley and rocky cliffs. The simple wood church was built in 1858 to serve miners at the Cliff mines. *Viewable by visitors from mid-June through Sept, daily 12-5. Donations welcome.*

◆ **Eagle River**, founded as a copper-shipping port in 1843, was named after the many eagles soaring overhead. Now a summer place with a tiny year-round population, it has several interesting sights the hurried motorist might miss. On M-26 south of the village, the worn monuments in the rustic **Eagle River Cemetery** attest to the many dangers and accidents that cut short miners' lives. As you pass over the bridge across the **Eagle River gorge**, pull over to the right, go over onto the old iron bridge, and look upstream for a view of rushing rapids, the ruined dam of the Lake Superior Fuse Company, and the dramatic wood arches supporting the new bridge.

Douglass Houghton, Michigan's state geologist, first drew attention to the Upper Peninsula's mineral riches. He drowned off the shore of Eagle River after he ignored the recommendations of his French and Indian guides and continued their canoe expedition in a storm. The **Houghton monument** by M-26 is boring. Much more interesting is a visit to the **Keweenaw County courthouse**, on the upper road that branches off to the right as you cross the bridge. It looks like a frame Southern mansion, with massive columns and portico. Inside, you can get a good **map** of county highways and byways. Government in this tiny county is an exercise in small-scale thrift and ingenuity. The jail next door, behind the sheriff's pleasant frame house, was temporarily closed for remodeling to bring it up to code so that the tiny county will no longer be urged to pay for transporting prisoners considerable distances and jailing them at approved facilities. One thing that hasn't changed is that prisoners eat good food prepared by the sheriff's wife for family and staff.

The **beach** at Eagle River is sandy and fairly warm but not as scenic as others farther north. There's a lively beachfront restaurant, and even condos.

◆ **Sand Dunes Drive** is the name of the beautiful eight-mile stretch of M-26 between Eagle River and Eagle Harbor. It parallels the sandy beach of the **Great Sand Bay**. Frequent pullovers encourage motorists to get out and take a swim or walk down the beach. The tilted shelf of volcanic crust drops off so rapidly under water, that the bay is up to 1,300 feet deep. On the opposite side of the road is the steep, dark, rocky forest, carpeted in pine needles.

Delightful **Jacob's Falls** cascades right near the road, 2 1/2 miles east of Eagle River. Next to the scenic pullout, tucked away in the piney hillside, is **The Jam Pot**. This memorably quaint little spot has the sweet simplicity of an earlier, gentler, more personal era of tourism. To this idyllic spot two monks (yes, monks - complete with hooded brown robes) have withdrawn from the world and their native city of far-away Detroit, to establish the society of St. John. They bake very good muffins, breads, cookies, brownies, and giant chocolate chip cookies, along with rich cakes, largely sold mail-order. And they make jams and butters from a big variety of local berries — apple-plum butter, wild bill-

Brother Peter in front of The Jampot bakery by Jacob's Falls. Just one of its muffins makes a satisfying lunch.

berry, strawberry, and more.

The muffins are huge — one makes a good lunch. The pumpkin muffin, full of raisins and nuts and iced with lemon frosting, wins raves for its flavor and texture. The cakes — things like walnut ginger cake, lemon pound cake, Jamaican Black Cake — are quite elaborate and costly. Take the Abbey Cake (around $30/4 pounds), described as "the perennial favorite. Rich, moist, and chewy, with dark raisins and walnuts in a molasses batter. It is generously laced with bourbon and will keep and improve for years." And at $4 to $7, the jams and jellies aren't cheap, either. Order forms are sent in back of a newsletter filled with prayers, scripture, meditations, and reflections about life (spiritual and everyday) at the monks' Keweenaw home. An excerpt: "When we hear the comment at The Jampot, 'Well, you certainly do live in God's country,' we are likely to respond, 'Everywhere is God's country.' If we are feeling talkative, we may also add, 'But it is easier to see Him in some places than in others.'" *Open daily May through fall color season in early Oct. No phone. Mailing address: The Society of St. John, Star Route 1, Box 226, Eagle Harbor, MI 49950.*

◆ **Eagle Harbor** is a quaint collection of ancient frame houses and newish cottages. They surround a shallow, protected harbor and **beach** that's one of Lake Superior's most reliably warm places to swim. It's the prettiest village in the northern Keweenaw, with just enough attractions to make it a lazily interesting place to stay: two good, homey restaurants with pie and takeout sandwiches for a picnic, easy access to Brockway Mountain Drive and other excursions, and two delightful local museums run by the Keweenaw Historical Society, an energetic group of old-timers and summer people who have produced some impressive exhibits. The protected, shallow **beach** at the harbor is pleasantly warm for Lake Superior.

The **Eagle Harbor Lighthouse and Museum** survey the harbor entrance. The red brick lightkeeper's house, built in 1871, is realistically furnished circa 1910-1920 and staffed by local people old enough to go back almost that far themselves. Outside are **picnic tables** on a sunny, rocky promontory with a fabulous view. You could spend rainy hours looking at all the stuff in the adjoining a mineral collection, paintings of local scenes, a fine exhibit on the Keweenaw's prehistoric copper culture, and an elaborate ritual costume of the fraternal order of the **Knights of Pythias**. The Eagle Harbor schoolteacher dreamed up the order here and founded it in 1864. The order's ceremonies, based on the Roman story of the friendship of Damon and Pythias, celebrate the virtues of brotherly friendship and self-sacrifice; the Knights' mock-Roman tunics are decorated with hundreds of metal discs.

A separate **maritime museum** building to the rear covers shipwrecks and fishing in great detail; another building deals with surveying, smelting, and mining. Many exhibits are dense stuff, too much for casual visitors. But the museum is the best single place on the Keweenaw to assemble an overview of the area's history. And the **museum shop** offers an outstanding selection of books about the Upper Peninsula and Lake Superior. It's worth a trip in its own right. *Follow signs from M-26 to lighthouse/museum. Open daily, mid-June thru Sept, 12-5. $1/person.*

Additional interesting material on the Knights of Pythias, including some fabulous fake jewels and embroidered satin robes, is in the **Rathbone School House** on a side street southeast of M-26 on the village's west side. *Open daily 12-5, mid-June through September. Donations welcome.*

◆ From **Eagle Harbor to Copper Harbor**, the view along 14 miles of lakeshore drive is the Keweenaw's rockiest and most dramatic stretch of shoreline. Four and a half miles east of Eagle Harbor, a roadside sign indicates **Silver River Falls**. By all means take the easy path through an overarching woods, both leafy and pleasantly piney. You'll hear and soon see the sparkling little river descending from a stone-arched bridge.

Rustic-style mileposts and directional signs are deployed throughout Keweenaw County. A Keweenaw County Road Commission employee cuts down replacement cedar posts in frozen swamps. In winter the signs are taken in and repainted. The picturesque signs, the lack of billboards, and the vast stretches of undeveloped land make much of the county seem like a vast park.

Alternately it spreads out over rocky terraces and rests in a series of pools.

Across the river, **Brockway Mountain Drive** (p. 766) climbs 600 feet to one of the most spectacular views you're likely to see. Save it for an excursion from Copper Harbor, and stay on M-26. Soon you'll come to **Esprey Park**, with picnic tables and grills, where stone steps go up to a rocky perch and a rustic gazebo. Just west of the park is a Michigan Nature Association preserve. Look for the small signs that say "protected area." Across the road is a posted **hiking trail** through a magically mossy forest.

In a few miles, the road runs right beside a place where big, bare slabs of ancient volcanic crust tilt right into Lake Superior. A wide shoulder lets you get out and explore the rocks and the tiny lichen, tough little flowers and stunted trees that find sustenance in cracks in these rocks. Six miles east of here, **Hebard Park** is another simple little park with picnic tables, grills, outhouses, and wonderful view.

Three more miles and you come to the village of **Copper Harbor**, Keweenaw County's tourism hub.

"ONE CANNOT FEEL HISTORY FROM THE AUTOMOBILE," . . . . . advises a fine little free historical guide put out by the Keweenaw Historical Society, "so take leisurely walks through our old and abandoned villages, around mine sites and historic landmarks, allowing time to reflect upon those who have gone before. Your visit will be greatly enriched at no cost."

THE LOW-KEY CHARMS OF THE KEWEENAW'S EAST SHORE . . . . .
Often when the scenic rugged, west-facing side of the peninsula is cloudy, the lower east side, protected by the high central ridge, is sunny. It's completely flat, and once you get away from the towns along Dollar Bay, there's virtually no traffic, which makes for wonderful, easy **bicycling**. People from Keweenaw towns and cities have their "camps" for fishing and hunting up here ("cottage" is too sedate a term) but there's little resort activity. . . . .
From Mohawk, turn east from M-26 toward the town of Gay. At the **Gay Bar**, a typical Yooper bar, you can get a Gay Bar T-shirt, subtitled "Gay, Mich."
. . . . .The scenic **shoreline drive** beginning at Gay passes many marshes, and shore birds are frequently seen. Wild blueberries can be picked from the road during most of August. . . . .There's a **roadside park** at Betsy Bay 7 miles northeast of Gay. Way across Keweenaw Bay, the Huron Mountains (the highest elevations in Michigan) beckon blue in the distance. . . . .The best swimming is almost 20 miles farther, at **Bete Grise** (locals say "BAY duh GREE"), east of Lac La Belle. Shallow depth makes for tolerably warm water for swimming. Eagles nest at Bear Bluff across Bete Grise Bay and are frequently seen.

For an even less traveled trip, go south from Lake Linden on Bootjack Road and Dreamland Road to get to **Jacobsville**, at the entry to the Portage Channel. Big red sandstone cliffs were quarried for many of the area's finest buildings. From the old lighthouse and breakwater, there's a fine view across the Keweenaw Bay to the Huron Mountains.

Brockway Mountain Drive

See glorious sunsets, soaring hawks, and a splendid view of the Keweenaw's rocky shore on the highest highway between the Rockies and the Alleghenies.

Most spectacular of all Keweenaw County's Depression-era relief projects is this nine-mile road that twists and climbs to one of the peninsula's highest peaks, a thousand feet above Lake Superior. At the windswept **Brockway Mountain Lookout**, you're so high above the Keweenaw Peninsula's rocky shore and the islands stretched out below you that the view seems almost like a living map. You can look down on soaring hawks and occasional eagles.

The mountain's western slope goes down to Lake Superior. It's the surface of the Keweenaw's uptilted, copper-bearing volcanic crust. Inland to the east, the broken edge along the north-south fault line becomes an almost vertical rocky cliff that drops down to the river valley below. Each spring, peaking in mid-April, hawks migrate northeast along the entire Keweenaw Peninsula. They gather by these cliffs to ride the updrafts out to the peninsula's end — a final boost before their long flight across Lake Superior.

The view from the lookout is so riveting, it's easy to forget about all the other remarkable features of this unusual road, the highest between the Alleghenies and the Rockies. The habitat toward the top is actually semi-alpine. The mountain's many varied ecosystems are home to many **wildflowers and berries** as well as trillium, orchids, wild strawberries, and thimbleberries — over 700 flowers in all, including many rare and endangered species, some found nowhere else in Michigan.

Here and all over the northern Keweenaw, the land seems like a vast park. Actually, most of it is onetime mining land now owned by the Lake Superior Land Company (page 752). In return for favorable commercial forest taxes, this land is legally open to the public for recreational use, including rock-gathering, mountain-biking, and berry-picking. The drive's stone walls — and the drive itself — are part of a Depression-era make-work project.

Be sure to stop at the **panoramic overlook** down onto
Copper Harbor near the drive's eastern end. For maximum
enjoyment, devote an hour or two to the drive and stop frequently. Bring binoculars, bug spray, walking shoes, and a compass if
you want to hike in the forest. Take a late-afternoon trip, and
you'll witness a **sunset view** that's hard to match. **Fall color
season** is even more glorious. It usually begins the second week
of September and lasts into mid-October.

*Drive entrances are 5 miles northeast of Eagle Harbor and half a
mile south of Copper Harbor. The drive is not plowed in winter. It's
open from the first snow-free days of spring (that's usually in late
May) up to the first snowfall. No admission fee.*

GUIDED FIELD TRIPS NEAR COPPER HARBOR . . . . . may be arranged
through Jim Rooks' Keweenaw Bear Track Tours. He was instrumental in
saving the **Estivant Pines**, the Upper Peninsula's last stand of virgin white
pines. They're one of his popular tour destinations, along with old mine sites,
birdwatching expeditions, geology or wildflower walks, cross-country skiing,
and more. Not for the impatient — Rooks has lots to say — but a good way to
focus on the details of the natural world around you. Fees are around
$15/person/half day, children (from 6 to 12) $7. Full-day tours are $25/
adult and $12/children. Call him in advance (906-289-4813) to arrange a
trip tailored to your interests, or sign up for a regular 9 a.m. or 1 p.m. walk
beginning at his wife's **Laughing Loon Handcrafts**. It's located at the northern tail of Highway 41 (Old Military Trail) that begins in Miami, Florida.
Get information about the Estivant Pines there or at Fort Wilkins. Look for
Walking Paths in Keweenaw, a guide to the Michigan Nature Association's 11
preserves on the peninsula.

FOR A REWARDING HIKE TO A REMARKABLE BEACH . . . . . start at the
west end of the parking lot at the Copper Harbor marina and look for the
trailhead to beautiful **Agate Beach**. The trail heads west through an evergreen forest close to Lake Superior's shore. In about 3/4 of a mile it forks.
Right takes you out along a peninsula that forms the harbor, to Hunter's
Point. Left, and you cut across the peninsula's narrow base to come to Agate
Beach, covered by pebbles and stones that sometimes include beautiful
agates. They're hard to distinguish from other translucent, quartz-rich rocks
because all are covered with little scratches that obscure the distinctive
banding that becomes apparent when agates are cut and polished.

Fort Wilkins Historic Complex

A remote Army outpost, built in the 1840s
to handle America's first mining rush

The 1843 Keweenaw copper rush, the first mining rush in American history, led to the building of this small fort. For three years the fort was the only source of law and order. The government's greatest concern was friction between native Indians and unruly newcomers, but little hostility actually broke out. By 1846 most of the small-time prospectors had left, and large mining companies had given and stability to the region.

This was a typical 19th-century frontier garrison, the most northern in the U.S., 600 miles from Detroit. The old fort became a favorite picnic spot among outdoor enthusiasts after the army abandoned it in the 1870s. The thickly forested site is uncommonly picturesque, on beautiful Lake Fanny Hooe (named after a pretty young lady who early visited the fort). When the old fort became a state park in 1923, less than half the structures remained. Some buildings were rebuilt.

What you see today is a stockade surrounding 19 buildings: kitchen and mess room, hospital, bakery, company quarters, etc. Some have been restored and authentically furnished by the state's first-rate Bureau of History as they might have been; others have brief, to-the-point displays about military life and the fort's archaeology and natural history. The first cabin you enter when visiting the fort has a good, small **natural history bookstore** and a display of live wildflowers.

Of the soldiers garrisoned here between 1844 and 1870, we learn that 8% died while in the army, half of natural causes, and 11% deserted. The officers' quarters have fancy lamps and furniture befitting their higher status. Their resident wives were supposed to bring civilization to the frontier.

It's worth beginning your visit by seeing the well-written **tape-slide show** in the visitor center installed in the second building. It provides a fine introduction to the early history of Keweenaw copper-mining. (Just outside the fort is an abandoned mine shaft from the 1840s.) **Living history** can be a real high-

Costumed interpreters give convincing performances as soldiers' wives (here doing the wash) and as the schoolteacher. They answer questions about everyday life with the accents and vocabularies of the real-life people they represent.

light of a visit. When you look in some buildings — for instance, the simple cottage of an enlisted man — you come upon a woman in period dress working away. Ask her questions about her life on the fort, and she answers in character — with a surprisingly convincing manner and accent. It's worth overcoming any embarrassment you might feel to come in for a chat; kids can really get interested in these conversations.

The big **gift shop** outside the fort suits all tastes and has numerous nifty activity toys, books, and games for children. Check here for a schedule of **summer evening programs and events**, and for information on **boat tours** to the **Copper Harbor lighthouse/museum**, managed by the park.

2 1/2 miles east of Copper Harbor on U.S. 41. (906) 289-4215. Park open 8 a.m.-10 p.m. State park sticker required; $4/day, $18/year. Park interpreters and living history on site 10-5:30 daily from mid-June to Labor Day. Buildings open mid-May through mid-October. Park open all year.

CAMPING AT FORT WILKINS . . . . . isn't terribly adventurous, but the location is most convenient. 162 modern sites are on big loops in wooded areas that back up on beautiful Lake Fanny Hooe (good for swimming) and are adjacent to the old fort, camp store, old cemetery, and other interesting sights. You can easily walk across the road and see Lake Superior, and it's not far to the town of Copper Harbor, either. Reserve in advance from July through mid-August, especially Monday through Wednesday.

A PLEASANT CRUISE OUT TO THE LIGHTHOUSE . . . . . leaves from Copper Harbor's Municipal Pier on the harbor and takes 15 minutes each way. Cost: adults $8, children $4. Call (906) 289-4215 for schedule after mid-May. Before mid-May, call the park office (906-289-4215). The 1866 lighthouse itself, part of Fort Wilkins State Park, is on a dark, rocky peninsula forming the harbor. There's no public right of way by land. So the short boat ride is the only way to visit this lonely spot and the small **maritime museum** in the lighthouse. A very simple earlier keeper's house, from the copper rush of the 1840s, is by the boat dock, and all sort of shipwreck artifacts line the walk up the hill to the lighthouse.

HEAVEN FOR ROCKHOUNDS . . . . . The public is permitted to visit and gather rocks and berries on the vast land holdings of the Lake Superior Land Company, which includes most of the northern Keweenaw Peninsula. Maps of agate beaches and old mines with rock piles can be purchased at the **New Keweenaw Agate Shop** on U.S. 41 in Copper Harbor. Mineralogist-owner Les Tolen has a splendid collection of mineral specimens (datolite, greenstone, and malachite are native to the area), lots of books on area geology, and rockhounds' tools. *Open daily from Memorial Day through mid-October. He may be away at shows other times; call first. (906) 289-4491.*

SHOPS IN COPPER HARBOR . . . . . especially for people interested in nature, are among the most interesting in the Upper Peninsula, an area unashamedly out of sync with trends and fashions. **Laughing Loon Handcrafts**, on First and Bernard a block north of U.S. 41 at the east end of town, is run by dedicated naturalists Laurel and Jim Rooks. It has the best local selection of books on regional history and nature, including *Walking Paths in Keweenaw*. (906-289-4813) . . . . . Right on U.S. 41, the **Thunderbird Gift Center** at the Minnetonka Resort (906-289-4449) is a rambling, old-fashioned souvenir shop with all the classics (rubber tomahawks, etc.), plus new and used books, antiques, and a fun, old-timey museum full of antique dolls and Indian artifacts.

© 1991, Bobbi Jean Litsenberger

Isle Royale

*Over 50 miles from the Michigan mainland,
this remote island is a superb place
for hikers or fishermen to confront true wilderness.*

For the person seeking the ultimate Midwestern wilderness experience, this 45-mile-long island is the leading candidate. The largest and most remote of all Great Lakes islands is a four-hour or six-hour boat ride from Michigan's Upper Peninsula.

This least-visited National Park gets as many visitors in a season (about 16,000) as Yosemite and Yellowstone get in a day. It's a place where you can stay in a lodge with meals provided and attend evening programs on natural and cultural history, or where you can camp in the backcountry and go for days without seeing anyone – it's your choice. Away from the park's hub at Rock Harbor, the only sounds you hear are natural sounds, except for an infrequent boat whistle or a daily airplane flight. You might well see a moose up close, or find fresh wolf tracks in the mud. You'll certainly hear the unforgettable laugh of the loon. Hikers will glimpse red foxes, which have become accustomed to people here and taken to hanging around campgrounds. (They should *not* be fed!) And canoeists can easily come upon beavers.

For the most part this has remained a pristine natural area. Several commercial fishermen have lived here in the past. The only known villages were short-lived, set up briefly by copper-mining companies in the late 19th century. Hundreds of years ago, Indians dug copper from hundreds of pits that can still be seen today.

The narrow island, only three to nine miles wide, is a series of long ridges that are really uplifted lava shelves – the mirror image of the Keweenaw's dramatic geology. The highest points are the edges of the upthrust, broken crust. This is the rocky, subarctic landscape of the Laurentian Shield, Precambrian formations that are from the earth's oldest geological age. A much-studied timber wolf population which crossed on an ice bridge in 1948 has dwindled to 15 in 1994, down from 1979's high of 50.. A moose herd which crossed frozen Lake Superior inthe early 1900s now numbers 1,800, the greatest density of moose in the lower 48 states.

Hikers have 166 miles of paths to follow, including the 42-mile **Greenstone Trail** following the island's central ridge. This five- to six-day trek is the most popular. Some hikers start out after taking a seaplane to the southeastern end. The trip's first part is through thickly forested terrain affording few views. **Mount Ojibway** (elevation 1,183 feet) is one of several peaks along the trail that provides splendid views to the Canadian mainland 15 miles away. Small **campgrounds** are along the trail three to 12 miles apart. There are 36 campgrounds in all, with 253 campsites, but only lakeshore campgrounds allow fires. Other campers bring their own portable stoves. A water filter is also needed, except in the two campgrounds at Rock Harbor and Windigo. They have water, fire pits, and showers. Backpacking novices are advised to get in shape, try out equipment beforehand, and plan carefully before embarking on a trip where they may be several days' hike from help. Camping is free. Campers should obtain backcountry permits on the island; sites aren't reservable.

Many come for the **fishing**. Pike are plentiful in lakes such as Lake Richie. Lake Whittlesey is known for walleye, and huge Siskiwit Lake for brook trout. Because the island's 42 lakes have

Trails along Isle Royale are dotted with 86 three-sided sleeping shelters with screened fronts.

Breeding loons need solitude. Because their nesting sites are at water level, the loon's reproductive success is threatened by boaters' wakes and by dams that change the water level. At Isle Royale, quiet is encouraged, and motorized boats are prohibited on inland lakes.

© 1991, Bobbi Joan Litsenberger

to be reached by foot, and boats have to be carried, none is heavily fished. Boats 20' and under and canoes can be brought over from Houghton on the Ranger III, and canoes can be transported from Copper Harbor. Some campgrounds are on islands reachable only by water.

For those who aren't into backpacking, a concessionaire runs **Rock Harbor Lodge**. Its 60 rooms cost $194 for two adults,, including meals. It is the headquarters for **boat and canoe rentals**, **fishing charters**, **sightseeing tours** (including a two-hour evening cruise/nature hike), a **restaurant**, a **snack bar**, and a **store** with camping supplies. Free **nature walks** and nightly **auditorium programs** are held here, too. Twenty nearby **housekeeping cabins** (maximum occupancy of six) rent for $126 for two people (add $5 if you're staying only one day). Meals are not included, though cabin guests are welcome to eat at the lodge restaurant and snack bar. Make reservations well in advance.

Introductory information about Isle Royale may be obtained by calling or writing the park at (906) 482-0984; 800 E. Lakeshore Dr., Houghton, MI 49931. Anyone investing the time and money in a trip to Isle Royale should also buy ahead of time a little book by ardent outdoorsman Jim Du Fresne to read on the boat. *Isle Royale National Park: Foot Trails & Water Routes* (The Mountaineers, ISBN 0-89886-082-2, $10.95) has interesting introductions to the island's history, flora and fauna, fish, and general logisti-

The rock formations of Isle Royale (here) mirror those of the Keweenaw
Peninsula's west-facing slope.

cal information. Detailed descriptions of hikes and trails, lakes and paddles will prove invaluable to anyone doing any walking or canoeing at all. (If you can't locate a copy, we at Midwestern Guides will keep some on hand to mail promptly, as a service to our readers. Send a $13 check made out to Midwestern Guides, 506 Linden, Albion, MI 49224. Add $1.50 extra for UPS instead of book rate.)

Late August and early September is the best time to visit Isle Royale. By then the sometimes irritating black fly population has dwindled, and so have the number of visitors. But the island is never crowded. Typically fewer than 300 people share the 134,000 acres.

The nation's most remote national park, Isle Royale is an improbable part of the state of Michigan. It's just 15 miles from Canada and far closer to Minnesota than Michigan. Legend has it that Benjamin Franklin secured it for the U.S. in negotiations with the British because he thought its copper would be useful in electrical experiments.

Open for visitors mid-April through October. Full services mid-June to Labor Day. Boat service from Copper Harbor (4 1/2 hours one-way), Grand Portage, Minnesota (7 1/2 hours), or Houghton (6 hours). Float plane from Houghton. For more details, write Isle Royale National Park, 800 E. Lakeshore Dr., Houghton, MI 49931. (906) 482-0984. Reservations for Rock Harbor Lodge during off season (502) 773-2191; in season (906) 337-4993.

Exceptional public golf courses

Michigan gives travelers one of the widest and finest selections of public golf courses in the world. We've picked some of the best, chosen to cover most parts of the Lower Peninsula. An excellent, much more complete guide is *Jack Berry's 1993 Guide to Michigan Golf* ($9.95). Prices below are for 18 holes. Courses are listed in the same order as the highlights in our book, beginning with the southwest corner of the state and heading east to Detroit, then north.

Hampshire Country Club — *Dowagiac. Southwest Michigan*
Gently rolling fairways and lots of trees make this long (7,000 yards from the blue tees) course a worthy challenge. It's a pre-qualifying course for the Western Amateur. *$14 weekdays. $16 weekends. plus $18 for cart. (616) 782-7476.*

Lake Doster Golf Club — *Plainwell. Southwest Michigan*
This course north of Kalamazoo is one of the tops in the state. It's a challenging, championship course, with water on 8 of the holes. The third, a short par 3, is one of the most beautiful and difficult in Michigan. From an elevated tee, you shoot to a green surrounded by water and sand. *$22 weekdays: $25 weekends. (616) 685-5308.*

Bedford Valley Golf Course — *Battle Creek. Southwest Michigan*
A traditional course with lots of sand and big greens, Bedford Valley offers a true test of golf. *$23 weekdays: $26 weekends. (616) 965-3384.*

Salem Hills Golf Club — *Northville. Metro Detroit*
Voted the 6th most enjoyable course in Michigan, Salem Hills allows fairly wide-open tee shots but its approach shots are demanding and its par 3s long. Toughest hole is the 11th, a 430-yard dogleg with a creek in front of the green. *$18 weekdays without cart. $29 with cart. Weekends $35 with cart. (810) 437-2152*

Pine Trace Golf Club — *Rochester Hills. Metro Detroit*
This Arthur Hills course was built in 1989. Its severe elevation changes reminds many of the finer resort courses up north. Lots of woods, too. Perhaps your best bet for a course in the Detroit

area. *6600 yards. $45 weekends. $40 weekdays. (313) 852-7100.*
Greystone — *Romeo. Metro Detroit*
Famed for its final three holes, widely regarded as the toughest
finishing holes in the state. The 16th is a par 3 to an island
green, the 17th has a tortuously narrow fairway, and 18th
entices you to shoot across the lake. *$37 Mon-Fri: $42 Sat & Sun.
(313) 752-7030.*

The Fortress — *Frankenmuth. Flint/Saginaw Valley/Thumb*
This Scottish links course has over 75 bunkers, with bent grass
tees, fairways, and greens. Oversized greens average over 3,000
square feet. *Mon-Thur $55: Fri-Sun $59. (517) 652-9229.*

Bay Valley Golf Club — *Bay City. Flint/Saginaw Valley/Thumb*
A pretty course, Bay Valley has 13 water holes plus the famous
14th Heather Hole. You have to shoot over a field of heather to
reach the green. *$52. (517) 686-5400.*

Timber Ridge Golf course — *East Lansing. Mid-Michigan*
Highly respected, this course was built in 1988 on hilly terrain
where in the 1940s a tree nursery was planted but never harvested. The 60-odd varieties of trees are now mature, adding to the
allure of the setting, where slopes plunge as much as 80 feet. *Golf
Digest* rated this one of the top 75 public courses in the country.
6060 yards. $45 weekends: $40 weekdays. (517) 339-8000.

The Pines at Lake Isabella — *Weidman. west of Mt. Pleasant*
Located in a quiet, isolated region on 875-acre Lake Isabella, The
Pines features rolling terrain and big, undulating greens. Number
9 is one of the hardest par 4s in the state — an uphill dogleg to the
right. Resorters can make this a busy course on weekends, but
before 1 p.m. on weekdays you can pretty much have the course
to yourself. *$20 weekends: $16 weekdays. (517) 644-2300.*

Saskatoon Golf Club — *Alto. southeast of Grand Rapids. West*
One of the most popular West Michigan courses, the Saskatoon
hosts more group outings than any other course in the state. The
four 9-hole courses are named by colors, and the newest, the
Gold, is the most popular. Its first three holes wind through
woods, then open up for the final Scottish-like holes. *$18 week-
ends: $16 weekdays. (616) 8652.*

L.E. Kaufman Golf Course — *Wyoming. south of Grand Rapids*
This is the best public course in the Grand Rapids region, well
cared for. Watch out for hole number 10 — the creek that cuts

diagonally across the fairway catches lots of balls. The 14th is pretty — pines line both sides of the fairway. *$16 weekends: $10 weekdays. Discount for seniors.* (616) 538-5050.

Grand Traverse Resort Golf Course — *north of Acme. North*

Every serious golfer visiting Michigan should play The Bear at least once. It's a beautifully laid out course. Some of the holes have a open-link-style Scottish flavor with sand hills, hummocks, and waste-high grass in the deep rough. Other holes wind through cherry orchards and woods. It's not as long or as difficult at Treetops, but it remains a very challenging course with 75 bunkers and tiered greens. 7000 yards. *Peak season (June 10-Sept 5) weekday $90. weekend $100. twilight $50.* (616) 938-1620.

Belvedere Golf Club — *Charlevoix. North*

This legendary course was built in 1927. It has hosted the Michigan Amateur 38 times. It features old-fashioned small greens. The emphasis here is on short play, with very challenging 3- and 4- par holes. 5-par holes give you a shot at a birdie or an eagle. *6700 yards. $50 Sun-Wed; $55 Thur-Sat.* (616) 547-2611.

Treetops — *Gaylord. North*

Arguably the most spectacular (and difficult) public course in Michigan. The name comes from designer Robert Trent Jones, whose sixth hole overlooks provides a breathtaking panorama of forested lands. Two other 18-hole courses at this complex are also spectacular. *$72.* (800) 444-6711.

Elk Ridge Golf Course — *Atlanta. between Gaylord & Alpena*

The trap on the par 3 hole number 10 here, plunging 120 feet from tee to green, is in the shape of a pig, a reminder that the owner of this exceptionally beautiful course is Lou Schmidt, owner of the Honeybaked Ham company. It's hilly, wooded, and full of wildlife, including elk. Most difficult: the 600-yard hole 18, where you have to shoot over wetlands to get to the green. *$60 between My 22 and Sept 6; $45 before and after.* (800) 626-4355.

Pine Grove Country Club — *Iron Mountain. Upper Peninsula*

Probably the best Upper Peninsula course. It's an old, traditional course which doesn't permit non-members on Tuesdays and Wednesdays. Mondays and Thursdays outsiders are allowed any time. Friday you can play before noon; Saturday & Sunday after 1. *$40.* (906) 774-3493.

Greg Wilcox's
Top Antiquing Areas in Michigan

1. Royal Oak—Birmingham. *Metro Detroit.* More than 20 shops in the immediate Royal Oak area with several more quality shops in Birmingham.

For more information: Duke Gallery, Royal Oak (810) 547 5511 & Watch Hill, Birmingham (810) 644-4775.

2. Allen. *Marshall to Monroe* Billed as the antique Capitol of Michigan. Over 26 shops in the area, more along U.S. 12.

For more information: (517) 869-2719.

3. Schoolcraft, Galesburg, Mattawan, Lawton. *Southwest Michigan.* Several quality shops around Kalamazoo.

For more information: (616) 347-9672.

4. Williamston, Okemos, Mason. *Mid-Michigan.* Known as the heart of antiques country. Williamston has over 110 antique dealers with many other collectible special interest shops in the area. Quality shops in Okemos; three large malls in Mason.

For more information: Longton Hall (517) 655-5621.

5. Petoskey-Harbor Springs. *Northern Michigan.* A hot bed of antiques in the summer. Several shops open all year.

For more information: (616) 347-9672.

6. Traverse City . *Northern Michigan.* Northern Michigan's antique capitol. Most shops open summer & winter.

For more information: Antique Emporium (616) 943-3685.

7. Tri-City Area. *Bay City. Saginaw & Flint.* Bay City Antiques Center and Saginaw Antique Mall are two of Michigan's top malls.

For more information: Bay City Antiques Center (517) 893-1116.

8. Marshall. *Marshall to Monroe.* Several quality shops and malls. More malls to east along I-94, in downtown Jackson. .

For more information: J.H. Cronin Antiques (616) 789-0077.

9. Grand Rapids. *West Michigan.* The center of western Michigan antique activity. Several local shops plus several in the outlying areas.

For more information: Antiques by the Bridge, Grand Rapids (616) 451-3430.

10. Pontiac Area Shops. *Metro Detroit.* Many quality shops scattered along I-75 North.

For more information: Water Tower Antiques Mall, Holly (313) 634-3500.

11. Southeastern Michigan (Ann Arbor-Saline-Ypsilanti-Wayne-Farmington). Several of Michigan's best shops are included in this area.

For more information: Hickory Hill Antiques, Farmington (313) 477-6630.

Greg Wilcox is publisher of Michigan Antiques Trading Post. 132 S. Putnam. Williamston MI 48895. (517) 655-5621. A free copy is available upon request.

SOUTHWEST MICHIGAN continued

Gardens
Fernwood 28-31
Barrett-Upjohn House 95

Greenhouses & Herb Farms
Bell's Flowers 96
Braeloch Farms 101
Herb Barn 70
Wenke's Greenhouses 96

Historic Buildings & Neighborhoods
Carnegie Library 33
Chapin Mansion (Niles City Hall) 32
First Presbyterian Church 87
Four Flags Hotel 33
Kalamazoo Train Station 84
Kellogg Biological Station Manor House 105-106
Ladies' Library 89
The Maples 59
Newton House 56
Niles Train Station 33
Octagon House 91
Park Club 88
Pears Mill 34
Ring Lardner Home   33
St. Luke's Epis. Church 89
South S.t Hist. District 90
State Theater 86
Stuart Hist. District 94-95
Vine Neighborhood 90-93
Warren Featherbone Company 26
Whitcomb Tower 63

Historic Museums
1839 Courthouse Museum 44
Celery Flats Interpretive Center 77-79
Fort St. Joseph Museum 31
Gilmore Classic Car Mus.100
Kalamazoo Aviation Mus. 79
Kalamazoo Public Mus. 88

New Buffalo RR Depot 16
Southwestern Michigan College Museum 59

Ice Cream Parlors
Carousel Ice Cream & Sandwich Shop 91
Caruso's 58
Four Flags Fantastic Flavors 33

Indians
Bronson Park Indian mound 86
Fort St. Joseph Museum 32

Industrial tours
Cook Energy Information Center 20-21
Simplicity Patterns 33-34

Lighthouses, Lights
North Pier 64

Museums, science
Southwestern Michigan College Museum 59

Nature centers
Fernwood 28
Love Creek County Park & Nature Center 44
Sarett Nature Center 68-69

Parks, local
Bronson Park 86-88
Island Park 32
Lake Bluff Park 60
Lions' Park 66
Madeline Bertrand Park 33
Pioneer Park 91
Portage Creek Park 78
Prairieville Township Park 106
Ross Township Park 106
Russ Forest Park 58
Silver Beach County Park 60

Parks, state & national
Grand Mere State Park 21
Warren Dunes State Park

Prairies
Dayton 34
Fernwood 30

Scenic drives
Territorial Road 46

Shops
Anchors 15
Attic Trash & Treasures 91
Buffalo Drugs 15
Caruso's Candy Kitchen 59
Country Mates 15
Designer's Exchange 88
Drier's Meat Market 24
Filoni Vestimenti 12
Flipside Records 84
G. C. Murphy 63
Gotta Have It! 91
Hearthwoods 14
Heritage Architectural Salvage & Supply Co 94
House of David Arts 67
La De Da's 88
La Grand Trunk 16
LeVerre Boutique 63
Lizards & Mice 86
Lyssa 15
Michigan News Agency 88
Midwest Fruit Package 52
Mole Hole 86
Okun Brothers Shoe Store 94
People's Food Co-op 86
Petals and Postings 85
Robinson Collection 94
Serendipity 10
Silver Balloon 63
Something's Brewing 86
Souk Sampler 95
Sweetwater Boating Supp. 15
Thieves' Market 91
Toy Company 63
Veni Sweet Shop 32
Whittaker House 14
Wild Birds Unlimited 44
Wolf's Marine 65
Woodrose Fine Imports 86

Skiing, cross-country
Madeline Bertrand Park 33
Grand Mere State Park 21
Kal-Haven Trail 71
Lakeshore Road 9
W. K. Kellogg Forest 104

METRO DETROIT

Recommended Michigan travel books

Buy them at book stores or order from us.

The following books are useful for Michigan travellers. Because not all are reliably available in every bookstore, you can also order them from us by mail. See the instructions on page 808.

Buildings of Michigan. *Oxford University Press, New York. 1993. Society of Architectural Historians Buildings of the United States series. 6 3/4" x 9 1/2". Hardcover. 603 pp. Illustrated, with 45 maps of cities and regions. $45 plus $2 shipping surcharge.*

No coffeetable picture book, this meaty, dense volume is the first in a monumental series commissioned by the Society of Architectural Historians. It presents an eclectic melange of stately homes and workers' housing, impressive office buildings, splendidly gaudy theaters, trend-setting factories, resort lodges and cottages, and local landmarks of all eras. All Michigan's famous buildings, past and present, are here: Cranbrook, old forts, the state capitol, Detroit's fabulous Deco office towers, Marquette's Yooper Dome, the Frank Lloyd Wright subdivision near Galesburg and Kalamazoo. So are many fascination but obscure places like Jude's sandstone quarry in Napoleon near Jackson.

Cities which were built up with considerable wealth, such as Saginaw, Detroit, Muskegon, and Kalamazoo, get their due. Neglected areas like the Thumb, north-central Michigan, all the U.P.'s iron ranges, and the southern tier of counties are explored in satisfying detail. That's what makes this an invaluable companion for backroads adventures and exploring Michigan cities. The interesting 53-page introduction is almost a book in itself on the historical background of Michigan architecture. More context is provided by introductory essays to cities and each of 17 regions.

KATHRYN BISHOP ECKERT *has been Michigan's state historic preservation officer since 1976. She is at once knowledgeable and wonderfully broad-minded about historic architecture.*

Jack Berry's 1993 Guide to Michigan Golf. *Momentum Publications, Troy, MI. 1993. 4" x 9". 154 pp. $9.95.*

Useful guide to over 500 Michigan golf courses open to the public. Fewer than half the courses are described in much detail, but readers get a good idea of the best ones in the state and in a specific area. Ratings for challenge level are a real plus.

JACK BERRY *is the seasoned golf writer for the* Detroit News.

The 1994-95 Complete Antique Shop Directory for Eastern Michigan & the Upper Peninsula. *Complete Antique Shop Directories, Lakeside, MI. 4 1/2"x 9". 240 pp. Many maps. $10.95.*

The 1994-95 Complete Antique Shop Directory for Western Michigan. *Complete Antique Shop Directories, Lakeside, MI. 4 1/2"x 9". Approx. 200 pp. Many maps. $10.95.*

These well-organized books have clear directions and many handy small-area road maps that show virtually every shop and mall in the state. They make it easy to survey an area's offerings without a lot of extra planning. Hours and phone numbers are included. Dealer specialties are only occasionally noted — a shortcoming that's outweighed by the books' simple, user-friendly organization and comprehensiveness. *Western Michigan* extends as far east as Jackson and Ingham (Lansing area) counties and north through Emmet County (Petoskey, Harbor Springs, and Pellston).

EDWARD LAWRENCE *is a Chicago-area urban planner who collects Arts & Crafts furniture and decorative accessories and sells them at the East Road Gallery in Lakeside, Michigan (north of New Buffalo). He and his wife, Jean, run Lakeside's Pebble House bed and breakfast, furnished in the Arts & Crafts style.*

A Guide to 199 Michigan Waterfalls. *Friede Publications, Davison, MI. 1988. 6" x 9". Illustrated, with 71 maps. 184 pp. $12.95.*

For backcountry hikers and motorists alike. One of the Upper Peninsula's special delights is all the waterfalls that punctuate its forests, tumbling over dark boulders in changing ribbons, sprays, and thundering foam. Good directions to waterfalls and picturesque old dam sites are provided — a real help in the case of many falls' remote locations and the two-tracks and foottrails leading to them. Many of these are nice spots for picnics and fishing. The falls are grouped by county. A helpful introduction to each county covers its natural and man-made attractions. Many falls are mapped. Tip: Falls River, near L'Anse, is the Penroses' choice for best U.P. river visit, with six waterfalls.

A Traveler's Guide to 116 Michigan Lighthouses. *Friede Publications, Davison, MI. 1992. 8 1/2" x 11". Illustrated, with 52 maps. 111 pp. $12.95.*

This helpful, unpretentious book is a good introduction to

Michigan lighthouses, operating and inactive, that can be viewed without trespassing on private property. The text explains the rationale for building each light, describes the setting today, and tells about major lifesaving events. Related side trips are suggested. To see lighthouses on remote islands and rocks, detailed directions and tips for arriving by boat are provided. Lighthouses almost always exert a special sense of place, whether they're part of a popular park or city fishing pier or isolated and surrounded by sand or rock. Often they're in view of major shipping lanes — a special treat if you can climb the tower. Indexes point out lighthouses with museums, those that can be visited inside, and those whose towers can be climbed.

RUTH AND BILL J. PENROSE and their children LAURIE and BILL research and produce their books as a team. They come from an Upper Peninsula mining family and share that devotion to place and past that marks modern-day Yoopers in diaspora. To them, searching out remote waterfalls and lighthouses provides wonderful destinations for family outings to enjoy forests and shore.

Natural Michigan: a guide to 165 Michigan natural attractions. *Friede Publications, Davison, MI. 1987. 7" x 9". 197 pp. Illustrated. $12.95.*

More Natural Michigan: a guide to another 141 natural attractions. *Friede Publications, Davison, MI. 1992. 7" x 9". 157 pp. Illustrated. $12.95.*

Both these books are statewide in scope, and most Michigan readers will find many natural areas close to their homes. *Natural Michigan* covers most state and national parks and recreation areas and most of the nature centers in southeast Michigan. *More Natural Michigan* includes more county parks and properties of nature conservancies; its appendices list places good for birdwatching, hiking, nature study, picnics, scenery, historical sites, cross-country skiing, swimming, camping, and scenic drives.

Birders like these books because they incorporate a huge range of places, some quite obscure, in two handy volumes. Be aware: sometimes the directions take you to the vicinity but not exactly to the promised spot! Bird-watching, plant, and wildlife highlights are regularly included, and hiking trails are generally described. No phone numbers are included, unfortunately.

TOM POWERS is a longtime librarian at the Flint Public Library. His book projects have combined his research skills with his love of the outdoors and interest in Michigan.

Michigan Fresh: A food-lover's guide to growers and bakeries. *Midwestern Guides, Albion, MI. 1992. 6" x 9". 288 pp. Illustrated with 20 locator maps. $9.95.*

The sheer variety and quality of Michigan's fruits and vegetables make this a valuable sourcebook. Chapters cover over 200 farm stands and U-picks, all of Michigan's farmers' markets, selected herb farms, organic growers and wine grape growers who sell to the general public, and 126 cider mills. Lists are enlivened with stories about individual growers and bakers, along with background info on the history and culture of various crops. Noted naturalist Ellen Weatherbee wrote a 13-page introduction to foraging for edible wild plants. The 76-page bakery section has informative mini-essays on 40 top bakeries state-wide.

Hunts' Guide to West Michigan. *Midwestern Guides, Albion, MI. 1993. 6" x 9". 233 pp. Illustrated with five city maps. $11.95.*

Every significant place along Lake Michigan's east shore from New Buffalo north through Muskegon and White Lake is profiled, and visitor destinations are described and evaluated. Includes recommended restaurants and lodgings, priced for all budgets. Readers and reviewers alike enjoy the historical and descriptive overviews that tell how each place came to be the way it is. Covers popular visitor destinations like Saugatuck, St. Joseph, South Haven, Grand Haven, and Holland and industrial cities as well.

Hunts' Highlights of Michigan. *Second edition. Midwestern Guides, Albion, MI. 1994. 5 1/2" x 8 1/2". 800 pp. Illustrated with 27 maps. $14.95.*

This book in your hands is by far the most comprehensive travel guide to Michigan. Because it appeals to so many kinds of interests, it makes a fun, useful gift for many kinds of people.

Hunts' Restaurants and Lodgings of Michigan. *Midwestern Guides, Albion, MI. 1994. 5 1/2" x 8 1/2". Approx. 200 pp. Illustrated, with locator maps. $9.95. Available in September, 1994.*

Recommended places to eat and stay at have been chosen for multiple factors emphasizing local color; individual personality; interesting, pedestrian-friendly location; and quality. Priced for all budgets. The best statewide guide available. (A new edition of Molly Abraham's *Restaurants of Detroit* is recommended for a fuller treatment southeast Michigan's fast-changing restaurants.) Detailed logistics, directions, prices, menu descriptions, and amenities.are included.

DON AND MARY HUNT *founded the Ann Arbor Observer monthly magazine, where Don is a regular contributor. For the past six years they have been exploring Michigan's cities, countryside, and shores, writing travel guides.*

Mackinac Connection: An Insider's Guide. 2nd Edition.

Mackinac Publishing, Mackinac Island, MI. 1992. 6" x 9". 159 pp. $8.95.

This chatty, informative book describes Mackinac Island's many facets from the perspective of a longtime summer resident who appreciates the island's natural setting and many odd details. It's full of helpful tips and candid info all lodgings, restaurants, shops, outings, events, walks, bike rides, and much more. Highly recommended pre-trip reading.

AMY MCVEIGH *is a freelance writer who also prepares training programs and promotional materials. A Mackinac Island summer resident since the age of six, she knows the island inside and out.*

50 Hikes in Lower Michigan: The Best Walks, Hikes, and Backpacks from Sleeping Bear Dunes to Oakland County. *Backcountry Publications, Woodstock, VT, 1991. 6" x 9". 253 pp. Illustrated, with hard-to-use topo maps of each hike. $12.95.*

This book excels in logistics and in evaluating hikes to help you decide where to go. Hikes are south of the 45th parallel (between Traverse City and Grayling), no more than four hours from metro Detroit. Five are overnight backpacking trips; nine are two miles or less. A one- or two-page description highlights each hike's plants, geology, aesthetics, wildlife, fishing, occasionally skiing, and just plain fun and adventure. Extensive trail notes follow. The introduction is full of helpful trail hints and tips on the best short and long hikes in each of six areas.

Michigan's Best Outdoor Adventures with Children. *The Mountaineers, Seattle, WA, 1990. 5 1/4" x 8 1/4". 240 pp. Illustrated with a map for each outing but no distance scales. $12.95.*

Seventy-five favorite outings suited to kids from 3 to 10 have been selected from years of hiking, camping, and canoeing trips. Most involve short hikes of under 2 miles. A few easy backpacking and canoe overnights are included. The emphasis is on scenic rustic campgrounds (no showers, no electricity, no flush toilets) in less-used state and national forests and parks. Adults without kids can also benefit from tips on finding beautiful, uncrowded beaches, lovely overlooks, and pristine lakes.. If your camping skills have atrophied since scouting days, read the introduction to avoid embarrassing yourself in front of your kids. The motivational psychology is masterful: emphasize alluring destinations, let younger hikers lead but rotate the title of leader, pause frequently to explore little things.

Michigan State Parks: A Complete Recreation Guide for Campers, Boaters, Anglers, Hikers & Skiers. *The Mountaineers, Seattle, WA. 1989. 5 1/4" x 8 1/4". 285 pp. Illustrated, with 42 maps. $12.95.*

Well-organized headings for all recreation subcategories (hiking trails, fishing, cross-country skiing, etc.) make this book easy to use and helpful. DuFresne's outdoor experience pays off, but his other books go into far more detail for trails. Campground descriptions help prospective campers find shade, a natural ambiance, and privacy. The locator map in front and quick-reference chart in back let you scan to find out what parks suit your needs. Also includes Mackinac State Historic Parks. Not totally up to date.

Isle Royale National Park: Foot Trails & Water Routes. *The Mountaineers, Seattle, WA. 5 1/4" x 8 3/8". 136 pp. Illustrated, with many maps. 1992. $10.95.*

A 34-page introduction to the island covers its history, flora, fauna, and fishing, and includes back-country tips. It gives visitors a good overview before visiting the nation's least-visited, least-touched-by-humans national park. The rest of the book consists of detailed notes to hiking trails and water routes. It passes muster with people who have hiked and canoed extensively on the island.

Michigan's Porcupine Mountains Wilderness State Park: A backcountry guide for hikers, backpackers, campers, skiers. *Glovebox Guidebooks, Clarkston, MI. 1993. 5 3/8" x 8". 160 pp. Illustrated, with 19 maps. $10.95.*

Follows the same format as the Isle Royale book but also includes chapters on waterfalls and skiing (downhill and cross-country). Appendix features backpacking itineraries. Sixteen trail-side cabins make hiking in the Porkies especially appealing.

Lower Michigan's 75 Best Campgrounds. *Glovebox Guidebooks, Clarkston, MI. 1992. 5 3/8" x 8". 160 pp. Illustrated, with 35 maps. $10.95.*

This is a terrific book for people who care more about a campground's natural setting and privacy than they do about modern conveniences. Many of Michigan's most scenic and least crowded campgrounds are in state and national forests, where lack of electricity and showers keeps away the crowds. One section covers 20 recommended modern campgrounds, another describes 45 rustic ones. Seven rustic cabins are also included.

JIM DU FRESNE *has spent most of his life camping and exploring the great Michigan outdoors. For some two decades he has been writing about wilderness and outdoor recreation. After years of worldwide adventure travel, he's back in Michigan raising a family, running a small travel publishing company, and writing columns for Booth News- papers on outdoor adventures with and without children. His Michigan outdoor books stand out because of their clear opinions and recommen- dations and the vast amount of outdoor experience they're based on.*

Camper's Guide to Michigan Parks, Lakes and Forests: Where to Go and How to Get There. *Gulf Publishing Co., Houston, TX. 1992. 8 1/4" x 11". 162 pp. Illustrated, with many maps of major campgrounds. $15.95.*

More a compilation of state and national parks and forests in Michigan than a guide based on actual experience. Offerings of each park or forest are described generally. This book is extremely useful because it includes *all* the hundreds of small campgrounds in state and national forests, with good directions and charts about number of sites, swimming, hiking, fishing, boat ramp at each campground. When camping in northern lower Michigan and the Upper Peninsula, if you know about these more rustic and obscure campgrounds, you can find spots on weekends on the spur of the moment and enjoy more privacy than in the popular state parks with their smaller campsites. Phone numbers and addresses of each ranger district are included, so you can request additional information ahead of time. (National Forests in particular produce some excellent handouts on local human and natural history, scenic byways, overlooks, etc.)

MICKEY LITTLE founded the Outdoor Education Institute at Texas A&M, where she is professor emeritus. She has compiled camping guides to several states. She loves to camp, canoe, and hike.

Northwoods Wildlife: A Watcher's Guide to Habitats. *Produced by the USDA Forest Service, St. Paul, MN. Published by NorthWord Press, Minocqua, WI. 6" x 9". 453 pp. Illustrated. $19.95 plus $1 shipping surcharge.*

Increase your chances of encountering wildlife or their signs by understanding the habitat approach to learning about animals and birds. This book describes them in the context of 18 kinds of wet- lands and shores, forests, and fields found in the Northwoods, that transitional zone between the broadleaf forests of southern Michigan and the needleleaf, boreal forest of Canada. (In Michigan the Northwoods begin north of Bay City and Muskegon.) Characteristics, behaviors, and sounds of each creature are satisfyingly long and interesting. There are plenty of tips for locating and observing wildlife. Appendices include a wildlife events calendar and wildlife-watching hotspots. (Brockway Mountain Dr., Whitefish Point, Isle Royale, the Porcupines, Sleeping Bear Dunes, Pictured Rocks, Seney Refuge, Hiawatha National Forest, and Wilderness State Park are in *Hunts' Highlights*.)

JANINE BENYUS is a freelance writer who writes books about nature and animal behavior for the general public, drawing upon scientific findings. She also wrote *The Field Guides to Wildlife Habitats* for Simon & Schuster/Fireside (in Eastern and Western volumes) and *Beastly Behaviors* for Addison-Wesley.

Regional County Maps. Universal Map Enterprises, Williamston, MI, 38" x 28". Two colors are used on older, cheaper maps; four colors for newer, $3.95 ones. Excellent indexes.
1. **Central Michigan:** *Clare, Gratiot, Isabella, Mecosta, Montcalm, Osceola counties. $2.50.*
2. **Eastern Upper Peninsula:** *Chippewa, Luce, Mackinac. $3.95.*
3. **Michigan's Thumb:** *Huron, Lapeer, St. Clair, Sanilac, Tuscola. $2.50.*
4. **Mid-Michigan:** *Barry, Clinton, Eaton, Ingham, Ionia. $2.50.*
5. **Mid-West Michigan:** *Allegan, Kent, Muskegon, Newaygo, Oceana, Ottawa. $2.50.*
6. **Northern Highlands:** *Alcona, Crawford, Iosco, Kalkaska, Missauke, Ogemaw, Oscoda, Roscommon. $2.50.*
7. **Northern Tip:** *Alcona, Antrim, Charlevoix, Cheboygan, Emmett, Montmorency, Otsego, Presque Isle. $3.95.*
8. **Northwest Michigan:** *Benzie, Grand Traverse, Lake, Leelanau, Manistee, Mason, Wexford. $3.95.*
9. **Saginaw Valley:** *Arenac, Bay, Genesee, Gladwin, Midland, Saginaw, Shiawassee. $2.50.*
10. **South-Central Michigan:** *Branch, Calhoun, Hillsdale, Jackson, Lenawee. $2.50.*
11. **Southeast Michigan:** *Livingston, Macomb, Monroe, Oakland, Washtenaw, Wayne. $2.95.*
12. **Southwest Michigan:** *Berrien, Cass, Kalamazoo, St. Joseph, Van Buren. $3.95.*
Though not particularly attractive, these maps are by far the most helpful and illuminating available. For backroads motorists and bicyclists, road surfaces are clearly distinguished. Identified recreation features include boat launches, campgrounds, canoe trails, ski areas, x-c ski trails, golf courses, parks, harbors, and beaches. Natural areas, prominent hills, and scenic lookouts are identified, along with odd things like Cheboygan's sawdust pile and Negaunee's mine cave-ins. On the reverse side, town street maps are

loaded with historic sites, industries, shopping centers, cemeteries, campus buildings, and more. Notes on local history are worthwhile. Spend 15 minutes studying these maps before setting out. You'll discover many interesting things you would have missed!

Atlas of Northern Michigan Cities: Lower Peninsula. *Universal Map Enterprises. 8 1/2" x 11". 28 maps, 50 pp. $6.95.*

A recreational bonanza, complete with inventories of facilities offered by local parks and beaches. Retail areas, historic neighborhoods, and industrial areas are identified. Towns along I-75 and the Lake Huron shore are well covered, but, oddly, nothing in Leelanau County is included. Local histories of each place. Street indexes. Maps are in one or two colors.

Michigan's Upper Peninsula Cities. *Universal Map Enterprises. 8 1/2" x 11". 20 maps, 50 pp. $6.95.*

Similar to Northern Lower Peninsula cities atlas. All U.P. cities of any size are included.

DAVID BROWN *is a cartographer who loves exploring off the beaten track and reading local history for tidbits for his map notes.*

To order

Send a check for the cost of the book or books you want plus $2 for handling and shipping. In the case of very heavy books, an extra shipping fee is mentioned after the retail price. We ship within 1-3 days of receiving orders. We use book rate (5-7 day delivery time_) for 1-2 books unless customers request UPS and add $1.50 extra. We ship UPS for larger orders. **Mail your order** to:

> Midwestern Guides
> 506 Linden Avenue
> Albion, MI 49224

Be sure your order includes:

◆ **Name and address** to ship to. Include UPS address if different from mailing address.

◆ If your order includes a **gift** to be shipped to another address, please specify which items go to which address. Include name of gift recipient, address, and greeting to be enclosed. **Add $2** shipping and handling for each extra address. We **giftwrap free of charge** and use paper from Gwen Frostic of Benzonia.

◆ **$2 shipping and handling** for each address shipped to. Include an extra $1.50 for quicker UPS delivery of small orders (1-2 books).

◆ **Check** made out to Midwestern Guides.

Thank you!